. . . And with a Light Touch

Learning About Reading, Writing, and Teaching with First Graders

SECOND EDITION

CAROL AVERY

Foreword by Donald Graves

HEINEMANN
PORTSMOUTH, NH

Heinemann
A division of Reed Elsevier Inc.
361 Hanover Street
Portsmouth, NH 03801–3912
www.heinemann.com

Offices and agents throughout the world

The author and publisher wish to thank those who have generously given permission to reprint borrowed material:

"Laura's Legacy" by Carol Avery. Copyright © 1988 by the National Council of Teachers of English. Reprinted by Permission.

Library of Congress Cataloging-in-Publication Data
Avery, Carol.
. . . and with a light touch : learning about reading, writing, and teaching with first graders / Carol Avery ; foreword by Donald Graves.—2nd ed.
p. cm.
Includes bibliographical references and index.
ISBN 0-325-00066-2 (pbk. : alk. paper)
1. Language arts (Primary). 2. English language—Composition and exercises—Study and teaching (Primary). 3. Reading (Primary). 4. First grade (Education). I. Title.

LB1528 .F67 2002
372.41—dc21 2001007445

Editor: Lois Bridges
Production service: Colophon
Production coordination: Vicki Kasabian
Cover design: Jenny Jensen Greenleaf
Cover illustration: Tiffany Hostetter
Photographs by Nathan Avery and Carole Beech
Typesetter: Publishers' Design and Production Services, Inc.
Manufacturing: Louise Richardson

Printed in the United States of America on acid-free paper
09 10 11 12 RRD 10 9 8 7 6

For
Kinsey Rochelle Avery
Adessa Denise Avery
and
William Rhett Avery
my "trailguides to the future"

Contents

Foreword by Donald H. Graves ..... **vii**

Acknowledgments ..... **ix**

Beginning ..... **x**

1. The Butterflies Are Being Born 1
2. The First Day of School 11

Environment and Tone **26**

3. Classroom Climate: A Foundation for Learning 27
4. Planning and Preparing 48

Writing **64**

5. Establishing and Managing a Writing Workshop 65
6. Mini-Lessons: Helping Children Craft Their Writing 108
7. Listening and Responding 137
8. From the Author's Chair 165
9. The Process of Publishing 181

Children's Literature **214**

10. The Why, How, and What of Reading Aloud 215
11. Reader Response 237
12. Children Take Literature to Heart 249

Reading **268**

13. Developing a Reading Workshop 269
14. Guided Reading and Literature Circles 298

15. Learning to Read 312
16. Learning Language: Phonics, Word Study, and Spelling 340

Expanding Literacy 372
17. Lessons from Kindergarten 373
18. Reading and Writing in Math, Science, and Social Studies 398

Considering Student Progress 416
19. Documenting Student Growth 417
20. Reporting Student Growth 449

Conclusion 461

Afterword: Laura's Legacy 464

Appendix A:
Conference Checklist 466

Appendix B:
Publishing Conference Record 467

Appendix C:
Directions for Bookbinding 468

Appendix D:
Reading Conference Notes (Whole Class) 471

Appendix E:
Reading Record (Individual) 472

Appendix F:
Strategies and Skills of Written Language 473

Appendix G:
Children's Books: Child-Tested Favorites 478

Works Cited 482

Children's Books Cited 487

Index 490

Foreword

I didn't realize how much I needed this book until I'd read it. Over the last three decades we've seen an explosion in research concerning young children learning to read and write. Researchers have invaded classrooms, observed children, formulated theories, completed dissertations, and written books and articles. Most of the writing about young children and their literacy has been written by researchers from the outside. Finally, we have a book written from the inside by a practicing teacher who may understand our researchers' theories better than we, as researchers, understand them ourselves.

"There is nothing more practical than a good theory," someone once said. Well, this is the most practical inside-the-classroom book about primary years that I've read. A practical book in this case doesn't mean cookbook recipes with first-grade activities. Rather, "practical" refers to the author's approach to teaching us how to observe children. Her premise is simple: Children are meaning makers; listen to them; observe the world through their eyes, and then help them express what they wish to say. We see the author in myriad learning situations with all kinds of children ranging from the Learning Disabled to the gifted.

Carol Avery sheds prescriptive teaching for listening to children. Many of us have written about the importance of listening but we haven't applied sound theory to the classroom. The soundness of Carol's interpretations of first-grade children is no accident. She's taught first grade for twelve years, been a high school English teacher, school librarian, and mother. She connects the child's fundamental urge to make meaning with the long-term view of what reading and writing are for—a lifetime of enjoying and learning to live in the world. This is no filmy-eyed work that ignores child problems. You will meet angry children; troublemakers crying, moaning, and swearing; and children of divorce. There are children with severe learning problems who at first don't want to read and write. We follow their progress from troubling moments through first scribbles and stuttering decodings to fluency.

There aren't too many texts that follow children from day to day over an entire year as they learn to read and write. Most texts, including my own, aren't always helpful to teachers who wonder what to do after introducing certain skills, or new learning procedures. This text documents children's learning right in the midst of a conference, then follows their gradual upward spiral to confidence and achievement.

With all of these individual cases, Carol doesn't neglect the overall classroom picture. "Books become the common ground that hold a class together," she says. There are numerous transcripts of children talking and learning together. We have that rare look at the understructure of her classroom—one usually lost to the casual observer or visitor—which shows the rock-ribbed tacit understanding children have about how a room works. In the author's room children learn to listen and help each other. Carol Avery shows us the details of developing a partnership with children, which, in time, becomes part of the understructure. Thus, new and experienced teachers, as well as academics who spend too little time in classrooms, can see how a classroom learns to take responsibility and enjoy reading and writing.

Carol Avery invites us to learn with her. This means that we will witness what doesn't work as much as what does. Most texts ignore how the author learned. We simply say it is a good idea to do this or use that approach without showing the process of dealing with the problems or bugs that go with new practices. Carol goes one better and shows real children in the process of learning to learn. As readers, we learn from Carol because of her own appetite for learning. It is the quality of her own reading, writing, and learning that cannot be underestimated as the basis for successful teaching. It is her partnership with children and the questions they ask that move her to read still more literature, peruse journals, and consult with other professionals.

This book is filled with a wide range of literature for children. The author knows children and books and demonstrates the ways in which she helps children to begin to meet authors and choose books appropriate to their ability.

And with a Light Touch is a liberating book. Carol Avery listens to children, their wantings and intentions, and helps them to become lifetime readers and writers. As Carol frees the children to enjoy their world, we learn with her how to become professionally free ourselves.

Donald H. Graves

Acknowledgments

The second edition of . . . *And with a Light Touch* could not have come to publication without the support, encouragement, and plain hard work of others. I am grateful to all who have helped along the way. I thank all the children, teachers, and administrators who have invited me to their schools. My experiences in their classrooms have played a major role in my professional growth. I especially wish to acknowledge those who played a direct role in the writing of this second edition: Barbara Borick, Cari Buckner, Cody Dobson and the teachers at North Park Elementary School, Michelle DeCamp, Tracy Downs, Alana Kempf, Chris Marana, Jean Nuttall, Sylvia Read, Barbara Scott and the teachers at E. M. Crouthamel Elementary School, Kimeen Scott, and Wendy Woodworth.

Lois Bridges provided encouragement, feedback, and friendship. I am fortunate to have had her as my editor. Her patience, encouragement, and vision kept me going through the ups and downs (and there were many!) of taking apart the first edition of . . . *And with a Light Touch*, and reconstructing this new edition. Her instincts are always on target and her honest and positive encouragement come at just the right moments.

There are others whose contributions made a big difference to this book; I am grateful to all of them. Ray Coutu made thoughtful suggestions as I began this project. Jennifer Avery provided computer expertise that I couldn't have done without. Carole Beech gave countless hours of expert editing and offered numerous helpful suggestions along the way.

I thank Vicki Kasabian and Lisa Fowler who patiently and expertly guided the manuscript through the production process as well as Denise Botelho and Anne Sauvé, who did an outstanding job with the final editing.

And finally, a special loving thanks to the family members who gave so much throughout all of the writing.

BEGINNING

The Golden Book Encyclopedia
The Golden Dictionary
The Golden Dictionary

CHAPTER 1

The Butterflies Are Being Born

The little boy yawned. His name was John and he sat at my feet in a circle of five or six of his first-grade peers for his daily reading lesson. Carefully, precisely, he printed a word in his workbook, looked up, and yawned again. And then I yawned too. I opened my eyes to find John watching me. We exchanged quiet smiles and waited for the others to finish writing the same word so we could continue the fill-in-the-blank exercises. I glanced around the classroom where the other three reading groups spent their seatwork time writing. They were all engaged in their work. And it hit me. The energy in this classroom was there: with the children *writing* at their seats.

Suddenly I knew: "It will work!" The *it*, a gentle suggestion by Rose Stetler, the reading coordinator, was to abandon the basal reader and "to teach reading through writing." When I'd first heard this notion the previous fall I'd thought, "That's crazy!" Now, on a morning in early March, I saw clearly that my first graders learned more about reading from the writing they were doing at their seats than they did from the carefully orchestrated lessons I presented to achievement-ranked reading groups. I knew at that moment that Rose's suggestion was anything but crazy. Writing was a powerful, efficient, and natural way to learn language.

Our district was easing writing into the curriculum, basing it on the research Donald Graves was doing in Atkinson, New Hampshire, in elementary classrooms. Because children in his research classrooms spent time writing every day, their teachers devoted less time to teaching reading. Despite this shift in time distribution, reading scores went up. "Writing made the difference," was the answer coming from this research. Hence the phrase, "learning to read through writing."

I had been following Graves' research as it appeared in the journal *Language Arts*. It all seemed so real, so different, from other research that I found myself thinking, "I bet my kids can do that." So, following the New Hampshire model for the past two years I had had my first graders writing, encouraging them to choose their own topics and spell as best as they could.

The first year I discovered that the children did far better with their own topics than with my story starters and, with concern for perfect mechanics set aside, they took off. They loved this writing so much that by spring of that year I had them writing daily as part of seatwork during reading instruction. Based on this success, the second year I started the children writing the first week of school in small groups, then continued daily writing as a seatwork activity. I enlisted the help of an aide and two mothers so that every day during the reading instructional period, an adult sat in the back of the room and listened to the children read their writing. Sometimes the adult lightly penciled in words or phrases that were undecipherable because of the phonetic spelling, but basically she listened and talked with the child about the ideas in the writing.

The results astounded me. I discovered that not only could first graders select topics, but also they could present coherent and detailed information about those topics on paper. I chose the best of their pieces, corrected spelling and punctuation, typed them, and bound them into little books. We had a whole shelf of these books, and they were the favorite reading material in the classroom. Though I felt comfortable developing writing among my first graders, I dismissed any hint of "abandoning the basal and teaching reading through the children's writing" as foolish and irresponsible. Now, on this morning in March, I saw a brief vision of a different way in the faces of the children. The next day I approached Rose Stetler about the prospect.

"We will need to do some planning and maybe get you some training," Rose responded, and then she went to work. She arranged a visit to Atkinson, New Hampshire where I saw writing in the first-grade classrooms that matched that of my own students. I returned home eager to encourage my students to write even more. I'd also learned of a graduate course, Teaching Writing in the Elementary School, which Mary Ellen Giacobbe and Lucy Calkins planned to teach that summer for Northeastern University. Mary Ellen was the first-grade teacher in Don Graves' study and Lucy was a research assistant. Within a few days, I'd sent my registration for the course.

I spent the remainder of the school year reading articles funneled to me by Rose and thinking about the following year. Sometimes I fought off misgivings: What kind of imprudent undertaking had I gotten myself into? But reading the stories from the New Hampshire research buoyed my optimism. I sensed that I had touched on something authentic both for the children and for me. I couldn't turn back.

On the last day of school that year, as the children hurried out the door, a quiet boy named George stopped to hug me. "Good-bye, Mrs. Avery," he said and he was gone. I felt a tinge of sadness. The reading program hadn't served George very well. He was in the low reading group and probably would stay there throughout his school career. I watched him leave and remembered the butterflies. In the fall George had brought a caterpillar to school in a jar. A few days later he brought a plastic box especially designed to hold caterpillars. His parents had gotten it for him, he explained, and he'd caught more caterpillars. Several caterpillars crawled around inside the box and from the lid hung a dozen or more green chrysalises, each with a fine strand of gold beads along one side. They were exquisite. We kept the box on the corner of my desk. In a couple of days the remaining caterpillars hung in tiny green and gold sacks. After a time the chrysalises turned black. Thinking them dead, I came close to discarding them or sending them home with George. Then one day in the middle of my teacher-directed reading lesson, monarch butterflies began unfolding from those seemingly dead chrysalises. George spied them first and cried out, "Look, the butterflies are being born!"

The principal, who had stopped in for an observation, sat with his pad and pencil. I glanced at him, struggled a moment, then looked at George and decided. "Let's watch the butterflies for a few minutes." We watched those butterflies unfold and dry their wings throughout the day. By the following noon a delicate sea of orange and black fluttered under the box lid. A couple days later we quietly, carefully carried the box outside. George lifted the lid and held it while, one by one, the butterflies took their leave and headed on their migratory journeys. George watched them until the last one was out of sight. He had known all along that inside those black chrysalises lived the developing butterflies. George knew lots of things that I didn't. I realized that there was much about George I didn't understand. I'd been too busy to see really, too busy "teaching." In that empty classroom, I felt a stab of guilt. My teaching had barely touched George's capacity as a learner.

This school year was over. Though the children had been different as they were every year, in many ways—except for the writing—the year had been like all the others before it. We'd read the same books, followed the same sequence of lessons, completed the same drill and practice exercises. Worst of all, the spread in reading achievement—the basic measurement of success in first grade—had widened. Every year brought children like John to the classroom, who ended as they began—on the top. And every year there were others like George, who for one reason or another moved through the system but never really became competent readers. This year, writing had brought life to an otherwise boring landscape by providing a forum where every child participated successfully.

A couple of weeks after school ended, I headed back to New England to learn more about this new phenomenon of teaching writing and, through writing, reading. The challenge of exploring writing kindled a renewal for teaching within me and put at bay an encroaching sense of burnout. I had no clue that I was embarking on a course that would change me as a teacher and turn me into a learner in my own classroom.

The burnout never returned. I would come to know that teaching begins with understanding—not getting the *children* to understand, but rather, about *my* understanding of each of them—what *they* understand, know, and care about and how they work in a classroom. I would realize that a significant aspect of teaching was listening to, honoring, and responding to children individually, and that I needed to be learning myself by reading, writing, observing, reflecting, and continually refining my classroom practice in light of the children and who they are rather than just the demands of curriculum.

This professional journey led me to write articles for professional journals, present at local, state, and national conventions, and write a book! Me, a classroom teacher, author of a book about teaching! Now, twenty years from this beginning, I find myself writing the second edition of *. . . And with a Light Touch*. Since the publication of the first in 1993, I've taught my own first-, fourth- and sixth-grade classes and demonstrated writing and reading workshops in many classrooms in every grade from preschool through high school. I've learned how the specific circumstances I told about in the first edition may be different, but the underlying theories and principles still apply. I can still say teaching doesn't follow a prescription; it's far more than implementing activities, programs, or plans. If a single thread runs through these experiences, it is that teaching requires listening and responding to the individual student and approaching the classroom knowing I am a learner there, not the final authority.

My teaching practice continues to evolve as I learn from children in classrooms and as I consider new ideas and practices emerging in the educational world. This second edition attempts to address my evolving beliefs and changing practices. One area of change is the teaching of writing. I continue to be amazed at what young children are capable of as writers. Children, especially those in the primary grades, when provided with a nurturing environment, write, revise, and edit with more thought, care, and sophistication than I ever imagined. I refine my role to keep up with them! Teaching writing requires showing children how to craft quality pieces of writing, a skill that goes beyond correcting mechanics. I learned early on the importance of teaching by demonstrating with my own writing. I've learned that showing children *how* to revise and shape meaning is fundamental to teaching them to write. I'm no longer nervous about being a vulnerable writer in front of a class, and I understand that showing children a perfect draft can be intimidating but that showing children my process as I work toward that draft is instructive. Also, I've continued to refine the way I handle writing conferences. I listen more, talk less, and ask better questions. I now better appreciate how critical frequent and effective conferences are in helping children develop as writers. And I've learned that being responsive to children does not mean "anything goes." I set high standards and expect children to invest their energies. In this second edition, I share strategies I've refined for the writing workshop to help children grow further as writers.

I also examine more extensively my read-aloud practices. I better understand now that reading aloud to children *is* teaching and that *how* I read and the *talk* surrounding that reading has a direct influence on children's growth as readers and writers. Daily read-aloud time cannot be shortchanged for it helps children understand the fundamental purpose of the written word. As a direct result of read alouds, children approach independent reading striving for comprehension and understanding. This attitude remains at the heart of reading for the children. There's a whole wide world of good books to share with children and I don't need to narrow my selections to the "best," or to those that connect with curriculum, or to ones leading to activities. There's much joy in finding and exploring the new together.

Like the rest of the educational community—and the country, for that matter—I've wrestled with the complex issues surrounding reading instruction. Teaching reading has become a political issue. Government-initiated reports cite "scientific" findings on how to teach reading even as almost anyone would agree that *their* child doesn't quite fit any scientific paradigm. And, competency in reading these days seems to be determined solely by test scores. At the same time, practices for teaching reading become more complex and more prescriptive. Guided reading and literature circles, for example, offer the potential of responding to individual uniqueness, but it's also possible for these practices to become complicated structures that come dangerously close to the rigidity of archaic reading programs. Teaching reading seems more perplexing—and confusing—than ever. If I've learned anything, it's not to jump on the bandwagon quickly or reject ideas outright, but to be thoughtful about change. This edition addresses my thinking as I consider current ideas and issues in light of classroom practice and the *children.* It is the educational needs of children—and what ultimately will be helpful for each one of them—that guide my teaching practices and that I hope readers will find on the pages of . . . *And with a Light Touch.* This edition is the continuing story of my metamorphosis as I listen to children and learn with them.

In a talk titled "The Enemy Is Orthodoxy," reprinted in *A Researcher Learns to Write,* Don Graves (1984) reminds us how easily we can slip into formulas for teaching. There is always a danger of creating a methodology that becomes written in stone, to be applied to all children. He cautioned against plans and procedures that become so ritualistic that the methodology, rather than the children and their learning, becomes our focus. I know this trap well. In the early years of my teaching I worked hard on developing "teaching practices." I cluttered my classroom, the curriculum, and my teaching itself with trappings: decorations for the room, activities and frills for the curriculum, myriad "creative" approaches. It was all very organized but very full. There was comfort in the certainty and the sense of control it appeared to bring. But I've come to see that control is an illusion; I never *really* had it in the classroom. Things just appeared under control. The complexity of individual human growth—and therefore our teaching practices—defies "control." All that clutter kept me from seeing the children and truly taking them into account. I cleaned stuff out—file cabinets and closets first, then preconceived plans and procedures. Eliminating the clutter cleared my mind. The temptation is always there to clutter our teaching with more or new practices. When I focused on children rather than practices, teaching became not only more challenging but also more rewarding and, more important, more effective for the children. I was able to let the children shine through.

Still, it's not easy. The enemy continues to be orthodoxy. As soon as I say "I do it this way . . ." I find exceptions or realize that "this way" has changed. I say that a mini-lesson for writing is no longer than five to eight minutes and then I present one in thirty seconds and another takes twenty minutes. This kind of tension is inherent in teaching but I think it nourishes a creative energy in the classroom. Guidelines, maybe, are what we need rather than absolutes. I strive to keep things simple, uncomplicated, so that the complex processes of learning can thrive. As I write this second edition, I am well aware that I may sound as though I'm creating another set of orthodoxies but, believe me, there are no intended absolutes here—except possibly one: the uniqueness of each child.

The uniqueness of each child is something Graves discovered in his research on children's writing. This research certainly made a major contribution to education in that writing opened up in elementary classrooms and today writing is acknowledged as a fundamental part of curriculum. However, the major finding of that research, and the implications for teaching based on that finding, are highly significant. In capital letters, in his book *Writing: Teachers and Children at Work*, Graves (1983) wrote,

> WRITING IS A HIGHLY IDIOSYNCRATIC PROCESS THAT VARIES FROM DAY TO DAY. Variance is the norm, not the exception. (270)

Almost every teacher I know can concur with this statement. In fact, most of us could substitute "learning" for "writing" and still agree. Teachers know this in their bones. Graves noted that many factors (self-concept, topic choice, organic factors, etc.) influence a writer's progress on a given day. As I launched writing workshops in my classroom, when doubts crept in, I took comfort in the knowledge that children wrote in "highs" and "lows," that I could not expect a steady upward spiral of growth, and that I must allow children the luxury of failure and the gift of time. I would remember a line from hearing Graves speak: "In a class of twenty-five on a given day, only five or six children may be working on 'hot' topics with the writing going well." In the final report on his research, Graves wrote about this variability and its implications for teaching.

> Many similarities were seen among the children when they wrote, but as the study progressed, individual exceptions to the data increased in dominance. In short, every child had behavorial characteristics in the writing process that applied to that child alone. It is our contention, based on this information, that such variability demands a waiting, responsive type of teaching. (1981)

"A waiting, responsive type of teaching." I believe this aspect of Graves' research is critical to teaching young children to write. Fortunately, when I was getting started with writing instruction, it had few of the trappings that surrounded traditional subjects, making it easier to develop this approach. Working with young writers taught me the effectiveness of a responsive approach and I incorporated it into all areas of the curriculum. For me, this means that I establish a classroom environment conducive for learning and then determine what to teach and when by observing and listening to children as they write. And I do *teach*! A responsive approach does not mean that I ignore curriculum or permit children to run the show! It does mean planning thoughtfully, with flexibility, and for depth of learning. It means organization and structure that children thoroughly understand. It means looking at how children learn throughout the school day and adjusting plans and structures to maximize their growth. Integration, I learned, does not mean teacher-planned activities, but rather, occurs within learners themselves as they take part in purposeful activities.

Previously, I'd seen differences as children wrote and in every aspect of their participation in classroom life. I hated attempting to blot out their differences and make them conform, but success with the curriculum and programmed teaching seemed grounded in uniformity. I much prefer the responsive type of teaching that Graves suggested because it honors individual differences, leads to an investment on the part of the child, and results in solid learning. Remembering to listen for the differences and gently encourage and coax the individual voices of the young writers in my classroom became a guiding principle.

As I've helped teachers implement writing workshops in their classrooms, I've noticed that success comes most readily when the teacher slows down and strives for this responsive approach. As I reflect on this, I see a "responsive type of teaching" as part of a rich instructional environment. It's an environment where the teacher listens to and observes each child, striving to understand the child's intentions and the knowledge that is informing the child's plans and actions. The teacher responds by questioning to clarify and commenting to validate the child's thinking. The teacher responds further by suggesting options, providing expertise, and urging the child to consider previously unexplored ideas. The learner takes risks and learning flourishes.

Graves became a profound teacher for me. His work totally revamped my teaching and his support and encouragement has been invaluable. In a panel presentation at an NCTE convention (whose date and time I've long since lost), Janet Emig spoke of not "killing off your mothers and fathers," meaning that we ought not abandon our roots, but learn from them as we strive to refine our teaching today. I've pondered Emig's message many times since that day. I've noticed a tendency in education to abandon sound research and proven practice for what's new, latest, or current. But our roots do define who we are today. In the first edition of this book, I recognized the role my early experiences in literacy, my mother's part in developing my love of books, and how my experiences as a mother shaped my role in the classroom. I talked about reading Jeannette Veatch and other educators as a college student. All these influences are still there. But other teachers came along in those early years of teaching writing and then reading in daily workshops and they become part of my "mothers and fathers." The strands of their influence are woven throughout the pages of this book. There are many of these individuals, but four of my earliest teachers stand out. In the order in which I met them they are: Donald Graves, Mary Ellen Giacobbe, Glenda Bissex, and Janet Emig.

Graves' research is as valid today as when he finished it. His belief in teachers encouraged me as it has countless others. He spoke at a nearby university in the spring of the year I describe at the beginning of this chapter. Everyone was hungry for information from him; the research he spoke of was such a breakthrough and so refreshing. In a breakout session I remember asking about the role of phonics in this approach and without hesitation he answered that phonics played an important role in children writing and then went on to talk briefly about how young children continually used phonetic sounds as they wrote. Whew! A sigh of relief. Phonics was too important in the school district to abandon it. On another occasion I referred to him as the "expert." He shook his finger at me and said, "You're the expert! Don't forget it." Graves has always been an advocate for teachers, espousing the expertise of classroom teachers over that of researchers and others outside the classroom. His book, *The Energy to Teach*, is another example of that commitment.

When I went to New England to study at Northeastern University about this new approach to teaching writing, Mary Ellen Giacobbe was my teacher. In our summer institute, she thoughtfully connected research to classroom practice and invited each teacher to develop his or her own writing workshops. She never provided a prescription, yet she advocated specific suggestions such as:

- Respond to the writer not the writing.
- Be careful with general praise and with praising too much.
- Build on what writers have accomplished rather than on what they haven't done.
- Look for growth over time.

All commonsense ideas, yet I found them helpful reminders whenever I was tempted to revert to archaic teaching formulas. In that summer institute I found validation of the ways I'd worked with writing in my classroom so far and inspiration to continue. Mary Ellen's expertise and insights into classroom practice and children echo throughout my teaching today.

In the summers following the Giacobbe institute I returned to New England and participated in "teacher research" (a whole new concept to me) led by Glenda Bissex. The experience of that year showed me how to closely observe and document what I saw children doing in my own classroom. In *GYNS AT WRK* (1980), Bissex documented her own son's early reading and writing. The book provided a model of close observation and helped me understand the nature of children's writing and the importance of letting children show us what they know and can do before we proceed in the classroom. I remember well one particular line from that book: "the logic by which we teach is not always the logic by which children learn" (199). This cautionary statement caused me to examine my teaching practices in relationship to children, eliminate clutter, and work toward becoming reflective about my practice. And, perhaps most powerful of all, Glenda provided an outstanding model of a teacher who listens and responds.

When I read Janet Emig's *The Web of Meaning* (1983), I discovered profound essays that opened my mind to thinking differently about teaching and learning. When I met her in 1987 at the English Coalition Conference, I soon learned that she believed in children, teachers, and the principles of a democratic society, especially for schools. Like the others above, both her work and her values influenced the teacher I was becoming. I certainly don't mean this brief listing to be exclusive, for there are many others. But through their work and their encouragement, these four people added significantly to my professional journey.

The first edition of *. . . And with a Light Touch* chronicled that journey. I told my story of moving away from programmed instruction to implementing writing and reading workshops, the stories of children learning in those workshops, and my own process of becoming a learner in my classroom. The writing helped me recognize how my teaching practices were rooted in my personal history and my best teaching was always grounded in observing and responding to individual children. Now, the second edition of *. . . And with a Light Touch* retains that story but updates it. In this edition, in addition to including ways I've fine-tuned reading and writing instruction, I share new stories from the classrooms I've been in, including some about kindergarten classrooms in a new chapter. While the context of these stories is still early childhood classrooms, I can safely say that the underlying principles are appropriate for other grades—even for working with adults.

That first year with writing and reading workshops, I explored, made mistakes, and learned. I believe that the trust I felt from administrators filtered through to the children. I continually revised and clarified my thinking based on observations and reflections. The year was one of the best teaching experiences I have ever had. Why? I've reflected on this question and always come up with the same answer. I had only a few basic preconceptions in my mind about *how* this writing and reading process classroom would operate: the children led the way. I listened, observed, and let them direct me in what and how to teach them next.

When I first began, I anticipated learning a methodology, a set of practices, a new teaching program. Rather than providing a prescriptive path, my teachers extended an invitation to claim my professionalism, to teach in the finest sense of the word. At first, I felt compelled to articulate my teaching and the children's learning through educational jargon and as a precise plan of action. (I found it easy to slip into my own orthodoxies.) After all, fellow educators understood the language of curriculum and the scope and sequence of programs, and these terms provided assurance for the big word looming on the horizon: accountability. Besides, there is a sense of security in knowing exactly what to teach and when and how. But, I don't believe that such teaching assures that every child will succeed. I will always remember George and the butterflies. For me, accountability is being responsible to children. *. . . And with a Light Touch* is grounded in this belief.

CHAPTER 2

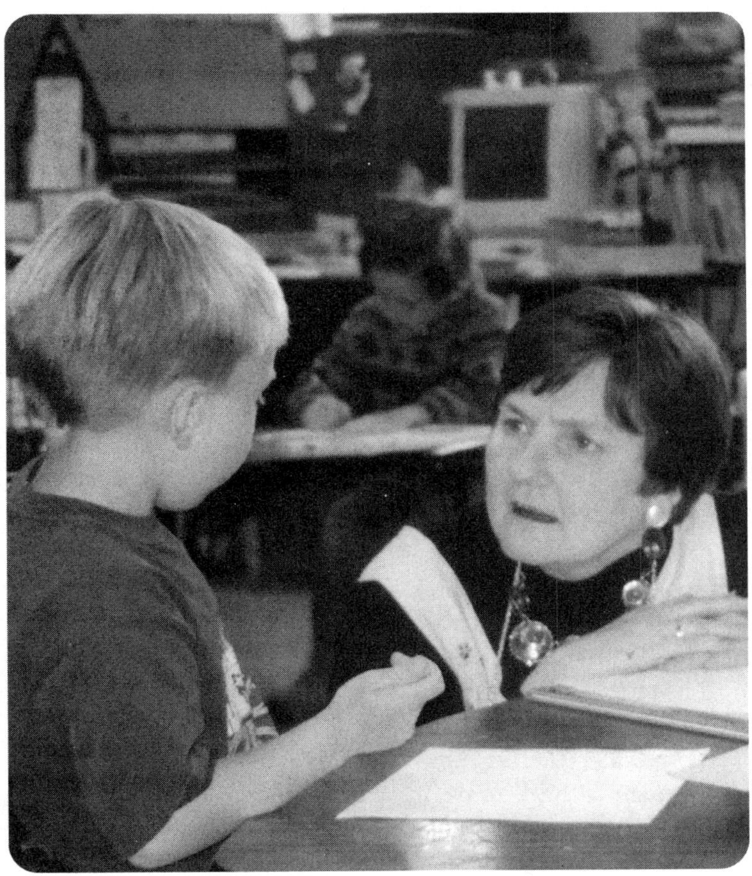

The First Day of School

For several years I worked with writing and reading workshops, honing my teaching practice. Then came a day when events in the classroom forced me to confront a basic reality of teaching: maintaining the dynamic energy inherent in the teaching-learning process results not from refined teaching agendas, carefully constructed curriculum, or fine programs and materials. Instead, effective teaching is based on continuous decision making by a professional in response to the current context of the classroom. Thoughtful decisions are well informed through experience and knowledge, but they are made in response to individual children in particular settings at given moments in time. Such decision making is rarely clear but, rather, infused with tension because we are working with human beings who are as diverse as they are similar. Establishing my own set of routines became my trap. But I'm getting ahead of my story.

On a warm September morning, the first day of school, I arrive at school early, carrying the student name tags I have made and a new children's book, *Cookie's Week*. The room doesn't *need* another book to begin the year, but I do. No matter how many September "first days" I go through, I am still anxious as school begins, aware that my anxiety is matched by the apprehension the children feel. So my trip to the children's section of a local bookstore over the Labor Day weekend became a means of quelling some of the jitters. Sharing a good book with children on the first day of school always relieves some of the tension inherent in a new group coming together.

I chose *Cookie's Week* because of the brief but captivating story line of a mischievous cat and her antics on each successive day of the week. I know the children will enjoy the humor on each page as Cookie knocks over flowerpots and falls in the toilet. The line on the final page—"Tomorrow is Sunday. Maybe Cookie will rest."—brings a satisfying conclusion. The repetitious pattern of the story, the large print, the small size of the book, all make it appealing for beginning readers. And the delightful pictures are by Tomie dePaola, one of my favorite illustrator/authors of children's books.

All these attributes will contribute to the children's involvement with this book. There is one more: I like it. I'm eager to read it to this new group of children, eager for them to like it too. The book represents a kind of connector, a material object that releases an intangible energy flow when we open the pages, read, and begin our year together.

Unlocking the classroom door, I enter and head for the windows to let in morning coolness to replace the stuffy air that has built up over a hot weekend. I begin laying out name tags on the front table. But all the while my mind is going over the plan for the day. On this first morning of this new year, I will begin establishing procedures for writing and reading workshops and for literature time. I've done this many times now and even wrote the story of one such first day for a chapter in *Stories to Grow On*. The procedures have worked well for me: literature time, writing workshop, reading workshop—three important components of my classroom. I want to be sure to get each one off to a good start today.

The children will come in shy and hesitant, as first graders always do, but as we begin the day on the carpet in a corner of the classroom, they will begin to relax. We'll chat informally and introduce ourselves; then I'll talk about some of the things we'll do this year. Surely, this is how it will go. I recall another group of children on another first day, and for a few moments I relive that time.

"Every day we will sit here and listen to stories," I say. Twenty-four faces light up. "Sometimes I'll read and sometimes you'll read. And we'll talk about what we read—what we feel or what the stories make us think about. But we'll do it every day."

As I open Marcia Brown's illustrated version of *The Three Billy Goats Gruff* (Asbjornsen and Moe 1957) some children say, "Oh, I know that story!" "It's a good one!" I read through the book, tapping my knuckles on the bench as the billy goats trip-trap across the bridge, and several children begin to tap the bookcase and the floor along with me. When I finish they cry, "Read it again." I read again and this time some chime in with the trip-traps and the ugly troll's roar, "Who's that tripping over my bridge?" I notice that Johnson, a Chinese boy who speaks only a few words of English, watches the other children as well as the pictures in the book and taps his knuckles with them. Upon hearing the troll's roar, he giggles in delight.

When I close the book, Dustin says, "I like that troll. He's funny!"

"Do you all think he's funny?" I ask.

"No!" says Meghan. "I think he's scary."

"He's like a monster," says Randy.

"The big billy goat wasn't scared of the troll and the little one tricked him. I liked that he tricked him," says Oliver.

The children relax and drop their initial reserve about coming to first grade. They are pleasant, cooperative. Most raise their hands before they speak. As the talk about the story continues, some children participate by voicing their ideas while others listen and display their interest through nods, smiles, and giggles. The responses of the children grow from literal comprehension of the text and also from personal experiences. As they talk, each child's comments prompt further ideas in other children. Their ideas differ, but by sharing they expand their understandings of the story and make new connections. They learn together.

After a few minutes I introduce Eric Carle's *The Very Hungry Caterpillar* by asking the children what they know about caterpillars. Most understand the metamorphosis of caterpillars to butterflies, and many report catching caterpillars in jars or cans. We talk briefly about the role of an author in creating a book. I introduce Eric Carle as the author of this book and then we read.

The children enjoy the repetitious language and the food the caterpillar devours. Cries of "Yum!" come from many as the story unfolds. They do not relate to the caterpillar feeling better after eating one nice green leaf, but are still enthralled with all the tasty, rich foods he consumed earlier. My typical adult response to the caterpillar's overindulgence is, I realize, not the children's view of the story. Another day I will tell them my response, but not now. Sharing my ideas too early could stifle some of theirs and be interpreted as the "right" answer. I want them to understand that there is no one correct reading of a text, that we all bring our own ideas and experiences to a piece of literature.

Before putting this book aside we look again at the illustrations, noting the holes in the pages that indicate where the caterpillar ate and talking about the varying page sizes. Why did Mr. Carle make the book this way? The children think, speculate, and share a variety of ideas—all affirmed.

I conclude the literature time by reading a few nursery rhymes. We come back to this rug and read and talk together two more times before the first day is through. We reread *The Very Hungry Caterpillar*, dramatize *The Three Billy Goats Gruff* with stick puppets, and discover several new books. The children carry home caterpillars they make from half an egg carton. (The caterpillar art project has been a successful first-day activity in my classroom for several years.)

Later on this first morning we begin our writing workshop. In order to respond individually to each child during the initial writing activity, I work with small groups of children rather than the entire class. I select five or six of the class to meet with me at a round table. The others will color a fall picture on a ditto—one of the few I will use throughout the year—at their seats. The picture requires little thought; I want them to eavesdrop on the conversations of the group at the table so that they will begin to think about what they will do when their turn comes.

I ask the children at the table to draw a picture of something they like or something important to them. The children open their crayon boxes. Danny spills the contents of his box on the table, looks through the colors, and selects a blue crayon. He swings the bright color across the bottom of this paper and a jagged line appears.

"Tell me about this, Danny," I say.

"Oh, this is the bay," he replies.

"The bay?" I ask.

"Yeah, the Chesapeake. The Chesapeake Bay. You know."

"Right, I know. The Chesapeake Bay. You've been there?"

"Well, that's where we keep our boat and that's where we go boating and crabbing and stuff."

"You keep your boat at the Chesapeake and go boating and crabbing. Well, how do you go crabbing? I mean, I love crabs but I don't know anything about crabbing."

Danny turns away from his picture to look at me. "Didn't you ever catch a crab before?" he asks.

"Never. How do you catch them?"

"Well, you can do it two ways." Danny's voice takes on an authoritative tone and he puts up one finger as he begins to explain. "One way is to just use a string and chicken neck from the side of the dock." A second finger goes up. "And the other way is with a trap. When my dad and I go crabbing, we use a trap."

"Thank you, Danny," I say and, noticing he has begun drawing again, I move on.

Across the table Trevor is drawing a dinosaur picture. I move around and stoop down beside him. "What's this about?"

"Dinosaurs," he replies. His lips purse and he presses hard with the crayon.

"Dinosaurs?"

"Yeah, dinosaurs. I know a lot about dinosaurs. I like to read about dinosaurs." I nod. Before I can respond further, Trevor returns to his paper and continues drawing.

Jan has been sitting watching and listening. Her paper remains blank. "I don't know nothing to draw," she says as I approach her.

"Nothing? You know nothing?" I respond with mock amazement that brings a grin from Jan.

"Well, I do. But I just can't think," she replies.

"I see. Well, maybe you can think of something you really like, something you did that you'd like to do again?" I nudge.

For a moment Jan is pensive. "I like that caterpillar book you read us," she says. I wait. We exchange smiles and then Jan picks up a red crayon and turns to her paper.

I continue listening and responding to the children at the table. Each time I come near Danny he is eager to tell me more about his activities on the Chesapeake. "Danny," I say after he finishes telling about the importance of running the motorboat through the channel, "You really know a lot about crabbing and boating and channels. I wonder, could you write some of those things here on the paper with your picture?"

Danny shakes his head. "I can't spell," he says.

"That's okay," I tell him. "Writers don't always spell correctly when they start to write. They fix it later. All you have to do is say the words you want to write slowly, listen for the letters, and write what you hear." With this assurance Danny is willing to try.

After the children finish this initial writing, each chooses a journal and learns where to store it in the class file. I explain to them that we will write every day in this journal. We discuss what to do with the first pieces of writing the children have just completed and decide to put them on the bulletin board. We block off a section for each child's writing.

Before we go to lunch on this first day of school, I ask the children to choose two books from those in the room and place them on their desks. When we come back from lunch I conduct my first mini-lesson for reading workshop.

"People read in lots of ways," I tell the class. "I'm going to show you some of the ways they read." I again pick up *The Three Billy Goats Gruff*. "Sometimes people read aloud like we did this morning when we read this book. They read all the words and use lots of expression. Sometimes they read silently like this, saying the words in their heads to themselves." I demonstrate reading silently. "Sometimes people read by looking at the pictures and telling the story by what they see happening in the pictures." I begin to go through *The Three Billy Goats Gruff*, talking about each picture, describing what I see in detail, constructing a story and forming questions about possible developments. "Often when people finish a book they go back and look through it again. Sometimes they read the book again. Good readers think about what they've read—what it was about, what it means to them, why they like it or don't like it."

The mini-lesson has taken only a few minutes. I explain to the children that this is our reading workshop and now they will read the books they have chosen just as I have shown them with *The Three Billy Goats Gruff*. As they eagerly open their books I begin to circulate among them.

I stoop down to Julie's desk and notice that she is pointing to the book title and making the sound of the first letter, *s*. "What is your book about?" I ask.

"I don't know," she replies shyly. She points to a small black fish. "I didn't open it yet, but I think it's about a fish because there's this black fish on the cover. Only, I know fish begins with *f* and this word starts with *s*."

"I think you're right. Julie, the title of this book is the name of that fish." Julie moves her finger under the word "Swimmy." "I bet you know the sounds *s* and *w* make."

Together, Julie and I make the consonant sounds and blend them together. "Swim?" Julie suddenly says.

"Pretty close! It's Swimmy!" Julie smiles, opens the book, and I move across the room to Matthew's desk.

"Tell me about your book?" I ask. The book is closed and Matthew is gazing around the room. Matthew looks at me for a moment. "I don't know," he says. I find the first page and ask Matthew what he sees. "A bear."

"Could the book be about that bear?"

"Yeah," he replies as he looks at me and smiles. I suggest to Matthew that he look at the book's pictures to see what happens to the bear. As he turns to the book, I move on.

When I come to Laura she tells me, "I know this word and this word, and these words but I don't know this word in the middle. 'Oh, a . . . we will go.'"

"This book's a song! Maybe you've heard it. Let's read together." I point to the words as we read "Oh a . . ." I make the sound of the letter *h*, pause, and continue, "we will go." Laura's eyes go to the picture on the page, back to the text, and then she reads "'Oh a-hunting we will go!' I got it now!" She goes back to the book. I move on.

The reading workshop continues this way for ten or fifteen minutes. When I sense the children becoming restless, I know it is time to end for now. To conclude the session I ask several children to tell the group about their books.

"I read the *Hungry Caterpillar* book," says Dustin, holding it high in the air. I am pleased that Dustin announces he has *read* the book. When I stopped at his desk he was retelling the story, his voice rising and falling with inflection, although not reading with word-by-word accuracy. What is important at this time is that Dustin sees himself as a reader and strives to form meaning from the text using a variety of resources: recall of the read aloud, clues from initial consonants, illustrations, and his own sense of story.

Now, as I come out of my reverie on this morning of another first day of school, I am ready to start another year. My procedures for the first day have worked well for several years. Each year there are differences because of the differences in children, but I have been able to adapt the same basic plan as each day unfolded. I am unsuspecting of the arduous day ahead of me.

The Children Arrive

Twenty-four exuberant children bound through the doorway in a matter of minutes. I feel their energy level as they grab their name tags and zip away for a look around the room. I hear their loud voices as they greet friends and examine books. "I had it first!" comes a shout. I see two children tugging at a book, but my attention is diverted by a parent at the door to meet me. After a brief conversation the parent leaves. I look back to where the tussle occurred a moment before only to see the book lying open, facedown on the floor. Two boys have found the blocks and are rapidly throwing them from the box to a heap on the floor. Another parent arrives, introduces herself, then adds, "I can see you've got your hands full. We'll chat another time." The blocks clack and the boys' voices turn to shouts as several more children join them. I move across the room to intervene.

"How's come?" they protest. "We want to *play*!" I maintain a calm and firm voice as I direct them to put the blocks away for now but I find myself wondering, "Whatever happened to those shy first graders?"

Somehow I get all the children in their seats and we proceed through the opening of the school day, including introducing ourselves and chatting together briefly. *Briefly* is all I can manage. The children all talk at once and no one listens to anything being said. We move to the story rug in the back of the room to start our first literature time. Getting everyone settled on the rug takes longer than usual, but finally we are ready to begin. I hold up *The Three Billy Goats Gruff.*

I open my mouth to speak and hear a loud voice, "I know that book. I have that. . . ." But before the sentence is finished another voice shouts, "My kindergarten teacher read that to us in my old school." As my eyes turn from the book to the children, I notice that a child who was sitting at my right is now on my left. In fact, several children have changed places on the rug.

"Stop it!" someone shouts. "He pinched me."

I go over the procedures for sitting on the rug, which I established only minutes earlier. There's a moment of quiet. I quickly open the book. As the children begin listening to the familiar story they respond with initial surprise then giggles at my deep voice rendition of the troll's "Who's that tripping over my bridge?" and join in with the repetitious "trip, trap" of the billy goats crossing the bridge. Their voices are loud and after each segment of the story I find it hard to pull them back to attending to the text with me.

"Read it again!" several of them cry when I finish. But I look at the clock and see that gym class begins in a couple of minutes. We line up—another complicated procedure—and hurry up the hall to meet the new physical education teacher.

Literature time resumes again on the rug after gym, math, and recess. In addition to *Cookie's Week* and *The Very Hungry Caterpillar*, I have chosen *Papa, please get the moon for me*, also by Eric Carle. *The Very Hungry Caterpillar* will be familiar to most of the children from nursery school and kindergarten. Carle's moon book is relatively new and I don't expect the class to be familiar with it. I've read it to several groups of children in the last year and found it to be a hit.

I read *The Very Hungry Caterpillar*. "What were you thinking when you heard this story?" I ask.

Elizabeth raises her hand. "Nature," she says when I call on her.

"Nature? Tell me more about what you mean by nature," I say as I think, "Where is this nature idea coming from? Kids don't talk about books with words like *nature*. Sounds like a prescriptive answer that a child *thinks* a teacher wants."

"I don't know," Elizabeth replies. "Just nature." Her voice carries a hint of baby talk that doesn't match her height and mature appearance.

"Okay. Any other ideas?" I ask. Two more children give me the "nature" response but neither can define the term. "Did you think of anything else with this story?" I ask.

"It made me think I'm hungry," says Ryan.

"Yeah, when's lunchtime?" pipes up another voice.

"Me too. I'm hungry." A clamor of voices takes over in anticipation of lunch. I capture the group's attention again by suggesting we look at Eric

Carle's pictures of the caterpillar's daily meals. The children are most interested in the conglomeration of sweets and rich foods consumed by the little creature on the final day before he makes his cocoon. In loud voices they all begin chattering about food, and it takes effort and time to draw them to the reading of the second book.

Papa, please get the moon for me has fold-out pages of the "very long ladder," of Papa climbing "higher and higher," and of the full moon. When we reach that page Brian says, "It looks like the moon's smiling."

"But I don't think he could really get up to the moon," says Greg.

"Yes he could," replies Brian. "If he had a long enough ladder he could." For a couple of minutes the children speculate about going to the moon on a ladder. Their ideas are good, but I'm bothered by the challenging, almost argumentative tone of their voices.

"What other ideas do you have about the story?" I ask, striving to put a gentle, wondering tone to my voice as a model for the children.

"Space," Jody says.

"Tell me about space," I say.

"You know, rockets and stuff."

"Oh, you like rockets and stuff," I respond.

"Yeah."

"Like what?" I ask.

"I don't know. I just like 'em."

While this conversation is going on, the attention of several of the children has drifted off. They unzip and zip again and again the velcro on their sneakers. They carry on conversations in twos or threes. They play with the long hair of one of the girls. One child has left the rug and wanders around the room. I decide to read *Cookie's Week* later in the day. We sing a couple of action songs, which serves to pull the children back together, and they return to their desks.

I begin my procedures for writing workshop. Individual boxes of crayons have not arrived and I was able to round up only six boxes, each with eight thick crayons—the kind toddlers use. I distribute coloring papers as I have done in past years, give directions, and group the children by fours to share each box of crayons. Then I call five children up to the round table in the front of the room. I have one box of twenty-four colors that I spill on the center table.

"How's come they get to go up there?" calls out a shrill little voice.

"How's come they get them crayons and we got only these?" protests another voice. Though I've already said so, I again assure the group that everyone will get a turn at the table and explain that our crayons haven't arrived.

When I ask the children at the table to draw a picture of something they like or know about, my request is met with blank stares.

"Whatjamean?" asks Laura.

"Well, like I might draw a picture of my cats because they are so much fun and I really could tell a lot about them. They play chasing games and get mad at each other and then they make up. Or, I might decide to write about trying to get in the cold ocean on my vacation in Maine." I am not comfortable providing such a precise model because I know the children will be likely to produce several cat stories and beach pictures.

Laura looks at me for a minute more but finally picks up a crayon and draws a large circle. "I'm gonna draw my cat," she says. She adds two triangles to the top of the circle for ears. "I knew it!" I think to myself.

"Mrs. Avery, what're we suppose to do?" asks a child in the large group. Many of the children at their desks are puzzled by the coloring worksheet. Only a few have begun to color the squirrels on the paper. Sharing the large crayons, the coloring process, the worksheet—all this baffles them. I go over the instruction again, then turn back to the table.

Laura adds a body to her cat. Monica draws a cat's face. Cory stands crayons on end in a curving line, domino fashion. Evan draws bands of color diagonally across his paper. Matt has now joined Cory making the crayon line.

"What will you draw?" I ask Cory and Matt.

Cory shrugs and Matt replies, "I don't know."

"What do you like to do? What's fun for you?" I ask.

"I play soccer," Matt answers.

"Oh yeah? Can you draw that on your paper?" I nudge.

"Ummm, maybe." I can see that Matt is not committed to this drawing, but he picks up a crayon and begins. I turn to Cory and try to start him in a similar manner, but Cory is still more interested in playing with the crayons. He grins at me for only a brief instant then continues standing those crayons on end. I feel my frustration building.

"I'm done," Laura announces. She has drawn a brown animal resembling a cat. I ask Laura if she can write about her picture. She hesitates for a moment but then slowly, deliberately writes IGNCAT above the drawing. Monica responds more easily to my suggestion to write, though she is concerned about spelling. When I turn back to Laura I notice she has erased CAT and written HRD in its place. "I changed my mind," she explains and then reads "I drew my hamster." Monica writes: I LOKe to PAey WiS BONES (I like to play with Bones). The girls go back to their seats.

Meanwhile, the occasional quiet chatter among the other children is now a crescendo that interferes with the conversation at the table. The children at their desks are not tuned in to what is going on at the large table, which is the whole purpose of the coloring activity in the first place. Several children have left their seats and are wandering around the room while the paper remains unfinished on their desks. I stop everything, redirect the children, and bring two more individuals up to the table.

Through my strong nudges (more like pushes, or even demands by now) eight children, one-third of the class, write at the center table this first day. With three days to this first week of school I'm right on schedule—each child will go through the initial writing experience during the first week. Lunchtime finally arrives.

Of course lunch runs overtime this first day of school and the children come back to the room fifteen minutes later than scheduled. Several of the boys have caught butterflies on the playground during recess and now each one races to be the first to present one of them to me. Looking down into the cupped little hands I see a pair of mangled wings and a slightly quivering body, the last seconds of life for the yellow-winged creature.

"See. A butterfly, like that book you read us. You know, about that caterpillar that ate all that stuff." Cory beams up at me as he speaks. In all, six or seven butterflies have become sacrificial responses to my reading of *The Very Hungry Caterpillar*. We put the butterflies on a sheet of construction paper on the back counter.

"Do we go home now?" someone asks. Before I can answer, the playground aide comes in to tell me that there was a lot of chasing and rough play at recess and one of my children is in the health room with a skinned knee. I talk to the class about behavior on the playground. I've planned this time after lunch for reading workshop, but we must be in music soon and the music room is upstairs at the other end of the building. So I lead the group in a couple of finger plays and then we begin the process of lining up to go to music.

When the group returns from music class we gather on the story rug again. I begin to reread *The Three Billy Goats Gruff* but never finish for the intercom comes on early with announcements for this first day of school. *The Three Billy Goats Gruff* joins an unread *Cookie's Week* on the counter, and we prepare to go home. Dismissal is hectic, but in a matter of minutes everyone is out the door and onto buses or walking the neighborhood sidewalks to their homes.

The day is over. I am exhausted, frustrated, disappointed. I wonder what the children took with them from this day. We didn't make caterpillars from egg cartons, draw self-portraits, read poems, or sing more than two songs. In fact, I feel as if I spent most of my day either getting the children ready to go someplace, settling squabbles among them, or stating and restating my expectations and directions. There was no reading workshop, and writing workshop was definitely *not* a positive experience for anyone! Throughout the day the children did not appear to listen to each other or to me. In fact, each child seemed to move and talk in the classroom as if he or she were the only individual there. The class behaved more like a group of three-year-olds coming to nursery school for the first time than a group of six-year-olds with some prior experience of working and playing in a group. I look at the crumpled butterflies on the construction paper and think about tomorrow and the months ahead.

Day 2

The second day is better—but not much. Crayons arrive and I start the writing workshop over (hoping everyone forgets the day before). This time I abandon the small-group procedure at the table and conduct the workshop with the entire group. Though I don't get to see every one of the children to provide individual responses as they work (there are simply too many children and too little time), I do get around to most of them, and my circulating among the students at their desks keeps everyone writing—somewhat. Though I'm not comfortable with my role of policewoman or taskmaster, I begin to recognize that for a while it will be necessary.

Since listening to stories had been the only strength of the first day, I integrate more read-aloud times. *Make Way for Ducklings* holds everyone's attention and becomes destined to be an all-time favorite for the year. I introduce the first reading workshop after rereading *The Three Billy Goats Gruff* and then demonstrating how one could tell this story by looking at the pictures. I show the class several other books that we can "read" this way. I ask who would like to read this book, and when the hands fly up, I begin distributing books to the children. When each one has a book I send the children to their seats to look through their books and read them. Although the reading time at student desks lasts only a few minutes, it is a beginning.

The children still clamor to be the first in line. At recess they fight over the playground balls and chase each other. They chatter continuously and interrupt each other all day long. And at the end of the day there are several more dead butterflies on the sheet of construction paper.

Reflections

Why did this school year get off to such a poor start? I spent months sorting through the reasons.

Schedule and Materials

Part of the hectic nature of the first day of school was the schedule. In addition to recess and lunch, the day was broken up with physical education and music classes. Sending the children off to a physical education class within the first hour of school certainly was unwise. The children and I needed that time together in the classroom. I should have canceled the class.

Trying to start a writing workshop with first graders without crayons is like trying to teach reading without books. You don't need a lot of materials to set up a writing workshop, but paper and crayons (or some other tool for drawing) are basic. For young children, making marks with color is important. To expect four children to share eight fat crayons and then pay attention to the interaction I led with their peers was naive on my part. I would have done better to have dug out the old colored pencil sets and sharpened them so that each child had a set of tools. But I didn't think of it—I had my own agenda in mind.

The Children's Backgrounds

Although not immediately apparent, as the weeks passed I realized the significance of the children's backgrounds in influencing the classroom dynamics. I have witnessed many changes in the children entering first grade through the years. Most teachers agree that changes in society, the family, and technology affect classroom life. This was certainly true of this group of children as I'll discuss in the next chapter.

Expectations and Orthodoxies

The beginning of each school year is always a time of come-down-to-earth reality. We carry in our heads images of the youngsters who left our classrooms a little over two months earlier. We think of that community and what those children could do individually and as a group. We forget the September days when that class first came together. Compounding this phenomenon for me was the fact that I was returning to the classroom after a year's sabbatical. Not only did I have more distance from the reality of day-to-day classroom life, but I also had spent much time writing and speaking about the accomplishments of my former first graders. I had formed expectations for these new students when I really needed to be open to seeing and listening and learning from them.

The beginning of writing workshop in my classroom had gone smoothly for several years. The success created an orthodoxy for me and I lost sight of the fact that it was not particular *procedures* that enabled the children's movement into writing so much as it was my own *observations* and then my *responsiveness* to them individually and as a group. I was in too much of a hurry on this first day of school and did not allow for waiting and observing. For a while I forgot that I, too, was a learner in this classroom who needs to keep growing. I neglected to be a reflective practitioner.

The lesson learned is that I can write no blueprint for teaching or learning that will be successful for every class of students. The dynamic learning I had experienced with the children in past years occurred because we worked in an *unprogrammed* manner. As architect of a new classroom community each year, I must always revise my plans and procedures in response to the students before me. I cannot force students into *my* mold of how the classroom will be run, but rather we must negotiate together.

Although I adhered to this belief in the past, I did not understand it as completely and profoundly as I do now. My role as a teacher is identified in my students. I ask students how and why they do things as they work in the classroom. I listen to what they tell me and observe not only the results of their labors but the processes they engage in as they read and write and talk together. As I listen and observe in the classroom I continually formulate my own theories concerning the learning processes of each of my students and our interaction together as a group. I plan instructional strategies based on my theories. And I test and revise those theories as children grow and change. The children are theory makers, too. Theory making, I believe, is a basic way we all learn.

"Theory into practice" is a much touted phrase in educational circles. Often this phrase is interpreted to teachers or by teachers themselves as meaning theory—the "best" or "right" notions about teaching and learning as professed by researchers or experts—is to be applied by classroom teachers, thus producing the "best" or "right" practices. I once believed this myself. When I removed programmed instruction from my classroom I began seeing—really seeing—children learning and I began *thinking* about my teaching. I realized that the children taught me and I learned from them just as much as it was the other way around. Practice changed in response to children. The work of outside theorists certainly informs my teaching. However, I came to believe that rather than theory *applied* to practice by classroom teachers, the theory of educational researchers *is transformed* into practice within the classroom setting and results in *new* theory—that of the classroom teacher.

This book shares my experiences and my evolving beliefs (my theories) about reading and writing and learning. It is never meant to be a prescriptive formula for no formula will work for everyone—or anyone. However, I think we teachers learn by glimpsing the experiences of other teachers. We see and then make adaptations to our particular contexts. *. . . And with a Light Touch* contains stories of children and me learning together, teaching each other.

The year that began so disastrously did come together, and stories from that particular group of children appear throughout this book. The next chapter relates stories of that group as we worked to form a community. It is the presence of community that influences—perhaps more than any other single factor—the effective functioning of this learner-centered classroom.

ENVIRONMENT AND TONE

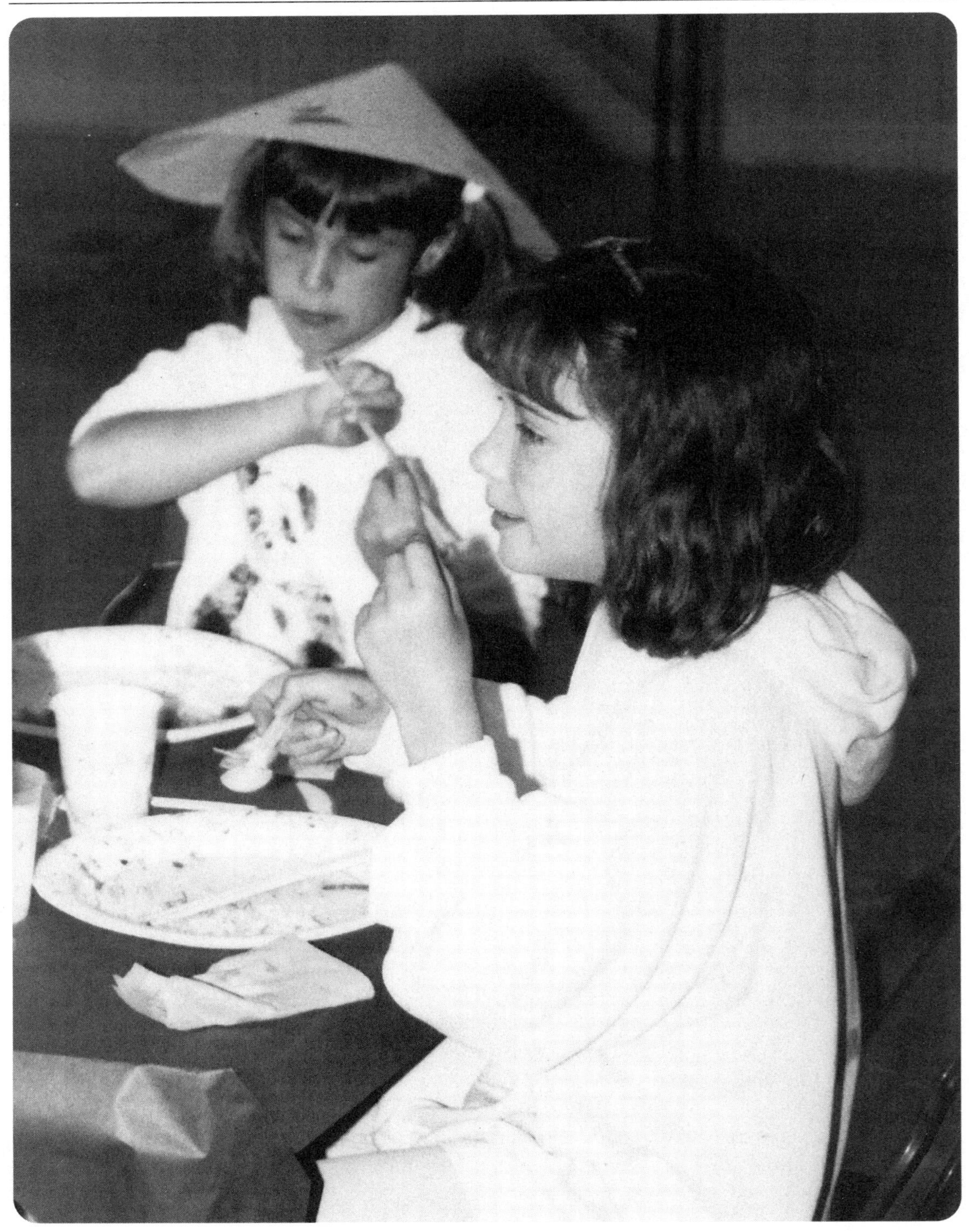

CHAPTER 3

Classroom Climate

A Foundation for Learning

Every teacher knows that the climate of the classroom is a critical element in children's learning and that classroom tone is set during the first days and weeks of school. I've learned that the entire tone of the year can be determined by the care, time, and effort I invest at the beginning. In part, this means establishing the structure, guidelines, and boundaries for all that we do. But there's more. There's an intangible aspect that includes the way we talk to each other, make decisions, and work and play together. And it is *we*, because although I am the one ultimately in charge, a significant aspect of creating the climate in my classroom is encouraging the children's voices, respecting and incorporating their ideas. I've learned that often children don't expect to be taken seriously, but when I do include the children in implementing, planning, and reflecting, they respond by becoming responsible and more thoughtful. This takes time, but it's well worth it.

Before school begins, I give considerable thought to organization and procedures, but when school starts, I adapt. I go slowly, listen and observe the ways the children learn and interact, and negotiate. I convey directions and expectations in a clear, concise, and calm tone and address problems in the same manner. We take time to get to know each other and accept our strengths, weaknesses, and differences. It's all about establishing mutual *respect*. The following stories and reflections come from the process of one classroom coming together as a community.

The Children

Laura cries as she wanders through our empty wing during lunchtime in this first week of school. At my desk, I hear her weeping and hurry to find out what has happened. She flings her arms around my hips, buries her face in my skirt, and sobs. The words heave out in desperate gasps when she finally speaks.

"I . . . can't . . . find . . . my class."

I lead her to the playground door where, spying the other children, she turns a quick smile to me and hurries off to play. She brushes the last tear from her cheek as she calls to a classmate.

Later I learn that Laura's trauma grew from a typical six-year-old's misunderstanding. Rain canceled our morning recess, but skies cleared by lunchtime and, after eating, the children went out to the playground as usual. But Laura remembered that I had said, "We can't go out to recess today because of the rain."

Being a child in school isn't easy—especially in September. There are places to be, teachers and other kids to meet, and so many new things to figure out and remember. Learning the ropes in a new situation is difficult. The episode with Laura is typical of the first days of school. First graders tug at your clothes or poke you incessantly with their fingertips, call you "Teacher, Teacher," or "Mom" and "Mommy" (and then blush with embarrassment), and sometimes "Hey!" or "Hey, what's your name? I forgot."

At 9:30 they want to know when it's lunchtime and by 11:00 they're yawning and asking, "When is it time to go home?"

In the middle of a math lesson they say, "Guess what? We're going to Hershey Park this weekend." or "Do you know my Uncle Bill?" or "My Mom might have a new baby. But it's a secret."

They forget where the bathroom is located, don't know that there are different bathrooms for boys and girls, or forget they *have* to go to the bathroom or don't *know* they have to go to the bathroom until . . . oh, ohhh.

They count on their teacher for everything: supplying tissues (including a reminder that they *need* a tissue), bandaging skinned knees, fixing leaking thermos bottles, braiding hair, finding a sweater that was stuffed inside a bookbag earlier. And they try to be subtle, as did one hungry little boy who, thinking of the snack Mom packed, said, "I think my banana bread must be rotting over there in my lunch box."

First graders can be enchanting and charming, and also puzzling and exhausting. During the first days of school they seem to move in their own little worlds, oblivious to others and unaware that they are part of a group. I watch them, listen to them, and think, "I've got to teach these kids to *read*?"

Every teacher knows teaching has become increasingly difficult because of the changes in children and their life situations. Children are definitely different than they were a generation ago. Even the youngest children in school must cope with stress brought on by changes in a fast-paced world. Many of them come to school withdrawn, angry, or with an "attitude." The most pressing difficulties result from the obvious changes in society and family structures. Technology, especially television and computer games, influences all of the children in varying degrees. The effect of technology seems to be moderated by the amount of parental involvement with the children, but the changes in society and family structures profoundly affect the lives of all children.

In this particular class are children from well-schooled professional families and those whose parents did not complete high school. Some come from wealthy homes and others live on welfare checks. They reside with both parents, a single parent, split their time between the homes of two parents, or live with a substitute parent. They tell stories of substance abuse in their homes, of theft to support these habits, and of good times on family weekends at cabins in the mountains or along the river. Typically, over half the children have moved to the area since their birth. And frequently, a class of twenty-five or so children includes at least one child who has been the victim of child abuse. Frequently, there is at least one child whose first language is Greek or Chinese or Spanish.

A standardized intelligence test administered to this group produces scores that range from 72–145 with five children scoring below 80. I don't give much credence to IQ testing, especially with young children. But I think the scores reflect the diversity among the children and provide an indication of the way each child might function within the traditional expectations of school. In this instance, the children with scores in the very upper end of the range come from homes of advantage. Every one of these children owns books, knows the experience of being read to regularly, and has been well fed and cared for since birth. The parents in these homes talk to their children and involve them in a variety of family activities. Each of the children at the very lowest end of the range comes from unsettled home situations, homes bearing various ills of society: child abuse, substance abuse, unemployment, etc. In several cases the parent or parents are conscientiously committed and involved in reconstructing a shattered family life. In other cases the child is one more problem the struggling parents face. The test does not reveal intelligence so much as it reflects experiences—the higher scores correlating with a student's potential to readily move into and adjust to the school setting.

Among the children in this particular group are:

- a child who tells me he goes home after school, unlocks the door, and watches TV until either the mother or sister come home ("When do they get home?" I asked. "Around 5 o'clock," comes the reply. The child leaves school at 2:30.)
- a child born in a distant part of the country who has never known his father and now lives with his mother and younger sibling
- a child who by court order no longer lives with the parents; the six children in this family are separated in different homes
- a child who recently has been hospitalized for injuries resulting from a parental beating
- a child of up-and-coming professionals; both parents put in long hours and take frequent business trips
- a child representative of the typical first grader of the past—each morning one parent escorts the child to the door of the classroom and says "Good morning" to me; the parent does not linger, but simply makes a connection with this part of the child's life.

Some children, like this last one, come to school from homes that have provided a secure structure in their preschool years. When classroom squabbles arise, this child rarely is involved but seems to rise above such incidents. The child presents a model of a confident, self-assured first grader that is not typical in this group. Children like this one easily move into the routines and structure of the classroom. They have developed self-control and self-awareness that provide them ready access to their talents, enabling them to focus on school activities.

But in contrast, many children coming to school today have spent their early childhoods in confusion, trying to make sense out of an environment that changes daily or even hourly. Adults in their lives spend little time with them. One set of parents told me that their work schedules permitted only one night a week when the entire family was together. Little in life for these children is secure or dependable. They project distrust and are continually on guard and constantly in motion, ready for the next unexpected encounter with the world. They are excitable, tense children. Such is the diversity of our classroom.

During the first days of the school year, the children and I begin to know each other. I listen and try to help them feel comfortable as we work out the procedures for the classroom. We can't hurry; building this community takes time. Years ago I read in *Freedom to Learn* by Carl Rogers (1969) that learners need "unconditional positive regard." My experiences with children confirm this concept. So I try to communicate my unconditional positive regard to every child, and hope in the process to demonstrate this attitude for peer interactions. It's important that every child know he or she is a valued member of this community.

Recalling Shared Experiences

"Remember when Ian got his hair cut and you didn't recognize him?"

"Yeah," says Ian, "I thought you might not let me back in our class 'cause you didn't know who I was."

The twinkle in Ian's eye and the grin on his face tell me he's continuing the playful interchange we had one Monday morning in mid-September when he arrived at school with a new haircut.

"Who's this?" I had gasped. "Do I know you?" In a split second Ian had picked up the playful tone and returned it. "It's Ian. Can't you recognize me?" Then he had switched to a reassuring voice and said, "Don't worry Mrs. Avery, it's Ian. I only got a haircut." And he reached out and patted my shoulder.

We've been in school a month now and this morning during the chatting time that follows the opening exercises, the children and I recall incidents from our first weeks together. As we recall shared experiences, there's a sense that each of us—myself and the individual children—invests a bit more in this classroom community. These stories are our history. Remembering helps us claim that history connects us one to another. Connections will provide a secure base for learning in the classroom. Taking time to talk about our times together contributes to building a sense of community. We are like a family that tells stories at family gatherings, stories that only family members can tell.

"I remember the day when the cat jumped in the window and we kept putting him back outside and he kept jumping in, jumping in. That was *funny*!"

"And when we went on the field trip in the woods to that—what was it called?—Gnome Countryside."

"We got to go on the rope bridge and we pretended we were the billy goats."

"And we built gnome houses out of rocks and little sticks."

"Nathan went with us. I got to be his partner and when we got back to school he read with me."

"Oh, remember how you forgot Nathan's lunch in the 'frigerator? But we all shared our lunches and then he had a *humongous* lunch!"

The children and I chuckle remembering our field trip. My eighteen-year-old son, on school holiday, had accompanied us. I was grateful for the extra adult when I took these "little squirrels" to the woods, and the children liked seeing me in the role of Mom. The day had provided us an important opportunity to engage in activities outside of the school setting.

"But some stuff's not so funny. When Megan's appendix burst that Sunday, that's a *real* important thing, and it wasn't funny," says Elizabeth.

"Yeah, she almost *died*! But she's gonna be back soon—in a couple of weeks. Our cards probably helped her get better quicker."

"I remember another thing not funny: when I said 'Fatty' to someone. I didn't know that wasn't funny, but *now* I know. I remember Mrs. Avery said, 'We will always be kind . . .'" Raymond recites my exact words with my precise inflection, from that morning of the second day of school. While coming in from recess, I had overheard Raymond call a child "Fatty." I had stopped cold, gone over to him, stooped to below his eye level, took his hands in mine, looked him straight in the eye, and said, "In this classroom we will always be kind to each other. That means that we can never call anyone unkind names," in a soft but emphatic tone. Raymond looked at me a moment and the room suddenly was hushed. He nodded gravely and replied, "Okay." We resumed class activity but everyone had heard and knew where I stood on this matter. Now he nods, acknowledging the gravity of that situation. I'm always a little awed when I hear a child repeat words I uttered some time—often a long time—previously. Frequently the words are ones from the first days of school, reminding me of the importance of those first interactions. Raymond also addresses his comments to the group and not just to me—a good sign. I've been working to encourage classroom conversations to be an interchange among the children—student to students, with occasional teacher comments; not a pattern of teacher to student, student to teacher, with *my* talk interjected between each child's comment.

"What do you remember about our school work so far?" I interject now in an attempt to shift the conversation slightly.

"Writing. I really like writing the best." Unanimous agreement on this. I'm not surprised. Every class has embraced writing workshop. If an assembly program intrudes on the schedule, they protest, "You mean we're not going to have *writing*?" I can imagine them responding in a similar manner only if I announced that we were skipping lunch. Why is this writing so important to them? I believe it gives children the opportunity to write about themselves and their interests and to share that self with the rest of the group. It's the element of *choice* (Veatch 1964, 1966; Graves 1983) that is critical to the children's investment in learning. This is true not only of the writing but also of the entire classroom. Giving children choices within a structured framework communicates trust in their capacity to make responsible decisions and become responsible learners. In addition, we learn a lot about each other through the writing, and there's a nonjudgmental acceptance of each individual that emerges when we share the writing and the interest in each person's topic.

"I like math too," a child remarks as the conversation continues.

"I like literature time and all our good stories you read us, like *Red Riding Hood* and *Corduroy* and *Rumpelstiltskin*, and the puppets we made."

"Like our teddy bears. We put them up because they're so neat." The construction-paper bears, now on the bulletin board, were a traditional, teacher-directed art project. However, as we cut and pasted circles together, I learned about the children's prior experiences with art tools. I could see that for some this would be an instructional lesson in using such tools. I was reminded once again of a basic supposition to bring to teaching: *presume nothing*.

The conversation continues as the children look around the room. We see our bulletin board on communities and the list we compiled on characteristics of urban and suburban life. We pause to recall favorite books. We admire the first-day photos of each child that now are mounted in their blocked-off sections of the bulletin board. I am about to conclude this class conversation when a child notices one more thing and we recall one more story.

"There's your monkey poster about mistakes, Mrs. Avery. 'We all make mistakes.' Remember when you took us to gym class, and we all sat ready for the gym teacher, only we were there too early?"

About a week into the school year, when the office buzzed me for the lunch count I hadn't turned in, I had brought out my old poster and talked about error. I want the children to understand that error ("making mistakes" in the language of the children) is a natural part of everyone's day-to-day life. So many children arrive in school believing they must strive for perfection, or that doing well in school means making few (if any) errors. These attitudes hinder children in maintaining the natural risk-taking behaviors that they exercised as learners in their preschool years. I remember Chris' comment when I asked one group of children what important things I should tell teachers in a workshop I was leading on the teaching of writing: "I think the most important thing is that we all make mistakes, and if you don't make mistakes you won't learn."

The Classroom: Learning to Work Together

The first days of the school year—especially with this group—were challenging ones for all of us. The children talked all the time, they clamored for my undivided attention, and, unaccustomed to a full day of school, they tired easily. We needed a relaxed pace and a playful tone to create a healthy classroom climate. The procedures don't all come together at once. In fact, I spent most of my energy in the first few weeks establishing routines and a *tone* that would help build a trusting community.

Writing Sets the Tone

After the frustrating first day of school I decide to start over. I gather all the children on the rug and begin a mini-lesson: instructions for beginning to write.

"Our new crayons have arrived," I say in a hushed tone. "And right now we're going to use them for the first time."

Several children clap their hands together rapidly but quietly and exchange enthusiastic looks. One little boy scowls and another says, "What if you don't *want* to color?"

Turning to this little fellow, I look him in the eye and say, "This year we will do a lot of things together because we are a group, and this is one of those things. You may use your pencil instead of crayons if you wish, but during writing workshop, we all write." I listen to my tone: quiet firmness, I hope. I can't allow the choice of not participating. This is not a do-whatever-you-please environment. Freedom of choice comes within the framework of meeting one's responsibilities within the group. As I finish the child nods and quietly says, "Okay." I'm glad for the opportunity to make this point clear. I expect participation. I expect children to follow group procedures.

"I'll give each of you a piece of paper like this one and a box of crayons. Then you may take them to your desk and draw. What will you draw? Well, that's for you to decide. Maybe you'll want to draw something you really like or something you like to do. What you draw is *your* choice. As you work, I will come around and you can tell me about your drawing when I stop at your desk."

Some children began to stir as soon as I utter the first sentence. By now, a few stand and reach for paper. "Hold it," I say. "There's no hurry. We'll *all* work until the big hand on that clock gets up to the twelve. So take your time and think about what you're doing as you work."

The children take paper and crayons and move to their desks. Their chatter subsides as they began drawing. I keep this first mini-lesson short due to the impulsiveness of many of the children. I've noticed already that as a group they seem in a frenzied hurry—always moving on to the next thing, never quite listening to everything that's said. Getting them to slow down will be a major accomplishment. I wonder how much the children understood from my directions. I'll determine tomorrow's mini-lesson by the way today's workshop goes, but my focus will be on establishing the procedures and tone.

As I move among the children, randomly stooping beside individual desks, I see a diversity of topics and hear a range of stories. I catch my first glimpses of the differences in their approaches to writing, hints of their individual learning styles. Lisa works quietly and spends a lot of time on the drawing of her taking her pet rabbit for a walk. She includes details such as eyelashes, barrettes in her hair, and a leash wrapped around her wrist that connects to the harness on her pet bunny. Natalie looks confused initially, but when she looks at Monica's paper and sees her drawing the beach, she proceeds with her own beach picture. Darren becomes frustrated with his drawing of a bike and converts the entire sketch to a house by drawing over it with black crayon and then drawing another bike, one that pleases him more, below the black house. One child fills the page with erratic scribbles. Another uses every crayon to make a design of sorts. At each desk I ask the child to tell me about their writing and I listen and smile and nod my encouragement.

My goal is to help the children invest in writing. I want them to believe that they can write—put drawings, letters, and words on paper that communicate. I want them to know that I'm interested in that communication. So, I set aside for now any concern for language conventions and listen to their ideas. I don't suggest corrections but rather, encourage expansion of their topics. A successful writing workshop (where children learn *how to write*) depends on the children's investment. My firm but accepting approach plays a major part in establishing the workshop climate.

We end writing workshop by gathering again on the rug. I've asked two writers to share their work. Unlike the literature time earlier, when the children clustered at my feet, this time they sit on the perimeter of the rug so that every child can make eye contact with each member of the group. There are a lot of wiggles during this sharing time, as one would expect from a group of six-year-olds. Yet the interest in their classmates' writing holds their attention and I carefully explain procedures as we proceed (see Chapter 8). This first sharing time was tentative, halting, but in a matter of days, the sharing of writing will become a significant part of building community.

The first full writing workshop was a little ragged, with the children not quite sure what to do, but we work at it each day, revising, refining, polishing. I direct my mini-lessons to procedures and we talk regularly about what goes well and what we need to work on. One day I pull out three rules for workshops (Giacobbe 1982) and ask the group what they think.

1. We work hard.
2. We work on writing or reading.
3. We use soft voices.

The children agree with these rules and we post them in the room.

Daily writing will be central to the classroom routine, the development of a nurturing classroom community, and, ultimately, the growth of each individual. Here, everyone is the most vulnerable and takes the most risks. In writing workshop the children share themselves with the group and receive affirming responses.

Routines Build a Secure Foundation

The routines of the school day begin to fall into place. We hang a calendar, learn how to read and write the date, and incorporate calendar activities into the opening of the school day. We also start Word of the Day (a word-play activity described in Chapter 16), devise a sign-in sheet for recording attendance and lunch count, and develop procedures for sharing within the large group. The opening activities contribute to our sense of community. Each morning we come together again and connect to each other through both the rituals of daily routines and conversational sharing. An important part of this opening is the reading aloud of a children's novel. We begin with *Charlotte's Web*, the first of a dozen or more children's novels I will read to the class this year.

Scheduling reading workshop after lunch works well. The children come in from the playground and are ready to settle down and read. Fifteen-minute blocks of time—even longer—aren't at all unreasonable in September, and soon the class reads for a half hour without any difficulty. As in writing workshop, I move randomly among the individual children and ask them about the books they are reading during this time. Our self-selection, self-paced reading routine forms the foundation for incorporating additional structures in the days ahead such as guided reading groups and listening to individual readers read aloud.

Helping the children focus and be successful is part of my task during the first workshops. I observe and respond to the individual child, helping that child discover a rightful place in the classroom community. For the child having difficulty writing, I encourage and wait; I try new angles to approach the child until I find what works. There's no one formula, but time and the child's capacity to learn are my allies. Helping children work successfully plays a significant part in community building, and taking time to build the structure and convey expectations in the beginning pays off later.

By early October, the children and I are settled into routines that provide the security of a structure we all trust. We've spent the last few weeks getting to know each other and working out a classroom climate that is becoming predictable and organized. The children helped put up the displays of their work on the walls and they've taken over tasks such as lunch count, attendance, and housekeeping chores. When they arrange the books along the chalkrails and the counters, the alignments they devise look somewhat peculiar—sometimes they stack the books in neat piles, sometimes arrange them according to colors on the cover, or line them up in step-fashion according to size. But if I ask for a particular title, any number of children can quickly locate it. Our routines have led to a comfortable and predictable environment.

Teacher Tone Enhances Climate

A month into the year I can truly feel the classroom is "ours," not just "mine." The children's ideas and contributions are everywhere. Among the many items on the back counter are Indian corn, playground rocks with "real gold" in them, a Phillies game program, tiny cars, and an assortment of walnuts, acorns, crumbling dried leaves, and withered dandelions. Even the butterflies from the first day remain. When I look at them now I think of the eagerness of the boys to please me, to present gifts, and win the favor of the ruler of their new kingdom.

The role of ruler does not appeal to me. Certainly I must lead and provide direction (there is someone in charge here!), but I'm not interested in establishing an autocratic reign. If I set up an authoritarian rule where I continually give directions and dole out assignments for students to complete, turn back, and receive my assessment, I will rob students of the right to develop responsibility for their learning. I'd prevent them from making an investment in the classroom community.

In an autocratic, teacher-directed classroom the teacher can become exhausted creating activities to keep children busy. I struggled with that model for years: I designed, the children completed, I graded. I spent more time on their work than they did! I plowed ahead, covering the curriculum with minimal input from students or little regard for their thinking. Children made minimal investment in either the classroom or their learning. I believe such an environment arouses anger in students, or indifference, or cultivates attitudes of "let's figure out what she wants so we can get it done." Such responses come when the teacher holds the controls, limiting or blocking children's natural curiosity and desire to discover more of the world.

I've been the benevolent dictator in the classroom, one loving the children, concerned about their welfare. However, I still held the reins of command, and the model was still one of teacher as authority, as expert pouring knowledge into the receptive vessels of children's minds. Communities developed in these teacher-directed classrooms, but frequently the community was one of children united in waging a "cold war" against authority. From time to time hostilities broke out, and I directed considerable energy into maintaining control—otherwise known as discipline.

Now, I direct my energies toward listening to and observing children, striving to understand their intentions and responding to their efforts to learn (Harste, Woodward, and Burke 1984). I can do this only in a well-structured classroom that invites teacher-student and student-student interactions. I cannot rule as an authority, nor pretend to be a peer, but I can be a sharer of information and a validator of experiences.

Even the way I talk plays a part in setting a tone that invites interactions from students and in building relationships that are the heart of any community. I avoid referring to myself in the third person when I speak—"Mrs. Avery wants . . ." or "Bring the paper to Mrs. Avery." I need to address six-year-olds just as I would any other responsible individual and I believe the artificiality of third person talk serves to remove me from the interaction. I want to speak in ways that communicate respect for children's expertise. I strive to keep the tone of my voice subdued—soft and even, avoiding a shrill or imperative tone. I attempt to convey honest responses in a manner that is neither coaxing nor demanding.

Certainly there are times when I, as the adult in charge, must exert authority. I strive to convey my respect to each child, but I also expect children's respect for me and for each other. When behaviors emerge that are unacceptable for our classroom I address them promptly—perhaps by quietly confronting a child as I did Raymond's name-calling or by using a tone of voice filled with outrageous humor as when I replied to a child's defiant "No!" "What?" I said, "I didn't hear someone say 'no.' Tell me I didn't. No, no, no, I didn't hear 'no' did I?" By this time everyone, including the defiant child is giggling. The tension's broken, the point is made and we move on working a bit better together. Working well together is, after all, fundamental to our year together.

Literature Connects the Community

Our "literature time" is a daily time period when I read aloud several children's books (mostly picture-book format), and we talk about those books and authors and illustrators. By the end of September the children form a repertoire of their favorite titles, ones they ask for again and again. Many of their favorites have repetitious and predictable story lines. The children listen for favorite lines and chime in when I read them. They also enjoy the delicious sense of naughtiness conveyed by the characters and story lines in many of these books.

Ian says, "I like the part in *Red Riding Hood* where the grandma says it was so dark [in the wolf's stomach] that 'I couldn't even read!'" The class agrees and then Jeff adds, "And the part when the wolf says, 'Your delicious—er, *de-*

lightful granddaughter.'" They all like the line from *Rumpelstiltskin*, when the title character stomps his foot and shouts, "The devil told you that!" At recess the children stomp their feet on the playground and say, "The devil told you that!"

The books become common ground, a part of the language and history of our community that we all know. The words live for us because of the *talk* surrounding this read-aloud time. Ian recalled a bit of history when he said, "Remember the day when you were reading *Henny Penny* to us and you turned the page and Ryan said, 'Uh-oh! They're gonna be supper-lupper!' We all laughed. That was really funny." The children and I remember and laugh again. The books bring us together. The children are also learning much about language and writing and reading as I weave in talk and demonstrations connected to various language skills. However, the curriculum is not my first focus during this time. I've learned that if I read and enjoy good literature with children, encourage and appreciate responses, the children benefit from all that books have to offer—including language skills. I find countless opportunities to bring up these skills in the context of our reading without mapping them out ahead of time.

One day during the third week of school, Elizabeth brings in a copy of *Jack and the Bean Tree*, autographed by author Gail Haley. The book is rather long to read aloud, and the rich language of an Appalachian storyteller makes it difficult for the children to follow. However, their familiarity with "Jack and the Beanstalk" and Haley's outstanding illustrations support the children's comprehension as we read. But most of all, their fascination with Elizabeth's explanation of how she got this book and that it had the *author's* name in her own handwriting sparks their interest. Creating awareness of authors and their writing processes is an important goal of our literature time. However, authorship takes a backseat this day as the children's reactions to *Jack and the Bean Tree* take us in an unexpected direction.

I read the description of Jack's hand opening, finger by finger, to reveal the magic beans. I see a couple of children, including Ryan, clench their fists and then open them finger by finger in response to the words they hear. A page later Jack's mother learns he has sold the cow for those beans and threatens to give Jack "a good whuppin'!"

"She's really mad," comments a child.

Then Ryan says, "I know what I'd give him. I'd give him the finger," and his hand goes up, middle finger extended, to demonstrate his point.

"Oooooh," comes a low moan sounding like ghosts sweeping through a lonely room. The children watch for my reaction, but I say nothing. My mind races. Now what? Ryan looks innocent. I bet he has no idea. Wait. See what happens. Maybe it will pass without anyone needing to discuss it further. But no such luck.

"You'd get in trouble," says one child.

"Troub-BULL!" A small chorus of comments surrounds Ryan.

"My brother does it," replies Ryan. A tone of innocence rings in his voice, as he looks to me for support.

"It's okay Ryan," I say. "But, I need to tell you that these kids are right. You probably would get in trouble if you did that. Most people think that to do that is rude or unkind. But I don't think you knew that did you?"

Ryan shakes his head in astonishment as he says, "Uh-uh."

"I bet a lot of people here didn't know about that. But now we do, so I don't think it's something we want to do in here, any of us. Do we all agree?"

"My mom said that's not nice."

"But we need to understand that Ryan didn't know. Now he does. We all do."

The tension diffuses, we continue the story. I have a feeling that the children might discuss this issue later among themselves, but I trust them to handle it on their own. I have made the point I needed to make, and I think Ryan survived without humiliation.

A few pages later in the book the class chimes in with the giant, "Fee, fi, fo, fum . . ." When the giant demands food from his wife, Monica says, "You can't order people around like that. My mom wouldn't do it either if my dad talked like that. But he would never talk like that."

For a few moments we discuss what would happen if we talked to people this way. Some children say they would be in a lot of trouble if they spoke to others—especially parents—this way, while others think they could get away with such talk. We listen to each other. I listen too and refrain from commenting on their remarks. My role is to encourage them to respond.

By the time we finish the book, we have spent more than forty-five minutes reading and talking together. When I began reading *Jack and the Bean Tree*, I anticipated contrasting it with other versions of the folktale, pointing out how Gail Haley introduces her version through the image and voice of a storyteller. As soon as I read the opening pages this day, I could tell the children missed the storyteller aspect. I had planned to talk about storytelling, about how we all tell stories, and that we can write them too. But it wasn't appropriate to go back and make this point after we finished, so I told myself I'd do it another day. Elizabeth left the book in the classroom until the end of the year. We reread it a couple of times, but I never returned to my original intent. Somehow it didn't matter.

Shared Rule Setting

At the end of the third week of school in one of my early years of teaching, I asked the children to come up with the rules for our class—the ones we would follow throughout the year. They talked through and dictated the following:

Our School Rules

1. We raise our hands for quiet.
2. We look at the person who is talking.
3. We don't bang on the soap in the bathroom.
4. We use only one paper towel.
5. We walk quietly in the halls.
6. We do not call people unkind names.
7. We don't kick, push, or fight on the playground.
8. We don't waste food.

We hung these rules in the classroom, but we rarely referred to them. The talk to arrive at them seemed more important than the rules themselves. I could trace the source of each rule to specific incidents or to directions given to the children. Rules three and four related to the principal's talk to the class about problems in the boys' bathroom. Number eight came from an aide in the cafeteria. I was struck by how quickly and with so little thought the children came up with rules that mirrored adult edicts. Since then I've come to understand that while children need adult input, they also need to shape rules from their own experiences and have a voice in creating the rules. So, now I try to keep rules at a minimum and develop those rules or guidelines with each group. I shape a classroom around the basic rules: We are kind to each other and we work hard. Actually, working hard takes on a light tone, a connotation usually not associated with work. The reason: we work together; we are a community.

Recess: Learning to Play Together

Not many days of school pass before problems develop at recess. During the first few days we talk about recess procedures. Then, as the children become comfortable on the playground, the tattling begins.

"Lisa won't play with me."

"Courtney fell." (I can see an uninjured Courtney jumping rope.)

"Jason pushed me."

Tattletales weary me. In some cases I sense that the tattler craves my attention, while other times I feel that the tattler is seeking to vindicate herself from any wrongdoing. What exhausts me is being set up as the all-knowing, all-wise Solomon, the judge doling out verdicts.

It might be easy to step in, to be seduced by these imploring innocents into summoning the accused, sorting out the problem, and pronouncing a judgment. I might even arrive at a reasonable and just solution. But I would create future problems: I would have established a procedure that would eventually back me into a corner and deny the children the experience of working through their own problems together. I would become a rescuer.

It looks like this: Jeri reports that Kyle took the ball from him. I talk to Kyle, confronting him with Jeri's accusation. Kyle denies guilt. I'm stuck with the word of one child against another. Frequently, information lies hidden beneath the surface, which I can't easily uncover, and there's no way to determine justice. I'm in a stalemate situation. To decide in favor of either child is to make a judgment based on incomplete knowledge. I could be wrong. To abstain only provokes anger over the injustice from one child and promotes irresponsibility for actions in the other.

If Kyle acknowledges he took the ball, I'm faced with providing retribution to Jeri. The standard teacher solution goes something like this: "Well, don't you think you should apologize to Jeri and give him back the ball?" or "Do you boys think you could share the ball? Now Kyle, what do you think you should say to Jeri because you took the ball away from him?" So Kyle mutters a weak "I'm sorry" and the boys go away with one child feeling vindicated, superior to the other. But both boys have learned that eliciting teacher intervention can lead to a power payoff.

How well I know these responses. I've heard myself and my colleagues come forth with them automatically, as though they were written in a teacher's manual. Yet I always felt that these procedures were ineffective because they lead children through the motions of solving problems but failed to address the underlying emotions of the children or help the children understand the interactions.

One day after recess several years ago, the class and I sat down to talk about all the tattling. "I'm feeling very frustrated with this," I told them. "I can't solve all these problems for you. And besides, I'm never sure exactly what's happened. Sometimes it's pretty hard to tell." The children acknowledged that this was true and they were quite aware of unjust decisions made by teachers. "How could we work this out?" I asked.

After considerable discussion, we decided that reporting a problem to the teacher on recess duty was appropriate if someone was injured, but that person ought to go to the teacher personally if possible, or the reporter would check with the injured person first to decide if help was needed. The person with the injury was to be in charge of deciding whether or not to tell the teacher, unless, of course, that person was seriously hurt. When there were troubles with another child, we decided that *both* people ought to come to the teacher together, but that they should try to work out their problem first. We just couldn't go to the teacher with *everything*. We had to make some decisions about what really needed teacher attention. If one person in a dispute was unwilling to involve the teacher, the other person could, but that person had to think first and decide if it was really important. For my part, I agreed not to step in and solve problems on the spot, but to listen and try to help people think about the problems so they might work them out themselves.

Of course, this discussion did not put an end to tattling. It did, however, start children thinking and taking responsibility for *some* of their actions. Some children easily adhered to the guidelines while others had more difficulty, but the number of tattles diminished.

I found children telling tales on others when they were so agitated they *had* to say it to someone. I started responding to such reports with statements to reflect the child's complaint and to acknowledge their feelings: "He took the ball away! You're pretty angry about that!" Often the child responded, "Yeah!" and walked away, the anger diffused. I realized that sometimes tattling was only a way of expressing intense feelings, and that when those feelings were validated a child could drop the issue. Other times I turned the problem back to the child with a comment such as, "How could you solve this?" or "What do you want to do about this?" I hoped such comments would carry the underlying message: This is your problem, not mine. I began to see results. One day two boys ran up to me, both of them shouting.

"He lost my car! I'm gonna kill him!"

"I didn't mean to! I didn't know it was his."

"Stop!" I shouted as I physically intervened to keep blows from landing. "Each of you tell me what happened. You go first. And you, you listen. You may not interrupt until he's done! Then you tell me and he can't interrupt you."

The story unfolded from each child, though I had to stop and remind each boy "No interrupting!" during the other's telling. By the time they finished, tempers had cooled somewhat. Suddenly the offending child spoke up. "I'm sorry. We could go look for it if you want." I'm sure my mouth gaped in shock at that moment.

"Well, okay. We're gonna go look. Okay, Mrs. Avery?" answered the other boy, and they left. I was stunned. What had happened? Listening? Talking? Being heard? All of these I thought. But what struck me most was the depth of sincerity in that apology. It was not the shallow apology that followed our usual teacher directives. This apology came from understanding someone else's distress and taking responsibility for one's own part in that distress. Because it was based on honest feeling, it was authentic. The honesty healed the wounds.

Now when first graders come up and begin talking to me simultaneously, I stop the talk with, "Wait, I can only listen to one at a time and I want to hear each of you. You speak, then you, and then you. No interrupting. We will all listen while each person takes their turn to talk."

Going through this routine one day, it became Max's turn to speak. "I forget what I was going to say 'cuz I was listening—I mean I got so interested in what these guys were saying I just forgot." Then he turned and started talking to the child beside him, a response to that child's talk. The two walked off together, leaving me forgotten in their wake.

Every year the talk about tattling and managing interactions with others on the playground becomes part of the important class conversations during the first weeks of school. The playground is that part of school where the children rely least on routines established and monitored by others. The playground activity is the underground curriculum of social interactions. The tone of the playground will carry into the classroom through the children's regard for others and through their own problem-solving abilities. And, like a recursive spiral, the tone of the classroom will be reflected on the playground.

One incident reinforced the recursiveness of this connection between playground and classroom. My mother's generation would have described Cory as "all boy." Tough, extremely active, and ever aggressive, he soon gained a reputation with the other children as a bully and a troublemaker despite his small stature. I began receiving reports of Cory knocking children down on the playground and then running away. "Thank you, I'll watch for that," I commented, but I had a difficult time seeing an infraction occur. Finally, another teacher saw Cory run up behind a child, fling his arms around the child's legs, then get up from the pile and run on. Cory wound up at the time-out desk in the principal's office. I walked in to hear a tearful Cory protest to our principal that he didn't do anything, he was only playing.

I knelt beside Cory and asked him to tell me exactly what had happened.

"I was just playing."

"Tell me *exactly* what you were doing," I said ever so gently. I counted on the slim threads of trust that had begun to run between Cory and me to bridge our communication now.

"I was playing football. I just tackled him, that's all."

I nodded and maintained eye contact with Cory. He looked at me with a penetrating gaze that searched for understanding. And I searched—seeking a connection to help Cory understand and to get us both out of this confrontation. Then the idea came.

"Cory," I began, "when football players play football, like Nathan does, they learn how to tackle. (My son, Nathan, plays football, and on our field trip Nathan took charge of Cory. Cory speaks of Nathan with awe.) But there are only certain ways they can do it. And they have to practice a lot, and they have to wear special equipment, and then they learn to do it so that people don't get hurt. They have *rules* about how to tackle. They only tackle in an official practice or a game. And the reason for all of that is so that people *don't get hurt*. We can't practice football on our playground because we can't do all those things that have to be done. People could *get hurt*, Cory, if we play football here."

As I spoke the tears stopped. Cory looked at me intently. I knew I had connected with him, though I was not exactly sure how. I was also unsure of my football theory. From everything I saw in Friday night games, those guys were out to tear each other's heads off. But I decided in this situation my interpretation of tackling would do.

Cory went back to the classroom to find his classmates anxiously awaiting his arrival. "What happened?" they asked.

"Nothin'," he replied. "We talked about football. That's all."

"Cory was confused about what we could do on the playground about tackling. But I think he understands better now," I added.

Cory smiled at me. "Yup," he said.

It was Cory's smile, not a smart-alecky "I won again" smile, but a genuine, grateful smile that prompted me to say, "Do you want to tell them, Cory?"

A brief pause. "Okay. See, I didn't know about not playing football on the playground. But Mrs. Avery told me about it, how Nathan does it and you gotta do special things. So now I know how come we can't play football at recess." By the end of his speech Cory's voice had taken on a confident tone, the tone of one teaching the class new rules about playground behavior.

Then a child in the room said, "We were worried about you, Cory. We thought you were really in trouble."

"I was. But I'm not anymore." Cory smiled.

Children are always quite aware of those among them who cause problems for the group. Yet singling out any one child for misconduct can threaten the community. The children identify with that individual: this could happen to me. Cory came through this incident with his dignity intact and at the same time he began to acknowledge the inappropriateness of his behavior.

Cory was still a handful, both inside and outside the classroom, but the frequency of reports of his roughhousing diminished. I think the key in reaching him was discovering *Cory's* perceptions and *his* intentions, without jumping in with assumptions and judgments of my own. It's taken me a long time, and lots of errors on the side of injustice, to come to this realization. When I initiated writing workshops in my classroom, I learned that withholding judgments, waiting and listening, working to understand the child's intentions, were key concepts in creating a responsive, nurturing atmosphere for writers (Harste, Woodward, and Burke 1984). The same principles hold true for other parts of the school day. Everything I say and do throughout the day sets the tone for the classroom.

Working through problems to resolutions that everyone can live with brings strong cohesiveness to a group and contributes to a tone that makes a class work. A couple of weeks after the playground incident, Cory sat at the center table and hesitantly read a book, the first complete book that he had attempted to read. A number of children noticed and gradually they clustered around as he read. When he finished they clapped spontaneously. "Good job!" "You're a good reader!" they proclaimed. Cory beamed at his classmates, then turned and beamed at me. This community was coming together.

REFLECTIONS

I've watched learning communities develop, and for some time I wondered when, and if, this class that started with such an ominous beginning would come together. I pondered this throughout September, and October and November and periodically throughout the year. This group came together in intermittent spurts at first, more slowly than most, but it did come together.

Working out our schedule and structure was one part of building a community. The children and I both needed to know *how* we would function and *when* we would do things. I took time to develop routines, making sure the children understood one part before I added more. Within the structure I made sure children had choices, as both Graves and Giacobbe advocate. True community requires that children be recognized as individuals and respected and valued as equals, people with rights, not as puppets to be controlled or manipulated. Giving children choices—about important things such as topic selections for writing, book selections for reading—communicates respect as well as trust.

Talk was a big part of forming this community. Along with the talk was listening. Don Graves has said that if there is one thing he would change within classrooms it would be *listening*. And he's not referring primarily to the children listening! I'm the one who needs to do the most listening. I worked on listening nonjudgmentally—listening to understand and taking it seriously. Children's talk is profound. I tried to replace pronouncements as to right or wrong with respect for children's thoughts. Through this kind of listening and talk, we negotiated problems, learned about each other, and came to accept and value our differences.

First grade is a child's first encounter with serious academics, or at least the time when school is taken with absolute seriousness by the significant others in their life. Children need honest, yet affirming, responses to their efforts. In a world filled with pressures that extend into our classrooms, learning must still be enjoyable and have a playful tone. We cannot jeopardize children's well-being by making learning drudgery, burdensome, and terribly serious. I want an environment that takes school seriously but is also relaxed enough for risk taking and laughter.

A critical element for this learning community was *trust*. Trust is valuing the learner as a human being, as one who has much to give, much to demonstrate, much to teach others. Trust is esteeming the learner so that self-esteem is enhanced. Trust is believing that all children can learn to read and write and that all children strive continually to make sense of the world. A trusted individual becomes a risk taker, and to engage in learning is to engage in risk.

A classroom community continually evolves throughout the year, and never two alike. Like a forest, a complex ecosystem, it grows and changes with each organism gaining sustenance from those that surround it. And like a forest, growth is indiscernible on a daily basis; we notice it only over stretches of time. We start as strangers and ultimately make a commitment to one another. Some years the commitment comes early and we know within a few days or weeks that this will "be a good year." Other years we struggle together. We are slowed by those reluctant to make a commitment, to trust the others. The community is shaped finally by *all* the individuals in the classroom. I cannot mandate it nor dictate its terms. It grows out of trust relationships between me and individual children and among all the children. Community begins on the first day of school as we start working and playing together, gradually developing a cohesiveness that helps create a nurturing climate in which to learn.

CHAPTER 4

Planning and Preparing

On an August evening, I stopped at school with two friends. We walked through darkened hallways breathing the smell of new floor wax. I unlocked the classroom door and flipped light switches. As though I had waved a magic wand, a medley of bright colors and shapes appeared before our eyes. Catchy phrases, posters, and pictures flashed from bulletin boards covered with brightly colored background paper. My favorite children's books lined the chalkrails and countertops. Disks of color, designed to resemble balloons and labeled with the color words, hung from the lights. Only one part of the room remained undecorated: a bulletin board set aside for self-portraits the children would draw on the first day.

After nearly two weeks of unpacking, arranging, and decorating, I had my room ready for the children's arrival. My preparations for the opening of school were akin to those of an expectant mother preparing a nursery and, like a mother-to-be, I was eager to show off the results of my efforts.

My friends gazed around and then, very gently, one said, "Gee, I think if I was a first grader coming here, I'd feel a little scared. I mean, there's so much to look at, so much I've gotta learn."

"Really?" I answered. "I guess things have changed since you and I went to school."

"Well, it's all very attractive. It's just that there's so *much*."

Looking back, I realize that the glitzy appearance of my classroom rivaled the fast-paced stimulation of television cartoons. I took room preparation seriously and sweltered for hours in the August heat to create that riotous display. I thought the definition of "dedicated teacher" depended on both time invested and elaborate appearance. Sometimes parents, administrators, and fellow teachers complimented my results, but despite all the effort I expended every year, no *child* ever commented on any aspect of the room's appearance.

My lovely room remained neat for a couple of weeks. As September waned, the room became messy and the displays tiresome. The hectic pace of day-to-day teaching left little time to create new fancy bulletin boards. To decorate the room I relied on the children's projects from art classes or bulletin boards from previous years, which I pulled from the closet.

I recognize now that all the preparations for school focused on establishing a classroom that belonged to *me*. I was the teacher and I believed the room decor was my responsibility. When my visitor indicated that perhaps my room was a bit overwhelming, I rationalized away the remark because I certainly didn't want to make changes in my perfect room at this late hour. But the next August I remembered her comment and decided to cut back on the decorating—I hung nothing from the lights! Change came slowly.

Structuring a Learner-Centered Classroom

My preparations for school have certainly changed. I want the classroom to be warm and inviting when the children arrive that first day, but not overwhelming. I've discarded the visual bombardment of laminated colors and shapes, posters, cute quotes, and oversized characters that once filled the walls. Except for the strip above the chalkboard where I tack the children's names, the bulletin boards are empty. In a few weeks these bulletin boards will display pictures of authors, children's art work, a mural painted by some of the group in response to *Charlotte's Web*, a collection of litter from our ecology study, and charts recording the children's ideas on urban and rural communities. Although these bulletin boards may not look as polished as those I spent hours crafting, they mean more to all of us. The first year I decided not to decorate the room for the opening of school, I admit I was nervous! Like a child asking permission, I sought out the principal to discuss my decision. He had no problem; the anxiety was mine.

I moved from interior decorator to professional decision maker and now prepare for the opening of school by anticipating what the children and I need for smooth operation of our classroom. Before school begins, I do what is essential to focus on the children during those first critical days, leaving as many tasks as possible for us to do together. Everything that goes in this classroom must contribute to our purposes: learning and literacy development in a supportive community.

What brought about this change for me? I came to realize that all the careful preparations of the physical environment do not necessarily create a classroom structure that responds to children's natural learning processes. Coming to understand the meaning of structure was a key issue in my professional growth. This changed me as a teacher, changed everything I did in preparation for school, and changed my teaching in the classroom. Donald Graves has often spoken about a classroom structure that is predictable (Graves 1983). Sometimes I hear teachers interpret predictability and structure to mean adhering to a tight and carefully orchestrated schedule and set of procedures. Traditionally, we in education have perceived a structured classroom to be one where the teacher is visibly in control, talking to children who sit quietly, listening and following the teacher's dictates. But Graves speaks of an invisible structure rather than this visible one. The invisible structure lies in the flexible operation of the classroom, worked out with the students and in which everyone has an investment. The predictability inherent in such an environment enables children to learn how to make responsible decisions and to engage in purposeful learning.

This change in the concept of structure has often led to misconceptions. Learner-centered classrooms have sometimes been perceived as having a "lack of structure." On the contrary, these are highly structured classrooms where children take responsibility for their work, their behavior, and their learning. They know the parameters, understand what is expected, and operate accordingly. They also know how to make appropriate decisions without relying on the teacher for their every move. This environment has high standards and high expectations for children's learning *and* their behavior—and the children know it!

The teacher's role in this structure is different. A teacher reminisced about the way she began teaching. "I was forever trying to catch errors," she said, "an octopus reaching out to grab hold of everything my students did wrong and stop it because I knew the right way. My role now is far more compassionate and, therefore, I believe more helpful." We use words such as *facilitator, nurturer, coach* to expand the definition of "teacher." As I establish classroom structure, I hope to provide the security that there is definitely someone in charge, someone who plans, negotiates, and shares expertise, but who is also a learner. This teacher is continually looking out for the needs of each and every student, and she's in touch with those individual needs because the classroom structure accommodates this.

One day a visitor in my room came up to me and said, "How do you operate without any structure?"

"Tell me a little more what you mean," I replied.

"Well," she went on, "the children move around the room. Everybody's writing something different. It just seems so chaotic. And when do you collect their papers? How can you manage all this without a structure? This must work for you, but I just don't see how."

Another visitor commented, "What incredible structure you have here. There's so much *organization*! I talked to every child and each one told me *exactly* what they were doing—and everyone was doing what they were supposed to do." The two visitors observed the same group of children on the very same morning.

Children need a structure. So do I. We need to know that every day after lunch we will read, that in the late morning we will write, that each morning there will be time to chat and share together. We need to know that we will receive responses to our work and that we will make choices throughout the school day about what we read, what we write, and how to proceed in our learning. We need to understand that we will make mistakes and know that this is okay because mistakes are a natural part of learning. We need boundaries and we need flexibility.

As I establish the classroom structure, I've got to remember that learning is a messy, nonlinear, idiosyncratic process. If I look honestly at the children, this fact is obvious every day! But maybe this fact is precisely what brings the temptation to organize, sequence, and manage learning. I keep things simple by eliminating clutter and keeping only essentials. And I'm very organized. Most important, I strive to be very clear in communicating with the children how the classroom functions so that their understanding is clear. This provides us a solid foundation to begin together.

SETTING UP THE CLASSROOM

When it comes to setting up the classroom, there are specific decisions I make to prepare the *physical environment* and the *academic environment*. (The following may seem obvious to seasoned teachers, but it is essential to setting up a learner-centered classroom. There's nothing sacred about this information and I'm forever tweaking it. Please skim and scan to suit your purposes.)

Physical Environment

I consider the materials and supplies we need and then plan the room arrangement.

MATERIALS AND SUPPLIES *Tools for writing*. I sharpen pencils (I prefer ones without erasers for beginning writers so that they quickly learn that it's okay to line-out and continue writing rather than strive for a "perfect" copy), write names on crayon boxes, and set out unlined white paper for writing on the first day. I've found that lined paper can frustrate young children's writing efforts because some kids feel compelled to use the lines but have difficulty. Unlined paper serves both drawing and writing purposes and creates a more natural and relaxed writing experience. It also allows me to see how children manage the blank space as they place letters on a page: left to right, right to left, top to bottom, helter-skelter. We'll mount these first pieces of writing on the bulletin board. On our September parent night they provide a glimpse of the writing of all the children in the room.

I borrowed an idea from Mary Ellen Giacobbe and made blank books of forty pages (8½-by-11-inch) for the children to use during the first few weeks of writing workshop. These books certainly aren't essential, but by using them, the children and I avoid struggles to manage several sheets of paper, to use the stapler, or to start a writing folder during the first days of school. In the past I made fancy books with wallpaper-covered cardboard, but now I give children oaktag to design their own covers and put together books with brads.

I set up five small cardboard file caddies—the kind that are purchased flat and ready for construction—to hold the children's writing. Once I used a plastic milk crate, but twenty-five or more children crowding around one container to retrieve and put away their writing books became chaotic. Assigning several children to each caddie eliminates confusion and also provides convenient units for me to peruse the children's writing, going through one caddie an evening.

Gradually, we will establish a writing center, a place to keep the paper and tools for writing, but the books of blank paper, crayons, and pencils are enough to start. Eventually the writing center will hold a variety of paper: unlined, lined, paper with lines on half of the sheet and a blank space for drawing on the other half, construction paper for covers. The center will include tools for writing and editing: pens, colored pencils, tape, scissors, stapler, staple remover.

Classroom library. From the first day, children's books saturate the life of our classroom. So, when I set up the room, a major focus is displaying lots of children's books. I'm particular about what I put out. I weed out old, shabby, or dull texts and strive for quality literature presented attractively. When children choose books to read, they initially go for attractive books and they will spend tremendous energy learning to read these books. I want them expending their efforts on quality material.

The genres of children's literature I display at the beginning of school include:

- ***Folktales and fairy tales***—stories familiar to many children. I choose several versions of favorite fairy tales with a variety of illustrative styles.
- ***Wordless picture books***—books that invite children to "read" the pictures, to tell their own stories.
- ***Predictable books***—those with repetitious language or plot sequences that encourage children to join in during an oral reading.
- ***Songs and chants in picture-book format***—the text in these books is already familiar to children and they can "read" the words easily.
- ***Poetry***—lots of poetry from Mother Goose to "easy-to-read" collections, anthologies, and small volumes on specific themes.
- ***Modern classics***—traditional favorites that are popular with children year after year, such as Sendak's *Where the Wild Things Are* or McCloskey's *Make Way for Ducklings*.
- ***Leveled books***—particularly books for children who have had little experience with books and books that will provide beginning reading material. I began reading workshop before "leveling" books became popular. Learning to choose appropriately was a reading skill we worked on, though we never spoke of "levels." The children became very good at choosing books they could read. They never saw themselves as ahead or behind one another as readers and there was no rush or competition to move through levels.

Not all of the thousand or more books that I've collected will be available in the classroom on the first day; I will set aside some titles to bring out as the year progresses. And undoubtedly I will purchase new titles as the year goes on, for the arrival of new titles fuels our continuing interest in reading and in good books. The essential idea of a classroom library is lots of books on a range of topics, genres, interests, and reading levels that are *accessible* to all the children.

Art supplies. I distribute scissors, paste, and crayons to each child during the first days of school. I also store art supplies in a cupboard where the children have access to them. I include crayons, colored chalk, scissors, paste, clay, construction paper and drawing paper, paint, and brushes. Gradually, I add an assortment of other items for creative construction: toothpicks, empty cardboard rollers from paper towels, buttons, lace, and fabric scraps. From time to time I share directions for constructing simple art projects, such as puppets.

Drama props and puppets. For imaginative play I gather a few items: hats, a telephone, a wig, a magic wand, aprons, etc. There's also an assortment of puppets. Children need very little to stimulate ideas; with imagination, a Raggedy Ann puppet becomes a fairy godmother or a witch.

Games, building blocks, puzzles. The games I choose (such as checkers) emphasize thinking rather than chance. I've collected an assortment of blocks and other construction toys, and I have a few puzzles (the kind that become group projects over a period of days or even weeks).

Media equipment. A lot of options are available including tape player, record player, headsets, computer, television, camera, video player. For the opening of school, I put out the record player and some favorite records for sing-along and creative movement, set up an audiotape of a children's book and connect it to individual headsets, and add copies of the book for the children to follow along as they listen. We use the computer for writing and researching in my classroom, never for electronic worksheets to practice "skills" out of context of authentic reading and writing. Once writers became fluent I introduce them to the computer and a rotating schedule allows for individual use on a daily basis. I want to provide the children with the computer writing experience but pen and paper, I've found, is basic for young writers.

ROOM ARRANGEMENT To set up the classroom, I incorporate the following:

- Writing center—a place for writing supplies and for the children's writing.
- Classroom library—shelves, tubs, chalkrail, a paperback book rack; I put books everywhere, many with their covers showing.
- Designated places for blocks, games, art supplies and a work area for art, drama props, puppets, computers, etc.
- Large-group gathering area—a place where the class can convene for read alouds, for sharing writing, etc. A twelve-by-fifteen-foot rug (our "story rug") designates this area in our classroom.
- Small-group conference area—a round table of child height serves for small-group meetings for writing or reading conferences.
- Places for children's interests—a counter to display the treasures they bring to the classroom and bulletin board space for each child; a sectioned-off area of a large bulletin board provides each child with a display space (photos taken of the children on the first day and stapled in the corner of each space identify its owner).

- Student space—individual student desks meet a basic need to provide each child a private space for storing supplies.
- Teacher space—my desk, a private space for my things. Like the student desks, it's off-limits to everyone but the owner. I've considered removing my desk to gain floor space, but I need a place for my things and to say, "Put it on my desk."

When I set up the classroom, I arrange student desks in two semicircles around a round table that serves as a small-group conference center and a place for me to work from for large-group instruction. The semicircular arrangement allows the children to make eye contact with others during our class discussions, a definite plus in building a community. I first saw this seating arrangement in my own first-grade class; Mrs. Kearney, in the 1940s, unbolted those old iron and wooden desks from the floor and fastened them to two-by-fours so we could move them around. She was years ahead of her time when she broke up the "little house on the prairie" schoolroom arrangement in favor of one that took the focus off the teacher in front of the class and shifted it to individual members of a group.

Later, I may move student desks together in pairs (maintaining the semicircles) to facilitate the natural talk surrounding reading and writing. Or we may move desks to "top-secret positions" for private work, such as a testing situation. But to start the year, I keep the desks separated. In September, first graders don't tune in to large-group talk when they sit with a partner. With some classes, children can manage pair seating rather quickly and with some groups it takes months. It depends on the individual kids and the tone of the class.

I sit beside the round table as I read a children's novel during the opening of the day or during large-group discussions. Years ago, when back problems prevented me from standing all day, I began sitting whenever possible. I discovered I enhanced communication and changed the entire tone by leaving an authoritative stance and moving to a position that invited natural conversation between the children and me. Such a little thing, yet how different from the edicts I remember from teacher training and administrator observations during my first years of teaching!

With student desks in place, I set up the rest of the room (Figures 4–1 and 4–2). I unpack my books, collect others from the school library, and display them around the room. Children need to see the covers of the books, not just the spines on shelves. I stand books on chalkrails, window ledges, counters, and shelving, and fill a paperback bookrack. The books project a welcoming appeal. When tempted to do too much, I remember Lisa, a first grader from years ago who one day in late March pointed to a word taped to the window and asked, "Mrs. Avery, why's that word on the window?" The word: *window*.

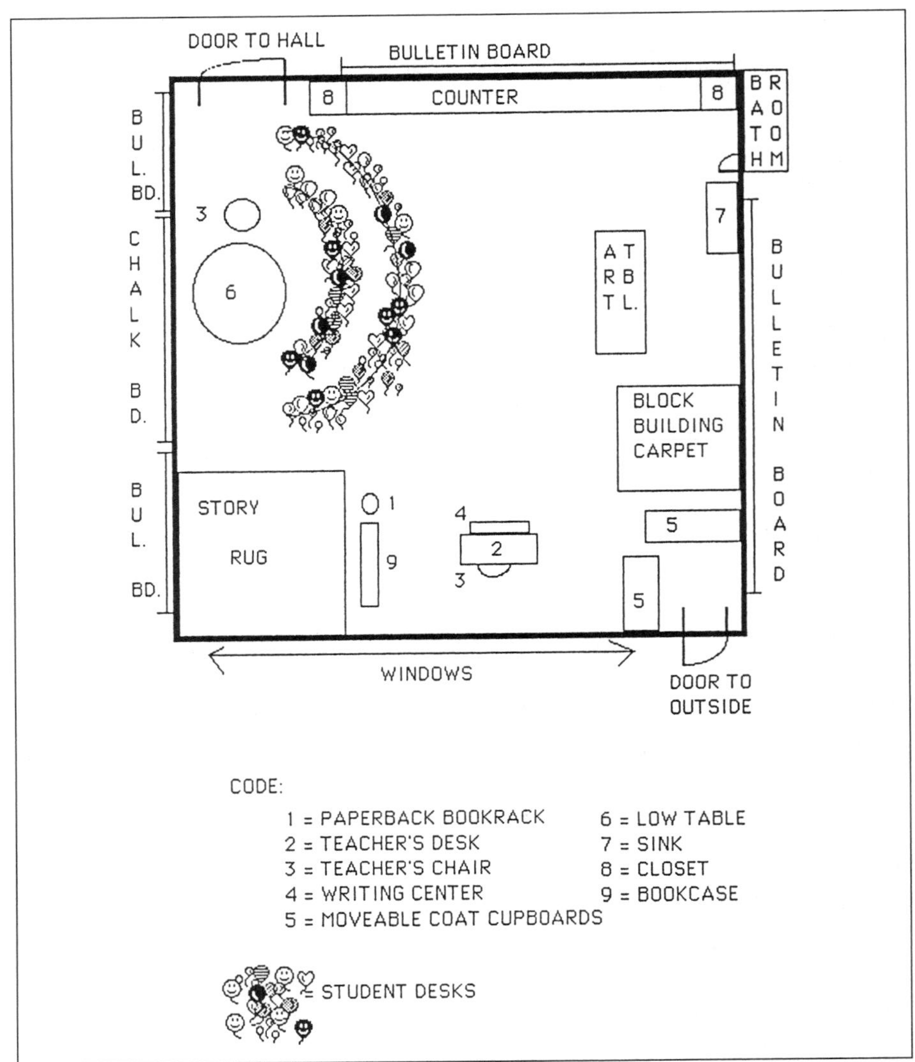

Figure 4–1

Classroom Floor Plan #1

I'd taped it there in August and Lisa had no idea what it said or *why* it was there. The children must understand the *purpose* of everything in the classroom, so now what goes up connects to classroom learning and usually is created with or by the children.

In the first few days of school I will spend time showing the children where everything is and outlining procedures for use. I keep instructions clear and simple and explain them a little at a time so that everyone knows how to make efficient use of our resources. Critical to room arrangement is *accessibil-*

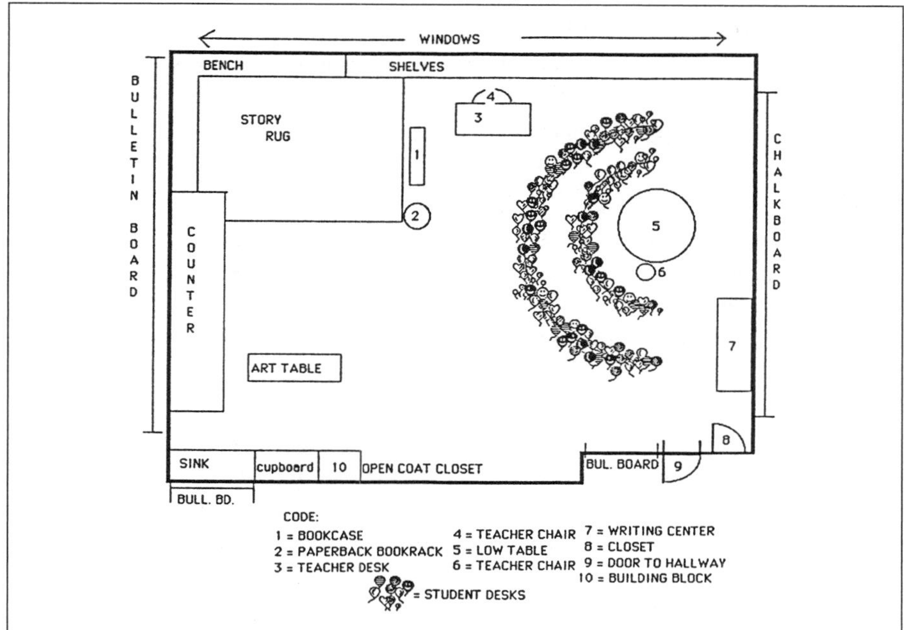

Figure 4–2

Classroom Floor Plan #2

ity. Accessibility means the room is designed and introduced to the children so that they know:

- where things are
- how to locate and use items and the appropriate time for using them
- the purpose of using materials
- how to make decisions for using class materials to enhance learning

I want children to use the classroom to the fullest. I want them to develop responsible and independent ways of using materials so that they don't have to wait for me or get permission. They need access to books, paper, art supplies, puppets, games, etc. But to accomplish these goals, I must take time in the beginning to introduce everything and discuss procedures for use.

Accessibility is more than being able to get to materials. In setting up the room so that children have access to supplies, I am simultaneously clearing the way so that we are accessible to each other: child to child, teacher to child, child to teacher. Materials, supplies, programs serve us, are under our control, rather than the other way around. Learning in this type of classroom emerges in the context of human interactions, sometimes involving materials, but never removed from relationships with others.

Academic Environment

The decisions involving the academic environment include curriculum requirements, time and scheduling, teaching strategies, and record keeping—always taking into account each learner's needs.

CURRICULUM When I initially planned for writing and reading workshops, I consulted the district curriculum guides, the scope and sequence charts from programs adopted by the school district, and assorted lists of skills considered appropriate for the grade level I taught. I compiled a list of all the concepts and skills I planned to cover during the course of the school year and referred to the list as a means of checking on myself. Was I covering the curriculum?

That first list contained specific skills under these categories: decoding skills, comprehension skills, attitudes and appreciation of literature, genres of literature, and study and reference skills. Initially, it was helpful to have this list for reference. Soon, however, I internalized the list and taught by responding to children, demonstrating specific content and skills and strategies as they were needed. Of course, I am still responsible for addressing the areas of the curriculum adopted by our school board. To do anything less would be to function as an irresponsible teacher—or a brazen revolutionary! But as the professional in the classroom, I am continually making decisions as to how to present curriculum. One result of a responsive teaching style is that curriculum in my classroom became integrated (see Chapter 18). But integration, I came to understand, was not merely connecting subject matter through teacher-planned units. Full integration occurred within each learner, as that learner constructed meaning from the classroom experiences. Facilitating this internalized integration required my expertise, my knowledge of content, and a keen awareness of the individual needs of the children. I needed to know the wide range of strategies that readers may employ while reading, be aware of techniques writers use to refine and craft writing, and stay abreast of new releases in children's literature. I had to be informed of new discoveries and information about social studies and science areas. Maintaining one's expertise on particulars related to curriculum is essential to being a professional.

TIME AND SCHEDULING Each year the principal distributes schedules of the times classes go to lunch and to special area subjects. The rest is up to the classroom teachers. I've learned that it is essential to provide chunks of time for the curriculum basics rather than splinters of time to address a fragmented curriculum. Each day I incorporate a block of time for:

- Writing workshop—time when we draft and craft writing
- Reading workshop—time to read, develop the skill of reading

- Literature time—time for reading aloud and talking about books
- Math—time to develop concepts and practice math skills
- Content areas—time to focus on science, social studies, and health. It's impossible to fit all into each day, so I designate a time block and focus on one.
- Free play or individual choice—a structured time when children choose from established options: art, puppets, reading, writing, puzzles, games, etc.
- Opening of the school day—a beginning to bring us together and start our day. Beyond the traditional activities, our beginning includes a word-play activity and reading from a children's novel.
- Handwriting—not a daily activity, but a part of the curriculum I address with two or three fifteen-minute, teacher-directed lessons a week

Identifying these parts of the school day, I map out the schedule (Figure 4–3). An important feature of the schedule is that it is both stable and flexible. I make adjustments as needed. If reading workshop is going well, I'll extend the time, knowing that another day I'll begin social studies earlier than scheduled. The exact time I move from free play into our opening each morning depends on the children's activity and the demands of a particular day. And while the schedule denotes chunks of time for particular areas, I've found that the various parts of the school day begin meshing one into each other. In literature time, we read about science and social studies topics and we discuss authors and their writing processes. Reading aloud before writing workshop often establishes a natural connection, and there may be a writing mini-lesson embedded during the talk about literature allowing writing to begin with a brief, focused reminder of something discussed moments before. Children's topics in reading and writing workshops emerge from books and topics discussed during other parts of the school day.

Teachers often tell me about all that they are required to cover in the school day and the way their day becomes dissected. In my experience, the class worked more efficiently when we had large chunks of time for the basics. First, we don't drop as much time moving from activity to activity and, perhaps more important, we incorporate skills, that are often separated, into actual reading and writing where the children more readily pick them up.

GROUPING CHILDREN I've found it a definite advantage to teach in a heterogeneous, self-contained classroom (one where all the children stay with one teacher all day except for music, art, etc.). In our workshops, I can present lessons to the entire group and then work with individuals in conferences or convene small groups—groups with flexible membership to avoid falling into the old ability grouping. Learning connections develop with ease and almost

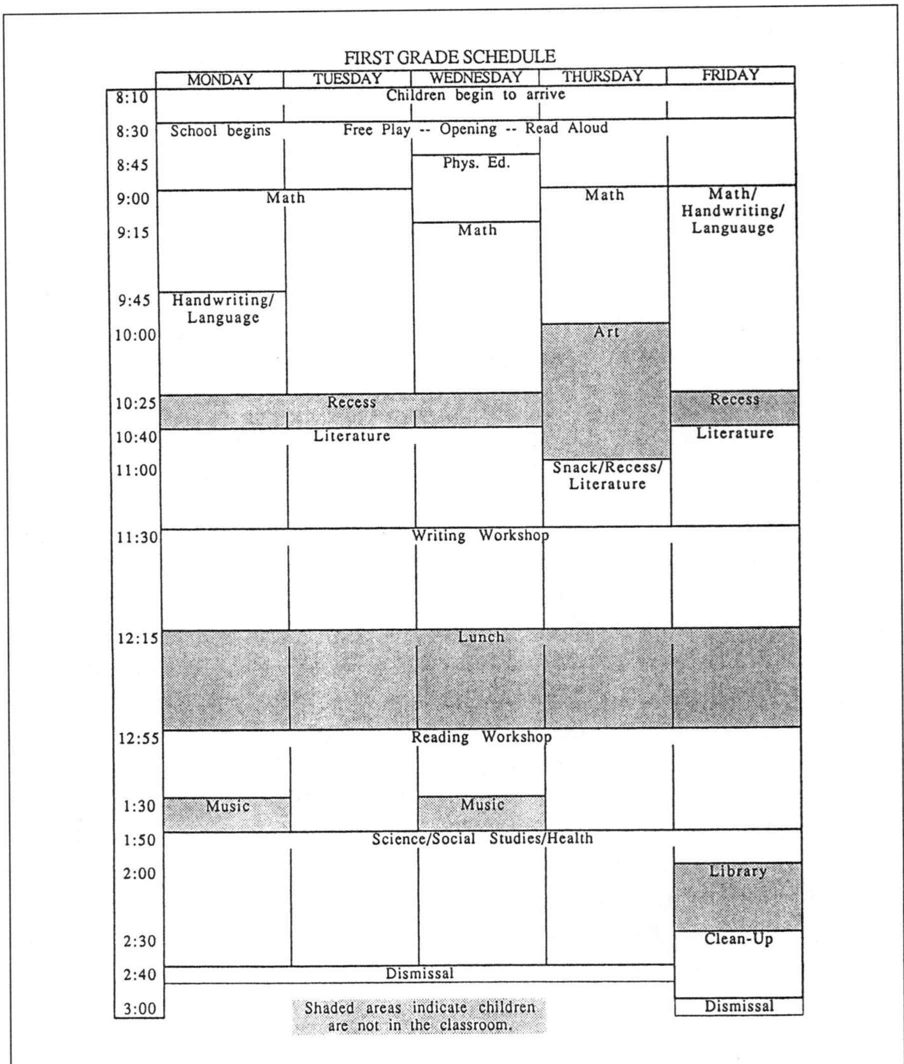

FIRST GRADE SCHEDULE

	MONDAY	TUESDAY	WEDNESDAY	THURSDAY	FRIDAY
8:10	Children begin to arrive				
8:30	School begins	Free Play -- Opening -- Read Aloud			
8:45			Phys. Ed.		
9:00	Math			Math	Math/ Handwriting/ Languauge
9:15			Math		
9:45	Handwriting/ Language				
10:00				Art	
10:25	Recess				Recess
10:40	Literature				Literature
11:00				Snack/Recess/ Literature	
11:30	Writing Workshop				
12:15	Lunch				
12:55	Reading Workshop				
1:30	Music		Music		
1:50	Science/Social Studies/Health				
2:00					Library
2:30					Clean-Up
2:40	Dismissal				
3:00					Dismissal

Shaded areas indicate children are not in the classroom.

Figure 4–3

First-Grade Schedule

effortless grace in a self-contained, heterogeneous classroom. I can teach meaningful wholes instead of dissected parts. I save time. I avoid the hectic pace that is so much a part of ability-group tracking that schedules teachers with different groups of children each day. I can establish a community of learners who know each other well, understand and *value* each other's contributions. All children learn much from their peers in such an environment.

RECORD KEEPING Before school starts I make up two folders for each child, one for reading and one for writing (color-coding the children's names designates writing or reading). Inside the reading folder I staple two papers for record keeping. A blank one is used for "Anecdotal Records" on which I write observations of a child's successes, comments, and interactions with books. The other sheet is the "Reading Record," a simple form (with room for five entries on one page) for my notes when a child reads a book to me. Similarly, stapled in the writing folder is a blank Anecdotal Record sheet and a simple form labeled "Writing Record." This form is designed to record notes from conferences (usually held with a small group of children) that I conduct when a child prepares a piece of writing for publication.

In addition, I draw up two record sheets to use with the entire class. One is a grid with children's names down the length of the sheet and days of the week across the top, forming a daily checklist that lasts two weeks. I carry this paper with me as I move among the children during writing workshop as Giacobbe advocated. A key indicates the various markings I use to indicate my perceptions of the child's engagement in writing as I talk with that child during a writing conference. The second record sheet is simply a piece of unlined eight-by-eleven-inch paper sectioned off into blocks, one for each child in the class. I use this paper to record anecdotal notes as I confer with individual children during reading and writing workshops. (See the appendices for record sheets.)

I label three more folders to hold these group records: one for the conference checklist and one each for the anecdotal records for both writing and reading workshops. I keep the group folders with the children's individual record folders in a small cardboard file caddie on the round conference table where it is easily accessible. My record-keeping system to start the year is ready.

LESSON PLANS I use a loose-leaf notebook as my plan book, adding pages I redesign each year to fit my schedule. I make a master weekly class schedule on two sheets of paper, filling in as much as possible. For example, under writing workshop I write: "Mini-Lesson" and leave a space to fill in the topic later. I duplicate the lesson-plan pages, punch holes in them, and place them in the notebook so that an open spread shows an entire week. I write a mini-lesson topic into the plan the day before I teach it. Planning any further ahead would defeat the responsive nature of the instruction. There's space to write notes for any particular part of the day—plans for a publishing conference, for instance. In addition to the plan book, I keep a folder in my desk for substitute teachers that contains a two-page description of the classroom and how it operates. I describe how writing and reading workshops are conducted, suggest a couple of mini-lessons the substitute might use, and explain the workshop checklists and record keeping. I've found that substitutes have no trouble working with the procedures and the children capably maintain the structure.

Social Climate

The organizational planning I've described here is necessary, but alone does not determine the effectiveness of the learning environment. There must also be an atmosphere (see Chapter 3) where everyone is valued and where social interactions nurture each member of the classroom community.

On the Saturday before Labor Day, a friend and I leave the classroom we had just prepared for the opening of school. It took us only a few hours, in contrast to the days I once spent at this task. We pause at the doorway and look around.

"It's mostly books," she says.

"Yes. Without them it'd be pretty bare," I admit and flip the light switch. The September twilight catches the long shadows of books the children and I will read together over the year ahead.

First Encounters

The night before school begins, I phone all the children to introduce myself to them, chat briefly, and ask them to bring a favorite book to school the next day. I reach two-thirds of the class. This task is time-consuming but very worthwhile. One mother told me weeks after school started of the importance of this phone call: "She went to bed with a smile, eager for the morning. Before you called, she had worried all day about going to school."

The phone conversations with the children are fun and fascinating. I ask how I might recognize them tomorrow and they eagerly tell me of their new clothes and their physical descriptions.

"I'll tell you one thing. I have dark brown hair and light shoes."

"I don't know what I look like. I'll have to ask my Mom."

When I ask about books, the children respond quite candidly.

"I got a whole pile of books up in my room."

"My Dad reads to me almost every night, except when he doesn't."

"I do a little books. I'd rather play computer games."

"I can tell you my favorite book. Storybook."

"I don't have no books, not really. I watch TV."

When I ask one little girl to bring a book to school, her shy voice changes tone and she cries out, "Okay! I'm going to pick one out right now!" When I hang up from the final call, I too am eager for the morning.

WRITING

CHAPTER 5

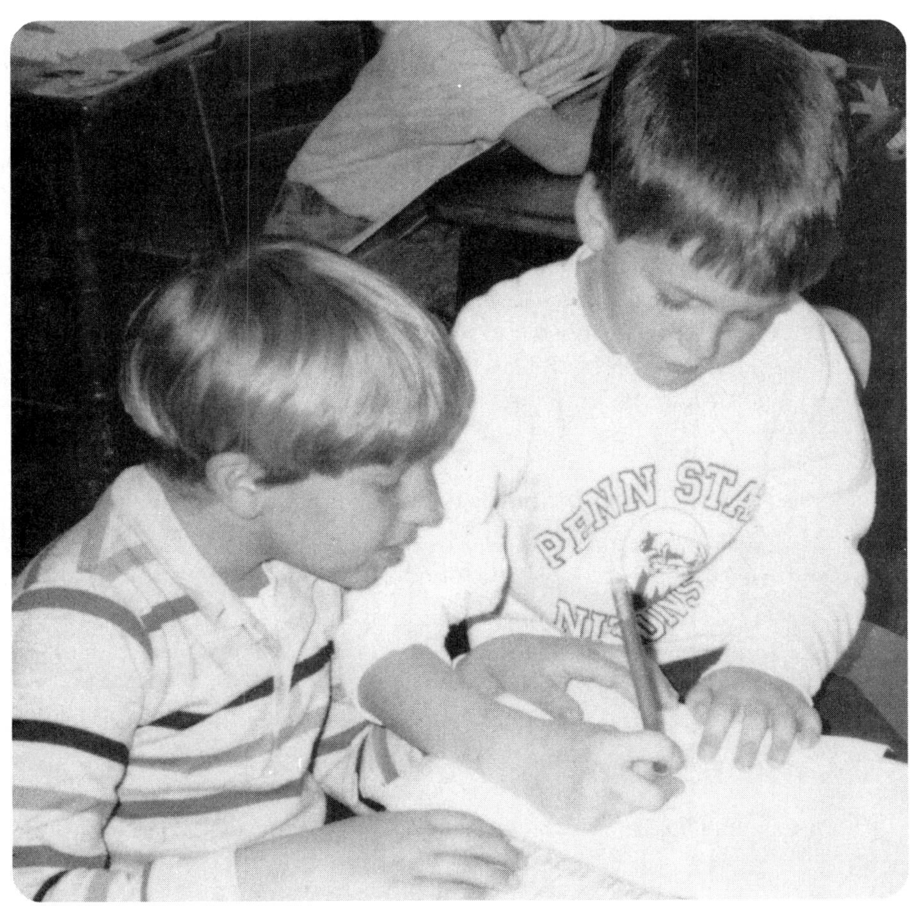

Establishing and Managing a Writing Workshop

My beliefs about children and writing are based on three assumptions: (1) young children *can* write, (2) young children *want* to write, and (3) young children possess knowledge, interests, and experiences to write about. The work of Graves (1983) on writing and of Harste, Woodward, and Burke (1984) on the literacy of young children professed these same assumptions, and my experiences with first-grade writers validated these beliefs. First graders may not use standardized spelling or adhere to all the conventions of written language, but they do understand that created symbols communicate meaning, and they are capable of communicating by placing marks on paper. All children have experiences to write about. They do not need to go on elaborate family vacations or own fancy toys to find topics. In my classroom Jody wrote about watching the trains go by his house, Megan about an old stuffed panda, Natalie about riding the school bus. The children write without assigned topics or classroom experiences designed to supply topics. I avoid measuring the children's writing against some preconceived concept of what they should or should not be able to do as writers. Such expectations handicap their efficient, natural learning styles. Don Murray says the role of the teacher of writing is to laugh and cheer. I try to remember his advice as I listen to writers talk about their writing.

Janet Emig (1983) uses the term "enabling environment" and in her essay "Non-Magical Thinking" lists four implications for presenting writing in school:

1. Although writing is natural, it is activated by enabling environments.
2. These environments have the following characteristics: they are safe, structured, private, unobtrusive, and literate.
3. Adults in these environments have two special roles: they are fellow practitioners, and they are providers of possible content, experiences, and feedback.
4. Children need frequent opportunities to practice writing, many of these playful. (139)

As I begin writing workshop, I try to keep her words in mind.

The First Writing Workshop

MINI-LESSON I once eased children into writing by asking them to draw, then gently suggesting they write letters to label pictures or convey short sentences. Now I'm more direct with an opening mini-lesson that demonstrates how to choose a topic and write. I use a topic from my own life—though ones the children can relate to—then draw and write, matching the general developmental level of the children.

The children are gathered on the carpet. I have just finished reading aloud. "We all have stories to tell and write," I begin, "just like the author of this book. I'm going to write one of my stories today. I'll show you how to do this. First, I have to think what I could write about. Let's see, I could write about the blueberry pancakes we had for breakfast yesterday. Or, I could write about when Adessa (she's six) slept over and the picture she painted. Or, I could write about my cats. There are so many stories about my cats. Now, I don't want to just write 'I have two cats' or 'I like my cats.' That would be boring. I need to think of *one time* with my cats. Hmm, I know, I'll write about when they were kittens and they played with the bows on the Christmas packages. They took them off and played with them." My think-out-loud strategy is designed to show the children a process of arriving at a focused topic. From the beginning I want to steer children away from broad topics that tend to produce limited writing such as "I like my cat."

The children listen intently. I turn to a twelve-by-eighteen-inch paper taped to the wall and begin drawing my cats and the Christmas bows. As I draw I talk to show my thinking. "This is my cat Snow and this is Cinder. I can remember and picture in my head when they had a red bow. . . ." I finish the drawing and write by stretching words out, listening for the sounds and writing letters: "So n Cnd pa y boz T ben ta r mis." (Snow and Cinder play with bows. They pretend they are mice.) I reread my writing, pointing to the letters I read.

When a few children tried to help me with spelling, I respond, "That's okay. I'll edit later. I need to think now." If we concentrate on spelling, we'll lose the focus of the lesson, which is showing children how to think and write for themselves. I'm demonstrating *how* to get ideas down and *how* to write words even though I can't spell perfectly. There are many times during the day when the children see me spell correctly, but in this demonstration I want to make writing accessible for them.

I keep this lesson brief, then turn to the children and ask them to think of something they can write about. "Of course, your story will be different from mine because you have your own ideas. When you write, I want you to stay in your seats. I will come to you. When I stop at your desk, I want you to tell me what you are writing about." I ask the children to raise their hands when they have their idea. I call them up individually to whisper their idea to me, give each child a sheet of paper and send her to her seat. This particular strategy heads off young writers getting to their seats with blank paper and not knowing what to do next. It also allows me to support the child who has difficulty coming up with an idea.

Two children are in this position today (the rest having moved to their seats and begun drawing), and I signal them to me and ask what they might write about. Sometimes, just the personal connection brings a response. If not, I tell the child to just begin drawing. "Something will come to you," I say reassuringly. What I will not do is suggest topics to children. I've learned that doing so only makes topic selection on subsequent days more difficult. I'd rather have children work through this struggle right from the beginning.

Doing so not only builds confidence, it's the beginning of learning a fundamental skill we need to write well. Also, my suggestions may lead young writers to topics they think I want, rather than what's important to them. There will be times when children are stuck for a topic, but we ride this out because in the long run working through such struggles strengthens the writer.

WRITING CONFERENCES With the children all writing, I move to their desks to begin conferences. I stoop down next to each desk, point to the child's picture, and say, "Tell me about your writing." Giacobbe had taught me that using the word "writing" defines the child's work—the drawing, scribbling, sprawling letters—as written communication. I am interested in the content, the ideas, in the writing, so I set aside concern for language conventions at this time. When each child speaks I listen, maintain eye contact, and nod to indicate I understand. I ask questions when I'm puzzled, but mostly I just listen, then respond by briefly summarizing what the child has said and conclude with "Thank you." I try to match my voice tone to the child's tone as another way of communicating encouragement. When Natalie speaks with eagerness, I respond enthusiastically. When Darren expresses frustration, I try to acknowledge it through an empathetic tone. To encourage each writer to want to write again, I must delight in their first efforts; it's important to value designs and scribbles with the same interest as more detailed work (Giacobbe 1982).

In the first writing conferences, I often ask the children to read to me what they've written. I want them to develop the habit of reading their words aloud and considering if they make sense. I teach them to run a finger under the words so they focus on *exactly* what they put on paper rather than simply retelling their ideas. When children have difficulty reading their words, I show them how to use various strategies: remembering their intended idea, using letter/sound clues, skipping to "words" they know for sure, and using context. Reading and reading one's writing and asking oneself, "Does this make sense?" or "What did I leave out?" is basic to becoming a writer. In a short time the children read on their own as they write, and we don't devote precious conference time to reading long pieces.

To encourage children to add writing to the drawing, I make gentle suggestions after listening to them tell about their drawing. Some shake their heads and I accept the answer for now. I ask Adam, "Could you write any of that story you just told me?"

Adam flashes a broad smile and says, "Yeah! Sure! I can do that. 'Cause last year we did writing—we drew pictures and we wrote about them."

Several other children respond to my invitation to write about their pictures. Later, when I examine their work, I notice that many wrote complete thoughts in sentence form. Once only a few children in a first-grade class could write a sentence at the beginning of the year. The difference is experience. The majority of these children had written in their classrooms the previous year. Only one or two children, who moved into the area over the summer, had not experienced writing in school.

Jody is one who hasn't written before. But he watches and listens to the children around him and imitates their behavior. When I ask him about his work he looks at me and says, "My model train. That's what it says."

"Could you point to the words and read it?" I ask.

He reads again, hesitating momentarily after reading "My" as he points to MI and then moves his finger back to the letter *M*, thus using it twice for the reading, and continues, "model train" (M I T O T O R A N) (Figure 5–1). I comment briefly on the train and thank him.

"I think I forgot an 'M'" he suddenly says.

"What could you do about that?"

"I don't know."

"No sweat. Think about it. We'll talk about that another day." Jody returns my smile as I walk away.

Figure 5–1

Jody's writing: "My model train"

I really don't have time to stop and address this issue with Jody today. Doing so would rob other children of interaction with me. But I do want Jody to know that we can and will confront this problem. Even more important, I want Jody to understand that he can work out solutions without me, and that I trust his ability to discover his own strategies. I hope my playful tone and spontaneous comment raise these possibilities.

Jody giggles and repeats my words as I leave his desk. "No sweat. Think about it. She said, 'No sweat. Think about it.' Okay, I'll think about it." He turns to the child seated beside him (who has listened to our conference) and repeats my words again. Jody looks at his writing, smiles and keeps talking to nobody in particular. Jody talks all day long. It's as though every thought that goes through his head must be verbalized. I'm coming to see that talking is a significant part of Jody's learning style. Children *need* to talk as they work. The classroom is rarely silent. Talk fosters learning through both the social interaction with others and the dialogue with oneself.

I learn a lot from Jody in this writing workshop: his fascination with trains, his capacity to learn quickly from his peers, his problem-solving ability, his willingness to take risks, his concepts about written language such as left to right progression of print and letter/sound correspondence. At lunch I will jot a few notes on my observations in my record-keeping folder on his writing. I'll write specifics (the train topic, his comments) rather than a synthesis. In just one writing workshop I've learned a lot about all of the children. Seems amazing, but it's true and fairly universal. One of the first things teachers tell me after beginning writing workshops is how well they know their children.

I don't linger with any child in order to talk with as many children as possible. The children spend close to half an hour writing—not long enough to see each child, though I do speak to twenty. At the conclusion, I announce that I will look at all the writing after school and tomorrow talk with children I didn't see today. I won't read everything the children write this year, but for the first few days I try to look briefly—no comments or marking of papers—at their work at the end of each day. In this way I get to know the writers and convey my interest in them.

LARGE-GROUP SHARING I introduce large-group sharing time (which we would call *sharing*) by going over rules that I learned from Judy Egan, a second-grade teacher in Atkinson, New Hampshire, during the Graves research. I have written these rules on eight-by-twelve-inch cards with a sketch to help the children read the meaning.

1. Look at the person who's talking.
2. Keep your hands still.
3. Be very quiet.

4. Listen carefully.
5. Think of any questions you have.

I go over these guidelines the first few sharing times. After that, I reinforce by holding up the card in the direction of an offender, a gentle reminder that usually resolves the problem. Later in the year the children take over the reminding. Inevitably, in every group there are one or two children who take on the role of enforcer of class procedures. That's okay—so long as they learn to do it tactfully. Shelly, for instance, assumed that role; she followed my model and held up the card to the offender, but never said a word. It worked, and probably better than if I had continued to do it.

Adam is one of the children I ask to share this day. He seems confident, but just in case he's uncomfortable, I check privately beforehand. I take a few moments to explain how the sharing time will work and go over procedures. Being very clear and specific builds structure.

Adam begins by reading, somewhat haltingly, "The Statue of Liberty. I took a cruise around the Statue of Liberty." Then he holds his picture up for the group to see (Figure 5–2).

Figure 5–2

Adam's writing: "The Statue of Liberty. I took a cruise around the Statue of Liberty."

"What do you see? What did you hear Adam read? Raise your hand and tell him," I said to the group. "Adam, you may call on people who raise their hands."

Adam proceeds to call on a child.

"I see the Statue of Liberty in your picture."

Adam nods. Silence. I see apprehension on Adam's face, reticent, cautious looks on the faces of his peers. "Any other comments?" I ask. More silence. Thinking of the words Adam read and looking at the boat in his picture I raise my hand. Adam calls on me and I ask, "You took a boat ride around the Statue of Liberty?"

"Yeah, we went to New York and we took a boat ride around the Statue of Liberty." A hand goes up hesitantly and Adam eagerly calls on this child.

"That's a good picture of the Statue of Liberty."

"Thank you," Adam replies. Another hand is up.

"Is that the boat you went on?"

"Uh-huh." Adam smiles.

"It's a good boat. What's that black circle thing?"

"Oh, that's the life ring. They have these lifesaver rings, so in case anyone falls in the water you just throw it." Adam explains with authority.

"Oh yeah, I know what you mean," replies the questioner.

"Yeah. They have them at the Statue of Liberty, so in case anybody falls in the water," Adam concludes.

I conclude Adam's turn by thanking him and leading the children in applause. Adam beams. Everyone had tuned in to the conversation about life preservers. We'd ended at a good moment when interest was keen. The workshop ends after another child shares writing.

THE FOLLOWING DAY As we continue writing workshop the next day, I demonstrate how to reread my cat story and continue it. I ask the children to begin by reading yesterday's pieces and making a decision whether to continue that writing or start a new idea. I'm establishing the expectation that we write every day, reread our writing, and may continue our pieces from one day to the next. Our writing workshop begins on the first day of school and ends on the last. The only other time in the school year when I will "begin" a workshop is the first day back in January. At that point the children have been away from writing for an extended time and I plan a lesson to get them back into daily writing.

Children amaze me with their ability to invest in daily writing. I think it's choosing their own topics without being rescued by an adult and then getting their ideas on paper that hooks them. There's a deep sense of accomplishment that is felt by writers of any age when they communicate what they care about through the written word.

The Process of Establishing a Writing Workshop

Certainly, there's no formula for starting workshops, but at the risk of sounding prescriptive, I offer a brief overview of my process.

Day 1

- Demonstrate how to select a topic and write on that topic, matching the developmental level of the children.
- Ask children to select a topic—something they know about, care about, or is important to them—and write, using the demonstration as a guide.
- Provide paper and writing tools so that children focus on writing. (Decisions about materials are handed over to children as writing habits become established.)
- Move among students as they write, listen to children's ideas, and convey an understanding of those ideas.
- Encourage children to read their writing.
- Refrain from correcting or providing "right answers" and turn questions such as "How do you spell . . . ?" back to the child for consideration.
- Conclude the workshop with one or two students sharing writing with the class and receiving responses to the content. Establish clear procedures and demonstrations for responding.

Day 2

- Demonstrate returning to writing by reading what was written earlier, and ask children to reread their pieces from the previous day and decide whether to make changes, continue the piece, or start a new piece.
- Continue brief individual conferences, striving to cultivate an attitude that writing is an ongoing process, that every writer has things to write, and that writers reread, rethink, and revise the words they put on paper.
- Conclude with a sharing time.

Subsequent Days

- Continue writing following the same structure. Demonstrate ways to make revisions with an emphasis on drafting, shaping ideas by including information, and making writing clear to readers.
- Observe children and note particular skills and strategies that can be presented in future mini-lessons.

Managing a Writing Workshop

It was Monday morning of the first full week of school, our fourth day together. Maggie arrived with a new set of colored markers and asked, "Can I use these when it's writing time?"

"Sure," I glibly replied, remembering that all writers, even young ones, have a preference for particular tools. When the workshop began, Maggie opened her markers instead of her crayon box. I felt a bit uneasy when I stopped to confer with her for she was obviously as absorbed in the markers as she was in the picture she drew. A few minutes later I looked across the room to see Maggie turning pages of her writing book and making sweeping circles and jagged lines on each page. I quickly moved to her desk. By now blood-red scribbles dripped from over half the pages in the book.

In an attempt to have Maggie confront the natural consequences of this action, I made some comment like, "This book is for your writing for the whole month of September. What will you do?" An undaunted Maggie twisted her mouth, rolled her eyes, then proposed several solutions: gluing in more pages, or maybe erasing the red marks, or finding a new book "somewheres." A day later I discovered Maggie with open paste jar and blank paper attempting to add pages to her writing book.

When I approached, she looked up from the paste jar and said, "I wanted to put more pages so I'll have enough."

"Good idea," I responded, "want some help?"

"Yeah, 'cause I'm having trouble. These won't stick too good." So Maggie and I worked with paper, staples, and glue and managed to insert several pages into the writing book.

On the second day of our workshop I had given the children a stapled booklet with forty blank pages, explaining that I wanted them to write only on the first page that day. Tomorrow we would turn to a new page. (I knew what some first graders might do when handed a book of blank paper and a box of crayons. Plus, I wanted to avoid the hurried, slapdash "I'm done" approach many children tended to use.) Maggie threw a kink into my preplanned organization. Absorbed in her new markers, she focused on the flowing brilliant colors and neglected the writing task. When other children saw her move beyond the first page, they wanted to do the same. I realized that the children needed firm guidelines from me to get the workshop started.

So, the next day I announced that we would use crayons and pencils for writing workshop, but for now no markers. I reminded them to write just one page a day. When the children thought they were finished, they were to look back over their work and think how they could make it better. Maybe something could be added to the drawing or some additional words inserted. "Take your time," I urged them.

The children slowed down. Flowers appeared around houses and vapor trails behind airplanes. Maggie pouted about markers for a moment when I privately told her my decision before school started, but she happily used crayons when it came time to write. Selecting writing topics each day was choice enough for these six-year-olds; they didn't need to face decisions this early about kinds of paper, markers, crayons, or pens. By limiting choices for a while, I hoped to focus attention on the writing and build the children's investment in the process of writing every day. Gradually, I would add options and guide children in making more decisions.

RESPONSIBLE CHOICE My idealized notions of student choice had led me to believe that I'd squelch creativity by denying Maggie her markers. However, sometimes I need to step in, give suggestions, even make decisions for a child. Tom Newkirk wrote about giving children choices: "It is not simply choice that we're after, but wise choice or intelligent choice" (Newkirk 1989, 184). I've learned that firm guidelines do not "squelch creativity," but may, in fact, nurture it. Boundaries free young writers to focus attention on the content of the writing. Of course, limiting the writing to one page in the writing book soon presented another dilemma. Within a few days Jason drew a picture on one side of facing pages and filled the other with sprawling letters. "Can I turn the page?" he asked. Obviously, he had more to write and needed the space. "Sure. That's fine," I replied. Then the child next to him hurried in order to turn his page. I stopped to talk to this child, to affirm his work—and to slow him down and prevent a potential bandwagon.

Such is the tension of rules, procedures, and guidelines. There are always exceptions; nothing is engraved in stone. Rules and procedures provide a flexible structure to support the children's development, to encourage involvement and risk taking. To be effective they need to be fluid. But make no mistake, there is a clearly defined structure here and the children understand how to function in it. As each class of children and I move through the first weeks of school, we establish procedures for writing workshop to meet both the needs of individuals and the welfare of the group. Though there are similarities year to year, each group takes on its own character.

TIME FRAME Every year, however, I use a workshop time frame similar to Giacobbe's that includes:

1. mini-lesson (five to eight minutes in length)
2. writing, with teacher conferring with individuals (approximately twenty to thirty minutes)

3. large-group sharing, where two or three children read their writing to the group and receive responses (ten to fifteen minutes)

The total time runs approximately forty-five minutes. In the beginning of the year this may be shorter, and later the time may be extended to an hour.

PURPOSE OF WORKSHOP In writing workshop we are learning *how* to write—a skill that goes beyond putting thoughts and ideas on paper. In some schools, daily writing is done only in "journals" where revision is not part of the process. For many young writers "writing is writing." I believe if children write in journals first thing in the morning, for instance, in their minds they have done their writing. When it comes time for workshop and revising and crafting our writing, these young children would lack energy for the process. A principal said to me, "I think we do a lot of journaling and freewriting in school and say we're 'teaching writing.'" I have to agree. Writing workshop goes beyond journaling in that we *teach children how to write*—how to put ideas on paper, but then also how to revise, clarify, and craft those ideas to communicate effectively.

Sometimes children write deeply personal pieces that are not meant to be crafted. I've found that in these cases the children often want to share feelings or information with someone. In that event, I listen and acknowledge what I've heard. One year, while writing a story for Mother's Day, Brenda wrote, "My Mommy feels sad because she says my Daddy doesn't love her anymore. He loves somebody else." I knew I couldn't let Brenda read those lines at our Mother's Day program. But that day I said only, "That sounds very sad for you." The next morning Brenda told me during writing workshop, "I lined that part out that I read to you yesterday because I think my Mommy will be sad if she heard that part." I'd been considering possible ways to lead Brenda to this decision, but she came to it on her own. We can generally trust children's sensibilities. I'm careful not to break trust with a child by discussing with others any highly personal information a child may write. (The one exception, of course, is child abuse, which, by law, teachers must report.)

WRITING MATERIALS Initially, everyone writes in a large book of unlined paper. Pencils without erasers make it easy for children to learn to line out rather than erase—a procedure that facilitates revision. The book contains forty pages and, conceivably, could last each child forty days of school. However, Lori's story spills over to four pages in two days, while Chris' piece is carefully executed on one page in three days' time. The way in which the children work—the pace and style—is a function of each child's personality.

Writing in blank books at the beginning of the school year offers several advantages. The book provides a sequenced record of a child's writing during the early days of the school year, which is helpful in getting to know the child and also in communicating to parents. With management tasks minimized, the children concentrate on putting their thoughts on paper, and I focus on responding to them. After just a few days, the children's stories become longer as they incorporate details and additional information. They experiment with spelling. I show them how to line out rather than erase when they wish to make changes and how to use carets to insert letters or words. They begin to experience the craft of writing.

Our writing center holds an assortment of paper and the children take responsibility for selecting paper, determining the number of sheets, and stapling. I've found that young writers, like most adults, favor smooth, clean, high-quality sheets when they start a new piece. A box holds staplers, staple removers, tape, scissors, and cans with assorted pencils and pens. The children have access to all these supplies (Giacobbe 1982). I'd like to say that this writing center is neat, organized, and well kept, but every year it quickly takes on a rather ragged appearance. Pencil cans become depositories for the lost and found crayons and pencils of the classroom. New pencils soon disappear to be replaced by badly chewed stubs. First graders eat the erasers and feed the wood to the pencil sharpener. When they get paper, they pull sheets from the middle of the stack like someone digging past the crust and first slices in a loaf of bread,

In earlier years, I taught first graders to use a stapler in order to staple seatwork papers. Now I devote a mini-lesson to explain how to line up paper, place the stapler, and squeeze gently. I present the lesson, see nods of understanding, but I know that the children still need to experiment and learn from their experiences. The first roll of tape lasts a maximum of two days, so we talk about wise use of materials and that the school cannot provide an unending supply of such items. The children understand and take responsibility for using supplies.

As the children use the last of the blank pages in their writing books, I phase in individual writing folders (ones without pockets work best) as a place for each child to store new writing (Giacobbe 1982; Graves 1983). Setting up folders takes several mini-lessons scattered over a period of time. We keep the folders in five small cardboard file caddies, which makes it easy for the children to retrieve and return the folders. First graders are not particularly good at maintaining writing folders. Soon, some folders are overflowing, with paper extending from all three open sides. During writing workshop, a folder topples from a desk and the paper scatters. "Oh no!" says the child and I think, "Not again." But I say nothing—usually. These are young children and they learn through their experiences, even from such minor things as spilled writing folders.

We continually negotiate our management problems. In a talk about the folders, we decide to clean them out once a month or so and file old writing in boxes where the children have access to them. Sometimes, like the time the pencils disappeared and we found them in one student's desk, the initiative for negotiation comes from the children. There are days when I think it would be easier to just impose directives on the group. But then I realize that I'd be back in the role of enforcer and the children would have little investment in my decisions. So we start with a few classroom procedures and negotiate others as the need arises. The classroom becomes predictable, yet evolving to accommodate the ongoing development of the children. The structure serves diversity among the children, and I work with them according to their individual needs.

One morning after problems with overflowing folders, the children used free-play time to organize their writing folders. They replaced one or two pieces of recent writing and gathered the rest in a folder made of construction paper in a box that we labeled "January Writing." Periodically, as writing folders became filled, we repeated the same activity. Keeping all the children's writing in the classroom until the year's end is important. The children need to look back at their writing from time to time to see their own growth or to turn to old pieces for ideas when they are stuck for a new topic. The accumulated writing also provides documentation to share with parents at conference time (Giacobbe 1982).

On this morning I watched Edward, a reluctant writer in September, carefully turn each sheet in his neat stack of papers. He examined each page, smiling and occasionally talking to himself and nodding. When he had finished, he brought the folder to me and said, "Anyways, I like to write, so don't lose this because this is real important."

That same morning I sat on the floor with Matthew, helping him sort through the disarray of papers in his folder, sequencing stories that long ago lost their staples, trying to teach him something about organization. I was lost, but Matthew knew how each page fit with the others. Amazing.

"I'm a pretty sloppy kid," he smiled rather matter-of-factly.

"Really?" I replied.

"Yeah, sloppy. I said that to my mom once—about me being sloppy. Guess what she said."

"What?"

"She said that's the way I came and I always been sloppy. Guess I'll always be a little bit sloppy." He grinned broadly. His demeanor and tone revealed awareness and acceptance of self. Then he shrugged his shoulders and added, "But I'm still a good writer, don't you think?"

"Right, Matt. You are a good writer." Edward, Matt, and all their classmates understood what was important.

Children Writing: The First Days

In watching first graders begin to write, I've noticed that each one works differently: different topics, different pace, different working styles. The stories of children over the first days of school show the diverse ways children move into writing and the range of teacher responses.

Chad

Chad is blue-eyed and strawberry-blond. His father is deceased and his mother has remarried. Chad's paternal grandparents are members of the Old Order Amish community of Lancaster County. Although Chad is not an active member of this community (his mother is not Amish), he maintains close ties with his grandparents. Chad is pensive, reflective, and thoughtful. He takes his time as he works. For the first seven days of school he writes about sharks.

DAY 1 In Chad's first drawing, three sharks swim amid a school of jellyfish (Figure 5–3). At first glance, I think that either the sharks pursue the jellyfish or attempt to flee from their stinging tentacles. But when I talk to Chad I learn both assumptions are wrong. Chad gazes at me and patiently explains that men go under the sea to watch sharks. "And there's jellyfish there, too," he adds, "because jellyfish swim underwater and these sharks swam into a whole group of jellyfish. There were jellyfish in the water when we went to the beach." The men watching sharks are not in Chad's drawing but they are clearly in his mind, and Chad drew the scene not from the perspective of an outside observer but from the viewpoint of the undersea explorer.

Chad turns to read his words. "Do you mind if I write what you read on this page so we remember it?" I ask. (In the beginning of the year, with the author's permission, I sometimes lightly pencil in children's words when they read their writing to me, not for children's recall but for mine, and also to share with parents.) Chad gives permission and begins to read.

"When people go in cages they have . . ." The words are scattered randomly on the page. To read, Chad hunts for each word, stabs the page with his finger as he locates the next word. He's stuck after reading "have" because blue crayon around the sea creatures covers the pencil marks.

"How did you decide where to write these words?" I ask.

Chad looks up, gazing into my eyes and replies, "I put them wherever they would fit."

"I see. Did you write them before or after you colored the water?"

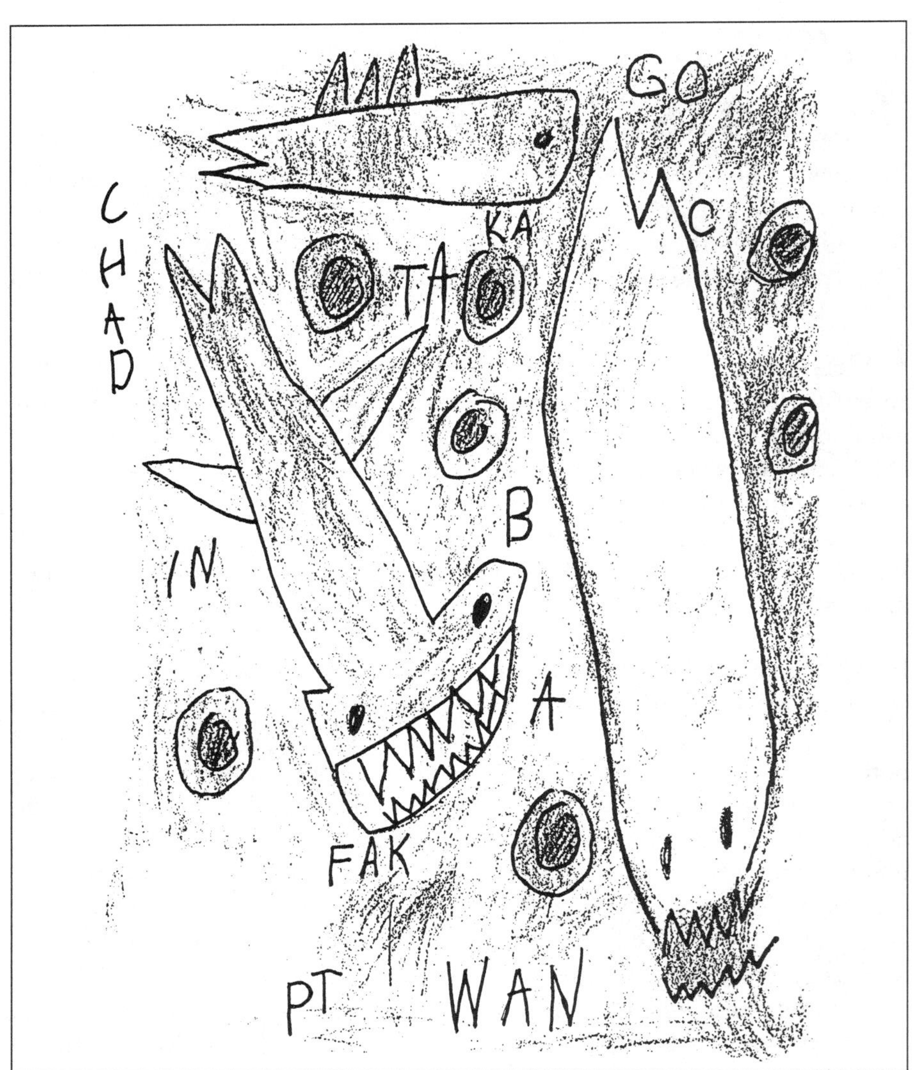

Figure 5–3

Chad's writing: Day 1

"I did the water after I did the words." I nod. Chad is having trouble locating his words because he's covered them with crayon, but I feel no need to comment on this nor on the random placement on the page. My "teacher" self thinks about left-to-right progression, but I keep still. I want to learn about Chad and his thinking, work on building trust between us, and make sure he wants to write again. To accomplish all this I've got to set aside concerns for conventions. No suggestions, no correcting, just listening, learning, delighting.

"You know a lot about sharks?" I ask.

"Yes, I do. I think sharks are very interesting creatures," Chad replies thoughtfully, maintaining that direct, serious gaze. His words seem carefully chosen.

"I think this is an interesting piece of writing. Thank you for sharing it with me," I respond and start to leave.

"What should I do now?" Chad asks.

"Well, you could keep working on the reading, if you want, or look over the whole thing to see if there's anything you'll change. It's up to you. Don't forget to write your name, though. An author always puts his name." I move on to another student.

At the end of the workshop Chad comes to me and says, "I found all the words and I remember what it says." I have no time to jot down those words and by the next day Chad has forgotten them. No matter. There would be lots of writing. Development would continue without reading or remembering every word.

DAY 2 Chad solves the problem that hindered his reading by restricting the blue crayon to the top of his picture (Figure 5–4). "I didn't put all the blue in as I did yesterday because I thought that would help me read it more easily today," he tells me. His pensive tone, his sophisticated speech is so atypical of first graders. He reads the writing, again searching the page for the words, sometimes pausing with comments such as "Wait a second. I have to find the next word." Chad reads, "One tooth from a great white shark might be twenty acres big. One shark in the whole world could be dangerous." Then he tells about the drawing. I learn even more than what is written as Chad tells about the sizes of sharks and their ferociousness.

DAY 3 Chad draws the surface of the water across the top of the page, then adds various sea creatures swimming beneath (Figure 5–5, page 83). Later he reads his writing, "A great white shark's favorite food is a sawfish. A shark would know how deep the horizon is." He uses some words more than once: "shark" appears on the page only once but Chad points to it and reads it twice.

"Tell me what you mean by 'how deep the horizon is'?" I ask.

"The horizon is the top of the water. You can look out and see the horizon when you're standing on the beach. Sharks live under the horizon, in the water. They know where it is, how deep the horizon is as they swim."

I understand. Chad's vocabulary, like all children's, develops as he comes upon words in conversation every day. He adds those words to his vocabulary, constructing the meaning by connecting the new word to what he presently understands and making his own sense of that word. Using "horizon," with his approximation of the meaning, was a way of playing with language, of refining meaning through use. I've regularly seen children develop language proficiency this way.

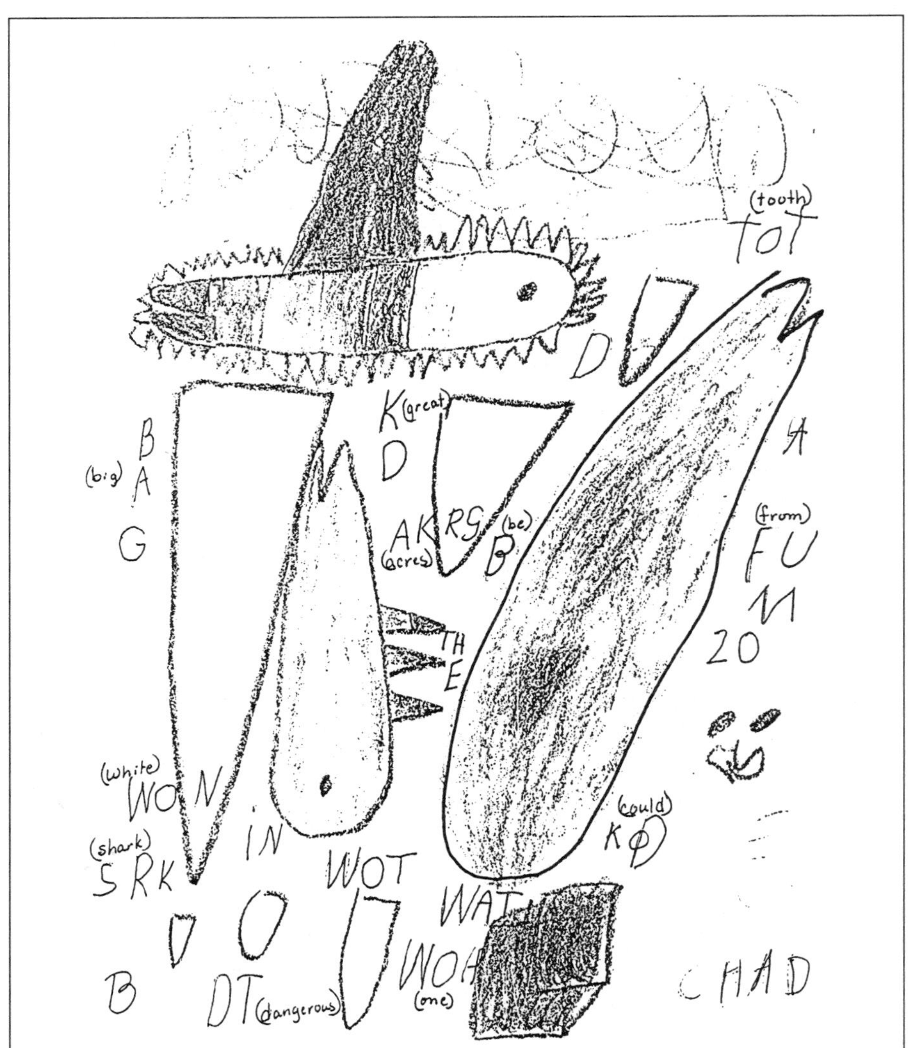

Figure 5–4

Chad's writing: Day 2, "One tooth from a great white shark might be twenty acres big. One shark in the whole world could be dangerous."

Chad continues writing (Figure 5–5) after I leave by adding the numeral one and the row of zeros to explain just how deep the horizon might be, and then, on the opposite page, a title: "SRKS."

DAY 4 Chad draws one large, black shark and the surrounding sea, then writes in left-to-right progression, "Sharks are dangerous. A great white is sometimes dangerous" (Figure 5–6, page 84). He inserts large dots between the words to establish boundaries. Like many children, he develops this strategy on his own to help him write and read his own words. I can see how these

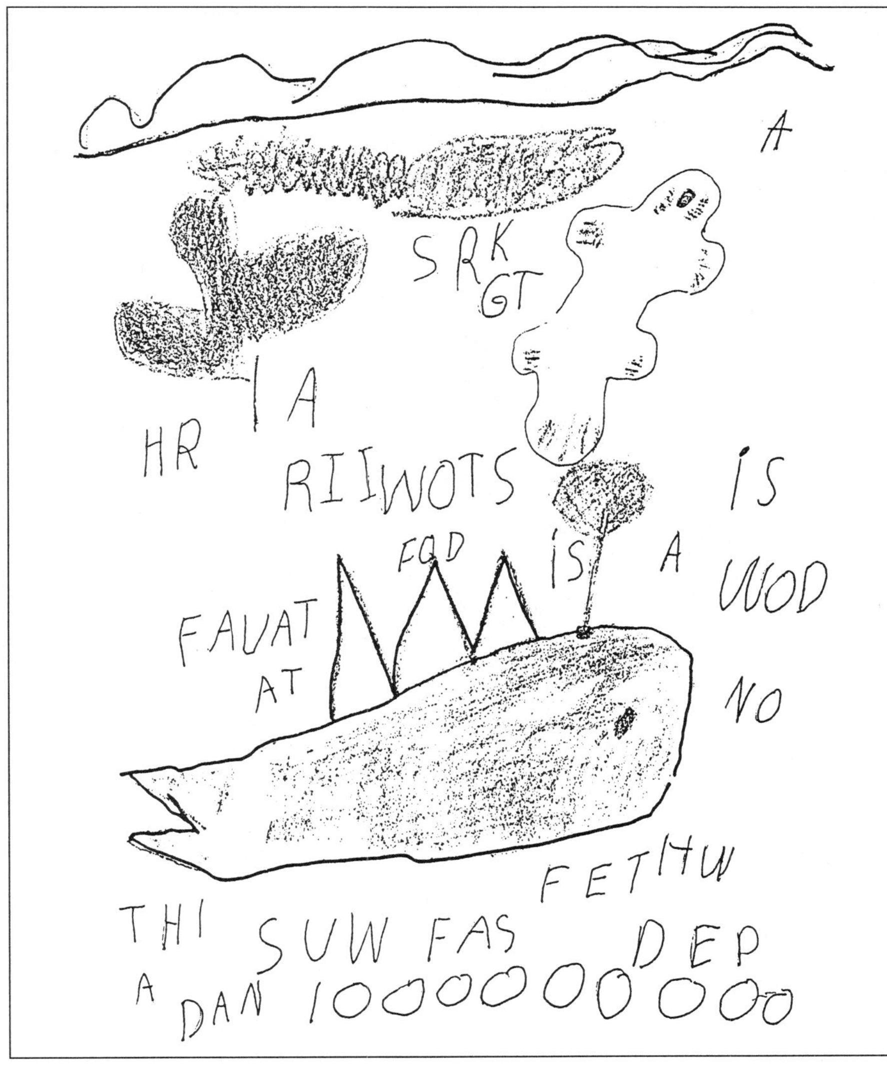

Figure 5–5

Chad's writing: Day 3, "A great white shark's favorite food is a sawfish. A shark would know how deep the horizon is."

dots assist his reading by helping him focus on each word. For Chad, the dots function far more efficiently than spaces between words.

DAYS 5 AND 6 With the discovery of left-to-right progression, Chad's fluency develops. His next story extends to two pages (Figures 5–7a and 5–7b, pages 85 and 86). Chad reads, "When a hammer head shark lays babies, it can lay 40 or 50 babies. If you kill a fish, the person who killed it can be in great danger because blood brings a shark. A nurse shark is dangerous." The story continues (see Figure 5–8, page 87). Chad reads, "A nurse shark is dangerous.

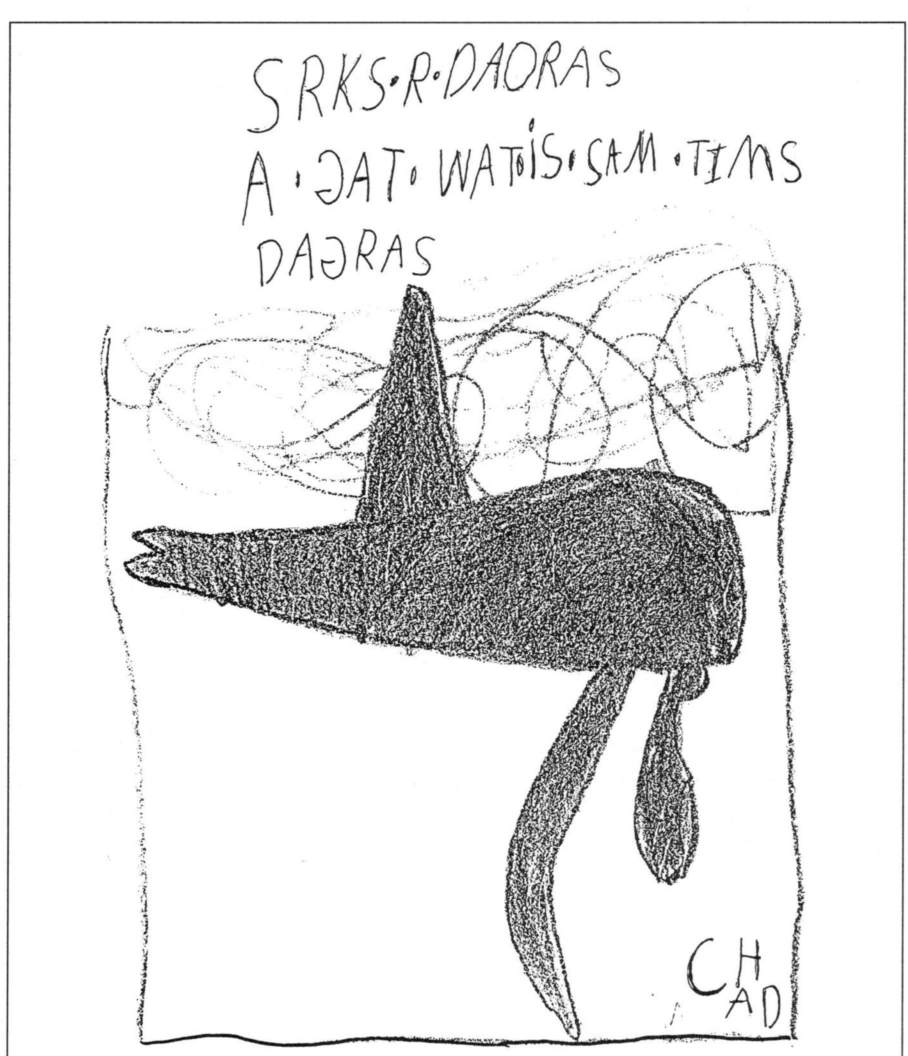

Figure 5–6

Chad's writing: Day 4, "Sharks are dangerous. A great white is sometimes dangerous."

Any person that's in the water may destruct. The person that's in the water can be killed." Chad carefully draws the pictures, correlating the details between illustrations and text. The nurse shark hovers above the distraught human, colored red—the color of blood. Above the shark and the human is a gray shadow, which, Chad explains, is the bottom of the fisherman's boat as seen from underwater.

DAY 7 "A shark can love each other. When a shark loves each other, they make a cave that's a hut" (Figures 5–9a and 5–9b, pages 88 and 89). Chad reads his piece and gazes into my eyes with the straightforward, gentle look that I believe is an extension of the honest heart that makes its way onto every page of his writing.

The saga of sharks ends. The following day Chad writes a short piece about travel: "People go across the ocean. They go from California to India." Then he launches into a series of pieces about rockets. When a hurricane threatens the eastern United States, Chad writes about hurricanes for several days. In the next few weeks he writes a series on each of the following topics: robots, the ocean, stars, and clowns.

On the day when grandparents are invited to school for lunch, Chad's Amish grandparents attend. Ten minutes into the afternoon I notice that Chad

Figure 5–7a

Chad's writing: Day 5, "When a hammer head shark lays babies it can lay 40 or 50 . . ."

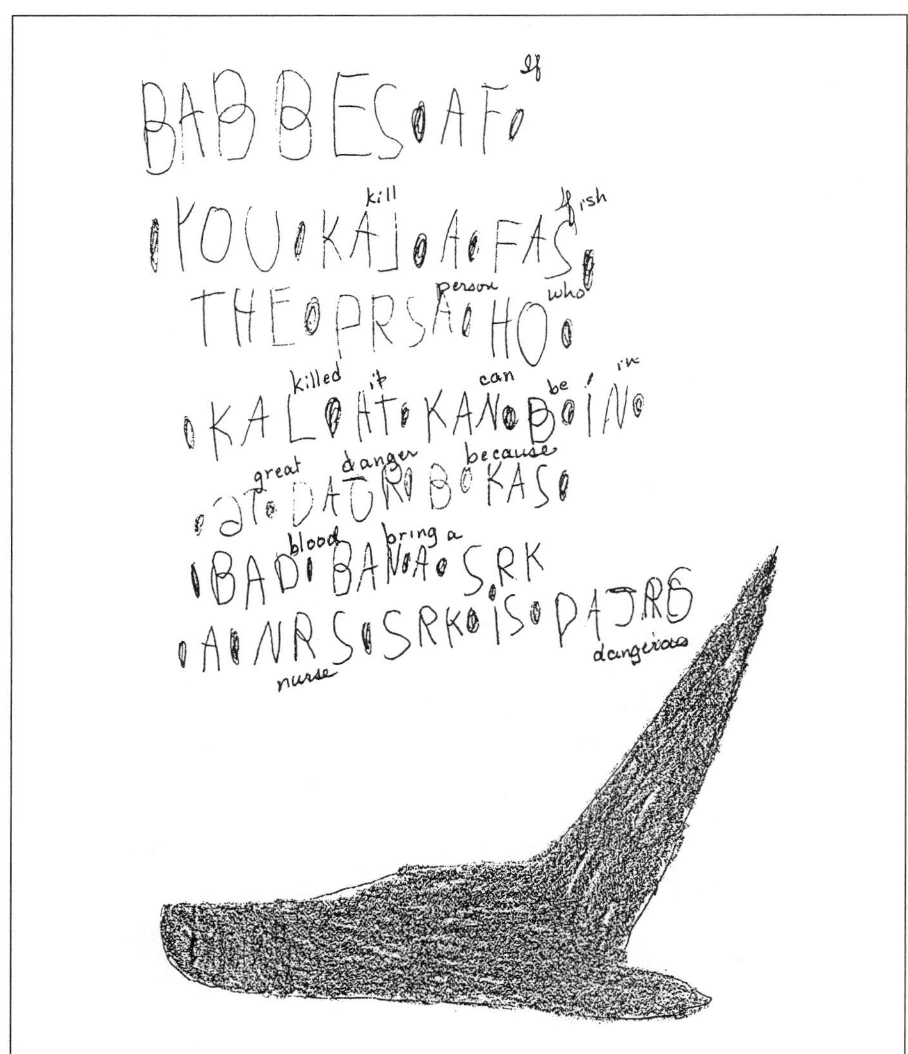

Figure 5–7b

Chad's writing: Day 6, ". . . babies. If you kill a fish, the person who killed it can be in great danger because blood brings a shark. A nurse shark is dangerous."

is missing. I send frantic messages to the office. A few minutes later a calm Chad appears with his grandfather. They've been touring the school. This gentleman with a white beard and dressed in the black garb of the Amish shakes my hand and bows ever so slightly. He thanks me for teaching Chad to read and to write. He tells me that he writes too. I look into his eyes and then into Chad's. I see the same gentle gaze and I understand, as never before, why our Lancaster County Amish are known as "the gentle people."

Later in the year, an illustrated *Stopping by a Wood on a Snowy Evening*, by Robert Frost, becomes Chad's favorite book. In March Chad begins to write poetry. One rainy, spring morning he hands me this poem:

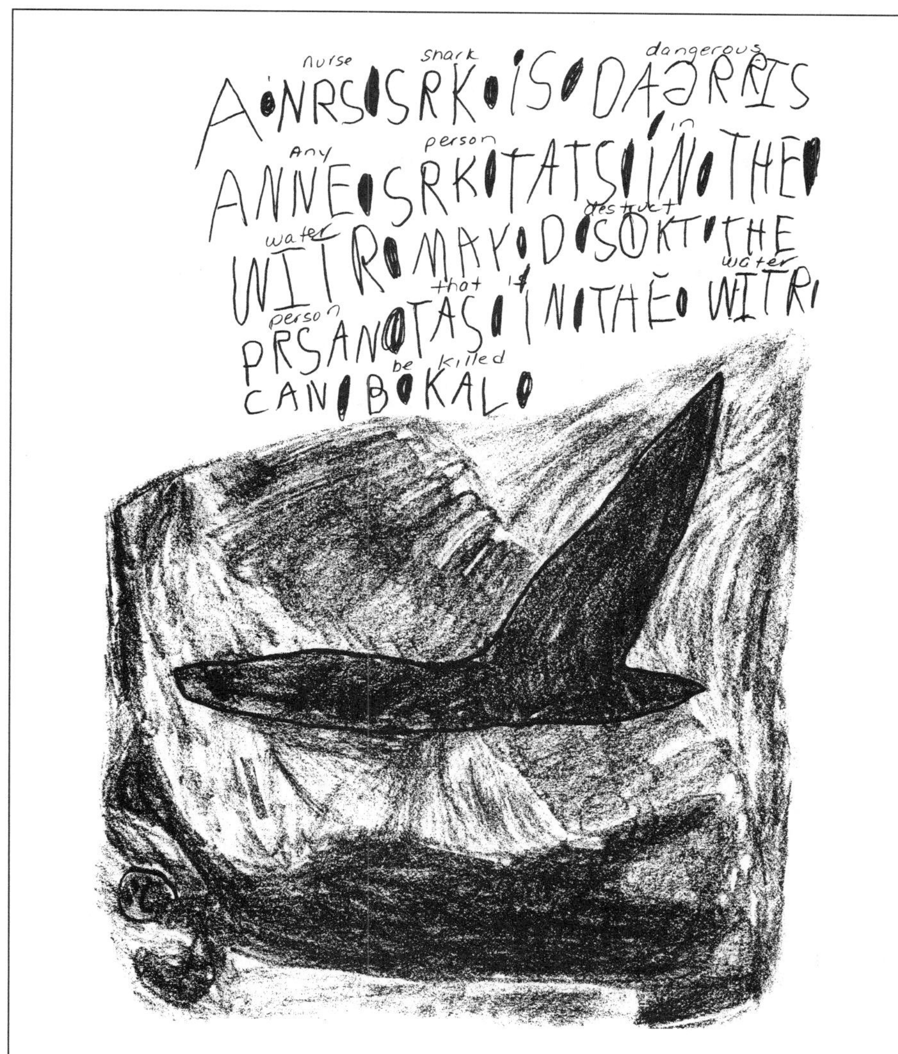

Figure 5–8

Chad's writing: Day 6, "A nurse shark is dangerous. Any person that's in the water may destruct. The person that's in the water can be killed."

> *Spring is dreary, dark and deep. And lots of children play with me. And a drafty wind sweeps the earth. And a drafty wind sweeps the earth.*

Chad says, "I'm going to be a writer when I grow up." No doubt he can reach his goal. But then, he already is a writer.

SARAH

Sarah's small size, brunette hair, brown eyes with long lashes, and creamy complexion give her a pixie look. She loves precision, which is evident in her

Figure 5–9a

Chad's writing: Day 7, "A shark can love each other. When a shark loves each other . . ."

neat desk, her deliberate pace at everything she undertakes, and her enjoyment of math computations, each number carefully formed. Sarah's parents are divorced. She lives with her mother and younger sister in a low-rent apartment complex. Her father resides miles away in Pittsburgh and Sarah sees him infrequently. Shy and quiet, Sarah is also one of the youngest members of the class.

DAY 1 Sarah draws a band of blue across the top of the page to make sky, then a similar green band across the bottom for grass. She adds an apple tree,

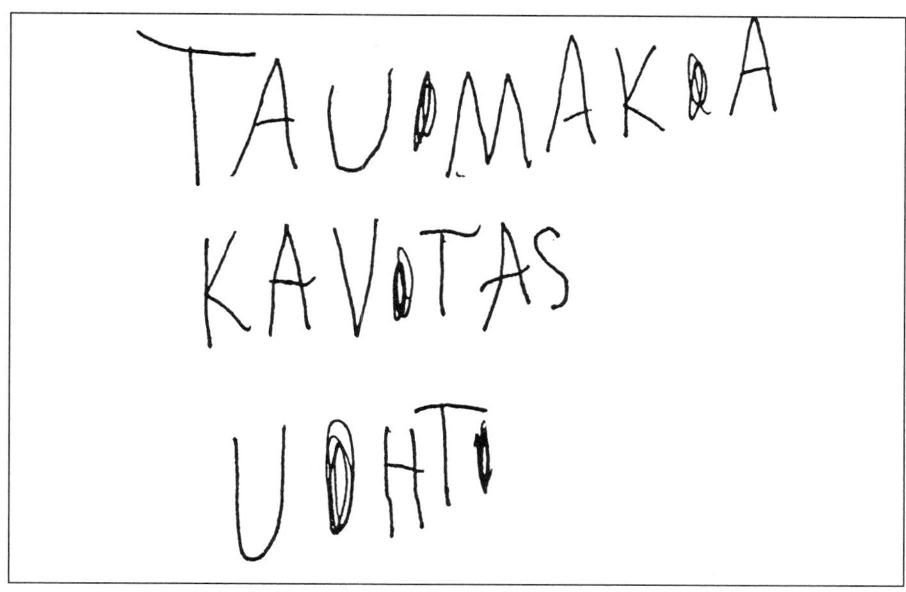

Figure 5–9b

Chad's writing: Day 7, ". . . they make a cave that's a hut."

sun, and a large flower. She works quietly, head down except to steal occasional glances at the child next to her. I stoop at her desk, she smiles shyly and says in a hushed little voice, "It's a tree and a flower."

"Oh, a tree and a flower," I reply in an equally quiet voice.

"An apple tree," she adds.

"Oh, and what else will you draw?" I ask.

Sarah shrugs, hesitates, then replies, "Me and my mom and my sister."

"Ahh, well, I'll be interested to see this after you do that." After school I look through the children's writing and see that Sarah penciled drawings of three people and added her name and date. She also wrote "I," a heart, "U" (the "I love you" message that many young children have learned) and added heart-shaped balloons on strings (see Figure 5–10).

DAYS 2–7 Sarah writes, then reads the "I love you" message. She spends most of her time drawing and seems to add words at the end of each workshop almost as an afterthought to fulfill a requirement to write. A close look at her succession of drawings reveals an evolving development: Each drawing expands on the one before it. Sarah begins each one with the tree, flower, sun, and people she included in her first drawing and then adds to the scene. A rainbow appears on the second day, a tiny house on the third, and on the fourth day the house enlarges as though through a zoom lens.

In our conference Sarah tells me she is playing outside her house with her sister. "Could you write those words?" I ask. Sarah looks at me. "Could you

Figure 5–10

Sarah's writing: Day 1

write 'I play'? Listen for the letters you hear." I repeat the words "I play" slowly, emphasizing each letter, then ask Sarah what she hears first as I repeat the words again.

"I?" she says.

"You got it. Write it," I answer. Sarah writes the letter *I*, looks up, and smiles. "What's next?" In a couple of moments Sarah has added "P A" and together we read her sentence: "I play" (I P A). "You wrote a whole sentence, Sarah," I say. She smiles shyly and goes back to coloring. On the following two days Sarah draws her house and writes "I P A" (Figure 5–11).

Figure 5–11

Sarah's writing: "I play."

DAY 10 Sarah draws a tree, a bush with flowers, the sun, sky, grass, and a person (Figure 5–12, page 92). All these elements appeared in prior pictures, but never in quite the same arrangement. She writes, "I Y T e G r e" and reads this line: I went to my tree to get a leaf.

"Sarah! All those words! And this picture—you tried some new things here," I say. Sarah smiles her shy smile and nods. Later she adds "A i e four i m," copying "four" from the chalkboard. I don't get back to Sarah to ask what the words say, but I don't need to know. I do know that this has been a breakthrough day for her.

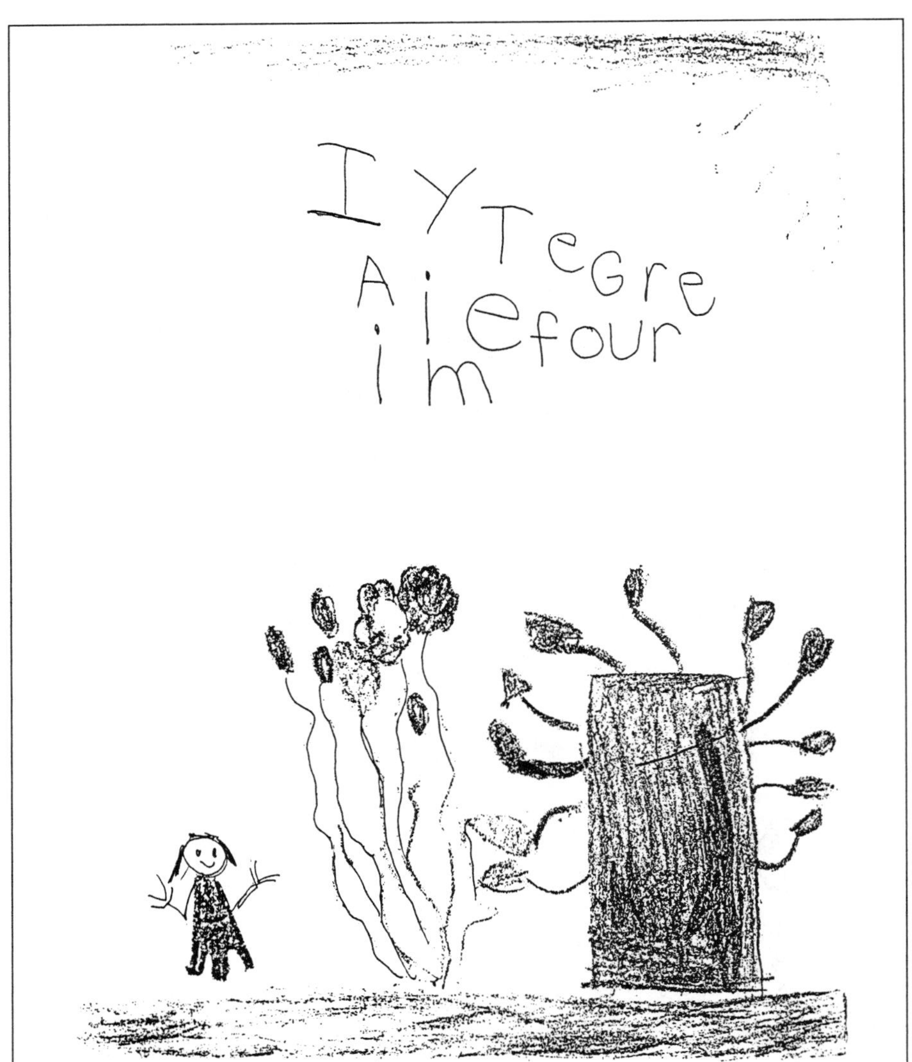

Figure 5–12

Sarah's writing: "I went to my tree to get a leaf."

Every day thereafter Sarah writes a different message. Her fluency increases. Only a week later she writes: I Y two B four I e e r A B two e N I r A B two I C D N I N two B N I Y N. She reads her writing, pointing to the letters as she does so, using them as clues along with her memory of her intended meaning: I went to bed. Before, my mom, she read a book to me. Then I read a book to my sister. Then I went to bed. Then I went (Figure 5–13).

In the following days and weeks Sarah composes pieces about visiting Kennywood Park on a trip to Pittsburgh, learning to ride a bike, picking apples in a local orchard, dressing as a witch for Halloween, missing the school bus. She fills the page beside each picture with rows of letters. As she writes

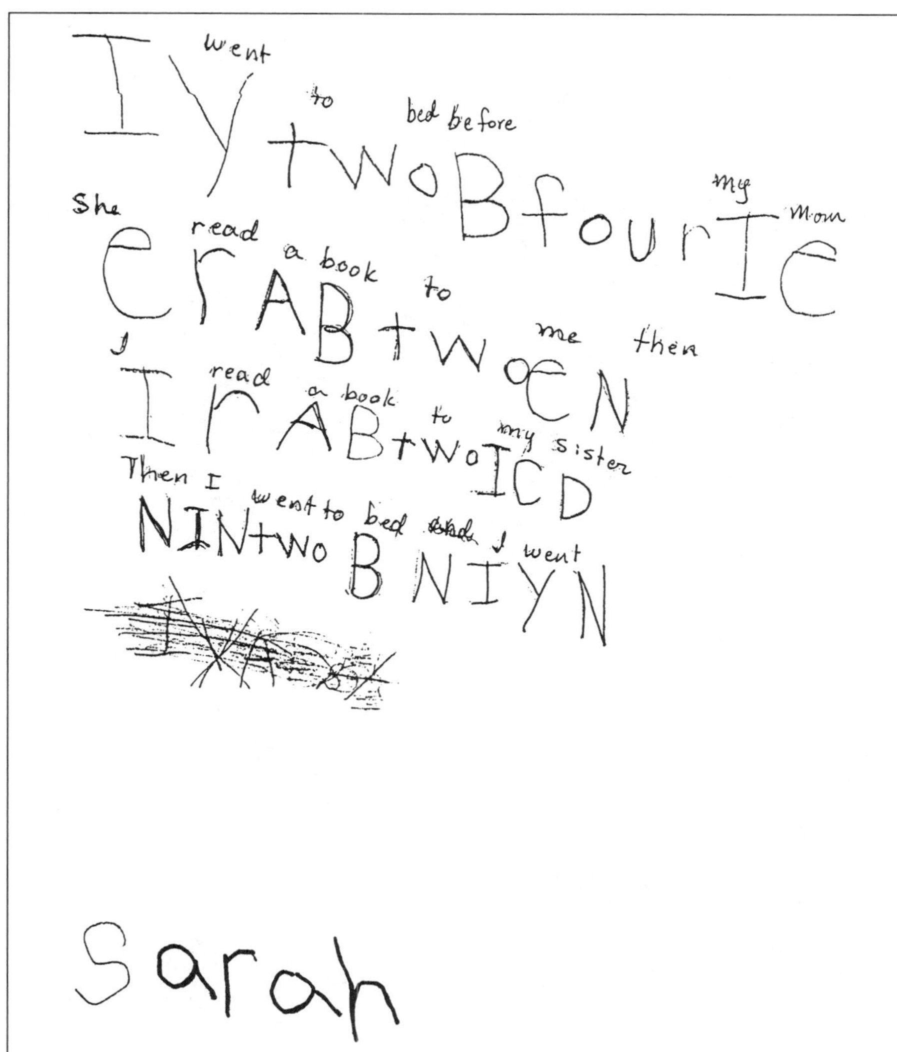

Figure 5–13

Sarah's writing in March: "I went to bed. Before, my mom, she read a book to me. Then I read a book to my sister. Then I went to bed. Then I went."

she whispers words to herself. She cannot always read her entire piece because she writes only one or two letters for each word and as the pieces grow in length she has difficulty remembering every word she has written. "I'll just tell you what it says," she says when she gets stuck.

Sarah works carefully and thoughtfully all year. In early March Sarah writes "Tiying My Shows" and illustrates the story with a picture of a house with Sarah sitting inside tying her shoes (see Figure 5–14). The story seems to sum up her learning process.

I lrnd to tiy my shows! I "tod" my littl sisdr that I can tiy my shows, she sed "yay!" Sarah can tiy hr shows. my Mom seaed "good" because wen I go

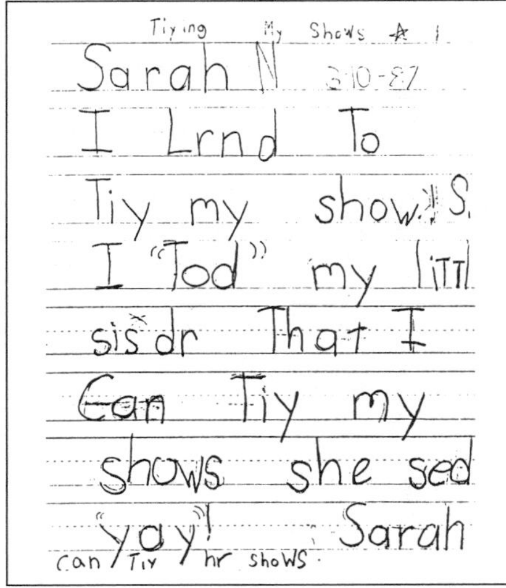
Tiying My Shows A 1
Sarah N 3-10-87
I Lrnd To
Tiy my shows.
I "Tod" my littl
sisdr That I
Can Tiy my
shows she sed
"yay!" Sarah
can Tiy hr shows.

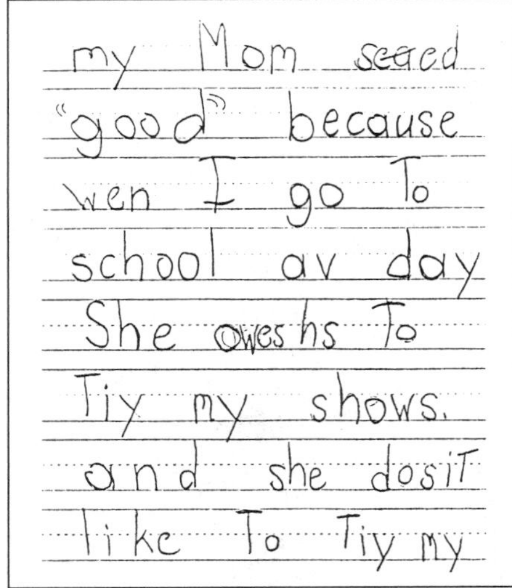
my Mom seaed
"good" because
wen I go To
school av day
She owes hs To
Tiy my shows.
and she dosit
like To Tiy my

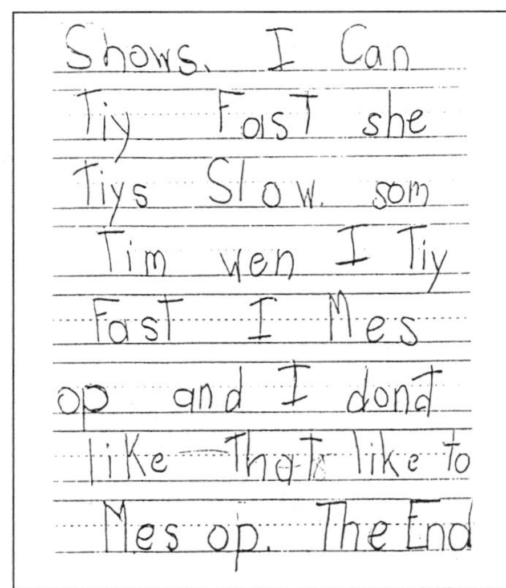
Shows. I Can
Tiy FasT she
Tiys Slow. som
Tim wen I Tiy
FasT I Mes
op and I dont
like That like to
Mes op. The End

Figure 5–14

Sarah's story

to school av day She owes hs to tiy my shows. and she dosit like to tiy my shows. I can tiy fast she tiys slow. som time wen I tiy fast I mes op and I dont like that like to mes op. The End.

Troy

Troy has dark brown eyes and curly brown hair. He is extremely shy, but on the playground he holds his own with the others despite being the smallest boy in the class. Troy's family lives only slightly above the poverty level. His father, who appeared at our parent conference in a muscle shirt with a bandanna on his head, is a laborer. I never met Troy's mother or had any contact with her. Troy moved before the school year ended.

DAY 1 Troy draws an underwater scene and labels the large fish with a letter *C* (see Figure 5–15). "That's for shark," he says, barely pausing to indicate the *C* as he fills the page with blue crayon. I wait. Troy continues to color.

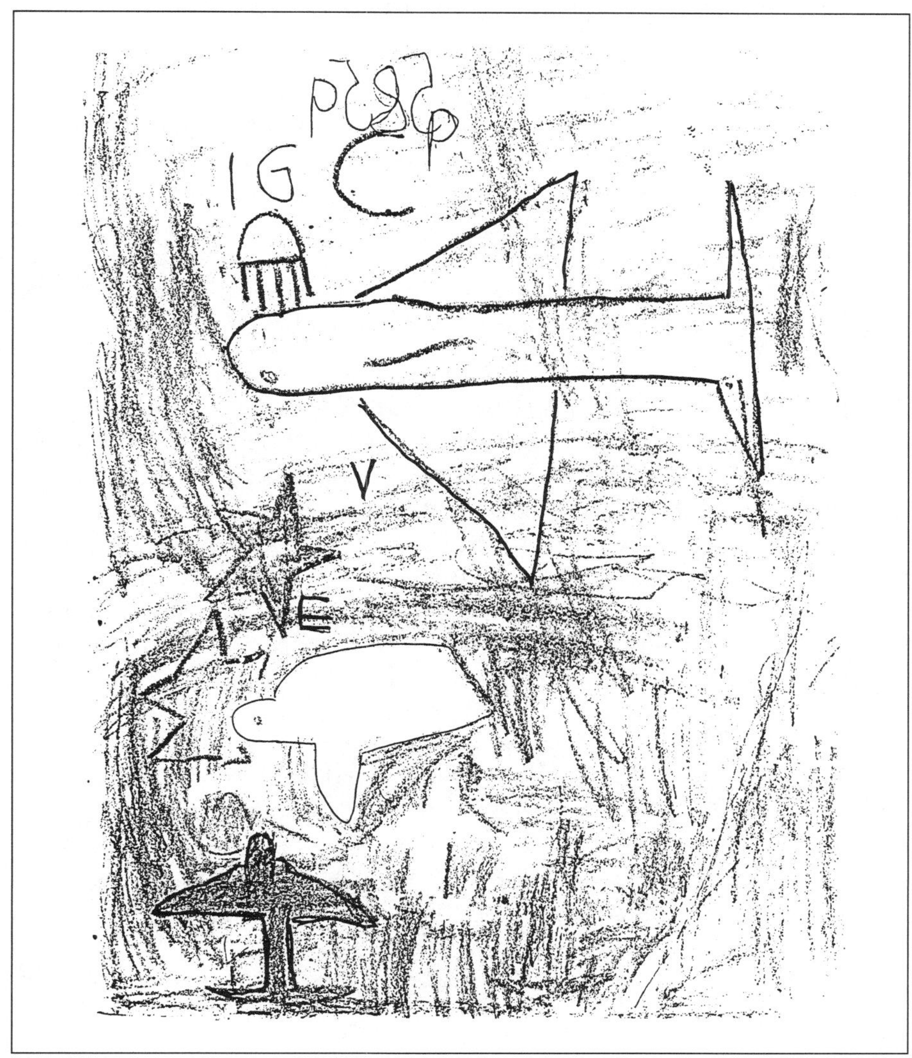

Figure 5–15

Troy's writing:
C = shark
IG = one jellyfish
E = eel
V = starfish

"Are these sharks too?" I inquire, pointing to the bottom of the picture.

Troy finally pauses. He seems somewhat startled by my interest. "Yeah, more sharks."

"What else is here?"

"Oh," Troy replies in an offhanded tone, "starfish, eel, turtle, clam. A jellyfish." He goes back to coloring. He has not yet made eye contact with me. "A jellyfish?" I reply quickly to keep his attention. "Yeah." Troy keeps coloring. "Will you write anything about the jellyfish or these other animals?" Troy glances up. I keep talking. "Jellyfish. What letter do you hear in 'Jellyfish'?"

Troy shrugs, then softly says, "Jellyfish." Pause. "G?" he suddenly asks, and picks up his pencil and writes *G*. As I leave Troy's desk I see him write *E* beside the eel.

DAY 11 For the next ten days Troy draws underwater animals and labels the pictures with the initial consonants, each day adding more and more letters to his work. Then one day he writes only one letter, a large *K*, on his picture (Figure 5–16). At first I think Troy has regressed or decided to rest from the steady growth. I am wrong. Troy tells me that he "made a big *K* for *all* these catfish." Instead of regressing, Troy is experimenting with writing and language, playing with concepts to figure out how language works.

DAY 14 Troy abandons picture labeling and writes a string of letters, which he reads: The archer fish is trying to catch the catfish (Figure 5–17, page 98). Without ever making eye contact, Troy tells about a family fishing trip. He describes his cat sitting on the bank watching the fish (upper right-hand corner of the drawing), the catfish (on the right), and the archer fish (on the left) with a butterfly under it. I ask Troy why the butterfly is in the water and he explains that the archer fish caught the butterfly by spitting at the butterfly to shoot it down. I am slightly puzzled even after asking Troy again, and I conclude that fantasy and reality mingle in his mind.

Two years after Troy left my classroom I looked at his writing and my notes from that day. Tracing his work onto a transparency for a conference presentation, I mused about the archer fish and decided to look the term up in my dictionary. I learned the archer fish has "the capacity of ejecting drops of water from its mouth at insects resting on objects over the water, causing them to fall so that it can capture them." I looked at Troy's drawing. A line extends from the mouth of the archer fish to represent the stream of water. My knowledge, not Troy's, was incomplete and my assumptions about his thinking were wrong. Troy continued to be my teacher two years after he left my classroom.

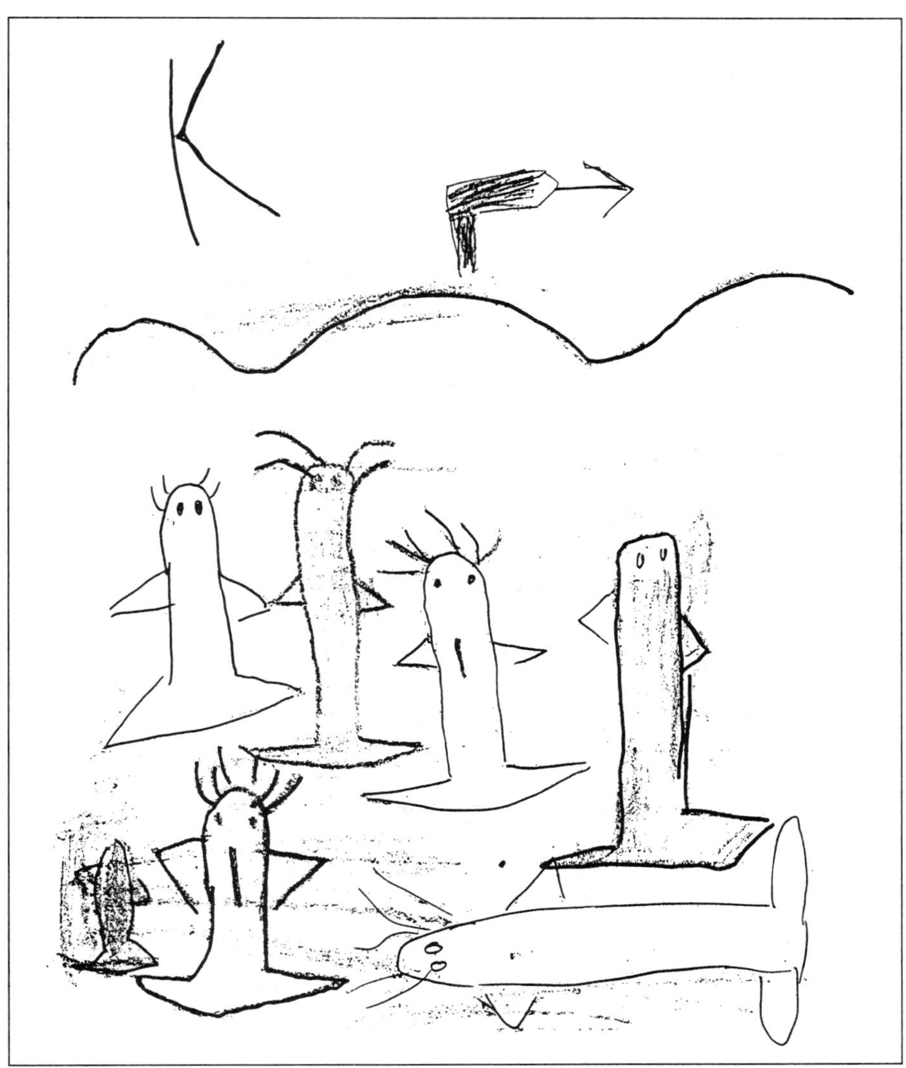

Figure 5–16

Troy's writing: K means "all these catfish."

RELUCTANT WRITERS

Some children come to the classroom reluctant to write. Usually, it's not just writing that is a problem; if we look closely we see the same behaviors in other areas of the curriculum. But because writing demands such active participation from the learner, the behaviors become obvious. Writing is one area of school that the child can't fake or move through halfheartedly. Writing requires an investment.

Figure 5–17

Troy's writing: "The archer fish is trying to catch the catfish."

The problem often doesn't surface immediately, for the child will draw and write *something*—a house, a rainbow, a design—during the first days of school. Soon the writing stagnates. For days the child draws rainbows or designs or just sits and stalls. Many factors influence classroom attitudes and performance; a child's life in the classroom can't be separated from the environment of his home, the interactions with others in his life, or his physical well-being.

Physical Issues

Ben drew designs and wrote very little in the writing workshop. He often seemed puzzled when I talked to him. Although he was agreeable and pleasant and even nodded in acknowledgment when I made suggestions, I saw little progress. Ben drew more and more designs. Occasionally, if I sat beside him, encouraging him while he worked, he drew a truck or a car. Eventually, Ben's parents and I considered his frequent ear infections, had his hearing tested, and uncovered a hearing loss. Ben did not follow through with tasks because he heard only snatches of classroom talk. He certainly didn't hear sounds in order to write corresponding letters. Fortunately, Ben's hearing problems were correctable, though it was late in the school year before the physical problems were cleared up. When a child struggles, I want to remember to consider the possibility of physical issues.

Writer Avoids Writing

Cory avoided writing. Every day he quickly drew something (usually indistinguishable) and only occasionally wrote letters or words (and those he frequently copied from the chalkboard). Then he spent the rest of the workshop goofing off. In an interview with Cory, he could not tell me of anyone he knew who wrote. One day as the workshop began, I plopped a little chair beside his desk and said, "I want to write with you today. I start with my name. How do you start?" I kept my tone cheery and genuinely interested. I wanted to learn what Cory thought and did when he wrote.

Cory looked at me in surprise. I started writing. Cory decided to take out his crayons, then a pencil. "Where do you put your name?" I asked. Cory wrote his name. "Oh, I see at the top. Do you write the date there too?" He looked to the chalkboard and copied the date. "Now, what do you do next? How do you get your ideas? Do you write about what you do after school? Or things at recess? Because I know you like to be outside a lot." Cory nodded, grinned, and began drawing. I went back to my writing and stopped to watch Cory for a while, then left saying I'd be back. I checked back every few minutes, provided support as he listened for letters to write, listened to him talk about his picture. The extra support this day helped Cory get into writing and he began taking the workshop seriously. Writing never became his favorite part of the day but he did become deeply involved in some of the pieces he wrote.

Carol Zartman, a first-grade teacher and an exceptionally good observer and listener, told the story of a little boy who struggled every day to write. "I just didn't know how to help this little guy. I didn't want to step in and take over, direct him in what to write, because I knew he'd never get involved. One day I wrote his dictated story and I saw how many ideas he had in his head. The next day I gave him a 'secretary,' a peer who took his dictation to get him started, then turned it over to him. It worked." The secretary wrote his words and also showed him how to get his ideas on paper, both through demonstration and explanation of how she wrote. After a short time, he wrote on his own without her.

Anyone who writes knows about stalling tactics. There are times when I'll do anything to avoid writing, including major household tasks I'd usually avoid. Children do this too. Joey sharpens his pencil, chats with Craig, pauses to browse through a book, and generally avoids getting down to work. Sometimes I confront this with a mini-lesson where I role-play the exaggerated behaviors of a stalling writer. When this doesn't work, I watch and wait and finally choose the time to confront him with a matter-of-fact reality. "You have a choice," I say. "You may write now or later at recess." It's amazing how many young writers decide to use the workshop time.

Emotional Issues

Sometimes emotional factors block a child's ability to write. Marcy cried silently every time the class did something new, whether it was writing or removing pages from the math workbook. She whispered only "I can't" when asked what was wrong. She stretched bland writing topics out for days. One day I presented a mini-lesson demonstrating brainstorming to find a topic. Again, the silent tears rolled down Marcy's face. I stooped in front of her desk and she said, "I can't."

"Do you live alone?" I asked in a no-nonsense voice.

"No."

"Who lives with you?"

"My mom."

"Write it down," I said. Marcy wrote "Mom."

"Anyone else?"

"I have a brother."

"Write it down." Marcy wrote her brother's name.

"Anyone else?"

"My cat." Marcy wrote "cat" without my direction.

Then she looked up and said, "I used to have a dad, but he died when I was a baby."

"Oh yeah?" I replied, barely audibly. Marcy started telling the stories of her dad, stories she had been told over and over again about the father she didn't remember. I listened. A few moments later, she wrote about her dad and at the end of the workshop, shared her story with the class. The tears stopped that day. Marcy confidently participated in all the class activities, especially writing.

However, more times than not, the emotional baggage children carry continues to hamper their involvement in classroom activities—especially writing—all year. Rich drew designs and wrote only a few words. Occasionally (with a lot of one-on-one urging and support on my part) he wrote a narrative. The only piece all year that I saw him initiate and become invested in was a story of his Christmas trip to Florida with Dad. A custody battle between Rich's divorced parents was brewing. Even though the issue would not surface for several months, the strain affected Rich's classroom performance and was evident in his rather cursory involvement in classroom activities, especially writing.

Marcy and Rich remind me of the vulnerability of all writers no matter their age. No writer knows what will emerge when she brings pencil to paper. Writers need environments where their first tentative explorations on paper not only will be accepted but also valued. Writers need to experience safety in that environment. Reluctant writers perhaps sense the vulnerability. They know instinctively that writing can be risky.

Learning Styles

Cassidy plays with a penlight during the workshop, shining it inside his desk, around the room, on his arm. His paper is blank when I stop to confer. When I suggest he put the penlight away, he begins showing me what it can do. His ideas are wonderful but I have difficulty following them.

"So you have penlights and laser lights. How are they different?" I ask in an attempt at clarification. He starts explaining differences. I interrupt before he goes too far and repeat the ideas I understand. "So your penlight is not a laser pointer because it doesn't have a red light?" He nods. "It has a white light? Can you write that? Write it right here on your paper so we'll know about this penlight."

Somewhat reluctantly Cassidy picks up his pencil and starts writing (Figure 5–18a). I wait a few seconds as he starts, then leave, saying, "Good job, keep going. I'll be back." A few minutes later I stop back and Cassidy tells me about making shadows with his penlight. Again I repeat his words so he hears them and leave. He continues writing. When I stop again, I tell him I'm confused how shining the light at the ceiling will make a shadow and he shows how he puts his hands together. "Oh, so you put the backs of your hands together, then put your thumbs together and put them up. Can you write that? How you put your hands?"

I leave and Cassidy writes the words describing how to make a shadow. In these conferences I've gotten glimpses into Cassidy's thinking and learning processes. He clearly preferred to show me rather than tell me about his penlight. When I put words to his demonstrations, he was able to write. He has a good vocabulary, but seems to prefer thinking visually rather than by using language. The following day I saw again how very important these conferences were for his success as a writer.

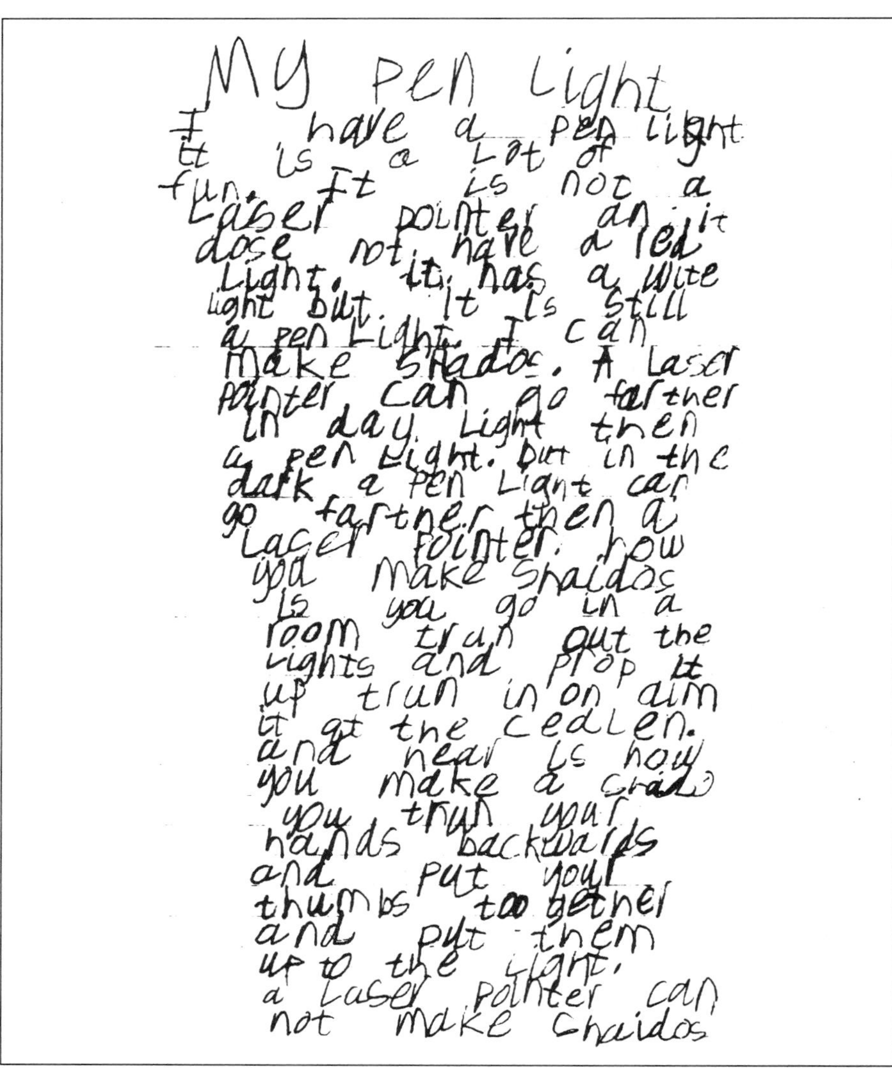

My pen Light
I have a pen Light
It is a Lot of
fun. It is not a
Laser pointer an it
dose not have a red
Light. It has a wite
light but it is still
a pen Light. I can
make shados. A Laser
pointer can go farther
in day Light then
a pen Light. but in the
dark a pen Light can
go farther then a
Laser pointer. how
you make shaidos
is you go in a
room trun out the
Lights and prop it
up trun in on aim
it at the cedLen.
and near is how
you make a crad
you trun your
hands backwards
and put your
thumbs too gether
and put them
up to the Light.
a Laser pointer can
not make chaidos

Figure 5–18a

Cassidy's writing

First Cassidy folds a paper boat. Then he writes, "How I make boats is I fold paper like this" (Figure 5–18b). He draws and numbers eight diagrams showing the paper after each folding. He's on diagram five when I stop to confer.

"I'm showing how to make a boat," he says and shows me the diagrams.

"Oh, I see. Now will you write the directions so that I will be able to know how you do each of these steps? How do you start?"

"You start like you start a paper airplane," he explains and then shows me with a sheet of paper.

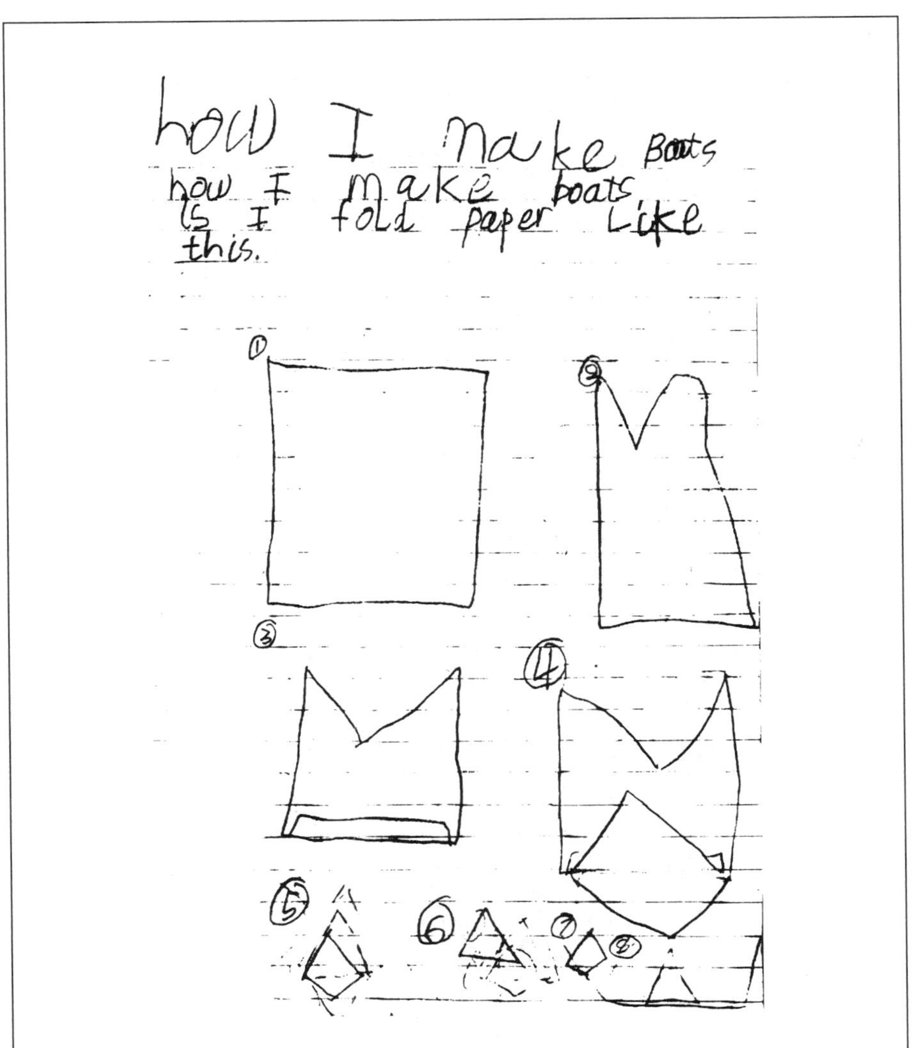

Figure 5–18b

Cassidy's diagrams of how to make boats out of paper

"You start by folding the paper in half—like you do when you make a paper airplane?"

"Un-huh," he continues folding, but with a bit of encouragement he begins to write words. With the support of frequent conferences that help him put language to his experience, Cassidy writes the directions (Figure 5–18c). In the last few minutes of the workshop he redraws his diagrams to "make them better" (Figure 5–18d). Clearly, for him drawings were the most important part.

Working with Cassidy, I came to see how he understood experience visually and spatially. Putting experience into words was more of a challenge.

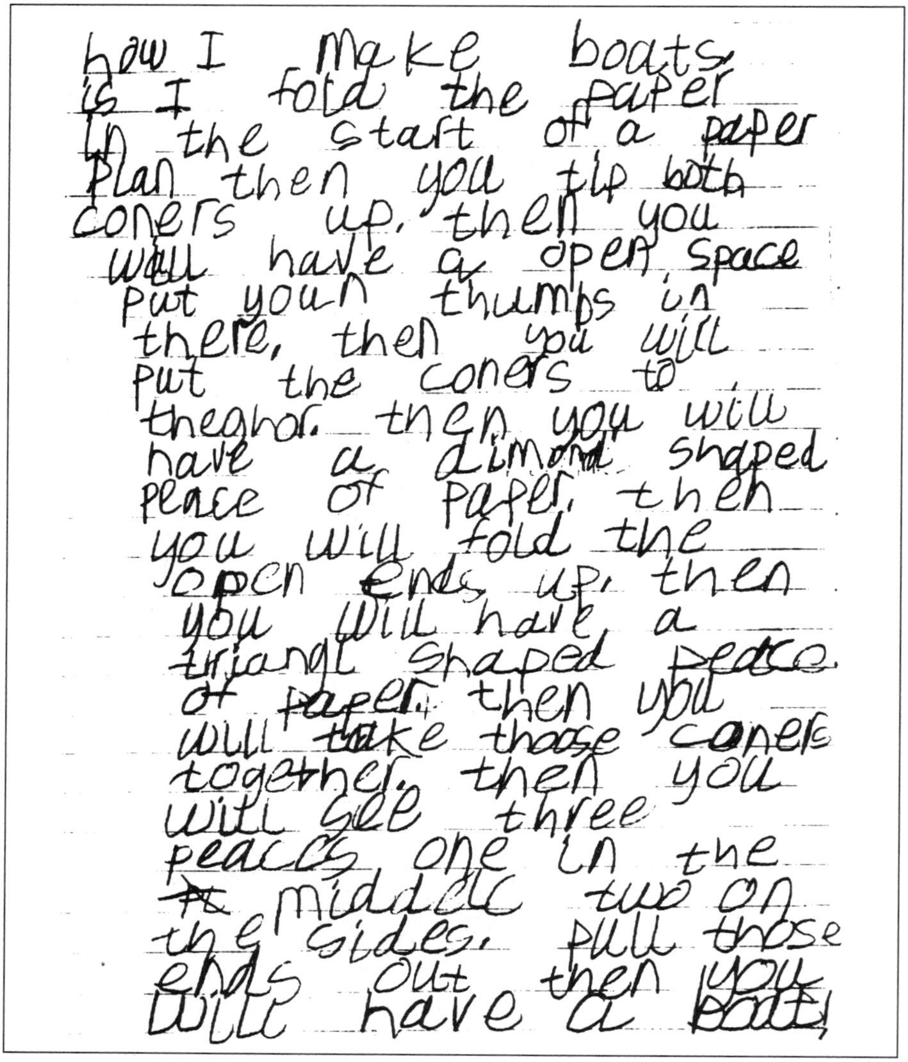

how I make boats
is I fold the paper
in the start of a paper
plan then you tip both
coners up. then you
will have a open space
put youn thumps in
there, then you will
put the coners to
theghor. then you will
have a dimond shaped
peace of paper. then
you will fold the
open ends up. then
you will have a
triangl shaped peace
of paper. then you
will take those coners
together. then you
will see three
peaces one in the
middle two on
the sides. pull those
ends out then you
will have a boat!

Figure 5–18c

Cassidy's directions for how to make paper boats

The support of frequent conferences provided language for his extensive knowledge and helped him write. As he gains experience writing, this scaffolding will be withdrawn and he will write independently.

The Struggling Writer

Jamal had written the same story about swimming "fifty-four times—every day since the first," his teacher said. In my first conference with Jamal I say, "Tell me about swimming. What do you do?" The pause before Jamal answers goes on forever. I wait.

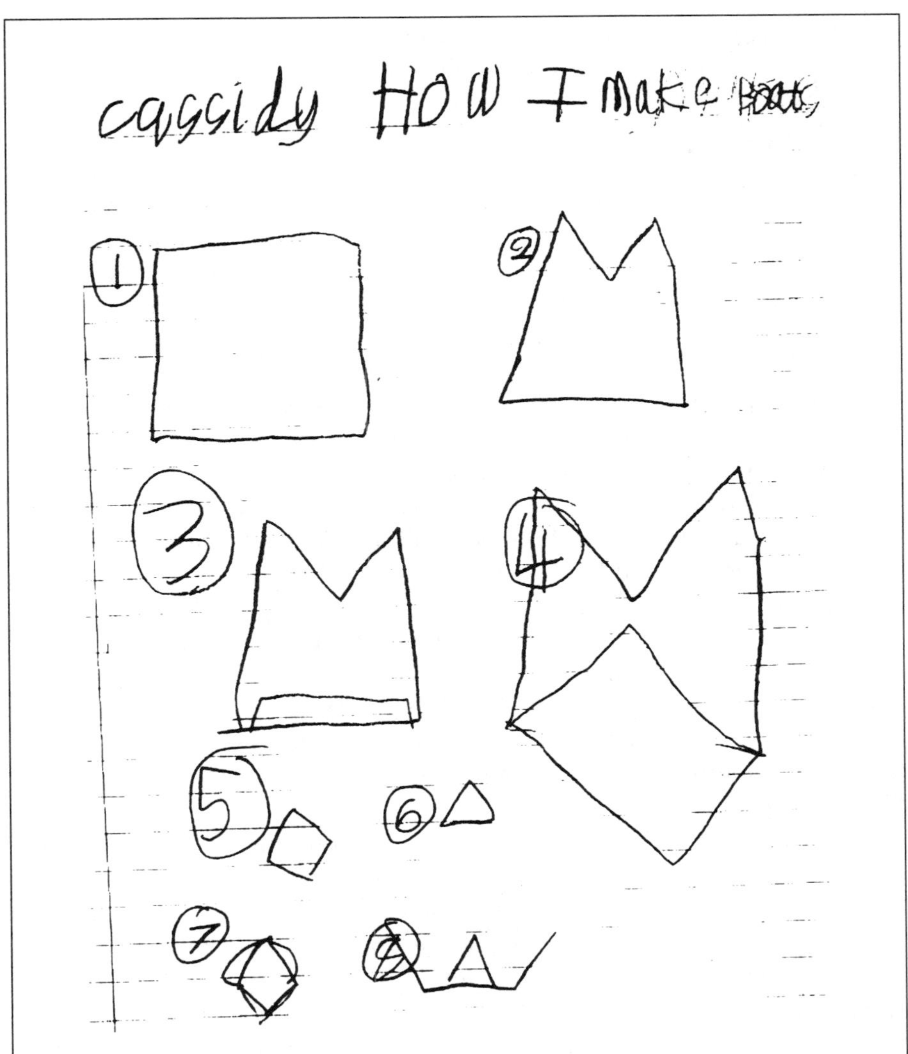

Figure 5–18d

Cassidy's revisions

"Swim and float," he finally says.

"Oh, I see you swim *and* float." His eyes meet mine for the first time. "How do you swim? How do you float?" Jamal glances away but I persist. "Tell me how you swim in the pool." Lots more silence and then Jamal begins to demonstrate swimming by moving his arms.

"Like this," he says.

"Oh, I see."

"And you float like this," Jamal bends over, pulls his legs up and grabs his legs below the knees.

"So when you swim you put your body straight and move your arms and when you float you bend over and then you float," I say.

"The pool floats you up," he answers.

"Ohhh, the pool floats you up?" I repeat his words with a questioning voice tone. I've found this questioning attitude often leads writers to elaborate.

"Yeah. You put your body straight and swim." He has repeated my words, "put your body straight."

"What's that like when you swim?" I ask. He's involved in our conversation and I want to extend this as far as he can go. He looks puzzled but I wait and repeat the question and wait some more.

"You move your arms like an eagle," he replies.

"Ohhh, you move your arms like an eagle. I see. Are you going to write that—how you move your arms like an eagle?" Jamal shakes his head.

"Why not? That's *so* interesting. You move your arms like an eagle. I can really get a picture in my head of how you swim." I say. "Can you write that?"

Jamal shakes his head but I'm not willing to let it go. "Give that a try."

"Okay," he says and I move on.

I check back later and see that Jamal has drawn a figure with outstretched arms, written his usual story, but not added anything. "Is this you with your arms like an eagle?" Jamal grins and nods. "Write it," I say, grinning back. "Get your words on paper right now." Though my words appear demanding, I keep my tone playful and encouraging. Jamal smiles and when I come back a couple of minutes later he has added two lines of letters that he reads as "like an eagle."

In my responses I've tried to get Jamal to become aware of his experience swimming and put it into words. He must have the language for his experience before he can write it. I had no idea what information would surface and it was important to avoid making leading suggestions. I want *him* to take the lead with the specifics; then I will follow with responses to help expand or clarify or focus that information. I know that what young writers first put on paper is the tip of the iceberg, there's always more beneath the surface. When he begins to get in touch with the information he knows, I confirm that I've heard his ideas and then invite him to expand with the question "What is that like?"

I'm pretty amazed at the simile he uses and see it as an indication of strong potential for this young writer. He's forging new territory and I want him to take the risk of writing what he's said, so I give some pretty strong nudges. To do so, I must continually read him, making sure that he's feeling confident, not overwhelmed, and that his motivation is not just to please me. I ask Jamal to share the writing to reinforce his risk taking. Working with Jamal has taken extra time this day; I'll take care not to let this become a pattern that will not serve him or his classmates. I know that after such a surge of effort he may "take a rest" and level off for a few days. That's okay. Progress forward is rarely lost.

There's no one strategy or set of procedures for reluctant writers. Honoring the thinking of writers and striving to help them commit ideas to paper is, I believe, the premise from which to begin. It amounts to listening, "reading" the writer, and responding honestly and supportively. Being in a hurry to solve problems or making assumptions of what the child is doing can get in the way. I try one approach after another, striving to find something that works. These children remind us of what all children need: honesty, space, caring, and our continuous efforts to help them help themselves.

Reflections

Managing writing workshops cannot be reduced to a how-to formula; management is an ongoing, complex task that develops differently within the context of each classroom. The pioneers in the teaching of writing wisely avoided giving us definitive directions even though we teachers long for concrete instructions and grasp at labels, recipes, and absolutes as we strive to get a handle on new teaching procedures. The danger is that our procedures become orthodoxy and handicap our ability to respond to children.

The challenge in implementing and managing a writing workshop is to develop fluid procedures that serve learners on a day-to-day basis. In writing workshop we work on our writing, struggle with evolving texts, develop writing skills, and learn to use writing as an effective tool for communication and learning. As a classroom teacher, I'm continually caught in the tension of an incredible balancing act. To manage all these ideas within the reality of the classroom, I've learned to trust my instincts, to consider the principles of outside experts, and to listen to the children and to my own needs. I keep working at this craft of teaching, making decisions, making mistakes, and struggling and learning. And when in doubt, I look to the children. For they always know, with the uncluttered wisdom of youth, which way to go. They continue to be my best teachers.

CHAPTER 6

Mini-Lessons

Helping Children Craft Their Writing

Six-year-old Chris wrote about a family trip to a local park. When I stopped at his desk he read his writing to me.

"I am near a pond and there is a duck and it caught a fish" (Figure 6–1).

I responded to the content, then, puzzled, pointed to his sentence, "Tell me about these zig-zaggy lines."

Figure 6–1

Chris' writing: "I am near a pond and there is a duck and it caught a fish."

"That's—what did you call it—'celery'? You know, like you did—when you want to put something in."

"Oh, you mean carets."

"Yeah, carets. I put those in because it means put a space here. Like you showed us, like you told us to do."

"Oh, I understand, Chris. You want spaces between your words so you're using a caret to show where you need them. Good thinking; I'm impressed. Do you think you will keep doing this? Or will you just remember to leave spaces without the carets?" I replied. Chris looked at his paper and thought a moment.

"Well, I really wanted to use them today, " he said, a hint of reluctance to give them up in his voice, "but maybe tomorrow I won't."

"Okay, whatever." I smiled and got up to leave.

"I think tomorrow I might just leave the spaces, but I don't know yet," he added and we exchanged smiles.

"Like you showed us, like you told us to do." The words ring in my head. In our mini-lesson moments earlier I had explained carets and shown children how to use them to insert any letters or words they discovered missing when rereading their writing. I had *shown* the children and *told* them how to use carets. Demonstrations, showing children how things are done, and explanations, verbal language that accompanies the showing, are basic components of teaching and are especially important in teaching children to become writers. The demonstration led Chris to experiment in his writing. This is the strength of mini-lessons in writing workshop. I present lessons based on observed needs among the children, watch to see if and how they understand the concept, then add further refinement either to individuals or the whole group.

Learning About Mini-Lessons

Lucy Calkins (1986) first introduced the concept of "mini-lesson" to the teaching of writing. She noted that this "ritual of beginning every writing workshop with a whole-group gathering brings form and unity to the workshop" (168). She also spoke of the simplicity and brevity of a good mini-lesson. My children knew that a mini-lesson marked the beginning of our workshop just as our large-group sharing concluded it. The information and strategies I presented were always based on my observations of the children writing.

By studying Graves, Giacobbe, and Calkins and through classroom experience, I've learned that effective mini-lessons are:

1. Short: usually one to five minutes. Many are brief reminders of under a minute; some are longer, such as when I demonstrate writing. In these cases, we start the workshop earlier so as not to take away from the children's writing time.
2. Focused: even though several issues may be apparent, I don't emphasize them all in one day.

3. Gentle in tone: light, informing, with humor and playfulness; these lessons are invitations, not mandates.
4. Responsive: the content is determined by the needs of the writers in the classroom and the topics are repeated in a spiraling fashion.

When I first initiated writing workshops, my mini-lessons addressed language conventions (ways to insert or delete information, spelling strategies, using punctuation, capital letters, etc.) and management issues (retrieving and storing writing folders, stapling, etc.) Although we did lots of writing, I soon realized that my selection of mini-lessons was inadequate. Drafting and editing did not make the children good writers or produce quality writing. We needed to draft and craft. Crafting involves editing *and* revising. The revision aspect had been missing.

Teaching children to write quality pieces that communicate effectively and even eloquently requires specific instruction. Introducing this concept early sets a standard for a writing classroom. I think I'm not alone when I say that in my own K–12 education I had minimal instruction in how to compose, that is, craft, a good piece of writing. In my senior year in high school, my English teacher required a composition due every Monday morning. It came back by week's end, thoroughly marked in red, with the requirement to "rewrite!" All this writing and rewriting certainly prompted thinking about how to write. But when it came to rewriting, it was our best guess about what to do because we had no instruction in shaping ideas, writing clearly and concisely, communicating our intended meaning, striving for eloquence and grace. Eventually, I developed my own strategies for writing and rewriting, but I really didn't know what made writing effective. I came to writing workshop in my classroom feeling woefully inadequate at teaching my students how to write. To help writers, I would have to learn more about good writing and how to communicate what I learned to young writers.

I know I couldn't have learned how to teach writing from a book or from a scope-and-sequence program. I had to write myself to expand my limited concepts about writing. I attended writing institutes designed for teachers. One of the best professional development plans I know is to attend a writing institute or writing project. Many of these are now held for teachers and even some school districts set them up. I know of teachers who form writing groups. One such group in Menominee County, Michigan, is made up of first-grade through high school teachers who come together at regular intervals to write and receive responses to their writing.

These days I see mini-lesson topics for crafting writing all the time in workshops. Like all of teaching, this took experience—plus a willingness to be a learner myself. Mini-lessons address concepts that require repeating again and again—though with different examples and perhaps a slightly different focus. I still teach mini-lessons on the conventions of language (see Chapter 16). However, the most significant mini-lessons deal with the qualities of effective writing and writing strategies. These lessons help writers value the importance of revision, leading them to become more skillful writers.

Possible Mini-Lesson Topics

Some mini-lesson topics are basic, others more complex. When I see children ending their writing because the page is full, I recognize the possibility for several mini-lessons on strategies for adding to a piece. When children rush to get paper or line up to use the stapler, I know I need to address procedures for managing materials. When children are stuck, not knowing how to proceed with a topic, I know it's time to present strategies such as abandoning a piece and moving on, or setting it aside for a few days, or talking with another writer, or rereading the piece. When a child incorporates conversation for the first time, I see the opportunity to share this new technique with classmates.

What follows is a list of the mini-lesson topics I presented during a particular school year. This list is neither inclusive nor exclusive, but is included here to provide an example of the range of topics addressed in a primary-grade writing workshop.

Procedures:

- writing the title, author's name, and date on writing
- establishing workshop rules
- defining the structure and sequence of the workshop (mini-lesson, writing with conferring, large-group sharing)
- using only one side of the paper to facilitate revision
- writing on every other line when using lined paper
- managing time in the writing workshop
- identifying ways to respond to writers
- using a writing folder and saving all writing
- suggesting procedures for editing one's writing
- establishing procedures for illustrating a published book

Strategies Writers Use:

- choosing topics
- using books as inspiration for topics

- considering genre and strategies for writing poetry, biography, autobiography, nonfiction, how-to books, fiction
- reading a journal (kept on a trip) and listing possible topics
- reading an old piece for possible revision or new topics
- choosing topics by hearing other writers' pieces (e.g., sleepovers, birthdays)
- anticipating an audience: imagine if it makes sense to a reader
- rereading for clarity and completeness
- sequencing information by cutting and pasting
- lining out to make changes rather than erasing
- strategies to correct spelling
- inserting information by circling a section and drawing an arrow to indicate relocation
- inserting information using an asterisk or caret
- reading one's writing and having a writing conference with oneself
- determining the focus of the writing
- writing from another point of view
- foreshadowing—providing hints of what is to come
- avoiding plagiarism
- reading old pieces

Qualities of Good Writing:

- writing to get "pictures in your head"
- adding information for clarity
- describing a situation through "show not tell"
- incorporating conversation
- choosing "good words"—effective and precise
- incorporating only *essential* details
- deleting unnecessary details and information for clarity and conciseness
- adding information for clarity
- focusing writing—too many stories in a piece
- writing effective leads
- writing effective endings
- considering connections between leads and endings
- omitting extra "thens"
- omitting extra "ands"

- eliminating sentences connected with "and" or "then"
- eliminating excessive and unnecessary adjectives (for first graders the word "very")
- using adjectives and adverbs effectively and sparingly—to enhance meaning
- writing effective titles

Conventions of Language:

- managing space: words too big (only two or three to a page), words too little (run into each other)
- using left-to-right, top-to-bottom progression
- inserting spaces between words
- using capital letters to start sentences
- using capital letters for proper names
- alphabetizing a list (in a glossary, for example)
- using picture dictionaries
- using exclamation marks
- using question marks
- inserting quotation marks
- changing "me and my friend" to "my friend and I" (compound subjects)
- using antonyms
- using synonyms
- using homonyms to refine spelling
- form for writing a letter
- using possessive ('s) using plurals (-s and -es)
- using consistent verb tense
- using "ing" endings
- using "ed" endings
- using commas to separate items in a series
- using commas in greeting and closing of a letter
- inserting punctuation at end of sentences (not at end of lines)
- using a colon
- using nouns as antecedents for pronouns
- using contractions

Even as I categorize these topics (all of which I've addressed with first graders), I realize that not all are focused, that some topics can be broken down to several parts for the purpose of addressing in mini-lessons. Topics also overlap and every topic (with possible exceptions in the procedural category) is addressed in several mini-lessons throughout the year, though never in the same way.

Ways to Present Mini-Lessons

The variety of ways to present mini-lesson topics is endless, but I offer some samples.

Direct Presentation

In direct presentation mini-lessons I convey information by telling the group in direct, concise fashion: "This is your writing folder where you will keep all your writing from now on . . ."

Role Play

I notice individual children procrastinating during workshop. I present an exaggerated role play of their behaviors by opening a writing folder, sifting through papers, dropping the folder, picking up papers, going to the pencil sharpener, stopping to talk to several people, sitting down and hunting through paper again, breaking my pencil, heading to the pencil sharpener, until suddenly writing workshop is over and it's time to share. "Oh-oh, I didn't write." The giggles break out midway through my minidrama, and when I'm finished the children quickly identify the point of the lesson.

Or I might use a role play for a lesson on punctuation. Children smack a period down at the end of each line on the page so the right-hand margin sports a string of dots down the side. I want to break the pattern quickly. I display a page of my writing on newsprint. "Now, I'm going to put in periods," and I read aloud and stab a dot onto the end of each line.

"No," they cry.

"What's the matter?" I ask in mock horror.

"You've got to *listen* to where the words stop, not just put it at the end of every line. It doesn't make sense," they tell me. I play the inexperienced writer, allowing them to be the experts who teach me. A playful tone and humor helps make the point. None of them will correctly punctuate their intricately constructed pieces of writing by the end of the year, but the lesson helps them work on punctuation.

Demonstration by a Child

Marlene learned about placing quotation marks in her writing when she published. She taught the class about quotation marks (with a little help from me) by using colored chalk to insert quotation marks in her own sentence on the chalkboard. She explained why she used quotation marks. Marlene was a far more effective teacher for her peers than I would have been.

Compiling Lists from the Group

The class periodically brainstormed knowledge from their experiences as writers. In one mini-lesson we listed some of our strategies for topic selection, producing a review in chart form that we posted in the classroom. The children often referred to the list when stuck for a topic.

1. Draw until you think of something.
2. Go to the list of "Ideas" in your folder.
3. Brainstorm a new list of topics—accept anything.
4. Look at your old pieces of writing—you might find something you abandoned that you can revise or write again because you know more about the topic now.
5. Talk with a friend (limit of five minutes).
6. Think of ideas other people wrote about, like birthdays or going to Hershey Park. Write your story about this topic.
7. Read one of your published pieces and see if it reminds you of another idea to write about.
8. Look around the room at the books and think of what they reminded you of when we read them.
9. Read a good book for a few minutes (ten-minute limit).
10. Just write "I don't know what to write today because . . ." until something comes to you.

The list prompted children to suggest other strategies they use to keep from being stuck. Mark told us that he made little notes at home or when he went on trips to help him remember things he would write later. Jonathan brought in his journal from his trip "up home." (When children go out of school for family trips, I staple a dozen sheets of paper with a construction paper cover, title it, for example, "Jonathan's Vacation Journal," and send it as the homework parents often request when they take their child out of school.) Jonathan read the journal to the class and later, during the discussion of topic selection, we went through it again and Jonathan came up with ten possible topics he could develop. Five minutes into writing he announced, "I just thought of another—seeing my old cat."

Teacher Writing in Front of the Class

Watching the teacher write and revise are among the most important mini-lessons because the demonstrations help the children understand how to improve the quality of their own writing. For example, I address the issue of focusing by composing a brief draft of two stories obviously connected together. One year I wrote about a family vacation in Maine and about taking Nathan to college after we came home. The children understood that the two incidents were really different stories and that a good writer would separate them. The children began to comment during the sharing circles: "I think you have two stories in this piece of writing." They reread their own pieces and focused on one topic instead of several.

Telling Past Classroom Experiences

I tell the children about the boy in my class several years ago who wrote about visiting his sister in Colorado. The piece began when the family got up in the morning, continued as they loaded the car, drove to the airport, got their tickets, boarded the plane, and flew to Colorado. But he wasn't done there. The story went on and on, telling about skiing, going to the movies, his sister's apartment. "'And then . . .' 'And then . . .' It got so boring," I tell the children, "because he told everything about his trip to Colorado! And when he was done, even *he* didn't care about it anymore."

I still remember how this youngster finally learned the concept of focusing. All my efforts to dissuade him from telling everything about his trip had failed. He wanted to publish it and insisted the entire story be included. As a last resort I sat him down with two of the more patient students and asked him to read the piece to them. It took a half hour! Meanwhile, I conferred with other students. Once in a while, one of the listeners caught my attention and rolled her eyes with an "I don't believe this" expression. I smiled an acknowledgment and, when he finished reading, joined them at the table.

"Well," began one child somewhat hesitantly, "it's a little long." I nodded. The other peer continued.

"I thought so too. I got tired of listening. I'd probably get tired of reading. It's longer than I can read!"

Then we talked about choosing information and focusing the piece. The young writer went back and eliminated whole sections of his story. He saved them for possible future stories, but for this publication, he pared the writing down considerably. He talked to the class later about this process and laughingly reminded everyone throughout the year about the time he wrote "everything into a very boring story." He became our authority on focusing writing and eagerly reminded the others of the problems encountered by writing too much. I tell this story year after year (without identifying the young writer). It makes the point.

Mini-Lessons on Editing Skills

When I first presented mini-lessons on editing skills such as punctuation, capitalization, etc., I provided sample sentences with errors and corrected them, explaining to the children the how and why of these corrections. Sometimes children helped me present these lessons. But I noticed that children made only occasional changes in their writing. They didn't reread and edit. I realized my examples were akin to the grammar-book format: skills out of context with the expectation that children would know how to apply them. What I needed to do was *demonstrate* rereading and applying the skill! So now I share paragraphs of my own writing, reread in front of the class, and make corrections for language conventions. I emphasize that even though writers may notice and correct some things as they write, an important final step is rereading and checking for these important aspects.

A Sample Mini-Lesson Topic: Leads

Experienced writers strive for effective leads, ways to capture the interest of the reader at the beginning of a piece. Young writers, however, tend to begin stories the same way every day. They quickly fall into patterns such as: "I went . . ." "I am . . ." "I like . . ." "We are . . ." The children chance upon these beginnings during the first days of school and stick with them.

Some mini-lesson topics need to be revisited over and over as children are ready to understand new concepts. Leads surely fall into that category, so I address the topic several times throughout the year. Once we start talking about leads, I point out the variety of ways authors begin their writing when I read to children. I reread strong opening sentences and comment that authors begin books in ways that set the tone for what follows. Writers hook the reader, I tell the children. Like a fisherman, the writer offers inviting bait, enticing the reader to read on. Concluding lines get readers off the hook, leaving them with a sense of completion. I point out various endings and we notice ways authors craft their work through leads and endings. For example, the playful tone in the opening lines of Walter Piper's *The Little Engine That Could* sets the scene and the famous concluding statement brings closure: "Chug, chug, chug. Puff, puff, puff. Ding-dong, ding-dong. The little train rumbled over the tracks. . . . I thought I could. I thought I could. I thought I could." To find examples of leads and endings, we simply look at children's books and notice the range of approaches authors use.

Of course, when we read a book for the first time, our purpose is always the enjoyment and meaning we take from the book. It's on the rereading that we look at the author's techniques. Having our literature time just before writing workshop turned out to be a boon. We read and talked about books, authors, and their writing, and then wrote ourselves. I often discovered mini-lesson topics embedded in these read alouds, and it took only a few seconds at the beginning of the workshop to remind students of a particular writing strategy.

In late fall, I wrote two leads, one a boring statement and the other a vivid description of the same event. I asked the children which was better and why. "The second," they agreed, "because it has more information," and "we can get a picture in our heads." ("Information" and "picture in our heads" became familiar terms, ones we used to talk about writing that "shows not tells," that created images for readers.) Another day I read leads from several books and we noted the differences. We had talked about these leads before, but taking a few minutes to look at them again renewed the children's thinking about improving their own writing.

In February I began a mini-lesson by writing three beginnings to a story about a skunk that went through our backyard the night before. I composed in front of the class by thinking back to the experience and describing it from three different approaches:

1. A warm fire made the room cozy. A strange smell suddenly filled the air.
2. "What's that smell?" I said.
3. I sat in the chair. For a moment I wondered what the smell was that filled the room this cold February night.

Then I turned to the class and said, "There are many possible ways to start a story. Here's three different ways. I wrote the first by thinking of my senses, how I was feeling: warm and cozy and then the smell. The second starts with what I said, a quotation. And the third tells what I was doing and thinking. All are about the same moment but they're just different ways to describe that moment." After discussing the three leads I concluded by saying, "Sometimes writers think about a good beginning when they start writing. Sometimes they come back and write a better beginning when they revise."

The children's writing revealed a growing awareness of quality writing. In April, Chris, who once had been concerned about carets and spaces, began his book about his mother: "Do you know what I think the best thing in the world is? It's not Disneyland or the movies. It's my mom!"

When I look back at the leads and endings of the children's writing, I see their involvement in crafting their work. Amy's "There's a Cat in the Bathtub" begins (after Amy experimented with three opening sentences): "Splash! Patches fell in the bathtub! The water was very deep." The story ends with the lines, "I kissed Patches goodnight and I went to sleep." Ellen followed the model of folktales when she wrote her own fairy tale, "The Very, Very Hungry Princess." Like a folktale, her story begins and ends with the predictable pattern: "Once upon a time, there lived a very, very hungry princess. . . . And she has never been seen again."

Mini-Lessons for Revision

All my learning about writing emphasized that writing is a process and that much happens in this complex and recursive process from the inception of an idea until the emergence of a final, polished piece. In schools, we've often "taught writing" by having students draft and then edit. Donald Graves reminds teachers that children direct their attention to the concerns the teacher addresses. If most mini-lessons address mechanics, children will be primarily concerned with editing. If we focus on the qualities of good writing, children will work on crafting well-written pieces. When children learn to develop their writing, they make a deeper investment in the finished product and take more care with mechanics in the final editing. Don Murray (1991) points out that "writing is rewriting" and that it is important to see the craft of revision (the rewriting) "in a context that *includes* editing but is *not only* a matter of editing." Even first graders can draft and craft their writing rather than just draft and edit.

Teaching revision begins the first day of school when I say to Josh, who starts to erase, "If you change your mind or decide you want something different, just line out the part you don't want and then keep on writing. All writers change their minds. I don't know of a writer who gets his ideas down just the way he wants them the first time." Josh gives me a dubious look but then flips his pencil around and follows my direction.

Later I talk with the entire class about revision. "All good writers revise. They change their writing. This year, we'll all do lots of revising as we write. Sometimes writers remember things they forgot or they decide to take some things out or to change the words. I'll help you learn how to do these things. We've just talked about one way: lining out when you change your mind about something you've written."

During the first days of school, I show children how to reread their writing and line out repetitious words or replace letters or words they want to change. I show them how to use carets to insert missing letters or words. These first strategies help young writers understand that writing can be changed. It's crucial to establish this attitude early. The point is not just correct mechanics, but for the writing to make sense and say what the writer wants to say. Responding to ideas and meaning in conferences further develops this attitude.

Learning with Jon's Writing

In early October of my first year with writing workshops, I learned from a child that helping children revise required both teacher responses and demonstrations. At the end of our workshop, Jon asked me to read his writing. "I think it's a really good piece," he said.

"Sure. Tell me why this is good, Jon," I replied.

"I don't know—'cuz it's long and it's about our vacation."

I read Jon's story (Figure 6–2) and wrote him a brief note: "I like this writing. What was the best part of the trip?" The next day Jon read the note, immediately wrote, then brought me the piece again. "I wrote some more about Hilton Head," he said. Figure 6–3 shows this addition.

At the workshop's end, Jon shared his writing. The children were confused because he had tacked the new information to the end of the initial story, throwing off the chronological sequence. I knew he had no idea that words could be moved. I explained that writers make changes—more than just a few words or letters—so their writing makes sense. I asked Jon to read his piece and locate the part where the added information actually occurred. He read and placed a large dot in his draft. Then I showed him how to read the piece, shifting to insert the ending section when encountering to the dot. Later, with the class watching, we cut the piece apart at the dot and taped the insertion in place. This presented a new problem for as Jon reread the newly constructed piece, children noticed that two lines didn't make sense. Jon agreed and crossed out the lines. As a final part of the writing, I showed Jon how to put commas between the sequence of state names. The typed book became the first published piece in the classroom.

Jon's revision marked a milestone for me. I saw how a child's writing could open up with one simple question and result in a major revision. My question, "What was the best part of your trip?" hadn't been calculated to evoke more writing from him, but rather asked because it came to mind when I read his story. He became quite involved with the additional information—as though he remembered something he'd forgotten. Now I understood what I had previously heard Giacobbe say, "*All* writers, children no exception, know more than what appears on the page they draft." Part of the intrigue of

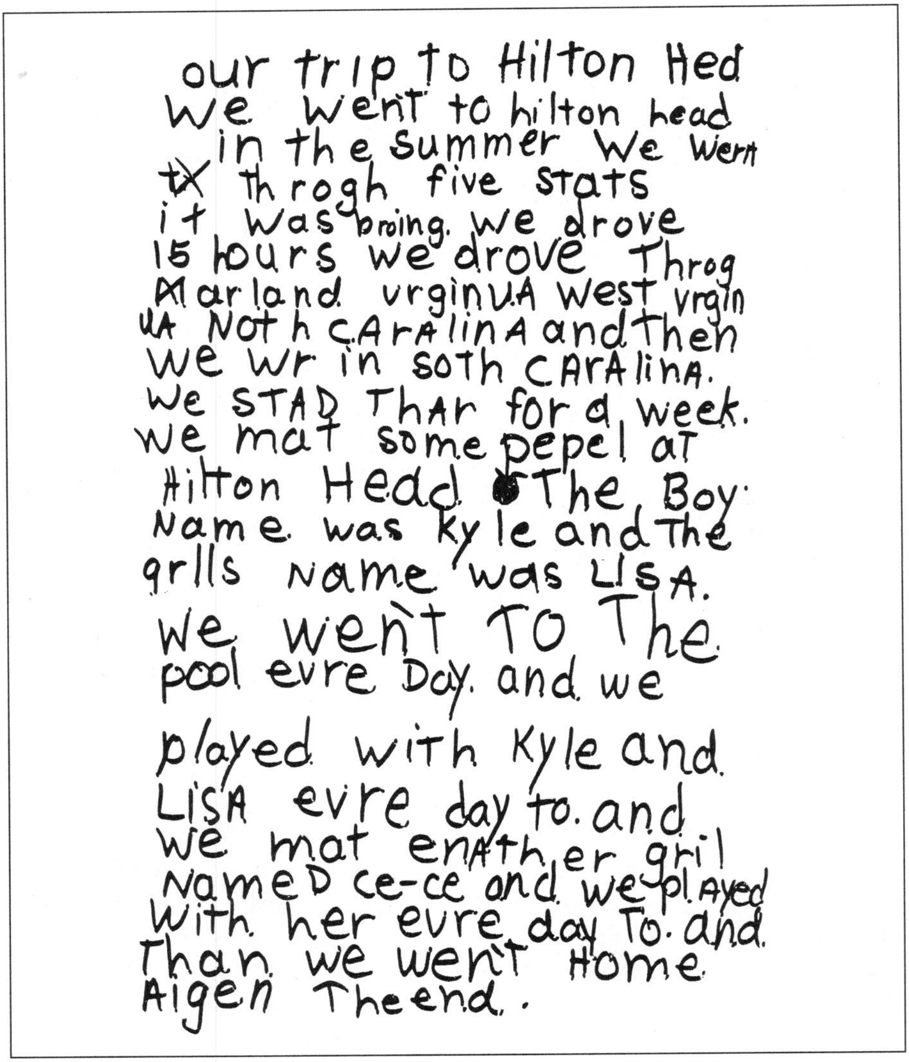

our trip to Hilton Hed
We went to hilton head
in the summer We Went
~~tx~~ throgh five stats
it was broing. we drove
15 hours we drove throg
Marland vrginUA west vrgin
UA Noth CArAlinA and then
we wr in soth CArAlinA.
We STAD ThAr for a week.
We mat some pepel aT
Hilton Hedd. The Boy
Name was kyle and The
grlls name was LISA.
We went To The
pool evre Day. and we
played with Kyle and
LISA evre day to. and
we mat enAther gril
NameD ce-ce and we plAyed
with her evre day To. and
Than we went Home
Aigen Theend.

Figure 6–2

Jon's original story

writing is getting in touch with lost or forgotten experiences, putting them into written language, and communicating to others.

Don Murray (1982) defines writing as "the process of using language to discover meaning in experience and to communicate it" (73). In the beginning there is only blank paper, says Murray, and at the end of the composing process there is a piece of paper that has found its own meaning. "This process of evolving meaning motivates writers" (18). It is revision that leads writers through this evolving meaning.

Revision is reseeing, rethinking ideas on the page and rewriting to better communicate the intended meaning. Revision is central to creating any ef-

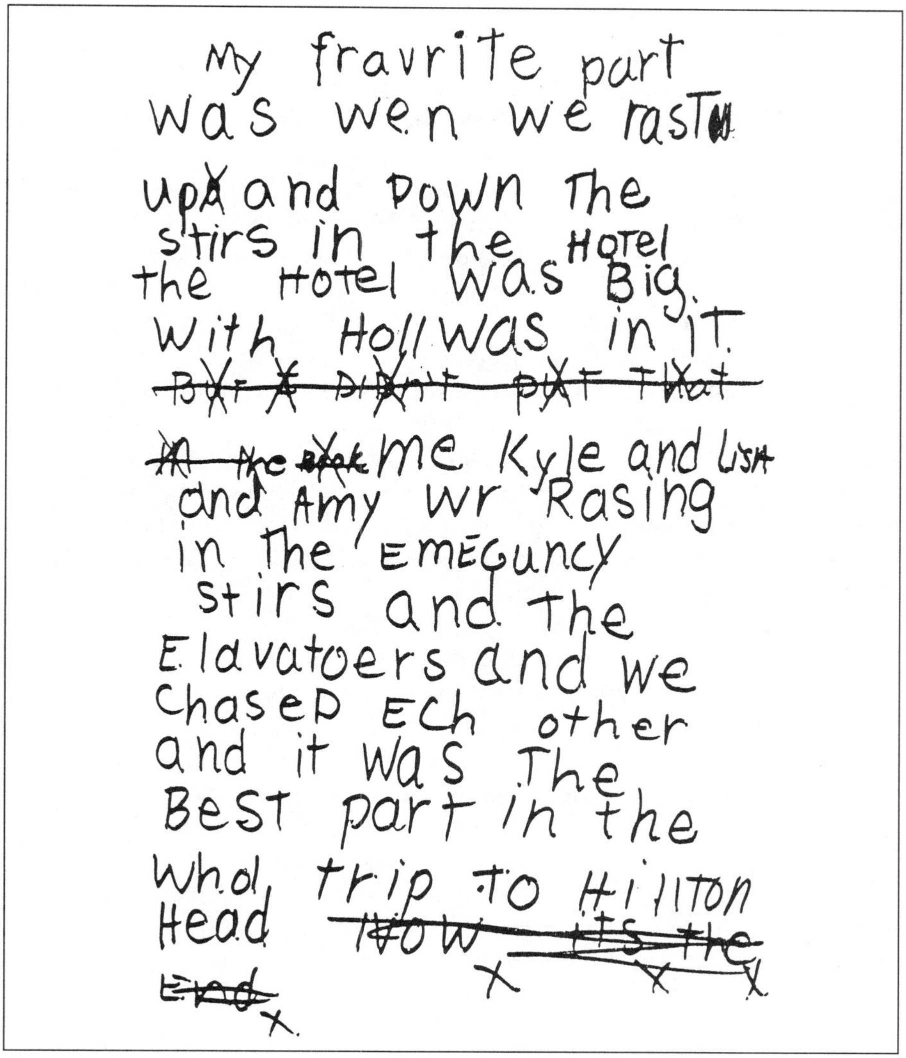

My fravrite part
was wen we rasT
up and Down The
stirs in the HoTel
the HoTel was Big
with Hollwas in iT.
~~But I Didn't put That~~
~~in the book~~ me Kyle and Lisa
and Amy wr Rasing
in The EmEGuncy
stirs and the
Elavatoers and we
ChaseD ECh other
and it was The
Best part in the
whol trip To Hi llTon
Head ~~Now its the~~
~~End~~

Figure 6–3

Jon's addition to his story

fective piece of writing; it's the heart of our writing processes. In a summer course with Glenda Bissex on revision, I learned to look for young children's revision over time. Rather than changing a piece of writing as experienced writers do, little ones begin again and redraw, refining their drawings and sometimes their words. When I looked at my children's writing, I saw that they revised by revisiting the same topics, adding more information and elaborating their drawings, thereby extending their ideas for readers.

The incident with Jon showed me that teaching children to write meant providing a climate where they could develop as writers and enriching this climate with mini-lessons on creating well-written pieces. I needed to *demonstrate* techniques if I wanted children to revise and craft writing. I was going to have to *show* them how.

It was scary at first, but I started writing in front of the class, plunging into a topic as the children did. I immediately noticed that the children imitated my writing. Not the exact story, but trying what I had done. If I began a piece with dialogue, for instance, they attempted a line of conversation to start their writing. I focused on ideas and content; they did the same. This is not to say that now everyone understood my demonstration. Sometimes days went by without a sign that anyone had heard a word. Then out of the blue a child would say, "See I did this like you did when you were writing the other day," referring to a mini-lesson when they saw me writing.

These mini-lessons are *writing demonstrations* accompanied by *explanations* that include my thinking and the decisions I'm making. I use the word "demonstration" rather than "modeling" quite deliberately. A model implies "*the* model," the right or perfect way. A demonstration shows others *how* to go about doing something, in this case writing. I'm demonstrating the way I work on writing and the writing is anything but perfect. I point out examples of good writing in children's literature as "models." I've noticed that while these models may be helpful in showing good writing, they are beyond the children's reach when it comes to trying them on their own. A writing *demonstration* is more accessible; it shows young writers strategies to try for themselves and provides a bridge between the writing of published authors and the children. My explanation describes what I'm doing as clearly as possible. At the end I often sum up what I've done as a means of helping children understand.

I believe that if the preponderance of mini-lessons consisted of the teacher writing, the effectiveness would diminish and also consume too much time. I suspect that the children remember these lessons because they connected to issues they experienced as writers and because they identified with the authenticity of a writer wrestling with ideas rather than showing perfection.

Mini-Lessons Beget Mini-Lessons

"SHOWING NOT TELLING" There are times in writing workshop when we seem to hit a brick wall; the writing stagnates and energy levels off. One late September, my class hit this wall as the initial enthusiasm for writing waned. Students drew and wrote a brief sentence almost as an after-thought. They rarely reread their words despite my urging. I knew they could do more; yet my strong nudges (which by now were verging on imperatives) produced no results. How could I get them involved?

I mulled over this question throughout the weekend. On Saturday, at a Connecticut conference, Glenda Bissex talked about the teacher as researcher—learning in one's own classroom. Our classrooms are our texts, she reminded us, and teachers look for the anomalies, those puzzlements when things don't quite follow the expected plan. Anomalies provide us with opportunities to grow by learning from our students.

On the flight home I thought again about my current anomaly. The children dutifully completed their writing but lacked investment in their work. Bissex had suggested that students may write to produce something to be corrected rather than something to be read. Perhaps these first graders did not think of their drawing/writing as *communication*, as something meant to be *understood* by others. In prior years, children had quickly recognized that writing held meaning to be shared with many readers. This group was different. These children, I theorized, lacked a sense of audience and, subsequently, made little investment in their work. How could I jar them out of this rut? After some thought, I decided to demonstrate writing in Monday's mini-lesson and involve the children as a responding audience. Because the writing would likely run longer than other lessons, I started the workshop a few minutes earlier than usual and made my drawing before class to save time and to downplay the drawing aspect.

On Monday morning, I began the mini-lesson by describing the sketch: the plane, the stars and moon indicating nighttime, the black earth below with lights resembling glowing campfires.

"You drawed a good airplane," someone remarked. I sensed that the children felt I was finished. Their response confirmed my prior assessment of the situation: drawing a picture was enough. Now to take them forward.

"Thank you. Now I'm going to write my story," and I wrote: I WT N A ARPN.

I spoke each word, stretching it out, listening for the sounds to determine which letter to write, just as the children did. When I came to "airplane" I commented, "I know *airplane* begins with an *A*. I've seen that word in lots of books." I reread the completed sentence, pointing to each word as I encouraged the children to do when they reread their words, then turned to the class and said, "Do you like my story?"

Silence. Then a child commented again on my drawing. "What do you think of my *story*? Does it make sense? Is there anything else you want to know?" They looked puzzled. "Let me read it to you," I said. "Writers read their writing, you know, in order to decide if it makes sense or if there's anything they left out." I read the sentence again.

"Where did you go?" someone asked.

"To Connecticut."

"When did you go?"

"On Friday night." I assumed the role of a child answering only what was required without elaboration.

"I went on an airplane to California once," came a response from Greg, setting off comments about airplane trips from several children.

"But about my story," I interjected, "I want to know if there's anything else I could put in it."

Jeff raised his hand. "What is it like to fly on an airplane?"

"Fun! I liked it." I was so much into my role right now that I replied with a typical child answer even though Jeff asked a leading question, one I could feel cracking into my writer's caution. His question was one that I'd asked in writing conferences, "What was that like for you?"

Jeff paused momentarily but then came right back. "Yes, but what was it *like* to fly on the airplane?"

Something in the way Jeff asked this question, not a routine question but an imploring, genuine question, coming from someone who really wanted to know, caused me to search for the best answer I could give. In my mind's eye I sat again in the seat awaiting takeoff. I described the moments I now relived. When I finished Jeff said, "Ahhh. Now I know."

"Should I write that? Do you think this would make my writing better, more interesting for someone to read?"

Jeff shrugged his shoulders. "I don't know. I guess. Yeah, why don't you write it."

I suddenly felt the choice I was forever turning back to writers. This was risky. I turned to the board and wrote:

> WE FASTN R STBLT The Pln
> WT TO the rNWayThn it srtd
> to GO FST I CD FL the Wels
> going rNd We rcd dN the rNWay
> and TN We WT up up up. I CD
> FL My Ers popt SO I SWllod hd.

I avoided perfect spelling since I was just getting some of the children to set aside their worries about spelling correctly as they wrote. When I finished writing I reread the entire piece then turned to the class and said, "Is my writing more interesting now? Do you think it's more interesting to listen to and for someone to read?"

"Yes!" came a chorus response.

I stepped back into my teacher role and asked, "When I read this piece, could you get any picture in your own head of me on the airplane?"

"Yes!" The group teemed with energy.

"I could see that plane go up, up, up!" commented Greg as his hand imitated the plane's ascent, and he punctuated his sentence with the sound of an airplane's zooming takeoff.

"Good writers try to include information so that readers will know just what it was like to ride in a plane, or play football, or whatever it is they're writing about. To do that, they think about the time they're writing about and put down the things that they can see in their heads, so then when readers read the writing they will get those pictures in their heads too. You could do this in writing—add information so that other people will know what it was like, so they will get pictures in *their* heads." The lesson was done. It had taken just under fifteen minutes.

In part, I had paraphrased Peter Elbow (1973) describing "movies of the mind," a way to explain how writers communicate meaning (the movies in their minds) through effective writing that allows readers to construct movies in their own minds. "Words," wrote Elbow, "don't transport the contents of my head into yours, they give you a set of directions for building meaning, we end up with similar things in our head—that is, we communicate" (152). We cannot hope to *tell* our meaning to others through words, we must *show* meaning through words that create images.

The focus of the mini-lesson had developed into "showing not telling," one characteristic of good writing. The lesson itself had a "showing not telling" character as well. Some mini-lessons are directive, *telling*, but this one was an active demonstration to *show* the children, to provide an experience with writing and audience. My writing emerged in front of the children and with the help of their questions. Their genuine interest encouraged me and I actually wanted to continue this writing and share it with these children. I wanted to *revise*. I hoped the children would feel this same energy, begin anticipating audiences for their writing and expand their pieces. That morning Greg wrote about his airplane trip to California, a piece he continued for two days. Even though the only change evident at first was in Greg's work, I sensed the children understood something new about writing.

REREADING AND REVISING On Tuesday morning I returned to the airplane story for the mini-lesson. I started by reading what I'd written the day before. "Writers can get into their writing by reading what they wrote yesterday," I explained. While reading the story, I experienced the plane trip again and, at that moment, remembered a previously forgotten incident. I quickly taped a new sheet of paper to the chalkboard and wrote:

Wn MN STD to gt of beks he ws
on the wrg pIN. So the pIN wnt
bk to the gat and he gt off.
Thn we had to wat to tk off.

I read my addition aloud and added that the man wanted to go to Rochester, not Hartford, but the captain made the announcement to the passengers after the man left the plane so as not to embarrass him. "I forgot to put that part in," I said. "But when I read this I remembered this whole part I didn't put in yesterday. I don't know why. I just forgot. That's the way writers work."

The children nodded and one child added, "You could still probably add that if you wanted to." Things were looking up in this writing workshop. Two days later a child asked how my plane story was coming. For Friday's mini-lesson I taped the three-page story to the chalkboard, read it, then noted that the last part was out of order. I reread and asked the children to help me find the spot where the incident about the man fit. They easily located it and I drew a large star at that place, circled the section about the man, and explained that when readers came to this star they should go to the circled part and read it next. Not one child picked up on moving information within a piece of writing. However, the class had been exposed to the idea and, when sequencing information came up in editing conferences two months later, the experience of this day provided a background for understanding the process.

The focus of each of the mini-lessons on the airplane story was very specific: showing not telling, adding information, sequencing information, reading one's own writing as part of the writing process. And the writing demonstrated additional tips for their writing such as:

- spacing between words
- listening for sounds and matching them to letters
- using drawing as a starting point for writing
- beginning to put periods in when the writing pauses
- recognizing words we can spell, such as *we, the, so, to*
- including details, specific information
- recalling visual spelling (*A* in airplane)

Each of these items might be the focus of a future mini-lesson. I noticed many issues as I wrote and read the piece, but to point out and reinforce *all* of them would overload the children. I know the children learned from the entire demonstration, not just the focused issue; they intuitively soaked up many other concepts. Children learn from all the demonstrations by others around them, both the formal and the informal ones that occur all day long. They take what makes sense to them, what touches their interest or needs at a given time, and incorporate that experience—*as they perceive it*—into their growing understanding of the world. In many ways, this mini-lesson contained something for everyone even though I will never know precisely what each child took away. The central issue of this mini-lesson, however, had been the connection between reading and writing. Stimulating an awareness of the dynamic relationship between these two aspects of written language would serve all learning in this classroom.

My airplane story marked a change. Gradually, the children expanded their writing. As they did, their investment increased. Conference reminders helped. "Do you plan to add those things you've just told me to your writing—like I did in my airplane story?" "Oh yeah, I think I will." Others watched their classmates writing more information and drew inspiration from their peers. Slowly, energy resurfaced in the workshop.

ADDING INFORMATION The children's writing opened up possibilities for more mini-lessons. Two weeks later I wrote in front of the class again. By now most of the children attempted to add to their writing. They did not always reread what they wrote and so repetitions, sentence fragments, and gaps in information appeared in their compositions. The writing was incoherent.

I imitated their writing with my own brief story: "I went to Park City. I had fun. I like Park. I think. We had fun. My son Nathan too. I had fun." Then I faced the group and waited.

"Aren't you going to read it?" a child asked with the same outrageous teasing tone I'd heard myself use with them.

"Oh, should I read my story?"

"Of course," everyone agreed, so I read my story, pointing to every word as I went. I could hear them suppress giggles behind me.

"It doesn't make sense."

"And there's too many *funs*.

"Well, what would you want to read in this story?" I asked.

"We could ask you questions and then maybe you'd get some ideas," someone suggested. The class quickly produced a series of questions that brought information. I acknowledged that I could include more information in the writing.

I concluded the mini-lesson with a summary statement. "To write something for someone else to want to read, the writing has to make sense, be interesting, and have good information. One way that writers work on this is by reading the writing and thinking about these things as they read."

A couple days later, I asked the class why they read as they worked on writing. They produced the following reasons, which we listed on chart paper in their words:

1. to remember it
2. to see if I want to revise it (change anything)
3. to see if I left anything out and to see if it makes sense
4. so I know how to read it in sharing circle

MAKING DELETIONS The following week, I saw children reading their writing and adding information to enhance their stories. Then I noticed children writing the same line twice. I watched carefully and realized the repetition resulted from the reading. A child wrote, stopped and read, then continued writing by repeating the last few words, the ones freshest in memory. To nail down the exact word that comes next could be very difficult! Time for another mini-lesson. I wrote a very quick story one Monday morning.

"My son Nathan broke his hand broke his hand at the football game. Someone stepped on his hand." (I chose not to use invented spelling in this lesson because I wanted the lesson to focus on the repetitious line.) Of course, the children quickly noticed the repetition when I read the story. I demonstrated a way to deal with this by drawing a line through the unwanted words.

When I stopped to confer with Max, he said, "I had some extra words—ones that were in here twice—so I lined them out like you did."

That same day Amy commented, "Oh, it doesn't make sense. They won't know why my dad was there." She added clarifying information to the end of her story which, of course, was out of logical sequence. I chose to wait a bit to address this issue because I sensed that asking Amy to move information now would discourage her. "One step at a time," I told myself. "She doesn't need to learn everything with one piece of writing."

This series of mini-lessons nudged the children into writing beyond drawing, expanded that writing, involved them in rereading their words in anticipation of an audience, and established writing as communication. I felt a renewed energy around writing. I had presumed a reading/writing connection that did not exist in the minds of these children. Mini-lessons taught and nurtured this basic concept—and led the children into revising their writing!

Demonstrating Revisions

When children begin writing, my first energies focus on encouraging them to put words on paper. To support their initial efforts I accept what they produce, conveying my delight and interest. I set aside my concern for conventions such as spelling, punctuation, etc., and focus on the content. Certainly, I address conventions in mini-lessons, and I may offer reminders in conferences, but I refrain from spending precious time in conferences correcting mechanics. I respond to a child's ideas and the writing's meaning. I try to establish trust so children will be receptive to exploring ways to improve the content of their writing.

Mini-Lessons to Develop Content

THE IMPORTANCE OF INFORMATION Young children often write one-sentence pieces that fall into a pattern such as "I like my dog" or "I love my Mom" or "We went swimming." Once in a while a second sentence follows: "She is nice" or "It was fun." I try to head this pattern off with the first mini-lessons of the year (see Chapter 5). The mini-lesson to address this is similar to my plane story. I write one or two sentences on a topic of my own and then ask the class to respond with questions. For example, I write "I like my cats," then explain to the class that this doesn't show readers very much about my cats. Then I write, "The cats slept in the Christmas tree." I take a few moments to talk about the difference between the two sentences. I'll point out that good writing gives specific *information* and we can often picture it in our imagination. If there's time, I'll expand the writing with more information. Including *information* becomes part of our language as we talk about good writing.

After one such lesson, Patrick added to his piece from "I like my dad" to three sentences about working with his dad. In a conference I asked him to tell me more. He then added several sentences explaining how he and dad plant and harvest corn.

Understanding the term *information* helps children expand a piece of writing. Sometimes children think they need to add "details." When I ask them to explain "details," they frequently say that it means putting in stuff like what color was your dog or what day did you go swimming. One child explained that revision meant "adding adjectives or names or how old someone is—stuff like that." Certainly details are important to writing, but before attending to details a writer includes chunks of information so that readers grasp ideas. Then relevant details become important and the writer makes decisions about adjectives based on how they serve a specific purpose in conveying the intended meaning. The color of the dog or when you went swimming may not be important to the meaning.

Information in writing gives readers a full picture. It also opens up the writing for the writer who recalls forgotten aspects of an experience. Writers relive experiences and deepen their understanding of topics. Recalling experiences and putting them on paper requires more than a superficial involvement with the topic.

DEALING WITH "LIST" STORIES "Show not tell" mini-lessons can help writers revise stories that are lists of attributes about a particular individual or lists of activities during a particular time or event. Here's an example.

> My brother is fun to play with and he is nice. I like to play with him. And sometimes he's mean. And sometimes he's crabby. And sometimes he's happy. And sometimes he's sad. And sometimes he's crazy. And all the time I play with him and all the time he plays with me. I love him so much. And I play hide and go seek together.

Initially, the children are pleased with this writing. After all, it's a whole page long! But the writing is boring to read (not to mention difficult to edit) and, I'm convinced, it becomes boring for the writer to produce day after day.

I believe there's potential in these stories. The problem is the significance remains hidden from the reader—and probably from the writer. In the story about the brother, for instance, I sense that this child adores her brother and that there's a lot more than what has made its way to paper. I want to encourage the child to discover something to reveal the relationship and its significance. A good way to do this is through a mini-lesson.

I wrote a brief story ahead of time that resembled the children's writing. I began the lesson by reading my writing to the class.

> One day I picked Adessa up at her house. Then I put her in the car. We drove to the park. We played on the swings. We fed the ducks. We fed some swans. We went to the wooden playground. We went down the slide together. We went to lunch before we went to the park. When we were done playing we went home.

Then I asked the class to question me about the writing. As they did, I responded as the writer, rather than the teacher, answering questions as I'd heard the children do. Some children asked "What did you have for lunch?" "What color were the ducks?" "What day did you go?" "Did you have fun?" The most effective questions got me talking about the day, telling more of what happened:

"What was the best part?"

"What was it like to feed the ducks and swans?"

"How did you go down the slide together?"

These open-ended questions elicited specific information and I felt a renewed energy for this topic; I wanted to write! I wrote the following story as the children watched:

> The trees had turned to yellows, oranges, and reds on the day I took Adessa to the park. The air was cool but sunshine made us warm.
>
> Adessa learned to feed the swans and ducks that day. I showed her how to throw bits of stale bread and crackers in the water. She stood on a rock at the water's edge. I held her hand. With her free hand she threw a cracker in the water. A swan darted over and in a split second the cracker disappeared.
>
> "Eee!" squealed Adessa. And she stomped her feet up and down in delight. Then she reached for another cracker. She knew how to feed the swans now.

As I wrote, I verbalized my thinking processes. I began by saying, "Let's see I think I'll just write about when we fed the duck and swans. We were in the park. I can picture when we got there. I know—that's what I'm going to write." And I began. I changed words, paused to think, wrote quickly when I knew where I was headed, reread parts when not sure what came next. I couldn't plan this ahead of time. In fact, I didn't even know what part of the first story I'd select to write about when I first showed it to the children. I concluded the lesson by pointing out the difference between "showing" and "telling" in writing and then issuing an invitation to the children. "When you read your writing today, you could think if you 'showed' your readers or just 'told' readers. You could start a second draft by thinking of one part of the story, picturing it in your head, and writing about just that part."

On subsequent days I returned to this writing for mini-lessons and we discussed specific qualities of the writing that enabled readers to feel as if they are present watching the scene. "Show not tell" mini-lessons lead to other topics for improving the quality of our writing such as:

- Focus: what one part of the writing is most important.
- Using conversation: people talking is a way of showing.
- Where the story begins: writers often include a lot of unnecessary preliminary information.
- How the story begins and ends: finding ways to get the reader into the story and leave the reader satisfied.
- Building to the most important part of the story: providing information and building tension.
- Developing the most important part: not all aspects of a story deserve equal attention.
- Finding other topics in a piece: often there are several topic possibilities.

It's tempting to use the same writing, such as the story above, with another class. However, doing so is not really effective. Authenticity is key to effective writing demonstrations. I can't "reuse" stories; the writing would lack the energy and the real struggles that are essential for children to see. Writing in front of the group was difficult at first, but I believe it's a key to helping children develop as writers.

FINDING A FOCUS In a fourth-grade classroom Joshua wrote a story about a soccer game. Unlike many children's writing, Joshua had a focus to his draft. In the first two sentences he set up the soccer game. The next sentence begins "Five minutes before the game was over . . ." and from there Joshua writes a moment-by-moment account, ending with how he scored the winning goal in the last seconds. With Joshua's permission, I shared his writing with his classmates and pointed out how he had focused the soccer story on the most important part of the game. The lesson went well but at the end Joshua provided the most instructive comment.

"Yeah," he said, "see my mom writes almost every day and sometimes I write with her. She told me it's like you put a spotlight on the most important part and you just write about that. You don't write all the other stuff." Then he added, "And I put the date in because it happened when I was in first grade and I'm in fourth now. So if you know the date you can figure out that the first graders were playing the fourth graders and we won."

Joshua spoke with the authority of a writer. He understood that writers make decisions anticipating their audiences. I use the "spotlight" metaphor regularly with children and tell them about the writer, Joshua.

The mini-lessons I've described show young writers how to develop topics. As they understand this fundamental concept, I work with strategies to improve the quality of their writing. For example, we look at the ways writers begin pieces of writing.

Mini-Lessons to Pull It All Together

Sometimes I use the mini-lesson to compile group-composed lists of the children's ideas. These lists help them articulate their growing knowledge and also serve as reminders that teach. In late fall, when Kristin published a book that the entire class loved, I asked them to tell me what Kristin had done to make her writing effective. As children contributed their ideas I wrote them on a chart.

Kristin's Story Had

1. good information
2. clear sentences
3. a title that fit the story
4. an interesting lead
5. a good ending
6. answered the question words—who, what, when, where, why, how

Through the years I've asked children periodically to list the attributes of good writing. This is a list from early spring.

Good Writing

1. has a good lead (hooks the reader)
2. makes sense
3. has a good ending (gets the reader off the hook)
4. makes the reader feel a response (happy, angry, sad) or think about something
5. has a good title
6. has strong information—to make it interesting
7. has a focus
8. is clear—so the reader understands
9. has interesting words
10. has good editing

Young children can craft their writing and they can articulate that craft. I had underestimated the children's capacity to understand, to assess, and to really work at improving their writing. They talked about the crafting process when I conferred with them. Lori said, "I don't think I did so good on my picture of people sitting down, but I really like my lead." And then she read, "One morning, bright and early, my mom and I went to breakfast. We went in and sat down. The waitress said that I looked cold!" Lori looked at me and said, "I spelled 'waitress' wrong. I put a D but it's supposed to be a T." She crossed out the D and wrote above it T R. "There, that's better." These young writers could juggle several concerns simultaneously. As writers and thinkers they could keep up with the best of them.

Learning About Quality Writing

To help writers, I honed my writing skills and my awareness of good writing. Grammar books weren't much help. Instead, I invested in the following activities which continue to this day.

1. I read about writing, starting with books Giacobbe advocated. Don Murray's *Learning by Teaching* and William Zinsser's *On Writing Well* helped me articulate qualities of good writing and the skill of teaching writing. Today, I continue to pick up books by authors on writing; each brings their own perspective to the craft such as Stephen King's

On Writing. I love two books written particularly for teachers, *Craft Lessons* and *Nonfiction Craft Lessons* by JoAnn Portalupi and Ralph Fletcher.

2. I notice techniques authors use, such as effective beginnings and endings, the structure of a piece of writing, word choices. I find myself talking about them with other readers and writers.
3. I work on my own writing. I try techniques gleaned from points one and two above, and seek responses from experienced writers. I learn from editors who make refinements in my pieces after I've taken them as far as I can. I'm grateful to the writer friend who wrote "Choose one or the other" when I used two verbs when one would do, and reminded me to "get out of the passive voice" when I'd slipped into old habits.
4. I watch children in classrooms, paying attention to what and how they write, and what they say about writing. I share what I learn with children and we talk about writing as fellow practitioners.

Reflections

Mini-lessons are crucial to teaching children to write, but mini-lessons aren't enough. All my experience in working with young writers teaches me that if children are to develop as writers they need *time* to write every day and supportive *responses*. Mini-lessons are a way we respond, though not the only way. Daily workshops allow children to explore and experience the strategies mini-lessons show them. They become confident writers who know how to manipulate words and manage language.

My teaching is rooted in responding to writers. I doubt if I'll ever use the specific format of the lessons I've described in this chapter again. The stories of these mini-lessons belong to classes of the past. New groups require their own lessons. The children will write new stories; I must present responsive lessons that are just as new. I share these lessons as examples that may evoke new lessons from teachers of other groups of children. Also, sometimes I find it helpful to look back at what I've done in other situations. Through reflecting on past solutions in present situations, I come up with new ways to tackle the present. Robert Frost said, "I am not a teacher, but an awakener." I liken the teaching that goes on with mini-lessons to Frost's statement. I am not teaching so much as awakening within young writers the stories they have to tell and providing demonstrations of ways to write those stories effectively. The writers in a literate community teach themselves, each other, and their teacher.

CHAPTER 7

Listening and Responding

A district administrator steps into our classroom and looks around. With a hint of alarm he asks, "Where's your teacher?" I sit on a tiny chair beside a child's desk in a sea of classroom activity. I'm listening to a writer. The six-year-olds find the incident amusing, and when the visitor leaves they bat the question back and forth in exaggerated outrage. "Where's your teacher?" "Where'd they think she'd be? On the playground?" The children deal with the issue, and the child answering the next knock graciously informs the visitor before the question comes: "My teacher's over there, but she's busy having a conference right now. Would you like to wait?" The children know writing conferences are important.

I spend most of writing workshop moving around the room, sitting so I can look directly at the writer—not hovering over a child, looking over her shoulder, nor even looking at the writing. I look the child straight in the eye and listen as the child tells me about her writing.

Around us the other children work on writing. Some begin a new piece; others continue a topic they've been working on for several days. One child, preparing to publish a piece, searches for spelling in a picture dictionary. Two or three pairs of children sit together, one child reading and the other listening to the child-authored writing. A child or two moves around the room to sharpen a pencil, get more paper, or just to move about because he feels restless. There's a quiet hum of "working noise." Once a quiet classroom indicated a well-managed classroom. I know better now and so do our administrators. We understand how crucial movement is and especially how important all that talk is.

Vygotsky (1978), the Russian psychologist recognized as a pioneer in developmental psychology, stated: "The most significant moment in the course of intellectual development, which gives birth to the purely human forms of practical and abstract intelligence, occurs when speech and practical activity, two previously completely independent lines of development, converge. . . . A child's speech is as important as the role of action in attaining the goal. . . . The more complex the action demanded by the situation, the greater the importance played by speech in the operation of the whole. Sometimes speech becomes of such vital importance that, if not permitted to use it, young children cannot accomplish the given task" (24–26). Vygotsky concluded that "children solve practical tasks with the help of their speech, as well as their eyes and hands" (26).

I watch children talk when they build with blocks, when they mark the check-in board in the morning, when they manipulate counters in math class, and when they gather their things to go home. They talk to themselves, to each other, to me. A few never seem to stop. In writing workshop they talk softly to themselves as they draw, or sound out words, or reread their writing and determine what to write next. They spontaneously speak to someone—anyone—near them (or across the room) as a particular thought comes to mind. And they talk to me as I move among them during the workshop.

All that talk contributes to the children's development, and the writing flourishes. Mini-lessons demonstrate strategies and skills for writers, but the heart of the writing workshop is the time when children write and talk and I listen and respond. An energy develops in that time that spills over to other parts of the school day. I believe that the talk surrounding writing is vital.

Learning to Listen

In the early days of writing workshop in my classroom, the children wrote and wrote and I responded. I set aside concern for convention and responded totally to content. Ignoring mechanics opened up the children's writing, and they fluently wrote one piece after another. I began using a handheld tape recorder as I conferred with the children to help me understand just what occurred in writing conferences. When I played back the tape, I heard myself doing most of the talking. I interrupted at the slightest pause, made strong suggestions, asked many questions—one right on top of the other. My heavy-handed approach, I realized, robbed children of the thinking that goes with writing. In professional presentations on implementing writing workshops I'd heard Don Graves say, "Shut up, listen, and learn." I needed to "shut up, listen, and learn."

When I said less, the children began using the writing conferences to think and to consider possibilities for their writing. I stopped groping for the right questions to ask and just listened. When I did ask questions, I asked genuine questions—ones that came naturally to mind because I felt confused or wanted more information. Instead of supplying answers, I turned issues back to the children by asking: What do you plan to do about that? How will you solve that problem? Given the opportunity to talk with a more patient and authentic listener, the children came forth with wonderful ideas that amazed me with their rationale, thoughtfulness, and creativity. First graders astounded me with their accomplishments as writers; they demonstrated an incredible ability to be thinkers and problem solvers.

Roving Conferences

Early March. Writing workshop. The room bustles with a quiet hum. I close the notebook where I write during the first minutes of every workshop, pick up the conference checklist (see Appendix B) and begin moving around the room. I stop at Tara's desk.

Tara rereads her writing and tells me about two revision strategies she is implementing. The energy in her voice reveals her involvement.

TARA: I'm writing about my birthday still, and you know how you said all that stuff up there you don't need? [Tara refers to the mini-lesson where I wrote and included extra phrases such as: This is the problem. Now I will tell you the problem.] I read this over and I found some of that and I just took it out.

MRS. A: Really? You found some of that?

T: Yeah.

MRS. A: That happens a lot—writers find stuff like that.

T: Yeah. And you know where I put the check marks where I didn't put things? I looked around my house and I found out some things my mom and dad got me.

MRS. A: Oh, so at certain places you put check marks because there was more information but you couldn't remember what it was.

T: Yeah, I found out what it was.

MRS. A: So now what are you going to do?

T: I'm putting it right in. I'm reading over so I can see if I have any of that stuff still in and then when I come back to this page I can put it in.

MRS. A: You have a lot of plans don't you?

T: Uh-huh.

MRS. A: Okay. Thank you.

I move on to Nickolas, who slouches in his seat. He chews the end of his pencil and appears to be daydreaming. His voice lacks enthusiasm when the conference begins. When I ask him a question about a part I don't understand, he sits up in his seat and speaks in a decisive tone of voice. I learn that he's been thinking through the specific information he'll include in the writing.

NICKOLAS: I'm still writing about, uh, ah, my hamsters, you know. And now I'm putting what we did to play with them. We made circles with our legs and that's what I'm putting now. [His voice trails off as he speaks. He only glances at me and stares at his paper.]

MRS. A: You put—I'm sorry, I didn't hear. You made a circled coop?

N: We made a circle with our legs.

MRS. A: You made a circle with your legs?

N: Yeah. Then we put the hamsters in the middle for a while.

MRS. A: You put the hamsters so they could move around in the middle of this circle between your legs.

N: Yeah. And [pause] we watch them on the spinning wheel.

MRS. A: Who sits and makes this circle with your legs with you?

N: My friends.

MRS. A: So you—I'm not sure about this—you put your feet together?

N: Umm.

MRS. A: Tell me, how do you do that?

N: We put our feet together and we have like about five people and you put your feet together and make a circle.

MRS. A: Ohh, it's not just two of you, it's five of you—a huge circle.

N: Then you need to put your hands down here [he stuffs his hands behind his knees] so they won't get out. Because then they can't go underneath your legs. So you have to put your hands here so they can't get out.

MRS. A: I see. So you're writing all this. You're describing all this now?

N: Yeah.

MRS. A: You're putting all that in so that people will get that picture.

N: Umm-hum.

MRS. A: Okay. Thank you.

Kelsie stands behind her desk, holding her papers. She's been reading to Amy, who is seated beside her. Kelsie's a confident writer and always open to suggestions to improve her writing. She also is comfortable rejecting suggestions that she finds inappropriate. Today she's writing a letter to author Arnold Lobel. In the conference I try to nudge her to think of her letter as more than a string of questions.

KELSIE: I'm starting a letter to Mr. Lobel and I've asked the question that we're stuck on—the question that all our class was wanting to know. Then I'm asking what's his favorite book is and how he likes it.

MRS. A: So—read that question. I'd like to hear the question.

K: Okay. "I don't understand why you don't put if they raked the leaves in *Frog and Toad All Year*, in 'The Surprise.'"

MRS. A: Oh. So now you're asking about the end of that story because we were puzzled and now you're going to ask him what his favorite . . .

K: Favorite things are.

MRS. A: Is there any information you want to *tell* him?

K: Well, I already put in that my teacher likes his books. And uh, I'm gonna put in that I like his books too, and what was his last book to make.

MRS. A: You know what Kelsie?

K: What?

MRS. A: I think he might want to know why you like a particular book. [Amy has listened to the entire conference and now she adds, "I think so too."]

K: Oh yeah. Okay, I might put that in too.

I move past a few desks and stop at Terri's seat. As a toddler Terri was labeled Learning Disabled. I've learned that she writes best if she verbalizes her ideas first. Rarely does she include information that she hasn't talked about. Conferences are critical for her.

TERRI: I'm writing about when I went to Chris' birthday party. And I'm gonna put in more information about it.

MRS. A: You're gonna put in more information about Chris' birthday party.

T: Uh-hum.

MRS. A: Tell me. Tell me what is going to be the most important information you . . .

T: Well, I got him a wheelie—a car that goes on its back wheels and the car does a wheelie, whatever.

MRS. A: The car goes on its back wheels and does a wheelie and that was your gift to him?

T: Uh-huh.

MRS. A: So you're going to put that in the story?

T: Uh-hum.

MRS. A: Is there anything else about . . .

T: I'm gonna put who he invited. I know all the guys—there were no girls except for his sisters. The party was mostly boys.

MRS. A: The party was mostly boys and the only girls were his sisters. Okay—and you!

T: Yeah, I'm not one of his sisters. I'm just his friend. But Christy and Chad didn't went. Christy can't go and I don't know what happened to Chad.

MRS. A: So, where are you in this story right now?

T: Well, I'm gonna put we played musical chairs.

MRS. A: You played musical chairs. And then, what are your next plans?

T: I'm gonna put then we got our prizes. I got a tablet and pencils.

MRS. A: You're gonna put about the prizes. You have to put in this part about the gifts.

T: Yeah, I do. And somebody's names and . . .

MRS. A: Okay. Thank you.

Marissa sits pensively and seems stuck. She's usually a rather fluent writer.

MARISSA: I can't decide what to write.

MRS. A: What's on your mind?

M: I could write about my brother getting stitches, but I don't think I should write that.

MRS. A: That seems important to you. You don't want to write about it?

M: No. Because . . . because it will make my brother feel embarrassed.

MRS. A: I see. Do you know that when writers write they don't have to show it to anyone. They have the right to keep it private.

M: Yeah, but he, he gets into my bookbag and reads all my papers.

MRS. A: Well, we aren't going to take this home right away and if you want it to be private you can make sure he doesn't read it.

Marissa tells me the story then she begins to write. A few minutes later I check back.

MARISSA: I just wrote the start. I don't want to write the next part cuz it's too sad.

MRS. A: That's okay. You know, I want to tell you that one way we use writing is to write the happy or sad we feel. Because then the sad goes on the paper and it's not all inside us. But only the writer decides whether to write this sad or not. So that's your choice.

M: Okay.

At the end of the workshop Marissa shows me her paper. Her usual smile has returned. On the paper is a drawing of the incident with no words. I return her smile and she says, "I just drew it." I nod and say, "Okay." Marissa had encountered one of the reasons writers become stuck: there is something they don't want to write about. The best way out of this is to acknowledge the topic in some way. Marissa's drawing did just that.

Bobby's face is contorted in frustration. He often is tense and nervous, but he loves to write and comes up with unique topics. Like Terri, hearing his own words helps him get them onto paper.

BOBBY: I'm writing a story and it's about a forest and it rains about . . . maybe—let me think—a couple of months and then it turns into a flood.

MRS. A: A flood?

B: Uh-huh.

MRS. A: A flood. It rains a couple of months and then the forest turns into a flood. Where did you get this idea, Bobby?

B: Well, [pause] I don't know.

MRS. A: No idea? [Bobby shakes his head. He still hasn't made eye contact with me.] How is the story starting?

B: Well, it's gonna start "Rabbit walked out and took his umbrella and he was soaked the minute he walked out because it was starting to pour."

MRS. A: He was soaked the minute he walked out . . .

B: Uh-hum. [Hearing his own words, Bobby finally looks at me.]

MRS. A: . . . because it was starting to pour.

B: Uh-huh.

MRS. A: That beginning really makes me want to read more. Thank you.

Bobby started writing as soon as I repeated the first sentence, so I concluded the conference. In second grade Bobby will be labeled Learning Disabled.

These six conferences have taken about ten minutes. Even though I spoke directly to a few children, others overheard and picked up ideas for their own writing. Amy gave her undivided attention to Kelsie's conference. The eavesdropping is not always obvious, but it occurs throughout the roving conference time. This is why I move around the room randomly. Mary Ellen Giacobbe calls learning by overhearing the "Dumbo effect," after the baby elephant with the big ears.

Both Graves and Giacobbe gave me suggestions for conducting conferences. Long conferences leave the child with too many concerns and prevent me from seeing many children, leaving a backlog of writers with whom I'm losing touch. Several strategies help keep conferences short: The writer begins the conference (thus eliminating the "hi, how are you?" small talk) by telling me the topic, where she is at the moment, and what she intends to do next. This information requires writers to keep their process in mind and provides the groundwork for my responses. Most important, the procedure allows the *child to do the talking in the writing conference*. By talking, the child thinks. By thinking, the child develops.

My role, as teacher, is first to listen. I listen for the *ideas* and the *energy*. What is it the writer cares about in this topic? What is important to the writer? I respond with comments and questions to let the writer know I care about the topic they are working on. I try to "up the ante" a bit by reflecting back to the writer what I've heard so that she may become cognizant of possible ways the writing might go. I'm not there to teach language skills or correct the writing even though writers will attend to these issues as they draft. In fact, I don't spend much time looking at the paper. Later, after the piece is completed and the writer has read and reread it, there will be time to address these issues.

Thoughts About Conferences

Keeping three procedures advocated by Graves and Giacobbe in mind helps me keep conferences running effectively:

1. *Listen* to what the child has to say.
2. *Tell* the child what I understand.
3. *Ask* the child to clarify or expand on what I don't understand.

Individual writing conferences function to keep the writer going, or in Lucy Calkins' term, to "nudge" them along. Questions help a writer discover for himself what he knows.

Author, poet, and teacher William Stafford (1986) wrote, "I never assess a whole paper or judge a person. Puzzlement in places, yes. Curiosity about further information, yes. Quirky, alive reactions, any time. . . . I want the students to know I am with them, that I do have reactions. But my reactions are only those that a friend would have during a conversation. . . . My way to be accountable is related directly, simply, honestly, nonthreateningly (and nonpraisingly) to my individual student" (93–94). Responding to first-grade writers is no different.

Conference Questions

In these short, frequent conferences with children, my goal is to help the writer. So I respond to the writer, not the writing, as Donald Murray says, and trust that if I help the writer, the writing will come. Sometimes I make suggestions, but I don't require that writers follow my suggestions. I don't have a list of questions in mind as I come to the conference. Still, I realize that I've developed my own predictable questions. Teachers observing me in workshops have compiled some of these questions.

Tell me about your story (piece, writing).

What is happening in your story?

How did you get that idea?

So this is about . . .

What part of the story will be most important?

What will be the best part of this piece?

How would this story begin?

So when you write this will you give information so the reader can see it like you saw it?

Will you put that information in your story? Because those are important things that your reader will want to know.

Can you tell me more? I don't know much about . . .

What was this like for you?

Are you going to start your words now?

When this happened, what do you remember most?

Are you going to include all these things in your story?

I think teachers have to develop their own questions. I put these here only to provide a sense of the questions, their open-endedness, the focus on content and the development of ideas, etc.

As children first begin to write I often say, "Read it to me." It's important for them to learn to read their own words. As pieces get longer, we move away from the reading because it consumes precious time. Instead I encourage the writer to tell me what's written in a sentence or so. I focus more on what is yet to be written because that is what is most likely to help the writer. In talking about plans or ideas to write, the writer rehearses these ideas and they become more vivid; more information is likely to make its way to paper. Also, because writers know that when I stop to confer they are to tell me about their plans, they tend to be continually thinking about what comes next. The moment when writers can become stuck is when they don't know what will come next. Conferences help writers keep going.

There are questions I avoid in conferences. I've learned not to ask questions that can be answered by yes or no or one-word answers. When a child writes about a dog, for example, it's easy to ask, "What color is your dog?" But the answer is not likely to develop the writing much and may not be significant to the meaning of the piece. It's better to ask broader, more open-ended questions. Here's a conference with Nicole as an example.

MRS. A: What was the best part about being with the horse?

NICOLE: Riding it.

MRS. A: Can you picture that? What do you see in that picture?

N: I get on. Grab the reins. Tell him to go.

MRS. A: How do you tell him to go?

N: I say, "Giddyup!"

MRS. A: Can you write that—how you get on, grab the reins, and say, "Giddyup!"?

We want details in the writing, but it's significant details that develop the key ideas that are important. If the color of the dog is important to the story, readers will ask that question because of the need to know. The children came to realize which questions helped writers and which tended to be trivial; we addressed these issues in large-group sharing when we listened to pieces of writing for meaning. The line in the classroom became "What color was the dog? Who cares?" followed by "What happened to the dog? That's what I want to know." When we listen to writers, we are listening for the ideas that led the writer to explore this topic in the first place. Our task is to help the writer get those ideas on paper.

I ask very few "How did you feel?" questions. The question just doesn't bring out enough information; the children answer "happy," "sad," "mad." A better question, I've found, is "What was that like for you?" To this query Megan answered "I jumped up and down and ran and kissed my mom." Her answer shows her happiness. "What was that like?" sometimes brings out similes in response. Joseph wrote about watching jet planes at an air show. I asked what they were like, he paused, then said, "They were loud like someone dropped a whole armful of wood on a hard floor." When Kelly wrote about visiting a local farm to pick a Halloween pumpkin I heard energy in her voice that had not yet emerged in the written story. I asked, "What was this like for you?" She paused, looked off absorbed in thought, then said, "Well, it looked just like someone took a huge bag of orange balloons and dumped it all over that field. That's what I kept thinking the whole time I was there." It wasn't choosing a pumpkin that Kelly remembered so much as the sight of the pumpkin field. Kelly's added description brought energy to her writing and the orange balloons became an example for other students of how to write description. The question took the story in a direction that was important to Kelly.

Another kind of question I'm asking writers in conferences is the process question. It's important for the writer to understand the decisions they make as they write, the how and why they write the way they do. So I'm often asking these questions:

> Tell me, how did you do this?
>
> How did you know how to do this?
>
> Why did you decide to put this in? (take this out? move this here?)

I start asking these questions the first week of school. At first, the children shrug their shoulders or reply "I don't know." But I'll say something like, "Okay. Think about it." Pretty soon they start saying, "And you want to know how I did it? Well. . . ." Articulating their decisions brings awareness, which in turn is likely to enable the writer to recall and use strategies again.

The most demanding hours of teaching I've encountered have been listening to and responding to writers. Listening means hearing the words, reading the body language and voice tone, being aware of the child's processes with past pieces and behaviors in the workshop structure, knowing the history of the current piece, and connecting all this to the present moment. I'm listening for the *energy*. Where do I hear energy from the writer? What is important to the *writer*? When I sense the energy, I acknowledge it with my interest and authentic questions. If I can tap that energy the writing will take off.

Often I find that I'm listening for the words that aren't said or yet written. Meaning, I know, is within the writer. A response may be a smile or a nod. Sometimes I can respond to a writer as I pass by the desk and we exchange glances and I know and the writer knows we've communicated—no words necessary.

Peer Conferences

My conferences with children are only part of the conferring that goes on during the writing workshop. Children chat with each other as they work. The conversations are natural sharing and learning—which is what conferences are all about. After a few weeks of school, I announce one morning as we begin to write, "If you need to talk to a teacher about your writing and this teacher (I point to myself) is busy, you could ask the teacher seated beside you. There are many teachers in this room. If one is busy we can find another" (Giacobbe 1982). The children nod. I'm merely confirming what they have already experienced. Their talk revolves around content; I've found that the children don't have enough experience to conduct peer conferences on editing. Some years we've designated areas of the classroom for children to meet and respond to each other's writing. The designated areas provided a place for more extended talk without bothering other writers.

Once in a while the children use the opportunity of talking with a peer to avoid writing. We address the problem in a class meeting, and the children usually solve it themselves. But one year this sharing became so intensive that writing was falling by the wayside. Children talked until there was little time to write, and then the next day they'd start out by talking with a peer again. To break this cycle I taped sign-in sheets in the sharing centers and required children to record the time they arrived and left the area. I never checked those sign-in sheets; but they thought I did, and the problem cleared up.

Record Keeping for Conferences

I maintain a record of conferences to help me respond to writers. The easiest is my conference checklist. At the bottom of the checklist I write the key to the marks I use so that a substitute teacher can use the form. This key provides a code for marking the box beside a child's name on a given day. *The marks note the child's engagement with the writing process at a given moment.* I'm not evaluating the writing. Nor am I assessing how well the child articulated her writing process. I want to remember how the writing is going. My code is simple.

✓ Everything is going well.

✓+ The child is sailing ahead, has plans, and the writing is surprising the writer and me.

– The writer is struggling; things aren't going well.

~ I'm not sure how things are going. They may be okay, but I want to keep in touch.

☺ The child shared in large-group sharing.

The checklist helps me keep track of whom I've seen or not seen during a workshop. I also can look back and quickly recall the tone of the conference from the day before. Knowing who has shared recently is important in selecting each day's sharers. When it comes time to choose sharers, first graders clamor to read to the class. (I hear lots of "I didn't share in a long time" statements—even from yesterday's readers.)

In the ten minutes of conferences with children at the beginning of this chapter, I noted the following on each child:

✓+ Tara—(Tara knew what she was doing and why.)

~ Nickolas—(Nick seemed to move into the writing at the end of the conference, but his uninvolvement a moment before leads me to keep a close eye on him.)

✓ Kelsie—(Writing going well, though I've seen better days with Kelsie.)

✓ Terri—(A typical day for Terri.)

–✓ Marissa—(Struggled and worked through the issue.)

~ Bobby—(I'm not sure how Bobby's doing—he may need another conference soon or he may take off.)

Looking at the conference checklist over a stretch of a few days alerts me to possible concerns. Take this example of Charles' checklist over a two-week period.

Charles	~	✓	~	✓	~ ✓	A	–~	~	~	✓☺+	

During the first week, the notations for Charles alternate between checks and squiggle lines; on Friday I talk to him twice during the workshop. The following Monday he is absent—significant because now he has been away from his writing for three days. Tuesday shows a dash and a squiggle line—two conferences and I'm getting concerned. On Wednesday and Thursday I record two squiggle lines. I feel out of touch with this writer and I sense he's struggling though I can't put my finger on the difficulty.

On Friday I spent a longer time than usual with Charles. We talked about HO trains, a hobby he shared with his dad. He knew a lot about this topic, but writing all the information was difficult. I suggested he manage his topic by writing about engines on one page, including everything he could think of about them, then on another page writing about the caboose, and so on, and then we could see what to do next. The strategy worked. Charles shared the writing with the entire group that day. The writing evolved into a "Dictionary of Trains," each page on a different aspect of trains. Charles successfully alphabetized the typed pages by laying them out on the floor and determining the sequence from the alphabet posted in the classroom.

An alternative form of record keeping for writing workshop is an anecdotal record sheet. This record has a block for each child in the class, with space to write brief notes. At the end of the conference I write down the child's topic and notes on what I learned: the child's intentions, a strategy the child used, the child's plans. I didn't use this record-keeping procedure during the conference session I've shown earlier, but if I had I probably would have made notes similar to these:

Tara: Birthday. Plans: Lining out "extra stuff." Checked at home and adding info. Used checkmark to add.

Nick: Hamsters. Plans: Describing circle with legs, play with hamsters.

Kelsie: Lobel Letter. Ask Mr. L ?'s—why didn't he tell if they raked leaves? Shared with Amy. Plans: Ask favorite things. Sugg: Tell about *why* like books.

Terri: Chris' B-day. Plans: Wheelie present, guests, prizes. Next: Musical chairs.

Marissa: Stuck—Incident with brother; put "sad" on page, illus. Only.

Bobby: Forest—Flood. Told me lead then began to write. Plans: ?

These notes provide quick, day-to-day reminders of the children's writing. I inform the class of the record keeping I'm doing. By telling the children that I'm noting their plans, they tend to take responsibility for remembering and carrying them out.

Responding to Problems

In writing conferences, I encounter writers dealing with a number of problems. The following examples demonstrate ways the children and I address problems.

The Writer Is Stuck

Being stuck looks different with different writers.

Ray was stuck. I watched him gather and staple paper, chatting with friends the entire time. He sat at his desk, went to the pencil sharpener, returned, and then wrote a few words. He flipped pages, looked around the room. I was pretty sure of the problem: he was beginning a new piece of writing and although he had his topic, he didn't know how to start. This was a pattern for him. I stopped to talk.

RAY: I'm gonna write when I went to my friend's. My title's "Sleep Over Night."

MRS. A: Are you making a title page here with the title and your name and date?

R: Yeah,

MRS. A: It's about sleeping over at your friend's house?

R: Well, we stayed up until midnight.

MRS. A: You stayed up till *midnight*?

R: Un-huh.

MRS. A: What was that like, Ray?

R: Well, uh, well he, well, when it was time to go to bed, well, uh, we were looking for ghosts—we were just staying in bed—and, uh, and it looked like there was a ghost at the door when we were going to sleep.

MRS. A: You were looking for ghosts and you thought you saw a ghost at the door when you were going to sleep.

R: Uh-huh!

MRS. A: What was that like?

R: And John . . . well, we . . . we, we were scared. John and me were sleepin', well John um . . . [Lots of stammering around. I've thrown him off track by my question. He stops to answer but now searches to recall his original train of thought.] I mean me and my friend were sleeping in the bed and John was sleeping on the floor. So, um . . .

MRS. A: So there were the three of you. Another friend and John.

R: Uh-huh, and when me and my other friend were in bed the ghost was just standing there and we were so scared we were hiding our pillows behind us.

MRS. A: Oh my gosh! Is all this going to be in there? How you were hiding the pillows and saw ghosts and all this business?

R: Uh-huh.

MRS. A: You won't forget any of it?

R: No.

MRS. A: Should be an exciting story.

Ray began writing about the sleepover. Talking got him going.

Edwin has been writing about his family's trip to Disney World and Atlanta. He's been trying to include everything and the piece is becoming a list of activities. Edwin has resisted suggestions to focus. Today he's been sitting reading his piece, chewing his pencil, talking to others, and not writing at all.

EDWIN: I've written fourteen pages.

MRS. A: Fourteen pages!

E: Yeah, all about me on my trip. 'Cept I don't know what to write today.

MRS. A: Are you ready to begin a new piece?

E: No. I don't know what—I don't want to.

MRS. A: Is there one part of this piece that's the best part, your favorite part?

E: [Shakes his head.] I didn't write the Atlanta part yet.

MRS. A: Un-hun. Okay.

There's a pause and then suddenly Edwin starts to talk. He speaks so animatedly and so fast that I can only understand some of his words.

EDWIN: We went to a dolphin show and my dad got wet. My mom and dad and my sister the dolphins . . . big splash and dad-ga-really wet.

MRS. A: Wow. So you got splashed and your dad got really wet! What did your dad say when he got wet?

E: I don't know. He said it in Chinese.

MRS. A: Oh, he said it in Chinese so you don't know what he said.

E: Yeah, and he turned his back and got all wet on his back.

MRS. A: He got all wet on his back? Are you going to write all this?

E: Yeah, I'm going to write. I got a keen idea. And I'm going to write about getting splashed and this is the first time I'll have people talking. I have a plan now.

In the next fifteen minutes, Edwin writes four pages focused on getting wet at the dolphin show. He adds a title to the section: BIG SPLASH! The question about his favorite part helped him recall the dolphin show and he bubbled with energy. Asking what his dad said led him to think of a way to include conversation, something he'd been wanting to try but wasn't sure how to do.

Mandy knew she was stuck. She'd been stuck for two days and she said so when I stopped at her desk. In this conference we struggled together to find a topic.

MANDY: I'm stuck.

MRS. A: Is this the same story you were stuck with yesterday?

M: Yes [a big sigh].

MRS. A: Mandy, I have an idea. See what you think about it. You seem to be stuck on this piece. What if you put this piece away for a while? Just put it in your folder, and you can come back to it after you've thought about it. Get out another piece of paper and just start writing and see if you can write about something else. You could write about something from your vacation journal.

M: Well, there's one thing I know about my birthday. It's funny.

MRS. A: Yeah?

M: And I hate my birthday being in April because there might be, you know, there might be a shower in April. And then May, that's a good time for birthdays because flowers grow.

MRS. A: Yes.

M: Lots of flowers. [Mandy's thoughts ramble and one topic leads her to another and another. The temporary inability to focus may contribute to the sense of being stuck. I try to get her to think about one idea.]

MRS. A: Yes. Okay, so what about your birthday would you like to write?

M: Well, it's very close to April Fool's . . . [Mandy continues to ramble. After several attempts to get her to focus, I determine that the birthday topic is going nowhere. I try another path in an effort to help.]

MRS. A: Okay [pause]. Okay, what do you want to write about now? What about Christmas? [She'd mentioned this in passing.]

M: Well, I didn't get lots of things.

MRS. A: What was your favorite thing?

M: I didn't have a favorite thing.

MRS. A: Um. You didn't have a favorite thing. Did you have a good time?

M: Yes, but there's something I just remembered. [There is sudden energy in her voice. Her eyes and her whole body perk up.] I got a record player from Grandma and my Aunt Snookie and the little needle—it broke off. Daddy had to buy a new one and he put, he put the needle that he bought back on, on the record player and now it works.

MRS. A: Could you write about that? The record player? And getting it fixed?

M: I think I will.

The story of the record player worked out for Mandy and eventually she published this writing. Selecting topics continued to be a problem for this child, although once she had a subject, she worked for days drafting and refining the writing. She maintained high standards for herself, which probably contributed to her dilemma in choosing topics. Each choice had to be a good one. Conferences helped her seek out topics, although she weighed each choice long and hard.

Madison finished a piece yesterday. Today she sits holding a pencil, her head laying on her desk beside the blank paper.

MADISON: I don't know what to write. I finished my story about camping.

MRS. A: Hmm, that's a tough time. I think one of the hardest times as a writer is when you've finished one piece and you don't know what to write next. I'll tell you something I try to do. I try to get the next idea before I finish a piece. That way it's in the back of my mind and I can get started putting it on paper. What are some of the things you do when you're stuck?

M: I don't know. I just have to think of things.

MRS. A: Well, you will. Something will come. Sometimes I just start writing. I just put the pencil on the paper, start it moving and keep it moving and something comes. But you have to keep the pencil moving.

M: [smiles] Okay.

I leave. A few minutes later she begins to write. I wait a bit and then stop back.

MRS. A: How's it going? Did you come up with something?

M: Un-huh. I started writing about my brother last night and then I remembered something else about him so I'm writing that.

MRS. A: So you know where you're going now?

M: Un-huh.

Many writers encounter the difficulty Madison faced this day. I support her by letting her know I understand her difficulty and offer possible solutions. I've learned not to fall into the trap of suggesting topics. I can't "give" children topics; they must depend on their own resources. This was difficult at first because I was uncomfortable when children weren't continually writing. Writers learn by working through all their struggles—including selecting topics and being stuck sometimes—as well as by the writing they accomplish. If I'm quick to rescue, I rob them of this learning.

Emery, a capable student, spent his time drawing but rarely put any words or even letters on his paper except his name. Seeing this pattern, I approached him hoping to convey my expectation for him to write.

EMERY: This is about skiing.

MRS. A: So you're writing about skiing. What will be the best part?

E: Probably when I went down Challenger—you know, Challenger, that steep slope?

MRS. A: *You* went down *Challenger*? Really? What was that like for you?

E: Scary!

MRS. A: Scary—scary how? Tell me what you mean—it was "scary" for you? [There's a long pause; I wait.]

E: Well. . . . I was going really fast . . . and it's steep.

MRS. A: Yes?

E: Yeah, and the wind was blowing past me so fast it made whistling noises in my ears.

MRS. A: Whistling noises in your ears! You were going so fast the wind made whistling noises in your ears. You *ARE* going to write that?

E: Umm, yeah, I might.

Emery did write about skiing—two sentences about the steep slope and the wind in his ears. My final comment, though a question, conveyed through a firm voice, strong eye contact, and nods that I expect this to be written. My voice also carried playfulness through a sort of outrageous humor. It's as though I'm saying, "Of course you'll write; that's what's expected and I know you can and I know you've been stalling and now's the time to do something." When I know the child and the context, I can determine when to give these strong nudges. It's all part of maintaining strong standards for the workshop.

Jared sat holding his head with one hand and his pencil with the other. I'd been aware for the last several minutes that he'd run into a problem. He'd begun the workshop writing up a storm, but now, suddenly, he was stuck.

JARED: Um, um, um, I'm writing about the USFL and I wrote all the teams but I'm figuring out um, um, what Washington's last name is.

MRS. A: Ohhh. You can't remember that. You've been sitting here thinking.

J: Uh-huh.

MRS. A: I'm wondering, Jared, if it would help if you went on and left a space for that, and then when it came to you, you could sit down and finish it—come back to it. What do you think?

J: Um-hum. [He hasn't looked up from the paper and the tone of his response tells me he's not sure this will work. I try again.]

MRS. A: What part is going to come next?

J: Um, um. [long pause] Who played um, in the game. Like urn, Philadelphia played Denver and um, New Jersey played Los Angeles.

MRS. A: Who played the first games . . .

J: Yeah.

MRS. A: . . . on the first Sunday.

J: Yeah. [Suddenly Jared begins writing, turning his attention totally from our conference to his writing.]

MRS. A: So you know where you're going now.

J: Uh-huh. [He never looks up. I leave.]

Jared needed to talk to discover what he knew in order to continue writing. He didn't pick up on my suggestion to leave a space for the information he couldn't recall. When I asked him what part was going to come next he got back into his topic again.

Most of the problems writers confront revolve around getting stuck. In the writing conference I listen to their struggles, ask questions, possibly make suggestions, but allow the writers to make their own decisions in working through the problem. The experience of that process is as important as the final product. Sometimes it's important to let them sit and think. I remind myself that we aren't into producing, producing, producing. We're about learning how to write and struggle is part of that. Writing is a restless activity, filled with shifting, moving, talking, moving about. I'm there to respond to the writer, to encourage and suggest solutions but not take over.

The Writer Copies Other Writing

Eventually plagiarism comes up with every group of children. A child picks up a book and copies word for word. I ask why he decided to do this and have to marvel at the underlying problem solving. Usually the child tells me with honesty, and even pride, how he figured out a good story to write. It's easy to just write the words in the book. I inform the child that this is something writers must never do and I bet he didn't know that. As I explain, the children react in amazement, and sometimes with a bit of chagrin. But the issue is critical for writers and we need to address it. Later, the child may join me in talking to the whole group about plagiarism. A significant discussion always ensues with the "experienced" child in a teacher role.

Sometimes child writers fall into retelling stories from television or movies. Eileen attended a local children's theater and was eager to write about the experience. She had loved the play, but when she wrote she discovered she couldn't manage the material. In an attempt to explain the parts she enjoyed, she got bogged down in retelling the play. It was October. I suggested she set the writing aside until a later time or that she just write about attending the theater without getting into the details of the play. She chose to go on to another topic. Months later she pulled this writing from her folder and said, "I think I know how to write this now. I'll just tell a couple parts I liked and why I like them because I can't write the whole play!" And she laughed at her earlier attempts.

The Writer Borrows from Popular Culture

In September, Thomas wrote superhero stories day after day. Was he copying the television tales? "No!" he insisted, and other children confirmed that his stories were original; he was borrowing only the characters and their unusual environments. The other children loved the stories and Thomas would have nothing to do with personal narrative, the genre favored by most of the class. Thomas and I both had difficulty reading his writing because he reversed many letters, neglected to leave spaces between words ("I just had my mind on the *story*," he'd explain), and frequently wrote left to right for a line then right to left for the next line. However, he could always retell his stories, finding words here and there in the written text for prompts. But I felt uneasy as the days went on because I could find no way to help Thomas. I waited for a change. Finally, I could stand it no longer.

"Thomas," I said one morning, "I'd like you to find another topic to write about today. I can't help you with your writing because I don't know enough about superheroes. And my job is to help you when you write."

"But Mrs. Avery," Thomas wailed, "I have this great story in my head today. I've gotta write it down."

"But what can we do? I can't help you and you have trouble explaining it all to me."

"How 'bout tomorrow?" he suggested. "Tomorrow I'll write something else."

It took two days before Thomas switched to his new topic: dinosaurs. He wrote about dinosaurs for weeks and became our dinosaur expert. I became captivated by the wonderful imagination he brought to these compositions, and I understood why his superhero stories had so enraptured his classmates. Superheroes opened the door for Thomas to write; I was glad I hadn't slammed it in his face through a premature response.

Video and computer games bring about other problems. One little boy, a delightful child and a solid student, received video games for Christmas. The effect was so gradual I didn't notice it at first. He began writing about Christmas and his presents and soon was into the games. The writing made no sense to me and, like the games, it never ended. When I talked to him he spoke only of the games. One morning his mother stopped in to drop off bookcovers she had made for us and I briefly expressed my concerns. A week later I noticed a definite change. This child began talking about playing soccer and getting ready for Valentine's Day. Later I learned that the parents had limited use of the video game machine to two hours on weekends. I was amazed and thankful. And I was keenly aware that the daily conferences allowed me to notice the situation.

After this experience I decided to ask children to eliminate computer games as writing topics. "I'm not sure that writing about these games helps you as a writer," I explained, "and I don't know how to help you write these pieces." I anticipated grief and complaints; instead I got agreement. "Those game stories are sorta boring, anyhow," commented one child. "Boring to write and boring to read," said another. Group consensus. Why had I waited so long? Because we all needed to wait that long in order to come to this realization.

The Writer Produces "Shocking" Content

Do I ever censor children's writing? Yes! I've never allowed blood-and-guts stories. Even first graders are capable of producing shock-laden material. Today's six-year-old is far more worldly than counterparts of earlier generations. When this kind of writing comes up, I simply respond similarly to Giacobbe and Atwell, "I am offended by reading that kind of stuff and so in this classroom, we will not write pieces like this." Most of the group sighs in relief. I also ban profanity, though most youngsters know instinctively that such language is not allowed in school. Usually the issue doesn't even come up. But then, sometimes it does.

Alex moved into our class in January. Such a bright child! Soon his writing provided a model that inspired the others to try new topics and new techniques. One day in March, individuals from the Pennsylvania Department of Education came to videotape our workshop. All went well through the minilesson and the roving conferences. I chose Alex for group sharing. He read about dad mowing the lawn and the lawnmower breaking. Alex continued, "Then my dad said, . . ." and quoted a string of words to turn a sailor blue.

Suddenly, every child's eyes were on me. The camera's red light glowed indicating it was recording every moment. Alex turned and looked at me, awaiting my reaction. Everyone awaited my reaction.

"Continue. Is there anything else?" I said.

"No, that's all I wrote," Alex replied.

"Okay, boys and girls, do you have any responses for Alex?" I knew I had to say something. The children probably wouldn't touch it, but as usual I would add my response—whatever it would be—after they gave theirs. I knew my response probably carried more weight, but I'd found that embedding it with the responses of a group allowed the writer to accept or reject it with grace.

Tentatively, Kevin raised his hand. Alex called on him and Kevin began to speak, looking over to me to check for affirmation as he proceeded. I nodded ever so slightly, not knowing what Kevin would say but deciding to trust his response.

"I, um, I don't, um I think that, well, you wrote this book, but if you published it, if you made it into a book for people to read, well, um, I wouldn't be able to take it home because my mom won't let me say words like that. So I couldn't read it." Kevin's voice started hesitantly, but as he spoke his back straightened and his voice gained strength. He looked at me and I nodded as he finished and settled back on the rug. Alex made no response except to call on Beth.

"I'm not allowed to say those words either. I really don't like to hear words like that," came her quiet comment. Now several children raised their hands and each child affirmed Kevin and Beth. A landslide was underway and I didn't want Alex to be buried, so I interrupted.

"Alex, do you hear what these children are saying?" He looked at me intently, striving to maintain his dignity. "I think they are saying that the words in this writing offend them and they don't want to read them. In fact, they'd be in trouble at home if they read them. Sometimes, Alex, grown-ups write words like this in their writing and then people have to make a choice about reading it. That's part of an important freedom in our country. But I think these boys and girls are telling you that in this classroom they don't want that writing. Their moms and dads don't want to hear it, and they're not allowed to read it or even say those words."

Alex nodded. "I can line them out," he said.

"Yes, you can," I replied. "You have an important choice to make."

"I think I'll probably line them out or I might just start a whole new piece," he answered.

The community provided the response. Alex had tested the limits of his new environment. But the structure was in place. The children knew how to respond even though we had never talked about this particular concern. Children's sensibilities can be trusted, and sometimes the most appropriate response is to wait.

GOLD STAR ADDICTION

"I'm done. Mrs. Avery, I'm done." Samantha stood beside me, lightly tapping my shoulder as I conferred with Mark. I tried to ignore her but she wouldn't go away.

It was mid-March and Samantha had been with our class for a little over a week. Although writing workshop was new to her, she was a capable student and was catching on quickly. Despite her progress, she frequently appeared at my elbow throughout the day, interrupting conversations with other children, smiling, presenting her schoolwork, and awaiting my approval. As the days passed and I attempted to wean her of the need for continuous affirmation, she became more insistent and demanding. Samantha was addicted to praise.

"Excuse me, Mark. I'll be back," I said, and turning to Samantha I took her hand, met her expectant countenance with a direct gaze that did not return her smile, and led her back to her desk. "Now, tell me what the *emergency* is," I said. Her smile, which had briefly turned to puzzlement, returned. She presented her writing to me saying, "I'm done. Did I do a good job?"

"What do you think?" I asked. Her smile evaporated.

"I don't know."

I pondered her reply a brief moment. She was right. She didn't know.

Tiffy, a quiet observer at the desk adjoining Samantha's, spoke up. "But, Mrs. Avery wants to know what the *emergency* is." Tiffy recognized the most immediate problem: interrupting a writing conference.

Samantha looked puzzled. Tiffy's eyes met mine with a look that communicated she understood what had initiated today's incident.

"Help me, Tiffy. Can you explain to Samantha?" On several occasions I had attempted to address the interrupting with Samantha. No change resulted. As with many classroom issues, I knew that a peer might communicate far more effectively than I could. It was no accident that I had placed Tiffy's desk beside Samantha's. The children regarded Tiffy as a peacemaker—pleasant, kind, and fair—qualities highly valued by first graders. I knew Tiffy would facilitate Samantha's adjustment to the classroom. I could not plan nor mandate such interactions, but only provide the setting for them to take place when moments such as this arose during the school day.

Tiffy responded to my query with a smile and a modest shrug as she said, "I don't know. I'll try." Then, turning to Samantha she explained ever so gently, "See, when Mrs. Avery is listening to someone talk about their writing no one's supposed to interrupt, not unless there's an *emergency*. Remember the other day when she said, 'Only if someone's throwing up or bleeding to death' and she hasn't noticed it? At the beginning she told everyone that and sometimes, at first, we forgot. I forgot and once Jason forgot."

Hearing his name, Jason looks over and grins. We all remember the day in September when Jason persisted in interrupting the writing conference until I turned and in a greatly exaggerated horror said, "Where's the emergency?" Jason had retreated quickly in momentary embarrassment.

Later, in large-group talk, we discussed my reaction and all the children, including Jason, felt comfortable with a rule about not interrupting teacher/student conversations, understanding that we needed this for the smooth operation of the whole school day. Although the surface reason for the rule was to help with management, the embedded intent was to develop independence in the first graders, both as writers and as learners. The outrageous tone of voice I used that day became a legacy, a tool employed to communicate a point firmly, while still maintaining an underlying humor. Voice tones became part of the communication history of our classroom, which we all knew and understood. But Samantha was new to our group. There was much about our communication, procedures, and tones that she did not understand.

Tiffy instinctively knew this as she continued talking softly. "What she means—what I think Mrs. Avery means—is that when someone's talking with her about writing, it's real *important* and she might not be able to listen so good if people interrupt her. You have to wait 'til it's *your* turn and then you can talk to her."

Samantha looked at Tiffy and then at me as she gave this matter thought for a moment. One could almost see the wheels turning in her head. "Oh," she finally said, slowly. "Well, what about when I'm done. Aren't you going to read it?" she asked me.

Before I could reply, Tiffy answered. "Mrs. Avery can't read *everything* we write. You gotta choose your best pieces to put in the basket for her to read and then you can publish that piece maybe. If you finish one piece, you just put it in your folder and then start another one. You read your writing and when you do—while you're reading it—you *think* if it's good or not and if it makes sense. Sometimes, if you read it on the next day, then you can decide if it's good and you might want to fix some parts to make it better."

Samantha looked at Tiffy, then at her writing. She turned to me and said, "Well then, what should I do now?"

"Well, you could read this piece to see if it makes sense, like Tiffy said, or you could start a new one and come back to this another day," I replied.

"She could read it to me, if she wants, and I could help her some," suggested Tiffy. Samantha looked at me, checking this possibility out.

"What do you think?" I asked.

"Okay," Samantha replied. "I'll read it to Tiffy."

I returned to Mark. Later I overheard Tiffy say to Samantha, "See you don't need to always ask the teacher if it's good. You can figure it out yourself." A puzzling concept for Samantha, I thought.

The contrast between Samantha and the rest of these children at that point in the year struck me vividly. These young writers wrote for themselves, not for grades, gold stars, stickers, or teacher praise. They understood the highs and lows, the ups and downs of a writer. They had developed an ability to assess their own progress and the quality of their own writing.

Samantha, on the other hand, worked for the goal of completing a task and submitting it for the approval of others. She was dependent on feedback and, since she was quite capable, she was accustomed to regular doses of glowing accolades. She lived under the illusion that she did everything well—even outstandingly. In this classroom Samantha was experiencing withdrawal from gold star addiction, a dependency that teachers foster in students when they heap rewards and praise on all the students' efforts.

One reason for gold star addiction is that we tend to give praise too liberally—too much, too often, too indiscriminately. Children come to believe that all of their efforts are "great," "wonderful," "super," and that they need do only more of the same. A child might resist risking new ways of thinking about or attempting a task because of the fear of error and the subsequent loss of reward. Indiscriminate praise tends to require escalation. The child becomes accustomed to stickers or stars or superlative comments and we lock ourselves into giving rewards regularly. When a piece of work comes in that is of slightly less quality we are trapped. What do we say? Do we give a sticker or not? The young child's perception is likely that reward means success, lack of reward means failure. We discourage the child (who may have put forth his best effort) if we decide we cannot give the reward this time, or we continue—albeit uneasily—with the hypocrisy. On the other hand, when a child shows improvement, we give a reward even though it may not accurately communicate the growth we observe. "Too much praise in the profession is diminishing and manipulative of the child," warns Donald Graves (1983, 215).

I recall watching children pull papers from the classroom mailboxes many years ago at the end of a school day. "Oh a sticker! Look!" cries one child while another hurriedly stuffs a stickerless paper into a bookbag. I remember feeling uncomfortable with both responses—the gloating and the shame—to my subjective judgments. I've given up putting stickers as rewards on children's schoolwork. First graders love stickers and I still give stickers. But I'll hand one out to every child in the room, not as a reward but simply as a gift.

As with all addictions, the substance that provides the glow, whether it is stickers, stars, or superlatives, becomes the essential end for the recipient. I've heard teachers say, "Kids will *kill* for a sticker." (And the statement that frequently follows is, "I can get them to do anything when I promise stickers.") Soon, however, the glow fades and we teachers become trapped into increasing either the frequency or the sparkle of the reward. We give two stars instead of one, hand out scratch-and-sniff stickers rather than plain ones, pile on the superlatives: "Wow! Terrific! That's great!" Children shift their focus from the learning task to striving for the reward, thereby increasing their dependence on us, the suppliers of reward, rather than developing the appropriate independence as individual learners that comes through realistic recognition of their own talents.

In *Children's Minds*, Margaret Donaldson (1978) states, "There is now a substantial amount of evidence pointing to the conclusion that if an activity is rewarded by some extrinsic prize or token—something quite external to the activity itself—then that activity is less likely to be engaged in later in a free and voluntary manner when the rewards are absent, and it is less likely to be enjoyed" (121). Over and over, I've seen young children strive for and delight in the accomplishment of learning tasks without the promise of either rewards or punishments dangled before them. I think of Lori saying, "I wanted to read *Charlotte's Web* because it's such a good book but it was pretty hard for me. I kept practicing and practicing reading and then one day I picked it up and then I could read it." I remember Traci racing in from the playground to report, "I just learned to jump rope. I jumped ten times without missing!" I see Jenny throwing her hands up in glee during a writing workshop and saying, "I did it! I wrote a whole sentence! I didn't think I could, but I tried, and then I did it." As their teacher, I encouraged and provided demonstrations, provided honest and specific feedback, and when they succeeded, celebrated with them.

Responses to children are never neutral. They are influenced by my experiences, interests, and knowledge, even my state of mind at a given time. But by listening and giving as honest a response as possible, I believe children will trust the response and also their own process. In every group of children I've worked with, every child has been able to identify the strongest reader, the most talented artist, the most gifted mathematician in the group. Children know each other's talents and have a healthy awareness of their own strengths in comparison. By providing specific responses to children we confirm what they already know, validate that awareness, and demonstrate our own respect of each child and the talents each boy and girl has to give.

REFLECTIONS

Learning to respond to writers means learning to *listen* to children. I think this listening/response is the heart of good teaching. I sure didn't do it when I began teaching, and even after years of working with children I still come out with some awful comments in response to what they've said. Usually it's because I've jumped to conclusions about their meaning or intentions. Listening and responding became a necessity. It's more than a skill, more than an approach. I think it's an attitude or classroom lifestyle that spills over from writing to every other part of the school day.

The following guidelines highlight my procedures for conferences.

1. Go to individual writers rather than have them come to you. Move to eye level, look the writer in the eye, and listen. Listen for meaning: the ideas, intentions, and energy of the writer. Take care not to interrupt or take over.
2. Respond by telling the writer your understanding of what is said. Repeating key words or phrases that appeal to you is helpful. Affirm

the writer through encouraging and specific responses; avoid general praise.

3. Ask about what is puzzling, seems unclear, needs clarifying, or what you want to know more about. Open-ended questions lead writers to talk about what is not yet written and can help determine the direction of the writing.
4. Set aside concerns for conventions. When students ask "how do you spell . . . ," turn the question back to them with a response such as "How could you go about spelling that word?"
5. Help beginning writers reread their writing. As pieces get longer, ask them to summarize the writing or read a sentence or two from the best part.
6. Keep conferences brief—under a minute each. However, in the beginning be prepared to take a little longer as students are learning how to take part in the conference. Deal with only one or two issues to keep from overloading the writer.
7. Move randomly around the room. Children benefit from overhearing conferences with other students.
8. Convey that this is serious, ongoing work but use a light tone.
9. View conferences as opportunities to learn from students.

Although I've moved away from a teacher-centered classroom, the nature of school gives me considerable influence. As manager of the classroom, influence helps me keep things running smoothly but, as a facilitator of learning, I must be cautious of my power. If I use a heavy-handed approach—one where I am always the expert and final authority—I could crush children's curiosity, intrude on their thinking, and interfere with learning. By sharing power with the children, we become a team and can relax, laugh, marvel together over what we discover, and we can learn. Sharing my expertise is basic to the teacher role. But how I share that expertise and the *timing* for sharing must be in response to the children, both individually and collectively. Determining how and when to "teach" creates the dynamic tension in good teaching and the precise reason why teaching can never be reduced to a set of procedures, practices, and plans. I've found that I must begin by irrefutably trusting the children's desire to learn and their ability to do so; I must respect children and try not to judge them. Trust and respect become the foundation that enables me to listen and then respond to the children with authenticity and a light touch.

CHAPTER 8

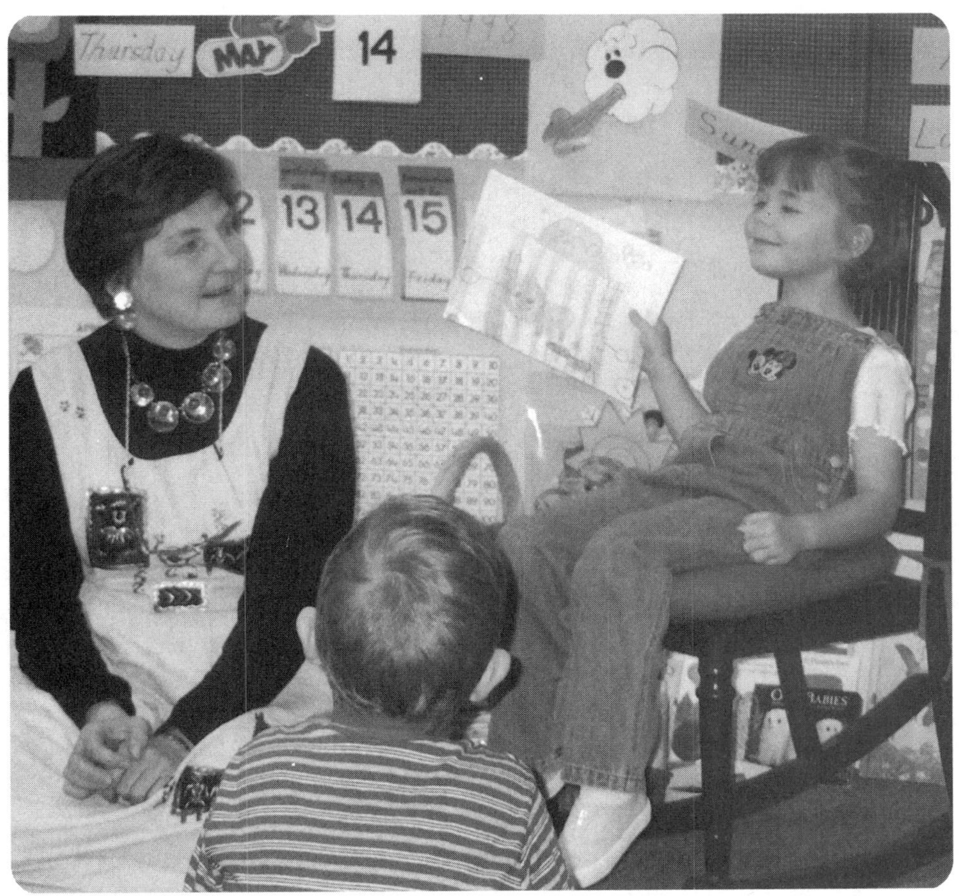

From the Author's Chair

"Can I? I didn't ever yet—well, almost never."

A clamor of voices bombards me with requests as soon as I ask children to gather for the sharing time that ends writing workshop. My conference record sheet helps me choose a child who hasn't shared recently. I also try to call on a writer who has had a particularly good day or one who has tried something new. But on any given day only two or three will share. Sharing time contributes to the supportive nature of our writing community and also provides a time for specific instruction.

It's a month into the school year and I've asked Amy and Darren to share. Amy has included direct quotations in her writing. Darren has happened upon a way to use the sides of his crayons to create an unusual visual experience. He is delighted with his work and sharing will enhance his status in this community. I look at my checklist to select a third sharer and notice that Erika hasn't shared for a while.

"Erika, do you want to share that piece about horseback riding?"

"Okay." As we move to the story rug, Erika confides that she's not sure she can read all her words. I assure her it's okay to read what she can and tell us the rest. I'm not concerned that she can't read it all; I see her use letter and context cues along with her memory of the content to read her writing. Her writing fluency expands each day and she's developing reading strategies.

We gather on the story rug; each child in turn sits on the author's chair to read her writing to the group. The children know the procedures for sharing at the end of writing workshop.

- The author reads, shows illustrations, then calls on responders (children or teacher) who have raised their hands.
- Responders begin comments with "I" rather than "you."
- Responders avoid using the word "should." (Both of these guidelines allow the responder to take responsibility for his or her comment on the writing. "You should . . ." or "You did . . ." imply that the responder knows the best way, which the writer has yet to figure out. Using "I think . . ." "I wondered . . ." "I didn't understand . . ." the responder takes responsibility for her opinion and allows the author to accept or reject the responder's idea.)
- Responders tell the writer as specifically as possible what they liked or learned by quoting words or phrases and avoid general comments such as "I like your story." Also, responders ask questions about parts that are unclear or about which they want more information.
- Individual sharing sessions end by applauding the writer.

Erika shares first today. She begins reading hesitantly.

ERIKA: One time I went with my dad for a ride and we—I'll tell you this part. It says, it says here we rode a horse—it was fun. I wanted to say "Giddyup" and they said to get down then. This is my picture of me riding a horse.

E: Karen?

KAREN: I learned that you went with your dad for a horse ride.

E: Un-huh. John?

JOHN: You wanted to say "Giddyup" but they said you had to get down then and . . . did you get to ride the horse?

E: Yes. I said that in the writing. Stacy?

STACY: How's come you *told us* some parts instead of reading 'em?

E: I . . . well, Mrs. Avery said it was okay just to tell it if I didn't—if I wasn't sure exactly what it said.

S: Oh. [Stacy nods and smiles, acknowledging her understanding.]

MRS. A: Sometimes we have trouble reading what we wrote. So I told Erika to tell us because she knows what it's about. It takes practice to learn to read anything. It's one of the things you work on when you write—reading what you wrote. [The children nod.]

E: Darren?

DARREN: I like your horse, and, um, I like your horse. You drawed good.

E: Thank you. Anyone else? Jody?

JODY: Well, what's that circle thing in the top of your picture? Is it a railroad or something?

E: That's a track where you can ride the horses only we didn't ride there. We just went on this path because the track is where they go fast but we couldn't go fast. So we didn't go on the track.

J: Oh, 'cause I thought it was a train track. Trains have tracks, too.

E: Mrs. Avery?

MRS. A: A track for horses and a track for trains. Two kinds of track, humm. Interesting. And I was wondering if you've ever ridden a horse before or if this was the first time?

E: No, I've ridden—well, this wasn't the first time I ever roden a horse, but it was the first time we ever went to this place.

MRS. A: I see. Well, what's it like to ride a horse? Probably some people in here haven't done that before.

E: Well, it's sorta scary at first and you're really high up and I can't get up myself. My dad helps—he lifts me up so then I can get on and you have to hold the reins. But at first my dad just held the reins and I held the horse's hair—the mane. I held the horse's mane.

MRS. A: So it feels scary because you're high up and someone has to hold the reins, and at first your dad did and you held the horse's mane.

E: Yeah, but then I held the reins. Josie?

JOSIE: Maybe you could put that in if you wanted to.

E: Yeah. Greg?

GREG: I was wondering why you decided to write this piece? Was it because you like horses? 'Cause I remember you were reading that book—what's it called? *All the Different Horses*?

E: *All the Pretty Horses*. Yes, and because we went to ride a horse.

MRS. A: Thank you, Erika. [Applause.]

Amy sits in the chair and reads.

AMY: I just learned how to ride a two-wheeler. This is the story. [Amy looks up from reading and comments. "I put that part—I wrote that in later. That's why it's so tiny a writing. I didn't think it would make sense if I just wrote the next part without that." She continues to read.] I was over at Josie's house and she just learned how to ride a two-wheeler. And she asked me if I could ride a two-wheeler. I said, "No, but I'm going to try." So I got on the bike. And then she said, "That is bumpy." So I went the other way. Then I said, "I did it, Josie. I learned how." Then she said, "Why don't you ride Emily's bike?" So I rode Emily's bike. Josie's bike was small. Emily's bike was the right size for me.

A: Laura?

LAURA: I heard that you learned to ride a bike, and you learned to ride Josie's bike.

A: [Nods to Laura.] Monica?

MONICA: I heard you read that you rode Emily's bike and I wondered, "Who's Emily?"

A: Well, Emily is Josie's sister. She's in second grade.

M: Oh, I see. And I was confused at the part when you said it was bumpy. I didn't get what you meant.

A: The *road* was bumpy the way I was going, so I went the other way.

M: Oh, now I get it.

A: Elizabeth?

ELIZABETH: I liked when you said, "No, but I'm going to try." And then you said, "I did it, Josie."

A: Thank you. Mrs. Avery?

MRS. A: I like that part, too. Amy, could you tell the group how you wrote those parts?

A: See, I was reading it over, and then when I talked to Mrs. Avery she asked if I put that part in—the part that said, "I did it, Josie," and I thought that was important for people to know that I did it, and so I wrote it, and I put circles and arrows like Mrs. Avery showed us. ["Ohhh" and nods from the group.]

MRS. A: Any questions? Amy revised by adding information she forgot the first time she wrote it—just as we talked about in mini-lessons. This writer also did something else. She included *conversation*. She thought of the words she said and wrote them, and I think it made it more interesting than if she'd just *told us* she learned to ride the bike. Don't you?

GREG: Yeah, you can *hear* her talking in her story. You know, like we talked about seeing pictures in our heads. Well, here we can hear people talking in our heads.

MRS. A: I like that. I hadn't thought of it quite that way before. Putting in conversation is something you could think of for your writing, so readers can hear the words in their heads. Thank you, Amy. [Applause.]

Darren is next. Writing has been difficult for Darren. He strings tiny, neat letters across a page but can't read a word of it. If I sit beside him while he composes, I am able to read some of his writing later, but I also notice that his mind switches from one topic to another and so does his writing. He loves drawing and carefully produces trucks, tractors, bikes, and buildings. One day he expressed frustration at not being able to reproduce the correct perspective on a barn. I provided him with illustrations and spent some time during free play showing him how to draw only two sides of a building instead of three. Today he holds up his work in sharing circle: reds, browns, yellows, blues, oranges, a blended spectrum that fills the art. Darren's work is unique. The exquisiteness of the page causes the children to gasp.

"How did you do that?"

"It's *beautiful*!"

"Neat!"

"I like them colors!"

"Wow! Darren, you're an artist!"

Darren beams. So far he hasn't said a word. The children seem to sense he's not ready to take charge of his sharing session, and they respond without waiting for him to call on them. Yet they maintain order. I marvel at their instinctive ability to manage situations with such grace. But I want to draw Darren in so I prompt him.

MRS. A: Darren, can you tell them how you did this?

DARREN: I just, ah, ah, I, um, with crayons.

MRS. A: With what part of the crayons, Darren?

D: The sides.

MRS. A: Can you tell us more?

D: I just, um, I used the sides—with no paper. Well, see, the paper all come off my crayons.

MRS. A: Ah, no paper on the crayons. Do you see, boys and girls?

VOICES: I did that before—but not like Darren.

What's the picture at the bottom?

D: A farm.

VOICE: Oh, it's a farm.

D: My granddad's farm. I go to my granddad's farm.

VOICES: I like the trees. I like the sky! All those colors. That sky's really neat. It's probably a sunset sky.

MRS. A: Can you tell us about the sky or the trees, Darren?

D: The leaves, um, they're all colors.

MRS. A: The leaves are all colors?

D: Un-huh, 'cause it's fall and that makes the leaves all colors.

MRS. A: Fall makes the leaves all colors. And you like those colors, Darren?

D: Um, I like the leaves all colors.

Darren squirms. His restlessness tells me he's done enough for now. We applaud Darren and get ready for lunch.

Making the Most of Group Sharing

The group sharing circle, another procedure learned from Graves, Giacobbe, and Calkins, is a ritual to end the workshop just as the mini-lesson is the opening. The children seem to appreciate the closure procedure as well as the opportunity to hear their classmates' writing.

Starting the Sharing Time

I begin our first sharing with some clear, strong statements: "Writers are going to read their pieces to us. We all know that the pieces have just been written, and the writers may make changes in them later. The writer has the easy part here; we have the hard part. We must *listen very carefully* so that we can tell the writer exactly what we heard or learned from the writing—or the parts that we really liked. When the writer finishes she will call on people who raise their hands. You may only speak when she calls on you. And, I want you to begin your response to the writer with the word "I"—such as "I learned . . ." or "I liked . . ." After we've told them what we learned or especially liked, then we can ask questions about anything we wonder about or want to know more about. Now, we aren't going to say things like 'I like your story' or 'I like the way you draw' because the writer won't know if you've really been listening. You could say that to anyone. We need to be specific—'I like the part when . . .' and then tell them the words you heard or something about that part. Does everyone understand?"

Granted, this is a lot of direction for some children to take in, but I'm prepared to shape the procedure and monitor comments as we move through it. When someone says, "I think you have a good story" I quickly interject, "Tell him *what* you liked in the story," I also participate with comments and questions of my own as models for the children: "I like the part when you said your dog rolled in mud" or "I liked the words 'tumbled into bed'" or "I wanted to know what happened after the milk spilled." I'm not just establishing the procedures and tone, I'm also teaching children how to listen to a piece of writing and respond. These are skills they need not just for responding to peers but also for learning to read and listen to their own writing.

Gradually, I work into a more backseat role—one where the children listen and take the lead, but I'm always ready to interrupt weak responses or demonstrate ways of responding to keep the sharing time on a developmental course. It must not stagnate, and achieving this is never easy. Basically, through my model, I'm trying to teach children to listen to a writer's meaning, to ask questions to clarify that meaning, and to examine the techniques the writers use to effectively convey meaning—all the while affirming the writer.

On this day, the sharing time provided an opportunity to expand writing skills, to enhance the sense of community, and to encourage and affirm writers. Some of the topics that emerged in this particular session were expanding the children's understanding of the word *track*, adding description, including conversation, inserting information, rereading one's writing for meaning, learning to read one's writing, connecting writing ideas to books, and using crayons differently. We didn't discuss every concept, but participating in the group sharing contributed to the bank of experiences that enrich the children's growing sense of themselves as writers and of their writing processes.

Sharing time also needs to nurture the writer. I supported Erika after she fielded Stacy's question about telling the story instead of reading it. In Darren's session, I spoke a lot because Darren hadn't become comfortable leading the sharing session. He would gradually develop this ability, and I would remove my support in proportion to his ability to take over. The critical encouragement for Darren as a member of the community came from his peers.

During the sharing, I often select a particular point to emphasize. We can't address everything; to do so would overload the children and frustrate their progress. In Amy's sharing, for instance, I could have responded to the question "Who's Emily?" by pointing out the writer's responsibility to consider if the reader will know what the writer knows. Instead, I chose to comment about Amy's inclusion of conversation, which Greg so beautifully described for us. The class would come back to his phrase "hearing talk in our heads" again and again during other discussions of children's writing. Stressing Amy's accomplishment provided opportunity for everyone to learn. There will be moments in the sharing when a problem in a piece presents just the right time to address a specific writing technique—a time when children are ready and will grow from the discussion. The writer must never feel embarrassed or uncomfortable. In fact, often the writer helps with the teaching by expressing in natural language a way to improve the writing.

Learning to hold back and ignore opportunities to address a skill was probably the hardest part of making the writing workshop a time for children to grow. In the end, the responsive approach covers more than any sequenced approach ever did. But with this responsive approach to teaching, I am continually making choices as to what to respond to and the appropriate timing for these responses. My decisions are informed not only by curriculum and my own knowledge, but also by my awareness of the children. As the professional in the classroom, I must respond to those "teachable moments" in a way that helps us all become excited about learning.

The Reluctant Sharer

Most first graders are eager to share their writing with the class. Only one year did I encounter a child reluctant to read her writing. At first I thought it was because she was unsure of being able to read what she had written. But as I watched this child I realized that she was genuinely frightened. She clearly communicated that no, this was not for her. I gave her time: time to trust the environment, the children, and me. In March I tried once again by asking her at the beginning of the workshop to share that day. She shook her head. "How about tomorrow?" I pressed. Reluctantly she agreed. But the next day she put me off until yet another tomorrow. On the third day I reminded her that today she had agreed to share, and throughout the workshop I stopped by her desk to encourage her. Together we read through her piece before she took the author's chair. I reminded the class that this was her first time to share and that I was sure they remembered how scary the first time was for them. When she stumbled on a few words I quietly provided them. The children listened, gently responded and applauded. The writer smiled. After this she accepted my invitations to share writing but never volunteered. The precise reason for her fear remains a mystery. However, what I learned from her was the importance of providing the necessary support for a child to be successful, to make the way easy.

Dealing with Rote Responses

During the first week of school I watched Lauren in the sharing circle. She held her hand poised to fly up the instant the reader asked for responses. Sure enough, up went the hand and Lauren gave the first response. "How did you get the idea for this piece?" she asked.

The question startled me because I'd never heard one of my first graders ask such a question during the first days of school. Lauren's question surfaced again and again and I noticed that she paid little attention to the answer. I waited for the right moment to ask Lauren the question that burned in my head: "Lauren, where did you get the idea for that question?"

"From last year when we did writing. I always asked that question." I understood. Lauren had participated in a writing workshop in kindergarten in another city. She had learned a formula, a routine complete with rote questions. She asked questions without thinking, without listening to the writer, without really wanting an answer.

Group sharing occasionally hits this snag. The children fall into a pattern of repeating questions they've heard me ask and spitting them out like robots. The sharing time loses its responsive nature and subsequently its effectiveness. Questions lacking authenticity produce answers lacking authenticity.

> Q: How did you get the idea for this story?
>
> A: I just thought of it, or Because I like my dog.
>
> Q: What will you do next?
>
> A: I don't know yet. I might add more or I might not.
>
> Q: How do you feel about this piece of writing?
>
> A: I like it.

Children can fall into a meaningless dialogue of routine questions and answers. What's more, they supply bland comments such as "I like your story," "I like your picture," "I think you have a good piece of writing." Programmed questions, answers, and comments lack the thoughtfulness of genuine responses and the sharing circle disintegrates to a useless ritual.

Lauren's formulaic question helped me understand that our central role was to *listen* to the writer and ask questions and make comments based on what we heard. It was as simple as that. Instead of striving to develop good questions, I needed to demonstrate good listening. If I listened and entered into the writer's space at that moment, I provide thoughtful responses. It boiled down to just plain hospitable conversation. When I listened, so did the children and they responded authentically. The children needed lots of demonstrations from me to learn to listen and provide effective responses. Sometimes, they tended to latch on to a response and repeat that same response over and over.

I found myself interrupting with comments such as, "I think someone already said that," or "Could you tell this writer the exact words that you liked best?" I spent a minute at the beginning of the sharing time reminding the group of our important task to listen carefully and tell the specific words or ideas we like or to think about the "really real" questions we want to ask.

Feedback ought to enable a writer to hear that the writing is on the right track—that the ideas are emerging. But *then,* the feedback also ought to help the writer to consider ways to go forward—ways that might not have been considered without the responses of others. This was the most difficult aspect of developing an effective sharing time. This took time. We all needed practice—lots of practice.

What Listening Is All About

One snowy January day, Jeremiah took his place in the first-grade author's chair and proceeded to read aloud. (See Figure 8–1.)

"Spread Eagle is a Lake. I saw an eagle! Me and my dad saw twelve fish. It is fun. I caught a big fish!" At this point, Jeremiah paused just briefly and

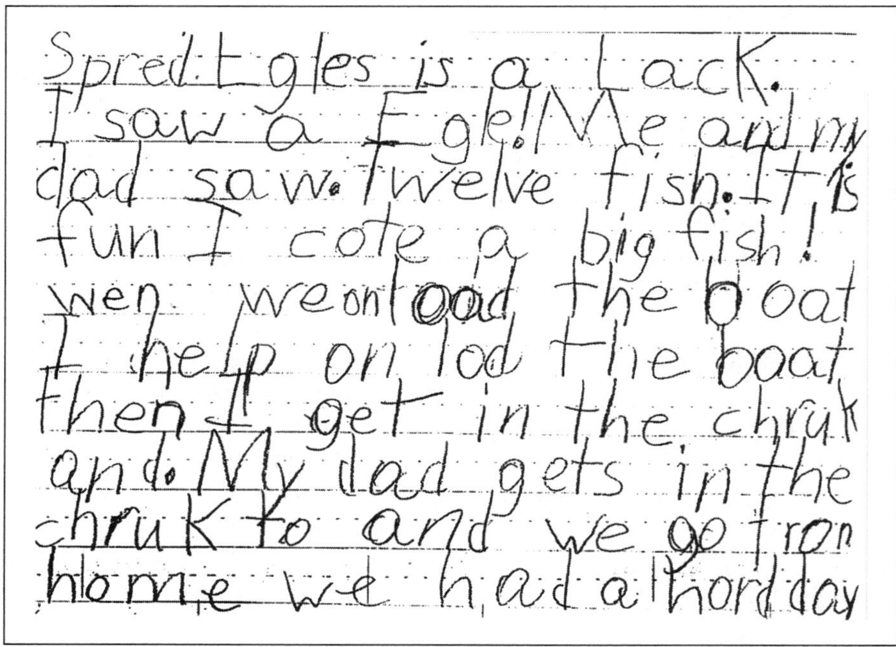
Spred Egles is a Lack.
I saw a Egle! Me and my
dad saw. Twelve fish. It is
fun I cote a big fish!
wen we onlood the boat
I help on lod the boat
then I get in the chruk
and My dad gets in the
chruk to and we go fron
home we had a hord day

Figure 8–1

Jeremiah's fish story

cast a glance around the group as if to say, "Did you get that part?" Then he continued, "When we unload the boat, I help unload the boat. Then I get in the truck and my dad gets in the truck too and we go home. We had a hard day."

Jeremiah's classmates respond to his writing by picking up my model. They let Jeremiah know about the parts that appeal to them: the eagle, the twelve fish, the hard day—and the big fish. However, catching the fish seemed almost lost among all the children's responses. I had sensed a lot of energy from Jeremiah when he read that part, so I raise my hand.

"I heard you say you caught a BIG FISH."

"Un-huh," Jeremiah replies; the same energy is back in his voice.

"Well, how did you do that?" I continue. "I mean I've only caught little fish, and that was a long time ago and I don't really remember much about it. How did you catch that big fish?"

"I just threw the line in and I caught the fish."

"You threw the line in—did you have to do anything first? For example, did you put corn on a hook? Because I know someone who told me they put corn on the hook." I maintain eye contact with Jeremiah throughout the conversation. Only Jeremiah knows this story. It would be easy to jump in with my projections, my expertise (no matter how meager) and take the lead. I want Jeremiah to take the lead here and to share all that he knows about catching that fish. I trust that he knows a lot.

"No. See we use a fly. You put the fly on the line and then the fish bites and then you reel it in."

"You put a fly on the line and the fish bites. You just drop this line over the edge of the boat? And then you reel it in?"

"You have to throw the line out," Jeremiah demonstrates the arm and hand motions of throwing a line out, "My dad helps me. He hold my hands and we throw it out together."

"Oh, I see. You have to throw it out. Your dad helps and you throw it out together."

"Yeah. You have to put your arms back and throw hard."

The story emerges with a detailed explanation of precisely how he waited for the feel of fish's nibble, reeled in the fish, landed it in the boat with a net—all with the help of his dad. He tells of specifics that I know nothing about. I conclude this bit of conversation (which has only taken a minute or two) by recapping the story in his words as best as I remembered them.

"Ah, I see. First you have to. . . . Then you . . . and then. . . ."

"Yeah," he nods, "I know *how* to fish. My dad taught me."

I nod in return and make one last comment, "I can tell you know a lot about fishing. You could probably write all that about catching that fish."

Jeremiah nods again and we all applaud.

Later, Wendy Woodworth, a staff development supervisor who had observed the session and who participates in an adult writing group herself, commented on what she saw. What amazed her the most was the conversation about the big fish. "I would have responded so differently. I would probably have told him how I know what he means because I've caught a fish too. And then I would have gone into *my* story of catching a fish. But you kept yourself out of it and were just interested in what he knew. And you got him to tell you *so much*."

Wendy helped me realize some subtle differences in responses to writers. Certainly, there's a place to tell writers about the ideas or memories that their writing evokes in us. But I think that this kind of response is appropriate at the *end* of the process, in response to the completed piece of writing. At that point writers want to know the full impact of the writing on others—on readers. Before that time, when the writing is still in progress, the writer wants to know if the emerging writing makes sense, what works or what doesn't work. The writer in the process of working through a piece wants supportive and honest comments that encourage by showing interest in what *he* has to say.

What I wanted to do was help Jeremiah see that he knows a lot more about catching that big fish than what he has written. I want to help him to verbalize this information so that he can become aware of all that's there and leave him with the notion that this is a possibility for writing more. Will he accept this invitation? He may not. The next day I may ask him during the roving conferences or, perhaps, as we begin the workshop, if he plans to write more about that fish—all the things he told us in the sharing time. But I will leave the decision up to him. He may not write this particular story, but he's experienced a lesson in realizing that the first words on paper are a beginning.

Many other lessons with this same focus will follow. Listening for the meaning behind the words is an important skill I want writers to develop. I want the writers to read their written words with an eye and an ear for hearing the ideas, images, and stories behind those words. I want them to question those words, get inside the surface meaning and decide how to convey a fuller meaning to an audience. With ongoing responses with this kind of focus, Jeremiah will come to read his writing and question his words so as to explore the "big fish" ideas for himself.

Learning to listen to one's own writing is a fundamental skill of a good writer. I've seen young children who are far better at this skill than some adults with whom I've worked. What makes the difference? First, they have *experience* as writers. They write a lot. Second, they've had responses from others during the *process* of writing, as they work to express their ideas, rather than when the writing is finished. They've been taught to write where the emphasis is on figuring out what one has to say and working to say it well. They've learned to stand back and read their own words as another reader might, to anticipate the questions, to notice the gaps, to rethink the ideas that the words convey. Such reading is the basis for revision. And, of course, they learn to tend to mechanics of writing because without those mechanics the reader will be at a disadvantage. To help writers learn to do all of this is what the teaching of writing is about.

What do I keep in mind as I approach this "teaching"? The key, for me, is listening to the writer. Here are some key underlying beliefs.

Remember that there's always more to the writer's ideas than makes its way to paper The words on the paper are only the tip of the iceberg. If the piece has content worth developing, information and ideas are still inside the writer waiting to be expressed. My job is to help the writer recognize this and then to step back and let the writer decide how much of that to share.

Listen for what's important to the writer I find myself thinking, "There's where I feel the energy coming from this writer." To do this, I've got to set aside *my* focus for the piece. I could easily mislead a writer into writing a piece for me. This might turn out okay, but a better piece of writing and stronger learning will come when the writer is writing what's important to him. In Jeremiah's story it was rather easy to sense where the energy was in the topic. His pause and his glance around the group as he read that one sentence communicated importance. It's not always that easy. To hear the words between the lines requires me to be still, to drop agendas, and just listen. When I do, I hear.

Ask questions—gently—to help the writer uncover what he knows I base my questions on what I hear in the writing and often ask, "Tell me more about that," or "What was that like?" I maintain eye contact. I strive to convey a nonjudgmental attitude. I've got to be *very* interested. *Genuinely, authentically* interested. And, I've got to convey that interest with everything I've got: facial expression, body language, and eye contact. It can't be faked. The writer will know in a moment. I nod and say things like, "I see," or "I understand now." I follow one train of thought with the writer as far as the child will take it. I must be ready to stop, sum up, and move on when I sense that writer has gone as far as he can or wants to go.

Help the writer express aspects of the writing that are not yet written A nonjudgmental attitude enables writers to take risks. It helps to recognize that the ideas are raw and the writer is working at putting nebulous ideas into words. These are beginnings rather than polished ideas. I find it helpful to tell back the ideas that I hear and put the pieces together in a sequence as they emerge for the writer. I try to keep the writer's language as much as possible rather than transcribing it into my own.

Invite the writer to develop these ideas in the writing I often end these discussions with writers by saying (again gently), "I think you could write this in your piece," "Do you plan to write this?" "I can see that you have a lot of ideas to write." These responses are intended to provide choice for the writer but at the same time to help the writer recognize that there is more to say. I want the writer to learn to follow the energy in the early drafts and to write what that writer knows and cares about. This is the writing that will bring the most investment from the writer and be the most likely to develop into quality pieces.

And Then . . .

My role in the writing workshop fell into a pattern that worked: I started with a mini-lesson, circulated among the children listening and responding, participated in the group sharing, and eventually published the children's writing.

I suppose I could have gone for years this way—establishing, reflecting, revising, and administering a writing program in my classroom. Then one day in November, after I'd left all the programmed instructional materials behind, an incident in my classroom changed my perspective on learning and teaching.

I returned from the NCTE convention in Washington, D.C., on the day before Thanksgiving, buoyed by all the stimulating presentations of the previous days. As the children settled into writing that morning, a tall, strawberry-blond, and rather shy boy came up to me and said, "Mrs. Avery, you always *tell* us about your writing, but you never *write* when we write. How come?" With the imploring honesty of a child straight out of Dickens, Chris stood before me, looked me straight in the eye, and awaited an answer.

I looked away briefly, then back to Chris and replied, "You're right, Chris. I'll write today." I vaguely remember turning to the whole class and announcing that Chris had asked about my writing and therefore I intended to write today, too, rather than circulating around the room. With no idea of what might come, I picked up a pen.

The night before I had driven my car around the mall in Washington searching for the newly dedicated (and as yet unlighted) Vietnam War Memorial. Dusk fell. I stopped to ask directions. Finally I parked my car and headed on foot, alone, into the darkness, away from the safety—if even uncertain safety—of big-city streetlights, into the unknown to search out this new memorial. Suddenly my feet sank into soft earth, and in a moment of horrified realization, I knew I'd walked on the newly tilled earth of the memorial itself. I was above The Wall, trespassing on the gravestone of long-dead friends and peers. Turning, I made my way along the monument's edge to ground level, and there in the darkness met several veterans who lighted matches so that, together, we might read the names on the narrow point of that angling marble. I walked deeper into that cavern of scooped out ground and touched a rose lying beside a votive candle. Moments later, I walked back through the darkness to my car to head home. My heart and thoughts were a wild collage of war and death and friends and struggles and life.

Now, the next morning during writing workshop, in this first-grade classroom, I said I would write. When I put my pen to paper, the words that came described the experience and intense emotions from the night before that still enveloped me. I wrote. Several children moved past me. One or two smiled or nodded, but no one spoke to me. They seemed to respect my need not to be interrupted, that what I was doing was important. I continued to write far longer than I initially had planned. When the time came to share, a child said, "Mrs. Avery's going to share her writing today." Panic.

"No, that's okay," I said. "I don't need to share."

"Yes," they chimed in. "You share."

"We want to hear your writing."

"You have to share, too."

I took a breath. "Okay, but I don't think it's anything you'll understand."

"That's okay," they replied and I heard buzzings of "Mrs. Avery's gonna share." "It's her turn." As we gathered on the carpet I thought that perhaps they might forget by the time my turn came. Of course they didn't. I began to read slowly, hesitantly. The children were hushed and perfectly still. When my voice cracked, Eileen slipped an arm behind me. When I struggled again to keep reading, Marlene lightly touched the hand that held the paper. I finished the reading. The hands went up and I proceeded to call on children for responses.

"I liked the beginning when you said the part about 'soft squishy mud . . . around your feet.'"

"I think it was scary the way you walked in the dark and you could see the lights only they were far away."

"This writing made me feel spooky and sad both."

"I think this is a good piece of writing and that it was hard to write this."

"Yeah, I'm glad you shared it with us."

I knew that my writing was filled with words and phrases that the children could never define if they encountered them out of context. I had not written the story planning to share it with anyone, let alone anticipating the children as an audience. Yet they had understood. The responses, verbal and nonverbal, from this gentle audience left me wanting to continue this piece of writing and wanting to receive their responses again.

I walked with the children to the cafeteria and then came back to my desk, my head reeling and my heart raw. Finally I began to write. I wrote to record what had just happened—the children's responses, how I had felt, now felt. I wrote to begin a reflection process on being a writer and a teacher of writing that would continue for weeks and for months. I had just experienced one of those moments in teaching, an anomaly, that surprises us, teaches us, invites us to change, to outgrow ourselves.

Prior to this I had been amazed by what children could achieve, but my amazement had been restricted to their academic accomplishments. I delighted in the ways they experimented and played with language. I marveled at their ability to transcend errors with grace, to use error as a natural path to further learning. I admired the energy of their learning, surging and receding again and again, yet always moving onward. But now I understood, because I had experienced through them the source of that energy—the heart and humanity of being a writer in a community. The children had taken me into that community in a new way. They taught me that academic behaviors are important, but that they develop best out of an intangible, unmeasurable essence created out of relationships.

CHAPTER 9

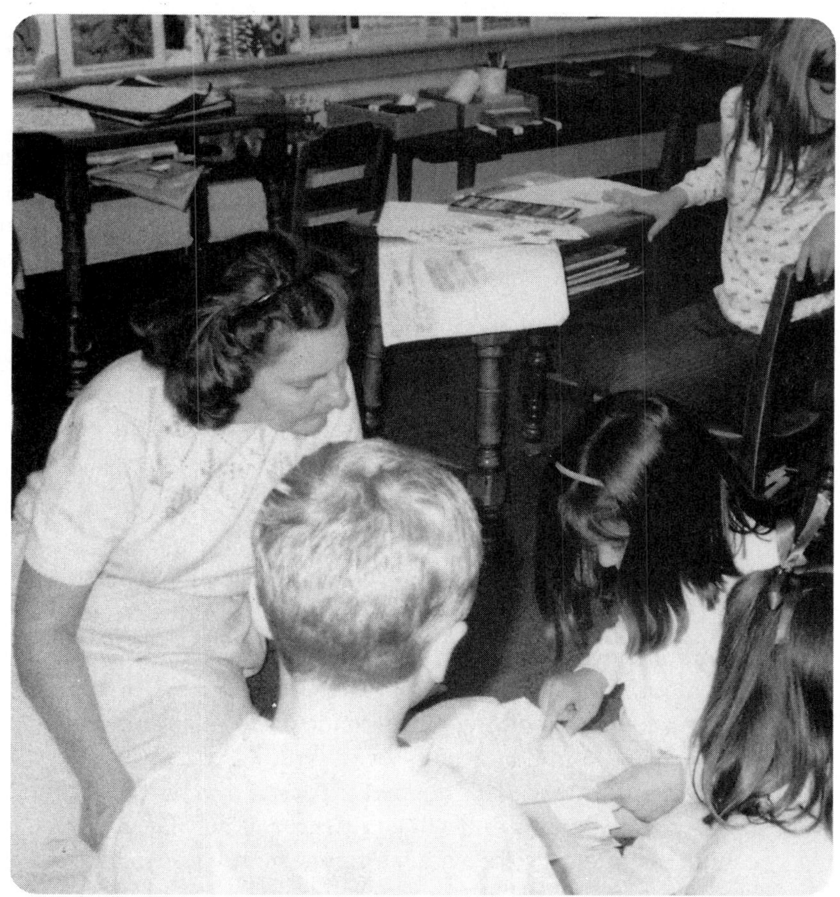

The Process of Publishing

When I first started children writing in my classroom, we published lots of little books. The process was simple: the children wrote, I revised and published. The children illustrated the typed pages and I inserted them in wallpaper-covered cardboard. These little books with the child's own words neatly typed pleased everyone: the children, their parents, and me. I thought those products provided proof of achievement. So I typed after school, before school, and in the evening at home to produce volumes of child-authored stories.

Gradually I became weary of the bookmaking. My student writers could dash out stories faster than I could produce book covers and type their pieces. Something had to change or we would burn out. Participating in writing workshops as a writer helped me see that the children had been "doing writing" but were not really engaged in the *process* of writing nor learning *how to write*. I realized that process and product were reciprocal elements of writing. Final products in attractive formats encouraged my young writers, but engaging in the process of writing, with all the struggles along the way, requires an involvement from the writer that makes the final product ever more meaningful.

As I worked on effective mini-lessons and developed my conference skills, the children thought about their topics in more depth and revised their writing. The emphasis on product diminished for both the children and me, and we became invested in writing to share meaning. Rather than being the goal of writing, publishing needed to serve the central purpose of writing, the process of making meaning and communicating that meaning effectively.

Our Publishing Process

The publishing process begins in late autumn after the children acquire a degree of writing fluency and appreciate that writing can be revised. I start by taking a couple of children through the publication process: helping them rethink, revise, and edit a piece of writing. Gradually, I take the entire class through this process. This deliberate pace allows me to respond to individual needs, establish procedures that will serve us all year, and, by beginning with confident writers, provide models for the more reticent. It takes nearly a month before every child in the room has published. Here's a general overview of the process.

- The writer selects a piece of writing, which she believes to be one of her best and which she wishes to share through publication, from the collected works in her writing folder. The writer rereads and revises and edits this piece again to refine it to the best of the writer's ability. It is likely that the writer may have some distance from the piece at this point and thus rereading is likely to produce some rethinking and clarifying revision. The writer gives this piece to the teacher as her "best work."
- I read the child's selected writing and plan for a "publishing conference." I make notes about content: ideas that are unclear, incomplete, or unfocused. I also note possible mechanics to teach the writer. I examine spelling, noting patterns in errors, strategies used by the writer, misspellings that the writer should know.

- I convene a small group of two or three students who have submitted pieces for publication. Either the writer or I read the piece aloud. Group members listen and respond to the *content* of the piece; their role is to help the writer with clarity, missing information or words, etc. I play a strong part in this responding too, especially at first, and gently nudge the writer to revise the piece for clarity, organization, grace, etc.
- Depending on the extent of content revisions, I address editing either in the last part of this conference or in a second conference. If the number of content changes is excessive, I may do an individual editing conference with the child. I may teach the writer something new or review something we've addressed in class. It's important not to overload the writer so I choose what to address depending on my sense of how much the writer can handle.
- After the writer has addressed revisions and editing from the conference, I ask the writer to read through the piece and underline three (this number varies according to the experience of the writer) correctly spelled words and circle three incorrectly spelled words that they think they can correct.
- After the writer makes all these changes, she reads the piece to another student from the small group as a final check. It is important to remember that all writers need a final editor and that expectations for student editing need to be appropriate to the experience level of the writer.
- The final draft is "published" by being typed with all remaining errors in mechanics corrected by the typist. (Recopying is an arduous and time-consuming task for young children and they are likely to make new errors. Therefore, I don't ask the children to recopy.) As children gain experience writing and know how to use a computer, the students may enter the final piece into the computer with an adult checking for correct mechanics before printing. The degree of responsibility the student assumes for revision and editing grows with experience; the "experienced writer" is not necessarily determined by age or grade level.
- The writer adds illustrations to the typed copy, which is then put into a bookcover, collection of writing, or other publishing format.
- The writer reads the published piece and celebrates with the class.

This is the process I used to provide our classroom with important reading material. Certainly, there are numerous ways to publish children's writing, including those that make use of technology as described in *Real ePublishing REALLY PUBLISHING!* (Condon and McGuffee 2001). For any process to be effective, it must be adapted to the individual child.

First Publications

Monica and Greg

On a morning in late October I approached Monica and Greg. "You've done a lot of writing. I'd like you to look through everything you've written and choose what you think is your best piece. I'm thinking that we can work on that piece a little more, see if there are any changes that might make it better, do some final editing, and then publish it by making it into a book."

Greg replied, "All right. But, see, today I was planning to write that piece about me and my dad, the one I was working on yesterday you know? So, I wanted to do that 'cause it's in my head right now."

"That's fine. No hurry. You can do this whenever you're ready. Let me know when you've chosen something." Greg went to work on his current topic for a while, then began reading through his writing. By the end of the workshop he had made a selection.

"Why did you choose this particular piece?" I asked.

"Because it's about our trip to *California*!" His eyes glowed with the memory of the family trip.

"So this was really an important topic for you."

"Yes! It's a good piece!" My question helps me understand Greg and his writing and also helps Greg begin to ask such questions of himself, thus developing awareness of his own decision-making process.

Monica spent much of the workshop reading through her writing and choosing the three-page story of Bald Head Island. When finished, she said, "That was really neat reading through all my writing. I kept reading things I had forgotten about and then I kept remembering more things I did and places we went and things like that."

Her voice trailed off for a moment and a pensive look came to her face. Then she looked at me and said, "It made me think about my life, sorta." In her quizzical countenance and voice tone I detected a new awareness dawning in her mind. "Do you know what I mean?" she asked.

"Yes, I think I do. Writing's like that—at least for me it is. Keeps me thinking about my life," I replied. Monica nodded and smiled.

That evening I read Monica's and Greg's selections. I studied each piece of writing and saw possibilities for helping each writer in the publishing conference.

PLANNING FOR GREG As I read Greg's writing (Figures 9–1a and 9–1b) I could hear him telling me about his California visit. The energy in the writing matched his enthusiasm for the trip. An articulate boy, Greg spoke in complete sentences that communicated a lot of information. His speech and his thinking followed a logical sequence. He wrote the same way, packing his written sentences with information. The grammatical structure "me and my mom" or "me and my dad" was part of his speech and so naturally appeared in his writing. He spaced his words across the page from left to right, formed the letters with a firm stroke, spelled a few words correctly, and used invented spelling to approximate others.

The airplane in Greg's drawing indicated the same thoughtful involvement. I marveled at the angle of the plane's wings, the inclusion of two engines and three flaps on each wing, and Greg's attempt to show the cylinder of the jet engines through penciled spiral lines. He included other details: a

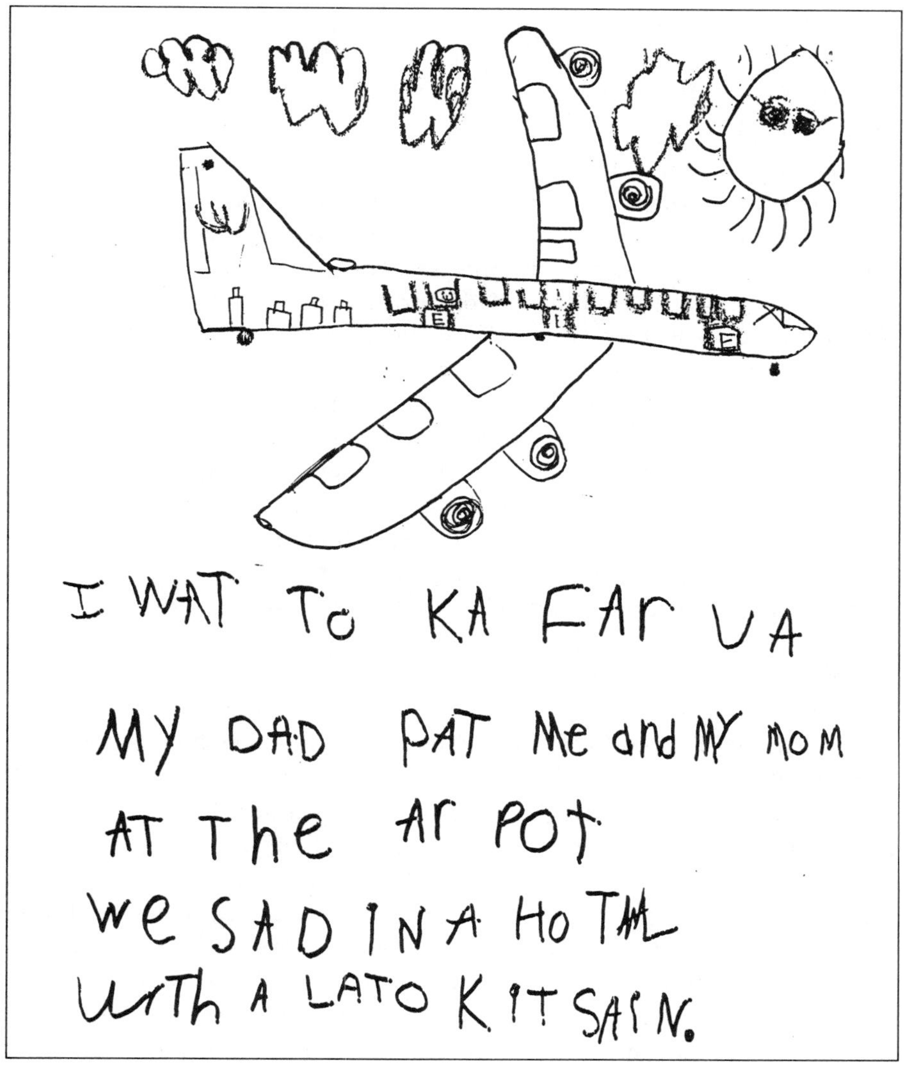

Figure 9–1a

Greg's writing

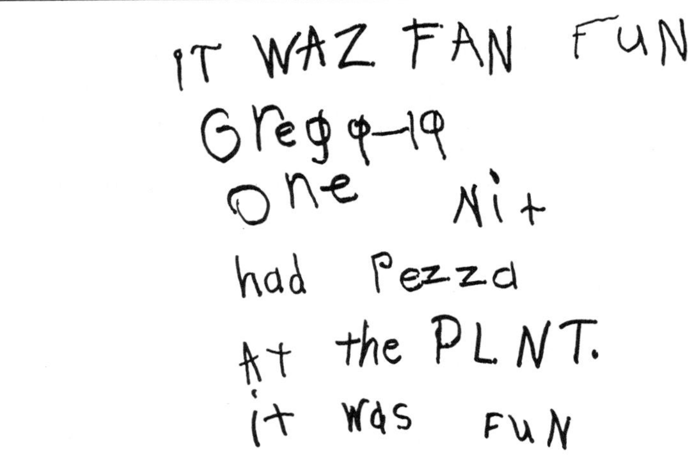

Figure 9–1b

Greg's writing

row of windows (one with a smiling face—probably Greg's) lining the fuselage; three exit doors, appropriately placed and marked with the letter *E* (I pictured Greg listening to the flight attendants before takeoff); and a rear baggage compartment filled with suitcases. The plane's tail sported an airline logo and a tail flap. Cumulus clouds and the sun—wearing sunglasses—completed the scene. I remembered Greg telling me that he drew the plane in yellow because it was the crayon "nearest to the plane's actual color." He had considered gray but decided it was too dark, not shiny enough.

Reading this writing—both words and illustration—evoked in me a deep respect for this writer. I would come to Greg's publishing conference prepared with possible ways to help him as a writer, but I would listen to him before making suggestions. Of course, I wouldn't expect Greg to revise, edit, and correct this piece of writing to perfection. But working together to refine the piece for publication would help Greg's development as a writer, a goal far more significant than developing a perfect product. Like all of writing workshop, *the underlying premise for the publishing conference is to help the writer rather than the writing.*

I noted possibilities for revision. Missing words were the most obvious: "My Dad picked me and my Mom [up?] at the airport" and "One night [we?] had pizza." Readers needed these words and I was sure Greg would want them included. I could address the "me and my Mom," misspelled words, or ending punctuation. Greg placed a period after "kitchen," a clue that he had begun thinking about punctuation. Any of these issues could come up during the conference. What we dealt with would depend on Greg and his limits for what he could handle with one piece of writing.

I read the piece again and listened for meaning. I understood three separate points: the family took an airplane trip to California, they stayed in a hotel with a kitchen, and they ate pizza at a plant. Then suddenly the story stops. As a reader, I'm left hanging, wondering why I've read this story. If I feel this way, other readers likely will too. I know Greg knows much more than what is on the paper. Helping him find the information that will bring the piece to a more coherent whole for readers will be worked out in the conference.

I jotted reminders for myself on a small Post-it note:

story stops
omitted words (up, we?)
sp. and punct.

I decided to address "me and my Mom" in a future mini-lesson for the entire class. The Post-it note went on the outside of the folder I maintain on Greg's writing.

PLANNING FOR MONICA I picked up Monica's writing and read the story of the family trip to Bald Head Island (Figure 9–2).

Monica wrote fluently, setting aside concerns for conventions and devoting her energy to putting ideas on paper. In her drawing the ferry skims the top of the water. In a conference she had told me about the beauty of that ferry ride and the sun on the ocean. Looking at her drawing now, I see shafts of sunlight streaming between the clouds. The detail in Monica's drawing indicates that, like Greg, she is a keen observer of her world. Only the topics differed: Monica noticed shafts of sunlight, Greg the parts of an airplane.

I reread the opening line: "I went on a boat. Actually it was a ferry." Monica's voice. I could hear her say those very words. The listing of family members, strung together with "ands" was Monica too. Replacing those "ands" with commas might be something to show her in the conference, but I needed to read on to get inside her writing. I knew this piece meant a great deal to her. I listened for the story between the lines. What was important to Monica? As I read on, I pictured the hills, Monica on her bicycle, and the golf cart. The story seemed somewhat disjointed but in these lines was something significant to Monica. On the Post-it note for Monica's folder I wrote:

golf cart—hills
commas in sequence
spelling and punct.

I was ready for the conference with Monica and Greg.

THE SMALL-GROUP PUBLISHING CONFERENCE The next morning we gathered at the conference table. Usually the publishing conference consists of

I WENT On A Boet
it. WOS AK SNLE A
FARE It tOK OS to
Bod he oiLNd I WNEt wis
MY mom ANd MY DAD
AND MY BROthR AND MY
GRiNomom AnD MY INt and
MY OKOL WEN WE GEt
thER thaY haD to
ONi LOWd WOt we
BROt thEN WE hAD to
GEt on the tRim thEN
that is WEN the tRIm
tAKS OS to the
BEchnAWS thEN WE hAF to
ONi LOWd ARe hAWS is NOS.

But the ILId hAS
Som hiWS ore OF the
hiWS IS VIARE hiYe
MY DAD WENt DAen
the hiL in A GOFCRt
hE WOS A Litit
SIARd I WOS EVIN SIARd
WIN I WENt DAWN
ON MY BOSIKOL I
hAd to WAlk the
BOSIKOL hAF WAIE DAWIN
the hiLe. I GOt
tO DRIV the GOFCRt
aND that WOS FUN.

I JeSt Went
to thes BOLdhed ILId
Somr It WOS
fun New
evin Betr I em
GOeF Krt. on the
LIKe It Sims
the I Kod dive
my the sILF GOeF Krt OL By
thenA Jrs Like But. one
or OWdr Kene 16
they ILId is dive
NIYS I Like it Ferey it
is fun ther.

Figure 9–2

Monica's writing

three or four children. This day we had only two, so I asked Max to join us. A third child would add another responder and Max had demonstrated skill in listening and asking effective questions. I started by explaining what we would do.

MRS. A: Monica and Greg have each chosen a piece of writing that they believe to be one of their best. They've read it through to see if it makes sense. But we all know that writers miss things when they read their own writing, so we're going to read these pieces and listen to see if each piece makes sense to us. Writers need readers and listeners to help them make sure that everything is clear. As we listen, I'd like you also to think if there's anything you want to know more about, anything that doesn't quite give you a complete picture in your head. Greg, will you read your piece?"

GREG: I went to California. My Dad picked me and my Mom up at the airport. We stayed in a hotel with a little kitchen. It was fun. One night we [pauses] oops, I left out a word. [He picks up a pencil and writes it in.] One night we had pizza at the plant. It was fun.

MRS. A: Okay. Responses? What do you think?

MAX: I think it's a good piece about flying to California and stuff. I was just confused about one part. You said, um, when you said you had pizza at the plant, well, um, I don't know, what is the plant? I never heard of a pizza place called "The Plant."

G: No, see the plant is a factory. We ate at the plant.

MAX: I don't get it. You ate at the plant. How come? How come you, um, ate at a factory?

G: That's where my dad was working—at the plant. See, he went there, he went to California for a business trip and then my mom and me, we, um, joined him. We flew out there later, after he was there, and when we got there we were hungry, so then we had pizza at his plant—where my dad worked.

MAX: Well, did everyone have pizza? Who had pizza? Like, was it everyone in the factory? And how long did you stay there, in California?

G: No, just me and my dad and my mom. See, the factory was closed but my dad could still work there. Armstrong, that's the plant. He had a key. And we stayed there three weeks. But not at the factory the whole time. We stayed in California three weeks.

MRS. A: Monica, what do you think about the piece?

MONICA: I'm confused. You said you stayed at a hotel with a little kitchen. Well, how come you didn't eat there?

G: The hotel had a little kitchen and it had a stove and a refrigerator and a sink. We ate our breakfast there. Just breakfast. Not our lunch or dinner.

MON: Ohhh. There's something, well, I think you said "It was fun" two times.

G: [reads his writing and notices the repetition] Oh, yeah.

MRS. A: What could you do about that?

G: I could line one out. [He locates the first one and lines it out.] That makes it much better. I don't need that twice.

MRS. A: I was wondering if there's any other parts you want to change. Like some of the things that you told us.

MAX: Yeah, like maybe people need to know it was Armstrong.

G: Yeah, I might change "plant" to "Armstrong."

MRS. A: Greg, it sounds like this trip to California was really special to you. You say you stayed three weeks. I was curious about what else you did in those three weeks.

G: Well, we did lots of stuff, but I didn't write all that because I can't quite remember it all. So I didn't put it all in.

MRS. A: Right. Putting *everything* in would probably get pretty confusing to write and for readers to read. You really have a lot of information here and I can tell that the plane trip and eating pizza at the Armstrong plant were important parts of that trip. But I felt the piece sort of stops. You go to California and then you eat pizza . . . [I let my voice trail off.]

MAX: Yeah, how did you get home?

G: Well, when we went home the airplane was crowded and so my dad had to sit in the back and my mom was mad because we couldn't sit together.

MRS. A: Could you add that?

G: Sure, cuz I still got some room.

MRS. A: Tell me what your plans are for this piece now, Greg.

G: I'm going to put in the part about coming home and fix some stuff about the pizza.

MRS. A: Sounds good.

We moved on to Monica's writing. I asked Monica if I might read her story so that she could hear it too. She agreed. When I finished reading the story both boys said they thought it was fine. "It makes sense," they said. I glanced at my Post-it note, then spoke.

MRS. A: This part about the hills is really interesting. This island really had steep hills, didn't it? What was that like, Monica?

MONICA: Well, I never *expected* that Bald Head Island would have such steep hills. I had to walk my bicycle and it was scary in the golf cart too.

GREG: Did you play golf?

MON: No, you have golf carts because they don't allow any cars on the island.

G: No cars?

MAX: No cars on the island?

MON: Well, see the island doesn't have roads, well, just dirt roads and you have to use your bicycle or the tram or you can use a golf cart. When my dad was driving the golf cart I got to drive it. He let me drive it.

G: How come you got to drive the golf cart?

MAX: Yeah, cuz only teenagers can drive. How come you could drive?

MON: Well my dad was driving the golf cart and he helped me drive a little. And then another day he helped me drive too and I got better and better at driving.

As Monica spoke, I heard in her voice the reason why this writing was special to her. The island was a place apart from normal life, located in the middle of the sea, with steep hills, without cars, a safe place where she enjoyed a privilege reserved for older people. Meaning went beyond the written words, the meaning was within Monica herself. Through writing, Monica had stayed connected to the magic of that special time.

MRS. A: I see. There were no cars on the island, just bicycles and golf carts and a tram. But your dad let you drive the golf cart and you did it more than once and you got better and better at driving. Can you put some of this information in your piece?

MAX: I think you could put in that you *learned* to drive the golf cart but you didn't drive it all by yourself.

GREG: Yeah, because you didn't drive it by yourself, just with your dad. And I think you have some "it was funs" in your writing too.

MON: Yeah. I can take them out. And I'll put in that there were no cars on the island and learning to drive the golf cart.

MRS. A: I'd like you to use colored pencils when you make these changes so I can see your changes. After you've revised I want you to read the piece to one of the other people in this group to see if your changes make sense. Then put it on my desk.

As the children left the conference table I overheard Max say to Greg, "That's a neat plane." Greg explained all the details on the plane, including the red dots, which were the lights on the outside of the plane. I had missed those when I looked at the illustration.

The publishing conference ended. It had taken approximately fifteen minutes. We hadn't dealt with editing; I sensed each writer had enough to deal with for the moment. I stuck my notes inside their folders, knowing that we'd get to these items later.

All of our work during writing workshop contributed to the effectiveness of this publishing conference. In mini-lessons, individual conferences, large-group sharing, and all our talk about writing and writers, the children had learned to recognize potentially unclear areas of writing for readers. They had developed poise and sensitivity in responding to writers. Now they capably carried these responding strategies into this small-group conference.

Greg inserted "up" and erased "we," replacing it with "me and my mom and my dad." He changed "plant" to "factory," then later erased and changed "factory" to "Armstrong." He added four sentences at the end (Figures 9–3a and 9–3b), wrote a dedication—Dadakcan to Dad and Mom—and circled the line to indicate that although it was written at the end of the piece, it belonged at the beginning.

Monica lined out both "It was fun" sentences and inserted the words: You rid in the goef kart be cos they are no crs a lawd on the Ilid. She lined out "I kod" and replaced it with "I now haw to," thus clarifying the writing as her audience had indicated in the conference.

With these revisions completed, I brought Greg and Monica together and said, "One of the last things writers do when they finish a piece of writing is check for correct spelling and punctuation. Now, of course I don't expect you to be able to spell all these words correctly, but I would like you to do some work on that. Remember at the beginning of the year I said we'd work on spelling later? Well, now is that time. I want you to go through your writing and underline three words that you know are spelled correctly. Then I want you to find three words that you know are misspelled but that you think you know how to spell and can correct, or that you can figure out how to spell by yourself or by finding the correct spelling somewhere. Can you do that?"

Both children attacked this task with confidence and enthusiasm. Greg underlined the phrase "me and my mom and my dad" and circled "arpot,"

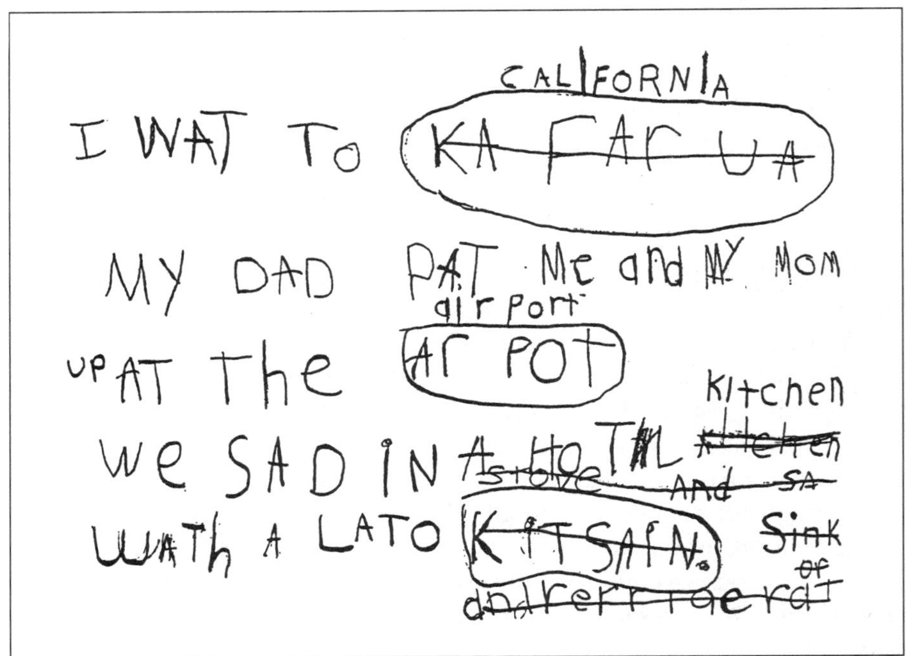

Figure 9–3a

Greg's revisions

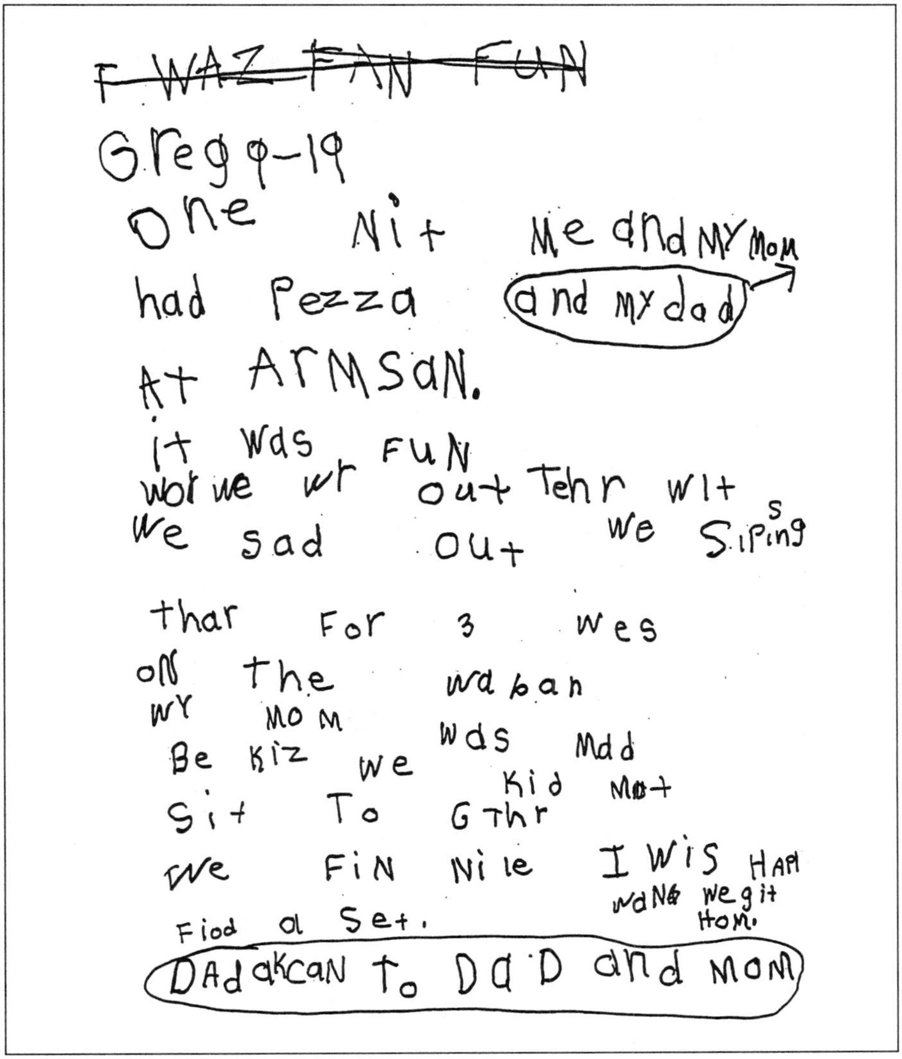

Figure 9–3b

Greg's revisions

"kitsain," and "Kafarua." He located "airport" and "kitchen" in the small picture dictionary in his desk. "California" presented a more difficult problem, and he came to me for help. I handed him the "C" volume of the *World Book Encyclopedia*. In no time Greg found the correct spelling. Monica underlined "the," "one," and "went." She identified "dawn," "wak," and "gofkrt" as incorrectly spelled. "Down" and "walk" presented no difficulty; she found them in the picture dictionary. "Golf cart" was more challenging. I could think of no resource in the classroom where she might easily locate the word, so I asked her if she knew anyone who might know how to spell "golf cart." "Probably my mom or dad," she answered. She wrote a reminder note for herself that read, "I ned to no haw to spel gofkret i ned to asesk my mom." The next day she came in with a slip of paper on which she had correctly printed "golf cart."

There was one final step for Monica in preparing her piece for publication. With the changes she made, the sentence "I jest went to Boldhed ilid thes somr" became an obvious interruption to the section about the golf cart. I met with Monica, read that part, and asked her what she thought. "I don't think it fits," she said. "Can I just take it out?" She lined through the words. We reread the section again and agreed on the improvement (Figures 9–4a and 9–4b).

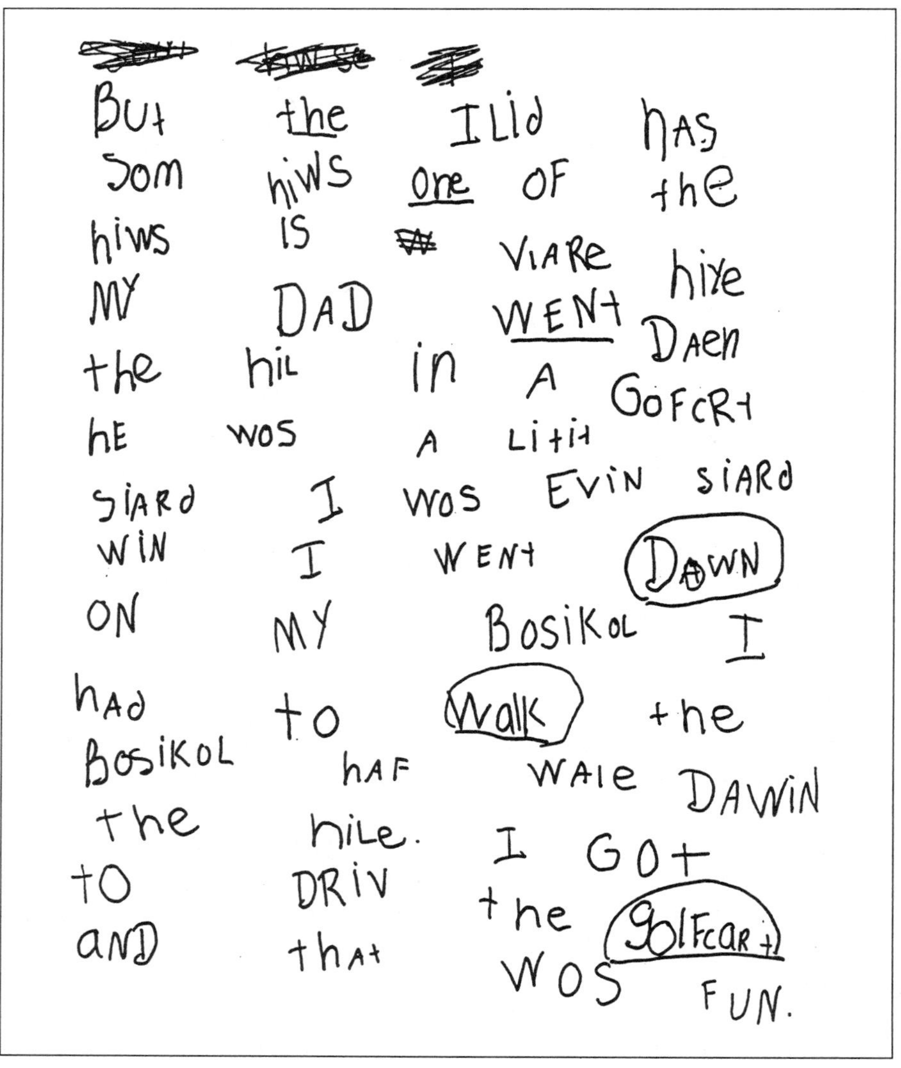
But the Ilid has
Som hiws one of the
hiws is viare hiye
my DAD WENT DAen
the hil in A GoFcRt
hE wos A Litil
siARd I wos EVIN siARd
WIN I WENt DOWN
ON MY BosiKoL I
hAd to Walk the
BosiKoL hAF WAie DAWIN
the hile. I GOt
tO DRiV the golFcart
AND that wos FUN.

Figure 9–4a

Monica's revisions

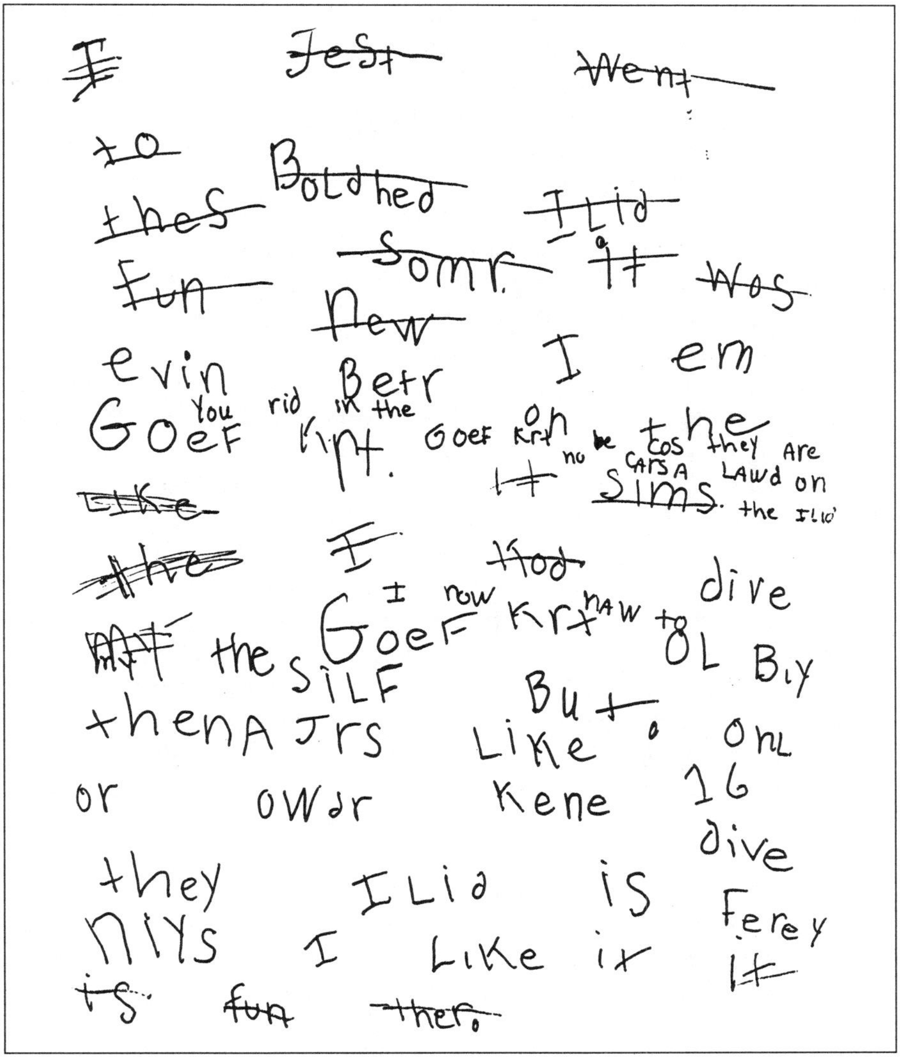
I Jest Went
to
thes Boldhed ILid
Fun Somr. It Wos
New
evin Betr I em
You rid in the
GoeF Krt. GoeF Krt on no be tos he they Are
CArsA LAwd on
Like It SIms. the ILid
the I Hod
I now kNAw to dive
My the GoeF Krt 8L Biy
siLF But.
thenA Jrs Like. OnL
or owar Kene 16
dive
they ILid is Ferey
niys I Like it It
is fun ther.

Figure 9–4b

Monica's revisions

Greg's piece needed one final revision too. When he corrected the spelling of "kitchen," Greg had added "with a stove and a sink and a refrigerator." The words were all spelled correctly, leading me to suspect that pictures in the child's dictionary inspired the line. Greg probably liked writing those words. But when he read the revised piece to Monica, she told him that every kitchen has a stove, sink, and refrigerator and that she didn't think he needed to put that in. Greg lined out the words before the piece came back to me.

The children's writing was ready for the typist. Both Greg and Monica had expended a great deal of energy, an indication of their investment in the writing. They cared about these topics and wanted them polished for readers.

But I sensed that they had reached the limit of willingness to revise and edit. They had taken their stories as far as they could and it was time to let these pieces go and move on.

The children sat with me as I typed their books, a possibility that semester because we had a student teacher. The child read the manuscript, I typed. As each page came out of the typewriter I handed it to the child to read back to me. We folded a piece of lightweight oaktag around the typed pages and fastened the edge with a row of staples. The typed draft was now ready for illustrating. I allowed each child one writing workshop in which to illustrate. Experience has taught me that writers procrastinate and some children will take days drawing and avoid beginning a new piece. Allowing one day validates the importance of illustrations and provides time for the writer to think about the next topic. (After that, children complete their illustrations during the morning free play or indoor recess.) When the drawings were completed, I used rubber cement to glue the completed story into a wallpaper and cardboard bookcover (see Appendix C: Directions for Bookbinding).

Before Monica and Greg finished the final editing of their writing, I started three more children on a similar process. Gradually over the next month, all of the children went through the publishing process. The nature of their revisions depended on the individual child, but the first issue addressed always revolved around meaning. Don't misunderstand. Certainly I am concerned about teaching children the conventions of written language. But I know that the key to developing writers is giving primary attention to the ideas one wishes to communicate to an audience. Writers who are truly involved with clarifying the content of their writing become very particular about the mechanics.

Each year there are children who come with so few experiences with written language that the publishing process with small groups is inappropriate. I usually work with these children on an individual basis to develop a piece for publication. Michael and Darren were two such children.

Michael

Nearly a month after Greg and Monica published their stories I asked Michael to select a piece for publication. He beamed and said, "This one." He pointed to the paper he had stapled only a few moments earlier. Several trees covered the page. He had written his name, the date, and "FAIHOT." "Fort," he said, pointing again. "Fort?" I repeated, puzzled.

"Uh-huh," he smiled, showing the black cavities in his teeth. "Me 'n Kevin buil-a-fot." The words slurred together in the mumbled baby talk intonation I'd gradually come to understand.

"Ohhh, this is about the day you and Kevin built a fort. I remember."

Michael nodded, grinned, and turned the page.

"What will you do here?" I asked.

"Umm. The fort." Michael began to draw.

"I see, you're going to draw your fort and then you will write about it?"

Michael nodded and went to work. I checked back with Michael several times during the writing workshop. He could not always read his writing if too much time passed, so I wanted to catch those words while they were still fresh in his mind.

When Michael moved from out of state and came to our classroom in late September, he had just turned seven. We'd all had trouble understanding him at first. In fact, he'd talked very little and looked away when any of us spoke to him. But Michael loved school. He loved the children, loved listening to stories, and loved writing. He spent the first week or so in writing workshop drawing or watching the other children work. I moved his desk next to a couple of confident students, and they naturally included Michael in their conversations as they wrote. Soon Michael started adding letters to his drawings, and then began matching those letters to the sounds in words. His cooperation and charm quickly earned him a place in the classroom community.

Michael completed two pages of writing during workshop that day. Above the drawing of the fort he wrote four lines, which he read to me word by word, pointing to each word and looking up to me for acknowledgment before he continued. "The day me and Kevin built a fort this is a fort." On the next page, he drew hearts and wrote four words. At first he had trouble reading them. We pointed to the words and I suggested he skip the first word and go on to find a word he knew. "Hearts! Stars!" he blurted out. "Now I know. There were hearts, stars" (Figure 9–5).

"Okay. Now let's read it all again." And so Michael and I read through his entire three-page, seventeen-word story (including the title). I told him I'd read it that evening and we'd talk about it more tomorrow. When I looked again at the writing, I noticed that Michael had put commas between many words; we had been talking about commas in the classroom. He correctly spelled "the," "me," "this," "a," and "day." I knew where "day" came from. Each morning we wrote the day of the week on the chalkboard and all the children knew the d-a-y spelling. "This" had been on the chalkboard. I couldn't be sure about "the" and "me." Perhaps Michael remembered them himself. The "si" spelling of "is" gave me a clue to his visual memory for spelling. But I was confused by the story itself. I understood the part about building a fort, but how were hearts and stars connected? I'd have to ask Michael.

In conversation with Michael, I learned the answer. Kevin and Michael built a fort, and then crawled inside and put heart and star stickers on paper. I helped Michael determine the placement of this information in the story and he added a line to the page with the fort picture: "Me and Kevin put stickers on paper" (Figure 9–6). "Raor" appeared twice because the first time Michael wrote he left out the word "on." When he read the sentence, he realized there

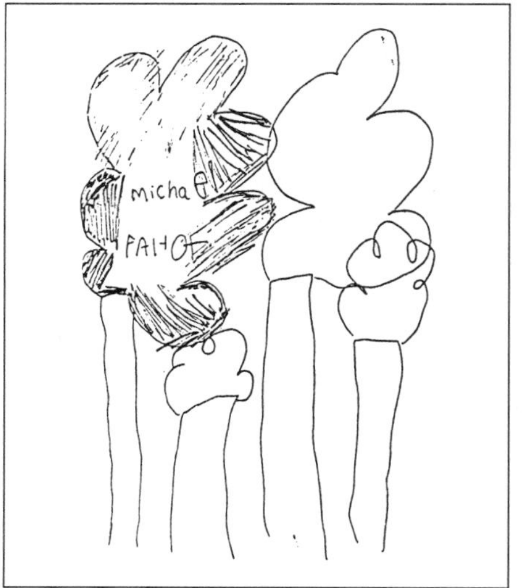

Figure 9–5

Michael's writing

weren't enough words and added another "Raor," though the "r" closely resembled a "p." After reading the entire story to me again, Michael added another sentence by writing down the side of the page beside the heart: "We put stickers on papers in the fort. I went home. Kevin went home" (Figure 9–7, page 200). Prior to this Michael had made few revisions in his writing. By spending a few minutes with him each day as *he wrote*, I better understood his writing process, his story, and his intentions. I could then help him take the writing further in ways appropriate for Michael. By the end of this process, I knew Michael had ventured into a lot of new territory as a writer. I wasn't about to require that he seek out words to spell correctly. There was plenty of time. Michael had been writing for just two months.

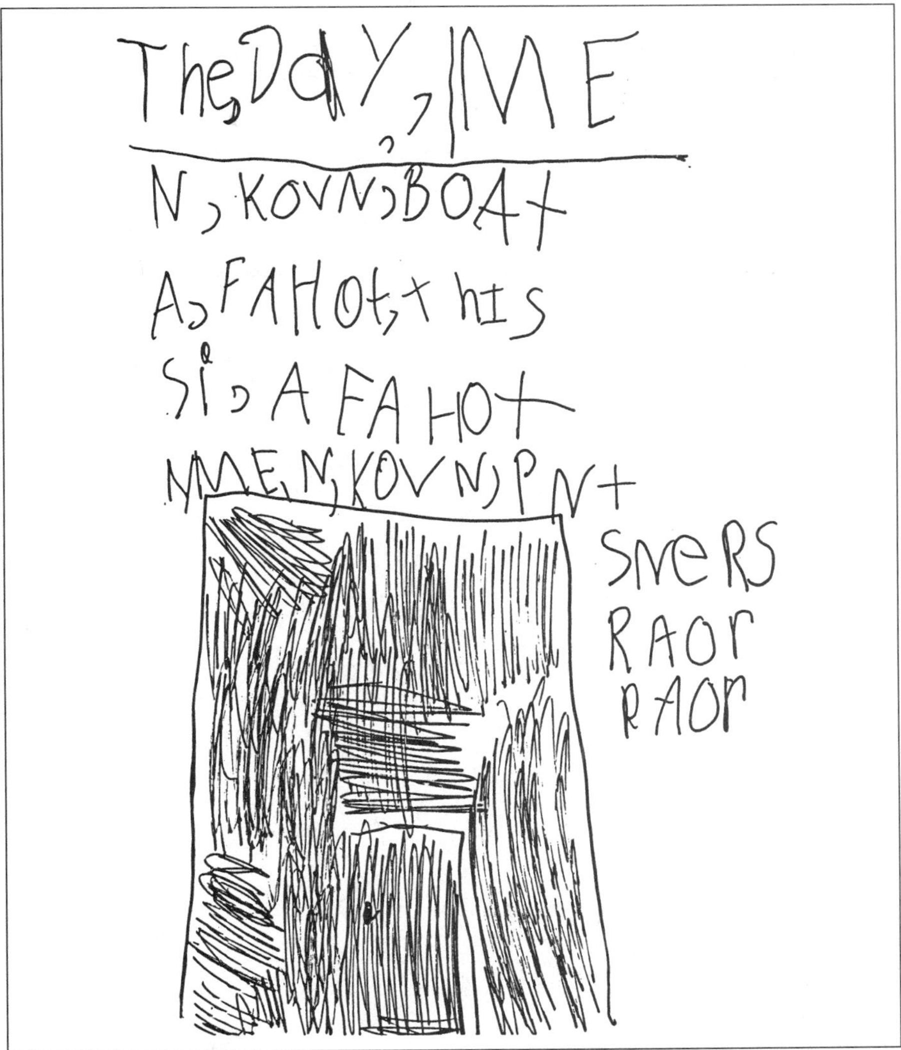

Figure 9–6

Michael's revisions

Darren

Darren wrote about visiting his mother's work. Like most of his writing, the words conveyed a jumble of thoughts, incoherent to any reader including Darren himself. I sensed that Darren wanted to publish his writing as he saw the other children doing, but he shrugged the idea off when I mentioned the possibility. "No, I can't, don't, I can't do that. I don't know how," he said. I sat beside Darren and together we read the piece using Darren's vague recollection of his ideas and clues gleaned from the letters he'd written. We unraveled the meaning as far as we could and then Darren told me what came next—just one sentence.

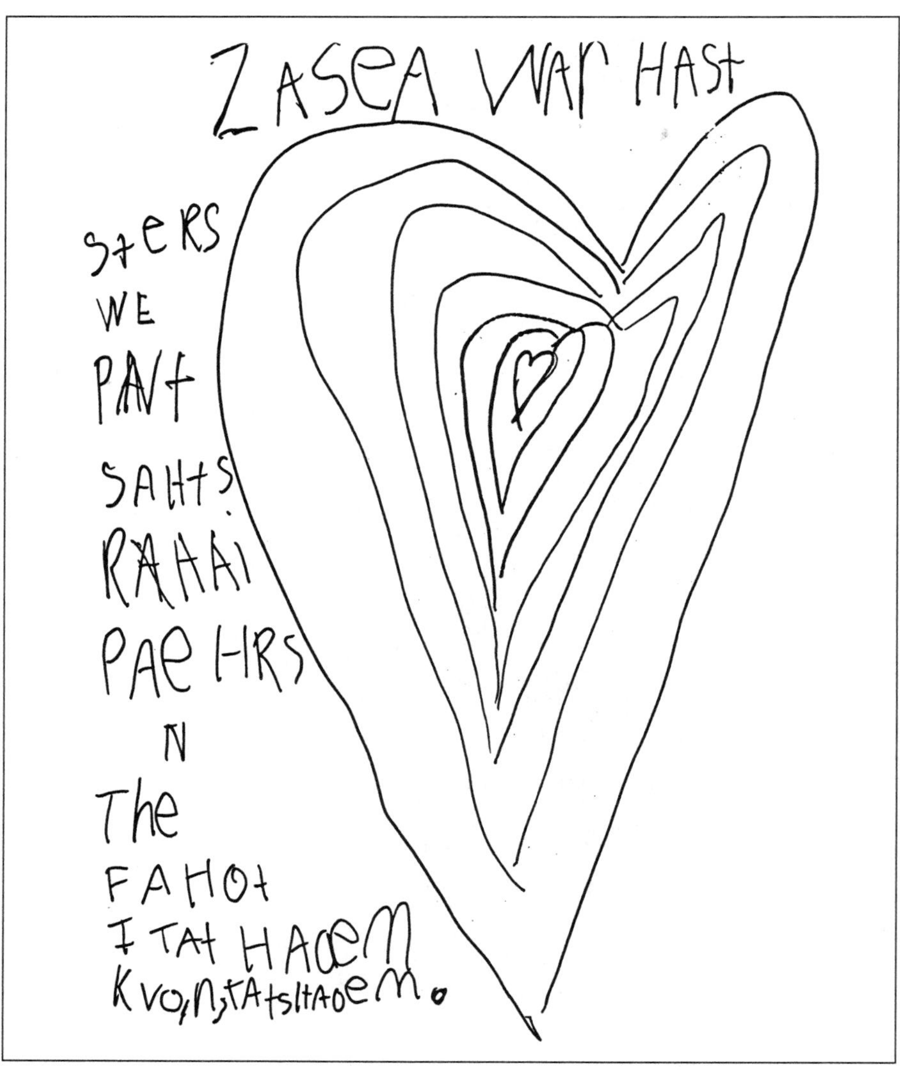

Figure 9–7

Michael's revisions

"Write that," I said. "Okay," he replied and then earnestly put the words on paper. I returned a few moments later and, with my help, he read what he had just written. He told me the next part and we followed the same strategy. Gradually, sentence by sentence, the written story emerged (Figures 9–8a and 9–8b). I read it to Darren. We both agreed that it made sense. Darren heaved a big sigh and said, "I done a lot didn't I?"

"You sure did!" I agreed.

"I think I spelled 'my' right, didn't I? See, here I spelled it 'mi' but I changed it. I changed it to 'my.'" I could only infer that he had become aware of correcting spelling from observing his classmates work through revision and editing.

"Am I done now?" he asked eagerly.

"What do you think?" I asked.

"Yeah, I think I'm done because I did a lot."

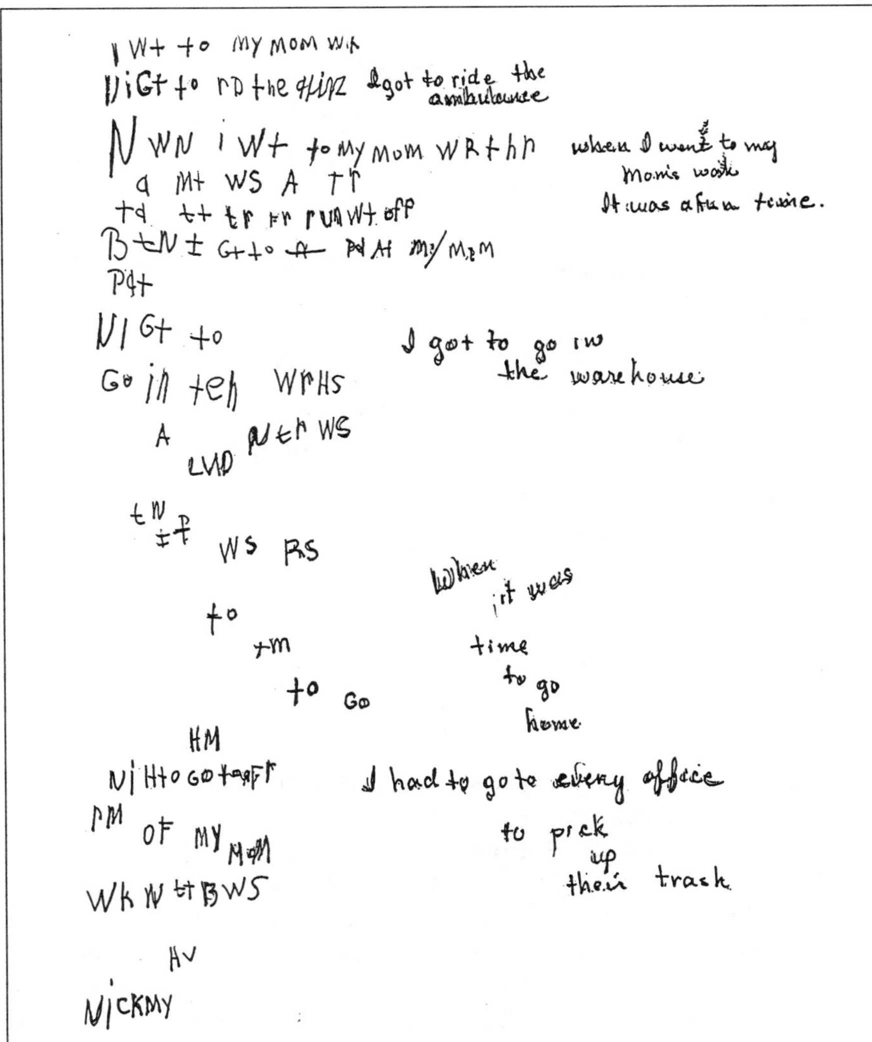

Figure 9–8a

Darren's writing: "When I went to my mom's work I got to ride the ambulance. When I went to my mom's work it was a fun time. I got to go in the warehouse. When it was time to go home I had to go to every office to pick up their trash."

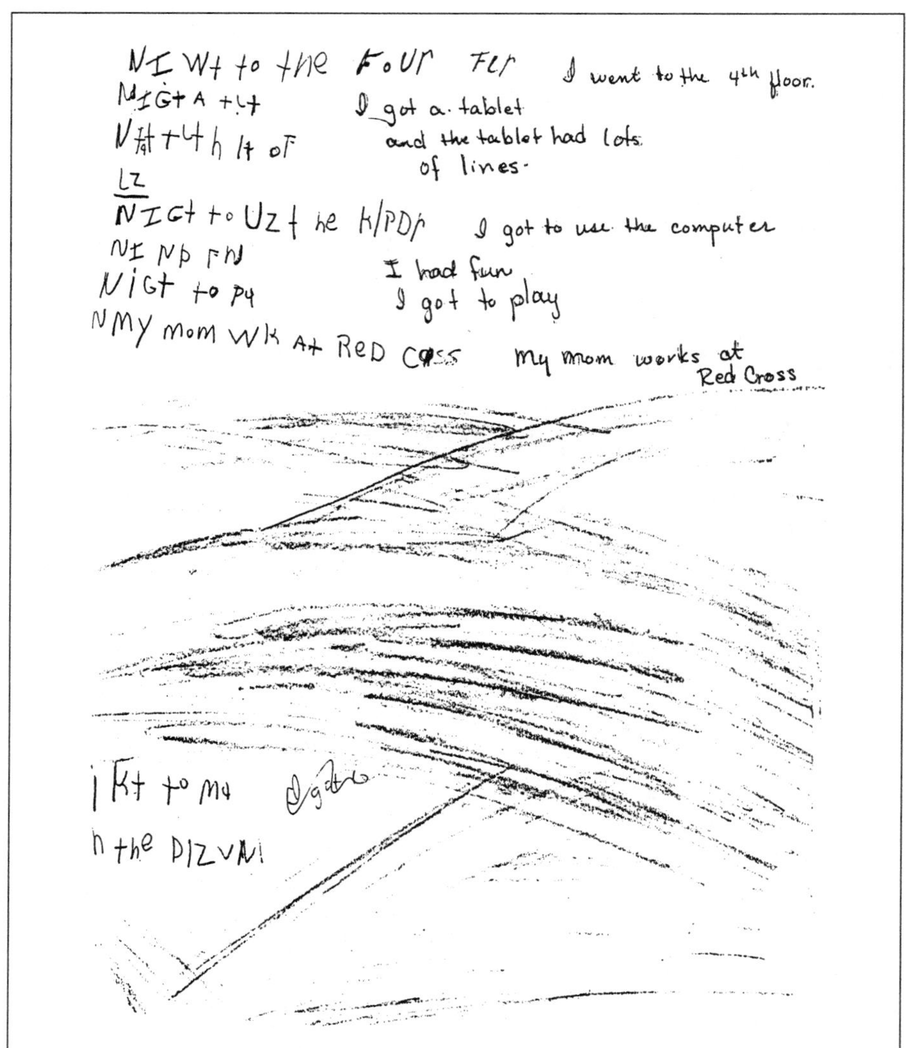

Figure 9–8b

Darren's writing: "I went to the 4th floor. I got a tablet and the tablet had lots of lines. I got to use the computer. I had fun. I got to play. My mom works at Red Cross."

"When I read your story it makes sense and I think other people will think so too. I think they'll like reading about your mom's work."

"Yeah, I did a good job," Darren said.

This process was a milestone for Darren. The support I provided for Darren and Michael was similar to that for Monica and Greg in that all the children worked to make sense for readers. The major difference was that I stayed close to both Michael and Darren to assist them through this process.

Later, Darren sat with me when I typed his book. Every sentence was connected to the next with "and." I suggested that we take some of them out and reminded him of a recent mini-lesson. Darren nodded and said, "I put words and then when people tell me I believe them." His comment seemed significant. Later I thought about his statement and realized Darren was telling me that he "put words" when he wrote but was aware that the story might not be clear to others. He counted on responses from other people and trusted that what they told him improved his writing.

Learning Through Publishing

Editing

Preparing writing for publication requires students to reread and rethink the piece and to make changes that refine the piece for their audience. As part of the publishing process, just before a piece of writing goes to the typist, I want children to do some editing. Sometimes I work with the child, especially if this is the first time the child is attempting a new skill. More often I ask the child to go through the piece of writing and do the best job possible. Early in the year, the task might be inserting periods and capital letters, but I don't expect perfection from first graders. Punctuating sentences in our English language is a very complex skill. If we always wrote in simple sentences, problems would be few, but complex sentences and phrases trip us up. We tell children to listen for the stops and insert periods, but the phrasing of sentences doesn't always lend itself to easily accomplishing this.

By their second or third publication, all the children do some form of editing, if only approximating a particular skill such as inserting periods or correcting one or two misspelled words. This is a list of the editing skills first graders used in one school year.

- determining the end of sentences, inserting periods and capital letters for first words in new sentences
- identifying questions and inserting question marks
- identifying direct quotes and inserting quotation marks
- inserting commas to separate items in a series
- capitalizing the first letter in proper names
- adding "s" for plurals
- adding "'s" to indicate possessive nouns
- identifying a few correctly spelled words and a few incorrectly spelled words and then finding correct spellings (The number of words varied in response to the child's ability to manage this strategy; usually, a

maximum of six words was the most any child tackled with one piece of writing.)

- leaving spaces between words
- leaving spaces between lines
- using legible handwriting

While these last three items could not easily be corrected on a draft, we discussed them in publishing conferences when writing became difficult to read. Students understood and worked on this with subsequent pieces.

Revising

The most significant work during the publishing process is refining and shaping ideas to improve the final communication. Young children *can* rethink and revise writing. In September, they lacked experience as writers and the writing community was undeveloped, but as we established trust and I demonstrated how to revise, they plunged into the high-risk activity of revising.

Revision requires sensitive responses from readers who convey their strong interest in the writer's ideas and in helping the writer communicate clearly. When the responder cares about both the writer and the writing, the writer trusts the responder. Even so, the writer is not going to make every change suggested—especially when revision is a new concept. The kind of changes I've found that children will make when they begin rethinking and reshaping writing include:

- adding missing words (usually they've been left out by accident)
- adding information to clarify the total content
- adding a title
- using arrows to move information to another part of the page
- using an asterisk or star to indicate where to insert information
- adding a title page
- adding a dedication page

With more experience, young writers wade a little deeper into the waters of the revision process and try changes and strategies such as:

- eliminating "then" or "and" at the beginning of every sentence
- brainstorming several possible titles and selecting one
- brainstorming several possible opening sentences and selecting one
- considering the ending (does the story just stop or does it need more information) and then revising that ending

- adding conversation to show not tell
- adding information to show not tell
- removing "and" and replacing with commas or periods
- adding an author's page (to give biographical information)

In the last months of the school year these young writers are immersed in the process of drafting, revising, and editing their writing. Because children work at various aspects of their individual processes on any given day, one might expect a chaotic environment. Not so. In fact, it's the range of activity that enables the workshop to function so smoothly. Everyone comes to count on responses from peers and from me to help them make their writing the best possible. The community establishes a repertoire of strategies, and children try out new ways of writing and revising that they observe within the community. Some of the more sophisticated practices they easily incorporate include:

- planning effective beginnings to hook the reader
- connecting endings to beginnings to get the reader off the hook
- revising a multi-focused piece into one that tells a single story
- removing irrelevant information (They labeled this the "junk writing" that needs to be thrown into the garbage can.)
- separating sections into "chapters" (which is really a form of paragraphing for first graders)
- supplying antecedents for pronouns or eliminating indefinite pronouns
- reordering information
- choosing different words for effectiveness or variety (for example, substitutes for the overworked "said")
- including a table of contents
- including and alphabetizing a glossary

As I saw the need for applying these revision topics in the children's writing, I addressed them in mini-lessons and in conferences and supported their use in publishing conferences.

Final Corrections

During the typing I corrected all spelling and punctuation so that the final product presented a perfect model for reading. I explained to the children that final pieces that are going out of the classroom to readers must follow the conventions of written language. "I will help you do as much as you can and then I'll fix the rest when I type."

"Yeah, 'cause we can't do all that!" a child comments.

"Not yet. But as you write you will learn to do more and more of these things for yourself. However, I think it's important for you to know that every writer needs a good editor, and so it's always a good idea to have somebody else check your writing when you've finished with it."

The children learn from seeing their own words in print. More than once I've heard a child say, "Oh, so that's how you spell *the*, t-h-e. I thought it was t-e-h." After Jamie's first publication she began leaving spaces between words, which greatly improved her ability to reread her writing and also led to spelling development. Children invariably pay close attention to the details of their own words in print. Usually I leave the child's language, particularly grammatical structures, as in Greg's "me and my mom . . ." At times, when I've corrected errors of this type, the child reads the writing and says, "Mrs. Avery, you made a mistake. This is suppose to say 'me and my mom.'" Or the child misreads the correction, substituting their own language. Valuing the child's language is important, and I also want the child to read words that correspond with the actual words on the page. This does not mean that we don't work on developing grammatically correct language. The language-rich environment of the classroom—lots of talk and lots of reading aloud—gives children experience with standard English. I'll present mini-lessons on these topics too. Some children understand and make the shift in their speech and in their writing and some do not. So, I'll present some topics several times throughout the year. Knowing the children and observing their language development influences the corrections I make. When I typed a story by Josie, I changed "me and my sister" to "my sister and I" because I'd heard her correct herself. I showed the corrected version to Josie explaining, "I think this is what you meant." "Oh, yes!" she answered. The decisions on correcting grammatical structures, like so many of the decisions to assist writers, are always based on the context of helping a particular writer at a particular time.

In the days before writing workshop, when I corrected errors, I effectively took the pencil out of the child's hand and imposed my authority on the writing. Urging children to develop their own writing required a new role for me: placing the authority for their writing in the children's hands. When I did, the children experienced what it meant to be a writer, took responsibility and learned!

The Authors' Party

The children stand in a line outside the classroom door. Their bodies wiggle with excitement but their voices are still. They know that seated inside on little classroom chairs are their parents, awaiting the special reading about to begin. Each child clutches a self-authored book. The last parent arrives, the two children who greeted guests and handed out programs move to their place in line; the children file into the classroom and seat themselves around the edge of the story rug just as they had practiced the previous afternoon. They all maintain a dignified poise. This is a special occasion and they've worked hard as individuals and as a community to come to this moment. The authors' party is ready to begin.

Nearly two weeks earlier we began planning to present the first published books to parents. Together we composed an invitation and wrote it during a handwriting lesson. The RSVPs started coming in. The children practiced reading their books to each other and to me so they would read "with expression," not just "dumb boring reading" as Stacy put it. One child wrote an invitation to the principal, another to the reading teacher, and then everyone added his or her signature to these special invitations. We decided on punch and pretzels for refreshments. I typed a program listing the titles of the books, and the children signed their names beside the appropriate title. We composed a greeting for the mistress of ceremonies to read and chose Elizabeth for this role since her mother would be unable to attend. And on the day of the program we rearranged the room, shoving child desks to one end, arranging chairs for the audience, and setting the author's chair on a small raised platform. We set up a microphone to project the young voices.

Elizabeth moves to the center and warmly welcomes the parents. "Welcome to our authors' party," she begins. She announces the first reader, who takes the author's chair and begins to read. I've warned the children that grown-ups may laugh at parts that they don't think are funny, but to pause for the laughter before continuing reading so that everyone gets to hear the entire book. Sure enough, ripples of laughter break out from the delighted audience. One little girl catches my eye and shakes her head in amused, tolerant disbelief. The children read books with titles such as "The Karate Test," "I Went to My Mom's Work," "Catching Caterpillars," "Trick or Treating," "The Tree House." Michael reads "Fort" and remembers to keep the book away from his face so we can hear his words.

Cory takes the author's chair, holding "We Catch Butterflies." He looks up, grins at his audience, and for a moment seems to forget what he's to do. Then he reads loudly, clearly, stopping to grin broadly after each page. I hear this story and remember that Cory was one of the boys who brought me butterflies from the playground that first day of school.

"Me and Michael went in the woods to scare my friends. Then we saw a butterfly. We caught it. Then we looked for more. We found pretty ones. We caught some of them, but we let them go again. Then we went to the park." When Cory finishes he looks over to me, smiles that broad grin, then looks back to his indulging audience. He takes a couple extra seconds, savoring this moment, before he realizes that he's done and it's time to move back to the rug.

The readings are nearly done when Elizabeth's mother slips into the room. Elizabeth's face sparkles when she spies her and she turns to me to check that I, too, have noticed. After Elizabeth reads her book, the final volume shared this day, she thanks the audience and extends our invitation for refreshments. Parents and children mingle, munch pretzels, spill punch, and then go home carrying the published books to share with their families.

Our Lending Library

The children will return these published books to the classroom tomorrow. Each book has a library card and pocket in the back. After the initial sharing at the author's home, the book becomes part of the classroom library for the remainder of the year. The children learn to read each other's books and teach each other how to read them. When they can read a book to the author (the authority on the book), they can sign it out for one night. The children become very particular about their book being read accurately, and I've overheard comments such as: "I think you need more practice before you sign this out, but I'll help you if you want." Class librarians take charge of carding the books each morning and reminding the forgetful; this classroom library is run by the children. I set up the procedures and then stay uninvolved unless specific problems arise. Through the years only one book has ever been lost. The children hold these books in high regard.

From now on, as the children's writing is published in book form, we'll hold much smaller authors' parties. The children will be the audience and two or three books will be presented at a time; we will conduct such an event perhaps once every couple of weeks. Of course, there are many other ways of "going public" with writing and the children published through letters, invitations, petitions—numerous ways of using writing to communicate. These processes involved rereading, revising, and editing in a process similar to the one they used for the publication of little books.

Publication brings deep satisfaction to a writer who truly engages in the writing process. But we don't need to publish everything that is written, nor do we need to publish in abundance. My first graders publish fewer books now than earlier classes, but their engagement as writers, and subsequently the quality of their writing, is far greater than that of other groups.

Reflecting on Our Writing Processes

One year in mid-November, I asked the children how they went about writing. Only a little over two months earlier they referred to writing as drawing, were concerned about spelling, chose unfocused topics. They progressed rapidly and now I wanted them to articulate their perceptions as a means of solidifying progress and of helping me understand their perspective on writing. In a few moments they produced the following list. I recorded the children's words on chart paper as they spoke.

How We Write

1. I sound out the words, like h-h-here. You try to see what letters are in it.
2. You think of the things you've done and think which one you want to write and make a story out of it.
3. You have to make spaces and make titles at the beginning.
4. I think of what I did and choose the longest story to write it.
5. You have to write your best—like your pictures are your best.
6. You can't just write one letter and say "I'm done." You write more letters and words.
7. You have to want to do the book. You have to *want* to write.
8. I know most of my words and you sound out words when you read it.
9. I write first and then draw pictures and read it over and see if it makes sense. It has to make sense to make a story. Then you could line out and write a different word that would make sense.
10. You have to *think* and sound out letters and write it down.
11. I always write first and then I do a picture if I have room.
12. You have to concentrate on what you're doing.
13. You put periods whenever you think the sentence would end.
14. I always make a picture so I don't forget what I'm going to do.
15. You can't write one sentence. It wouldn't be interesting.

Most children understood the process of putting information on paper by drawing and sounding out, and they had begun to think about broader issues: making choices, ascertaining that the writing made sense, realizing the commitment of a writer. Throughout the year we continued to talk about writing and how we wrote.

In May I asked the same group of children, "What do good writers do?" The hands flew up. One comment stimulated another and I went for more chart paper—four times! The children produced the following list.

Good Writers . . .

1. know how to "spell" without being perfect (on first drafts)
2. write the words down (their thoughts) before they "go out the window"

3. think about things to write; think of a story when they're going somewhere or doing something so they won't get stuck and get out of the habit of writing
4. think about what will make sense to other readers
5. don't write a 1,000 pages to be good because long doesn't mean it's better
6. have to make a good beginning and a good ending
7. don't write lies (When Matt contributed this idea I stopped and asked him to tell me more. He explained that a writer can't just make things up because nobody will believe him—a writer's got to write what he knows about, like what he did or "stuff like that.") We added a second sentence: "They write what they know about."
8. have to make it interesting; they make choices to put in what readers really want to know about
9. make decisions—you can't write about everything in one story
10. look at the pictures to figure out the words if they can't read their writing
11. number the pages to keep them in order so the reader isn't confused
12. put in lots of strong information
13. use their own ideas; they don't copy other authors' writing
14. think of a good title, one that hooks the reader; one that matches the story, like Stacy's golfing story
15. keep their writing because they know all their writing is important
16. draw pictures that go with the story (In "The Trouble with Tyrannosaurus Rex" the author didn't match the pictures with the words. She forgot where to put the animals.)
17. put their name and date so they know when they wrote it
18. line out instead of erasing in case they change their mind and want it back again
19. revise after, before, and during the writing as they write to make sense and to make it clear and interesting
20. think about what they could do with their story to make it better
21. read their writing to see if there's missing words or ideas
22. read other authors' writing
23. choose good words that make the writing better
24. write every day
25. don't publish everything they write—some stuff is boring, junky—and they don't revise everything either

26. READ all kinds of writing: good books, poems, fiction, nonfiction
27. make spaces between words; use periods and commas, quotation marks, question marks
28. work hard!
29. read their writing to other people to see if it makes sense and to revise

The children learned what writers do because they wrote every day. This list represented more than behaviors; it reflected understanding about the process of a writer writing. At first I asked the class, "What makes good writing?" Though this question was worth thinking about, when I asked "What do good writers do?" the children had more ideas and contributed more thoughtful responses. The latter question focused on the writers and their learning rather than on writing.

Do all of the children like to write? Most do. But every writer in the room experienced days when they didn't want to write. Courtney commented, "Writing is very hard work on days that you don't know what to write about. But on easy days it is easy because I know what to write about." Jeremy said, "All it is, is time and hard work! Sometimes it's easy, but lots of times it isn't. But I still like to write." Most of the children learned to push through the barriers that made writing difficult by sticking with the writing, learning to trust that the words would come. Kelly commented at the end of one workshop, "Yesterday I only wrote a couple of words. My mind just wouldn't get thinking. But today I kept writing and writing and writing! I didn't even know it was time to stop when you said it was sharing time."

Some children had more trouble. Jody usually spent a day of restlessness when he finished a piece before he could begin another one. Cory said he liked to write, but if he missed a day or two of school he had a hard time getting back into his writing, and I sensed that without the discipline of the daily workshop, writing would easily drop out of his life. Darren loved to draw in writing workshop and he loved the *time* the workshop provided for him to dream and imagine and "live in his own world," but he consistently said he didn't like to write. I suspect that his difficulty getting coherent thoughts on paper contributed to his feelings.

Still, every class of children has loved writing workshop. The children protested if workshop was shortened, let alone eliminated for even a day. I don't think this is because they found writing easy or enjoyable every day. Part of the appeal, I'm sure, grew from having access to each other, being able to learn and build relationships together. But there was something more. I think the children found writing to be rewarding because it tapped something deep within them, an innate desire to learn, to know, and to understand. After writing about China, Leslie said, "I thought I only knew a little bit about China but I found out I know lots of stuff. I just forgot I knew some of it." Oliver talked about his brother's birthday: "I just had to write all the birthday things down so I could stop holding them in my head and then we could always remember them because I wrote them down. And when I started writing I wrote some things that I forgot about!" We write to learn and to discover. We write to forget and we write to remember.

The children frequently referred to imagination when they talked about writing. They were able to tap into their imaginations far more readily than I've seen many adult writers do. During a mini-lesson in January I referred to a book by Ruth Brown entitled *Our Puppy's Vacation*, noting how the author told the story of going to the beach from the point of view of the puppy. I mentioned that Ruth Brown used her imagination to think what the vacation was like for the puppy. Near the end of the workshop I talked with Monica. She had come to me earlier and asked if she could read her writing to me when she finished. I had said I'd see her just before sharing time. Then she read her story, "Over the Rainbow," which had nothing to do with point of view, the focus of the mini-lesson, but had everything to do with the purpose of writing.

> I wonder. I do wonder, what it would be like over the rainbow. Would it be another world? Would it be the same? Would there be little people? Would it be a forest? I would like to walk over the rainbow. And when I would get to the top, I would like to slide right down it. But! before I got to the bottom, I would stop, look, and if there was a pot of gold at the bottom, I would slide right into it. I really do wonder.

By the end of the reading, her voice had taken on a tone of awe and wonder. When she looked at me I saw a deep pensiveness in her eyes. I felt us encircled by a quiet sense of mystery and magic, which the writing had tapped somewhere deep within this child. "Tell me about this. How did you write this?" I asked quietly.

"I don't know exactly. It's really strange. When you said how writers use their imagination . . ." Monica interrupted her thought to respond to my puzzled look. "In the mini-lesson—you said writers use imagination." I recalled my passing comment, nodded, and Monica continued. "When I started thinking about that—about imagination—and I've been wondering about rainbows a lot and so I just used my imagination and I really got into it and the words just came out of my head. I didn't know I had those words. They just kept coming out. I keep thinking and thinking about it."

Janet Emig (1983) wrote:

Literacy is not worth teaching
if it doesn't provide access;
if it doesn't sponsor learning;
if it doesn't unleash literal power;
if it doesn't activate the greatest power of all—the imagination. (178)

I think Monica and her classmates understand. They write.

CHILDREN'S LITERATURE

CHAPTER 10

The Why, How, and What of Reading Aloud

In my childhood elementary school in Waterville, Maine, our teachers read to us every day—everything from the Bobbsey Twins to the classics. When a teacher finished a book, we clamored to read it ourselves. The memory of my teacher's voice accompanied my own reading, enhancing meaning, adding expression, and filling in unknown words. In third grade Mrs. Howard read *Tom Sawyer*, and to this day I carry images of Tom whitewashing a fence, of Tom and Becky lost in a cave, of Tom, Joe, and Huck prancing into church to attend their own funeral. Mrs. Howard explained key words such as "whitewash." When we read *Lassie Come Home*, she clarified "licking his chops." Mrs. Howard's read alouds introduced me to Meg, Amy, Beth, and Jo in a book I would read over and over again.

Remembering school read alouds, I am struck by the realization that no teacher ever bombarded us with questions, follow-up activities, or book reports. Our teachers read; we read. Our teachers pointed us in the direction of good books while we gossiped about the "best parts," checked out books from the town library, and saved allowances to buy a few precious books of our own. The pervasive message from our teachers was "keep reading and enjoy it." We did. Not until seventh grade in another state did a teacher ask for a book report, which I remember as a rather dull activity compared to the lively engagements I'd been experiencing.

When I became a first-grade teacher, I read to my class every day—a children's novel to begin the school day and lots of picture books in a chunk of time we called "literature time." Later, when I gave children's literature official sanction with a forty-minute time slot, I found that not all my colleagues valued reading aloud. A teacher responding to the curriculum I wrote for state department requirements, said, "Reading aloud every day is unrealistic." An administrator who came to observe the class while I was reading to the children announced, "I'll come back when you're teaching." These responses, while disconcerting, turned out to be helpful because I explored why reading aloud was important and reflected on my own practices when I read to children. I realized that both the literature and the way I conducted the read-aloud sessions provided a foundation with written language that touched every aspect of the children's learning—and was indeed "teaching."

Research on Reading Aloud

Educational research validated reading aloud years ago. Tunnell and Jacobs (1989) found that regular "reading aloud seemed to be a must. Daily reading aloud from enjoyable trade books has been the key that unlocked literacy growth for many disabled readers" (475). In *Awakening to Literacy*, Teale (1984) cites numerous studies supporting the value of "storybook reading." Holdaway (1979) advocates "shared book experience" as a "major input part of the program . . . that could last up to an hour in length."

Gordon Wells, in his longitudinal study of children's literacy development (1986), found that of all activities that gave children an advantage for school education, the "sharing of stories" became the most important. Children who succeeded in school had heard many stories in their early years. Jonathan, in Wells' study, came to school having heard over a thousand stories while Rosie had heard relatively few. Jonathan easily moved into school learning while Rosie struggled. The children's early patterns continued through the conclusion of the study when they were in fifth grade. Wells believes that stories are particularly important because:

> 1. In listening to stories read aloud . . . before they can read . . . children are already beginning to gain experience of the sustained meaning-building organization of written language and its characteristic rhythms and structures. So, when they come to read books for themselves, they will find the language familiar.
> 2. . . . through stories, children vicariously extend the range of their experience far beyond the limits of their immediate surroundings. (151–52)

Reading aloud is important for the children's literacy development but also *how* I read is critical. Recent research suggests that "the way the teacher conducts read-alouds significantly affects children's literacy learning"(Teale and Yokota 2000). Reading aloud is anything but a peripheral activity. In my classroom, reading aloud is an integral part of reading and writing instruction, a time to address reading and writing strategies and processes as we read and talk about books and authors. For organizational purposes, we call the daily chunk of time devoted to reading aloud and talking our "literature time" but, in truth, this read-aloud time is also reading and writing time. I don't believe my reading and writing workshops would have produced strong results if it not been for "literature time." If it's done well, reading aloud is a key component in children's development as readers, writers, and learners.

Read Alouds as Demonstrations

Years ago Jane Hansen asked me, "What do you do when you read to children? I know you do more than just read." Jane's question stayed with me and I came to realize that what I do other than "just read" is *talk.* I read to children and we talk, and the talk is genuine because it's responsive to the children. I'm convinced that the responsive talk is precisely what makes read alouds such a rich teaching context. I share a range of literature with children but I'm also providing demonstrations of *how* to read and *how* written language is constructed. Reading aloud becomes a way to "guide" reading and writing development. The demonstrations are more than holding up a book and reading it aloud. The reading aloud is embedded in an interactive process that permeates our classroom.

A few highlights from my reading of *Fran's Flower* by Lisa Bruce to a group of four- and five-year-olds provide glimpses of what this looks like. I've learned these children have limited experience with books in their homes so I begin by talking about the front and back of the book, then show how we open the book and turn pages. I read the title, sweeping my hand under the words and emphasizing the /f/ sound at the beginning "Fran's" and "Flower" ever so slightly. The children watch all of this closely and when they spontaneously repeat the title, I point out the letter *F* in both words and tell them these words begin the same way because of the same letter. I repeat the title and we listen for this /f/ sound for a few seconds. We even take a moment to notice how our teeth and mouth formed the beginning of "Fran" and "flower." Next we talk about the cover illustration briefly and our ideas about what the book will be about. When I open the cover, we pause to look at the end pages, illustrated with flowers and bees. The children have a lot of comments.

"Bee. Flower. Does bee begin the same as flower?" I ask. Several children say, "NO!" while others looked puzzled. The differences tell me the range of knowledge regarding discrimination of initial sounds.

We read the title page quickly and begin the story. I start by "reading" the first illustration and eliciting the children's ideas. Then I read the words and go back and check out the picture again. "I wonder who Fred is?" I muse. (He's mentioned in the words but to identify him as a dog we need to read the illustrations.) When one child says Fred is the bee, the others point out why they think Fred's the dog. "We'll have to read more to be sure," I say. (A page later we verify that Fred is the dog.) The children miss the tip of a plant in a flowerpot, which is important to the story, so I say, "Oh, Fran said she wants to grow a flower. This must be it. I wonder what she's going to do with it." The children have no response and the brief silence and slightly puzzled looks on their faces indicate that thinking this way about the book may be new to them. Before we move on, I repeat the words *Fran, found, flowerpot, filled, Fred*, pointing out that they all begin with that /f/ sound and the children begin repeating these words. The time spent on this letter-sound relationship is *brief.* I point it out and we move on; the central focus must be the story itself.

As the story develops, Fran's flower doesn't grow so she feeds it pizza and other food. "You won't believe what she feeds it next!" I comment before I show the page. I use an outrageous voice tone designed to convey the silliness of Fran's idea and to encourage the children to experience this silliness. I'm teaching them to get in touch with their thoughts about what happens in stories and express their responses—in this case amusement. My comment also brings out ideas from the children that the plant needs water and sun.

A few pages later, when Fran is "fed up," I ask what that means. When there's no answer, I suggest looking at her face. "Angry!" a child says, "She's angry!"

"Yes, 'fed up' is a kind of anger," I confirm, and we talk about feeling 'fed up' by having them think about how they would feel if they had a plant like Fran's that wouldn't grow no matter what they did. A couple children begin talking about times they or family members were "fed up."

Our talk continues this way as the story unfolds. The children notice the plant growing from page to page and the large flower at the end. "It looks like a bullseye!" one says. When we finish reading, I return to the first page and explain that they could read this book by going through the pages, looking at all pictures, and telling the story. I show how by demonstrating a page-by-page retelling.

We spent twenty minutes on this picture book of less than two hundred words. The talk surrounding the story was as important as the reading of the story itself. This talk involved the children in the story and explored reading strategies. I demonstrated *how to read*—how to decode, question, and think about a book as one reads while maintaining the engaging experience of listening to a story. I'm teaching reading by making the process visible throughout the read aloud. I'm demonstrating reading strategies and skills in an authentic context, blended in the way accomplished readers blend as they read. I'm guiding reading development. Such reading is appropriate for older readers as well as young ones; we adjust the specific demonstration to match the development of the readers. As readers develop decoding strategies, more of the talk centers on meaning making.

The substance of this class talk has these characteristics:

- This talk is not children answering traditional teacher questions; it's a sharing of ideas, questioning text, making connections, striving to understand a multitude of perspectives.
- An important part of this talk is *listening* to each other and *thinking* about other's ideas.
- The talk takes off with open-ended questions that stimulate *children's* ideas and build on those ideas rather than being channeled toward the teacher's thinking or the teacher's agenda.
- This talk follows no curriculum, adheres to no plan for literary analysis or integration with other topics, nor is it geared to pre-planned questions gleaned from some literature guide. It occasionally veers off on meaningful tangents just like natural conversation.
- The talk is grounded in the experience of that particular reading and is shaped around the children's responses and thinking at the time.

I take part in the talk too, both as a member of the group and also as the one in charge, managing the whole thing. I have expertise to share, but I'm not the final authority. It's a delicate balance to strike; it's teaching with a light touch. The result, I am convinced, influences the children's academic growth and strengthens our classroom community thinking.

Managing Literature Time

Literature time begins on the first day of school. The children gather on our story rug and I read several books. We'll read as many as three or four titles (later in the year, as our talk expands, we're more likely to read one or two). Each day I'll introduce at least one new book. We'll repeat many books, reading them again and again, for it is in the rereading that we truly learn how to think about books and develop comprehension skills.

The children listen and talk and talk as I read. It's not long before they have favorites. They love Robert McCloskey's *Make Way for Ducklings* and listen with unfaltering attention. They notice every detail in the brown and white drawings. The boys make the screeching sounds of cars coming to a halt as the ducklings cross the street. They all giggle at the rhyming names of the ducklings, not because they rhyme but because "their mother must get them all mixed up when she tries to call them." I show them photographs of the little statues of Mrs. Mallard and her ducklings in the Public Gardens in Boston and tell them about seeing children sitting on the ducklings and talking to them.

"I'd talk to them too," says Matt. "I'd tell them I like their book. And do those ducklings ever go in the water?" His questions unleash a crescendo of voices.

"Wait! One at a time." I struggle to make myself heard through the din. During these first days of school it seems I'm forever working to get the children to talk one at a time and to listen to each other's comments. "Everyone may talk," I explain, "but one at a time. You begin, and then you, and then you. No one may interrupt and I want you to listen to each other."

After a child's comment I ask, "What do you think about that idea?" and listen to one or two peer responses before I continue. We begin to establish ways to listen and respond. In the beginning, the pattern of talk is teacher-child-teacher-child. To develop responses that probe deeper than one child's comment, I turn to another child and say, "What do you think about that?" If there's no answer I'm likely to turn back to the first child and say "I'm not sure she heard you. Would you repeat that?" Then I'll go back to the second child after the comment is repeated. Or, if a child shrugs off my appeal for a response I'll say, "Think about that. We'd like to know what *you* think." Quite often that child will volunteer an answer a few minutes later.

Children quickly learn that this is a *group* discussion and I expect each child to *listen* to others' ideas as well as expressing one's own. Slowly the pattern shifts to child-child-child-teacher, with my input receding each day. More and more, my job is to select the next speaker so that a few children don't dominate and to help children stay on topic. Eventually the children respond to each other and my role drops back to a few occasional questions or comments to nudge thinking or to ensure that everyone has the opportunity to speak.

One McCloskey book leads us to another and another. Sharing my own responses extends theirs. When we read *Blueberries for Sal*, I stop at the words, "Kerplink, kerplank, kerplunk," McCloskey's language that imitates the sound of berries falling into an empty tin bucket. I say, "Listen to those words. I love the sound of those words. I wonder how Mr. McCloskey thought of them?" The children listen to the words, enjoy the sound, but are puzzled. Plastic has replaced metal buckets and they have no experience of picking berries. I explain about metal buckets and their imaginations take over.

"Oh, I get it," says Max. "It's the sound of the berries hitting the bucket. Neat!" As the story continues the children giggle at the plight of Little Bear and Little Sal and understand the mix-up with mothers before the characters do in the story.

Rereading favorite titles encourages new ideas and connections to other books. When we read *Mrs. Wishy Washy* the second time, the children chime in with repeating "wishy washy, wishy washy." They request a particular version of *The Three Billy Goats Gruff* because they like the picture of the troll. "He's more like a monster," says Jody. The group agrees. When we read Robert Munsch's *Love You Forever*, they laugh uproariously at the role reversal of the son rocking the mother. When I finish reading the book Aaron says, "It keeps going on like the other book, like *Henny Penny*. It keeps going on and on."

"Yeah," says Jeff, "she'll grow up and then he'll get old and then his daughter will come and rock him." Aaron and Jeff caught the pattern and made connections between two books. The pondering looks, then nods among the children indicate that the boys have helped everyone understand.

I read nursery rhymes (which some groups regard as "baby stuff") and let these rhymes lead us into poetry. Sometimes children respond with blank stares when I first read poetry, but after a couple of rereadings of lyrical or humorous verses, faces light up and they cry, "Read it again!" Judith Viorst's "Mother Doesn't Want a Dog" is always a favorite as is "A Thousand Hairy Savages," by Spike Milligan. I begin reciting it as the children line up to go to the cafeteria and the class chimes in. Later we'll do the same with William Carlos Williams' poem "This Is just to Say" for this lunchtime ritual. The children also love e. e. cummings' poem "Maggie and Millie and Molly and May." I know it's the alliteration that the children find playful and intriguing.

Popular books are ones with repetitious lines or books that are songs. After reading *I Know an Old Lady Who Swallowed a Fly* to the group, I point out two different versions. The group's attitude is "So what?" I quickly drop my plan to compare the two versions. When I read *Oh! A-Hunting We Will Go*, the children sing the refrain. "You can probably learn to read this book because you already know the words," I say. Looks of surprise cross their faces, hands fly up, and pleading requests come, "Can I have that book?" "Can I read it?" "Can I?"

During literature time I introduce books that children can learn to read, such as predictable books or books with a strong story line told in a few words. We also read more complexly written stories, ones that children can "read" by retelling, using illustrations to remind them of the story. I haven't leveled all the books in the classroom because I want the children to know they can pick up any book and look through it, and I want them to learn how to choose their own reading materials by taking into consideration their interest and the readability. I've also found that children will work to read a difficult book—one that leveling might disallow—because of particular motivation. Learning to choose appropriate books for one's own reading is an important skill for readers of any age—even the youngest. We'll work on the skill of choosing books as part of reading instruction. The books I read aloud contribute to the development of this important skill.

We become a community that reads together. The books—stories, poems, and nonfiction—become a common ground of shared experiences that knits our community together. I focus on the children's natural delight in listening to and talking about stories, and I strive to maintain the role of a responsive teacher while at the same time teaching children about genre, authors, literary conventions, and so on. The benefits of this important teaching time spill over to every other aspect of the school day (especially reading and writing workshops), weaving an intricate web connecting every aspect of the curriculum.

Suggestions on *How* to Read Aloud

"When you read a book aloud," my first graders tell me, "you have to read it with expression—so people will want to listen. Otherwise, it gets boring."

"And you have to take your time. You can't hurry 'cause people can't listen as fast as you might read."

"You gotta stop and let people think, let them talk some, in between."

As usual, the children had it down. They knew what made reading aloud enjoyable. Each teacher develops her own style as she reads to children. I offer some tips of things that have helped mine:

1. Begin by choosing a book you *want* to read. It doesn't have to be one you've read before; you can let children see you experience the first reading. Enter into the reading with passion, a deep investment, and anticipation.
2. Introduce the book with a few comments—tell something about the author or why you selected it even if it's just "I've never read this book before and I'd like to know what you think of it."
3. Talk about the end pages, title page, dedication page of some books, but definitely not every book.
4. Use an expressive voice that picks up the tone of the story and the voices of the characters.
5. Use timing for emphasis. Pause for listeners to digest, contemplate, consider ideas.
6. Watch expressions on listeners' faces and adjust the reading in response to the audience.
7. Vary your approach with different readings. For example, sometimes read straight through without comment from either yourself or the listeners. Another time, pause and elicit responses through open-ended questions such as, "What do you think about that?" Sometimes share your personal responses taking care not to thwart the responses of listeners who may look to you as the authority.
8. *Invite* talk about the reading and demonstrate talk by thinking aloud in order to:
   - predict then confirm or disprove the prediction as the book unfolds
   - make connections to other books
   - make connections to personal experiences
   - consider characters and what makes them tick
   - express likes and dislikes about the book
   - consider the author's language, style, and strategies

   However, avoid addressing all these areas with every book.
9. Accept all ideas expressed, demonstrate the value of everyone's contribution, and strive to understand the thinking behind the children's ideas. Invite all students into the conversation.
10. Allow for interruptions from children to share connections or ask questions.
11. Turn students' wonderings/questions back to the group for their input. (The teacher doesn't have to be the provider of all information. Encourage children to share their perspectives.)
12. Ask questions to which you do not know the answer.

13. Repeat well-turned phrases that appeal to you and tell the listeners why you like them. Point out interesting language or construction that the author uses. Ask the children what they think is the meaning of particular words.
14. Take your time. Enjoy the reading and the talk!

Teale and Yokota (2000) write that "done thoughtfully, reading aloud becomes a critically important means of teaching background knowledge, vocabulary, comprehension strategies, and knowledge of written language so crucial to becoming skilled and willing readers during the primary years and beyond" (15). They point out that research shows significant variation in the ways teachers read to children. These differences, in turn, affect children's reading growth. It's important to do more than read and ask the traditional teacher questions that channel children's thinking to a particular interpretation.

Many different individuals read to my children throughout the year: mothers, grandmothers, peers, older students, student teachers, the principal, the reading teacher, other classroom teachers. Each has a unique style. One reader evoked criticism from the children because he read too fast. On another occasion, children expressed delight in the voice tone of a particular reader. However, the children were disappointed with a guest reader who did not seek their responses to the reading. In contrast, when a child reader stopped suddenly in a story she was reading aloud and asked, "What do you think about that?" I saw the listeners perk up, catch the twinkle in the child's eye, and begin thinking of unexpected events for the story. The children knew what worked. Taking time to talk allows the listeners time to pause, think, and "catch up" with the story. It leads to deeper engagement in the reading which, in turn, helps develop comprehension.

Shared Reading

Shared reading is a time for children and teacher to enjoy books together but with the added bonus of children *seeing* the text as the teacher reads. My experiences with shared reading grow out of our read-aloud time quite naturally with the biggest difference being the children taking a more active role in the reading itself. Big books work well for shared reading. In this reading demonstration, the teacher points to the words on the page thus showing children how print is arrange. Children may follow along and chime in with words or lines as the teacher reads. The teacher may also point out specific structural components of written language. But the main function of shared reading is the enjoyment and pleasure of reading together (Clay 1998; Holdaway 1979; Routman 2000; Parkes 2000).

Big books were not available to me when I launched reading and writing workshops and our daily literature time. However, I occasionally printed poems on chart paper and the class and I often read them together as part of our opening exercises. We'd talk about rhyming words and how they were spelled similarly and sounded alike. When a Halloween poem had a strong line shouted by trick-or-treaters, I pointed out quotation marks, and the capitalization of the line for emphasis. The children soon memorized these poems and they often read them, pointing to the words, during free-play time or during reading workshop.

Many of the first big books that appeared on the scene lacked the quality of writing and the wonderful stories we savored in our literature time. Many excellent books are now available in big-book format though not all titles lend themselves to this format. The key is to remember that the time is meant to be one of joyful sharing of literature. If the focus is on "teaching" a skill, the children will recognize the agenda and the possibility for a joyful experience fades.

Books for Children

Children's author Katherine Paterson (1990) lists three properties the scientist ascribes to beauty: simplicity, harmony, and brilliance. Paterson applies these attributes to the art of children's books and describes Patricia MacLachlan's book *Sarah, Plain and Tall* as a "beautiful book."

> Simplicity? . . . the book is complete in itself—direct, and without superfluous words. Harmony? You'd have to look far to find a book in which the parts—character, setting, and plot—so gracefully conform to one another and to the language of the whole. Brilliance? . . . we aren't talking about cleverness but about clarity—about the light that the book sheds not only on itself but beyond itself, to other stories and other lives. Don't you keep thinking of it? Don't you compare other books to it? Don't you know the prairie better now? And what it means to care about another person? (158–59)

Paterson believes this test of beauty applies to the art of children's books, "for the stories that have endured, the stories to which we turn as we seek to shape our lives, are all beautiful in this sense" (159).

Children are good at recognizing beautiful books. They remember words and phrases. Jeff says, "I been saying those words at home at lot," and he goes on, in his best witch's voice, to quote a line from a Lillian Moore poem. They remember characters. Jenny hugs herself and says, "I just *love* Templeton [the rat in E. B. White's *Charlotte's Web*]. He's *so nasty*!" A husky laugh ripples from her before she quotes the rat, "What do you think I am, a rat of all work?" and then another deep laugh. Children remember books that touch their lives. Josie loves stories about grandparents and older people; her favorite is Barbara Cooney's *Miss Rumphius*, and she regularly works on learning to read it for herself. Darren requests rereadings of Carol Carrick's *The Accident* again and again and he keeps the book in his desk for months. We all have books that have endured for us because they helped us to understand ourselves, others, and our worlds a little better. They are the books we turn to as we seek to shape our lives, and undoubtedly they are different for each of us.

In my classroom I introduce children to many, many books. Some will qualify as "good literature" and some will never make any list of great books. But by hearing lots of books from a range of genres, styles, and even literary quality, young children will find ones that endure for them because of their simplicity, harmony, and brilliance. Children return to these books because they touch their lives in mysterious and magical ways.

The books children find to shape their lives may not be highly acclaimed. Robert Munsch's *Mortimer*, the story of a child avoiding bedtime, is a book youngsters request again and again. Yet *Mortimer* doesn't make any list of great literature. When Maurice Sendak's *Where the Wild Things Are* was published, much of the adult world rejected it for children, arguing that it was too frightening. Children love it. I've seen many preschoolers identify with Max, who temporarily escapes the troubles of his real life to an imaginary world where he controls all the frightening wild things. The children's embracing of Sendak's book made it a classic. Children often know good books because they quickly sense powerful meanings. Sendak (1990) himself observed how his own niece saw immediately that *Higglety Pigglety Pop!* was a book about death when reviewers missed that basic point. "It's the way children dive into symbology or metaphor," says Sendak, "they get it. They may not like what they get, but they know how to go right to the heart of the matter" (56). Children have taught me that I must read lots of books to them and let them decide what is best and what they want to hear again. If I determine which are the best books, using adult standards, I may well miss some books that will touch their lives.

Of course, the books I choose for the classroom and those I select for reading aloud influence what children read. Though children eventually discover books on their own, young readers first move toward the ones I read aloud. Even later in the year, the books read aloud remain the focal books in the room. So I choose books carefully but not cautiously. I apply no readability formula or leveling tools other than seeking out a few books in September and October that will be manageable for beginning readers because of the shorter length, perhaps predictable language patterns, and the physical format (avoiding small print or too many words on a page). The first year of reading workshops I searched for easy-to-read books because I was tied to the notion of controlled vocabulary. One day I handed Chris a folktale retold in a controlled vocabulary that I thought would be easy for him. Later I checked with Chris, asking him what the book was about. "I don't really know," he said, "I think it's 'Jack and the Beanstalk.' The pictures look like it is, but there's not enough words to tell." At that same time Chris fluently read books with words such as "astronaut," "forest," "happened," "wizard." So much for controlled vocabulary. Children continually astound me with the reading material they are able to tackle.

I choose books that I enjoy and that I anticipate children will like. I make some poor choices, books that bomb or receive a lukewarm response (though they may have been a great hit with another class). But by introducing a range of quality and variety of books, I hope to develop the children's reading tastes and skill in making choices.

Considerations in Selecting Books

Choosing books for the classroom is an important task for teachers. As the professional in the classroom I need to know good books and how to seek out new ones. The following are some of the characteristics I consider when selecting books for my classroom.

1. Tried-and-true favorites: books I love and that other classes have loved and books that have become classics.
2. Books representing a variety of cultures and peoples and that avoid stereotyped roles for individuals. I strive to achieve a balance of male and female protagonists.
3. Books that connect with specific curricular areas. For example, I'm always on the lookout for new books on China, ecology, or dinosaurs.
4. Books that provide good reading and match the interest and reading development of my students. For beginning readers, for example, I look for books with predictable or repetitious phrases, books with a strong story line in a few words (but that also avoid a controlled vocabulary), books with easy-to-read print. Some of these books may be leveled books as a way of assisting the most beginning readers in learning to select appropriate books.
5. Books representing a range of topics, child interests, and genres.
6. Books that are well written: the language flows, the book has rhythm, rich vocabulary, well-turned phrases, wonderful images. The book is a pleasure to read aloud!
7. Books by favorite authors. Children await the next book by a favorite author just as adults do.

8. New books: not only newly published books or books unfamiliar to the class, but also books with different or unusual formats, illustrations, or presentations. Someone has taken a risk and tried something new.
9. Books with attractive format:
   - print is easily read, not embedded in the illustrations or compressed tightly together
   - text correlates with the illustrations on the page
   - illustrations are high quality, with a diversity of artistic styles
   - cover is appealing (though we know you can't judge a book by its cover, one of our first invitations comes from the cover)
   - paper quality is sturdy
   - size of book is easy to hold and read (not too small or too big)
10. Book jackets that give information about the author or the process of writing this particular book is a nice addition, though certainly not necessary.

When I taught fourth grade I learned some things about selecting books that apply to all grade levels. The range in reading achievement of my fourth graders made book selections complicated because many students chose books that were too difficult for them. I attacked the problem by filling my room with picture books on a broad range of reading levels and using these books for our read alouds. I told them the "E" on the spine of these library books meant this was a book for "everyone"; I knew, I said, because I'd been a librarian who put some of those E's there. The books caught on; reading picture books became "cool."

Another difficulty I encountered that year was locating books in which my Puerto Rican students could find themselves and their culture. One of the first books the class loved was *Zomo the Rabbit*, the West African folktale illustrated by Gerald McDermott. "It looks like Puerto Rico," Cynthia said one day. "Yeah, I like it. It's Puerto Rico," her classmates concurred. I scoured bookstores and libraries looking for books with Puerto Rican characters. At a national convention, I went to all the children's book exhibitors and asked for their titles with Puerto Rican characters or culture. Vendors handed me books on Hispanic culture but these were Southwestern or Mexican cultures. "We're not Hispanic. We're Puerto Rican," my students proudly told me. Now, when I go in bookstores, I see many titles that would have filled this need. I saw firsthand that year how important it is to have books in our classrooms that connect with the culture and life circumstances of the students in those classrooms.

Series books serve an important function as children crack the code and really get into reading. For some students this begins by the end of first grade. Readers need lots of practice at this point in their growth and I found that if I could get a reader hooked on one book in a series, she'd continue with the others. Series books provide readers with practice that develops fluency, characters who become familiar, plot structures that help readers see how story lines are constructed, and a sense of accomplishment and success. "I'm on book 23!" reported a third grader reading the Magic Tree House books.

I began my own professional development in children's literature during an undergraduate children's literature course. Our text, *Children and Books*, by May Hill Arbuthnot (1964), like a similar one by Charlotte Huck that I love, provided a rich introduction to the depth and breadth of children's literature. However, the most valuable part of the course was reading several hundred children's books. I maintain my knowledge of children's books by reading and talking with others (especially children) about my reading. I maintain a file of bibliographies clipped from journals or picked up at conferences and workshops. I watch for the "notable lists" printed each year in *Language Arts* or *Reading Teacher* and I regularly read reviews of new books in journals such as *The Horn Book.* Of course, nothing substitutes for holding a new book in your hands, opening the cover, relishing the pictures, tasting the words. One of the best ways I know to keep in touch with new publications is to visit a good bookstore. One teacher I know plans a bookstore visit once a week. She's established a rapport with the proprietor who pulls out new arrivals when she comes in the door. Visiting a bookstore will lead to buying books of course, but one advantage in owning children's books is that they go with you rather than staying in the classroom during the inevitable transfers that teachers make.

Building a Classroom Library

My classroom library started as a collection left over from my sons' childhoods plus the books left in the classroom by other teachers. Actually, those old classroom books were dregs; the teachers didn't want them and, eventually, neither did I. On a shoestring budget, my classroom library grew through the following tactics:

- I scoured garage sales, used bookstores, and an annual used book sale in our community.
- By using bonus points and some of my own funds, I purchased books through mail order book clubs.
- I requested donations from parents and friends, with a clearly stated "no strings attached" policy: I wanted to be able to discard at my discretion.
- I asked if monies previously allocated for workbooks be channeled to books for the classroom library. (When I first made this request, it was denied; the decision was later reversed.)

- At back-to-school night, I suggested giving a book to the classroom instead of gooey cupcakes for birthday treats (one paperback is less expensive than two and a half dozen cupcakes). Many families chose this option and we'd receive books inscribed, "To Elizabeth's first-grade class in honor of her seventh birthday." We celebrated the birthday by reading the book and remembered the day throughout the year during rereads.
- I purchased books myself.
- I checked out several dozen books from the school library on a long-term basis.

It didn't take long to build a classroom library. I didn't need lots of books nor did I need multiple copies for first graders. At the beginning of the year, young children "read around" in lots of different books, noticing words here and there, reading the pictures—generally acquainting themselves with books as meaning-conveying objects. When the children begin reading entire books, the books are short and so one child doesn't tie up one book for long stretches of time. Eventually I collected extra copies of some of the most popular books (such as Arnold Lobel's *Frog and Toad*), but my limited resources initially prevented this luxury. The important thing was to have a selection of *quality* books to accommodate the diversity of children.

Literature Genres

Many of the picture books for young children are stories. Sometimes stories have gotten a bad rap as in: "Oh, it's only a story," or "You're just reading a storybook." Gordon Wells observed the significance of stories: "Making sense of an experience is to a very great extent being able to construct a plausible story about it. . . . Storying becomes the means whereby we enter into a shared world, which is continually broadened and enriched by the exchange of stories with others. . . . Storying is . . . the way in which the mind itself works" (1986, 196–97). The great teachers throughout history understood the significance of stories. Stories are the path to learning. I chose stories for most of the classroom read alouds because the children craved them. However, I also incorporated other reading.

Poetry

During literature time and at moments throughout the day I read poetry aloud. I hope to make children poetry readers and so we just read and enjoy.

"Listen to the sound. What sounds do you like?" "What pictures come to you?" are questions I ask to invite responses. Sometimes we get up and move (dance or mime) to a familiar poem as we recite it together. I display posters with favorite poems and copy poems on chart paper for reading together and for children to reread on their own. The children have construction-paper folders in their desks and I provide copies of favorite poems for them to keep in poetry folders. The children select these folders to read during reading workshop; the familiar lines and rhythms support their reading.

When I read lots of poetry and invite children to respond to the rhythm, sound, and images that poetry evokes, children begin writing poetry. I've never been comfortable with the formulas for writing poetry that the old language arts texts suggested. The children's poetry follows the model of the poems they hear and only a small portion of their finished poems rhyme. Courtney published an entire volume entitled "Poems." On the final page, with the heading "Author Speaks," she wrote: "When I read poems, they make me feel something inside because they are so graceful."

Wordless Picture Books

For years I tried to incorporate wordless or nearly wordless picture books in my classroom. I urged children to tell stories, but they rendered bland versions with "and thens . . ." as they turned each page. When I understood reading as constructing meaning from the page, wordless picture books took on new significance. I explained to the children that in this kind of book the author/illustrator invites readers to use their imaginations and tell the story in their own words by reading the pictures. Then I opened Tomie dePaola's *Pancakes for Breakfast* and demonstrated (with a not particularly exciting rendition) how to look at pictures and tell a story. "Your stories will be different from mine and I'm sure a lot more interesting," I said before I handed the book over to the children.

Early in the year the children told original but simple stories. As they became conscious of story construction through listening to lots of stories, their stories took on more vitality. Children crafted each telling, expanding on each version, yet taking care to make it different from those told by peers, by reading illustrations carefully and looking for undiscovered details. They practiced their stories in order to present them to the group. Frankly, I was amazed at their intricate and imaginative storytelling.

In late February, Jeff presented his version of Molly Bang's *The Grey Lady and the Strawberry Snatcher*. With the ear of a true storyteller, he adjusted the pace, volume, and tone of his voice throughout the telling. "Once upon a time there was an old lady who bought some strawberries. 'Umm, what delicious strawberries! I'll take them home to my family.'" He turned the page and continued. The drama picked up as Jeff built to the climax of his story with the pace and tone of his voice. When he finished, a delighted audience asked questions.

Stacy asked, "How'd you think up that story, to make up with the book?"

"Well, I was thinking of a different story that was kinda boring and then I thought of this one. How I thought it up was, the minute I heard it, the minute she started reading it (referring to my introducing the book to the class earlier), I started making up my own story for it." The reading of wordless picture books is as diverse as the readers who bring meaning to those books.

Informational Texts

Recent years have brought an increase in quality nonfiction books for children and children love these books! Many of the informational texts that I read in my classroom connect with our social studies and science units, but I certainly don't restrict my choices to these topics. When I choose nonfiction books, the key criteria is accuracy of information. I also look for books that are well written, presenting information interesting and appealing formats.

Certain authors have a reputation for merging accuracy with an appealing presentation. Two examples that come to mind are Patricia Lauber and Aliki. One year I read Lauber's *Volcano* to the class over several days as part of our literature time. The children talked about volcanos the rest of the year. In our dinosaur study we frequently found conflicting information in books, which led us to check the copyright dates. Aliki's several books about dinosaurs became popular with the children, and they noticed that she had revised her books to keep up with current knowledge.

Novels

My family got a television set when I was ten. My students are shocked to hear this; they can't imagine a world without television. "But," I add, "we had the radio, and every day when I came home from school there was one half-hour program that I listened to—a different one every day." I tell them about "The Lone Ranger," "Sargent Preston of the Yukon," "Sky King," "Superman," and how I sat beside the radio and made the pictures in my head as I listened to each story.

"As I read this book without pictures on every page, this is what I want you to do: make the pictures in your head just as I did when I listened to stories on the radio," I explain to introduce longer children's books, the ones the children call "chapter books." As part of the opening of each school day I read aloud a section (usually about a chapter) from a children's novel. Can first graders sit for this kind of reading? Yes! This read-aloud time becomes an important part of the beginning of our school day. We talk for a moment about where we left the story and the talk and ensuing reading play a part in bringing our community together to move into another day.

In contrast to literature time when the children sit on the story rug, during novel read alouds the children sit at their desks and I sit at the conference table. We talk about comfortable ways to sit for long stretches without having to move restlessly: keeping hands still, and if they tend to get into trouble have the hands hang on to each other; feet flat on the floor; sitting straight; desks cleared and leaving things inside the desks alone. This may seem rigid but I've found it works in getting wiggly first graders to focus on listening. In a matter of days the procedures are established. "Listening positions," I announce as I pick up the book, and the children straighten in their seat and look at me beaming, ready to listen.

Each morning, before we start the next chapter, we recall events in the plot as it unfolded the day before, and sometimes speculate about what will happen next. During the reading we stop to talk about the story or to discuss unfamiliar words that confuse us or hinder our understanding. For example, when I read *Mr. Popper's Penguins* none of the children knew the term "icebox." I explained. When I explained "tripod," we made connections to triangle and tricycle. If I set up this procedure early by stopping and talking about a specific vocabulary word or two, the children feel comfortable to ask about words they don't understand as we encounter them. "I don't get that. What does . . . mean?" We stop and work out meaning. Over the course of the year we may read a dozen novels.

I begin every year with *Charlotte's Web.* At the end of the year the class votes from the list we've compiled throughout the year and chooses one book to read again. I've done this every year to demonstrate the importance of rereading books that most touch our lives. Every class has chosen *Charlotte's Web.* In the September reading, first graders identify with Wilbur, the helpless little piglet who depends on Fern to take care of him. By the time we read the book again at year's end, the children identify with Charlotte, the good friend and good writer. There are always mixed feelings about "poor old Templeton," E. B. White's "rat of all work."

I'm always on the lookout for new books to read aloud. A good review or two is enough for me to try a book with the class; I don't have to read it through first. Occasionally I start a book that I abandon. For example, several years ago I began a highly recommended book that just didn't read well aloud. One day I simply started another book. The children seemed not to notice—maybe they were grateful! Today I'd do that differently, though; I'd talk to the children and get their opinion first.

Like all the books shared in the classroom, we stop and talk about passages and lines that are worth savoring. Take *Charlotte's Web* for example. When I read about the children swinging on the rope in the barn I urge the children to imagine themselves on this swing. "Read it again!" Matthew cries at the end.

"I could feel my stomach jump to my neck." The children giggle at the geese and goslings repeating everything three times, and they delight in the complaining Templeton rescuing Charlotte's egg sac. When we read the chapters describing twilight and dawn, we recall our visits to the planetarium where we learned about the rotation of the earth as the cause of day and night; we also remember Barbara Berger's beautiful book *Grandfather Twilight.* Charlotte called the meeting of the barnyard animals together by announcing, "Attention, please. Attention, please." When I use the same phrase to get the attention of the class a child says, "I know who said that. Charlotte." The line becomes a familiar one that I use again and again throughout the year. "Yes, Charlotte? I mean, yes, Mrs. Avery?" replied a child one day with a twinkle in his eye.

Occasionally, after completing a novel, I suggest that the children think of a part they especially liked and that they paint or draw an illustration and write a short passage telling why they like that particular part. I put these pictures together into a class book, type the written words, and paste them on the page opposite their picture (which is the back of the preceding picture). The book then circulates to the children's homes on an overnight basis. Parents write responses on a page labeled, "Reader's Comments." A book of watercolor illustrations and responses after reading *James and the Giant Peach* were laminated and turned out especially lovely. One parent wrote, "This is one of the most beautiful books I've ever read—I loved these pictures!" When I read the comment to the class the next morning a child piped up, "Probably they're good because we made those pictures in our heads when you read the book."

And What About *The* Book List?

During one school year I listed all the books I read aloud to the children. I recorded titles the first time I read a book and made no attempt to note the numerous rereadings. The list was an eye opener; I saw that I shared with children only a small fraction of the books I knew and loved. At the end of October many wonderful Halloween and autumn books remained unread. How important my teacher choices were! The list showed how easily I could get into ruts. It also helped me see the total picture leading me to incorporate new authors and genres.

Lest anyone think I'm recommending creating a list of books[1] to read each year, this was not my purpose. In fact, such a list is anathema to a good liter-

1. Please note that I am not referring to bibliographies that suggest books on particular topics, or new books, etc. I *love* bibliographies—lots of them.

ature program. Much of the joy of our literature read-aloud time derived from the spontaneity and responsiveness of our selections. One book naturally led to another and another. The children requested favorite titles and authors again and again. I read books that connected to interests that surfaced in the class. Our processes of selection provided children with a model of the way readers select reading materials and how choices lead to further choices.

Keeping a list for one year was instructive. In addition to adding more variety of authors and genres, I noticed my list was lean on books reflecting a range of cultures; there were few books about Native Americans, for example. I found books to fill this void.

Sometimes I still feel twinges of disappointment when I pull out a book of which I'm particularly fond and the children say, "Oh, we read that in kindergarten." Then I remember I want children to know good books and say, "Wonderful! I love to read good books again and again. Let's read this one again. Just remember for some folks here this might be the first time they've heard it."

Good books bear rereading, and while I want the children to value rereading favorite books, it's also important to respect my colleagues and their choices. A unit on Japan is part of the third-grade curriculum and so I generally stay away from Japanese folktales; our first-grade China unit provides a taste of Eastern culture. On the other hand, I read *Charlotte's Web*, as does a second-grade teacher in the school. Rereading a book provides a different experience.

How sad to establish a list of grade levels for books or to "save" books. It's impossible to do anyway; children find books on their own through the library, bookstores, friends, and siblings. The world of English studies has a canon, a list of the books that everyone "should" read. We all experienced this canon in our journeys through school—everyone in tenth grade reads *Silas Marner* or *Julius Caesar*, for instance. A canon, or a list of books to read, immediately becomes inclusive and exclusive. To make such a list we include particular titles, genres, cultures. But the very nature of choice also excludes possibilities. Not only may we close the door to riches beyond our own current experiences, but also we may unwittingly restrict reading to the "tried and true," thus eliminating new choices.

I believe a function of reading instruction is to help children diversify, read what they like to read and move on. One reading experience leads to another and another. The interactions among a community of readers promote this behavior more effectively than an imposed list. Lists presume to know and then direct interests and sequences of reading behaviors without taking the growth of the individual reader into account. Inherent in any reading list lies the danger of orthodoxy. The list of books emerging for each class must be ever fresh and new so that the stories of children learning may likewise remain fresh and new.

Reflections

Charlotte Huck once said that one sure way for teachers to include literature in their classrooms was to say, "Research now proves that the more literature children are exposed to and the earlier they are exposed, the better will be their reading scores." Test scores are not why we read literature in my classroom. We read for greater reasons, reasons such as these below, which Charlotte Huck so beautifully articulated when she talked about the transforming power of children's literature:

- To make more human, to help us see the world from inside the skin of persons very different from ourselves . . .
- To develop compassion and insight into the behavior of ourselves and others . . .
- To show us the past in a way which helps us understand the present—not only the facts but to help us feel . . .
- To develop the imagination . . . literature helps us entertain ideas we never could have had . . .
- To take us out of ourselves and return to ourselves, a changed self. (1986)

Children listened to and talked about literature in my classroom. It filled their talk, influenced their behaviors, connected to all of their learning. Literature became the foundation of classroom life and I saw Charlotte Huck's transforming powers of literature present among the children. There's no particular list of books, no magic formula. Bring a broad range of books into the classroom, allow children to find their favorites, and read aloud to them.

CHAPTER 11

Reader Response

With daily writing workshops and read-aloud times in place, echoes of children's literature appeared in the children's writing. Words and phrases from children's books popped up regularly, and children began writing fictional stories borrowing characters from books by professional authors. Eileen, a child in that first class, wrote "Babar's First Tooth."

> Babar was a baby elephant. He lived in a beautiful house with his brothers and sisters. Babar was the smallest elephant you have seen. Babar had no teeth.

Babar's brothers and sisters called Babar names because he was little. Babar felt sad. Babar didn't pay attention to them at all.

One day Babar grew a tooth. He ran inside to tell his brothers and sisters, "I grew a tooth."

"We don't care if you grew a tooth."

"But it's my first tooth."

"We don't care!"

Babar went to his room. He started to cry. His mother and father came up to his room. They said, "We're glad you grew a tooth."

Babar stopped crying. He dried his eyes. He said, "I don't care what they say."

Babar marched downstairs. He said, "You better quit it!"

"Why should we?"

"Because I said so." Babar taught them a lesson.

"Now are you going to call me names?"

"No. We're not."

"Well good!"

Babar's brothers and sisters are playing with Babar now because Babar taught them a lesson. The End.

Eileen talked of how she got the idea for this book.

"See, I was looking through some of my Babar books and I got an idea to write about Babar's first tooth. In the back of the book it was talking about how teeth grow 'cause his little boy had eight teeth and he lost one of them and the boy was sad so he got a new tooth so I thought to write a 'Babar's First Tooth.'" Then Eileen read the lines that she felt were the best part of what she had written: "Babar's brothers and sisters called Babar names 'cause he was little. Babar felt sad. Babar didn't pay attention."

In a parent conference, Eileen's mother spoke of her daughter's apprehension about first grade and learning to read. Eileen's second-grade playmates teased her because they could read and she couldn't. The parents urged Eileen to ignore these taunts and reminded her that soon she too would read. Eileen's story, written shortly after she began reading, was not only about a young elephant acquiring a tooth, but also about her own growth. A book evoked a personal connection in the life of this reader. For Eileen, writing was the process for expressing that connection.

Eileen's classmates lauded it as "one of the best stories they'd ever read!" Good stories beget more stories, and in discussing Eileen's book, the children talked about times when they too had experienced taunts by older children. Their connections were far deeper than any I elicited through questions or follow-up activities to children's literature. Such *engagement* with books evokes responses that not only lead readers back to reading again and again, but also connects readers to their communities, and helps them understand experiences and make sense of their very existence.

This engagement with language, literature, and meaning began appearing regularly in my classroom, the result, I believe, of our reading and writing environment. The children read and wrote every day. They chose their books for reading and their topics for writing. And every day the children heard lots of literature read aloud and had an opportunity to talk about that literature. During that read-aloud time I avoided directing children's thinking toward adult answers. I trusted children's capacity to learn. They never let me down.

THE READER-RESPONSE EXPERIENCE

When I read the work of Louise Rosenblatt (1938, 1978), I found a theory about reading that articulated the intangibles I saw as my first graders read and wrote about and talked about their reading. Rosenblatt describes reading as an equal transaction between a reader and a text in which meaning is constructed in the mind of the reader. The particular meaning and the way in which the reader constructs that meaning are unique to each reader. Rosenblatt (1978) says:

> The reader brings to the text his past experience and present personality. . . . The reading of a text is an event occurring at a particular time in a particular environment at a particular moment in the life history of the reader. The transaction will involve not only the past experience but also the present state and present interests and concerns of the reader. (12, 20)

Readers bring to a reading event not only knowledge and understanding from life experiences, but also current hopes, wishes, dreams, biases, concerns, expectations, attitudes, and feelings that affect or create meaning. Certainly, readers must remain attuned to the text and responsible to what is written there, but diverse interpretations will emerge among readers due to the different emphases of different readers. And every reading or rereading is a unique experience eliciting a unique response.

Rosenblatt uses a continuum to help us understand the range of purposes for which we read. The purpose of a particular reading experience ("transaction," to use Rosenblatt's term) falls somewhere along this continuum according to the reader's "focus of attention during the reading event." At one end of this continuum is *efferent reading*—reading in which the reader's attention is focused on what will "remain after the reading," what will be carried away from the reading: information acquired, questions answered, etc. Rosenblatt provides an example of efferent reading: a mother whose child has swallowed poison reads the poison bottle for the sole purpose of discovering the antidote. The mother certainly does not pause to think, "Oh, that's awful tasting stuff. He might not like that," or "Interesting, they wrote that in alphabetical order." Her concentration is only on gleaning specific information to deal with the emergency. In less urgent examples, Rosenblatt notes, we also read newspapers, cookbooks, and history books with an efferent approach. Efferent reading answers questions of who, what, when, to whom, in what sequence, and so on.

At the other end of the continuum is *aesthetic reading*—reading in which *"the reader's attention is centered directly on what he is living through during his relationship with that particular text"* (25). In addition to "images or concepts or assertions that the words point to, [the reader] pays attention to the associations, feelings, attitudes, and ideas that the words . . . arouse within him" (24–25). This aesthetic reading leads to more open-ended questions, such as "What were you reminded of?" or "What were you thinking and feeling as you read?" Rosenblatt says the aesthetic is a more "literary" reading of a text.

A reading experience is rarely either/or—efferent or aesthetic—for as we read, we move along the continuum. We shift our focus of attention, at times responding with an efferent stance (gleaning specific information from the text), and a moment later, a more aesthetic one (pondering what that information means to us, how we respond). We adjust our reading purposes from that of obtaining information to considering the personal response the reading evokes within us as we move through a text.

I read the newspaper, for the most part, in an efferent manner, to learn what is happening in my community and the world. I read headlines, scan and skim news stories, putting together a composite update of recent events. I could give up this reading in favor of watching television news. In fact, some days I do. However, my purpose for reading shifts as I read the newspaper. Sometimes I read human interest stories or articles about people I know or parts of news stories that evoke responses, which in turn cause me to shift my reading away from a mere gleaning of information. My reading often slows down when I come to this kind of reading and I find myself reflecting on specific details and making connections to my own experiences or beliefs. I've moved along the continuum and am reading for aesthetic purposes.

For the most part, reading instruction has leaned toward the efferent position, one with right or wrong answers. We define purposes for readers by "setting the purpose" when we introduce a new book. Reading instruction in school tends to favor the *literal* reading of a text, crowding out the *literary* reading. It's easily tested and so we often base comprehension on a literal recall of facts. We ask who did what, when, how, to whom, in what order, and on and on.

Our literal approach to reading begins early in school. We read a story to our students such as *Goldilocks and the Three Bears*, for example, and then we ask questions correlated to specific reading skills.

- What did Goldilocks do first when she went into the bears' house? What did she do next? (In our educational jargon, this is called sequencing.)
- Why did little bear's chair break when Goldilocks sat on it? (making inferences)
- Why did Goldilocks run away? (cause and effect)
- What is the main idea of this story? (I'm frequently confused when this one appears in tests and teacher's manuals. I usually have to look up the correct answer in the answer key. One preprimer test provided a three-sentence story with a picture and then asked children for the main idea.)

All these questions have "right" answers (our answers, or "school" answers), and we expect children to provide those answers, thus demonstrating they are good readers. Even with more open-ended questions, a notion exists of what is the best answer.

One day in my own classroom I asked, "How do you think those bears felt when they came in and saw what Goldilocks had done?"

"They probably thought it was pretty funny," a child replied.

The traditional teacher response is to redirect the child's thinking, "Well, look at the picture. Do those bears look like they're laughing?" or "Would they *really* laugh if someone broke their chair?" And the child pulls back his reply and begins seeking out the one the teacher wants by searching her face, listening to her hints, and then submitting a more acceptable answer.

But on this day the child continued, "It's just like my little brother the other day. He sat down on his chair and it fell apart just like that, and he started laughing and we all laughed because it was so funny." The child went on to explain that part of the chair had become unglued, so the whole chair was weak, his brother was too heavy, and when he sat down it fell apart. Maybe that happened to the bear's chair too, he proposed; maybe it needed to be glued. This child connected the story with a memory and led him to some specific speculation as to why little bear's chair broke.

"It's the *experience* that's so important," Louise Rosenblatt said to me as we sipped iced tea on her back porch. I told her about Jeff.

"Jeff was reading to me and came upon the word *disgusted*. 'My Mom keeps saying that word a lot but I don't know what that word means.' I asked Jeff what he *thought* his mother meant. 'I'm not sure, but I think she's angry,' he said, and his voice tone switched from unsure to definite in that answer."

"Yes!" said Rosenblatt. "That's it. That's the experience."

Jeff understood the meaning of a word based on his experience with that word and brought that meaning to the story he read. The reading experience further developed his understanding of the word. I did not refine his definition; he'll continue to do so in his own time and through further experiences with reading and talking with others. Jeff's response to one word provided me with an example of a child learning to read aesthetically.

I want to help children learn how to read with more than mere decoding skills and literal comprehension. I want to help them develop Rosenblatt's aesthetic approach, to *experience* literature through personal meaning making and then deepen that experience in reading communities of discussion and acceptance. If Jeff learns to read this way with one word, then he will bring broader issues to his reading and come away with a thoughtful understanding that further enhances his understanding of not only the text but also his own life. This is the power of literature. It is not merely knowledge that we are after (though that is important and will develop too), but also *understanding*. Experience and reflecting on experience leads to understanding.

Schools and teachers have been accused of producing individuals who *can* read but who choose not to read. Reading instruction that focuses on literal recall with correct answers (an efferent approach to reading) may be one reason for this disinterest in reading. Mark Twain said, "The man who does not read has no advantage over the man who can't." First graders showed me that it is aesthetic reading that hooks readers. I found that children who read for aesthetic purposes as well as efferent ones become readers who *choose* to read.

After reading Rosenblatt I realized that all the talk that surrounds our reading aloud time, our "literature time," was a major factor in the children's reading development. Children talk to express *their* ideas, not to answer my questions. In the rich conversation that develops, they shape and make meaning. The talk extends everyone's understanding of a particular text. It increases the children's involvement with particular books, increases their natural responsiveness to literature, and leads them further into books and reading. However, I learned that it's not always easy to establish this authentic talk—not as simple as bringing the children together, reading a book, and asking for their responses.

Learning to Talk About Books

Literature time on the first day of school usually went well. I had come to count on this time as a way of establishing rapport with a new group of children. Then came the discouraging first day I described in the beginning of this book. If this group enjoyed listening to stories, they kept it well hidden. That first day the children had poked, pushed, and jostled for position on the rug. They had responded to the reading of *The Three Billy Goats Gruff* in tones of impatience and annoyance—not delight—because they were familiar with the story.

Then there was Elizabeth's comment about "nature" after I read *The Very Hungry Caterpillar.* This wasn't child talk, the way a child really talks about a book among peers. This was *school talk,* the kind of response a child gives in a school setting. I could see my work was cut out for me: to show these children that rereading books was important and could uncover new ideas, and to help them take the risks of honest communication.

On the second day I read *The Very Hungry Caterpillar* again, and this time when I read about plums I commented that I liked plums and didn't get them very often when I was a child because plums didn't grow in my area. The children began to voice their own likes. "Umm, I like chocolate cake," said one child, and then a succession of "umms" followed from the group with the mention of each food item. When I finished reading I said, "I really like the picture of this butterfly."

"Yeah, I do too," said a child at my feet, and I knew that she'd agree with whatever I said. But I continued, "It sorta reminds me of the butterflies that have been around our playground at recess."

"Yeah, we catched some," said Cory. And a conversation on catching butterflies and recess broke out. Greg said he knew how butterflies grow and he explained that the butterfly is first a caterpillar and then it makes a cocoon and then "hatches" into a butterfly. It was a small beginning. The children had responded to this book with slightly more natural talk and made a few connections.

To help children learn to talk about books in this way I need to handle my role gingerly:

- sometimes offering my ideas, but quickly diminishing their importance;
- accepting unconditionally the children's spontaneous thoughts;
- asking children what *they* think and then welcoming those responses;
- striving to understand and delighting in their ideas; and
- in the beginning, being cautious about expressing my own opinions.

Though my role is to be someone in charge, helping to manage and coordinate all this talk, I can't afford to be the expert with the final answer, nor the judge valuing one idea over another.

Our community grows around this literature time of reading and talking. The books become a repertoire of common experiences. I approach the entire process of teaching literature with an attitude of trying to *understand* the children and their ideas rather than attempting to change them to my views. When I do this, the children express their opinions more freely. I nod and reply "I see," or ask questions to help me understand. I presume that the children's logic makes sense and that if I don't understand, it is my problem, not theirs. I continually learn new ideas from them. As part of the talk and as a way of clarifying for myself and validating for a particular child, I often restate their ideas and then comment, genuinely, "I'm impressed!" or "I hadn't thought of that."

I ask questions for which I don't know the answer, questions that arise from the situation and the interactions among the children. Those questions become very specific because I've listened and I'm asking about what I didn't understand. Such questions prompt thoughtful answers. Sometimes, at first, children responded to such questions with "I don't know." I once supplied answers to "I don't know" responses. Then I began to suspect that "I don't know" really meant "I don't know what you want me to say, teacher." I began responding to "I don't know" with "Think about it" or "Let me know if you think of something." Often the best questions are ones that can't be answered immediately and, by leaving them unanswered, I encourage children to mull over ideas.

Of course one could argue that some readings are "better" than others. For example, a "better" reading of *Goldilocks* recognizes that the three bears are outraged rather than amused by Goldilocks' breaking and entering. However, it's the *experienced* reading that brings this response. Part of my role is to provide children with experiences with books and to encourage them to read and write. I still ask some questions or make comments to direct children's attention to inferences or details that they might otherwise overlook. This becomes part of the growing experiences they have with literature.

While I want children to become aware of the ideas books stimulate for them, I've discovered that, initially, questions such as "What does this make you think of?" are just too broad. (That's probably part of the reason I got that "nature" answer. I asked a vague question; I got a vague answer.) The children have better responses if I share my authentic responses to a particular line, a particular character, or a particular situation. My comment about plums during the reading of Eric Carle's book was specific and honest. I can't write or plan these questions ahead of time; they've got to come from me at the moment that I'm reading to the class, for then they will be honest responses to this particular reading. The children intuitively know this. I'm demonstrating how a reader responds. This kind of talk is very real: genuine and of the moment. It puts me in mind of a line I read somewhere once: Honesty and openness evoke honesty and openness in return.

CHILDREN'S BOOK TALK

With time, patience, and many invitations to respond, even the class that in the beginning had been so unruly, becomes adept at talking about books. They consider possible interpretations and make sense of what they don't understand by pooling their knowledge. They move back and forth along Rosenblatt's continuum between aesthetic and efferent as we read and reread books. Knowing that it's okay to express their ideas, it's only a few days into school when the children speculate when we read *Snow White* as to how to defeat the wicked queen. "Color the apple *yellow* and give it to her," is an idea they all like. When we read Eve Bunting's line about leaves chasing each other in *Ghost's Hour, Spook's Hour*, Matt says, "Yeah, I see them playing tag. I play tag." When the little boy in this story says that his *dog* was scared, the children giggle knowingly and Laura says, "He [the boy] was too! He just didn't want to say. He's too embarrassed." It is mid-October when we read *Where the Wild Things Are*, and a discussion ensues about what the wild things will do at the end of the story.

"Max doesn't want *them* to eat dinner because they're man-eating—they'll eat *him*!"

"Why are they man-eating?"

"They have sharp teeth and sharp claws like meat-eaters."

"They won't [eat him] because they're friends."

"They'll dance all night. That's what they'll do."

"No. They don't want him to go because he trained them with their eyes and they didn't want him to go." Each child's comment reminded me of an interest or experience particular to that child: dinosaurs, good friends, and staying up late at night.

A week later they loved Alvin Schwartz's *In a Dark, Dark Room and Other Scary Stories*, but after the story where a sweater appears on a grave Lisa says, "I don't get this one. It doesn't make sense." I ask the others what they think. One child replied and started a string of responses from other children, each thought stimulating the next response.

"I think the mother died."

"Maybe he was alive in the car ride and *then* he died."

"But the Mom said in the story that he'd been dead a year."

"I think the sweater sunk up on top of the soil."

"Maybe it was spirits." The notion of spirits hushed the group and they lapsed into shudders and spooky "oooo" sounds.

I held the book so all could see and allowed the children to do the talking, interjecting only to help manage the conversation from time to time (for example: "I think Emily has something to say. Let's listen to her idea.") or to give an occasional nudge ("What about this part of the picture?" or "Tell me what makes you think that"). I was glad I kept quiet. It was important to leave questions hanging, unanswered with no closure. Sometimes I have fought with myself to provide closure by presenting final answers, but as a learner and a reader with the children, I enjoyed turning the page and saying, very honestly, "Hmm, wow, interesting. Lots of ideas to think about here."

Chris Van Allsburg's *Two Bad Ants* is a book where illustrations and text are mingled and readers must tend to both to obtain a refined meaning. For example, the ambiguity of what ants see from their ground level allows lots of discussion by the children. We talk about different possibilities, permitting individual interpretations to stand, sometimes arriving at consensus when the facts and inferential information seemed overwhelmingly in favor of a particular conclusion. For the most part, the children remained open to new information and interpretation.

With every reading of this book, the children refined their ideas, clarifying and supporting their individual positions during the group talk. Then one day a substitute teacher read the book. The next morning the children pounced on me as soon as they came in the door.

"*She* said it was sugar."

"*She* said it was coffee."

"*She* said it was the kitchen."

"*She* said it was English muffins."

They were clearly annoyed with the absolute answers and what's more, they didn't want to read the book again. The magic came from considering possibilities, figuring out meaning from those possibilities, revising, refining, clarifying that meaning, and doing it all through reading and rereading of the book in a community that talked and accepted a diversity of ideas. Each reading was a new experience. With absolute answers the magic was gone.

Despite their protests I reread the book again that day, but pointed out that readers must be true to what author Van Allsburg writes, that when an author has written and illustrated his book with clues as Van Allsburg has done, he invites us to use our imagination and figure things out for ourselves. The children once again became involved in the book. Reading with a totally efferent purpose was a reading they could easily give up. Reading that blended aesthetic responses along with the efferent led these young readers back to this book again and again.

Making Meaning

Meaning is within people, not in texts. We construct meaning anew with each reading. A teacher told me of comments relayed by her English teacher who studied with Robert Frost. Through the years Frost's famous poem, *Stopping by a Woods on a Snowy Evening*, has been the topic of seminars and discussions, with a focus on its meaning. Frost reportedly told his class that he had no idea what the poem meant to him when he wrote it, that he could only say what it meant to him at the present time.

Patricia MacLachlan (1990), author of *Sarah, Plain and Tall*, says, "as a writer I trust fully that my readers will come to my books with their own pasts, their memories, their own views of the world. I am always delighted when readers make my books theirs with their interpretations, and I am just as delighted when my books raise questions rather than just provide answers" (220–21). The reading these authors describe is reading that creates readers who will come back to books again and again to seek meaning for their lives. They will be able to figure out answers for themselves using reading both as a comfort and a resource.

When children "make books theirs," to use MacLachlan's phrase, it's important to remember that their interpretations will not match ours. My students loved *The Piggybook*, by Anthony Browne, a story where Mom does all the work in the family. One day, however, Mom leaves and returns only when the family agrees to share responsibility. The book comes to a close with everyone happy. Then we turn to the final page for an added twist: Mom fixes the car. The children were puzzled by this final page.

"I don't get why the author wrote that last page. The book ends here when the Mom was happy."

The children brought to the reading their experience from an era when Moms may indeed fix cars and they didn't see the twist that older readers might. Eventually I shared with the class that adults often laugh when they read the last page and explained why. The children shook their heads in amazement. "Grown-ups sure have different ideas sometimes," piped up one little fellow.

Most adults love Elsie Minarik's *A Kiss for Little Bear*, in which a kiss for Little Bear is passed along. But Emily expressed disgust. "Too much kissing in this book. YUK!" she said after she read it.

Children pick up on the specific language authors use. Jon giggles and repeats James Marshall's line in *Goldilocks*, "'. . . your delicious, er, delightful granddaughter,' I just love that part. I think I know why James Marshall wrote that. I think he wanted you to know that the wolf is a tricker!"

This is the aesthetic reading of which Louise Rosenblatt writes. For these children, talk about characters, plot development, and themes occurred as more than abstract analyzing of literature. Such discussion developed as children became involved with literature and wanted to understand more of what that literature offered. The primary response was Rosenblatt's aesthetic, a response that connected to their lives. Aesthetic response led to consideration of details and specifics in a piece of literature because the children wanted to understand more fully.

Robert Coles, in *The Call of Stories* (1989), writes that the task of those who teach literature is "to engage a student's growing intelligence and any number of tempestuous emotions with the line of a story in such a way that the reader's imagination gets absorbed into the novelist's" (63). At one time I was so wrapped up in teaching reading that I defined "reading" as a repertoire of behaviors rather than considering reading as a meaning-making process that continues through a lifetime, a continuing process of learning to read that never really ends and that engages intellect and imagination. I want my classroom environment to lead children into a lifetime of reading by becoming aware of *all* the purposes for reading, not just the efferent ones of carrying away information. It is the aesthetic purposes that capture minds and hearts and lead individuals to reading throughout their lives.

CHAPTER 12

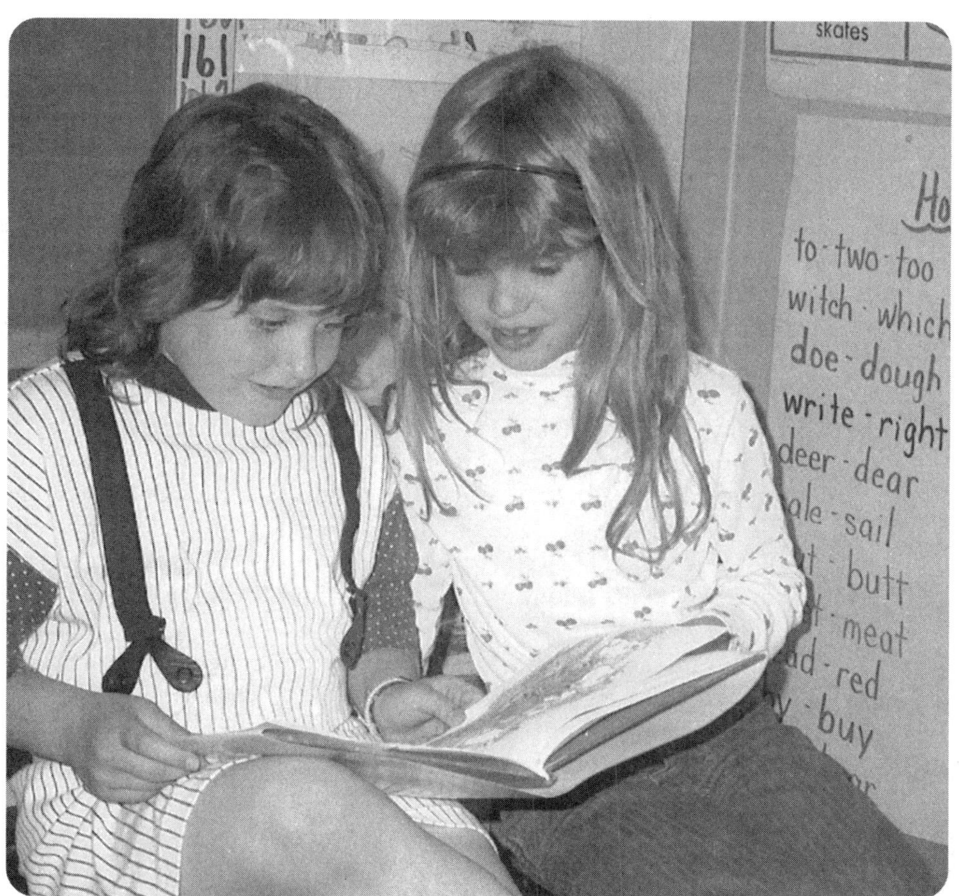

Children Take Literature to Heart

Soon after I moved away from the basal reader, I purchased a creative activity book on Arnold Lobel's Frog and Toad books. Well, it sat on my desk for weeks, months. Occasionally I flipped through it, but nothing appealed at any moment. A year later I sat down to figure out why I had never used this wonderful resource. Many of the ideas that emerged in our classroom conversations about these books had been formatted into worksheets. And, the puppet patterns paled next to the puppets the children and I had created together. What struck me as so creative now appeared as busywork. Why had I initially been so enchanted with this book? It presented a bridge between the workbook culture and the dynamic responses of children reading real books. At that time I thought I needed that bridge to make the shift. I never used the book because the classroom talk as we read and reread Lobel's books provided richer, more in-depth study.

In a similar manner, I initially was tempted to select books for reading aloud with an eye for how I might "use" a particular title. I came dangerously close to abusing children's literature. When I first saw Mem Fox's *Koala Lu*, I thought of using this book about a tree-climbing competition in conjunction with our annual field day. I would read the book and then we'd have a discussion about winning and coming in second and that everybody can't win a blue ribbon, etc. Fortunately, the children saved me from such didacticism. When I read *Koala Lu*, the children talked about climbing trees! What's more, their conversation reminded me of the time I looked out a second-floor window to see my three-year-old son Nathan swaying back and forth in the top of a young sapling—at my eye level! The children and I talked on and on about tree climbing from both a parent's and a child's perspective, a conversation far more meaningful than my plan to connect winning or losing to field day. If the *children* had made the field day connection, then of course the book could have facilitated a discussion on this topic. I might have even brought it up at some point, as long as I guarded against the impulse to use the book to "teach" a lesson.

The outward rationale for my need to "do something" with literature was to connect children with good books; the inward need was to assuage the fear that I really might not be teaching. I found myself falling into the trap of an activity-oriented curriculum that was sometimes "fun" but usually didn't extend children's learning as intended. Activities shifted the focus away from the richness of the literature to the activity itself and the children did not necessarily make the connections I presumed they would. Children completed activities for me or for a final product rather than turning to the literature for the sake of the meaning and insight it shed on their own lives. Activities roadblocked personal meaning making.

I led the children through an art activity after reading Burton's *The Little House*. The children completed the activity, but I could not detect that they had made the connections to ecological issues and urban/suburban environments that I envisioned. The final products looked uncannily similar. On the other hand, Aaron's sequel to Eric Carle's *The Grouchy Ladybug* became a play the children presented for their mothers at our Mother's Day program. The planning and presentation was steeped in meaning for everyone. In the course of a class discussion on entertainment for the program, the *children* suggested dramatizing Carle's story *and* Aaron's. The idea, planning, and implementation all came from the children. For instance, one child went through both books, listed all the characters, and went around to all the children and negotiated who would take what parts. Another drew the program cover. Still others helped classmates learn their parts. Of course the children needed my guidance with this production and specific resources from me at times, such as help in drawing the costumes they made from butcher paper, but the production grew out of children's needs and purposes.

Under the guise of curriculum integration, I came close to falling into the trap of creating rigorous follow-up activities that shifted the focus away from actual reading, with all the meaning making and connections inherent in that process, to the activity as an end in itself. This was part of my process in weaning myself from heavily programmed instruction. I had to make a choice. I chose to read and share books with children and to listen to their ideas rather than imposing mine.

Our Folktale "Unit"

For many years I justified classroom practice with statements such as, "The children loved it" or "We really had a good time." While child engagement brings child enjoyment, it does not necessarily follow that enjoyment brings lasting engagement. I strive now for depth of engagement from children along with enjoyment. Our folktale "unit" is one example of such engagement.

On Monday morning of the third week of school, I put photocopied finger puppets of the characters from *The Little Red Hen* on the children's desks and write the following note on the chalkboard:

> Dear Girls and Boys,
>
> Good morning! Please color the puppets on your desk.
>
> Love,
> Mrs. Avery

The children begin arriving and I greet them at the door. "There's a note on the board to read," I say. These first arrivals look at me, slightly puzzled, but put away their lunch boxes and sweaters and stare at the board. I move beside them. They look at me, then the board, then back at me.

"Can you figure any part of it out?" I ask.

"I know this says 'Love,'" says one child as he points to the word.

"And this says 'Mrs. Avery,'" says another with a big grin directed my way.

"You got it," I answer. "How'd you know that?"

"'Cause I already knowed the word 'love' before I came to school. I can even write it."

"Ah, I see," I nod.

"And I just figured 'Mrs. Avery' because you probably wrote it," says another child.

"I knew 'Mrs. Avery' because it's up there," comments another child pointing to our names on the bulletin board above the chalkboard. "I just looked up and saw it was the same."

"Good thinking. Let's read the rest. It starts like notes or letters begin," I say as I point to the first word and start to pronounce "dear" by making only the /d/ sound. The children are puzzled. "Dear," I read and continue across the line slightly enunciating the first letter of each word as a clue. When I get to "boys" a child calls out, "Boys! It's gotta be boys."

"Right! How did you know?" I ask the question that by now is familiar and the children giggle at the obviousness of the answer. I read the rest of my letter aloud, pointing to the words as I read. Before they go to their desks I tell them that they can help the children who sit near them read the note when they arrive.

As other children come in, the first arrivals and I help them through the written message. Soon everyone is coloring the puppets and chatting about the weekend. I move among them and hear Josie telling about sleeping over at her grandma's, Ian awing others with the story of his trip to Baltimore and the submarine he saw with "real teeth and mouth painted on it," Jeff talking about the ball game he played with his dad. Their talk is natural, relaxed, and loud. It seems they all need to talk, and I find myself wondering if they're listening to each other's stories.

I didn't plan the blackboard note as a reading lesson or the finger puppets as an activity for a folktale unit, even though my morning letters on the chalkboard will become part of the class routine and we will read lots of folktales. My primary goal this morning, which grew out of a strongly felt need on Friday, was to start our week off calmly and orderly. The way children enter the classroom in the morning sets the tone for the day, and this group had burst in boisterously each morning. A third of them ride the same bus and by the time they arrive at school they've become involved in an assortment of frays spilling over from older children. Unlike classes from other years that read, wrote, or created art projects in the morning, this group had difficulty managing this morning time independently. For a while I decided to provide a morning activity to assist the children in building a structure for working independently.

Some children don't enjoy coloring. Watching this group, I know some of them would rather play with blocks, but they go along with the coloring. Cutting out the little puppets and taping them together gradually brings a bit more involvement. (I suspect using tape has something to do with this.) The children admire Ellen's beautiful coloring job and the compliments prompt several youngsters to go back and add more coloring to their own puppets.

At literature time later that morning, we open Paul Galdone's version of *The Little Red Hen.* The repetitious language brings the children into the story and they chant along as I read. We come to the end and Elizabeth dramatically says, "My mom would just *die* if she had to do all that work! She comes home from work and flops on the sofa and says, 'I have such a headache!' "

"My mom wouldn't do all that work either," says Monica. "But my dad would help her, we'd all help her, and then we'd get done."

Elizabeth and Monica's comments stimulate the other children and they talk about distribution of work, Dad's cooking dinner, their own jobs at home. "Fairness" comes up, a concept highly valued by justice-minded first graders, and after some discussion the children unanimously agree that "it's fair that the little red hen didn't share at the end because those other guys didn't help."

"But," adds Ian, "if she had chicks, she would share with them because they are her children." The group supplies instant consensus with Ian's statement.

I found the children's discussion fascinating. They began by relating this familiar folktale to their own experiences, expressed strong attitudes about right and wrong, talked among themselves, arrived at a value statement, and concluded by acknowledging a commitment to that value. What's more, they did it without my input. I maintained an observer role and refrained from interjecting my opinion. In fact, the only comments I made were occasional questions such as "What do you think about that?" or "Oh, yeah?"—comments coming out of my own pondering that also served to encourage reflection within the children's minds. I am convinced that this frank and searching discussion would not have occurred if I had taken on the traditional teacher role: censoring, directing, and imparting didactic opinions.

The candid responses continue when we move on to the next book, Paul Zelinsky's *Rumpelstiltskin*. Stacy cries out, "Oh, I just *love* that story. Know why? Because I like when he says, 'The devil told you that!' That part's so *good.*" The last two words loll out of Stacy's mouth as she emphasizes her relish of the story.

"Yeah," chimes in Aaron, "and I like when he guesses his name and he says, 'Stringbones.' "

A chorus erupts as the children repeat, "Stringbones, Stringbones." They savor speaking the unusual name over and over.

At the end of the day I arrange the children in small groups, demonstrate how to use the finger puppets to tell *The Little Red Hen*, then ask them to retell the story themselves in their groups. I move from group to group and discover several complications.

The first problem arises as the children decide who will take what character. Some heated discussions take place while each group works this out. In one group, a single child takes the lead and assigns roles to the others. The mandate falls flat as mandates frequently do. "No!" comes the direct response from one child, "we get to decide too." Others agree. The first child tries to rationally present his reasons, but the group overrides him. After a few moments the dictator relinquishes control. He looks at me and sighs as though to communicate, "Can you believe them?" I shrug my shoulders to say, "Don't look at me," and move to another group.

This second group has selected character roles but is now stuck, unable to get the story started. I help the narrator get them going. All but one group has this same difficulty even though we've read the story several times; the children solve the problem by using the puppets, not to retell *The Little Red Hen* but to tell their own stories, which are blends of fantasy and reality with the cat, the dog, the mouse, and the little red hen (who, by the way, isn't red on most of the children's puppets).

"Once upon a time a hen was going to have a birthday party. 'We have to get ready for the party' she says. 'Everyone's got to help.' Now you say, 'Not I,'" Jackie cues the next child.

"No," comes the reply, "I got a better idea," and then, slipping into role, he says, "I'm going to watch TV. Do it yourself." And so it went. The children produced imaginative stories and negotiated the plot as each story developed. Only one group stuck with *The Little Red Hen* and they struggled to recall, sequence, and retell the precise story. It was also the least involved group and I saw the children glance around the room, puzzling over the energy the other groups displayed.

We included a folktale almost every day in our literature time and the children requested many for rereading. In their discussions the children made connections and noticed characteristics of folktales. When we reread *Henny Penny*, Brian noted that these characters "didn't use their heads—they didn't think." "Like in the *Gingerbread Boy*, those guys didn't use their heads either," said Matt.

"In the *Billy Goats*, the troll didn't use his head with the big billy goat. That was pretty stupid to get in a fight with *him*," commented Max.

"But the big billy goat used *his* head. He *really* used his head," Jeff said, and his eyes twinkled with awareness of the double meaning. He looked around at his peers.

"I get it. I get it," they said and giggled and repeated Jeff's words.

By the time we read a second version of *The Gunnywolf* in mid-October, the children had developed a rather sophisticated awareness of folktales.

They immediately compared the second version to the first, noting differences such as the jungle becoming a woods, the mother character a father. When we came to the end of the second story I asked, "What will happen?"

Ryan, so good at humorous one-liners, immediately recalled a line of poetry we all knew and piped up with, "Gobble, gobble, gulp, gulp, munch, munch, munch."

At the end of literature time that day I pulled out a sheet of chart paper and suggested to the children that we list the characteristics of folktales—what helped us recognize a story as a folktale. In a few minutes the children contributed the following ideas:

- There's usually a bad guy (villain) like a wolf, witch, troll, ghost.
- The characters don't use their heads.
- It usually ends with a happy ending.
- They often begin "Once upon a time . . ."
- They have patterns—like at the beginning they're all right (the characters), in the middle they get into mischief, at the end they get out of mischief.
- They have special numbers—like things happen in threes or there are three characters.
- They sometimes have animals for characters.
- They're "retold." We don't know the author.
- They repeat words a lot.
- Some people use their heads good like the little girl in *The Gunnywolf.*
- They usually run away a lot—like the Gingerbread Boy or Goldilocks.
- People forget or don't follow directions or break a promise and then they get in trouble.

We reread our list and put it on the wall. From time to time throughout the year, I saw the children look it over and chat about particular points.

This focus on folktales is as close to a literature unit as I get. Once, I gathered books on a theme and we spent a week or two reading them. The limitations of this unit approach stifled our thinking and our involvement with books and reading. I felt compelled to read those books on friendship or farm animals every day to the exclusion of a title I longed to read. More important, the children displayed a diminishing interest in the books. "Read this one," I'd hear from a child as she handed me another title when I picked up my theme selection. Units or themes now focus on introducing a particular genre of literature, such as we did with folktales or on the broader themes that compose our social studies or science curricula.

Children's Literature and Children's Writing

Author and teacher-educator Mem Fox says, "Writers don't improve their craft unless they have a real purpose, a real audience, and a real investment in their writing" (1990, 471). The responsive nature of writing workshop required highly tuned listening and observation of children. As I developed my skill in "kidwatching" (Goodman 1985), I noticed a richness of language development and learning connections emerging from children that caused my activities to pale in comparison. Children became more than just fluent writers who wrote longer and longer pieces. These children crafted their work and they learned much about that crafting process from my mini-lessons, from exposure to lots of good books, and from their *personal investment* in those books. As writers, the children picked up words, phrases, organization, and structure; they borrowed characters and explored genre. As learners, they explored ideas, discovered meanings, employed imagination, and made connections to their own lives—all through writing and talking, with children's literature as a fundamental foundation for it all.

Jody wrote about a firecracker that was a "dud," the word E. B. White used to describe the unhatched goose egg in *Charlotte's Web*. Lori ended her Christmas story of Santa's visit to her house with lines reminiscent of Clement Moore's famous poem: "Then Santa went up the chimney. He called all of his reindeer. The first one he called is Rudolph, the red-nosed reindeer was the first one that he called. Then Santa went off the roof and he said to all a merry Christmas and to all a good night!" Megan thought of the idea and then wrote a book patterned after Bill Martin Jr.'s *Brown Bear, Brown Bear, What Do You See?*, reminding me how once I would have had everyone in the class write such a book as a follow-up activity. How often, I mused, we take an idea that works for one child and turn it into an assignment for everyone, establishing more orthodoxies.

Stories such as Eileen's "Babar's First Tooth," where young writers borrowed fictional characters and wrote their own story, occurred often. Children also wrote personal narratives using Arnold Lobel's characters, Frog and Toad. Kristen wrote her own Frog and Toad book, for example, with three chapters: Frog and Toad Get a Cat, Frog and Toad Go to the Beach, Frog and Toad Play in the Snow. All three stories are about Kristen and her sister, fictionalized via the characters of Frog and Toad. Jeff used Frog and Toad to write a fantasy adventure entitled "Frog and Toad Meet the Volcano." The story begins, "Bang, swoop! went a volcano. It was erupting. 'Now what should we do? Let's go see where it is' said Toad." In Jeff's story, Frog and Toad climb a volcano, survive its erupting, only to discover after fleeing that they have ended up in Volcano City. The story concludes with a line reminiscent of the ending of Sendak's *Where the Wild Things Are*: "But just then the world changed and they were back home."

This is the way fiction emerged in the classroom. In the beginning of the year I sometimes banned fiction writing. The reason: children got into "fiction" with unreal characters who moved from one event to another. The stories never ended and when I pressed in conferences the child replied, "Well, this is fiction." Young writers needed more experience as writers and exposure to fiction as a genre before they plunged into writing fiction for themselves. With this experience first graders began writing fiction with complex characters and effective plots.

Literature often stimulated topics for writing because of the connections children made when we read together. Particular books reminded children of personal experiences. When I read Robert McCloskey's *Blueberries for Sal*, children talked of being separated from Mom. Josie wrote "I Was Lost," recounting an experience shopping with her mother and sister. When Mom went for the car the girls waited for what seemed like such a long time that Josie felt lost and began to cry. Ryan wrote a story about losing Mom in the drugstore. "I couldn't find my mom because it was so high in there," he wrote describing the stacks of merchandise. Jeff wrote "I Sneaked Out the Door" after we read Robert Kraus' *Where Are You Going, Little Mouse?* about running away from home. The children became so attuned to finding writing topics in books because of the personal connections they made, that when stuck for a topic all they had to do was look around at the books in the room to be reminded of something to write about.

The same book often stimulated both nonfiction and fiction writing. Chris wrote about ladybugs after hearing Eric Carle's *The Grouchy Ladybug*. This nonfiction piece explored his own theories about ladybugs.

> Some ladybugs are red. Some are yellow and some can be brown. I think ladybugs can fly. I think they have black spots too. I think they live on trees. One time I caught a ladybug and it was yellow and I kept it for a while then in a few days after, it died. Then I caught a red one and it died because I flooded it and it drowned. Then I asked my mom. I said, "Can ladybugs be different colors than brown, yellow, and red?" She said, "There can be gray ones too!" I said, "What color spots do they have?" My mom said, "I don't quite know right now. Go ask Daddy." Then I went to my dad. He said, "Go jump in a lake." So I jumped in the pool instead because I had my bathing suit on. My brother wanted to go in the pool too, but my mom said, "No."

Two months later, Chris wrote a fiction piece patterned after *The Grouchy Ladybug*. However, instead of a ladybug the main character is a honeybee.

The class was involved in a social studies unit on China at the time and Chris integrated information from that unit into his story. Here is an excerpt: "He came upon a giant panda bear. 'Wanta fight?' said the bee. 'If you insist' said the panda bear scooping some honey out of a tree and swallowing a few bees. 'Oh, you're not big enough' said the bee and kind of scadadelled out of there. He came to the Great Wall . . . "

Several years later, when children brought the term *sequel* to our writing workshop, Adam wrote "The Grouchy Ladybug Goes to the Sky," the story of events after the ladybug's encounter with the whale in Eric Carle's book. It seems the ladybug broke *his* wing when he was hit by the whale's tale at the end of Carle's story. In Adam's story, the ladybug commiserates with the fireflies about not being able to fly. The fireflies search out the whale and have a talk. The whale reports being unaware of having hurt the ladybug. Reporting this back to the ladybug, the fireflies convince him to try to fly one more time. The ladybug's wing has healed and he flies. Adam's story concludes, "He was flying. He soared higher and higher. The wind was in his face. He was the happiest ladybug in the world."

Greg entered school with an interest in the *Titanic.* According to Greg's parents, this fascination began at age three when Greg watched a National Geographic special. Greg's parents bought him books on the *Titanic,* which he shared with classmates. He and his dad read an old book on the *Titanic* I loaned them that had belonged to my grandfather. Then in the spring, Greg wrote "The Death of the *Titanic,*" which he dedicated "To all who went down on the Titanic" see Figure 12–1. He spent nearly two weeks drafting his piece and another week revising and editing. He organized the writing into chapters that alternated technical information with the human-interest story. He included a glossary at the end because "there's some words in here that some people might not know. So I explained them in the glossary." He also alphabetized his glossary (Figure 12–2) according to his invented spelling. Here is the story as it was published in the classroom.

The Death of the Titanic

Chapter 1 Getting Ready to Go

The *Titanic* is getting ready for its maiden voyage. Finally, everything is ready. Bands play. No one even guesses that this also will be its last trip.

Chapter 2 The Wall

If the *Titanic's* front got torn off the bow section, one part, the back, called the stern, would still float because there was a wall in the middle. But the bow would sink because there wasn't one in the front. But the stern could still go.

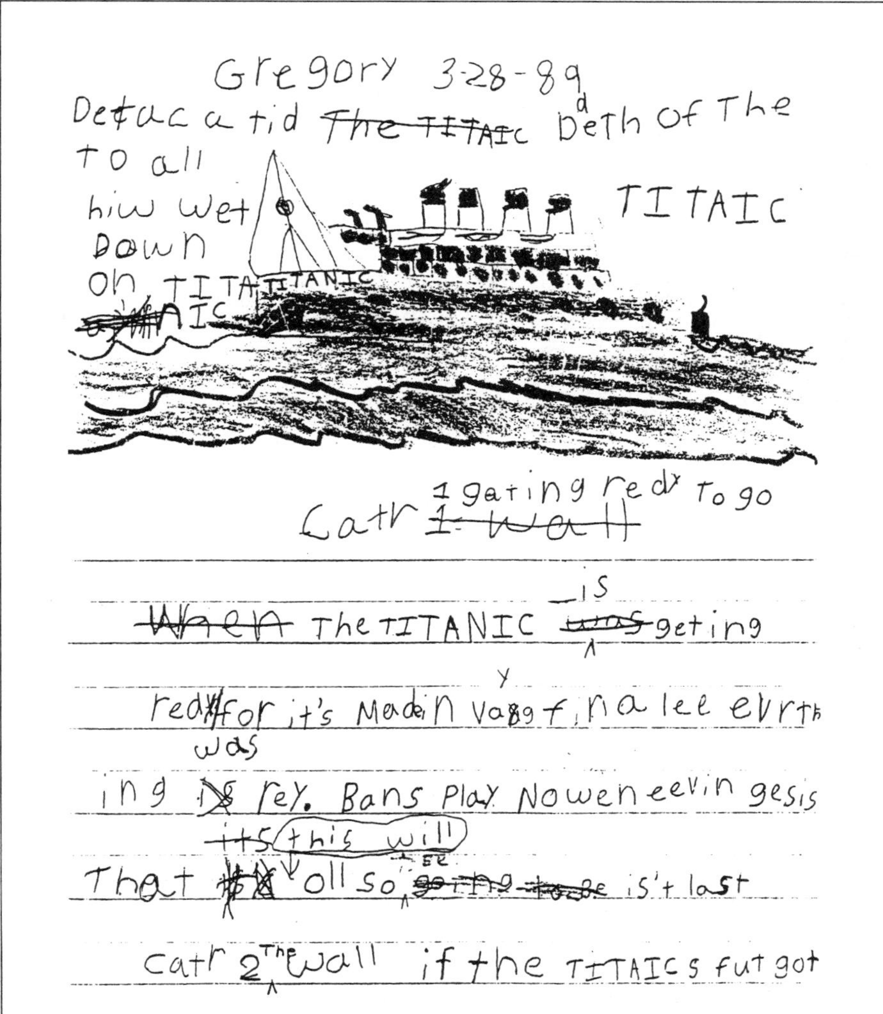

Gregory 3-28-89
Detuca tid to all hiw wet Down on TITAIC
Deth of The TITAIC
TITANIC
Catr 1 gating redy To go
The TITANIC is geting
redy for it's Madin vag finalee evrth
ing was rey. Bans Play No wen eevin gesis
That this will oll so be is't last
Catr 2 The wall if the TITAICs fut got

Figure 12–1

"The Death of the Titanic"

Chapter 3 Iceberg
When the *Titanic* had gone a little over half way to New York, the *Titanic* got into icy water off the coast of Canada. The sea is smooth as glass. The air is bitter, bitter, bitter, bitter cold. It is a good night to be inside but the lookout stays high in the crow's nest. Suddenly he sees a dark shape! It's a mountain of ice! And the *Titanic* is heading right for it! The lookout rings the alarm and calls, "Iceberg straight ahead!" The Captain tries to turn the ship but it is too late. The ice scrapes across the ship's side. Then the Captain runs down below to see if his ship is hurt. Soon he learns the terrible truth. The ice has hurt the ship

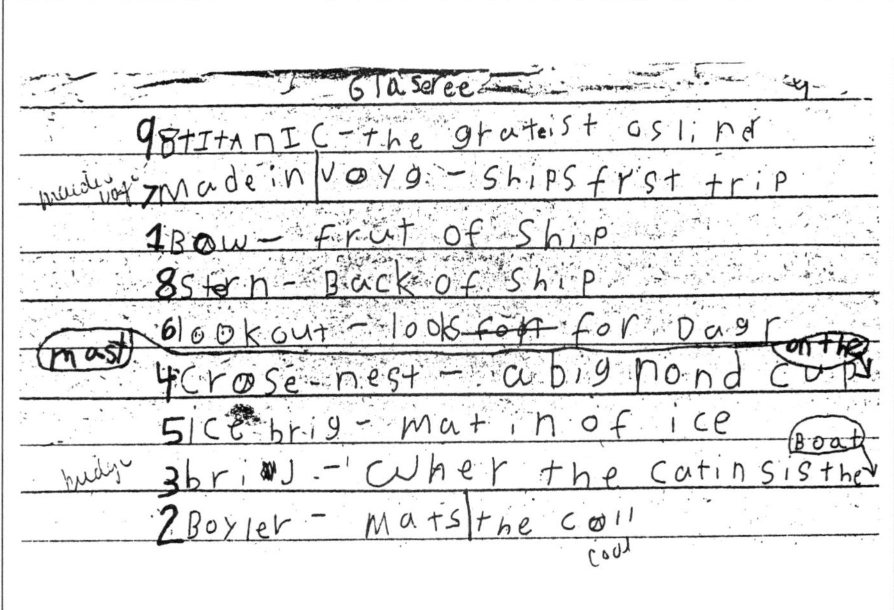
Glaseree
9 8 TItAnIC - the grateist oslind
7 Made in voyg - ships frst trip
1 Bow - frut of Ship
8 Stern - Back of Ship
6 lookout - looks for Dagr
4 Crose-nest - a big nond cup
5 Ice brig - matin of ice
3 brij - wher the catins is the
2 Boyler - mats the coll

Figure 12–2

Greg's glossary

badly. Over five watertight compartments are filled! That is too many. The *Titanic* is going to sink! Nothing can be done. Now the Captain gives his order. "Ready the lifeboats! Wake the passengers!" The Captain is worried. There are only enough lifeboats for half and there are 2,227 people on board.

Chapter 4 Water-Tight Compartments

The bottom of the ship was divided into sixteen water-tight compartments made with a switch on the bridge where the Captain steers the ship. A water-tight compartment is a place with two sides but no top so when it gets filled, it overflows into the next one. Two, three, or even four can be filled. Still the *Titanic will* float.

Chapter 5 Explosion in the Boiler Room

When the *Titanic* was sinking, the Captain wanted to keep the lights burning as long as they could. But when you leave the boiler door open you run the risk of water getting in and it changes to steam which makes a big BOOOMM!!!! Sparks flew up the smoke stacks. Outside the *Titanic*, sparks filled the air. Then the stern stood up toward the stars and sank.

Chapter 6 Rescue Ship
Soon the sky grew lighter. Thirteen small lifeboats remained of the greatest ocean liner in the world. It seems as if the help will never come. Suddenly, a light flashes and another and another. It is a ship! The *Carpathia*! It has come from fifty-eight miles away and its top speed is 8 m.p.h. Everyone is saved but the sea is rough and it takes many hours. Finally, it is done. Everyone is safely on board the *Carpathia*.

Glossary

Boiler—melts the coal

Bow—front of ship

Bridge—where the Captain steers the boat

Crow's Nest—a big round cup on the mast

Iceberg—mountain of ice

Maiden Voyage—ship's first trip

Stern—back of ship

Titanic—the greatest ocean liner

Ellen captured an essence of good picture books when she wrote "The Very Hungry Princess." In addition to the title echoing *The Very Hungry Caterpillar*, Ellen's modern fairy tale reminded readers of Robert Munsch's *The Paper Bag Princess.* Ellen acknowledged that Munsch's book influenced her. The text reads: "Once upon a time there lived a very, very hungry princess. Her name was Chickie. She loved dog food. She would eat it right up. Crunch, crunch, crunch. She always picked the right prince, but she had terrible table manners. Then as you see? She'd [at this point Ellen goes to a new page] . . . disappear in the night. And she has never been seen again." When I came to type Ellen's revised and edited piece, I questioned her because the piece did not make sense to me. Ellen told me, "You have to look at the pictures when you read this book because the pictures go with the writing. Without the pictures it wouldn't make sense." I was still confused. Her sketchy drawings didn't seem to help and I pressed Ellen further. "Well, I think you're having trouble because the pictures are still in my head," she said. "When I publish this, I'll draw the pictures that go with the words and then it will make sense." Sure enough, Ellen's drawings completed the story. In the bedroom of the princess she drew all the things the princess "likes" and on the page where the prince comes into the story she included his interests of playing the piano and reading. I remembered that James Marshall did the same in the illustrations of the bears' rooms in *Goldilocks;* our class discussed those illustrations in literature time. The last two pages of Ellen's book were designed to lead the reader to believe that the princess disappeared into smoke, but turning the page we see that in fact she took off in a spaceship! Ellen confided to me later that she didn't tell why the princess disappeared because she thought readers could figure that out for themselves. "Was it because she was tired of always picking the wrong prince?" I asked.

"That could be one reason," Ellen answered.

When we read Marc Brown's and Levrene Krasny's *Dinosaur's Divorce*, Susan candidly wrote the story of the breakup of her family. In her story she recalled a specific incident of violence that she had witnessed. With the permission of Susan's parents, we published the piece and both parents celebrated their daughter's writing. The writing also evoked much discussion in the classroom and several other children wrote stories of the divorces in their families.

In all this child writing, I recognize elements of autobiography—connections to the lives of the children, their interests, concerns, and experiences. I saw many examples of children gleaning meaning from good literature and connecting it to their own lives through writing.

Author Study

Many years ago, when I asked a group of first graders for their ideas about an author, the children said, "He made the book." Then they speculated that the author literally "made" all of their books by painting, writing, and sewing together each and every copy. Today, children understand authorship and are familiar with authors and illustrators and their styles. I introduce authors and illustrators during literature time and we notice their styles and discuss their processes. The connections children feel to these individuals deepens their appreciation and understanding of good books and good writing.

First graders notice an illustrator's style before they notice the writing style of authors. Tending to the work of illustrators establishes a natural bridge for examining the individual styles of authors. Also, a major purpose of author study is to provide the children with models of skilled writers and illustrators and to share tips and techniques of their processes. We are learning vicariously from experts about how to write.

During the first week of school, I pull out a picture of Eric Carle when I read his name on the title page of one of his books. "He grew up in Germany and he didn't like school much," I tell the children, relating tidbits of information about Carle that I've picked up from publishers' brochures, book jackets, and a magazine article. I add that he makes the pictures for his books by painting brightly colored tissue paper and then cutting and pasting the paper. "I read that he has drawers full of colored tissue that he's painted for his illustrations." The children suck in their breath, imagining such a sight. We put Carle's picture on the bulletin board beside us. We've read several of his books by now, and the children notice on this day that he often has the sun or the moon somewhere in his books. One year I bravely led a group of children through painting tissue and making collage pictures, Eric Carle style. The project was a major undertaking and one I didn't repeat. Such an activity is the rare exception in connection with author study. It's enough to add authors' pictures to our bulletin board and to share information about the people and their processes.

Through the years I've built a file on authors by collecting journal articles and publishers' brochures. Book jackets provide information and several reference books are available on authors, which any librarian can quickly locate. The author bulletin board continues to grow throughout the year with pictures of our favorite authors, many of them photocopied from book jackets or brochures. On the day of our authors' party, when the children first publish, I add each of their pictures to the bulletin board of authors. Author study is a rather simple, yet ongoing way to acquaint children with authors' and illustrators' styles.

Books provide models of strategies writers use and, in our talk as we read their books, I share information that I've learned about authors and their processes from conferences I've attended and my own reading. For example:

- Carol Carrick wrote *The Accident* about the death of their dog and *The Foundling* about their new puppy. This might have been one story, but they recognized that this was really two stories in one and wrote two separate books.
- Tomie dePaola's *The Art Lesson* is autobiographical but he didn't write a biography that tells *everything* about his life. Instead, he focused on one incident and told everything about that event. He also changed the teacher from a second-grade teacher to a first-grade teacher because it worked out better in the construction of the book and didn't change the meaning.
- Steven Kellogg's books about Pinkerton are based on escapades with his own dog. Kellogg wrote about a topic he knew well.
- Patricia MacLachlan's idea for the title of *Seven Kisses in a Row* came from her husband's ritual of giving their daughter seven kisses in a row at bedtime.
- Ann Turner first got the idea for *Dakota Dugout* as she pulled waxed paper off the roll and thought of oiled paper for windows. Then she

asked herself who was looking through this window, where was this person, and why was she there. She answered the questions from her own imagination, then researched life on the prairie to write her book. When she wrote *Nettie's Trip South* she felt the writing wasn't working and her writing suggested she try the piece in the form of a letter.

- Maurice Sendak's wild things in *Where the Wild Things Are* started out as horses. The wild things remind him of visiting relatives when he was a child.

All this talk about authors and their processes connects to writing and reading. Certainly the children realize that they themselves are not famous authors, but they identify with the processes of authors and try new techniques or strategies they hear about these authors using. Children who write every day identify with the ups and downs of writing. Frequently, mini-lessons for writing workshop are quick reminders of an author's strategy that we discussed in literature time.

The depth of involvement in writing led to the celebration of child authors in the classroom. "Celebrating Author . . ." focuses on one child at a time. I read the child-authored books and we make a poster about the child as author with the child writing about family, favorite reading, and adding a drawing. I interview the child about writing and reading, typing the words as they speak, then put these comments on the poster along with a photo. The interview was an important aspect of "Celebrating the Author" because the children articulated some of their own processes as readers and writers, boosting self-awareness of those processes.

Sometimes children write to authors. Chad wrote to Maurice Sendak in late fall. He loved *Where the Wild Things Are* but was puzzled over a line in the book. "That part about out of a week and over a year, I don't get it," Chad said. "I been thinking about it and thinking about it and that just doesn't make sense to me. What does the author mean?"

"How could you find out?" I asked.

"Well, I could ask him only I don't know where he lives."

"You could write him a letter," I suggested. Chad looked interested. "If you write and revise it like you do when you publish, I'll send it." So Chad wrote to Sendak. Besides his question, he told Sendak that he was an author too and that he had just published his first book. Chad wanted to send a copy of his published book. I typed his letter, Chad signed it, and we sent it off with the original draft, one of Chad's school pictures, and the published book. Several weeks later Chad received a postcard reply from Sendak explaining that the line in question meant that Max used his imagination. On the postcard, Sendak lined out a word and used a caret to insert, a new word, as Chad had done in his draft.

The children write to authors on their own initiative when they have a question or become so involved with a book that they want to connect with the author. Jody wrote to Aliki because he loved her dinosaur books so much that he had asked for nothing else for Christmas. She wrote her reply to him in England but explained in the letter that she would mail it when she got back to the United States so he would get it sooner. After he read the letter, Jody ran to the globe to find England!

I've never given a class assignment of writing letters to authors. Only a few children choose to write to an author over the course of a year, but almost everyone who did received a personal reply, and all of the class participated in the experience of opening and reading those letters. Author Ann Martin (1989), writing about letters she receives from children, makes an observation about the class assignment letters. "For the most part, these letters are short, follow some prescribed form, and lack spontaneity or imagination. Many actually end with, 'P.S. If you write back I'll get an A'" (31). To be meaningful to both the receiver and the sender, the letters children write to authors need to spring from real purposes that the *children* feel.

"Just Read"

The connections that are the basis of learning must take place within the children themselves. Teacher-planned connections belong to the teacher. In a responsive classroom, children become risk takers, make decisions, and take responsibility for their learning. They become involved in books and reading, in writing, and in learning without the embellishments of activities. My role is to set up the environment where connections can begin and then to nurture those connections as they naturally develop. The best way I know to do this is through lots of reading and natural talk in a classroom community.

There is also a push to teach skills with literature. Of course I am responsible for teaching my students the skills necessary for them to learn how to read, make sense of what they read, and appreciate literature. But there's a place for caution. Exposing children to a literature-rich environment may help them understand the structure of written language, literary conventions, characteristics of specific genres—all the demonstrations that books can provide—so long as the focus stays on the *readers.*

There is a fine line when it comes to teaching with literature. I want to take care not to cross that line. When I first obtained big books, I tried skill instruction as the accompanying guide suggested. I stopped reading and started talking about some traditional skill—I think it may have been rhyming words—when Natalie, seated at my feet, tapped my knees to get my attention and then quietly said, "Just read, Mrs. Avery." I looked to the other children and they nodded in agreement. The skill lesson had nothing to do with helping readers understand or enjoy the book.

Professional writers have voiced their concerns about the manner in which children's books are used in the classroom.

- Natalie Babbitt speaks out on her concern that "real stories are being used in the same way that the old texts were used. . . . A good story is sufficient unto the day. It is complete as it stands. If it has something to teach, let it teach in its own sufficiency. Let it keep its magic and fulfill its purpose. In other words, let it be." (1990, 697, 703)
- Lee Bennett Hopkins answered the question of a major publisher who asked what they might do to get kids to study a book thoroughly by replying, "Leave it alone. Let teachers read it aloud, have children read it on their own, and leave it alone." (1991, xiii)
- Louise Rosenblatt writes: "It is teachers who need to be clear theoretically about efferent and aesthetic reading. As they commendably seek to present more 'literature' in their language arts curricula, they need to be careful not to 'use' the appeal of such texts simply or mainly for their efferent purposes of teaching grammar or 'skills'" (1991, 447). Rosenblatt also writes, "The great problem, as I see it, in many school and college literature classrooms today is that the picture—the aesthetic experience, the work—is missing, yet students are being called upon to build an analytic or critical frame for it. No wonder they so often fall back on published 'study aids' which give them all the (efferent) answers required." (1980, 394)

When I think of responses to literature I think of Chris closing the book he's finished reading, hugging it to his chest, and staring into space with a quiet smile on his face. I think of overhearing Josie, holding Aliki's *The Two of Them* and whispering to Monica, "This is a really good book. The cover looks sad, but it's not sad inside. You liked *One Foot, Now the Other* (dePaola) and *Marianne's Grandmother* (Eggar), you'll *really* like this one." I think of Ryan coming to me in a somewhat demanding manner and saying, "Do you have any other books like this one, because this is a really good book. I like this book and I want another." There was no need for me to require these children to do something to demonstrate their involvement or to prove to me that they read, or even to extend their reading.

Children's literature authority Charlotte Huck (1986) wrote, "If you want to develop readers, you have to read to children, give them time to read real books, and opportunity to discuss them, respond to them, value them" (69). These authors and experts on literature know what's important in regard to children's literature in the classroom. Natalie was only six, but she and her classmates also knew: "Just read, Mrs. Avery."

READING

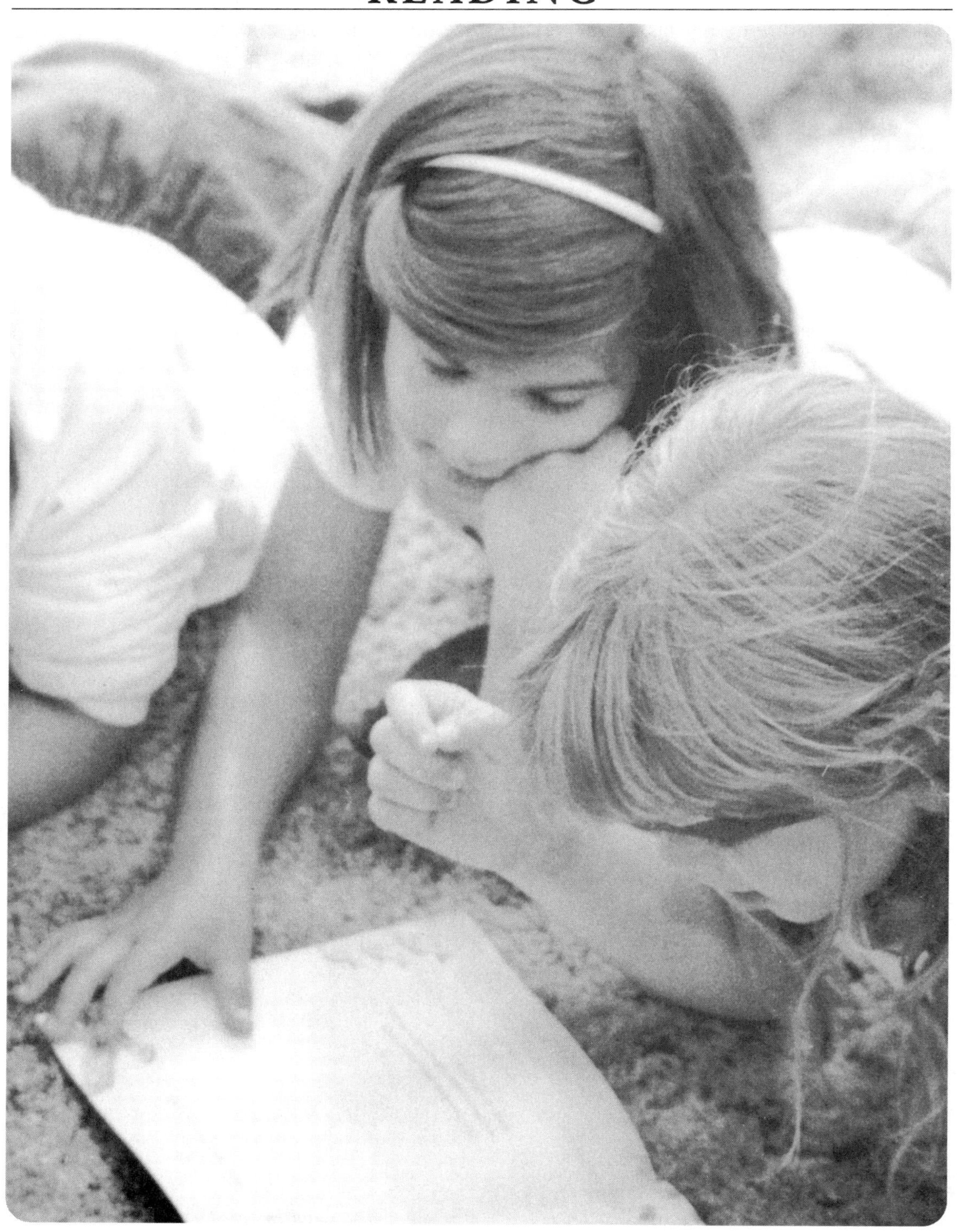

CHAPTER 13

Developing a Reading Workshop

"Can you read?" I asked my first graders during individual interviews the first week of school. The children shrugged, shifted uneasily, or looked surprised before they answered "no" or "not yet" or a hopeful "I'm almost learning to." When I asked, "How does somebody learn to read?" Nearly every child replied, "By sounding out."

"How does a reader sound out?" I asked.

Matt answered, "I don't know, but that's how people learn to read. I know *that*!" Matt's reply was typical of the children's answers.

Two children who said they could read gave different replies. One answered, "I looked at signs—you know like 'Stop'—and I asked my mom 'What did that say?' and she told me and so I could read."

The second child said, "Well, I don't know how other people do it, but I can tell you how I did. My grandma and my mom read to me and I started asking, 'What's that word?' and they'd tell me and then I started remembering and then I just learned to read! I started with little words and then I got into bigger and bigger words."

Certainly phonics is an important reading strategy for beginning readers, but the children's notion of *one* pathway to reading bothered me. I knew that good readers need a range of strategies even from the beginning and that no one way was appropriate for every child. I felt an even deeper concern with the underlying attitude that accompanied the "sounding out" belief: learning to read is difficult. I heard it in the grave tone of children's voices, saw it in their eyes, noticed it in their restless squirms.

In my early years of teaching first grade with a reading program, we devoted large chunks of our energy, time, and focus to perfecting the *skills* of reading—talking *about* reading—and the children spent little time *reading*. No wonder children thought learning to read was hard.

Research demonstrates that the amount of time spent on independent reading has a direct influence on growth in reading. Children who ranked in the 98th percentile as readers spent 67.3 minutes a day reading. Those in the 70th percentile read only 16.9 minutes a day and those who read 1 minute ranked in the 19th percentile (Anderson, Wilson, and Fielding 1988). More recently, the National Research Council produced a report, *Preventing Reading Difficulties in Young Children* (Snow, Burns, and Griffin 1998). The report is a "synthesis of research on early reading development . . . to provide an integrated picture of how reading develops and how reading instruction should proceed." The committee reached consensus on a number of items including the following:

> that reading should be defined as a process of getting meaning from print using knowledge about the written alphabet and about the sound structure of oral language for purposes of achieving understanding. (vi)

While the committee found that early reading instruction should include information on letter-sound relationships when children do not have this knowledge, they stated that instruction "must also maintain a focus on the communicative purposes and personal value of reading" (vi).

First-grade instruction, they stated, should provide instruction and practice with sound structures that lead to phonemic awareness and also instruction on becoming familiar with spelling-sound correspondences and common spelling conventions. They found that beginning writing with invented spelling helps children develop these understandings and that effective teaching includes focused instruction on conventional spelling and sight-word recognition. The committee strongly stated that instruction should include independent reading, including reading aloud.

Reading and writing workshops in my classroom incorporate all these instructional strategies. In my reading workshop, a large chunk of time is devoted to *reading* real books with the focus always on making meaning. Through focused lessons, skill instruction is connected to the process of making meaning as readers read and writers write. In these explicit lessons I tell children that this (skill or strategy—including letter-sound relationships or recognition of high-frequency words) is something that will help them read or write and I demonstrate just how this works. I continually guide reading development, as children work with these strategies, in individual conferences, small-group sessions, and in short, focused, large-group instruction. Children "practice" and develop reading skills during actual reading rather than with workbooks or skill sheets.

That first year, initiating a workshop approach for reading instruction raised my anxieties. What if children didn't learn to read? But as that year unfolded, my anxiety gave way to amazement. The progress of children in former first grades paled in comparison to the solid achievement of these young readers. Children learned to read by reading every day in a structured workshop that permitted me to present skills and strategies at times that were most helpful and meaningful for the individual child. This responsive approach required that I have a solid grounding in reading skills and strategies, a willingness to set aside preconceived notions of the "best" practice, and most important, the patience to observe and listen to children and then provide appropriate instruction.

As the teacher, my responsibility is to establish and maintain a structure that provides a secure foundation for learning and, within that structure, provide children with the specific information that will enable them to learn efficiently. But the key ingredient in making this work is a "waiting, responsive teaching style." I learned to teach by observing and responding rather than proclaiming and asserting.

Structuring the Reading Workshop

Working with writing workshops helped me develop the reading workshop. The two paralleled each other in their structures and in the way children worked within those structures.

CHILDREN SPEND TIME READING I begin reading workshop by establishing a daily time for self-selection of books and self-paced reading—a time for young readers to browse through books, to become comfortable with the process of becoming a reader, and to sink into the luxury of real reading. I move among the children for brief conferences similar to those of writing workshop where I demonstrate specific strategies a reader needs at a given moment while always maintaining a focus on making meaning. Gradually, I add additional structures to support learning needs. Literature circles provide a means for children to deepen their comprehension of a particular book through discussion. Guided reading groups offer a scaffold to support readers as they explore books and work on reading strategies. But the heart of reading workshop is the children spending *time* reading.

This time is far richer than our former Sustained Silent Reading (SSR) because children receive responses as they read and I integrate specific help with reading strategies and skills. Writing workshop and literature time also contribute to children's reading development by providing opportunity to use written language actively and engage in talk that deepens comprehension.

I once believed that first graders couldn't sustain long periods reading, especially in the fall months. The children showed me differently. The first few workshops last approximately ten minutes, but in a matter of days we work up to twenty, and within weeks, thirty minutes. By midwinter, there are days when the children sustain forty or fifty minutes and protest when I announce it's time to stop. Some days, when reading is going well, I extend the time, borrowing time from science or social studies, knowing that on other days these studies will require more time and I can borrow from reading.

I found that having a solid length of time was necessary. At the end of only fifteen or twenty minutes, children had just begun to sink into their reading; longer stretches enabled them to become deeply immersed and increase their investment. I learned that children need *lots* of reading time on a daily basis to learn to read and to want to read.

CHILDREN MAKE CHOICES Readers in workshops choose their reading material and make other choices too. They choose *how* they will read, whether it be by "reading" the illustrations, as Sarah did with *The Very Hungry Caterpillar*; or reading captions under illustrations and ignoring the remainder of the text, as Greg, Brian, and Michael did with a book on the *Titanic*; or singing the text, as Laura did with *Oh, A-Hunting We Will Go*; or practicing until able to read every word accurately. They may choose to reread, to move among several books, or to abandon reading they have begun in favor of something else. They choose the kind of books they will read, including the level of difficulty, the genre, and topic. They set their own intentions and purposes, such as reading to learn about dinosaurs with *Bones, Bones, Dinosaur Bones*, or to laugh at the plight of Big Anthony in *Strega Nona*, or to indulge in the imaginative world of *Rumpelstiltskin*, or to identify with the sibling rivalry in *Mufaro's Beautiful Daughters*. They also choose the strategies they will use to figure out words in order to get at meaning. They choose how to respond to what they read and they know that they are not required to "do something" after completing everything they read. Of course, they learn to do all of this with specific instruction and guidance from the teacher. Merely putting children and books together will not assure that they will learn to read!

Learning to make all these choices develops with direction and support. I don't just turn children loose. I establish structures and boundaries to foster wise choices; I provide direction to enable children to expand their choices into uncharted areas. I teach specific skills and reading strategies (including phonics) and help children integrate these into their reading processes both through teacher demonstrations and individual conferences with children as they read.

Teaching children how to make choices surrounding reading helps them become initiators of their own reading activity, choosing to read outside of school as well as within the reading workshop. Parents are the first to testify to this. In November conferences I hear frequent comments such as, "He's trying to read everything in sight. But he also knows what he likes to read best." At the end of the year, parents write comments such as this one by Jenny's mother: "Jenny carried from school to home her desire to learn. She reads everything she can get her hands on." And Stacy's dad wrote, "A conservative estimate of the number of school books and those purchased by me through a book club which Stacy has read *and enjoyed* would be about 250. A celebration in itself."

CHILDREN RECEIVE RESPONSES A major way in which reading workshop differs from SSR is that the reading workshop involves interaction with others. Beginning readers need responses *as they read.* Early in the year, teacher conferences provide encouragement and demonstrate ways to crack the print code while maintaining a focus on meaning. As young readers acquire decoding strategies and develop a vocabulary of words they recognize, responses enable them to articulate their ideas, thoughts, and feelings about what they read. This responding requires me to listen first, thus providing an audience for a child's ideas and wonderings, then offer suggestions or ask questions. Guided reading sessions planned in response to observations of children, provide a sub-structure for responsive teaching. Not all responses come from me; soon the children learn from my model how to respond to one another. They figure out words together and talk about the books they read. Later, literature circles grow out of these discussions. Responding involves the entire reading community—teacher and children.

A single, precise description of reading workshop threatens to become a formula that robs the workshop of its essential characteristic: responding to children within the context of a particular classroom at a particular moment in time. This literate teaching environment is intricately complex.

Starting Self-Selected Reading

Reading workshop begins on the first day of school. The first graders come in from lunch recess and settle in their seats. On their desks lay books each child selected before lunch. "I know you can all read," I begin. Immediately the children look away. Some begin searching in their desks for something, anything; others look around the room or stare at the floor. I can almost read their thoughts, "Oh-oh, I'm in trouble. She doesn't know." Or "What do I do now?" Or "I didn't think you had to read until after you've been in first grade." I point to the narrow strip of bulletin board above the chalkboard where I've mounted all our names. "What does this say, Beth?"

"Beth," she answers.

"How about this, Jason," I say, pointing to his name.

"Jason."

"See, I knew you could read." I continue pointing to names. After five or six successes, I point to the name of a shy child or one likely to be unsure. Hesitantly she answers—correctly. The children recognize names of friends or siblings. "There are other things I bet you can read too," I add. I write "I ♡ you" on the board, then run my hand under it and ask, "Who has an idea what this says?"

"I love New York!" cries one boy.

"Good try! But, it's tricky. Let's look closely," I reply as I point to the first letter and say, "This letter is an *I* and it says . . .

"I!" a child says.

"Right. 'I,' and the heart means?"

"Love?"

"Right again. 'I love . . . '" I run my hand under the words again to focus the children's attention to specific letters and say, "This looks like New York." (I write "New York" on the board as I speak.) "It has some of the letters—*Y* and *O*—but New York has an *N*. Hear it?" I emphasize the *N* in "New." Then a child says, "I know! It's 'you'! I love you! That's what it says."

"How did you know that last word, 'you'?" I ask in mock disbelief.

"I don't know. I just did. The other part said 'I love' so that part had to be 'you.'"

"Good thinking! 'You' is what makes sense, isn't it? New York would make sense too, but it needs an *N* and there's no *N* here. There are other words you can probably read too." I show the class a stop sign and they respond by crying out, "Stop." "For the next few minutes everyone will read the book they chose. One way you can read it is to look at the pictures and think about the story that the pictures tell. You may even find some words you know.

While you read, I'd like you to stay in your seat and not exchange your book for another. If you finish it, go back to the beginning and go through it again. You'll probably notice something you didn't see before. I'll come around and you can tell me what your book is about. I may not get to everyone today, but if not, we'll do the same thing tomorrow and I'll try to see you then."

This was the beginning of one reading workshop. Through the years I've started our workshop in similar ways, yet each one differently and each one in response to the children's comments and to what they communicate through their attitudes about reading. One of my initial goals is to help children view themselves as readers and to see reading as easy rather than difficult. In the days that follow, I strive to develop the concept of a reader as someone who makes sense of what they read, whether that be written language, pictures, or environmental print. Some years we collect words from environmental print and make a scrapbook. The children delight in reading Wendy's, Burger King, McDonald's, Tastee Cakes, Crest, K-mart, Kellogg's, Captain Crunch and noticing the differences in these names. They begin to see reading as easy and that sounding out is not the only way to learn to read.

Within a few days, the children learn the routine of coming in from lunch recess, selecting a book, and settling into reading. Some children want to select a stack of books and then hurry through them, believing that quantity means success. Helping them slow down and reread instead of going on to another and still another book encourages more thoughtful choices and, eventually, leads the child to probing beyond a superficial perusal. To manage this, I ask them to choose two books and to take their time. I point out that good readers reread their books and that when they finish they can go back to the beginning, read again, and notice things they missed the first time.

During the first week or so of reading workshop, the children sit at their desks and I come to them for brief conferences. I limit getting up to change books at first because some children will continually be up and around the room. As children understand my expectations, I allow them to sit on the floor and move to various parts of the room. They love the corners and cubbies of the room—under my desk is a favorite place! However, they must be within my eyesight; no crawling behind the coats, hiding behind a movable divider, etc. When this procedure is working well, I allow the children to read in pairs. At first I do the pairing, putting children together where one is strong enough to help the other. The children work out how they will read together. Frequently, they decide to alternate pages, with one child reading and the other following along. We read in pairs only one or two days a week at most. This cooperative learning is helpful but it can also lead to dependence and a loss of focus on reading. Later in the year, I sometimes ask a particular child to teach another to read a book that the first child knows how to read. This is a strong learning situation for both children.

With patience, persistence, and perseverance on my part, the children settle into reading. Many students begin selecting books with discretion. I'm able to conduct interviews with individual students and listen to them read a bit to me, procedures that help me learn about each child as a reader. I'll continue to do some roving conferences each day. I deliberately keep the structure uncomplicated in the beginning so that everyone learns that the major focus of reading workshop is reading. "Self-selection/self-pacing" is fundamental; each student takes responsibility for selecting reading material and reading it.

At first I planned for reading workshop to end with a formal sharing time, just as writing workshop does. Then I noticed that children shared their ideas and recommendations for books in very natural ways during the workshop, in literature time, and throughout the school day. Incorporating a sharing time in the workshop seemed redundant, a stilted repetition of what was occurring naturally. Eliminating a daily formal sharing also provided a bit more reading time. Occasionally we closed with a *brief* sharing and, frequently, that sharing consisted of a child telling the group about a particular strategy she had used that day.

The low hum of children's voices reading to themselves or with a partner pervades the room in reading workshop. First graders want to hear the words they read; silent reading is an advanced skill for far more experienced readers. Later in the year, many of the children read silently, shaping the meaning in their minds from the words on the page, but at the year's end the majority may still read by whispering softly to themselves. Moving away from the notion of silent reading was only one of the many traditions surrounding reading instruction that I left behind.

Responding to Readers

Conferences during the reading workshop are similar to my roving conferences in writing workshop. As the children read I move among them, stooping beside individuals. The focus of these conferences is on meaning and strategies to get at meaning. I listen to the child read and comment about the reading, providing feedback essential to that child's reading development. The feedback may include:

- demonstrating particular reading strategies and helping the child implement those strategies
- asking comprehension questions that deal with literal recall, predictions, synthesis, and implied meaning, making personal connections
- encouraging the child by validating efforts and successes

- stating an expectation of continued reading and use of the strategies demonstrated

When I approach a reader I often ask, "What is this book about?" or say, "Tell me about your book." Children make an opening statement and the conference is under way. Like writing conferences, in these brief conferences I listen and ask questions to bring out the child's ideas. I also may remind students of specific strategies we've addressed and encourage the child to try them. If a child seems confused with my opening comment, I guide that child into examining the illustrations with me and we chat together about what we see. "Read to me," I might say to a more experienced child, and the child reads a few words. If she stumbles on a word, I suggest or demonstrate an appropriate strategy or simply supply the word, depending on my knowledge of the child's reading development. There are no hard and fast rules; I listen and respond to nurture the reader. I "read" the child and the situation, using intuition and professional knowledge gleaned from prior experiences with children learning to read and my knowledge of this particular child. In all reading conferences I am guiding reading development.

Beginning Reading Conferences

These conversations took place in a September reading workshop with first graders.

"What's this book about?" I ask of a child with Bill Martin Jr.'s *Polar Bear, Polar Bear, What Do You Hear?*

"A bear."

"Ah, do you know which one of these words might be 'bear'?" I ask, running my finger under the first line of the title. The child pauses to look closely at the words, then points to "bear."

"You're right. That says 'bear.' How did you know that?"

"It has a *B*."

"Sure does. 'Bear' begins with *B*. This bear is white. What do we call those white bears, the ones that live at the North Pole?" The child looks puzzled, but the question is addressed to anyone within earshot.

"Polar bears," comes the answer from somewhere in the room.

"That's it. Polar bears," and I turn back to the book and the child I still crouch beside and ask her if she might find that word *polar* on the cover. She looks and then points to the word. "How'd you know that?" I tease.

She giggles as she says, "I just knew it. It begins with *P*."

"Yes it does. Read with me." We point to the words as we read together, "'Polar bear, polar bear.' Look at that! You read it all! Go on and look at the pictures and read some more." My goal has been to suggest a strategy and urge the child to apply the same strategy to the next pages on her own. The repetitious language of this particular book will help a beginning reader. Most books will not provide this support, but the strategy of using the pictures and then connecting with words and initial sounds can work for many texts.

Word-by-word accuracy does not concern me at this time. Nor am I concerned with presenting reading strategies to individual readers in a specific sequence. The central focus now and throughout the year is deriving meaning from the illustrations and print on the page. I demonstrate strategies; I urge the child to try them independently of me, trusting the child's capacity to select those strategies most helpful for him. I must encourage the child to risk, to plunge in and try, and so I try to maintain a playful tone and communicate my confidence in the child's ability to figure out things himself. Of course, to maintain credibility with learners, I've got to accept—indeed delight in—the results, whatever they may be. Initial efforts won't produce perfection. I believe that children develop language usage, whether it be spoken or written, by approximating the correct form of language in the beginning and then refining that language through usage. *Responding*, part of the craft of teaching, means "reading" the child in a particular context, enriching the context in a playful way, and gently inviting the child to explore new possibilities.

When I stop at another desk, a child reads hesitantly. "Read with me," I say. Then I point to words, the child points, and we read together. At times my voice drops out and the child takes over. When the child pauses I pause. The child looks to me when he's stuck. "How could we figure this out?" I ask. He shrugs his shoulders. "Let's read the rest of the sentence." So together we go on. "Now go back to the beginning and let's think what will make sense." We read from the beginning to the problem word, I pause for the missing word, then read the rest of the sentence. "What makes sense there?" I say as I point to the word again and begin forming the initial sound.

"Ball!" His eyes brighten.

"Right! Let's read the sentence again." We start from the beginning and read the entire sentence with the newly discovered word.

I stop beside another child, who reads an entire sentence to me. "I'm impressed!" I say, "You read that all yourself. How did you do that?"

"I don't know," she answers with a shrug and a grin.

"That's something to think about. How *did* you do that?" Children will give me the "I don't know" answer at first, but I keep asking. By leaving it unanswered, leaving it with the child and knowing that the child will internalize the question, one day when I ask they'll say, "I don't know" and then proceed to supply an answer. Soon they'll have a ready answer when I ask such a question, and eventually they'll say, "And you want to know how I did it?" and explain. Becoming aware of the process one uses and putting it into words serves to further enhance learning.

At Jared's desk I help him read the pictures. "What's happening in this story?"

"I don't know."

"Well, what's happening in this picture?" I ask in mock amazement, implying that he knows. Jared tells me about the illustration. Then I move to the next picture. "And this one?" More explanation from Jared. "Ah, so here the bear was . . . and here he . . . You can read these pictures. And you told me you didn't know how to read," I tease. Jared beams. "You can do this yourself, I bet. You don't need me to read this book and figure out what happens." Jared smiles.

And so I move around through the room, stopping and lending expertise, sharing a strategy, encouraging, helping children discover the power they have to think for themselves by working *with* them and then leaving them to explore on their own. It works. To encourage young learners takes time and patience and a playful tone. I keep reminding myself: Let's not take ourselves too seriously here. Everyone will learn to read in good time. I'm here to help, but I trust the children to do this without becoming dependent on me.

I spend only a half to a full minute with each child, thus keeping responses focused and short. Overloading the reader could easily occur because I see so many things I could teach at any particular moment. If I stay only a short time I'm not tempted to address everything, and I also prevent the child from depending on me for answers. Actually, I'm rarely giving children answers but rather helping them find answers for themselves; the children quickly pick up this model and use it with each other. Later, when Sara asks if she can teach Erika to read a particular book, I'll remind them that good teachers don't tell people the answers, they help them figure them out for themselves. I overhear Sara say, "Okay, now skip that word and read the rest. Now come back and read it all and figure it out." Or Justin, "Here, just cover up the end. Now what word is it?"

"Smile?"

"Okay. Now put the 'ed' on it. What's it say?"

"Oh, 'smiled.' I get it."

I frequently use a handheld tape recorder during these conferences (and play the tapes back as I drive home in the afternoon) to capture the patterns of our reading conferences.

Conference Questions and Comments

The conferences start with the child reading or talking about what he's read. In response to this beginning by a child, I ask questions such as:

- What do you think about that?
- Tell me what's happening in this book?

- What's that remind you of?
- What were you feeling when you read that?
- What were you thinking when you read this?
- What do you suppose will happen?
- Why do you think that happened?
- Why do you think [this character] did that?
- Did you ever know anybody like that?
- What's the most important part of this story to you? (or exciting, funny, etc.)
- Are there any words that gave you trouble in this book? How did you figure them out?
- What's another way you could figure out that word?
- What went through your mind when you read that?
- What is the best part of this book so far?

Sometimes I make comments to demonstrate responses, such as:

- Listen to those words again!
- I like the sound of . . .
- I like the way the author says . . .
- You won't believe this next page . . .
- Uh-oh! Guess what?
- I don't know about this . . . What do you think?
- Let me show you something that might help.

These questions and comments (and these are only a sampling) are similar to those I make when I'm reading aloud to children, and they always come after *listening* to the child. I raise them primarily to encourage the child to make her own observations, ask questions, form hypotheses, and modify understanding as she reads and works toward an acquired meaning. I hope that my responses help the child work independently, take risks, and develop her own strategies to get at that meaning.

I demonstrate one possible strategy to keep the child in touch with meaning. I keep these demonstrations short and move on. I can't demand the child use any particular strategy nor expect a child to do it my way. Rather, I want to share expertise and have the child determine what she needs to do. When I convey my confidence in children and trust their decision-making processes, I find that they usually exceed my expectations. It's like a parent showing a child how to stack blocks, asking the child, "What will you build?" and then leaving the child to experiment on his own for a while.

Teaching at the Point of Need

Roving among readers during the workshop becomes standard procedure. The pace and tone is similar to that of writing workshop, and the children soon know that I will be there to help if they are stuck or to listen to their ideas about what they read. As the workshop becomes an established procedure in the classroom, more specific instruction occurs in the brief, focused conferences. The following interactions between the first-grade children and me from one February day are typical.

Jeff is reading *Ben's Trumpet.*

JEFF: I was stuck with this word "stoop" but then I thought of "soon" and it has the double *O* in the middle like you showed us, so then I thought it's "stoop"!

MRS. A: Ah, so you got this word on your own by thinking of "soon."

J: Yeah, I could've looked up there—you know, at those double *O*'s on the wall, but I just thought of "soon" first.

MRS. A: Good thinking. What do you think of this book?

J: It's got a good beginning. I gotta read more before I can really say.

MRS. A: Okay. Thank you.

Aaron is reading *Building a House.*

AARON: [reads smoothly then stops when he comes to "cement"] I like this book because it's about building a house and I think it would be neat to do that—build a house.

MRS. A: You'd like to build a house?

A: Yeah.

MRS. A: Read to me a bit. [He backs up and rereads what he has just read, stopping before he comes to "cement."] Go on. I'll read with you. [We reread the last sentence together up to "cement."] Tough word. But look at the picture. And let me give you a clue. The *C* in this word makes the *S* sound, not the *C* like in "cat."

A: [He looks at the illustration. I begin uttering the *S* sound. He looks at the word, at my face, at the picture, at the word, and I hear him barely utter the "ent" from the end of the word.] Cement! Right? [I nod.] Cement. I just figured it out because that makes sense.

MRS. A: Good going.

Darren is reading *The Very Hungry Caterpillar*.

DARREN: . . . comed a teeny and very hungry caterpillar. [He stops reading to look at me.] I'm reading *The Hungry Caterpillar*.

MRS. A: Good for you. What do you like about this book? [I ignore the fact that his reading is not perfect.]

D: Um, um, I like he eated all them things. [He reads on and is stumped by "though." I supply the word. He continues reading but reads "pears" for "plums." Before he turns the page, I step in.]

MRS. A: Look at that word, Darren. It begins with *P* like "pear," but is this a picture of pears?

D: Um, I don't know. I mean yes, I mean no. I mean they're not pears. I don't think they're pears.

MRS. A: Right, these are not pears. These are plums.

D: Oh. I didn't know that.

MRS. A: And there's a second letter—*l*. Remember the "pl blend" we talked about?

D: Oh yeah. [Looks up to the bulletin board where "pl" is posted with the other "l" blends.] /Pl/. . . plums.

MRS. A: Let's read again. [We return to the sentence and, pointing to the words, reread and make the correction.] Good for you. Looking to the second letter will help you and the pictures will help you sometimes too, so remember to look at them.

D: Yeah, 'cuz anyway I like the pictures.

MRS. A: Un-huh! Have fun.

Jody is reading *The Karate Test*, authored by a classmate. He reads "wait" for "watch" but corrects himself after reading a couple of words further. He reads "knew" for "know," but the text still makes sense and sounds correct to the ear, so Jody takes no heed of the slight error. He reads "but" for "because" and quickly goes back to successfully correct the word.

MRS. A: How did you do that?

JODY: Well, "but" didn't make sense, so I looked and I thought "be-make" but that's not a word [he laughs] so I knew what the *C* was so I said "because."

MRS. A: Oh yeah? Interesting.

J: Yeah, because I put the two letters at the beginning together and usually I can figure them out.

MRS. A: What if it doesn't make sense?

J: Then I try again.

MRS. A: Sounds good. Tell me about this book.

J: Well, Jeff wrote it and I thinked I wanted to read his book. He does karate and it'd be neat to do karate. I might ask my dad if I can do karate but he might not because I don't think he ever done it, done karate.

MRS. A: So you chose this because Jeff wrote it and because you'd like to do karate too.

J: Yeah. When I read it to Jeff, I'll take it home and read it to my dad.

MRS. A: Okay. Thanks, Jody.

[I decide not to correct the misreading of "know" at this time but make a note to point it out in a mini-lesson that will address the letter-sound relationship and the context of past or present tense.]

Josie is reading Susan Jeffers' illustrated version of the Robert Frost poem, *Stopping by a Woods on a Snowy Evening.*

MRS. A: Oh, you're reading *Stopping by a Woods.*

JOSIE: Um-hum. It's very quiet. It's a quiet book; just sounds like you should read it softly. I like the pictures in the book—like snow's falling down everywhere. [She shows me the last illustration in the book.]

MRS. A: Ahh, yes. Nice. Quiet.

J: One thing about this book. He's the only thing that's colorful.

MRS. A: Ah. I hadn't noticed. Why do you suppose the artist did that?

J: Maybe because it was snowing so much, and if she made the man colorful you would see the man because he's the one who's talking.

MRS. A: Oh, so the artist wanted you to look at the man because he's the one who's telling this story.

J: Yes.

MRS. A: Thank you, Josie. When I read this book again myself, I'll think about what you said.

J: Mrs. Avery?

MRS. A: Yes?

J: You know that chapter book I was reading, the one you gave me?

MRS. A: Yes?

J: Well, I put it on your desk. It was okay, but it was kind of boring and a little bit hard, so I decided to put it back.

MRS. A: I'm glad you did. I think you're enjoying this book much more.

J: Un-huh.

Since the reading conferences in the first week of school, children make meaning from illustrations and from those mysterious marks on the page known as words. They develop a wide range of skills: context, visual cues, phonetic cues—all leading to making sense of the text. Their vocabulary develops as we talk about meaning and also through the listening and talking in literature time. The reading conferences play a major role in using a range of reading skills while children maintain a meaning-making focus and deepening comprehension. When I work with children unaccustomed to these conferences, I frequently find they provide quick replies to my questions and are not used to thinking beyond the literal meaning. To overcome this I ask open-ended questions and leave those questions unanswered when I leave the child. These conferences with second graders are typical.

Kelsey is reading a book about a box of lizards escaping in a classroom.

MRS. A: Would this happen in this classroom?

KELSEY: No.

MRS. A: Could you imagine this happening in this classroom? [Kelsey looks puzzled.] What if this did happen here? [No answer. I wait; still no answer.] Hmm, think about that as you read. [I move on.]

Ryan is reading a Henry and Mudge book. He tells me a bit about the story—a literal retelling of events.

MRS. A: Do Henry and Mudge get along?

RYAN: Yeah. [It's obvious he's giving the answer he thinks I want to hear, and he provides no reasons for his answer.]

MRS. A: What do they do that shows they get along? [He has no answer and looks baffled.] Could you read this book and find things that show ways that you know they get along? [He nods slightly and I leave.]

Dwight is reading a Magic Tree House book.

MRS. A: Where are they off to in this book?

DWIGHT: [Pause] They're traveling to a faraway place from the treehouse.

MRS. A: [I know that this is the plot of all the books in this series.] What's the most important thing that's happened in this book? [He has no answer, so I ask him to read a bit to me. He struggles to read one sentence, barely coming up with half of the words.] Is this book too hard? [Dwight nods.] Why don't you get one that's easier. [Dwight smiles and goes to find another book.]

Matt has come across the lyrics to the song "America" in an anthology.

MATT: I can read this; it's the song we sing every morning. But I can't read this part. [Points to the second stanza. We go through it together but the vocabulary is difficult even though he can decode the words.] Rocks and rills? What are *rills*?

MRS. A: Good question. Do you know any place where you might find out?

M: A dictionary?

MRS. A: Good choice. But I'll tell you I think you'll need a teacher's dictionary to find this word. Do you think you can try to find it there?

M: I don't know. [He goes off to get the dictionary. I return a few minutes later; he's having difficulty. I find the correct page.]

MRS. A: It's on this page. See if you can find it.

Matt finds the word, we discuss the meaning briefly, and I point out how it's located alphabetically. At the end of the workshop, he shares his experience and the definition with the class.

Reading is more than word recognition. Reading is gaining meaning and understanding. Learning the words and strategies for figuring out those words is for the sole purpose of making sense of the text. To help children do this I must keep my focus on *meaning* throughout conferences—and from the beginning of their processes of learning to read. We are learning how to crack the code *and* developing in-depth comprehension in an integrated process.

In order to respond to children as learners and to teach with a responsive teaching style I must *wait* and *listen*, then think and reply. Learning this style took time, self-discipline, and some self-reprimanding. Every time I came to the conference with preconceived notions of what I ought to teach, I missed the learner. When I listened to the tape of Josie's comments about the Jeffers/Frost book, I heard a metaphor for listening—and subsequently responding. To respond I must be quiet and "read softly." I think of Josie's words: ". . . it was snowing so much and if she made the man colorful you would see the man because he's the one who's talking." He's the one who's talking—*the one who's talking*. Josie's words echo in my mind and I know that to connect with learners, to be a good teacher, I must listen to the one who's talking—the child.

Choice in Reading Workshop

Choosing What to Read

Children select books for reading workshop from the dozens displayed around the room. On the first day the selection processes are as varied as the readers' personalities. First grader Jared picks a book about a cat and returns to his seat. He flops his arms over the book and watches the other children. A few seconds later he opens the book, quickly shuffles through the pages, closes it, and heads to exchange this book for another. Lucas and Brian sprint for *The Very Hungry Caterpillar.* Brian wins and shouts, "Look, I got the one you read to us." Amy walks around the room, picks up and rejects a couple of books, finally settles on *The Napping House.* She slowly heads back to her seat, opens the book and smiles at the contents as she walks. Danny walks directly to a dinosaur book, grins, and says, "I know which one I want." Melinda sits shyly at her seat until I take her hand and lead her to the counter and make suggestions. Ryan picks up a poetry anthology and says, "I got a big book. See how thick it is?" Jason asks, "Where's that book about the billy goats—the one you read us?" Jenny stacks six books in her arms, until I remind her that one is enough. "Ohhh," she protests, I want to read them all." Jessica stands with a finger pressed against her chin as she ponders her choice between two books. Finally she says, "This one," and picks up a richly illustrated fairy tale.

Children select books with varying degrees of thoughtfulness and for a range of reasons. Watching first graders select books provides clues about each child's experiences with books and with making decisions. Learning to make decisions is an important part of this classroom. Children will be selecting their own reading material, and from the beginning of school I work with them as they learn to make choices.

Jackie chooses books with ease. Her mother has read to her since birth and Jackie is familiar with lots of titles. She selects books for her family's read-aloud sessions each evening. She knows how to read the pictures for a sense of story, understands the role of print in conveying the story, and grasps details of format such as the left-to-right, top-to-bottom flow of print. She needs little assistance from me other than to guide her to choices she has not yet found. Jenny also has experiences with books but she wants to read them all and hurriedly. Part of this is her personality, for I've noticed that she wants to be first, to hurry through any task, and to claim success if she has done "a lot." I respond to Jenny by asking her to choose one and set the others aside for later. "Good readers take their time," I say. "Look through this book carefully and, if you finish before our time's done, go back through it again and look for things you missed the first time."

Jared has few experiences with books and he opens his book from the back cover. Within thirty seconds he announces, "I'm done," and gets up for another book. To help Jared with his random selection process, I direct his choices by selecting two or three titles and then say, "Choose one of these." When he has difficulty deciding, I hand him one title saying, "Try this one. It's a favorite of mine. I think you might like it too." In the next few days I'll do some mini-lessons on how to choose books, suggesting that the children select books that appeal to their individual interests and look interesting and possible to read, either through pictures or text. In addition, I'll observe the children and help them individually.

As children begin learning to read entire books, they sometimes have difficulty choosing books they can manage. I address this minor hurdle by recommending specific books to children. "Try this one. Let me know how it goes," I say. Sometimes a child comes back a few minutes later and says, "This book's too hard," and then we look for another together. Other times the youngster plunges in and later reports, as Stacy did, "You know that book you gave me? Well, it's a really good book. I can read it!"

A few children believe that they must always read challenging books, as one little boy announces while searching the room for such a book for himself. "It's all right to read some hard books and some easy ones too," I say. "Every good reader does that. Good readers choose different books at different times. At night in bed I like to read easier books." I suggest that the way to decide is to read a little of the book to get an idea of how hard it is. I make a comparison to the three bears: "Some books are easy. Some books are hard. And some books are just right. You have to decide which one you want and remember to mix them up. It probably wouldn't be a good idea to read all hard books or all easy books." The children catch on quickly. One day Julie says, "I can read this book, even though it's a pretty hard book, because you read it to us. When I finish, I'll choose something easier to give my mind a rest."

In a group brainstorming session in the spring my first graders compiled a list of their strategies of how to select a book that very much paralleled the strategies adults use for book selection.

How to Choose a Book

1. Ask another person, "What book have you read?"
2. Look in the book to see if it's a book I like—the pictures, the title—or to see if it's too hard or sometimes too easy.
3. I read the first page and if I get stuck on too many words it's too hard. It's like a test. If it's too many easy words, like *Arthur's Nose*, put it back and get *Ghost's House, Spook's Hour* and it's in between.
4. I ask the librarian for really good books that I know or sometimes I ask for good books.

5. I like books by certain authors—like Jane Yolen.
6. Read a little and see if it's interesting.
7. Look for books I've listened to.
8. Ask somebody what a book is like—what they think of it.
9. I look for books with big words (big print), like *Mortimer*.
10. Look around the room for books that look really interesting to me.
11. I look at the cover, the title, and the pages to see if it looks good.
12. Sometimes you change your mind later (after you put it back) and get it.
13. If the cover and title sound neat I try it and if I don't like it I put it back.
14. Pick books by authors I like or books I think are funny.
15. Everyone likes different books to read. They have to be interested in it.

Not every child used all these selection strategies; a strategy that was significant to one child was less important to another. But the same was true for adults. Readers choose books through a range of strategies, and validating individual strategies is important.

Choosing to abandon a book is just as important as choosing to read it. With so many good books available, I want children spending their time with a book they find satisfying. From the beginning, I teach them to set aside books that they don't like or that are too difficult or that they just can't get into; they can always come back to a book later.

I also make basal readers from the district's adopted reading program available as choices for the children's reading. The children quickly dismiss the preprimers. One little boy summed up the reason one day: "Who would read this book? I mean, I don't get it. It just keeps saying the same words over and over. It doesn't make any *sense*." However, the "first readers" intrigue the children for a time because they are "thick books." Children choose these books because when reading them they perceive themselves as accomplished readers. After a time, as one by one the children discover that these books contain only a few stories that match their individual interests, the enthusiasm for these "thick books" wanes. One day two children decided to read a story together. One picked up the paperback version and, not finding a second copy, the other located the same title in the basal reader. Soon they realized they were reading different texts. The children were outraged. "How could someone do that to an author's story!" they demanded. "You can't change what an author writes. It's his *writing*! Only the author can change it."

"How did you choose this book?" is a question I ask over and over. In the beginning, the children often respond with "I don't know. I just picked it." I nod without comment or sometimes say, "Umm. That's something you might want to notice next time—how you choose your book." When children have heard the question over and over they begin answering.

"It looked kinda good when I saw the pictures, so then I tried it and I thought I'd like to read it."

"Melanie told me it was a good book and so I thinked I'd like it too."

"I really like James Marshall books so I figured I'd like this one."

"I tried out the words, I read a little bit, and I thought I could learn to read it."

"'Cause it's funny. I like funny books."

"I have a cat so I just wanted to read a book about a cat."

The school librarian reported that the children use their knowledge of books to choose their library books. "They ask for specific titles or authors. These kids know what they want," she said. Readers who have learned to make choices take responsibility for those choices and actively seek out the books they want to read.

Choosing How to Read

Children make other choices surrounding their reading. Selecting their own reading material helps them develop a range of purposes for reading and a commitment to the reading. They explore reading strategies, moving among many purposes and strategies as they read and making choices appropriate to the material and their interests. The heightened self-awareness is evident in the comments they make when I ask how their reading is going.

Melinda and Elizabeth read a book over and over. "We're practicing this book so that we can read it to the class with lots of expression—so people will want to listen," they say.

"I been reading this book of riddles and I'm just skipping around 'cuz that way I find the funniest ones. I don't read it one right after the other. That got boring to me," Jeff comments.

Michael, Matt, and Greg pore over a thick volume on the *Titanic*, seeking out interesting pictures. "Look, it's a clock. Oh, it's the same one as here, in this picture, before it sunk." They read the caption under both pictures and confirm their observation. It takes all three of them to figure out the words in this one-sentence caption, using the picture, letter-sound connections, and most of all, their ideas of what makes sense. When I ask what this book is about, they flip to the cover and read the title. Title, pictures, and captions serve their meaning-making needs. The text is far too difficult for them at this time and they pay it no heed.

"I'm trying to read *Charlotte's Web* because I love this book and I been wanting to read it for a long time. There's some words I don't know, but I can still read most of it," says Lori.

Jody browses through a book about trains, a passion of his. He chooses a section about old locomotives and painstakingly reads the first sentence, then shifts to the labels on the drawing of an old train. "I'm reading the parts of old trains. It's like when I been on the Strasburg Railroad and I remember some of them parts and some I don't."

Kelly spends the entire workshop engrossed in her book. "This book's so good I was just reading and reading to find out what was going to happen to the girl. I didn't even hear you say reading time was over," says an amazed Kelly.

Jason and Edward read poems from their poetry folders. Jason comments, "Me and him are reading poems in our poetry folders because we both like poems. We know how to read all of these," Jason points to one stack, "and these are a little hard, and these we don't know [about] yet. We didn't try them."

The children read difficult books because these are books they are longing to read for themselves. They read rapidly and they read slowly according their interest, experience, skill level, and the pace of a particular story. They reread favorite books, read parts of books, or practice reading texts because these strategies connect with the needs they feel or the meaning they desire. Underlying all of the purposes for reading is meaning that connects to the reader's experiences or needs. The meaning-making purposes of reading influence the strategies readers use as they tackle unknown words.

Elizabeth says, "I skipped that word because it was too hard and I just keep reading and then I figured out what it was."

Stacy and Emily come upon the name Mr. Vinegar in a story they read together. "What's his name?" they ask me when I stop to confer with them. After I tell them, Stacy says, "Oh, because we didn't know so we just said, 'Mr. Whatever.'"

Greg carries his book to the chalkboard and gazes at the list of vowel digraphs we've compiled over the course of several short whole-group presentations. "Hmm," he says, "a-i says *A*." He looks back to his book, hunts for a word with his finger, and then puts the digraph sound between an *M* and an *N*, reads the surrounding words, and then suddenly says, "main! That's it, main." He heads back to his seat, reading as he walks.

Amy covers up the first four letters of "whenever" and then says to herself, "Ev . . . ever. Whenever."

Max comes to me, leading a small group of youngsters. "Mrs. Avery, we need to ask you this word. We can't figure it out and we asked lots of people, even Monica." I tell them the word and Max says, "Ohhh. We thought of a couple words it could be but those didn't make sense." The small group and I chat about why the familiar strategies didn't work in this particular case. "That's the way it is," I explain. "This language of ours just doesn't always work the way it seems it ought to. You learn one rule and then right away there's an exception to that rule. You just have to remember that rules don't always work and keep trying out different ways."

"Yup," grins Max. "Thanks," he says, and the group goes back to their reading. I muse over his words ". . . and we even asked Monica." No one ever proclaimed Monica to be the best reader in the room, but the children knew each other's strengths and where to turn for help. From the beginning I urged them to try to solve difficulties and answer questions on their own and use me as the last resource. These children knew how to make decisions because they worked in an environment where they continually made choices and learned from both error and success without penalty or extrinsic reward.

Initially, children look to me to provide the answers for the dilemmas they encounter, whether it be choosing books or knowing how to begin reading those books or learning individual words. I supply solutions to those problems, for this is certainly not a guessing-game environment. However, I provide solutions in the form of tips, suggestions, or invitations by demonstrating possible methods to solve particular dilemmas. As I work with individuals, I show children how to apply those methods as they read. I want to avoid presuming that a particular solution is appropriate for any individual. Children become skillful readers when presented with many strategies and with opportunities to choose those most effective for them. I continually suggest new and untried books and reading strategies for their consideration and they learn to make thoughtful choices.

Children's author Katherine Paterson (1990) wrote, "I believe in freedom of choice as much as anyone. But the young don't know the rich variety of choices that are available. Someone they trust must be wise and bold enough to hand them something they would never have known to choose" (150).

During the early days of reading workshop, I was uncomfortable letting children make their own choices; I saw the needs of one as the needs of all. Programmed instruction had lulled me into believing that success depended on every student reading every story and learning every skill in specified sequence. Really letting go of that was one of the hardest things I had to do! At first I required children to read their own choices as well as the stories from the basal program. I was caught by my own conceptions of how learning to read had to be: quiet, orderly, with everyone on task as I defined that task and as I could witness that behavior. When I let go of that notion and taught children how to make choices about what they read, how they read, and why they read, the world of real reading opened up in my classroom.

Mini-Lessons for Reading

Writing workshop begins with a brief mini-lesson, and initially I planned to do the same in reading workshop. However, I soon discovered that many mini-lesson topics had been covered during the discussions about books, genre, and authors in our literature time. Other mini-lesson topics were embedded in writing workshop or in language lessons during other parts of the school day (Chapter 16). I found that reading workshop mini-lessons were often brief reminders of skills addressed earlier, presented now as a review with suggestions on how to apply them during reading. Like writing workshop, I discovered topics for mini-lessons as I observed children reading. I often shared with the class a particular strategy I had observed a child using the previous day.

In the Giacobbe/Atwell (1985) workshop, I learned more tips on reading mini-lessons. Most reading mini-lessons became brief reminders, suggestions, or tips to assist readers. These might be a particular strategy for getting at unknown words or suggesting a particular author or genre. Like writing workshop, the first mini-lessons address procedures and basic ways to begin reading. Some of those first topics include:

- procedures for selecting books
- how to "read" books (reading illustrations, retelling, etc.)
- the importance of thoughtful reading and *rereading* rather than moving through several titles
- how to hold books, open them, and turn pages
- the concept of *word* and how words are put together to make sense
- the directionality of print on the page and connecting one picture to another
- using soft voices when sharing with a person nearby
- the underlying premise that reading must make sense

Once children understand how the workshop operates and have a clear notion of beginning reading strategies, the need for daily mini-lessons diminishes. Mini-lessons for reading workshop are short—two or three minutes in length—and these lessons occur once or twice a week.

One kind of mini-lesson is a "book talk" in which I present a genre of literature, or the books of one author, or a specific title. For example, I gather several poetry books or biographies or wordless picture books, share them quickly, then offer them to children. Or, when I read a book by an author such as Pat Hutchins during literature time, I suggest other titles by Hutchins at the beginning of reading workshop. In a book talk to introduce a particular title, such as Arnold Lobel's *Owl at Home*, I might begin by saying, "Some of you liked reading *Frog and Toad* and Pat Hutchins' *Good Night, Owl*. You might like this book about an owl by Mr. Lobel. It's called *Owl at Home*." I read the table of contents or perhaps a few lines from parts of the book to entice readers. Then I offer the book to the class.

Some mini-lessons present strategies for reading. For example, on the chalkboard I write, "We went to the . . ." Then I cover the next word and write, "to get a book." We read the sentence together and I ask the children to suggest words that could make sense in this sentence. They list "shelf," "store," "library," "desk," "school," "house," "bookstore," "table." I uncover the first letter of the hidden word to reveal the letter *S*. We eliminate some possibilities. I show the last letter, or perhaps the second, and we quickly arrive at the covered word. I recap the process of using context and letter-sound clues to figure out unknown words. Another important mini-lesson is one where I demonstrate reading using a big book for all to see and "thinking" aloud so the children can watch my process and the strategies I use to make meaning. In other mini-lessons, I might remind the class of a particular skill addressed earlier in the day, during writing workshop, for example. Sometimes, I suggest to the children that if they notice words with a particular phonetic element (a blend, a vowel pattern, a punctuation mark) to point them out to me when I stop to confer.

Partner Reading

Children become natural teachers for their classmates and they often choose to read books together during free-play time in the morning. Sometimes they read in partners during the reading workshop. Once again, there's no prescription for reading in pairs. Some children naturally pair off or work by themselves, managing the decisions with ease, and constructively carrying out the format they choose. Other classes have difficulty, and I need to build the structure for them by assigning partners or deciding which days they may read with partners. Once the pairing is accomplished, children easily develop procedures without my direction. Sometimes a pair of children alternate pages as they read, with one reading aloud while the other follows along; then they reverse roles. Sometimes they read softly together. Still other times the stronger reader reads a book while another follows along, or one child reads a sentence or two and then the partner repeats, echo fashion. And sometimes one reader works on learning to read a book with instruction from a child who has already read it. Though the reading is central, a significant bonus of partner reading is the talk that develops between the two as they discuss the meaning of what they read. The children become responders to each other's reading process. The social aspect of this learning is a definite asset for everyone.

During a reading workshop in early March, children read with partners and I move among them, stopping to listen a moment and generally be available to lend assistance.

Greg and Matt sit at Matt's desk with Marc Brown's *Arthur's Valentine.* Greg reads and Matt supplies words occasionally. I quickly realize that Matt knows how to read this book and is teaching Greg. When they stumble on a word, their eyes go to the pictures where they find a clue, figure out the word, and continue. They turn the page and look through the illustration before reading the words. Greg reads "2B or not 2B" carved on a door. "Hmm," he says, "That makes no sense."

"Yeah, that's what I thought when I read it too—makes no sense. So I just skipped it, 'cuz I didn't really need it—for the story you know." Greg nods and they continue reading. I move on. I've heard them read, noting strategies they were using. They acknowledge my presence with smiles and keep reading.

Amy and Max read Robert Munsch's *Mortimer* by alternating pages. "We're practicing. Tomorrow can we read it to the class?" Amy asks.

"Maybe," I reply. "Any problems?"

"No," says Max. I notice that Max mouths the words silently as Amy reads. When Max reads, Amy's eyes follow the words.

Laura and Kelly read *The Three Billy Goats Gruff* curled up under my desk. The repetitious language helps Laura and she reads fluently, pointing to each word. The remainder of the text is more challenging and Kelly suggests she skip one word and read on. Laura does this but is still stuck, so Kelly supplies the word. "I just got this book today," Laura says, "and I'm just starting to learn it. I know some parts already!"

Monica and Natalie sit leaning against a wall. A stack of books—all with short texts—rests on the floor beside them. "We read *five* books!" says Natalie. "I read the pictures and Monica taught me some words too. It's easy when you're with someone you like."

LISTENING TO READERS READ

I found it important to listen to individual first graders read books to me that they have practiced to a smooth, expressive fluency. This is a significant teaching and learning time—make no mistake. I'm not merely sitting and listening passively as a child reads. Rather, I observe everything about the process: the fluency, expression, responses, comments, even the child's body language during the reading. I take notes throughout this time—an abbreviated running record (see Chapter 19)—and I engage the child in conversation about the reading and the process of learning to read this particular book. It's an important time when the child informs me about their reading development.

This reading parallels publishing in writing workshop; the reader polishes a piece for an audience. This process motivates young readers to practice some books, encourages them to work on new words rather than skipping them, and promotes fluency, which enhances comprehension. Rather than just reading more and more books, children read and reread several books, a definite asset to reading development. When a child satisfactorily reads a book to me or another adult, the child may take the book home overnight.

The listening begins this way. A few days into September I notice that Jackie reads *The Napping House* with no errors. "Can you read all of this book?" I ask in amazement. Jackie nods and beams. "Well, practice by reading it over a few times so that you can read it smoothly like I did when I read it to the class. Then I'd like to listen to you read it to me," I say. A couple days later Jackie tells me that she can read this book "really good" now. "Okay," I say. She sits beside me and reads, and I take notes of any miscues and comments she makes. When she finishes the reading I ask, "How did you learn to read this?" (I ask this question of all readers when they share a book they've learned to read.)

"I don't know. The cat part was hard. By sounding out," she answers.

"Oh, the cat part was hard and you sounded out. Did you do anything else?" Jackie shakes her head.

"Umm, that's something for you to think about next time—how you figured out the hard parts." I ask her another question: "What ideas came to you when you read this book?"

"Sleeping. At nighttime I don't want to go to bed and morning I don't want to get up."

"Oh, so you thought about how it is when you go to bed and when you get up," I acknowledge. Jackie nods and we both smile. I tuck a letter to Jackie's parents in the book and hand the book to Jackie to put in her bookbag. The photocopied letter reads:

> Dear Parents,
>
> Today your child is bringing a book home to share with you. I hope you will enjoy listening to your child read and that you will talk about the book together. Before you return this book to school please take a moment to write any comments or questions you have. I welcome your perceptions of your child's learning process.
>
> Have fun!!
>
> Sincerely,

I'll send a copy of this letter home with every book throughout the year. Some parents answer, some never do. Whatever parents choose is acceptable. In

Jackie's case a reply comes back with the book the next day. Jackie's mom has written:

> Carol,
>
> I enjoyed listening to Jackie read *The Napping House*. Jackie liked when the bed breaks while I enjoyed the cat being scared. We talked about the last illustration and agreed the rainbow and playhouse were interesting.
>
> Jackie is excited about first grade and likes (loves?) Mrs. Avery.
>
> Fondly,
> Pam

Before the day is out, I answer Pam's letter and send the reply home with Jackie. I photocopy the reply, staple it to Pam's note, and file the stapled letters in the folder where I document Jackie's reading process. Parents are responders to their children's reading and the letters help bridge the chasm that can so easily exist between home and school.

Taking books home provides children with an extra incentive, although the intrinsic rewards of learning to read provide sufficient motivation. Some children want to take a book home as soon as they've read it once or without reading it to me. Carrie comes to me as soon as she sees Jackie taking a book home and asks if she can read her book and take it home too. She begins to read, but the reading is halting and full of miscues and errors. I suggest that she practice a day or two as Jackie did. She scowls her disappointment but then brightens and says, "Okay." Two days later Carrie reads her book without errors and with great animation.

Through our school volunteer program, two adults come in each week for thirty to forty-five minutes and help by listening to children read before books go home since I can't hear everyone more than once a week or so. One is a first grader's grandmother who in her professional life taught both high school English and first grade. The other, the mother of a former student and a former preschool teacher, understands the process of our classroom. I had shown the women how to keep records as the children read, ask open-ended questions, and help a child explore a range of strategies to overcome possible struggles while reading. Both women proved to be natural responders who nurtured the children's reading processes. Their contribution gave me time to be accessible to more children during reading workshop and permitted children more one-on-one time to read and discuss an entire book with an adult.

Listening to children read became an important instructional process in my classroom. It provided children with one-on-one time with a teacher and it gave me another opportunity to closely observe the children' s reading development. As children became more accomplished (usually in late spring), I found that they no longer needed to read entire books to me. I asked them to read a selection from a book and then talk with me about their responses to their reading. At this time also, literature circles replaced this structure and children were well on their way to more independent reading.

REFLECTIONS

I spend much effort during the first days and weeks of school establishing our workshop so that each child—and I mean every one—understands and carries out the ways we work in the workshop environments without continual teacher monitoring. I strive to communicate clearly and carefully our structures and expectations. I believe a fundamental element in the success of creating the environments is treating children with utmost respect: asking for their input and using their ideas, negotiating what both they and I can be comfortable with, and stepping in quietly, discreetly, to monitor every little deviation from what I want to happen. I'm careful to communicate reminders and reprimands in a playful (but clearly no-nonsense and clear) tone rather than a demanding, demeaning, or especially a coaxing voice. The children learn that they have a lot of choice within this structure but that I expect standards to be maintained. Because I take time to create this environment, the children develop an inner discipline, and we begin to layer the workshop with additional structures.

CHAPTER 14

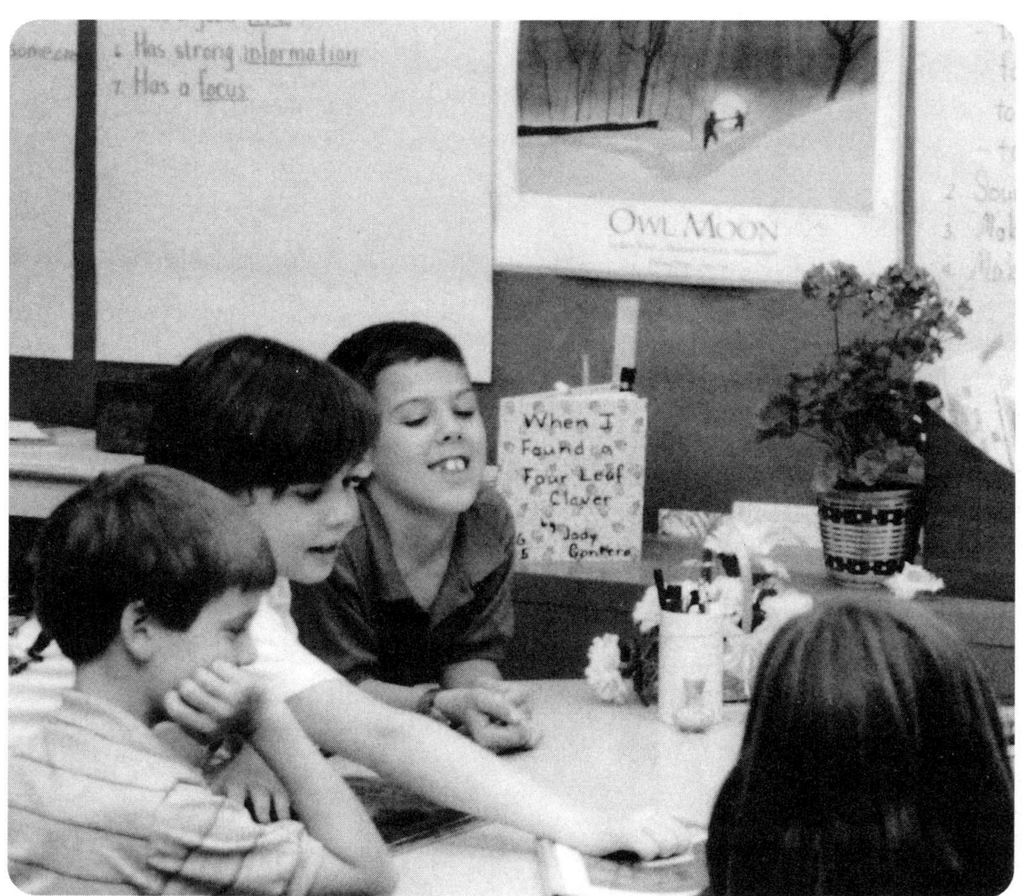

Guided Reading and Literature Circles

Guided reading groups and literature circles are elements within independent reading which is the heart of reading workshop. Independent reading provides the foundation (and the backdrop) for literature circles, guided reading groups, individual conferences, and interviews that add to the depth of reading instruction. I've never relied on centers to provide this backdrop; I'd rather have children *reading* than doing activities *about* reading because lots of practice reading is fundamental to becoming a reader and continuing to grow as a reader.

GUIDED READING

At the beginning of a reading workshop I announce that I want to meet with Jared, Brett, Annie, and David. The workshop structure is well established and the children function without my constant supervision. They know that when I meet with small groups they are to carry on their reading as usual and not interrupt. The time spent building these structures and clearly communicating my expectations pays off; the children make good use of reading time and I'm able to focus attention on small groups without distraction. So the class plunges into reading and the four children and I gather on the carpet for a guided reading session.

A "GUIDED READING" SESSION

I've chosen a book with a patterned text that will support the children's reading; repetitious language and rhyming words limit the range of decoding strategies needed to read this book. Though the book has a rather superficial story line, it does have a slight twist at the end, giving it some semblance of story—and something we can discuss for inferences. My choice of book must have more than labeled illustrations or plotless descriptions. Such books might be appropriate for very young children, but the thinking process of first graders is far beyond such readings. Reading is about making meaning, which is one reason we've moved to literature for reading instruction. I want even the briefest of texts to have a meaning that stimulates the mind of the reader.

I pass out the books and the children eagerly tear into them. I notice they bypass the cover entirely and flip through the pages. They glance quickly at the illustrations as though trying to decide whether this book is going to be of any interest. One child counts the number of pages. Another turns pages front to back while another flips randomly back and forth. They appear to rely on the illustrations for any meaning, though their glances are brief. From my initial observation, I begin to form some theories about their notions about reading and I respond accordingly.

"Let's all turn to the cover of the book. Like this," I say as I place my copy in front of me. Accomplishing this is complicated and it takes an extra minute to get everyone together and focusing on the cover.

"When readers begin a book or when they choose a book, they usually look at the cover and think what this book might be about, will this be something that interests them. What do you see on the cover?"

"Kettles."

"Pans."

"For cooking."

"Yes," I say, "Pans for cooking. What else?"

"Paper bags."

"Yes, and the picture will help us read the title. Let's put our finger on the title." I put my finger under the first word. Two children readily put fingers on the title but neither finger is near the first word. A third child watches the others then places a finger in imitation. The fourth child has not appeared to be attending and now does nothing in response to my request. I stop and show each child how to point to the title.

"As we read, we'll move our finger under each word. That will help us look at that word and see the letters so that we can read it," I say. Then I read the title *Bags, Cans, Pots and Pans*, and move my finger under the words. I notice that fingers rest on top of the words and that the fingers of two children do not match the words accurately. Instead their fingers sweep along in a "guessing" attitude. We read the title again and I place a finger on each of these children's books and, with a deliberate action, move word by word through the title. I comment briefly that the picture and the words go together and give us ideas about what this book is about. Most often I would continue this type of discussion as we go through the pages of the book, but today I notice that this particular group of children is having a difficult time attending to the task and staying with me. I decide to read the book and look at the illustrations as they follow along.

"Now I'll read the book and you can follow along. Use your finger," I say. I read aloud and slip a finger onto a child's page from time to time to help guide individuals to the correct place. I comment briefly on the illustrations to help build a complete sense of the story, but I notice that the children do not flexibly move between text and illustrations. Focusing their attention on the words and staying with me commands most of their attention.

When I finish this seven-page, forty-eight-word story (which is about a family packing a van for a trip and ends when they declare that they need a "big, new van" with the implication that there is too much stuff for their current van), I comment, "Oh my goodness. They have a problem. I wonder what they might do." The children make no comments after my remark and I sense that they didn't completely follow the story line and may not be accustomed to thinking about meaning as they read. However, it's important to demonstrate a reader thinking about what is being read, if only briefly.

"Let's read it again and this time you read with me," I say and the children eagerly flip to the beginning of the book. We read through it together and again I monitor the finger pointing. Two of the children do this quite well by now and read with me, pausing only occasionally for me to say the word first. The other two struggle more with both pointing and enunciating words and one child utters a word now and then. I hear her voice only on the page with four sentences that begin with the same three words and end with one different word.

We come to a page where the words "flags" and "fans" break from the repetition pattern. The children struggle with these words. The illustrated flags are little, triangle-shaped flags and thus not easy to "read" in the picture. The children use the initial /f/ sound but read "fans" for "flags." Fans are the easiest pictures to note on the page but "flag" appears in the text before "fan." Thus the children readily jump to an incorrect conclusion in reading the word. This aspect of the text provides an opportunity for me to assess reading strategies. It is also a fine teaching opportunity.

"Whoops, that's not 'fans.' Look at all the letters. The pictures help but sometimes we need more than the pictures and more than the first letter. Look at the first two letters. See: *fl*." This doesn't appear to help anyone so I tell them the word *flag* and point out that it begins with *fl*. "Good readers look at all the letters and the pictures," I add as a little reminder. We reread this page with the corrections and finish the book. I make a mental note to do more with the *fl* blend another time soon and connect it with this group's reading.

"My goodness," I say. "You're beginning to learn to read this *whole* book." It's a delightful moment, as I've intended to elicit through my voice tone. The children smile and comment on their own success briefly before we continue. "This time you read it together and I'll listen." I get them started and quickly drop out. With two children I must still monitor the pointing and with one I keep my finger above each word and she points below. When we get to the end of the book I ask, "Why do you think they need a big new van?" The children's answers beg the point implied through text and pictures.

"They probably want a new van."

"They're going to buy a van."

"They want another van."

"But *why*?" I ask.

"'Cause they *want* a new one."

It's clear that they've missed the idea that all the things won't fit in the van. My theory is confirmed when I suggest this idea and we revisit the text briefly. The children respond with amazed "oh's" and "ah's." Now they understand. Pointing out the key idea is a way to lead emergent readers into anticipating inferential meanings as they read.

I ask the children to read the book once more, keeping their fingers under the words they are reading. This time I am silent and "listen in" to individuals as they read. I'm ready to support if one child gets stuck. Two children are fluent and at the end I send them off to their seats to practice. "Read this again and again so that you know all the words and can tell me what happens in the story," I say. I help the two remaining children finish the story, send one back to practice independently and spend an extra minute with the fourth child until I see she can work independently.

The entire time spent on this lesson has been less than fifteen minutes and this one went longer than most because we took a few minutes extra establishing procedures on starting to read. At the end of reading workshop, I hear

Brett say, "I read this book five times! I know it all. I can read it with my eyes shut!"

"Yes," I reply, "but I want you to look at the *words*! Good readers look at the words!" He grins and assures me he will. A day later I bring the four readers together again and they reread the book while I "listen in." They all read successfully and the beams of pride on their faces confirm the success they feel.

The lesson with this group was filled with instructional opportunities that we call "teachable moments": handling a book, reading the title, predicting, pointing to words, picture clues, letter-sound correlation, consonant blends, inferences, etc. These arise within the context of reading and require that I pay close attention to what the children are saying and doing. I must strike a delicate balance. Touching on everything or dwelling too long on one point will bog us down. I must keep the focus on the central act of reading, acquiring a meaning, and enjoying the process. I must make choices. When I take a moment to explain something, I must also keep the momentum of the reading going. Those choices are based on my knowledge of the reading process for emergent readers, a sound grounding in reading strategies and skills, and most important, on an understanding of individual children at this particular moment. The more I work with them, the more I know each child. Still, my decisions throughout the guided reading lesson are based on what I observe with the children at that moment.

Later in the workshop, I stop to see David. Spanish is the language of David's home and I had noted in the guided reading session that he listened for the voices of others and his words came a split second after the other readers. Now he tells me that he has read this book five times and can read it now! He has opened a Henry and Mudge book, but it is clear that this book is quite difficult for him. I go through two pages with a mini–guided reading lesson: first I read and point to the words, next he reads and points with me, then finally he reads and points while I listen. "Now practice these two pages," I tell him.

"Okay," he agrees and goes to work. Later, as the workshop ends he comes to me jubilant and says, "I can read it! I'm going to read this book for the rest of the year!"

Purposes for "Guided Reading"

In the example above, my purpose was to gently "guide" several children through an initial reading of a book so that they might learn to read it independently. I'm scaffolding children's learning as they first look at the cover, then open the book and anticipate the story, and read the pages. And *always*, we're thinking about the meaning of what is read.

Guided reading groups are one means of demonstrating the nitty gritty, the fundamental processes (often taken for granted by accomplished readers) one uses when one reads. I show children *how* to read a particular book by reading and articulating some of my thinking and processes as I read and they follow along. For example, I say things such as:

- "Does that make sense?"
- "Does this sound right? I better read it again."
- "If it doesn't sound right or make sense I know I've got to stop and do something."
- "If I read to the end of the sentence, it may help me figure out what makes sense."
- "I'll ask someone; we might figure it out together."

I may invite readers to read along with me, imitating what they have just observed me doing. I also invite readers to read as I listen in and finally, as I see that they're ready, I send them off to read on their own. The stage has been set for the reader to practice independently. Of course, the procedure varies with each reader or group of readers; flexibility is paramount in responding to the needs of individual learners and guided reading procedures must always be responsive to children if they are to be effective.

Children come to school with varying degrees of experience in handling books, hearing stories, and noticing the words on the pages of books. Some children know how to look at the cover and begin to think about the story within. They may even make connections to other books they know. Other children skip the cover, hastily flip through the pages, and reach for another book. Guiding these children through a reading experience helps them move into the reading process with success by providing an experience that unveils aspects of reading that the children may not have picked up in their preschool experiences. My goal is to provide demonstrations and encouragement so young readers feel supported when they first read. This "guidance," followed by practice, leads to independence.

Guided reading groups can help beginning readers over the initial hurdle of cracking the code and move them into fluency. I see guided reading groups as a procedure most helpful in first grade, some in second, and a little in third. Of course, this is not absolute. These groups can work for any grade level where we want to guide learners through new strategies. I modified guided reading procedures with struggling fourth-grade readers. By this age it was important that these children not see themselves as separated from their classmates into the "cans" and "cannots" with regard to reading. So I used guided-reading strategies on a one-to-one basis in reading conferences or with pairs of students or blended guided reading techniques into literature circles. Rather than meeting in formal groups, I usually just spent a bit longer with a particular child during the reading time or met with them in the morning when students were arriving. Maintaining a casual tone was important for this particular class.

Guided reading groups can also provide a structure for demonstrating ways to read various genres: newspapers, magazines, nonfiction. Basketball playoffs were going on when I worked in a fifth-grade classroom and the boys were quite pleased when I read Bruce Brooks' *NBA by the Numbers.* In small groups they huddled over the book during the reading workshop, reading not only the text but also the details in the color photos. They examined the pictures of players' feet and identified the specific players by the shoes! The next day they brought in catalogs of sports equipment to verify their point. When I asked which shoes they'd want to buy, they immediately selected the most expensive. I guided their reading through the catalog page, comparing prices and quality. They suddenly realized that "those shoes are a rip-off!" Another student read the syndicated children's newspaper section, the Mini-Page, on basketball, which included a cookie recipe. When he misread the amounts for ingredients I guided him through reading the recipe and later shared these strategies with the entire class. The validation of the boys' sports reading led them to bring in basketball cards. We read them together, with the boys teaching one another and me how to read this particular genre. Their examples reminded me how important it is to build on children's interests if we want them to become readers. The goal, after all, is to *be* readers, not just know *how* to read.

Much has been written about guided reading practices (Mooney 1990; Fountas and Pinnell 1996; Routman 2000; Calkins 2001; Opitz and Ford 2001). In my own experience, I have found that guided reading offers many advantages for students. I "guide" children's reading throughout the reading workshop, not just through guided reading "groups." My brief conferences with individuals during the workshop are one example. I'm not inclined to establish daily guided reading groups for everyone in the class or to level all our books. Creating ability-ranked reading groups and moving them through a sequenced level of books was one of the weaknesses of the basal programs I left long ago.

Planning for Guided Reading Groups

The most effective guided reading lessons aren't thoroughly planned in advance the way basal lessons once were. I can't choose a book just to address the difference between /f/ and /fl/, for instance. To do so would most likely eliminate the responsive nature of the reading experience. If however, I choose books that provide children a secure reading experience and at the same time a bit of a challenge, a rich reading environment will ensue. The children engage and I find numerous opportunities to teach. I address reading strategies in the group session, others in follow-up conferences, still others in lessons for the entire class. I know the topics I point out during a particular session will most likely not be mastered immediately. The children need many experiences and lots of practice.

As children gain experience as readers, they may select books for guided reading groups, a practice that ensures I don't take over their developing strategies for choosing books. I strive to keep membership in groups flexible so as to avoid the trap of homogeneous grouping. The frequency of guided reading groups is determined by observed needs and tempered by student interest. Even my role in the group shifts according to what the children need; sometimes I take a strong leadership role while other times I facilitate by allowing the children to take the lead and I interject to provide information or expertise as needed. I certainly don't want to re-create the old practices of homogeneous reading groups that meet daily to move through a predetermined sequence of reading material! Long ago, I experienced the limitations and dangers of such approaches.

As we implement new practices, there is a temptation to impose labels and establish exact procedures, mandating that everyone adhere to the new "right" way. It's easy to focus on *practices* rather than *learners*. I think this is one of the biggest challenges for teachers. Graves (1984) reminded us that the danger is orthodoxy. I believe that to best help children, we must incorporate flexible practices in light of our own classroom contexts and remember to *keep it simple*. In *Reaching Readers*, Opitz and Ford (2001) write of guarding against a "guided reading dogma." They go on to say "we need to be cautious when an educational practice, like guided reading, begins to develop the trappings of an orthodoxy" (1) and point out that "there is more than one way to implement guided reading practices" (14). Their book provides thoughtful ideas for teachers to consider as they work with guided reading.

Guided reading sessions, like literature circles, can be rich additions to reading workshop. When we listen to children and observe them as they read, we see their successes and areas where they need guidance. Guided reading offers teaching methods for responding to children. And, teaching responsively provides an authentic and stimulating learning environment.

Literature Circles

Literature circles begin in my first-grade classroom in the late spring. The children naturally talk about books they read during reading workshop—it's not at all unusual for children to pause in their reading and read a section or comment on something they were reading to a child next to them. When children read in partners they discussed illustrations and story lines continually. Talking about reading was well established in this classroom. So bringing several children together in a "literature circle" to share responses to books evolved naturally.

Beginning Literature Circles

My role in literature circles is to start the discussion, facilitate it as necessary and occasionally nudge it toward unexplored topics. I often begin with an open-ended question such as: What did you think about the book you read? What did you like about this book and why? The children are quite accustomed to providing specific answers and referring to the book to substantiate their ideas. After all, we've been doing this for months in our literature time.

In our first literature circles, children shared different books (I had few titles with multiple copies). The conversations tended to be about how the books or characters in the books were similar or different. Because children often read books other children brought to the book discussion, they were able to make these comparisons rather easily and they enjoyed batting around ideas. One of the benefits of these discussions, besides the obvious thinking that developed, was that children often reread books or chose to read books that others brought to the group. As Max left the group one day he commented, "I've read this book but I didn't read that book. And now I'm going to read it and decide if I agree with what Greg says or what Alex says." In literature circles children also discussed a book's construction: vocabulary, favorite phrases, beginnings and endings, even the shape of the plot. Jody commented on *Harold and the Great Stag*, "This book's like the letter *G*. It starts out like an *O* but instead of coming back to the beginning it goes in and then stops—like a letter *G*." Talk such as this is a direct outgrowth of the talk from our literature time.

First-Grade Literature Groups

The few multiple copies in the classroom provide opportunity for literature groups when several children have read the same title. In a first-grade classroom (not my own), I meet with four children who have read *The Tiny Family* by Norman Bridwell. I begin our discussion by asking, "Did you have any struggles, words you couldn't figure out as you read this?"

"Yes," says Megan, "'clothes.' It doesn't work to sound it out."

"Cloth-es," Craig says and Shannon corrects him.

"You're right. Sounding out won't work with this word. What do you do if sounding out doesn't work?" I ask.

"Go back and try it again," suggests Shannon.

"Yes, and when you do, one thing that will help is to think what makes sense. Use the first sound and the picture that will help you too." Quickly I demonstrate how this will work with this word. "Were you all able to read this book pretty easily?" I ask. The children nod and I continue. "What did the book make you think as you read?"

"It's good."

"I liked it."

The responses are limited so I keep going. "Well, tell me more. Tell me what you liked. Why is it good?" I open my book and then the children open theirs. With further nudging they talk about illustrations and a few incidents from the story. It takes a considerable time to get them away from literal retelling. When I ask what they think about things they give me one-word or two-word answers. Finally I ask, "Well, what would it be like to be little like this tiny family?"

Somewhat hesitantly the responses come. Megan says she would go down an ant hole if she was this little and explore all those tunnels. Craig says he'd be careful because you could get crushed by the big people. Shannon thinks it's like *Jack and the Beanstalk* and the others agree. For a brief moment they talk about this connection. I interject only to validate their ideas by expressing interest in what they say.

"You know what?" I say, "You've just done something good readers do. When they read, good readers think about other books they're reminded of. I bet you'll do that some more when you read." The children nod, pleased with this accomplishment. We conclude.

Getting talk going in this group went slowly. They children talked most easily about their decoding strategies. It will take experience talking about their reading before they consider more than a literal retelling. However, first-grade children are quite capable of this talk if we as teachers place an emphasis on it.

In another classroom, a group of four children has read *Patrick's Dinosaur*. When I gave out the books the previous day, I asked the children to read and then write a few sentences about what was on their minds after reading. "This will help you remember what you thought until tomorrow when we talk about the book together. The group convenes and we begin by reading what they wrote. "You all had different ideas," I observe, "tell us more about your thinking?" And the discussion is off and running.

At first their comments are a retelling of the story. I acknowledge this important aspect of comprehension, but I also want the children to make connections and extensions as they read. As we continue talking and look through the book together, they begin to discuss why Patrick has a dinosaur. Is it real? Where does it come from? What would they do in this situation? The discussion helps a child clarify his thinking; he thought the dinosaur had escaped from a zoo "or something." The other children point out that this couldn't be so and refer to the text to prove their point. The talk has begun to bring out the questions they had when they first read the story. The talk in literature circles leads them to recognize questions and ideas as they read, and bring new questions to future discussions.

One day in the spring Brian, Cory, and Greg discussed *Owl Moon*. Jeff joins the discussion toward the end. Throughout their conversation they make connections and deepen their understanding of the book.

MRS. A: Tell me what you think about *Owl Moon*.

BRIAN: I think it'd be neat to go owling because then you might be able to capture one. You couldn't really keep it for a pet. I wouldn't want to have him for a pet 'cause it just would wreck up the whole house. You don't know what it could do.

COBY: The owl could bite!

MRS. A: The owl could bite?

B: Yes! It could hurt you.

MRS. A: What did you think about this book, Cory?

C: I like the part with the boy and the man and they're standing there looking and they hear an owl. [Cory begins making whoo-whoo sounds. The other boys join in.]

MRS. A: What do you think, Greg?

GREG: Well, my favorite part is when they get to see the owl flapping its wings.

MRS. A: Tell me about that.

G: Well, I'd like to see an owl flap its wings, but I wouldn't like to take it as a pet because it could fly around the house and break glass and stuff like that. But I would like to see it in the woods. [More owl sounds from Cory and Brian.]

B: I like that part too.

MRS. A: Why do you like that part, Brian?

B: Because it's real neat.

C: It's real neat because I like how the owl's claws and its wings are colored. I'd like to see his face. [Cory has opened the book to the page that illustrates the back of the owl and the father and child shining a flashlight on it. The boys all talk at the same time as they examine the illustration.]

MRS. A: Is this a boy or a girl?

C: A boy.

B: It's a boy.

G: A boy.

MRS. A: What makes you think it's a boy?

C: Because it looks like a girl. It looks like a girl, but it's *not* a girl. It has a girl hat, and a girl's skirt, and girl's boots but it's a boy!

MRS. A: It has girl things but you still think it's a boy?

B: Yes! That silver wings part is like it's talking about giving you a clue about an owl.

MRS. A: What do you think, Greg?

G: Well, I think when they say silver wings they mean the moonlight reflecting on the owl's wings.

MRS. A: I see. So you think the ending is talking about what it looks like.

B: Yes. It's sort of a fairy-tale ending—a happy ending.

G: I think the ending has to do with that they saw an owl.

MRS. A: Oh. What do you think it means that you don't need words or warmth or anything but hope?

B: You don't need warm or stuff like that. All you need is hope that you'll see an owl! Like it says. [He points to the words in the text.]

MRS. A: Okay. Is there any other part of this book that you really like?

B: Yes. You have to go to the forest to find an owl. You just won't see an owl at night flying around the school.

MRS. A: [Jeff, who has been listening to the conversation, sits down at the table.] Jeff, what do you think about *Owl Moon*?

JEFF: Well, it's a good book and through the book it goes whoo whooo.

MRS. A: You all like that part. Why do you like that?

J: Well, it's pretty neat how they say it. I read this book to my dad a lot and he liked it a lot too.

MRS. A: Jeff, is this a boy or a girl?

J: You can't tell, but it kind of looks like a boy. I think it's probably a boy.

MRS. A: Is there anything else important about this book?

J: Yes. It's got a lot of information in a story about how you do owling. It's in a *story*.

B: You have to go owling at night because owls are nocturnal. They won't go out at day because they're asleep.

J: What are these things up here? [Jeff points to the man's cap.]

G: Well, see there's this special kind of hat—I forget what country they used it in—and there's these flaps you can put down over your ears when it's winter and you go out.

J: And you can fold them up. They're Russian.

C: Ohhh, I know what it is—just like this hat—it has bumps you can pull the whole thing down so it can cover your ears so your ears are not cold.

MRS. A: Okay boys. Thank you.

The children learn to talk about books, focusing on ideas about characters, about incidents or information in the book, and about how the book connects to their own experiences. They address the total book—both pictures and text. In fact, they pore over the pictures, frequently noticing details I miss. As they talk together, they stimulate further ideas and extend their thinking about their reading and the ideas they find in books.

Structuring Literature Circles

In my first-grade classroom I convened literature groups by calling together a few students who had recently read the same book. We sat down together and I started by explaining that this was a place to talk about our books much as we did during literature time. What was interesting in their book? I had no trouble getting this talk going and once it started I shaped it by making sure everyone participated with no one student dominating. I asked questions from time to time, keeping these questions broad and open-ended.

Which character did you like? Why?

How did characters change from the beginning to the end?

What did this book make you think about?

What other books did this book make you think about?

What do you think about . . . an event in the story, an action of a character, etc.? What would *you* do in this situation?

Have you ever known anything like this to happen?

What was the best part? Why?

Were there words or phrases in this book that you really liked?

Was there anything confusing, or that you didn't understand, in this book?

First graders are quite good at addressing these questions by late winter and early spring because they evoke talk that is typical of all our talk about literature. Literature circles are a time to expand understanding of one's reading. This means moving beyond literal recall of story lines and also considering the ideas of others. Developing these extended comprehension strategies is important to becoming a reader.

Reflections

When I began teaching children to read I felt mystified with regard to the process of "cracking the code." How did a child do this? How had I done it decades ago? What ought I, as teacher, do to best help each child? After working with several hundred children as they became readers, I can emphatically state that I've seen no two children learn to read in exactly the same way. Children use a broad range of strategies and the way in which they employ these strategies, integrate them, internalize them is unique to each child. The structures of guided reading and literature circles can best support children's reading development when we remember to maintain a focus on the learners themselves.

From my experience of watching several hundred children learn to read, I've come to believe that comprehension needs to be central to reading instruction for all children from the very beginning. Young children do not deal with nonsense when it comes to learning. They are highly sophisticated learners who strive to make sense of the world and dismiss what they perceive to be irrelevant. But if we nourish the purpose for reading by involving children in deep understanding of *what* they read, children invest in learning to read and work hard at cracking the code. They have a better chance of success. When children experience reading as a meaningful activity that connects to their lives, they are inclined to read more. To teach readers the nuts and bolts of decoding while maintaining a focus on comprehension, I've found that it's essential to understand how each child uses specific strategies and what they're interested in and care about as learners and readers. Like teaching writing, teaching reading requires a "waiting, responsive type of teaching."

CHAPTER 15

Learning to Read

I believe that all children, except those with severe brain damage or dysfunction, can learn to read. I also believe that for each child the timing of when that child begins to read, the pace of reading development, and the strategies the child finds helpful will be unique to that child. There are no reading groups in my classroom. Without groups, I witnessed children learning to read as I never had before. Differences of age and school experiences fell away. Children—all of them—expended tremendous energy to learn to read. They worked together, learned from each other, and applied a range of strategies to get at the mysterious world of print. *The significance and timing of any particular strategy was unique for each child and no two children learned to read with identical processes.* It became obvious to me that methodologies arbitrating the sequence and timing of reading strategies hindered rather than helped children's learning. The heavy body of research and documentation on reading lends considerable insight into reading development and strategies that readers use, but in the end the process is different for each individual.

Unlike writing, which leaves a paper trail, reading development is more difficult to document because so much of the process remains hidden within the reader. I wanted to understand not only the children's development in decoding and literal comprehension but also their development as aesthetic readers (Rosenblatt 1978). I listened and observed as children worked at learning to read passages in books and in their own writing. (Reading words, lines, or passages they had composed in writing workshop contributed to reading development in a major way.) I regularly listened to children read entire books they had mastered, recording how they read: the miscues, expression, fluency, use of fingers for pointing, and strategies used to figure out words. I asked questions such as: How did you figure that out? How did you learn to read this? What struggles did you work through? What did this book remind you of or make you think about as you were reading it? I recorded the children's replies. Of course, I couldn't record everything, but note taking during reading workshop served two functions. First, it helped me see clearly the progress of individual children and thus greatly aided planning for instruction as well as determining responses to help readers. Second, over time it provided documentation of the children's individual processes for learning to read.

Wanting to Read—A Prerequisite to Learning

Many first graders today come to school eager to read and most have experience writing and reading their names, letters of the alphabet, or even a few words. Other children have few experiences with books and are baffled by the paper-and-pencil and book-reading activities of school.

Kurt was eager to learn but had little experience with written language in his home. He spoke little and always in one or two syllables. In reading and writing workshops he watched other children and, somewhat hesitantly, imitated them. Then one day in February he said, "I wanna *reeead*!" Though he had been reading a few books prior to this, he had not really been involved with them. Then came a change. His reading skills did not take off suddenly, but he began to approach books with vigor, as though a light had suddenly been turned on.

Kurt illustrates that to learn to read and write—and probably to really learn anything—you have to *want to learn.* Kurt had been going through the motions, imitating peers because he wanted to be included among them. His initial motivation was social and he became part of the community, doing what the community did: read and write. That experience led him to discover that reading was something he really wanted to do. All of my lessons would not have made Kurt a reader had he not decided to learn to read for himself. Instruction must be grounded in purposes felt by the learner. Inevitably, for most children the day comes when they "crack the code" and discover how written language works. But that moment always comes after the child's decision to want to learn to read.

The Children's Strategies

Each child acquires a complex, unique, and integrated set of reading strategies as they read in an environment rich with demonstrations of making sense of written language. *The timing and the ordering of those strategies are different for each child.* Though I continually introduce, suggest, or remind children of ways to approach reading, I must leave decisions on using specific techniques up to the individual. Often no child uses a particular approach immediately and certainly not every child in the room will find every strategy helpful. Children are naturally efficient learners, dealing with what makes sense to them at a given moment and ignoring that which, from their perspective, is nonsense. Allowing children to choose their own strategies in an environment where they are surrounded by demonstrations permits children to maintain and expand their efficient and natural learning capacities.

While there is no one sequence to the development of reading strategies, I have observed some particular techniques that children exercise as they learn to read.

Retelling Stories and Using Memory

Some children "read" books to me during the first days of school by talking about single illustrations, by retelling the stories in sequence using the illustrations, by reading words here and there that they recognize, or through a selection and combination of these strategies. Children who talk through a book, even if they omit most of the actual text, are participating in a natural process of beginning reading. The books they choose to read in this fashion usually are ones I have read to the class.

Familiarity with a text and memory of phrases help readers. It is easier to read or retell any book for which one has a context rather than a book filled with unfamiliar names and places, or with an unfamiliar story line. Children use memory of a particular book to recognize words. For example, when I asked Adam how he learned to read *Cookie's Week* he said, "I remembered you reading it and when I came to words I didn't know I could just hear you saying them, so then I knew the word." Children made similar comments even after becoming fluent readers.

Of course, as they begin reading, children use strategies other than memory of a text to figure out words, but memory plays an important part in the initial process. Children read and reread books, and those repeated experiences with words *within a meaningful context* contribute to the development of a sight-word vocabulary. Children may not recognize words they have been reading in a book when presented with these same words in isolation, but recognizing words in context is part of the developmental process of meaning making. Requiring children to know all the words before reading is like requiring children to know how to spell before they are permitted to write.

Even after children become fluent readers, they continue to rely on familiarity with books—usually ones read to them at home or at school—to select reading material. Familiarity with a text helps make a book or part of a book predictable, a characteristic that helps beginning readers. Also, patterned language, such as in *Cookie's Week* or *Ten Little Bears*, supports beginning readers. However, some books are too predictable, using so many repeating lines that children rely on memory exclusively. The book does little to support growth in the reader because it fails to provide opportunities for the child to explore other strategies or even to look closely at the words. Sometimes these books are written for the specific purpose of creating predictable texts and many are rejected by children because they are not fun to read.

Pointing to Words

When children read books, I suggest they point to the words. Pointing directs a child's attention to the words and actually helps children learn individual words by focusing on those words as they read and reread particular texts. Most children naturally point when they begin browsing through books whether they discuss illustrations, pick out a few words, or read entire books. Pointing is similar to the pointing parents and preschoolers do as they first explore books together; it is a way of focusing on particular aspects of the book. I've noticed that the few children who do not point are those who have had scant experiences with parent-child story times. For these children, I point as I read and they soon pick up on this strategy.

As children begin reading entire books, I encourage them to follow along by pointing. Observing the way a child points provides glimpses into that child's awareness of individual words. At times children move their fingers under each word, accurately pointing to the word they read aloud. Carrie read *Cookie's Week* with this kind of pointing. When she read "garbage can" for "trash can" she noticed the miscue and made a correction without prompting. Pointing helped her focus on the individual word, thus enabling her to notice the mismatch with the initial letter (*t*) and the initial sound /*g*/ she read. Other children make general sweeps across the printed line, often indicating memorization of the text. Sometimes children point by *covering* the word they are reading; I quickly show them how to move a finger under the words.

Cory moved his fingers under the lines of *This Old Man* when he read it. His errors did not interfere with the meaning, but he obviously was not attending to individual words. Most children go through a period when they rely on pointing in a word-by-word fashion but, as they become fluent with a particular text, their fingers begin to glide under the words. Eventually, on their own, most children abandon pointing to words except when they come upon a difficult word. When Jody came upon the word "decided" his finger suddenly pointed to the word while he focused momentarily on it. On numerous occasions with fluent readers, I observe a child's finger dart to a position below a challenging word, hear the child read that word, and then see the finger retract. Adults (including myself) do the same thing occasionally, especially when reading aloud. Sometimes I ask a child, "Can you read this now without pointing?" as a nudge toward moving away from pointing if I sense that the pointing is no longer needed. The pointing strategy enhances the initial meaning-making process by helping children focus.

Learning to Read New Words

As children read new texts and reread others, they begin developing, *in an integrated fashion*, strategies to figure out individual words. The following strategies help many children learn to read unfamiliar words.

PICTURE CLUES From the beginning, children look at the illustrations in books with intense interest, an activity that takes on almost a ritual quality and that continues throughout the year. Newkirk and McLure (1992) described first graders as "milking" the illustrations. As children begin tending to the words on a page, they connect the ideas in pictures to the meaning conveyed by those words. Even after they abandon memorization as a way to read, they glance at illustrations when they are unsure of a word. As children become accomplished readers, they naturally ease out this strategy for word identification but still spend considerable time reading the pictures and discussing illustrations with their peers. Reading the pictures, noticing details in the illustrations, and making inferences and predictions from those illustrations seems to be a significant activity, one that leads to reading written text with the same attitudes toward comprehension.

CONTEXT CLUES Sentence structure and word order, expected word meaning, words surrounding an unknown word, and illustrations all help readers. The children's entire experience with language—written and oral as well as with books—enhances the development of reading. They expect a text to make sense and they use their knowledge of how language is constructed to make sense of written passages as they read. Since the structure of written language is not identical to spoken language, reading aloud to children is critical in helping them develop an ear for written language so they can then use context clues.

VISUAL CLUES The appearance of a word—the shape, length, specific letters, and patterns of letters—helps when reading. Children often make comments such as David's, "I learned 'something' because it's so long and it has *ing* at the end." We share such comments in the classroom, making one child's experience available to all the children. A variety of experiences with written language, from both outside and inside the classroom, contribute to a child's using visual clues.

PHONETIC CLUES Children say they sound out, meaning that they use phonetic clues, especially initial consonants. I observe children developing an awareness of patterns in the structure of words as they write and read and then applying those patterns when they come upon unknown words. Rarely do I observe children sound out an entire word; the context usually provides supporting strategies so that the child figures out the words by using only *some* phonetic clues. When I asked Jody how he sounded out he explained, "I looked at the *bl* at the beginning and the *t* at the end and then I got it."

MULTIPLE CLUES Children employ their own multiple approaches to deciphering words, such as asking another reader, skipping the word, testing and rejecting possibilities for meaning, reading other words around it for clues, and using the strategies listed above. Time and choice are the children's allies in developing their strategies. When Monica first attempted to read *Mufaro's Beautiful Daughters*, she had the option to decide to give herself more time. Monica talked about her process. "This book was once too hard. Then I tried it and there were only three words I didn't know. My reading had gotten better by reading so much. When I get stuck I think really hard—like once I forgot 'stop.' I thought really hard what could I use for it. I look at the vowel in it. It's easier for me to use the vowels now but sometimes they don't always work for me. I get nonsense words. So I try other ways. Like 'approaching'—I thought of hundreds of words and then one pops in my head. I read the page and it usually works out. I figured out 'silhouetted' that way." Monica decided when to read this book, when to set it aside, when to return to it, and what strategies to use to decode.

Practicing

When children tell me how they learned to read a book they often talk about "practicing." Practice did not just mean time reading, but for beginning readers, meant rereading and working at perfecting reading, much like one learning to play the piano plays a particular piece again and again. This practice involves learning all the words, thinking about meaning, and reading fluently with the expression that fits that meaning.

Adam smiled and told me, "I keeped on practicing and I had a little bit of words from you and on most of the words I tried to get it [to] make sense, so then I knew what the words were."

Jody said, "I was just practicing. When there were words like 'spilling' I hardly knew what they were. I skipped it and went on."

In a voice brimming with pride Stacy answered my question about her reading approach. "How? When I got [this book] and was practicing reading it. I tried it a month ago and I couldn't read it and now I know more words and I got the hang of it. Now I can read it with lots of expression because I really know it!"

Glenda Bissex (1980) sees "practice being as crucial for reading success as for playing basketball or piano or any other skill" (170). In observing her son Paul's reading development, she noted that one important form of practice was rereading books. She writes, "Perhaps it gave Paul, as a beginning reader, clearer feedback on his own progress; he could tell he was reading the same book more fluently than before. . . . Personal selection of materials was important for this kind of practice" (171).

Children have the freedom to decide if and how long to practice by rereading a book, though occasionally I urge a child to reread when I feel such guidance to be in the child's best interest. Once in a while a child chooses to stay with one text until able to read that book fluently, but most children set books aside, sample other titles, or read with friends and return to the original book from time to time until that book can be read with ease. Practice in learning to read a book means working on a particular title (alone or with other children) with some regularity, but interspersing that reading with other reading materials. Only one child ever complained about rereading a book. "I got tired of this book because I read it so many times—over and over." When I asked, "What could you do if this happened again?" she giggled, then replied, "Get another *book*!"

Writing Helps Reading

Marie Clay (1998) states, "Writing can contribute to the building of almost every kind of inner control of literacy that is needed by the successful reader. And yet there is no predictable sequence in which the shifts will occur!" (130).

"You can read your writing because you wrote it and you know what it says," Mark said one day. The children concurred. When children read words they have just written, they focus on meaning and then use phonetic and context clues to read. They transfer these processes to reading other materials with relative ease, though the pace of this transfer is unique to each child.

Early on, many children's reading of their own writing is an approximation of the exact text. Some children go through a period when they write pages and then are unable to read it all. Both cases parallel the stage when children "read" books by retelling a familiar story using the pictures as a guide. To help children with reading in both reading and writing workshops, I urge children to look at the words and attempt to figure them out. "Remember what this story is about and then let the letters and pictures help you," I say. I applaud the success of reading even a few words and don't require youngsters to figure out entire passages. With time, experience, and nurturing support, children naturally incorporate context, visual, and phonetic clues to decipher their own writing. They transfer these strategies to the reading of books by professional authors.

A child's published books are the easiest reading material in the classroom for that child. The books of classmates follow next. The children are familiar with these books because they hear them read in sharing sessions during the writing process. Seeing their own and their classmates' writing in print—with conventional spelling, punctuation, etc.—helps children develop a vocabulary of words they can both read and write.

That insight from years ago that "it will work," that children could learn to read by writing, turned out to be credible even if somewhat simplistic. When children compose in daily writing workshops, read their writing, share, receive responses, revise and edit for the purpose of meaning making, they naturally integrate multiple strategies for working with written language that carry into their reading processes. Reading and writing mingle, complement, and augment each other as children learn written language.

Becoming Good Readers

On a spring morning, after several years of close observation and documentation of first graders learning to read, I asked my first graders: "You are all good readers; what do you do that good readers do?" I wrote their responses on chart paper. The class produced the following list.

Good Readers . . .

1. . . . know how to pick books they can read;
2. . . . know how to pick books they like;
3. . . . know when to abandon a book because it's too hard, boring, too easy, not interesting;

4. . . . tell other people about good books;
5. . . . figure words out by:
   a. sounding out but it doesn't always work
   b. asking another person
   c. skipping and coming back after reading the sentence and then seeing what makes sense
   d. looking at the letters for clues
   e. sometimes sounding out the two beginning letters
   f. using the pictures to help
   g. covering up half the word to figure it out
   h. the shape of the word
6. . . . read to other people;
7. . . . listen to other people read;
8. . . . write because reading and writing match;
9. . . . like certain authors and pick their books;
10. . . . write to authors;
11. . . . talk about authors and poets and illustrators;
12. . . . go to bookstores and buy good books like *Two Bad Ants*;
13. . . . *read* a lot!;
14. . . . don't always know all the words because they're still practicing when they get a book;
15. . . . look for books. They don't just grab the first thing they see;
16. . . . think about books when they're not reading them;
17. . . . know how to tell people about good books;
18. . . . look for new authors;
19. . . . spread out and read *lots* of authors;
20. . . . pick books they've never read before;
21. . . . go to the library and reread favorite books again and again;
22. . . . read to find out things they want to know about;
23. . . . go to the library; and
24. . . . *love* to read!

Much discussion and agreement surrounded the compiling of this list. When Matt contributed "looking at the letters for clues" (5d), a discussion ensued in which the children said that "first you have to look at the words. After you look at the words, you notice the letters." Some children had already developed this particular strategy when they entered first grade. Others acquired this strategy through involvement in the classroom. I realized that "looking at the words" was a critical breakthrough for each reader.

When Max contributed item 19, "Good readers spread out," I thought at first he spoke of the way children liked to spread out on the floor throughout the room as they read. "No!" he protested, amused at my ignorance. "Good readers read different things—they read different authors. They don't just stay with the same kinds of books or authors. Add 'pick books they've never read before.'"

After we finished our list we reread it and at the end I asked Monica what she meant when she said, "Good readers write because writing and reading match" (item 8).

"Well, it's like this," she began. "It's kinda hard to explain, but when you write, you write about your life—you know, things you did or things you know something about—and that makes you think of things you've read. And, when you read, you think about things in your life and then you want to write about them to get them all down and then you can read about your life too." She paused and then her face lit up. "It's about your *life*!" she continued. "Reading and writing match because they're both about your life. They both make you think about your life."

The children listened and acknowledged that indeed this was true. I was dumbfounded. Monica expressed what many adults might have forgotten or perhaps never experienced: Reading and writing are tools for meaning making and meaning making is a *life* process.

The Children Reading

What follows are glimpses of individual children learning to read in reading workshop in my first-grade classroom. The first two vignettes are of rather typical first graders who began reading with ease, though not at the same time or in the same way.

Jackie

The second week of school Jackie read *The Napping House.* Her only error was substituting "sleeping" for "slumbering." Before she took it home to share with her family I pointed out the difference in the structure of the two words and explained that "slumbering" was another word for "sleeping." "Oh, I never heard that word before," Jackie commented. (Children told me that it was hard to read a word if "You don't know that word." When I asked the class what they meant, they explained it was easy to read words you had *heard* before and you could usually figure out the meaning when you read "the whole thing." Children added that they usually knew words because they'd "heard the book before," referring to the reading aloud of books in the classroom.) Jackie liked the part of the story when the bed breaks "because it's funny" and she liked the rainbow on the last page. "It's neat. I like rainbows." Jackie was on her way as a reader.

She continued to learn to read entire books with little difficulty. She figured out unknown words through picture clues, the sound and rhythm of the language, letter clues, familiarity with the text (i.e., she'd heard the book read aloud), and the anticipated meaning—what made sense. She integrated this range of strategies in an efficient, mutually reinforcing manner. In a September interview she said she could "read a little" and that she learned because "every night we have story time and my mom reads to Emily and Maggie and Andy and me." In an interview at the end of the year I asked Jackie how she learned to read. She replied, "I started reading these little books my friend has, like one about a bus ride. Then I started reading harder ones and then I read them for a while and then we started having reading time every night and when I got to first grade I could read hard books." She added, "When I came to first grade I didn't really know how to write but I got the hang of it through writing because we write every day."

Over the year, Jackie took home more than thirty books that she had read to me or to a reading workshop aide. In addition, she read nearly all the books published by her classmates and numerous other trade books. Her comments during her reading of *Marianne's Grandmother* in April showed the integrated nature of her reading, writing, and learning processes and her thinking. Jackie said,

> Marianne's grandmother is making the dress to see if it fits her. . . . It's kinda like the story that I published about my grandfather only she tells what she used to do with her grandmother. . . . What I wonder is how old Marianne was. Sounds like she's five or six. It doesn't sound like she's eight because she asks lots of questions. . . . This reminds me of a book Elizabeth wrote and it's like *Nana Upstairs and Nana Downstairs* because in *Marianne's Grandmother* the grandmother dies and in *Nana Upstairs and Nana Downstairs* the grandmother died. They're alike because Tommy visited his grandmother every Sunday and she visited her grandmother. They do things together and my grandma and I do things together too.

Jody

Jody brought *Cookie's Week* to me during the third week of school and asked to read. He read the first four pages from memory without looking at the words. Then he began to stumble. I pointed to the words and said ever so gently, "Here, let's look at the words." But the attention Jody gave each word as he tried to figure it out caused him to lose touch with the ideas those words were meant to convey. I suggested we read together. We read through the book, pointing to the words, with Jody's voice trailing mine. "We read it," I said when we came to the end; Jody smiled. I urged Jody to "practice" reading it and reminded him to look at the words as he did so, then read it to me in a few days. "Okay," he replied good-naturedly, "because I still needed some help." Ten days later Jody read *Cookie's Week.* He made several miscues but all of the words he read maintained the meaning: "upset" for "knocked," "was" for "were," "shut" for "closed," and "trash" for "trash can." Three days later he read *This Old Man* without errors, pointing accurately to the words as he read, and said at the end, "This book's easy!"

Two weeks later he read *Building a House.* Pointing to the words was a big help and if he got off track he paused to find his place. The two miscues, "long" for "large" and "done" for "built," maintained meaning. He quickly corrected "done" to "built" when I asked him if this was what he meant to say. When I asked how he learned to read this book he said, "By sounding out and listening off of you and I asked Monica and also Stacy helped me a little." This book had been a challenging leap for Jody, but he had wanted to read it from the first week of school. His interest stemmed from his father's occupation as a carpenter and Jody said, "My favorite part's where they're up on the roof 'cause that's what my dad usually does—put the shingles on." Jody continued as an avid reader and writer from that point on. Like Jackie, he read many books in the classroom throughout the year. He read twenty-five of those books to me or the reading workshop volunteer and took them home to share with his family. When I talked to Jody about reading and writing in September he said, "I can read—sorta. Well, not really yet." He spoke at length about his mother as a reader and writer. "The last time we went to the library, she read every book in the whole library!" he said, and then added, "And she's always writing a letter to our Aunt Judy." In May, Jody talked extensively about his reading and writing. Here's one excerpt from those remarks:

> In the beginning I picked up books like *Cookie's Week* and I just started practicing it and I got it. Before I went to school I could read just one book of mine—a little book. I sound out some of the words, but some I don't sound out. I ask somebody. I know how to pick books. It's like yesterday—it was not too warm and not too cold. *Arthur's Teacher Trouble* was like that. It's right in the middle—not too hard and not too easy. I pick a book and stay with it. If I don't know some of the words, I skip to the next word and see if it gives it to me or I use the pictures to give it to me. It's important that you read something every day. If you don't read and write every day you get out of the habit of it. Reading is fun, funner than writing, but writing

> is fun too—especially when you finish a piece because you worked hard.

Jackie and Jody's prior experiences with written language, primarily home experiences and attitudes cultivated in their homes, influenced the pace and timing with which they moved into reading. Not all children come to school with these experiences.

Our school district provides support through the reading teacher to first graders identified by the classroom teacher as likely to be "at risk." By providing this support at the beginning of a child's school career and continuing for as long as needed, we've found that a child is more likely to become a successful reader. In Jackie and Jody's class, I identified seven children in September for extra support. This number was larger than in any of my previous first-grade classes. Luci Steele, our reading teacher, arranged a half-hour time slot three days a week to see these children. We wanted this time to be in the classroom, but when Luci came to reading workshop to focus on these seven children, what sounded great in theory turned into mass confusion in practice. The children lacked the inner structure to attend to tasks within a large group without continual teacher direction. We revised our plan and had Mrs. Steele work with the group in her own room, following similar workshop procedures, for three days a week. The other two days the children worked in reading workshop, and I usually paired them up with other children. The procedure worked. The children learned to adapt to the workshop structure and Mrs. Steele addressed individual needs as the children developed as readers.

Three of the seven children left before the school year ended and new children (often with similar problems) took their place. The following fall, only two of the seven returned to our school. The transient nature of their family lives influenced their school lives. Each of these seven children brought complex personal histories that affected their learning. Without delving into the details of those private histories, here are the stories of three of those seven children.

NATALIE

Natalie attended kindergarten in a rural community in another section of the state. "They didn't teach you nuttin' there," she declared in a September interview, then added, "I can only write my name. It's hard to learn, especially when you're my age." The comments seemed to indicate Natalie's perceptions of herself as a learner. However, Natalie wrote eagerly every day and her writing became her first reading material. "My kitten was the best kitten in the world before we moved," she read, taking on an official reader's tone as she read the intended meaning from the randomly selected letters she'd written. She looked me straight in the eye and said, "Do you like it?"

"Yes," and before I could say more, Natalie continued talking, telling me about the kitten they left behind when they moved just before school started.

Natalie could *sing* the alphabet, but she was lost when it came to identifying letters beyond those in her name. I encouraged her to think about what she wanted to say and to put down letters that might make those words. "They don't have to be perfect. Your *ideas*—what you want to tell other people—are the most important part." She readily accepted my suggestion. With concern for correctness set aside, Natalie wrote fluently by writing strings of letters across the page. Most of her pieces were fantasies about butterflies and flowers, unicorns and puppies. She continued to read these pieces using the pictures for clues and running her finger under the letters she had written. On several occasions I suggested she listen for letter sounds but her face clouded before she'd reply, "That's too hard for me to do." I backed off. Give her time, I reminded myself.

Natalie loved books and stories. In reading workshop during the first days of school she flipped through books over and over and sometimes told the story softly to herself. At the end of September she brought me *The Very Hungry Caterpillar* and announced, "I can read this book all by myself." She sat beside me and told the story from beginning to end by reading the pictures. Her version only vaguely matched the actual words in the text. When she finished she beamed at me and said, "I did it, didn't I?"

If the discrepancy between her achievement and that of her classmates occurred to her, it did not seem to bother Natalie. She worked diligently and conscientiously. It didn't matter to her (or me) that her handwriting was haphazard across the page or that her drawings were at times masses of scribble lines. She happily went about her work and made friends with everyone. Her only distress came from being teased at the bus stop by older children who called her "fatty." Natalie's parents supported the school program and their daughter's learning. "We don't expect her to be at the top of her class or anything like that. We only want her to learn, be happy, and enjoy school."

When Natalie brought back the books Mrs. Steele sent home with her twice a week, she read each of them to me before she returned them to her. "I need to read to you," she'd remind me on busy mornings. In mid-October she commented during reading workshop, "I know how to recognize 'snail' and 'sun' from each other. 'Snail' has all those letters and 'sun' has three."

Natalie began learning the individual letters of the alphabet with instruction from Mrs. Steele, from classroom language lessons, and from strategies she devised herself. She wrote the alphabet with her friend Stacy during play time: "Me and Stacy are practicing handwriting," she said. I noticed her locating particular letters by softly singing the alphabet song and pointing her finger to each letter of the alphabet posted on the wall. "I'm just finding *M*," she said. I suggested we put an alphabet strip on her desk but she scowled and shook her head. Natalie didn't want to be different from the other children. I thought of putting an alphabet strip on every desk as I had done other years. I made the suggestion to the children. "NO WAY!" came the unanimous reply. "That's *baby* stuff. We did that in kindergarten!" Thank goodness I asked, I thought.

In early December Natalie told me, "Writing's fun! Reading's fun! I'm learning so much stuff." One day she told me she was writing about a trip to McDonald's. "Me and my family," she read, and then added, "now I'm going to write 'went.'" I looked at the writing. "Me" was there and MI was clearly intended to be "my." WaLe for "family"—the *W* could be an *M* reversed and I could hear Natalie pronouncing "family" as fam-a-lee, thus the aLe. She was beginning to listen to the sounds of letters! I sat beside her for a moment.

Natalie said "went" and looked at me, puzzled. I repeated the word and exaggerated the /w/ sound. Natalie watched my mouth, a look of concentration on her face.

"What letter do you hear at the beginning of 'went'?" Natalie shook her head but kept looking at me intently. "It's a *W*," I said, "but it's a tricky one because *W* sounds like *Y*."

"Should I write a *W*?" Natalie asked. I nodded. Natalie wrote.

"What else do you hear in 'went'?" I asked.

Natalie repeated the word several times, then suddenly said, "*A*!"

"Write it! Anything else?"

"*T*!"

"That's the last letter in 'went,'" I said as Natalie wrote. "What comes next?"

Natalie reread her sentence, "Me and my family went . . . to. Is t-o 'to'?" she asked.

"Sure is," I replied. Natalie wrote.

"McDonald's comes next," she said. "That's a long word. I don't think I can do that."

"Well, let's give it a try," I suggested. "I'll help you. You know when you've seen the McDonald's sign?" Natalie nodded. "Well, picture it in your head. What letter do you see at the beginning of McDonald's?"

Natalie squeezed her eyes shut in concentration then suddenly said, "*M*! I see *M*!"

"You got it!" I replied with an enthusiasm to match Natalie's. "Anything else?"

Natalie closed her eyes again but this time she said, "I don't know. It's all jumbled together."

"Well, then let's listen to see if we hear any letters. McDonald's," I repeated slowly.

Natalie repeated the name slowly. "Is *A* next?"

"Write it," I replied.

Together Natalie and I worked through the spelling of "McDonald's" with Natalie writing MaktallLS.

"Did I spell 'McDonald's'?" she asked when we finished.

"You sure did. How did you do that?"

"I listened and then I just wrote the letters!" she replied in total delight.

At this point Stacy walked by Natalie's desk. "I could help Natalie, Mrs. Avery. I could be her teacher and show her how like you did."

"Okay, Stacy. Just remember what we said about good teachers."

"Yeah, I know. Good teachers don't just *tell* people the answers, they help them figure it out for themselves. Don't worry, I can do that. So then Natalie will be able to do it herself," Stacy stated in her most grown-up tone.

Natalie beamed. "Yup," she said. Stacy took my place beside Natalie. Later, when I looked at Natalie's writing, I noticed she underlined the word "McDonald's" in her piece and put a star above every letter—a strategy I often used with the children at the end of handwriting lessons when I asked them to assess their own handwriting by marking with a star the letters they felt were best. All our lessons with letter-sound relationships had begun to click with Natalie—a big step for a child who had not known the alphabet just three months prior. I had made several attempts to connect letters with words with Natalie and she had consistently rejected my offers. On this day I had spent slightly over five minutes and from there she took off; I had waited and watched for three months for this "teachable moment." This piece of writing became Natalie's first published book.

A week later three literacy events occurred for Natalie. She brought in a newspaper clipping and read the headline to me, "Santa is a Christmas state of mind." Then she zestfully explained her process: "I looked through the whole paper to see if I could find anything I could read. Then my dad helped me find this picture of Santa and I knew 'Santa' and I knew 'is' and 'a' and 'Christmas' and then he helped me to read it all!" The next day Natalie read *The Bus Ride* to me. She read the book smoothly and her finger moved under each word as she read. When she came to "rhinoceros" she stumbled, then said, "rhino?" and looked to me for help.

"Rhinoceros," I said.

"Oh, I don't know that one. Is this a rhino or a rhinoceros?" she asked, pointing to the picture. I explained the words.

Natalie nodded and said, "'Cuz I didn't know they mean the same."

A couple days later Natalie read the typed version of her story about McDonald's at our author's party. She'd had no trouble learning to read it and explained why: "'cuz I wrote it so I *knew* what it says!"

In the winter months Natalie read other books with predictable language patterns, such as *Cookie's Week* and *All the Pretty Horses*, a book that had been her favorite since September. She began experimenting with punctuation and quotation marks when she inserted them where she thought they might go. In mid-January I read aloud "The Snowball Fight," a piece she planned to publish. "You can read what I wrote? How'd you do that?" Natalie startled me with her questions, questions I had asked *her* all year. She sat looking at me, waiting for an answer—just as I'd done with her for weeks. She really wanted to know!

"Hmm, let's see." I paused before I answered to ponder just how I *had read* her writing. "Well, I looked at the pictures, and I used the letters you wrote, and I remember how kids spell some words because I've seen them before—so that helped me figure some words out—but mostly, I think mostly, I kept thinking about what you were saying and what made sense."

Natalie looked at me, pondering this answer with a serious countenance, and then replied, "Yup, that's kinda how I do it too."

At the end of the school year Natalie worked on reading Lois Ehlert's *Planting a Rainbow*. This book was a challenge and the first time she read it to me her reading was halting and she missed many words, such as "seedless," "watch," "again," "select," and others. I suggested she choose another book and come back to this later or practice this one some more. Five days later Natalie came back and read *Planting a Rainbow* smoothly and with no errors! When I asked how she'd done this she replied, "I *really* wanted to read this because I just *love* this book with all the colors. So after you told me some of the words I went back to my seat and read it over and over until I just remembered them!"

During the last week of school I asked the class what they remembered from the year that had helped them learn. Natalie said, "I remember the day I spelled 'McDonald's' and you told me I did it right so then I could spell. That *really* helped me. I'll tell you one thing," she added, "I just love to read and write." In an interview during the last week of school, Natalie commented on her reading and writing.

> How I learned to read is I learned "the" because you wrote it a lot and I saw it. The books that you read to us I learned all the words because I heard them over and over again. They [the words] were just up there in my head. My favorite books are Tomie dePaola books. I like his pictures and the way he says things. When I write, I know some of the words and I sound out some. In the mini-lesson I do what you said, then I get my story real well. My best piece is "When I Got My Duck." I just like the way it sounds and feels to me. In writing, I like to get the feeling inside before I write. Then I say what I want to write and see if it makes any sense.

Darren

One morning in mid-September Darren handed me a flat box as he walked into the classroom. "What's this?" I asked.

Darren looked puzzled and said, "I don't know." We opened the box, found cupcakes, and Darren said, "Oh yeah, it's my birthday." A moment later Darren joined the other children who were putting paper candles with their names and dates of birth on cardboard birthday cakes, one for each month, that were spread out on the floor. When I joined them, Darren looked at me and said, "I don't know what to do. When's my birthday?"

"When is your birthday?" I asked.

"I don't know. I don't remember, I mean, I don't know when my birthday is," then he shook his head as though trying to clear his thinking in some way. "I get confused . . ." He smiled as his voice trailed off.

"Didn't you just tell me today was your birthday?" I asked softly.

"Today?" Darren looked startled.

I led him to my desk and looked on my class role. "Yes, today. It says right here. Today's your birthday."

Darren looked at the cupcakes and at me and then said in a puzzled voice, "Yeah, today's my birthday. I'm seven years old today."

If Darren seemed puzzled, so did I. During the first days of school I attributed his frequent confusion to the many recent changes in his life. His mother had remarried and the new family unit had moved into the school district over the summer. But now, in late September, the confusion continued and the range and complexity of his behaviors fell into no discernible patterns. His comments in class brought impatient protests from the other children. DARRE-NNN, they'd chorus until I'd remind them that we needed to listen and try to understand Darren's ideas. When we discussed ways animals prepare for winter, Darren suggested that a bear would go to a store to buy a winter jacket. "But bears don't wear jackets," said Matt, "They have their own fur."

"Oh, I never thought of that," Darren replied and the look on his face told me that he truly hadn't considered this idea.

When the class sat at their seats, Darren constantly fidgeted, cutting paper into slivers inside his desk, falling off his chair, or writing on his desk, chair, or his own arms with pencil or pen. He frequently left his seat just to walk around the classroom. "Darren is in a state of constant movement," I wrote in my observational notes at the end of September. When I gave directions to the class, Darren began the particular task only after he noticed the other children beginning. "What are we supposed to do?" he'd ask in a startled voice. Eventually, he came to rely on imitating other children or requesting assistance from me in order to accomplish basic tasks such as finding a page in the math book. When the children took turns telling math stories to illustrate addition facts, Darren volunteered, but when I called on him he suddenly became bewildered and said, "I can't. I mean I don't know." A few minutes later he raised his hand again and then repeated the story Emily had just told.

In a September interview, Darren told me that a good reader was one who could "read fast" and that his favorite book was *The Mouse and the Motorcycle*, which his mom had read to him. He hoarded books in his desk as though they were precious possessions that he might never see again if he put them back on the shelf.

One day a child cried, "Darren has about twenty million books in his desk!"

"I just wanted to read them," Darren answered as he pulled them out.

In reading workshop Darren spent most of his time reading with or watching other children. I began to surmise that he *wanted* to read and hoarded the books he wanted to read, but that he truly didn't know how to go about reading. My individual conferences seemed less helpful to him than what he learned from the other children. He imitated them by choosing their favorite books and turning the pages as he'd seen them do. He stayed with reading most when he read with a partner, a collaboration in which the partner child read and Darren closely followed that child's moving finger. Throughout this reading, the pair stopped to talk about the book. The process resembled a parent-child storybook reading at bedtime.

In October Darren read one of the books from Mrs. Steele's room to me. This book, about a mother bird teaching her baby to fly, had few words (mostly "up" and "down"). Darren pointed to each word and read accurately, but when I asked him what he thought of the story, he looked baffled. "Who are these birds?" I asked. Darren shrugged his shoulders. "Are they related?" Darren looked puzzled so I rephrased my question. "Do they know each other?" More puzzlement. "Could they be brother and sister or . . ." before I could finish Darren interrupted. "Yes!" he said obviously glad to have an answer.

"Are they brother and sister? Or could they be a mother and her baby?"

"Yes, I mean no. I mean, I don't know," he said. I asked if the birds in the first picture were the same ones in the second illustration. He told me no. After I went through the book and told the story from the pictures to Darren he replied, "I didn't get that." I wasn't sure he understood even then.

When Darren wrote in writing workshop, he spent most of the time drawing—his favorite activity—and he told me he could write but he couldn't spell. I suspected that when Darren said he couldn't spell, he meant that he didn't understand the connection of letters to sounds or that letters on a page represented words. During a couple of writing workshops I spent a few minutes with Darren, working him through the process of listening for sounds in words then writing letters to represent those sounds. After this, letters began to replace some of the wavy lines in his writing. However, I never heard him attempting to reproduce the sounds of letters when he wrote. All the words he wrote seemed to come from visual memory. I noticed that he frequently copied words from the chalkboard, and he wrote entire words randomly to convey his meaning, even though these words were not the ones he intended them to be. When he had no visual recall, he either wrote letters randomly or reverted to the wavy lines. In no time, and sooner than many of his peers, Darren developed a vocabulary of words he could spell correctly. He couldn't always read these words, but when I read them for him he'd say, "Oh yeah, that's right." However, even when he remembered how to write a word, he could not consistently read that word and rarely read words together in any way that communicated meaning.

One of Darren's favorite activities in school was handwriting instruction and, even though he often substituted uppercase for lowercase letters or became confused about which line on the paper to write, he produced beautiful papers with precisely executed letters. He recopied handwriting lessons and even the texts of the short books he read for Mrs. Steele, both in free-play time at school and at home, and frequently presented these papers to me. "I'm playing office," he told me during free-play time, and added that this was like his dad's office. He sat with a toy telephone held to an ear and wrote numbers and letters on his clipboard. "I'm filling out claims," he said. He became deeply involved in his play and engaged other children in elaborate scenarios portraying office scenes. If others chose not to play, Darren created imaginary office visitors.

Darren especially loved to draw houses, barns, and buggies. His drawings had a distinct, artistic style, different from that of any child I'd ever seen. The other children marveled at his talent and his sensitive use of color. They enjoyed Darren not only for his artistry but also for his pleasant attitude and sense of humor. "Darren's really weird," one child confided, "but I like him a lot even though he's weird!" The comment spoke for all of us. We didn't understand Darren and his behaviors at times were trying, but we all found him delightful and so interesting. Even so, Darren's unique behaviors and thinking patterns led me to discuss this child with the principal and the school guidance counselor. We considered the possibility of a learning disability. The district psychologist talked with Darren and administered some screening tests, but these tools provided no insights.

In writing workshop, despite the outstanding artistry and correct spellings, the content of Darren's writing confused readers. He wrote words and phrases, repeated them, drifted from one topic to another, and rarely could read more than a word or two of what he'd written. When we published his first book in mid-November, I eliminated the small-group conference because I believed the procedures would only confuse Darren. He read a sentence; I typed. When I asked him for a title, Darren said, "What do you mean?" I explained titles to Darren by showing him several books. "Oh, okay," he said and immediately proposed the title, "When I Went to My Mom's Work." In the days before our author's party, Darren practiced reading his book over and over. Some days he forgot what the words said and asked for help. His peers and I focused on context clues to help him remember what the pages said. Darren successfully read his book at the author's party.

Learning to read his published writing seemed to inspire Darren to read a book from the classroom library. During the first two months of school, Darren spent reading workshop browsing through books, noticing words here and there that he recognized, sitting with peers as he listened and followed what they read, and generally gaining experiences with books, readers, and reading. Now he settled with one book, *The Bus Ride.* He had been reading books with a few lines of highly predictable language for Mrs. Steele, but this was the first time he volunteered to read a book to me from the classroom collection. He became stumped on the word "then" and said "en" and he substituted "bunny" for "rabbit." He moved his hand under words as he read, as I had encouraged all the children to do to help them focus on individual words, but I noticed that he pointed to different words than those he spoke. At first glance it seemed he had memorized the text. However, closer observation revealed a complex integration of strategies. To read the book he relied on the book's illustrations, the predictable pattern, and memory from his many experiences with this book. Those experiences began early in September and included hearing peers read the book, looking through the book on his own, and working to read it both with peer assistance and independently. He made no use of letter-sound relationships, a pattern I consistently saw during conferences in reading workshop. Still, Darren had made tremendous progress from the beginning of September.

When he read *It Didn't Frighten Me* two and a half weeks later, his finger trailed behind the words he read during the repetitious refrain in the text, but he pointed accurately to the words in all other lines of the book. He had memorized the refrain and didn't need his finger; his finger helped him focus on words that did not repeat, and the focusing helped him attend to each word and read it accurately. A month later Darren read *Catch That Frog,* from the old Scott Foresman Unlimited Series. He substituted "in back of" for "between" and "over" for "under," and when I directed him to the illustrations he was clearly confused by these concepts. However, when he read "went" for "jumped" he immediately corrected the error and turned to me and confided, "I knowed that word 'jumped.'"

Sequencing information and connecting one part of a story to another continued to be a major difficulty for Darren, both in his writing and his reading. In December he wrote about going to visit his grandpa's farm. The story jumped from one incident to another, leaving readers to fill in the gaps. When peers questioned lack of clarity, Darren seemed puzzled. The story made sense to him. I chatted with Darren about the piece during writing workshop, getting him to tell me the information that was in his head but not on the paper. When he told me a missing part, I urged him to write it and showed him where it would fit in the text. I moved on to other students while Darren wrote, then came back and read the inserted information, trying to help Darren grasp the meaning for himself. We continued through the story the same way.

About the same time he read *Building a House,* by Byron Barton. He read "Then put up walls" for "They put up walls." When I asked if this made sense, Darren replied no. We corrected the error together, but Darren made a similar error in the next sentence. I wrote in my notes during that reading, "Not listening to himself for *meaning*!" It appeared that if the words flowed he perceived himself as reading, but that he gave little consideration to the words making sense. However, he had begun to think of the story as a whole, and at the end told me that he would like to grow up and be "one of them guys who make houses like this." Then he went through the book and told me about the pictures and how he would like to do these jobs.

When Darren came back from Christmas vacation he wrote a coherent and (from all I could determine) sequenced story of visiting Longwood Gardens over the holidays. He read *Beyond the Hill* and said, "It's talking about mountains and stars and that kinda stuff," but his puzzled countenance told me the story was baffling to him. His mother wrote that when he read this book to her, he talked about the stars in the book and the stars he saw during the planetarium visit.

In March, when he first began reading *The Happy Day*, a book about approaching spring, he said, "The bears are dancing and they start crying when the flowers are coming up because they're gonna die. That's what I think." Later, when he polished his oral reading of the book, he read it to me before he took it home. On this reading he talked about spring. It seemed that Darren required many experiences with a text, not only to learn to read but to *understand* what that text was about.

About this time Darren began having sudden outbursts, which were untypical of his pleasant, somewhat carefree behavior of the fall months. One day Jody found a piece of Darren's writing in his folder. "Why'd you stick your writing in my folder?" Jody demanded.

"Well, I'm so sorry," said Darren in a voice that mocked Jody's.

"Don't stick your writing in my folder," Jody replied.

"I didn't do it, Jody!" Darren yelled. He grabbed his writing from Jody and began pacing around the room, muttering to himself. The outburst startled all of us. It took several minutes before Darren's rage subsided. He began talking about being mad when he couldn't find his book or pencil or during minor interactions with other children. He began writing about anger and his stories were coherent for the first time!

One day he and Jackie began to coauthor a story entitled "Ben's Dog Got Run Over." Jackie wrote with Darren for one day and then Darren continued on his own, checking in with Jackie from time to time to read the developing piece aloud. In this story, the dog of a boy named Benny is run over. Benny cries "all day and all night and all day in school." When the other children learn why, they too cry. At one point in the story Benny says, "I am mad my dog died." When Benny tells his mom that he will kill the man who ran over his dog, "she sended him to his room and with no supper and he was grounded and he had no supper that night." The next day Darren revised the piece to read "he had a great supper that night." When I read Darren's writing I saw many allusions to his favorite books. Two of those books had been *Ghost's Hour, Spook's Hour,* by Eve Bunting, and *The Accident,* by Carol Carrick. The characters in the former are a boy and his dog, and the latter (a book Darren reported as his favorite) is about a dog being killed by a truck.

In another story Darren wrote about a character who is mad and "slammed the door in his face." Then one day Darren produced the following story without pausing to line out or even reread as he wrote, a procedure he had not done *all year.* "There was a boy. His name was dummy because he was a dummy. The next day he went to school and everybody made fun of him. He laughed at himself. The people in school laughed harder and harder. 'What's wrong?' he asked. 'You are dumb.' The next day he got very angry. He said, 'Goodby' to his mother and left in a hurry and wrote a note to his teacher. It said, 'Bye, Mrs. Bounds.' I am mad because everybody makes fun of me and it was so very (sic) that the teacher wasn't even there." Darren read the piece to me. I listened, retold the story to Darren, and then gently inquired, since Mrs. Bounds was our art teacher, if this story was about her or anyone we knew. "No. See this is the other school, my other school, not this school, just another school. I just used Mrs. Bounds' name because I like art." Darren's displays of anger subsided after this writing, but none of us ever discovered what had been upsetting him.

Soon after this incident Stacy chose to write about her parent's divorce after hearing *Dinosaur's Divorce.* Stacy and Darren were good friends and soon Darren chose to write about the divorce of his parents. He graphically described events that occurred and, although the piece seemed disconnected and Darren himself acknowledged he didn't understand all that had occurred at home, I understood most of his story. Darren spent days on this writing and seemed particularly satisfied with the ending, where he related that his mother and stepfather did not fight. He now read all of his writing without assistance from me, not only immediately after writing it but also on subsequent days. He had a strong grasp of the meaning embedded in his words and used that meaning as well as all the other strategies he had developed to read what he had written. When he read incorrectly, he caught the error within a few words and went back to reread and self-correct.

Darren now saw himself as a writer and a reader and identified with professional authors. He wrote letters to authors Eve Bunting and Carol Carrick to tell them how much he enjoyed their books and how many books he himself had published. Carol Carrick wrote a personal letter to Darren and told him how many books she and her husband, Don, had published and then commented that Darren would soon be ahead of them.

One day in May, Darren picked up Thomas Locker's *The Boy Who Held Back the Sea.* When I stopped at his desk during reading workshop he read perfectly. "What's happening in this story?" I asked. The old patterns of confusion with meaning appeared as Darren first looked at the pages, then replied, "I don't know," then pointed to an illustration and said, "a boy who lived in the town, he acted like that boy."

"Tell me more about the boy," I said. Darren shook his head as though trying to clear his thinking. "My head doesn't work sometimes," he said. During the last days of school Darren read *A Kiss for Little Bear.* His reading was a close retelling of the story but not an accurate reading. "It gets all mixed up for me," he said.

With books that he read several times and had heard read aloud, Darren began to understand the stories. It was difficult to tell if his comprehension developed from reading or from hearing class discussions. On a word identification test administered by Mrs. Steele, Darren scored a 1.9, placing him on grade level. I knew that a test of his reading comprehension could likely produce a lag behind word recognition. I also knew that Darren would never be a typical student and that his future teachers would be as baffled by him as I was. I also knew that Darren brought a particularly unique view of life to a classroom community and a special talent as an artist. He would always provide an unusual perspective to situations and offer contributions that would not occur to others.

Michael

During free play three weeks into the school year, the principal brought Michael, with his mother, to the classroom. Michael, a tall blond boy of seven, smiled shyly. Large spots of tooth decay blackened that smile. He clutched a small pencil case that held colored markers and two pencils. He mumbled a few words when I said hello. I called one of the boys over and asked him to show Michael around the classroom. "Sure," he replied, and the two boys went off together.

Michael had moved to our community from a distant state where he had lived with his grandparents and mother, who was separated from his father. A reconciliation between the parents had brought Michael, his mother, and younger sibling to Lancaster. He had not begun first grade before he moved, though he had attended kindergarten. Later he would bring in paperback books his teacher had given him and a small photo album from his kindergarten year that she had made and brought to his home before he moved. At Christmas this teacher sent Michael another book.

With his former teacher, Michael had obviously established a love for stories and books. Literature time was his favorite time of day; he loved listening to stories. "R-EE-D!" he'd say and then sit in rapt attention as I read. During reading workshop he hugged books to his chest, turned the pages and looked at pictures, and watched other children reading. He also watched and then imitated them during writing workshop. At first he drew and wrote only his name and the date. Then he added a few letters, and slowly those letters began to match the sounds he intended. His oral language handicapped him, for Michael mumbled or spoke in baby talk, and he spoke only in one-word utterances or sentence fragments. His writing and reading developed slowly.

The support of Mrs. Steele, his working in daily writing and reading workshops, and the continuous interactions with other children served to nurture his language development. When possible, I spent extra moments beside Michael as he read or wrote, helping him develop specific strategies. Michael could compose stories orally and, with my help, he put a story he told me into writing. It became his first published piece (see Figures 9–5, 9–6, and 9–7). At the November parent-teacher conferences I urged Michael's father (his mother was working) to read to his son and to talk with him about books or any experiences they had together. Michael's father told me his work schedule allowed only one night a week when the entire family was together. Michael's mother was at home with the children in the evenings he said, but acknowledged, "I've never seen my wife read." In a later meeting Michael's mother said, "I don't do so good at reading myself. I can't read, really." Once she had told me this, Michael's mother began writing notes (using invented spelling) to me when he brought books home. When she was hospitalized during the winter, an unknown hand wrote a note and Michael's father added his signature at the end.

In early January, Michael read *Brown Bear, Brown Bear, What Do You See?* It was the first book he had read from the classroom library. He said that his friend Kevin had suggested it. He read "beautiful children" as "boys and girls"; when I pointed out the correct words he shook his head, grinned, and said, "Boy, I hate that word because it's too hard for me." I was delighted that he had spoken an entire sentence! He spoke as if he had marbles in his mouth, but it was an entire sentence. I asked him to repeat his words more clearly so I could understand and he did, then smiled. The garbled language seemed to indicate a degree of uncertainty about his performance. With encouragement of that performance, he abandoned the undecipherable talk. Michael moved on to other books with predictable language patterns, such as *It Didn't Frighten Me*, and books written by classmates, such as Darren's "I Went to My Mom's

Work." He rapidly began developing a vocabulary of words he knew upon sight and specific strategies to figure out unknown words. He used letter-sound clues as well as context. Meaning always led the way for him. He viewed written language as having meaning and used strategies that he first used in writing to decipher words written by other authors.

Near the end of the year Michael read a book about dinosaurs. When he read to me, his only error was "points" for "plates." Referring to a small and rather helpless-looking dinosaur, he commented after the reading, "Tyrannosaurus *cannot* eat him!" Then he added, "I like that I can read now."

"How did you learn to read?" I asked.

Michael shrugged and said, "I don't know. I just kept trying and my friends helped me and I look at the words now."

Michael's family moved before he began second grade, and he did not return to our school the following September.

Reflections

At the end of one year a parent wrote, "These children believe they can read anything! My daughter sits down every night with the newspaper and she actually reads it. I've seen her confidence grow [through] her effort and desire to learn and even more important to understand." This parent's child was one I would have assigned to the "low group" had she been in my class a year earlier. This is not to say that the typical "low group" children suddenly make miraculous strides and match all their peers in school learning, but they do achieve solid success as learners. It's impossible to compare their growth to "low group" children in my former classes and prove that this group achieved more. However, I *know* that these children were far better off in this community of learners than other children I taught through a reading program, not only in their achievement but also in their investment in learning. The workshop approach permits children to work with their peers and to learn from each other. The models of more experienced language learners helps the less experienced ones. The children do not view themselves as superior or inferior to one another. Rather, they value the talents of their peers. The children regarded Monica as an excellent reader, marveled at Darren's artistic talent, loved Michael's tales of playing in the woods and his knowledge of small animals, and appreciated Ellen's insightful and sensitive responses to their writing. At the end of one year, a parent noted one of the most positive aspects of her son's first-grade experience: "Respect and appreciation for his classmates' talents and interests." Alone I could not meet all demands within the classroom. Gradually children learned to look to peers as a resource. We became a community learning together.

Glenda Bissex (1980) writes, "It has become increasingly clear that language acquisition is not merely imitative but systematic and creative, in the sense of the child constructing the rules for himself." As to how much the child depends on instruction in learning to read, Bissex suggests that "the 'truth' perhaps will be found to vary widely among beginning readers, some virtually teaching themselves while others depend more on instruction" (134). In my experience with first graders, some children, such as Jackie, arrive at school already reading or on the brink of beginning. With a conducive environment and a few guidelines they read, relying on their experiences with written language and learning processes they've developed long before they came to school. Other children, for whatever reason, do not seem to have processes for learning written language in smooth running order (according to the expectations of school) when they begin school. Programmed reading instruction did not serve these children well. Rather than allowing the children to build on the systematic and creative processes they already possessed, the program required the children to adapt to its procedures. The structure of writing and reading workshops and the classroom tone allowed for direct teaching and for all children to continue their natural learning processes.

Teachers recognize that "low group" children need more time, more demonstrations, more explanations, more direct instruction. Schools often deal with this need by separating these children from their peers and giving them more worksheets, more skill and drill—the very activities that had not been working for them all along. Because this remediation often focuses on skills as ends in themselves rather than as strategies for learning to use language, the children aren't able to connect the exercises to actual reading and writing. I found these children need experiences where they can develop strategies in the context of making meaning. These experiences are best acquired in a community of their peers. These children also need more frequent responses and guidance as they read than do children with more experience. Those responses must come while the children are engaged in reading and writing.

Reading workshop accommodated an individualized pace and provided opportunity for more teacher time for responding on a one-to-one basis. I'd place a small chair beside a child's desk and ask, "Okay if I sit here and watch how you write [or read]?" The children soon accepted my presence as part of the classroom procedure. In those few minutes beside a child, I observed *closely* and interjected occasional requests. My role was coach, supporter, and teacher, providing *very specific, direct instruction* and expecting the child to continue independently of me.

Jerome Bruner refers to the natural manner in which parents nurture children as "scaffolding." Scaffolding supports the child as learner, helps that child extend learning, and is gradually removed as learners work independently. Children such as Nicole, Darren, and Michael worked well with the same procedures as their more experienced classmates, and in the same environment, but they required more support as they acclimated to school learning and moved into reading and writing. The scaffold of the workshop approach gave them this support.

After several years of documenting first graders learning to read, I know *every child learns to read differently.* Just as Donald Graves stated that writing demands a "waiting, responsive type of teaching" (1981), so I believe that reading requires a waiting, responsive teaching style. When I began teaching writing with this responsive approach, I realized that it was not enough to establish an environment and let children write. To help writers develop, I had to be familiar with strategies that writers use and to develop an ongoing awareness of the qualities of good writing. Similarly, to teach reading with a responsive teaching style, I had to bring to the classroom expertise about reading strategies, a knowledge of available reading materials to accommodate individual interests, and an awareness of the many purposes for reading. I had to strive to incorporate all of these aspects into the structure.

With the mask of a reading program removed, I could see—really *see*—classroom learning for the first time. Because the children were not all completing the same workbook pages or reading the same story, I discovered individual learning processes. I began to observe and listen closely. From the children I've learned that every child's learning is continually evolving and that learning is an intricate composite of each child's personality, heritage, previous learning, environment, and group collaborations. Children may share common interests and attributes, but these characteristics combine and operate differently within each child.

How *do* children learn to read? Defining the process of learning to read with precision is complex. It strikes me that a major handicap to reading instruction may be that we have attempted to articulate learning to read with such precision that we create inflexible orthodoxies. Every classroom teacher who has taught with a reading program is well acquainted with these orthodoxies, which are impossible to apply to every student with any degree of effectiveness. I have come to tolerate ambiguity in the classroom and in the learning process. The children have helped me understand that learning is messy, jumbled, nonlinear, and often unpredictable and that they learn well in a literate environment where they talk, listen, write, and read. Learning to read is complex but need not be complicated if we trust children's capacity to learn.

CHAPTER 16

Learning Language

Phonics, Word Study, and Spelling

The children's names are the first words examined closely when school begins. I use them to begin the first reading workshop (Chapter 17) and we notice them as we explore the room together the first morning. Each year is a little different, but the names are the beginning. The children recognize their own first names and I ask, "Are there any that begin with the same letter?"

The children quickly notice Jared, Joseph, Josie, Jackie, and Jeffrey. Then there's Monica, Matthew, and Michael. "Mrs. Avery," someone points out. "It has an *M*."

"It has an *A* too, like mine," says Aaron.

"Avery and Aaron. They don't sound alike," says Jeff.

"You're right; they don't," I reply. That's because *A*'s a vowel and vowels work differently than other letters.

The children look mystified, but I leave it at this today. Most of the children seem to have a good grip on letter-sound relationships at the beginnings of words. They've learned this skill in kindergarten. Later we'll label children's mailboxes and put nametags on their desks. I'll spread out the names on the floor or a table and, before we put them to their intended use, we may group them by the first letter or last letter. We may count letters or go through the alphabet and count how many of each letter are present in all the names. Perhaps I'll ask the children to clap the number of syllables in each name.

Throughout these playful games, we're considering strategies for reading the names of classmates. We'll examine the names and talk about their structures and how letter sounds help us read and remember them. I'm building awareness of how words are put together. This is the beginning of working with words, phonics, and spelling in this classroom.

Most of the children come to first grade with phonemic awareness, an understanding that speech is composed of a series of individual sounds, and with some knowledge of phonics. That is, they understand that letters connect to sounds to form written language. Many can identify the particular sounds represented by consonant letters and apply this letter-sound relationship to the beginning of words. They know that letter *d* makes the sound that begins words like *dog* and *donut*, for example.

During the first days of school, the children and I review the letter-sound relationships of consonants, keeping this review in the context of reading and writing. Karin Dahl points out that "phonics in context" takes into account:

- the context of children's needs and their emerging phonics concepts,
- the context of their developing language knowledge, and
- the context of reading and writing activities. (Dahl et al. 2001)

In my classroom, maintaining these contexts is central to all instruction I do on the structures of written language.

Even though these lessons are review for many children, I still present them as though it's new to them. This direct teaching consists of showing an alphabet letter, relating its sound and *immediately* giving examples. "This is letter *b*. It makes the sound like /b/ as at the beginning of *boy*, *boat*, or *bear*. Can you think of other words that begin with the same sound as *boy* or *boat*? You can use this sound when you write and when you read."

We post an illustrated alphabet—a bear above the letter *B*, for example. The children gain experience with alphabetical order, letter recognition (upper- and lowercase), and letter-sound relationship. I make sure they know the name of each animal so there's no mix-up when they refer to the alphabet to identify a letter-sound connection. We chat about using letters and sounds during writing and reading and I remind the children that this alphabet is there to help.

I ask the children to bring in words they recognize from cereal boxes, toothpaste, candy wrappers, or other items they see frequently. As the words come in, we consider how each is structured. How do we know this says "Crest" and not "toothpaste?" I ask, and the children look at the beginning letters in each word. When we read "Frosted Flakes" they notice both words begin with *F*. I point out the second letter and contrast the initial sounds of "Frosted" and "Flakes" and notice the slight difference brought by the second letters. And what does the *S* at the end of "flakes" do to the meaning? Lots of questions; lots of word exploration.

We create an environmental print scrapbook, and the children browse through it, reading the words and continuing their conversations on word structures, noticing words that begin or end with the same sounds and letters.

Investigating words becomes a way of thinking in this room, a way of having fun exploring words. I want the children to be curious, observant, and fascinated with words. The specific lessons addressing the way words are put together are always connected to strategies that readers and writers use to take advantage of word knowledge.

Working with Phonics and Word Structures

So much is written about phonics instruction that it would seem that phonics is the primary path to learn to read. The National Research Council, a government-sponsored panel on reading, studied reading instruction and recognized other components.

- The NRC report said that first-grade instruction should provide "explicit instruction and practice with sound structures that lead to phonemic awareness . . . familiarity with spelling-sound correspondences . . . and their use in identifying printed words . . . and instruction should promote comprehension by actively building linguistic and conceptual knowledge in a rich variety of domains." (Snow, Burns, and Griffin 1998, 194–95)

- The National Reading Panel stated, "Phonics should not become the dominant component in a reading program, neither in the amount of time devoted to it nor in the significance attached. It is important to evaluate children's reading competence in many ways, not only by their phonics skills but also by their interest in books and their ability to understand information that is read to them." (*Report of the National Reading Panel* 2000, 2–97)[1]

Lucy Calkins says, "Children need opportunities to construct their own understandings of sound-letter correspondences and of spelling patterns. These understandings will develop best when the learning students do as they write also becomes a resource for them as they read" (2001, 201). Children use phonics on the first day in writing workshop when I urge them to stretch words out, listen for sounds they hear, and write the letters that match the sounds. As a second strategy I suggest they write letters they remember from seeing words. "For example," I'd add, "if you've seen McDonald's you know it begins with an *M*."

When I watch children write, I hear them repeat a particular word over and over to themselves, listening for letters and perhaps searching for a visual recall of the word. They connect the names of letters to the sounds they hear when they repeat words to themselves. "Ball, ball, ball—*b*! Yes, it's *B*. I know it's *B*" I hear Dylan say to himself while writing. Then he continues by saying the last part of the word, "alllll" and writes "*ol*." Pleased, he moves on to the next word. I'd always had a gnawing sense that our sound-out approach to phonics was not necessarily helpful to children. I don't often see children sounding out by using a letter-by-letter approach. More often, they use the initial letter, then meaning, and the remaining letters in a chunk. Countless examples of children writing—and reading—in the classroom confirm this.

The children's knowledge of letter-sound relationships enables many of them to listen for sounds and write in invented spelling without much difficulty. Still, some children spend most of their time drawing. Sarah drew her house and a tree outside. To nudge her into writing I asked, "Oh, your house. What letter does house begin with?"

Sarah looked at me and shrugged, "I don't know."

---

1. For perspective on *The Report of the National Reading Panel* I recommend *Resisting Reading Mandates: How to Triumph with the Truth* by Elaine M. Garan, Heinemann 2001, and the September 2001 issue of *Language Arts*, National Council of Teachers of English.

"Hhhhhhousss," I stretch out the word to show Sarah how to do this. She listens intently then says, "*H*?"

"Yes, it's an *H*. Write it," I say.

Sarah smiles and writes the *H*. I ask her what she will write for the tree. She identifies *T* after repeating the word as I did for house. "See, you can do this," I say and leave.

Of course, not every child responds as readily. Some need more time and experience in classroom writing and with activities such as our environmental print project. But writing is when children are most actively involved in using letter-sound relationships for themselves, and part of my role is to nudge them to try writing letters and then words. We continue to address specific phonetic issues throughout the school day all year long.

Phonics Lessons

As part of morning exercises, we mark the calendar and write the date and day of the week on the chalkboard. This brief activity, like countless others throughout the day, provides opportunity to examine words. I ask questions such as: "What letter does September start with?" "What other words begin like September?" "When we say 'Monday' what letter do we hear first?" Soon we notice that all the days end with "day." Later, we'll talk about the sound of "*a*'s name" that is made by *ay* and we'll combine the ending with other letters to get *may, bay, way*. These incidental and somewhat spontaneous lessons are brief, but they serve to keep phonics and the ways words are constructed in the children's minds. Frequently, extended phonics lessons grow out of these briefer ones.

Consonant Blends

The children's knowledge of consonant letter-sound relationships is refreshed by writing daily, and it's not long before I can introduce blending consonant letters.

"I've noticed that all of you are using the sounds of letters when you write. I want to show you something that will help you do that even better. You know the sound that *f* makes and the sound that *l* makes." At this point I may elicit from the children a few examples of words with these initial sounds. Then I continue, "Sometimes two letters can come together and we blend those letters and we can even say them so they sound like one sound. If we put an *f* and an *l* together they will blend to the sound we hear at the beginning of the word *flag*."

I write "flag" on the chalkboard and ask the children to repeat the word, to stretch it out, to notice how their tongue moves as they repeat "flag." I ask for other words that might start the same way and they come up with examples: *flower, flew, fling.*

At this point I assess the children's understanding by listening to the way they talk and what they say. Do they convey confidence? How readily do examples come? What do facial expressions tell me? I must determine whether to pause for the day or whether to extend a bit further. Frequently, I find that by extending, I actually help the children consider the *concept* of blending rather than just learning a new sound. "There are other letters you can put the *l* with and do the same thing. Let's try *p*. If we put *p* with *l* we get another new beginning for words." Often at this point, a child comes up with *play.* "You get the idea. This is something you can use when you write or when you read today."

At this point, we may take a moment and brainstorm more words that use these blends. I'll invite the children to keep their eyes open for words with *fl* or *pl* to add to our list. I'll write *fl* and *pl* on a piece of sentence-strip tagboard and connect them by tape one above the other on an inch-wide strip of construction paper, leaving a long tail to add blends (*gl, bl, sl, cl*) later. I hang the strip on the bulletin board next to the calendar and each morning for a while we'll review the "new sounds" as part of our opening. When writing workshop begins this day, I'll remind the children in a brief mini-lesson of using these blends as they write and demonstrate how with a couple of examples. At the beginning of reading workshop, I'll demonstrate them again. Now equipped with this concept, the children begin to recognize blends everywhere.

In the next days and weeks, we'll add more blends to our repertoire. They'll be placed on the bulletin board grouped according to letter: *l* blends, *r* blends, etc. We'll write words with blends during handwriting, play board games with them, write words using them on individual chalkboards. The children learn to recognize the sounds that particular blends make, but more important, they understand the *concept* of blending letters. They begin using blends in writing and reading and they'll point out this usage when I stop to confer. Using blends during reading and writing is the whole point of knowing them.

Jane Braunger and Jan Lewis, in examining research on literacy development, state that "Children develop phonemic awareness and knowledge of phonics through a variety of literacy opportunities, models, and demonstrations" (Braunger and Lewis 1997, 5). In all of my instruction with phonics I strive to provide the children with a range of experiences but always to connect them to the essential purpose of using these phonic elements in reading and writing.

Digraphs

Teaching digraphs (*wh, th, sh, ch*) follows much the same pattern as teaching blends. Digraphs in words are discussed as we compose sentences during "Word of the Day" (see below), read books aloud, encounter question words, or even when we read the children's names (Shannon, Theron, Whitney). I'll introduce each digraph individually and point out tips to help identify them when listening for sounds. *Wh* begins like the question words, *what, when, why*, etc. *Sh* is like the sound when you put your finger to your lips for quiet. *Ch* is like the chugging train, and when you say a word beginning with *th* your tongue goes between your teeth. We have a lot of fun trying out these sounds together and then we add a strip of them to our bulletin board. Like blends, we refer to them and practice them in numerous ways throughout the day.

Vowels

Traditionally, first graders learn vowel sounds several months into the year. However, in the first week of school Marlene wrote a sentence across the top of her writing: "OOSOORB OB SOT." In our conference she pointed to each letter as she precisely read, "I am outside under a rainbow and beside a tree" (Figure 16–1).

After I responded to the message she communicated I asked, "Marlene, tell me about all these *o*'s."

"Those aren't *o*'s," she replied, smiling at the silliness of my question.

"Oh, they're *not o*'s?" I replied.

She shook her head and said, "They're circles."

"Circles. Well, why did you put circles in your writing?" I asked.

"Well, you see," she patiently explained, "I didn't know what letters make those sounds so I put circles in." I didn't quite understand at first. Seeing this, Marlene said, "See, like this." She reread her piece, commenting as she started that she forgot to write the *I* at the beginning. As she hit each word with her finger I saw that the sounds she couldn't identify were all short vowel sounds: *a* in *am*, *o* in *outside*, *u* in *under*, *a* in *a*, *a* in *and*. Marlene could distinguish the vowel sounds but had no knowledge of what letters to write.

I had never considered teaching vowel sounds to first graders in September, but the next day I introduced the short /a/ sound to the entire class. I began by explaining that Marlene had come across sounds when she was writing that she didn't know and that these sounds were made by letters we call vowels. "Today," I said, "we're going to talk about one of those sounds—the one made by letter *a*." I went on to explain the sound at the beginning of *apple* and demonstrated how to identify the sound and write, using a few examples with *a* as in *apple*, and as a middle letter as in the word *cat*. I concluded

Figure 16–1

Marlene's writing

the lesson by giving Marlene a piece of red paper and asking her to draw and cut out a large apple. The finished apple (with a large *a* written on it) went up on the board as a tool to remind children. "Look at the apple and think of the beginning sound, when you think you might need to use an *a*."

Gradually, I introduce the other short vowel sounds in similar fashion. I discovered that other children besides Marlene were ready to incorporate vowels into their writing and reading strategies. Of course, many children were not ready to use these sounds and could not distinguish between the short vowel sounds. I certainly didn't expect everyone to be accountable for their use at this time, but introducing them helped everyone in the long run because children gradually became aware of them and eventually picked up on the vowel concept.

In time, I introduce the long vowel sounds formed by the "vowel, consonant, silent *e*" pattern. Later, we work with the *r* controlled vowels: *ar, er, ir, ur, or.* And still later in the year, usually early spring, I introduce vowel digraphs: *ai, ay, ou, oi, oy, oo, ow, ea, igh, ie.* We take time to compare the sounds with other vowel sounds we know and to sort words according to sound, not spelling, as in the words with *ea, ow,* and *oo.* Each of these two-letter combinations goes on our bulletin board. We review their distinguishing sounds, and the children can use them during writing and reading. They become part of the knowledge about words that the children and I address just as we had done with blends and digraphs.

Other phonetic structures come up as the children write and read. For instance, a child runs into a silent *k* as in *knight* or a silent *w* as in *write.* Or, "copy-cat" letters like the *c* as in *circus* as opposed to *cat,* or the *g* in *giraffe* as opposed to *game.* It becomes quite easy to provide lessons that explain these nuances of language and it's meaningful to the children because someone in the class encountered a need.

The experience with Marlene reminded me to be vigilant in observing what children need to take writing or reading further. While occasionally, children encountered language issues in reading, most often it was writing where issues first surfaced. The need for vowel sounds, for instance, became apparent in children's writing before they absolutely needed them in reading because the children used a range of strategies to figure out words and make meaning while they read. Writing had a way of zeroing in on various aspects of written language.

I'm not advocating introducing vowels early in first grade; on the contrary, I'd be inclined not to be in a hurry to do so. I do think it's important as a teacher not only to be familiar with curriculum, but also to have a solid grounding in the way our language is structured. With knowledge of phonic and structural components internalized, I was able to recognize opportunities to teach specific skills in context rather than relying on a sequenced list. An important aspect of teaching language skills for readers and writers is listening and observing children to determine what possible strategies may help them at a given moment.

My classroom experience demonstrates that phonics instruction is a helpful strategy but that children differ in the degree to which they use phonics. Clarence searched my face for any hint to confirm that he'd found the correct answer as he attempted to replicate a specific letter sound. He did not hear precise discriminations between short vowel sounds at all and barely those of consonant letters. (He also had difficulty carrying a tune when the class sang together.) Clarence did use letters as clues when he read. One day I watched him come to a word beginning with the letter *B*. He tried out several words that began with *B*—words that he *knew* started with that letter. He happened to hit upon the correct word, *balloon*, by looking at the picture. A *visual* memory of words beginning with *B* rather than an auditory one helped Clarence. I had to admire his resourcefulness. Clarence learned to read.

In contrast, Shelly relied on letter-sound relationships as her dominant strategy for tackling unknown words. She quickly mastered the sounds represented by letters or combinations of letters and loved the precision and patterns they provided. She became frustrated by words that failed to follow the rules and dealt with these by learning them and giving them her own category. "I know *because* now. It's *different* from the others," she said. Shelly enjoyed math computations and begged for extra math worksheets, which she completed with neatly formed numerals. Her desk was always organized. She appeared to view the world of phonics with the same precision.

I present phonics to children as one of *several* strategies good readers use. Opportunities for phonics instruction pop up continually throughout the school day. Mills, O'Keefe, and Stephens (1991) provide a detailed description of an approach to teaching phonics throughout the school day in their book *Looking Closely*. The children's investment in our "word play" confirms that it's important to present a balance of strategies and to connect all strategies to the purpose of making meaning.

WORD STRUCTURES

Children's writing opened up the need to get into the structure of words. True, readers use word elements, but they are most relevant and essential to learn for the purpose of writing. In no time at all, we need to work with onset and rime. *Onset* consists of the letter or letters before the vowel. *Rime* is the vowel and what follows. Children learn to recognize and pronounce the onset and patterns of rime. It's easier to put onset and rime together than it is to go through the individual sounds. So, instead of sounding out */c/-/a/-/t/*, a child recognizes the *at* ending and puts the *c* in front of it and pronounces */c/-/at/* (Moustafa 1998; Strickland 1998). Teachers have recognized this for years and have taught this strategy by introducing word families.

Recognizing rhyming words naturally leads to writing them and noticing how many adhere to a patterned structure. So, it's a small step to point out to children that if you know how to write or read *cat*, then you can figure out how to write or read a lot of words that rhyme with *cat*: *rat, hat, bat, sat*, etc. The children and I collect the ending part of rime and post them. A few examples are: *-at, -un, -ent, -ank, -ack, -ink.* The children also notice that vowel digraphs and a word ending such as *-ing* can be used to form new words. The children learn to pronounce these rime chunks and also discover that our language is full of patterns. "Words are like math," Jeff said one day, "Math has patterns and words have patterns, too!"

Word endings are a structural aspect of words that I usually teach early in the year because children begin writing an *s* or sometimes a *z* to make plurals. This concept is often addressed in a writing mini-lesson.

Sometimes I'm able to build on the work of an individual child as I did when Wendy used the *-ing* word ending in her writing: "I AM MACIGN A PICR" (I am making a picture). In our conference, Wendy explained, "This is me and I'm making a picture of me making a picture of me making a picture. See, I saw this in a book my Mommy read to me. It keeps going on and on. And see, I wrote the 'I-G-N.' My Mommy told me about the 'I-G-N.'"

"Oh, I see. This is a picture of you making a picture of you making a picture. And you know about the 'I-N-G,'" I answered, deliberating stating Wendy's new concept correctly.

"No!" she replied. "The 'I-G-N.'"

The firmness in her voice told me to leave it alone for now. Correcting is not teaching. Instead, I made a mental note to bring up *-ing* endings at another time. In the next couple of days I found ways to incorporate *-ing* into the writing I did in front of the class and emphasized it a bit more each time. Then I presented a writing mini-lesson on *-ing* referring to Wendy and the fact that she had already used this ending in her writing. Wendy commented, "Yes, my Mommy showed me I-N-G, so I knew how to write it."

The word ending *-ing* became the first on our bulletin board that included other endings such as *-ly, -s, -es, -ed.* Some years we get into suffixes such as *-ful, -ness* or into prefixes such as *un-, re-, dis-.* A study of word ending easily expands to include root words and the fact that "words can grow" as in *bake, baking, baked, baker, bakery,* etc. Such a lesson centers on showing how all these words connect to a central meaning with the endings slightly changing that meaning. I also address other structural components such as: compound words, contractions, homonyms, synonyms, and antonyms.

In pointing out these structural aspects of language, I want to be careful to respond to what children can handle without overwhelming them. I want them to find words, see how they work, and be fascinated by them. I keep it playful and exploratory, and I encourage the children to notice examples. They often become genuinely excited as they discover patterns and share new structures with each other. I've got to keep clear of the old "skill and drill" approach if I want to maintain the energy and interest they have in our language. I've found that the best way to accomplish this is to teach in response to the children's development and with a light touch.

Demonstrating Strategies

The first year I taught without a reading program, I referred to a list I had compiled of first-grade skills to make sure I didn't miss anything. Gradually, I internalized that list and decided what to teach and when to do so by observing children. Now, when I look back at this list, it's obvious that I addressed many skills that go beyond those listed because some of the children were ready for them. What I'm really teaching are strategies for reading and writing. The skill checklist was essential in the beginning, but it was also important to put my first attention on the children and their dynamic processes of learning to read and write. In this way, I taught readers how to go about reading by demonstrating strategies rather than teaching them isolated skills with the expectation that they'd know what to do with them. What do I mean by "strategies"? I like Regie Routman's (2000) explanation: "Strategies are the thinking, problem-solving mental processes that the learner deliberately initiates, incorporates, and applies to construct meaning" (130).

I assess continually what readers and writers are doing and understanding and, on that foundation, demonstrate specific strategies at moments when children are likely to incorporate them as they read and write. It's a matter of timing as well as demonstrating. Whether these demos are whole-class or small-group lessons or responses to individual students, children pick up on them, try them out, and integrate them into their current knowledge of reading and writing processes. All the while, the children and I focus on making meaning because that is the purpose of the strategy.

Connie Weaver (1988) writes that the difference between skills and *strategies* is a crucial distinction as these terms pertain to reading instruction:

> In the word-centered skills approaches, children are taught to use their stock of sight words, their phonics and structural analysis skills, and their understanding of context in order to identify words. Concern with comprehension typically comes later, after the selection has been read. But in a meaning-centered strategies approach, children are actually taught to use their developing comprehension of a text in order to help them identify the words. They are taught to use context of all sorts to *predict* what will come next, to *sample* the visual display, using a minimum of graphic/phonemic cues to confirm or modify their prediction and to tentatively interpret a word, and to use following context to *confirm* or *correct* this tentative interpretation. . . . Meaning is the beginning and the end of reading, and the means as well. (145)

In our classroom, many demonstrations consist of the ongoing daily reading and writing activities of the children and myself. Others are focused presentations that are responsive in nature, take children's work seriously, and maintain a playful tone. They are invitations for children to try something for themselves.

Demonstrations in Read Alouds

When reading a book to children, I focus on meaning and also demonstrate how to read. Such demonstrations naturally surround the reading. Occasionally I comment or interject questions to point out the clues the book provides to get at the meaning. While I didn't have a big-book format when I read Molly Bang's *Yellow Ball* to first graders in September, the large print and limited number of words on each page enabled the children to follow the print with my direction. The reading was, in essence, what is called a "shared reading."

I began by holding up the book and reading the title while I pointed to the words. A large yellow circle suspended in the sky over the ocean dominates the cover. "Sun" a couple of children said quietly when they saw the cover. I responded, "This does look like the sun, but this word is "ball" and it begins with *B*. If it had an *S* it could be 'sun.'"

Then one little guy commented, "Or bus. At the end."

"Oh yes, if there was an *S* at the end of this word it might be the word 'bus.'" I acknowledged his contribution by repeating his idea and putting it into a complete sentence. Some children talk in phrases or one-word responses; helping them develop oral language goes on throughout the day, especially when we talk about books in the large-group setting.

I read the author's name and noted that "Bang" begins with the same letter and sound as "ball." On the dedication page I asked the children where this story will take place and they quickly identify the setting as the beach. "The pictures tell us that, don't they?" I acknowledged. *Yellow Ball* has twenty pages with a twenty-eight-word text. On the opening two pages a little boy holds a large yellow ball and two other children hold out their arms ready to catch the ball. I read the two words on the page spread: "catch, throw." "Who can tell how the story begins from these pictures and these two words?"

"Throw the ball," commented one child.

"Who will throw the ball?" I asked.

"That little boy."

"Oh, the boy will throw the ball and then what will happen?"

"He's gonna catch it," replied another child.

"Ahhh. So the story begins when the little boy is throwing the ball and the other boy—and the girl perhaps too—are going to catch the ball."

"Yeah," said still another child, "they're gonna play hot potato."

"Hot potato?" I said. "Tell me about hot potato." For a moment or two the children explained how to play hot potato.

On the next two pages, four pictures show the ball drifting into the water while the children play on the sand. I asked who could tell what's happening in these pictures, and as I spoke I pointed to each picture in sequence, left to right, top to bottom. I said nothing about the order, just went through the sequence by pointing a couple of times. A child told a story to accompany the pictures as I pointed to each illustration. When she finished, I read "Uh-oh" from the bottom of the second page. The class responded with a series of Uh-ohs and I ran my finger under the word and read it again with them. "You can read this, can't you?" I said. We continued through the book this way, with the children telling the story from the pictures and me validating their ideas by repeating their words, sometimes forming their fragments into entire sentences. I ran my finger under the words when I read and invited the children to reread with me.

"The fish is looking up at the ball and the ball is *above* him," I noted on one page, emphasizing "above" written under the picture. Then I did the same for the other three pictures and accompanying words on this page spread. We speculated as to why the water is green in one picture and blue in the other three. A child suggested that "Maybe because it's *under* the water, and the sun above makes it a different color." "Good thinking. That's certainly possible," I commented. We continued through the book, reading the pictures and the few words telling the story. The ball goes out to sea, is caught in a storm, the ocean becomes quiet, and the ball comes ashore on a page where a rosy sky meets the water. I asked what time of day this might be to have this kind of sky. A child suggested sunset. We looked at the previous page with the ball floating on a moonlit ocean.

"It's dusk—when the sun comes up," suggested another child.

"Oh, you think it's dawn, when the sun comes up," I say, restating the comment but substituting "dawn" for "dusk" without making an issue of this minor error.

"Yup, dawn," replied the child.

Some children were confused about sunrise and sunset and we talked about the difference. The children speculated as to whether the illustration showed sunrise or sunset and concluded sunrise because the previous page showed the moon at night. "Or it could be sunset or sunrise on another day if the ball stayed out in the ocean a long time," another child contributed.

"Yes. Good thinking," I responded.

One child told the end of the story to accompany three illustrations: a woman and a child walking along the beach, the pair finding the yellow ball, and the child picking up the ball. "Hug" I read under the third illustration.

"He hugged it and they went home," concluded the child. We turned the page to see the child sleeping with the yellow ball under an arm and the final word, "Home."

"You're right!" I responded. "They went home. And that's the last word in this book, 'Home.'"

I had spent fifteen minutes on a first reading of this book and, through demonstration, incorporated many traditional beginning reading skills.

- "reading" the illustrations
- left-to-right directionality of written language
- top-to-bottom and left-to-right movement through pages of a book
- word-decoding strategies of beginning and ending sounds
- letter-sound relationship
- sequencing
- cause and effect
- vocabulary development
- sentence structure
- setting and characters
- predicting

Yet, throughout the reading the focus remained on making meaning from Molly Bang's illustrations and brief text. I did not plan the demonstrations, and I'd certainly not choose a book and read it aloud for the primary purpose of demonstrating reading strategies. When I first held up the book, my only purpose was to present a new book I liked to the children. Skills came up as strategies to get at meaning, and we never allowed them to dominate, to take over or take away from the central purpose of reading. Children will employ these strategies in the same way when they read books on their own because children naturally imitate from the demonstrations around them.

Later, after children begin playing with these strategies, I nudge their development as readers further by helping children identify a specific strategy they might use. I'll also label the skill at some point with a specific lesson that shows the skill and describes it. Children have begun to use this skill at this point, and the lesson validates and articulates their knowledge. *The skills never take on a life of their own independent of the meaning-making process.* When we teach them as strategies in the context of reading and writing, we keep skills in perspective.

Spontaneous Demonstrations

Opportunities to point out how language works come up throughout the day. Simple unplanned demonstrations of language usage occur when I point out a particular aspect of written language. For example, as I write a sentence on the board I say aloud, almost as if I was talking to myself, "Of course, I'll use a capital letter because this is the first word in a sentence." Or I might talk aloud about the ending punctuation or some other aspect of the sentence to help children "see" my thinking. The talk is incidental to the task of composing the sentence, but gives children one more opportunity to find a useful strategy for themselves.

When we read the directions in the math book we come across a one-word sentence: "Subtract." I might ask a question such as: "How do we know that word is 'subtract' and not 'add'?" "What does the writer do to show us this is a sentence?" "How can this sentence have only one word?" "Did you notice the *tr* blend is in the *middle* of that word?" We take a moment to discuss a particular point and go on with the math lesson. I believe every teacher is provided countless opportunities during the day to point out strategies to make sense of written language.

Word of the Day

As part of our opening every morning, we play "word of the day," an activity I devised that demonstrates a number of language skills. I select two children to come to the front of the room where they each select a word card from the dozen or so cards spread fanlike in my hands. I've preselected the cards somewhat. Since we're in September I include words such as these: *me, my, I, a, the, go, in, on.*

Each child reads the word on the selected card, figures it out using phonetic clues (usually initial and final consonants), or asks another child. The idea is to identify the word quickly, using the most efficient strategies. (This is not a test to determine children's sight-word repertoire or their phonetic decoding skills.)

On a day in September, the words are *get* and *the.*

"Who has a sentence that uses *get* and *the*?" I ask.

Emily raises her hand and suggests, "Get the teddy bear."

I place the word cards on the chalkboard edge and Emily begins to dictate the writing of her sentence. I carry out her directions.

"*G*," she begins, "no, I mean *capital g, e, t,* space, *t, h, e,* space." At this point Emily stops to reread. "Get the . . . teddy bear . . . *t*, period, *b*, period. I put periods after the *T* and the *B*," she adds, "because I know there's more letters, but I don't know how to write them yet."

"Good enough, Emily. Let's read the whole thing and see if there's anything we'd revise." I point to the words as Emily reads her sentence aloud and when she's finished I say, "If we were going to publish this for lots of other people to read, we'd have to finish the spelling of teddy bear. Would you like me to show you how we'd do that?"

"Yes," says Emily.

I draw a line through "t.b." and write "teddy bear" above it adding, "This is the way a writer makes changes; they line out, then write the new words or ideas."

"Only I don't think I could spell 'teddy bear' yet," says Emily.

"Of course not. Someday you will, but until then there are other ways—like writing *t.b.* And later, you could revise by getting help from someone else or by looking it up in a book." Emily nods and smiles.

I underline *get* and *the*, the two words of the day. "*The* begins with a *th*. Say it with me. Notice where your tongue goes when you say /th/ at the beginning of *the*." The children repeat "the" over and over, and we note how our tongue goes between our front teeth. "When you're writing, you might want to remember how your tongue goes between your teeth when you say the /th/ sound in *the*. Can you think of any other words with that sound?"

The children think a moment, then hands go up.

"That."

"Think."

"Theron, anyways, that's my name," says Theron.

"Right! We've got a great way to remember the sound for *th*—just remember the beginning of Theron's name."

The two words remain on the chalkboard ledge throughout the school day and the sentence stays until we need the chalkboard again. Tomorrow I will put the words in a box that holds all the previous words. I never *drill* the children on these words, the phonetic sounds, mechanics of composition, or revision strategies that we've just addressed, nor do I ask them to copy the sentence. (The time it takes first graders to copy is just not worth it and depletes their interest in the activity.) The lesson is short and spontaneous. Each day we address whatever issue arises through the draw of the words and the sentence a child contributes: punctuation, patterns, and irregularities of phonetic elements, capitalization, etc. There's always something to talk about, and over the course of the year we address many conventions of written language.

BEGINNINGS OF GRAMMAR INSTRUCTION Of course, the sentence we write during the "word of the day" activity always must make sense. During the first days of school, the children often suggest sentence fragments when I ask for a sentence. When children selected the words *my* and *red*, another student volunteered, "My red car."

"Ah," I said, "but what about your red car? For this to be a sentence, you must tell me something about your red car."

The child thought a moment. "My red car . . ." I said, restating the child's line with the words hanging, waiting for completion.

"... is fast," he replied. We went on to talk briefly about sentences. The children quickly develop an intuitive "sentence sense." This is the beginning of grammar instruction.

Eventually, I taught children the terms "noun" and "verb" during this time and later addressed "adjectives" and "adverbs." First graders picked up an understanding of parts of speech as we constructed sentences each morning. When I presented mini-lessons on the effective use of adjectives and adverbs, the children understood and I avoided the old way of teaching adjectives, for instance, by having writers sprinkle them throughout their writing—a practice that can lead to weakening the quality of the writing.

Sometimes during "word of the day," a child comes forth with a sentence that goes on and on and on. "Whoa!" I say. "Let's shorten that a bit. We'll be here all morning writing that long snake of a sentence." They laugh and help the child revise before we write.

The children examine what they have dictated and I begin asking, "How would you revise or edit that? Are there any changes you want to make?" The child looks at the sentence and corrects spelling, punctuation, words that were left out, spacing between words (for if a child does not tell me to put a space in, I leave it out). Other children begin raising their hands with suggestions, and when the composer of the sentence has taken it as far as he can, he calls on classmates for their suggestions. Sometimes revisions and editing create errors. The ensuing discussion enables us to examine the reasoning behind specific ways of writing or spelling or correcting written language. We always end with a correct version.

"Word of the day" shows children conventions of written language in a nonthreatening, enjoyable way. I often saw children initiate language skills in their own writing that we had addressed during this activity. The children saw strategies for *how* to make revisions and editing changes in writing. This activity also helped children refine their sense of syntax (sentence structure) and semantics (sentence meaning), which, in turn, contributed to writing and reading development (Clay 1998). A crucial factor in these results was that *the sentences always came from the children and were not predetermined ones that I proposed*. And because the sentences were the children's language, we addressed editing skills that children encountered as they wrote.

Charts and Lists

Carrie writes "two" for "to" as she composes. I explain the difference between the words to Carrie and then suggest we tell the entire group. A short while later Carrie helps me explain homonyms to the class. On a large sheet of chart paper I write the three forms: *two, to, too*. I comment that there are other words that have two meanings and many of them are spelled differently. Jason suggests *for* and *four*. With a different colored marker we add to the chart. We collect homonyms from that point in the school year. Sometimes a child comes upon one in reading and, checking with me, adds it to the chart. Some children bring in lists they've brainstormed with family members at home and we tape these papers to the chart. One day John says, "I've got one: 'fish' like you 'go fish' and the fish that you catch." We take a moment to discuss the different meanings and I point out that *fish* has two meanings but one spelling and so doesn't quite qualify for this list.

We add other charts too, such as ones for compound words and contractions and ones related to a particular topic, holiday, or season. We draw a chart and title it "Words Can Grow." I write "bake" on the roots of a plant that extends to the top of the chart, with branches bearing "baker," "bakery," "baking," etc. Sometimes, the children made similar charts.

We also create charts over the course of several mini-lessons, such as this one on punctuation:

Punctuation

- ***Period .*** To end a sentence (says "stop").
- ***Exclamation Mark !*** To show a lot of emotion (anger, excitement), a lot of expression.
- ***Question Mark ?*** To ask a question.
- ***Comma ,*** To separate words in a series; in the greeting or closing of a letter; to signal the reader to pause.
- ***Quotation Marks " "*** To show someone talking.

At the end of the mini-lesson on periods, I started the chart with the brief statement about a period. The chart grew on subsequent days as I addressed other punctuation. The chart served as a reminder for students as they wrote and I referred to it during later mini-lessons.

Some charts, such as ones on good writers and good readers, list ideas from group brainstorming sessions. All of the charts hang in the room throughout the year and I refer to them regularly as issues come up. Children use them as resources when they write. Because we create the charts together, the children experience the purpose of each, and thus find them useful. On the last day of school, as we clean out the room together, I distribute the charts, the lists of blends, picture reminders for vowel sounds—all the language reminders we have used all year—to the children. "Who wants the compound word list?" I ask. I take it down, roll it up, and it goes home with Suzanne. Next year I'll make new charts with the next group of children—charts that will be meaningful for *those children.*

Word Games

We play word games at the large chalkboard and sometimes with individual chalkboards the children hold at their desks. The games are ones that teachers and children have played for decades, such as starting with a root word and then adding letters to form a new word. Or I might dictate four words that rhyme for the children to write on their individual chalkboards and then we note the structural similarities. I find it rather easy to come up with playful activities such as these, but I also know that a little goes a long way. If I pull the individual chalkboards out too frequently the novelty fades, the children moan, and the play diminishes to drudgery; once a month is enough to maintain children's interest.

I try also to diffuse any tone smacking of testlike competitiveness. "He's copying mine," a child protested one day. "That's okay. In fact, it's great. One way to learn is by watching others," I responded, and I suggested that we move desks together in pairs so that the work could be more collaborative. So much of what we do in schools is set up as a testing situation. The purpose of using the chalkboard is to experiment with written language together and to learn through the experience. Errors and working together need to be part of that process.

Handwriting Lessons

I teach handwriting to first graders through teacher-directed lessons where I write on the chalkboard while the children write at their seats. At the beginning of the year I demonstrate the way to form uppercase and lowercase letters on lined paper. From then on, handwriting is a matter of practice. I've learned that I can take children through a daily fifteen-minute handwriting lesson or spend fifteen minutes two or three times a week and obtain the same results when it comes to producing legible handwriting. I want children to be aware of situations that call for one's best handwriting. A writer can't attend to producing lovely handwriting while drafting a piece of writing because the focus is on communicating ideas. However, writing that's to be read by others requires an attractive presentation. The purpose of good handwriting is to enhance such writing. Therefore, we learn to form letters and then practice for legibility. I emphasize the purpose of handwriting with invitations or notes we send home.

Rather than a repetitious drill of letters or copying items such as poems, I engage the children in the handwriting by incorporating other learning activities such as these.

- Word play: We write *bike*. I ask children to change one letter to make a new word. We write *hike* at a child's suggestion and go from there.

Another day we may write rhyming words, or contractions, or any one of numerous possibilities.

- Language usage: We write a definition of quotation marks or the rule for forming a plural or possessive, followed by a couple of examples. To prepare for addressing valentines, we write the names of the class members, alphabetizing them as we write.
- Phonics: I write *stop*, point out the *st* blend and then ask children to volunteer other words that begin in the same way. Or we write words with a particular vowel sound or a word ending.
- Onset and rime: I write *man* and point out that if you can read this word, there are several other words you also know. I demonstrate how to change the first letter, and invite the children to give me additional words in this "family." I believe it's important to teach word families by starting with what one knows and building on that knowledge rather than presenting a "family of words." In that way, I'm also teaching a reading strategy.

Instead of collecting and correcting handwriting practice papers I ask the children to look over their work and circle letters or words they feel are done well. Often I walk around the room and place a sticker or a stamp on all the papers while the children are attending to this self-assessment. Practicing handwriting has less drudgery when children are involved in more than copying letters from the chalkboard.

Demonstrations During Mini-Lessons and Conferences

In mini-lessons I remind children of a particular language component that we've previously addressed and remind them to use this when they read. I might point out two words—*book* and *food*, for example—remind them of the two sounds the *oo* can make and suggest that if they encounter a word with *oo*, they try both sounds. Or I might write *meet* and *meat* on the board and remind them to look at the beginning and ending letters, but also remember to use the middle letters. "You got to look at *all* the letters. If you look at just the beginning, you might just guess and get it wrong," children reminded each other.

I learned an important thing about teaching language skills in minilessons when I presented a grammar lesson to a ninth-grade writing class at the request of their teacher. The lesson was about pronouns and antecedents and, since I had not yet met the class nor seen their writing, I had no idea of how they used or misused pronouns. Nevertheless, I presented a brief lesson, and at the end, the students had gained little. I had tried to teach without any information about the students, their strategies, or their writing. I learned that teaching grammar—or anything—without a meaningful context weakens the lesson and student motivation can wan quickly. If lessons are tied to *student* work, with examples similar to that work, and with the acknowledgment that this is something we've noticed and want to demonstrate in order to help, we have a better chance of connecting with the student.

As I talk with a child during a reading or writing conference, I may remind them of one of the conventions of written language or a strategy to figure out a word by simply showing them how it will apply to what they are doing at the moment. "This is something that might help you," I'll say as a form of introduction, and then present whatever I have to say. I may point out what they are doing right with a comment, "You got that sound right. Continue. Say it slowly and listen to yourself."

Sometimes while working with a child, I'll point out a particular strategy—a phonetic element, for example—and comment, "You may run across this as you read today. If you do, you'll know how to use this."

Occasionally, class discussion will turn for a few minutes to a specific phonetic structure or perhaps to a punctuation mark in the books the children are currently reading. "Do you find any question marks in your book?" or "Can you find a word that begins with a *kn*?" I'll ask. As children spot examples, I write them on the chalkboard and we talk about using these strategies as we read. Often, days after such discussions, children tell me about a particular strategy that they've used: "See, I found the *oo* like you showed us and so I knew this word."

Opportunities for spontaneous instruction on language come up throughout the school day. I keep such instruction short, focused, and playful. The idea is to help children continually become aware of how language works by pointing out or reflecting on some of the examples that come up.

Developing Spellers

The practice of allowing inventive spelling with young writers carries a concern that children may become poor spellers. The National Research Council's report on reading states: "the use of invented spelling is not in conflict with teaching correct spelling. Beginning writing with invented spelling can be helpful for developing and understanding of phoneme identity, phoneme segmentations, and sound-spelling relationships" (Snow, Burns, and Griffin 1998). I discovered that conventional spelling develops when children write every day and receive explicit instruction on how words are structured. The writing of Jan, Danny, and Trevor over the course of the school year is typical of this spelling development.

On the first day of school Jan wrote *A* for *apple*, *O* for *orange*, *P* for *pear* in her self-selected writing topic about Eric Carle's book *The Very Hungry Caterpillar*. Under a picture of his family's boat, Danny wrote LF.JKT (reversing the J) and read "lifejacket," adding, "When you're on the boat it's real important that you wear your lifejacket." Trevor drew dinosaurs and wrote ONE TIME LOG LOG AGO BCEOSU. WEAID AS HIVE AS TEN ELAFN. (One time long, long ago brachiosaurus weighed as heavy as ten elephants.)

All three children expressed reluctance to write because they couldn't spell. "That's okay," I reassured them, "no one expects you to spell correctly right now. We'll work on spelling later. What's important now is your *ideas*. You can write saying the words you want to write slowly to yourself and writing the letters you hear." I wanted to start children taking risks through invented spelling. Mary Ellen Giacobbe taught me this way of responding to children's spelling.

I delight when children write as these three children did that September morning. This early time in writing development is no time to correct errors. An enthusiastic and accepting response encourages writers and paves the way for them to continue. When Jan read "apple," "orange," and "pear" to me, I replied: "I'm impressed! How did you do that?"

Jan grinned. "I just remember seeing them in my alphabet book."

When Danny wrote "lifejacket," he stopped after every letter to ask, "Is that right?"

"Looks fine to me," I commented. When I asked if he wanted to write anything else he declined and I accepted his decision.

Of the three children, Trevor was most concerned about correct spelling. "I can read, you know," he said in response to my urging to set aside concern for correct spelling and it seemed as though he was telling me that he *knew* that words were spelled one way and only one way. He became very frustrated with me when I would not spell for him. "Is there an *N* in 'long'?" he asked.

"What do you think?" I turned the question back to him because I knew that if I spelled one word I'd end up spelling the dictionary. Reluctantly, Trevor wrote "log" and continued.

When he read his writing he asked, "Is there an *E* in 'weighed'?" and before I could respond he answered his own question, "I think there is," and immediately inserted the *E*. "Is that right?" he asked.

"Yes, there is an *E* in weighed," I answered.

"Yes, but I want to know if that's the right way to spell 'weighed'?" he demanded.

"That's not the perfect way, but I can read it and I know that you will learn to spell 'weighed' and lots of other words correctly by spelling it the best you can and by going back later and editing it as you just did." Trevor looked at me dubiously a moment, then seemed to accept my answer.

"I put periods after 'brachiosaurus' and 'elephants,'" he said. "You want to know why? I'll tell you. See, I don't know how to spell those words so I put periods to make them abbreviations."

Mary Ellen Giacobbe (1991) writes of her students: "I learned that all children can write and that I must value their temporary spellings as clues to their thinking. Their inventions are windows of their minds—a way they reveal their thinking about how our language works" (26). Sandra Wilde (1997) writes, "When kids are inventing spellings, they are teaching themselves about phonics." These three children had just given me a glimpse of their thinking and experience with language and their knowledge of phonics. I would learn more from each of them as time went on.

Writing samples from late November/early December show how their spelling had evolved since September.

On December 5, Jan wrote: MY DAD GOT ME CHRISTMAS CARDS THEY HAVE CARE BEARS MY DAD GAVE THAM TOO ME ON SUNDAY THEY WERE 3 97 (read by Jan as "three dollars and ninety-seven cents") I AM GOING TO GIVE THAM OUT ON THE DAY BEFOR. . . . Jan's story about the Care Bear Christmas cards continued for several pages. She spelled most of the words correctly. When I commented on Jan's development as a speller at our parent conference in November, her mother said, "Yes, the other day she wanted to spell 'McDonald's' at home and I just told her to close her eyes and see it in her head. Then she could spell it." My amazed look caused Jan's mother to comment, "That's how I spell."

About the same time Danny wrote:

My Sidr and Hr Frend I wos
thar to we wor paing up
frot and wen I kam dan
to gat my drtgun wit eight
drs I wax wrd then I wut
in sid to tell my Mom to sk to got
my sidr to hulp me find my Drt
gun with eight durs my sidr shu
me sum plass wer I didt lok fur
my dar gun my sidr and I wnt
in to tull my mom at my sidr . . .

My sister and her friend (I was
there too) we were playing up
front and when I came down

to get my dart gun with eight
darts, I was worried. Then I went
inside to tell my Mom to ask to get
my sister to help me find my dart
gun with eight darts. My sister
showed me some places where I didn't look
for my dart gun. My sister and I went
in to tell my Mom that my sister . . .

Danny's story continued for several pages, telling of the dart gun that was never found. He correctly spelled several words consistently: *I, and, then, to, my, Mom, find*. He copied *eight* from the classroom wall. His willingness to risk with temporary spelling allowed him to develop close approximations of the correct spelling of other words, which served not only his writing but also his growing awareness of correct spelling.

Trevor wrote about baseball in late November, correctly spelling most of his words. The piece begins:

> Base-ball is a fun Game. You have something called a bat. And there is some one called a picher who throws something called a baseball! And then you try to hit the base-ball and run to little things called bases. 1st 2end 3td And if you get to home plate you're team gets one point. if you miss the ball. . . .

Freedom from concern for correct spelling enabled each child to write fluently and focus on ideas. Spelling, like all other language skills, continued to develop as these samples from late spring show.

Jan loved unicorns and in May she wrote this fictional piece.

> THE UNICORN
>
> Once a pounatime thre was a unicorn and her name was Joy and she was good because she did what her mom said/says [Jan wrote "says" over "said" when she reread the piece. The change reflects her growing awareness of the correct grammatical structure even though "says" reflects her spoken language patterns]. One day her Mom told her to dean ["clean" was revised to "wash"] wash the dishes so she washed the dishes and dryed the dishes. then her Mom said "thank you."

Jan's story continues for several pages.

Danny wrote a story entitled "My Life," spelled "My lighf," an error that reflected phonics instruction of /igh/ as a long /I/ sound.

> When I was three or four weer old. this is war I was. I was in a stor with my mom. When I got lost. this lady came and pit me up and omost tock me to the lost and fond ofist. When my mom soall that I was not thair. she ran to fin me. then she fond me. The end.

In late April, Trevor wrote a piece about penguins. He began his draft with a dedication page: "Deadacated to Hector and Justin an enimie in football." The body of the work begins:

> Penguins are fasinating creatures. They are birds. The adelies have a misoin in the fall. The Adoult-Adelie's go on the misoin. The Adelies live around the South Pole. The misoin is to go to the South Pole They pick a serten Penguin. They pick the stongest penguin. The Penguin swim from there [changed to "their" during editing as a result of teacher instruction] home land to the South Pole. There they try to find their mates from last year. Their mate is the penguin thet had the baby. The penguin thet swam to the South Pole is. . . .

Trevor misspelled more words in this piece than he did in his baseball writing. However, he had become a writer willing to use the words he wanted rather than only the ones he could spell correctly.

Factors Influencing Spelling Development

I believe three factors intertwine to influence spelling. The first, and perhaps the most important, is *writing every day in a writing community on topics of choice.* Children care about their writing topics because they choose them and they want the writing to communicate to readers. They know, because I emphasize it, that good spelling helps readers and so they take care with their spelling. They reread their pieces and edit for correct spelling. The amount of *time* we devote to writing permits practicing writing words and refining the spelling of words. The children frequently talk about spelling as they write. This conversation overheard between three children during a workshop is an example:

"How do you spell *city*, with a C or an *S*?"

"It's a *C*."

"No, I think it's an *S*. Listen s-s-sity."

"No, it sounds like *S* but it's really a *C*. I remember seeing it."

"*C*? *S*? *C*. I'm gonna write *C*. I think it's *C*."

A second important factor is *the proliferation of written language in the classroom and the amount of reading the children do*. Children see and hear examples of written language in chalkboard writing, in books they read or hear read aloud, in the writing done by peers, teachers, and authors from beyond the classroom walls, and in the charts and posters the class creates. Children report remembering words and thus are able to write them. I correct the spelling of all words when I type children's final drafts for publication, and children pay particular attention to these corrections.

The third factor is *teacher instruction and the standards we set* in the classroom for quality work. It's important to address careless or sloppy work habits. I've heard too many intermediate-grade teachers report that their students say, "This is my writing. I can spell any way I want." Invented spelling is not an excuse to be careless but rather an invitation to use knowledge of phonics, patterns, and structures and to *think* about spelling and to spell words the best way possible. I explain to children that spelling is for readers and, therefore, before turning in a piece to be read, it is the writer's responsibility to have as much correct spelling as possible.

From the beginning I demonstrate the place of conventional spelling and gradually help young writers take responsibility for their spelling. I address spelling as part of our ongoing word study and build on the children's successes. For example, I point out patterns in words: If you know how to spell *cat*, you can easily learn to spell a whole list of words that follow the same pattern. I add that we cannot count on these patterns to spell all words.

I affirm children's explorations with spelling. One day Chris said, "I just learned how to spell 'little.' See, I sounded out /l/-/i/-/t/. That's *l* and then *it*. But I didn't know how to write the rest. So I kept saying 'l.' Then I thought 'camel.' I said 'camel' and 'little' and they end the same. They have the same sound so then I could write *el*, l-i-t-e-l, little!"

I smiled as I searched for words. "Chris," I began, "I'm really impressed with your thinking. I think it's amazing the way you discovered that. There's just one thing."

"Yeah?"

"Well, even though it seems that's the way to spell 'little' it's not right. *But that's not your fault.* It's this crazy language of ours. It doesn't always work the way it seems it should," I explained.

"Oh," replied a somewhat subdued Chris.

"Would you like me to show you how to spell *little*?" I asked.

"Yes," Chris replied with renewing enthusiasm. I wrote the word on a scrap of paper and Chris revised the spelling in his draft.

Our "Word Wall"

The first year of writing workshop in my classroom I noticed early that when children wrote every day there were some words they used over and over. As they wrote these high-frequency words, they began arriving at spellings for them that were not always accurate. Or, they used one letter and went no further; for example, *am* became *m* or *mi* became *my* for some children. During the first few days they paused to think about the spelling of *am* but after a few times writing the word they settled in on their spelling. I decided to provide a scaffold to help them spell.

To begin the workshop, I asked the children if there were any words that they wanted to write a lot but which they weren't sure how to spell. The hands flew up and a whole range of words poured out. I reminded the children that I wouldn't spell for them but that I would help them learn to spell for themselves.

"For example, someone mentioned *my.* I've seen it spelled a couple of ways as you write and I'm impressed with how you've figured it out. Let me show you the correct way to spell *my.*" I wrote *my* on a small piece of sentence-strip oaktag. "Most of you know that it begins with *m* but the second letter is tricky. It sounds like an *I,* but it's really a *Y.*"

The children contributed more words until we had five: *my, a, go, like, to.* I wrote each word on a piece of sentence strip and posted them on a closet door that was in easy view of the entire class. "When you write, you can use these words to check your spelling. You could look here when you first write one of these words or you could check at the end. Good writers always go back and check their spelling when they finish. This is part of something we call editing."

Today this would be called a "word wall." We simply called it "our words." And they were "ours." They *always* came from the children; my suggestions were based on observing the work of learners. I didn't want children to continue misspelling the same words in the same way for weeks at a time. One reason for starting this procedure had been to address possibility of misspellings becoming solidified.

We added to our word list occasionally if I thought the children were ready to contribute more words. From time to time, we took particular words down because the children felt they now knew them and didn't need the reference anymore. What I didn't want to do was create a humongous list where children would have difficulty locating a particular word. The process of using the words to write needed to be quick and efficient. Posting words on the wall needed to be purposeful and meaningful to the *children*.

One day, rather early in the year, I asked the children to spell *because*. In the next few minutes I wrote on the chalkboard ten spellings from ten different children:

becos
becalls
becase
becouse
bekoue
becoe
becuke
bekos
becas
bekis

As children spelled, they made comments such as, "I think it has an *S* in it." "I think there's a *U* or an *O*." "I know it begins with *be*." After compiling the list, I wrote *because* correctly and explained that it was one of those words you just have to learn. No pattern will give much help. "Let's put it with our words," a child suggested, and so I wrote *because* on a piece of oaktag and mounted it on the closet door, reminding the children it would be there when they needed it. I suggested that if they came across other words that didn't fall into a pattern, we could put them up too. Periodically a child would suggest a new word, which I would then add to our collection of irregular spellings. Soon our list included: *was, said, were, does, been, friend, done, once, come, want, have, they*. We posted *would, could,* and *should* together at the request of several children. "Those words are hard to find in your pictionary," commented Matt.

A few weeks after the lesson with *because*, Laura said in a writing conference, "I know how to spell *because* now. You know how? I just wrote it so many times!" Laura had not written *because* over and over as a study technique to prepare for a test, but rather she had written it when she needed it for her writing, referring to the correct spelling on the classroom wall.

Using Spelling During Editing

Correct spelling was essential for the children's published books, which went beyond our classroom, and we addressed spelling as part of the publishing process. I discouraged children from looking up words until they finished a piece of writing. Some children wanted to look up every word during the drafting stage, which severely inhibited their composing process. Drafting is a time for a writer to maintain a focus on ideas. When it came time to correct spelling, I never expected a child to spell every word correctly but they all knew I expected them to assume responsibility for correcting some misspelled words. Before children could submit a piece for publication, I required that they go through it and correct words they knew how to spell. I couldn't assume they knew how to proofread; it was important to *show* them how in mini-lessons where I used my own writing. In these mini-lessons I taught children to read, look at every word, and think, "Does this look right?" "Does this word sound right so it makes sense in the writing?" or "Does this word follow a pattern that I know?"

After we met in a publishing conference and the child made revisions, spelling was one of the last issues I asked writers to address (see Chapter 9). The number of words each child was asked to correct depended upon the individual's experience and developmental level. Obviously, I wasn't going to require correct spelling of a child who strung letters together with no sense of the boundaries of words. To make final corrections, the children used their desk pictionaries and sometimes larger picture dictionaries and children's dictionaries available in the classroom. They also looked numerous other places for words: books, posters, charts, even T-shirts.

How Do We Spell?

From the children I learned that spelling develops through visual as well as through auditory means. Experience with written language—reading, writing, and thinking about language as we explored words—aided spelling development. The children's fascination with words led them to notice the similarities, patterns, and differences in the ways various words were constructed.

In late spring in one of our class brainstorming sessions I asked the children, "How does a writer spell?" The group compiled the following list, which, like our other charts and lists, I recorded and hung on the wall as a reference for them.

Spelling

1. You could sound out—but that might not always work.
2. Ask other people.
3. Look in your pictionary or dictionary.
4. Look for the word in the room.

5. Look in a book.
6. Ask Mom or Dad or sister or brother.
7. Look on a map or globe (for state or country).
8. Look in the newspaper.
9. Look on a shirt.
10. Look on a crayon.
11. Try to remember words.
12. Remember little words. "I learned *hit* because *it* is in it."
13. Use a word a lot. "I learned *go* that way."

As we finished the list Bradley announced, "I got a humongous mind and I just keep words there."

REFLECTIONS

At Kendall Demonstration Elementary School, on the campus of Gallaudet University in Washington, D.C., I worked with classes of deaf children. One group of six- and seven-year-olds, comparable in age and interests to my first graders, could knock the socks off many of their peers throughout the country when it came to reading and writing. It was February. They wrote clear, organized pieces of writing that were for the most part spelled and punctuated correctly. They read voraciously. One child was reading the books of Laura Ingalls Wilder. These children are deaf (most since birth); they do not learn language auditorially and obviously phonics is not part of their instruction. However, they are immersed in language-rich environments in their homes and at school, their first language being American Sign Language. They learn language by *using language for meaning-making purposes.* Their example inspires me to maintain that stance for all language instruction in my classroom.

Direct instruction has never left my classroom; neither has skill instruction. However, direct instruction no longer dominates the day and skill instruction takes the form of demonstrating and informing students of specifics that are always connected to purposeful use. Every day we do some of the things I've described above to learn language skills. But this instruction does not consume huge chunks of the school day nor does it dominate over reading and writing. Rather, these specific ways of working with language are mingled with reading and writing throughout the day and they exist to serve reading and writing development. If there's one guideline that's crucial in their effectiveness it's: *Keep it simple*! It would be easy to clutter teaching and the children's learning by being concerned with skill development for its own sake.

EXPANDING LITERACY

CHAPTER 17

Lessons from Kindergarten

On a Monday morning in early February, kindergarten children gather on a classroom carpet and begin their day by sharing stories of their weekend. Tracy Downs, their teacher, listens, asks questions, and listens some more. She nods and repeats their stories in full sentences, but using their words; the children beam and nod at her understanding. She pulls out a book, *In the Rain with Baby Duck*, and reads.[1]

1. This chapter on kindergarten is meant to be read within the context of all of . . . *And with a Light Touch*. The examples and ideas here grow out of the rest of this book and will no doubt be better understood within that fuller context.

When she pauses to ask a question about family traditions, the children continue some of the stories they had been telling earlier. "You could write that," she says.

"Yeah, when the bear came my mom said, 'Looks like you'll have a bear in the house,' and I said, 'You're crazy!'" Madeline says.

"You *do* have a story to write," replies her teacher. After reading some more she asks, "Why does Baby Duck feel sad?" She calls on Lance, who is listening closely but does not raise his hand.

"'Cause his feet got wet," Lance answers. The children begin telling stories of getting wet feet, of being in the rain, of wet clothes in the snow. Lance tells about the time he and his brother went out in the rain in their bare feet and ran around and around the house.

Tracy repeats his words so that he hears it as a whole story. "So it was raining and you and your brother ran around the house in your bare feet and that was a lot of fun."

"Yup," says Lance.

"That's a good story, Lance. You could write that story today in our writing workshop." This reading and talking continues a couple more minutes until the book ends. "Turn to someone sitting beside you and share with your partner what you'll write about." The children chat for a moment and the teacher hands out their writing folders. They head to their tables, open the folders and crayon boxes, and begin drawing.

Tracy and I move among the tables, sitting and talking with the children as they draw and write.

"What are you writing about?" I ask Austin.

"I went down Big Blue," he replies.

"What was that like?" I ask, striving to convey interest through my voice tone.

"Fun."

"Fun how? How do you go down this big water slide?"

"Lie down."

"I see. You lie down and then slide all the way down?"

"Yup," Austin looks up and grins.

"Will you write that?" I ask. Another shrug. But a few minutes later he writes, "I go down Big Blue."

The conferences with these kindergartners continue in similar fashion. I talk to one or two at a table and then move on to another table; I've found that talking to one child at the table tends to involve them all if only through overhearing my conference with one child. I also know that I can't see every child every day, a reality that is difficult for five-year-olds to accept. So I often comment on the work I see others doing at the table before I move on: "All those letters, Stephen"; or "Interesting picture"; or "I see you're really writing a lot."

About a third of the class draw with no letters except their names. Greg's picture is just like the child's next to him. "I'm copying hers," he says. I ask, "How come?" and he shrugs and smiles. "Copying," I've come to realize, is sometimes an important learning strategy for kindergarten children. Doing so seems to allow them access into untried areas and gives them confidence before breaking out on their own with their own ideas. Molly is concerned about "messing up" and has turned to a new page. Adam asks for help, "Can you help me make the graveyard, /g/, /g/, /g/?" Together we find the *G* on the alphabet on the wall. Some children write sentences or phrases: "INSI" for "It is snowy," "MINM" for "Me and my Mom." When I ask if they plan to write more, they clearly communicate that they are finished. I accept their answers. West writes about snowboarding and tells me he jumped off a ledge; he has written "I amsbowbohdng I jomp on L." "What letter comes next?" I ask, and "stretch out" the word *ledge* by saying it slowly so he can hear all of the phonemic parts. West writes an *A*, then, noticing that he's used all the space at the bottom, writes *J* above the entire message.

Katie is merrily drawing without a specific focus. A picture of her with friend Daria emerges on the page and she writes with ease. When I ask her to read to me, she points to the letters and reads, "Me and Daria went on picnic. We had salad, donuts, and cookies," (SLD DNT Ke). She fills in the missing words "we had," "and" when she reads but doesn't seem to notice that they're not on the paper.

After about fifteen minutes, the noise level in the room begins to rise, a cue that it's time to draw this section of the workshop to a close. The children stack their folders on the tables, and Tracy and I pick them up as the group moves back to the carpet for sharing. We've asked Lance and Austin to share their writing: Lance because of the energy he feels for his story and, unlike previous days, because he has written letters on his drawing; Austin because he has written an entire sentence. The recognition of this selection reinforces their successes this day and provides examples for their classmates.

Lance takes the author's chair in front of his peers, holds up his paper and tells the story he had told earlier about running around the house with his brother in the rain (Figure 17–1). This telling, in contrast to the earlier one, is smooth, confident, and organized. "I wrote 'rain,'" he concludes proudly. Among the raindrops on his page are the letters "RN." The group responds with brief comments and questions. These kindergartners are only beginning to listen to each other's stories and Tracy has a procedure for their responses: one "I learned . . ." statement, one "I liked . . ." statement, and one question. She prompts the children to follow this structure, "Tell Lance one thing you heard." Lance calls on three children as Tracy prompts each response. Lance nods as each child speaks. The children are learning to listen to each other's stories and their responses are brief. But this doesn't matter. Lance is pleased.

Figure 17–1

Lance's writing: "Rain"

Austin takes the chair and reads his sentence about the ride on Big Blue. The group follows the same pattern of response. They've learned to listen and respond with "I" statements, but their questioning is rather superficial. The workshop for this day ends with the children doing some stretching exercises to "get their wiggles out."

In the next days, I will work beside Tracy and Barbara Borwick, teacher of the kindergarten class next door, in planning and implementing the writing workshops. We will determine our teaching strategies through our observations of the children and their work. We gear the specific lessons around directions we believe the children are ready to try. We decide to provide a writing demonstration in a mini-lesson. The next day we draw on the white board and then write a brief sentence. We use invented spelling as part of the demonstration and show how we listen for the sounds of letters as we say a word we want to write. We go to the small word wall for words such as *and, the*, and *on* to show one strategy for spelling. We use the alphabet on the wall to check how to write a specific letter. We also emphasize the importance of reading what one has written to see if it makes sense, and we continually read and reread as we write.

These are strategies we want the children to use as they write, and we know that merely *telling* the children is not nearly as powerful as *showing* them how to go about writing. We notice that after the specific lessons many children use these very strategies as they write. After noticing that writing a sentence seems too difficult for some children, we write by labeling a drawing with one letter or a sounded-out word and explain that this is another way writers get their ideas down. Our goal is to help each child find a comfortable way to write; we have no expectations that any two of them will be alike in their understanding of written language nor of how to write. In the following days we notice the ups and downs of the children's writing and how the mini-lessons (which present new concepts and repeat concepts previously shown) nudge them into new areas.

Gregory draws but declines all urging to write. On the fourth day, when he tells me he has drawn a Ferris wheel and that he jumped off in his parachute, I ask if this is true. "No," he says, "I'm just pretending." I decide to nudge a bit more today, so I ask what letter he hears when he says, "Ferris wheel." He repeats the word a couple of times then says, *F*. A nearby child also says *F*. I ask if he can write an *F* and he does (Figure 17–2). Then I ask about the letter for parachute. "P-p-p-p. How do you make a *P*?" he asks and turns to the alphabet on the wall. "It's under the pig," I say. He finds the pig and then writes *P* on his paper. Then, without prompting, he says "Guy" as he points to the figure at the bottom of the Ferris wheel. He looks to the alphabet again, "Jack-o-lantern?" I tell him the jack-o-lantern is a *J*, he wants a *G* like the gorilla. He writes the *G* and shares his writing in the sharing time.

The mini-lesson on labeling pictures had lowered the bar for Gregory; he took the challenge with teacher support during the conference. The next day he draws a plane headed for the ground and wrote "MDMDMD" (Figure 17–3). I overhear him reading his words to the child beside him: "May Day! May Day! May Day!" Then he starts another piece by drawing a picture of a burning house with a fireman throwing a person out of an upstairs window to safety.

Madeline is the class social butterfly. She is never at a loss for words and has a comment on everything the teacher says, a story to match every tale told by a peer, and boundless energy as she flits from one activity to another. In writing she hurries to draw page after page as if finishing her writing book

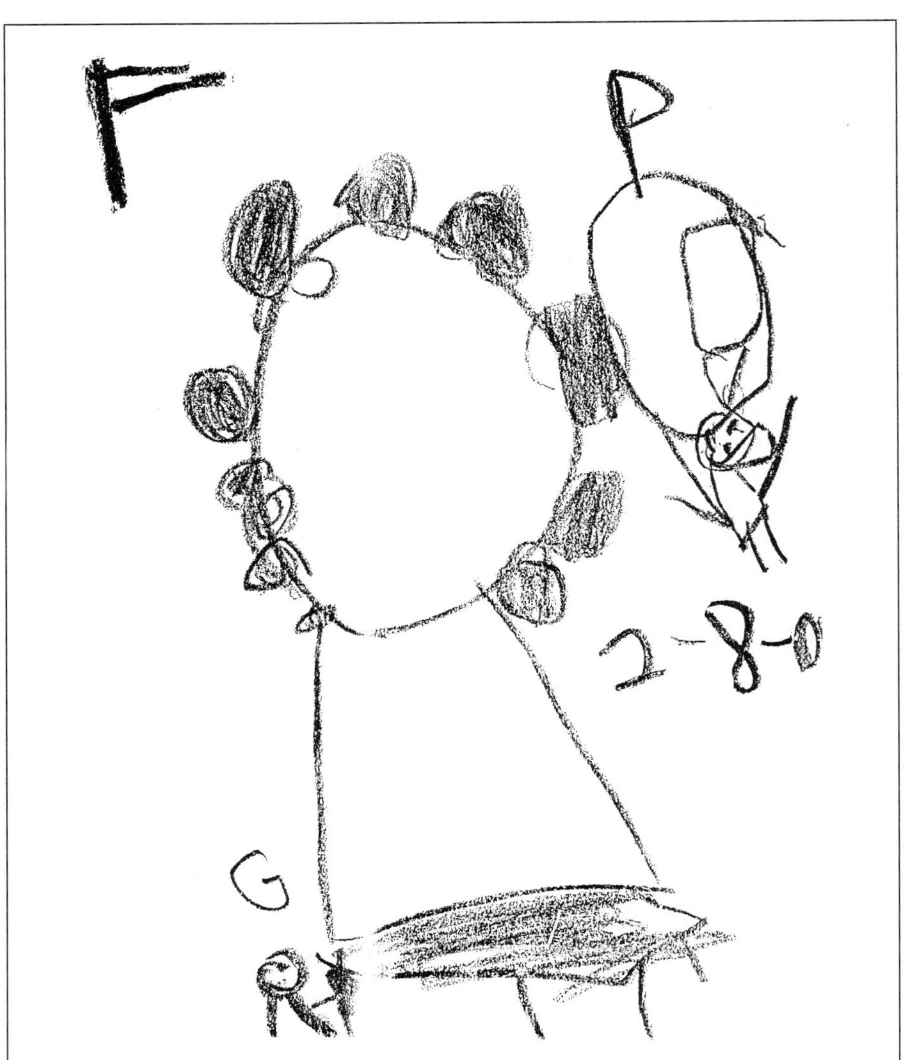

Figure 17–2

Gregory's writing:
F = Ferris wheel
P = Parachute
G = Guy

is one of her goals. She resists nudges to write letters other than her name or names of family members. But after several days of observing this behavior, her teacher goes directly to her when the writing time begins. She sits with Madeline as she draws and nudges her to write. Out comes "DADISGCIF-FVDISWTW" (Dad is drinking coffee then he went to work) (Figure 17–4, page 380). This is a major breakthrough for Madeline; the specific direction from her teacher at the right time leads her through this writing. It is a step forward for this child and she writes more in the following days.

West draws tables in a restaurant and explains he is eating French fries at the lodge. He writes "I Am In the LOJ." For the next three days he draws

Figure 17–3

Gregory's writing: "May Day! May Day! May Day!"

intricate pictures of walking through the parking lot when leaving, driving the tree-lined road to exit, and coming into his own driveway at home. Though there are no words, his pictures tell a story.

Katie says, "My dad dropped me in the water once. We were on the Appalachian Trail and he dropped me on the ice. I fell in." She looks up and smiles her cheery smile. I restate her story and ask if she can write that. "Yeah, I can," she says confidently. She writes "water" and then reads, "My Dad dropped me in the water." I ask if she can write those words. She looks at the paper then adds, "Dad dropped me at the water." Her words are randomly placed on the page but I encourage her by maintaining a focus on her idea

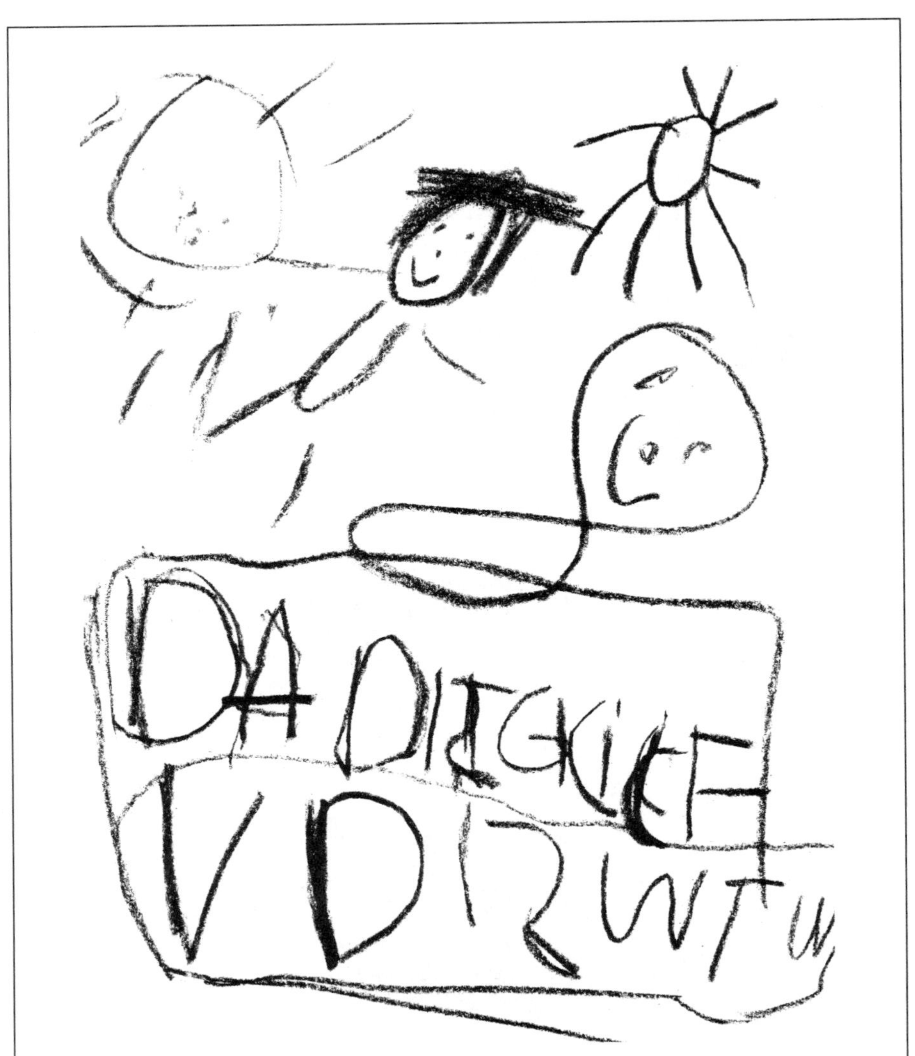

Figure 17–4

Madeline's writing: "Dad is drinking coffee. Then he went to work."

and what word comes next. The following day I see her early in the workshop as she is rereading her words from the previous day and ask what happened when she fell in the water. She tells about her mom giving her a coat and then going home and taking a bath. "Will you write this?" I ask. "Yeah, I should," she replies, flashing her big smile, and goes on to write "Me Mom g h c" (My Mom gave me her coat) (Figure 17–5). I notice that she still places her words rather randomly on the page with only a vague sense of moving left to right and top to bottom. As she reads she merely hunts for the next word she needs

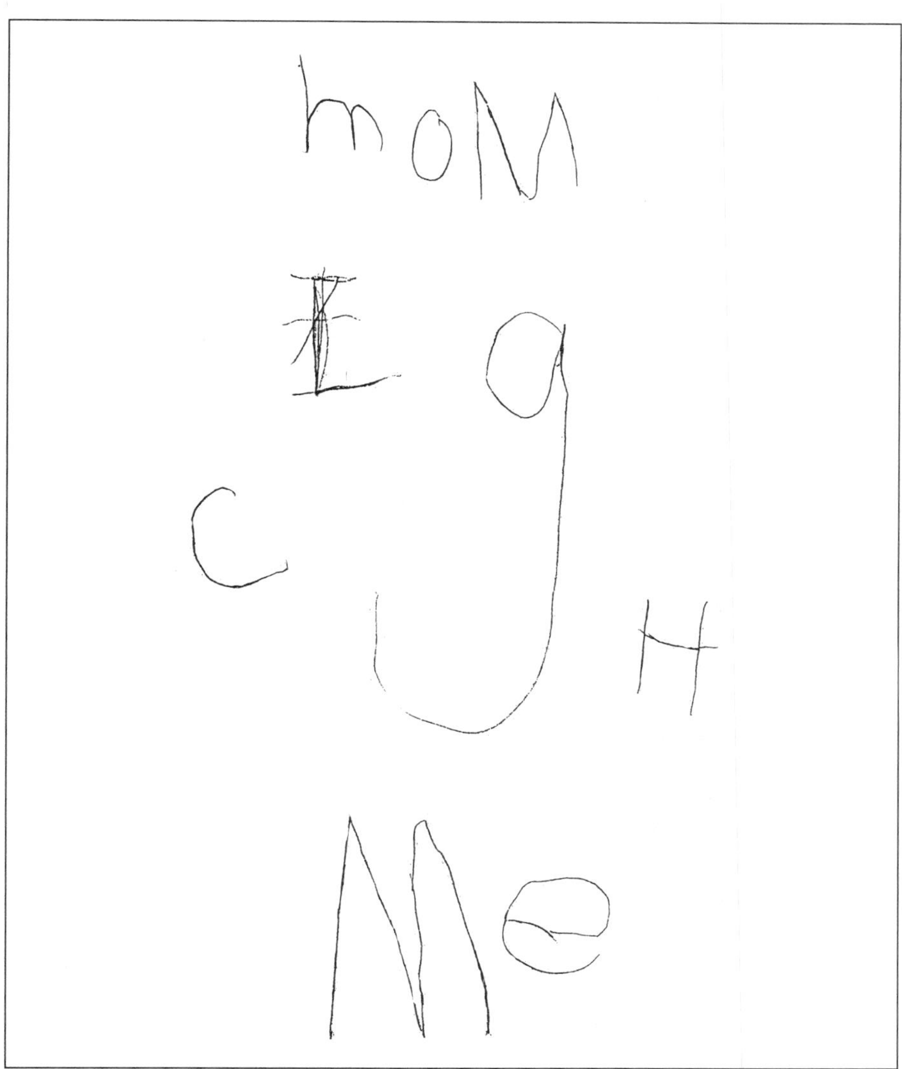

Figure 17–5

Katie's writing: "My Mom gave me her coat."

on the page. I make a mental note of this but say nothing to Katie. Later, we can address this in a mini-lesson, but at this point in the writing it's important to keep the focus on Katie's intended message and celebrate the big steps she's made these two days.

There are also children who continue to draw and talk without adding letters or words (Figure 17–6). Jared draws a detailed picture of a cabin and in sharing provides extensive description: the ladder to the attic where there are boxes and spiders, the woodstove burning with smoke going through a

Figure 17–6

Jared's writing

pipe and out the roof, the lights on beside a woman sitting in a massage chair while her sister is in the "washing room" doing the washing. The opportunity to explain his illustration in sharing is important for this young writer. As he communicates through speech and his drawings, he is working toward the day when he will add words to his work. Another child, Kerry, draws a circle with eyes and mouth and four lines extending out for arms and legs. A line represents a stage. As he draws he says, "I sing a song. This is the stage" (Figure 17–7). It's important to talk to Kerry *as he draws* for he has difficulty talking about his drawing a short time later. Kerry enjoys the writing time. It's important to see him *as he is working*. The conferences and observations as the

Figure 17–7

Kerry's writing

children work, the sharing time, and the writing itself all come together to provide pictures of each child's unique development.

The children are making strong progress in their literacy development. Tracy, Barb, and I all see the strategic role writing plays. We note progress in letter recognition, letter-sound relationship and the identification of letter sounds, phonemic awareness and, above all, a deepening awareness that one's ideas can be conveyed to others through words on paper—that meaning resides within the written word. In fact, both Barb and Tracy note that, because of writing, their classes' achievement at this point in the year matches the end of year performance of last year's groups.

Kindergarten Writing Workshop

Like workshops at all levels, kindergarten workshops require a solid structure grounded in consistency, predictability, and, most of all, active involvement on the part of the teacher. The most successful workshops I've seen occur on a daily basis in kindergarten classrooms. Barb and Tracy have their kindergartners all day and they give a full hour to the writing workshop, beginning with reading a book of quality literature, then presenting a mini-lesson, writing, and finally sharing. Teachers with half-day kindergarten sessions feel a greater time pressure, but I know of many who give a block of thirty to forty minutes for a workshop. At first, this time seems too much of a chunk to give for writing in a half day. But teachers who do so quickly see the benefits and recognize that writing provides active involvement in all of the prereading skills so central to the kindergarten curriculum. What follows are tips I've learned for implementing writing in the kindergarten classroom.

Structure and Materials

TIME Reading aloud naturally blends into writing workshop; the children are gathered close to the teacher and reading aloud stimulates children's thinking of personal connections and knowledge. Many teachers, therefore, blend the read-aloud time and the beginning of writing workshop. A *brief* minilesson with the children still seated on the carpet begins the workshop. Children move to tables with a clear expectation to begin drawing. Within a day or so, they realize that as they work their teacher will come to their table and will be interested in knowing about their work. This writing time may last only ten or fifteen minutes and the teacher knows when it is time to call for the sharing. One sign is when the children's voices begin to rise—an indication that they are moving their focus from writing to talking. Of course, the children talk as they write—and it's important that they do—but there's a point when voices become louder and it's easy to tell they are ready to move on.

The teacher chooses one or two children in random order to share and keeps track so that everyone eventually gets a turn. Two sharers provide a stimulus for the entire class (children will pick up on skills and ideas of others), as well as a boost for the sharing writers. Initially everyone may want to share, but it's important to keep this aspect of the workshop relatively brief. The focus is on developing writing and learning from each other rather than indulging every writer. Like all workshops, the first ones go slowly. However, children soon understand what is expected and they move into writing smoothly and work longer. It becomes possible to move through a writing workshop from mini-lesson to sharing in a little over a half hour.

MATERIALS Kindergartners need unlined paper but each teacher will experiment with different textures and types. Tracy, for example, found that her children put more effort into their drawings when they used manila drawing paper rather than white copy paper. Barb makes booklets of blank paper and gives a new one to the class at the beginning of each month. The booklets help with managing lots of pages and provide sequencing and organizing tools for the writing. Some teachers use folders (those without pockets are easier to manage). Whatever the management of the children's writing, it is important to keep it all in school in some sort of sequenced order; this writing is clear documentation of children's growth. Crayons are basic. Some teachers provide markers though occasionally children seem to focus on the marker as a toy rather than a tool. I like pencils without erasers; it's easier to teach children to line out to make changes rather than erase; lining out fosters risk taking by showing that error is a part of any strong learning process.

CONFERENCES Conferences are crucial for young writers, and in kindergarten this is especially true. When children sit at tables, it's easier to stop and talk to one and communicate with the others if only briefly. In these kindergarten conferences I listen for the child's meaning and look for the moment to encourage and nudge the child to extend his efforts a bit further in getting words on paper. It's a "scaffolding" kind of response: I suggest ways, work *with* the child for a brief moment or two, and then move on so that the child can continue independently. The focus is on developing the *how,* the process of getting *ideas* on paper, and it's important that the child experiment with doing so on her own without me. To be effective, I must "read" the child by listening carefully to her words and voice tone and observing her body language so that my response is just enough and not too much. I must keep the conference short by stopping to listen and then moving on—get in and get out. I trust the child to figure things out from a small amount of teacher provided information. Young children are powerful learners; they rarely disappoint this trust.

Sometimes our concern over getting a finished product leads us to stay with a child too long and do too much with them. I've seen well-meaning adults sit with a child and help them sound out every word as the child writes. Because of the finished product, we may delude ourselves into thinking we've "taught," but we must ask what did the child learn? Often, this child is quite able to work independently and, in fact, may grow more by doing so. Some children may become dependent on adults to get words down and become unwilling to risk working independently. Also, when we support children this extensively, we can no longer look at their work and know what they are able to do on their own. And, it is possible to overwhelm a child as happened with Stephen. I worked with him briefly one day to get him started listening for sounds and writing letters. Soon after I left, another adult sat with him and helped him complete two lines. This "help" continued the next day. On day three when I stopped to talk to Stephen again he told me he was only going to draw today. When I asked why, he told me, "Yesterday I wrote a lot of words and so I don't want to write any today. I don't always want to write words because I don't stop. So I won't write words today, but tomorrow I will." Stephen wisely drew the line for himself. Not all children will do so. I'm convinced we teach best in conferences when we teach with a light touch.

Kindergarten Mini-Lessons

It would be easy to move away from mini-lessons in kindergarten. One teacher who did so soon recognized how very important they were to the children's writing development. "I didn't see quick results so I thought those lessons weren't doing much. But after I stopped I realized that the kids had been getting a lot from them after all. Now I do one every day—even if I'm just repeating something I think they all know. But I keep them *short*." Kindergarten teachers know instinctively that mini-lessons must be short. The way to accomplish this is to keep these lessons focused and to show children through examples rather than a lot of explaining. Writing demonstrations by the teacher are particularly helpful for young children because the children learn much by watching others, then trying for themselves. But it's also important to vary the lessons; a writing demonstration every day would soon lose its punch. Short daily lessons are essential to the writing workshop in a kindergarten classroom. Here are some of the topics for kindergarten mini-lessons:

- Begin to write by thinking of an idea and drawing what you picture in your head.
- Write about something you know or have done or like.
- Identify the initial sound in a word, the ending sound, a sound in between.
- Match the sounds you hear in a word to letters.
- Identify individual letters and the sounds that go with them.
- Label a drawing with a letter for initial sounds or with entire words.
- Place spaces between words.
- Write a whole thought or sentence about a drawing.
- Use capital letters at the beginning of sentences.
- Use a capital letter to begin names.

- Place a period at the end of a sentence.
- Locate letters (in the room) you want to write so you know how to write them.
- Use a word wall as a spelling strategy.
- Write *I* as a capital letter.
- Use *ing* as a word ending.
- Use *s* as a word ending.
- Remember words you know how to write.
- Use words you don't know how to write and spell them the best you can.
- Listen for the sounds in words as you say them slowly ("stretch" them out).
- Match letters to the sounds you hear when you "stretch" out a word.
- Listen for the parts of words that you know (*-at* ending as in *cat*, for example).
- Read what you wrote and think if it makes sense.
- Point to words as you read your writing.
- Reread when it doesn't make sense.
- Look at a drawing and add to it.
- Revise by adding to your drawing or your words.
- Draw a sequence of pictures that tells a story.
- Think about a story's beginning, middle, and end.
- Develop a focus (not just "my dog" but "one time with my dog").
- Develop the most important part—the focus.
- Write top to bottom, left to right, return sweep.
- Write the date on every piece of writing.
- Reread what you wrote yesterday to begin today's writing.

Revision in Kindergarten

Revision is re-seeing, rethinking what one has written and making appropriate changes in content to clarify ideas in the writing. Revision is a complex thinking process, yet kindergartners who write and learn to read their writing revise almost from the beginning. As a child looks over a drawing, she decides to add another person to the picture. A child reads what he's written and finds the letters don't match the reading, so he draws a line through a letter and writes another. This is revision, a thinking process in which writers make changes so that the ideas on the page more closely convey their intended meaning. As we watch young children revise, we notice that sometimes these early revisions may not improve the clarity of the final writing. However, the process of going back and thinking about the work and deciding whether or not to make changes is significant and, I believe, important to development even if it means temporarily setting aside the notion of a better product. It's the development of the *process* that is important here. True, we want good products in the end, but if we put the emphasis on product without process we shortchange child writers of truly learning how to write. In turn, if we develop strong process, children will become good writers who produce some excellent final products.

I watched my granddaughter Adessa at age five make a major revision in her writing as she sat beside me drawing and writing while I wrote on the computer. Earlier that day she had asked why one of my cats did not have a tail; I told of the accident when the cat was very young. Adessa began her writing by drawing the front door of my house, the mailbox (important to her because she loves to get the mail), and a car in the street. Then she wrote: SNdr RN AT The dOR-And-A-KR-kAM RiT — THS WA (Cinder ran out the door and a car came right this way) (Figure 17–8a). At this point, she stopped, saying she'd finish tomorrow. Sure enough, when she returned the next day, she reminded me that she had to finish her story. We read it together and I expected she'd continue writing. But instead she took another sheet of paper and redrew the original drawing, including many more details. After she finished the drawing she wrote the rest of the story, which she then read to me: "The car ran over Cinder's tail and grandma got her to the vet" (Figure 17–8b). She added, "I didn't write all those letters 'cuz my hand was getting tired at the end and I didn't have any more room. Anyways, want me to tell you about my picture?" And with that she launched into a long explanation of everything she had drawn, even the sun watching the accident about to happen. I saw in her work a very accurate depiction of my house, the sidewalks, driveways, and streets. Adessa's major revision was in her *illustration* and, to a lesser degree, in adding more words. Watching her work and listening to her comments reminded me that, for young children, drawing may be more significant than writing letters or words and that encouraging revision in the drawing will develop this habit of thinking about one's work. Also, drawing allows the child to think and plan what may then be written. Revision in the young child's work will come through redrawing or rewriting or adding or, occasionally, crossing out. Encouraging this process through teacher demonstrations in mini-lessons and in conferences is important for the development of writers.

In one workshop I demonstrated reading my writing, had another idea, and decided to write a second sentence. During the conferences, I stopped and asked Austin to read what he had written. He read, "I went to West's party and went on the Boogie Board" (IWTWWET A WONTHE BEOD) (Figure 17–9). Then I asked what else he did at the party. He pointed to his

Figure 17–8a

Adessa's writing

Figure 17–8b

Adessa's revision

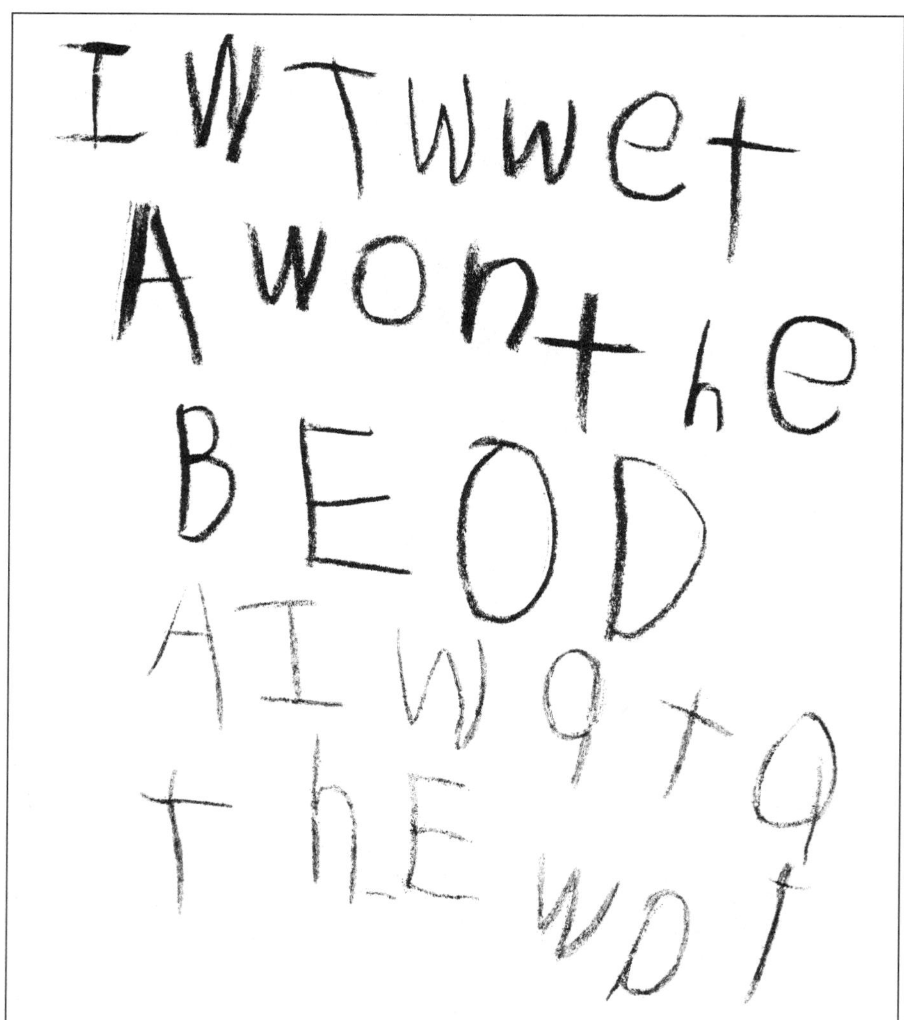

Figure 17–9

Adessa's writing: "I went to West's party and I went on the Boogie Board. And I went on the whale."

drawing. "That's the big, floating whale," he grinned, and I asked him to tell me about it. He did; I ask if he could write that. He nodded and wrote AI WatA the spi (And I went on the whale).

A child won't always add on as Austin did. Many times when I've asked a child if they plan to write something more that child will say "no." I've got to accept this answer and wait for another day. (Of course, if a child *always* says "no" I must observe closely and determine new strategies such as working with them for a while to bring that child along.) Even though a child rejects my suggestion, that suggestion plants the seeds for later development. Much learning goes on in children's minds before we see it manifested in their work and play. This is one reason why it's important to have a *daily* workshop; each workshop builds on the previous ones—often in ways that we may not see at first.

Listening intently and conveying my genuine interest helps a child be open to new ideas and ways of doing writing. I've got to set aside any need for a perfect or even approximate product and be involved with the child and his work. There's an energy that grows out of this genuine interest that opens a child to trying new ideas. He invests in the writing, thinks about it more, cares about it and makes decisions about it. It is this *ownership* that leads writers to truly invest in their writing, improve their writing, and grow as writers.

Publishing Kindergarten Writing

A small group of kindergarten children huddled around an 8½-by-11-inch booklet. "Here's my page," one cries, "I'll read it. 'I saw cows. Cows make milk.'" He carefully points to each word as he reads. The other children listen and watch the pointing intently. Then they eagerly turn the page to look at the drawing and words of another classmate. The children are reading a "classbook"—a book of "published" writing on their field trip to a local farm. When they returned from the visit, each child wrote about a part of the experience. The teacher then typed up their sentences and pasted them on each child's page. Then she organized the pages in a chronological sequence of the trip, added a laminated cover, a blank page for "reader comments," and a library card and pocket in the back. The kindergarten class had published a book. Of course, the teacher read it to the class when it was finished and now the children love reading it on their own. The book also circulates to the children's homes overnight and parents write comments on the page included for that purpose. Each morning when the book comes back, the teacher reads the new comment to the class.

Publishing in kindergarten does not involve the amount of revision and editing that is required for older children. But seeing their words in print brings the same sense of accomplishment and pride to these young writers that any published author feels. A class does not need many of these books; one a month is more than enough. When to begin publishing depends on the experience level of the class. I'd want to be sure that every child is feeling confident as a writer before venturing into creating a published product. Like publishing at any level, the product results from the development of a process, and for this reason, it is important not to rush products. And, of course, a class book need not be on one topic. The children might select a favorite piece—one they think to be their best—for inclusion in a class book. I'd caution against having them redraw or recopy their work, however. To do so would be frustrating for many children. Better to make the process a celebration of the good work they've done.

WRITING LEADS TO READING

I've watched three grandchildren learn to write before they learned to read—that is, if you define reading as the decoding of words *and* getting a meaning. All three "read" very early in the sense that they held books, turned pages, told stories in a reader's voice tone while looking at pictures—long before they went to school. And I watched Rhett, the youngest, read in every sense of the word before he entered first grade. Rhett was five when he sat in my lap and read Jane Yolen's *How Do Dinosaurs Say Goodnight?* It was the first time he had seen the book. Some words he knew: *the, and, is.* Others he figured out by using illustrations, contextual meaning, syntax, visual appearance, and initial letter-sounds in a seamless blend. When he needed more than the first letter, he went to other letters in words, using sounds, but always keeping what made sense in the forefront. He made a stab at expression and reread sentences when his voice tone didn't match the meaning of words he'd uttered. When he finished, he said, "Let's read it again." This time the reading was fluent in every way. Perhaps, the most important ingredient in his reading was his motivation to read a book on dinosaurs—a topic that has been his passion since he was three.

What led to Rhett's reading? First, he's been read to since he was a newborn. At eighteen months his favorite book was *Little Elephant*. He sat on my lap, I read, and talked about the photo illustrations, pointing out details. When I'd read "Can you see me?" referring to the baby elephant underwater, he'd turn to look up at me and giggle. When I read "Where's my mother?" he'd turn the page and say, "There she is!" We read the book over and over again for weeks and he kept refining his understanding. He noticed more in the photos. He gradually realized that the baby elephant was underwater and stopped turning to make the familiar comment. He picked up the book during play, turned the pages, and studied the illustrations. In these early years, Rhett also spent time with crayons, pencils, and paper and filled pages with scribbles and drawing. His sister (eighteen months older) provided a strong model. He learned the alphabet and some letter-sound correspondences from his sister and his mother, but all of this teaching-learning was done very informally. At four he began stringing together letters to write "words" and before he was five wrote "The Crayon Book, written by Rhett and illustrated by Mommy"—even though Mommy's role was limited to stapling the pages together. The book's beginning reflects his awareness of how stories often start: "A green frog lived a long, long time ago." The book continues as an attribute book, listing various creatures and their colors, then switches to activities in his life. He read it with great authority. When he came to a page that he couldn't recall he simply said, "This page is for you to make up yourself." It is not surprising that Rhett began reading and writing before he entered school. All of his young life he has been surrounded by reading and writing as meaningful, social, and playful activities.

Children come to kindergarten with many experiences but not every child comes with lots of experiences with books and written language. Our task as teachers is to be sure we never look at children without such experiences as deficient, but to create a literate-rich environment in our classrooms where *all* children can experience reading and writing as meaningful, social, and playful activities. Certainly a daily time for reading aloud to children is a must for kindergarten. The first priority in this special time is sharing the best in children's literature with lots of opportunity for talk by the children stimulated by a teacher's open-ended questions and accepting responses (see Chapters 10–12). Teachers also read big books to children and incorporate specific strategies that bring the children into the reading of familiar lines and show children the flow of print on the page, etc. It's important to keep these strategies well blended into the reading and not let them dominate the fundamental purpose of reading—enjoyment of story and language. It is also important to select big books carefully; many of these books are written for the purpose of "teaching" and lack the high quality that is available in the many wonderful books for children (Teale and Yokota 2000). Literate-rich environments are filled with print (Au 2000). In Barb's and Tracy's room, the children see many examples of print resulting from class activities: Daily News, word walls, labels of room areas, word families, story retellings dictated by the children, etc.

Kindergarten children also spend time daily "looking at books," as Barb and Tracy call it. The children begin by browsing through books in partners or alone, retelling stories they've heard, "reading" the illustrations, and talking together about the books. They imitate authentic reading behaviors and begin noticing letters and words they recognize. They are truly beginning to read. Teachers are actively involved with the children during this time, moving among them, asking questions, chatting about books and stories. This important time (which may be several five- or ten-minute slots inserted into the kindergarten day) forms the beginnings of reading workshop.

Barb describes the development of their reading time: "I use reading—looking at books—as centers and in five- to ten-minute intervals throughout the day. At the beginning of the year, as I read to the children, I teach them how to hold books, talk about the parts of a book, etc. Then as time goes on, throughout the year, children read—some read the pictures, some look and read familiar words, use picture clues, beginning and ending sounds, etc. We also have third-grade reading buddies that read to us every week. We read to them by late winter, but at the beginning they read to us and we learn left to right, top to bottom, etc., as well as just listening to increase attention spans and to love reading and literature!" Barb's room is filled with "book basins," plastic tubs of books organized by topic or title alphabetically. Books about ghosts are in the "G" basin, for example. The children have access to hundreds of books. Some are books written to be easily read by beginning readers, but the vast majority are high-quality children's literature. Many books circulate to the children's homes through Barb's "lending library." She slips books in plastic bags and the children take them home for the night to read with their parents.

Kindergarten teachers teach letter recognition, phonemic awareness (knowledge that words are composed of chunks of sounds represented by letters), and phonics (letter-sound relationships) (Moustafa 2000; Dahl et al. 2001). The most effective teachers I've seen present these concepts in ways that connect to children and their knowledge of the world such as building on names in the class in the ways Lucy Calkins describes (Calkins 2001). They teach these skills totally within the context of authentic reading and writing activities rather than with drill and practice exercises and worksheets.

Barb Borwick lists some of the topics she incorporates into writing and reading activities in her classroom.

- letter recognition, formation and sound for each letter
- rhyming
- classifying and sorting letters, words, and pictures
- listening for and identifying sounds in words
- sound blending
- knowledge of authors and illustrators and what they do
- parts of a book, holding a book, turning pages, and the left to right, top to bottom, return sweep of print
- concepts of "word" and "letter"
- comprehension of stories through discussion, retelling, and open-ended questioning
- sequencing stories—recognizing beginning, middle, end
- retelling stories in one's own words
- reading by using pictures, then words, then sentences

When Barb presents these concepts, she emphasizes to the children their use in reading and writing. She and Tracy incorporate language concepts throughout the day: as they read to children and talk about books, as they write with the children, as the children read and write. Barb creates six centers in her room, and twice a week the children participate in these centers, each child moving through three centers a day. The centers consist of:

- *Fine-motor activities* to develop hand muscles for holding pencils and crayons
- *Number activities* to write numbers and develop skill with one-to-one correspondence, counting, number concept
- *Art activities* relating to skills addressed in the classroom (example: letter recognition) and to develop creative expression and fine-motor skills
- *Reading corner* with bins of books and pillows to select and enjoy books alone or with a peer
- *Writing activities* to develop letter recognition, concept of words and sentences, questions (Children sort letters, words, put sentences together and write.)
- *Games* to develop cooperative work and play with peers (Games include manipulative skill games and self-checking games, among others.)

All the centers involve the children in manipulative, pretending, and playful activities—no worksheets! It's a time to talk and think together and to move into reading and writing. Teachers play a crucial role during center time by moving among the children, asking questions, responding to children, and encouraging their thinking.

Reading to children, talking about what's read, "looking at books," learning how written language is put together, seeing lots of print, and engaging in lots of talk are all important in creating the literate environment essential for learning to read. Children with the benefit of a daily writing workshop have an additional advantage: as they write they are mentally and physically engaged in activity that supports their development as readers and in ways that are meaningful, social, and playful. As Barb puts it, "There is a fine line in the difference between reading and writing." When children write, and read their own writing, they employ all the intricate strategies that we want them to use as readers. Children use these strategies in a highly integrated fashion that is totally centered on meaning making. Some ways that writing supports reading include:

- awareness that thought and knowledge can be conveyed through print (functions of written language)
- letter recognition and letter formation
- letter-sound relationship
- phonemic awareness—recognizing the sounds of speech, words, and attending to them

- awareness of word structures and differences in word structural patterns—rhyming, etc.
- understanding of the directionality of print on the page
- awareness of word boundaries—spaces between words
- understanding that written text is supposed to make sense
- reading for meaning—does the written text make sense
- rereading for meaning when a text does not make sense
- using context clues when reading a text
- using letter-sound clues when reading a text
- developing a sight-word vocabulary
- developing a concept of story—beginning, middle, end, concept of tension and purpose
- developing an awareness of audience and the notion of the transactional aspect of a reader with a written text, that readers negotiate meaning as they strive to understand the intentions of writers

I've seen young children develop these concepts when they write in a daily writing workshop. Of course, the development is anything but sequential. Rather, children's learning is messy, nonlinear, and recursive. They may demonstrate a particular strategy or skill or awareness one day and then show no signs of it for an extended time. But, if the writing continues each day, and children are allowed to form their theories about written language, test those theories as the write, and revise them as they gain experience as a writer and reader of their own writing, their language development will flourish.

Reflections

Janet Emig has said that it was the teachers of the youngest children who had to really know how to *teach.* I've heard her speak of education in terms of "from K (kindergarten) on down." As I've worked with kindergarten children and watched their teachers, I've seen just what she means. Successful kindergarten teachers understand what it means to teach with a responsive teaching style. They must know what to teach, and how and why, but they also must know and understand *who* they teach. They internalize the curriculum, plan for the school day, and then begin revising those plans as soon as they're with the children. They dance a delicate and graceful dance with the children: teaching and listening, observing and teaching, always based on the moment and on what children show them. And, what is more, no two children are alike. One of the strongest lessons from kindergarten is the model of what it means to be a teacher. Kindergarten teachers really do know how to *teach children*.

CHAPTER 18

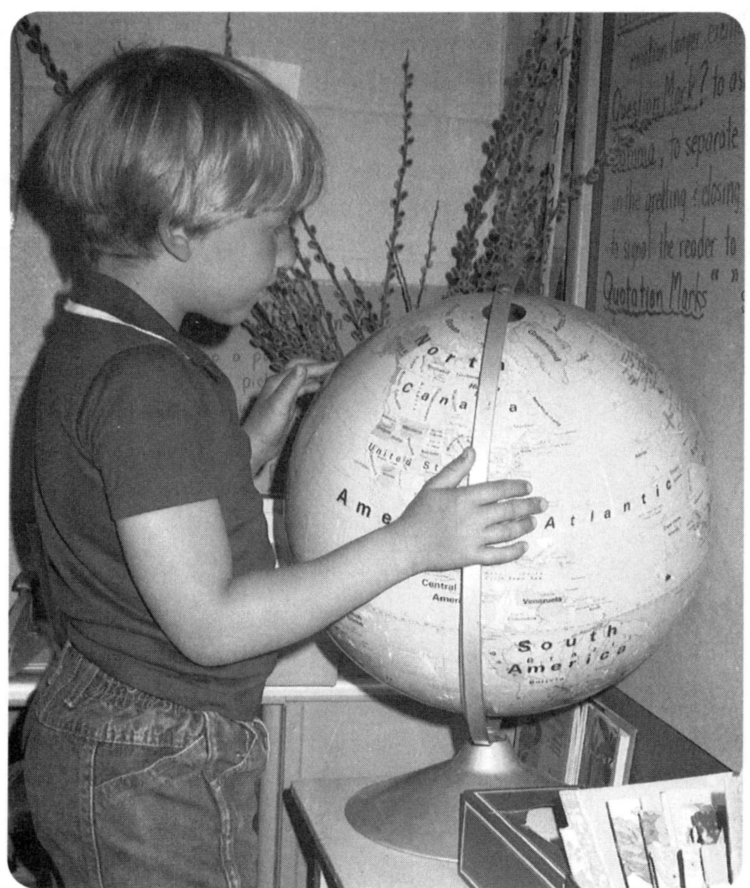

Reading and Writing in Math, Science, and Social Studies

When I first taught elementary school, I maintained a file of articles, informational resources, and activities connected to science and social studies topics in the adopted curriculum. Every year I opened my file and taught about dinosaurs or China, for example, by conducting a range of preplanned activities. The children had "fun" and they were *active* learners (these were activities after all), but something wasn't right. I knew it in my bones even as I shared my fossil collection.

With writing and reading workshops in place, the children talked about writing as the best part of the day, cried out in dismay if reading workshop was shortened, spoke with anticipation of books we'd read and talk about in literature time. My dinosaur lessons became flat in comparison to the energy surrounding reading and writing. When I took a good, hard look at it, I saw that the activities lacked children's *involvement* and *thinking,* which were a part of the rest of the day. I began searching for ways to incorporate reading and writing—and the thinking that comes when children have responsibility for their learning—into other parts of the curriculum. Like winter snows melting to reveal new life in spring, so moving away from my tried-and-true teaching practices revealed the dynamic nature of learning.

Writing to Think and Learn

Short and Burke (1991) write: "If a curriculum is truly learning-centered, then that curriculum is based on inquiry and the search for questions that matter to us, whether we are adults or children" (55). I wanted children to experience writing as a tool for raising questions and seeking answers.

As I thought about writing in curricular areas I realized that, just as they did in writing workshop, children needed time to explore ideas and talk with peers and opportunities to share, rewrite, and revise their writing and their thinking. Most important, the children had to have a large part in forming questions, investigating ideas, and drawing conclusions so that they could experience the involvement that surrounded our workshops. What follows is the story of a first-grade class from February through June as we began incorporating writing into curricular units.

Planetarium Visits

Our class was scheduled to visit the high school planetarium four times during February. Immediately upon returning from the first visit and before any discussion, I asked the children to write what they remembered about the trip or what was important to them. Writing *before* discussion is important for it gives learners an opportunity to discover their thoughts before they speak (a particularly enabling factor for reticent children). Writing first also commits writers to a stand, and allows them to discover their own thoughts without first being directed by others—including the teacher. Toby Fulwiler (1985) believes that "more personal writing is a direct route to more autonomous thinking."

Since the children had been writing for several months, they were comfortable with my request. After a few moments of writing the children shared with a partner, and then a few children read their writing to the entire group.

I wrote with them and then moved among them as the pairs chatted. Some children wrote about riding the bus. One or two wrote pieces that began with our departure, included one sentence about the planetarium, and ended with our return. The majority of the writing consisted of one or two short statements such as: "We learned that the sun is a star." "There are nine planets." "Comets are sorta like stars but they're not stars." I was struck by the brevity of most of the writing, a contrast to the fluency displayed during writing workshop. But the writing was enough to start discussion. In the large-group discussion we composed questions we had, which I recorded on chart paper. For example:

> What is the difference between a comet and a star?
>
> Why are some planets hot and some cold?
>
> If the sun is a star, why can't we see it at night?

Before our next trip we reread the questions, and when the children arrived at the planetarium they posed their questions to the planetarium instructor, who started answering, then stopped in puzzled amazement and said, "You kids certainly have a lot of questions today."

After each visit, and also after reading books or viewing filmstrips on astronomy, we followed the procedures of writing, sharing, discussing. Sometimes we wrote again after the large-group discussion. With each writing, fluency increased; the children became comfortable writing to include new information. I wrote with the children. Each of us kept our writing about the planetarium in individual construction-paper folders, which we called our "planetarium logs." This writing differed from the pieces done during writing workshop in that we did not revise or craft the writing in any way.

The planetarium logs were one of several learning logs that the children maintained on different topics of study. The logs were tools for inquiry—allowing children to frame questions and to seek answers. I didn't collect and read them and I certainly didn't grade them. Our learning logs were never intended to be finished products or pages of note taking. Learning logs are places to think and discover meaning.

After the last planetarium visit I asked the children to read through their logs and write a new piece about something of interest to them. The final writings were not just assorted facts strung together, as children had produced in previous years when I asked them to write at the end of a unit. Most of the writing revealed the children's search for answers to questions they had raised.

Jared, who had been fascinated with planets, wrote: "There are nine planets. Mercury is the planet closest to the sun. Mercury is hot. Earth is not hot because earth is not close to the sun. Venus is another planet. Mars is another planet too. You could not live on some planets because they are too cold or too hot. Only earth."

Billy, the child who wrote one sentence about comets after the first visit wrote: "When comets get near the sun it makes a tail. The tail turns away from the sun. Comets are as big as Manheim Township. Comet's orbits looks like a cigar!!!! Comets go very fast! I like comets."

The astronomy unit established writing as an expected procedure for science units, and when we began our study of dinosaurs, the children easily wrote after viewing filmstrips or listening to me read about dinosaurs. The sharing time was sometimes done in pairs, sometimes in small groups, or occasionally in the whole group. Children wrote additional ideas in their logs during and after the sharing. I expanded my role by moving among them as they wrote, asking "How do you know this?" "Why is this important?" "What do you think?" The children began posing the same questions to each other. They pooled their knowledge and hypotheses. The group became interested in two particular questions in regard to dinosaurs: Why did the dinosaurs die? What color were dinosaurs? The children suggested many theories during writing and sharing. They were not content with absolute answers but excited to discover many possibilities.

At the end of the unit (a misnomer, for I discovered that this kind of learning never ends; once inquiry begins, it continues), I asked the children to read through their logs and write about dinosaurs using all they knew about good writing: strong leads, interesting information, focused ideas, clarity, making sense to other readers. They plunged into these pieces.

"This is fun!" said Katie.

"Listen to my lead," said Jeff.

"Can we do this tomorrow?" asked Jon.

When we set the writing aside that day, Courtney had written: "Roar! Roar! Roar! This is the sound of the ancient dinosaurs. They ruled the earth many years ago. They were terrible. We still don't know what color they were. They just guess green. But soon the dinosaurs started to die. No one knows for sure how they died. Some scientists say it got too cold. Some scientists say the land coughed and volcanoes blew up. Some . . ." (Figure 18–1).

Amanda wrote: "Boom! A star fell to the ground. The dinosaurs died. Dinosaurs lived millions of years ago. Dinosaurs could be pink or red or yellow or green or white or blue or orange or even polka dotted . . ." (Figure 18–2). Most of the children chose to continue writing and revising these pieces during writing workshop on subsequent days.

Writing in Math and . . .

Writing and sharing became a norm as we worked with various areas of the curriculum. In math the children used manipulatives and worked in teams to come up with various combinations that could be written as addition facts. They talked as they worked and wrote about how they discovered the com-

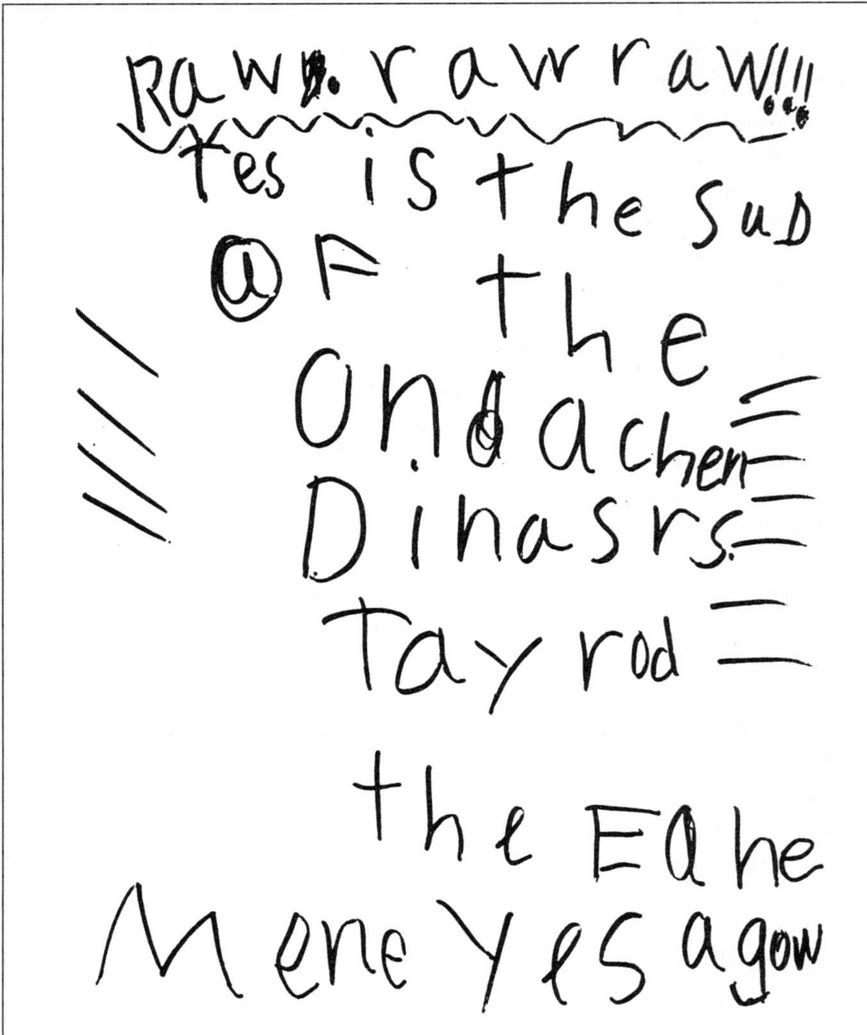

Figure 18–1

Courtney's writing: "Roar! Roar! Roar! This is the sound of the ancient dinosaurs. They ruled the earth many years ago."

binations they found. We shared the written ideas in the large group, noticing patterns, and articulating strategies that children found helpful. Throughout the year I ask children to explain in writing how to add or subtract. Janelle wrote about addition: "Addition is adding means + the plus sign means you join 2 numbers and you get a big number like 8 + 3 = 11 and here's another one 2 + 8 = 10. Melissa had 9 cookies and her mother made two more cookies and now Melissa has 11 cookies" (Figure 18–3).

The day before presenting a lesson on the addition of double-digit numbers, I asked the children to try to solve the problem 31 + 42 and then to explain how they did it or to simply state they didn't know how and why.

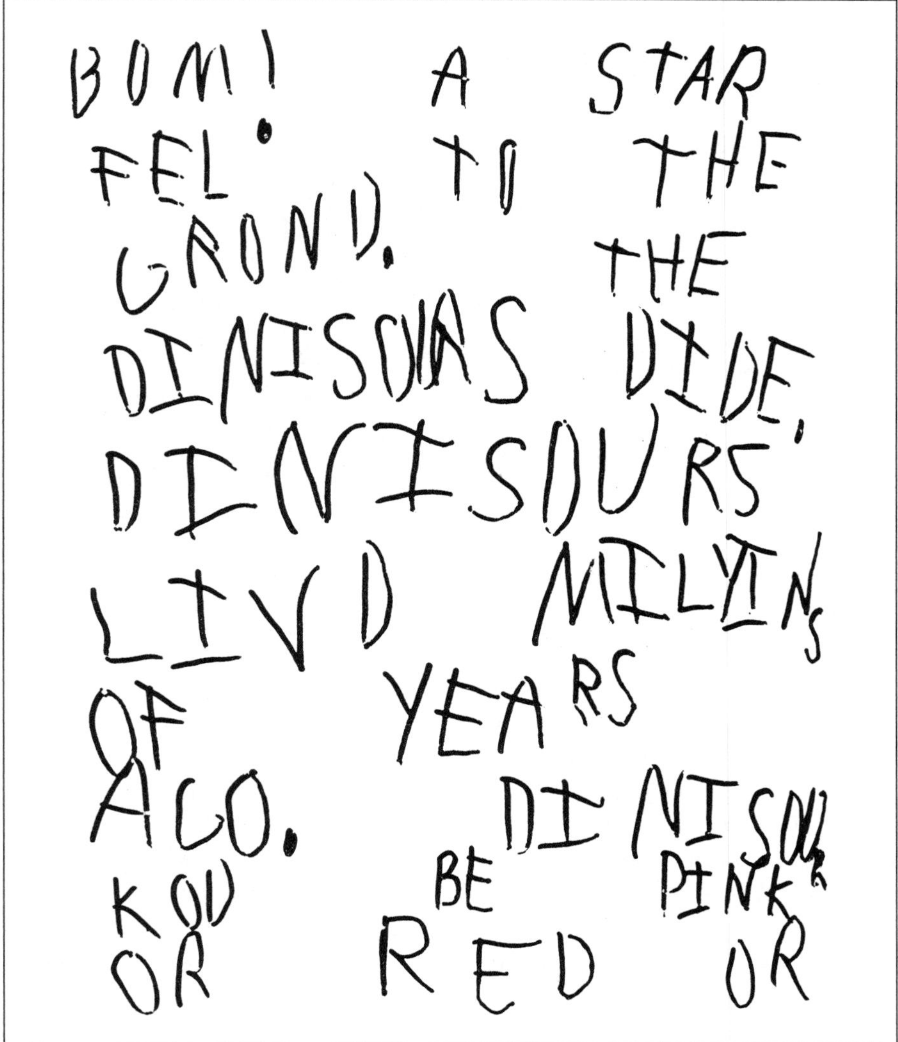

Figure 18–2

Amanda's writing

Patrick wrote: "I added 3 and 4 That was 7 and then I added 2 and 1 that was 3—so it was 73."

Billy wrote: "I don't know what this is because there are too much numbers."

A few days later, after instruction, children completed the same problem, wrote about their learning process, and then looked at their first explanations to see their own concept growth.

In March I brought forsythia branches to school to force blooming and asked the class to observe and write and talk each day on their theories about these sticks and what they might be. Each day the children recorded the

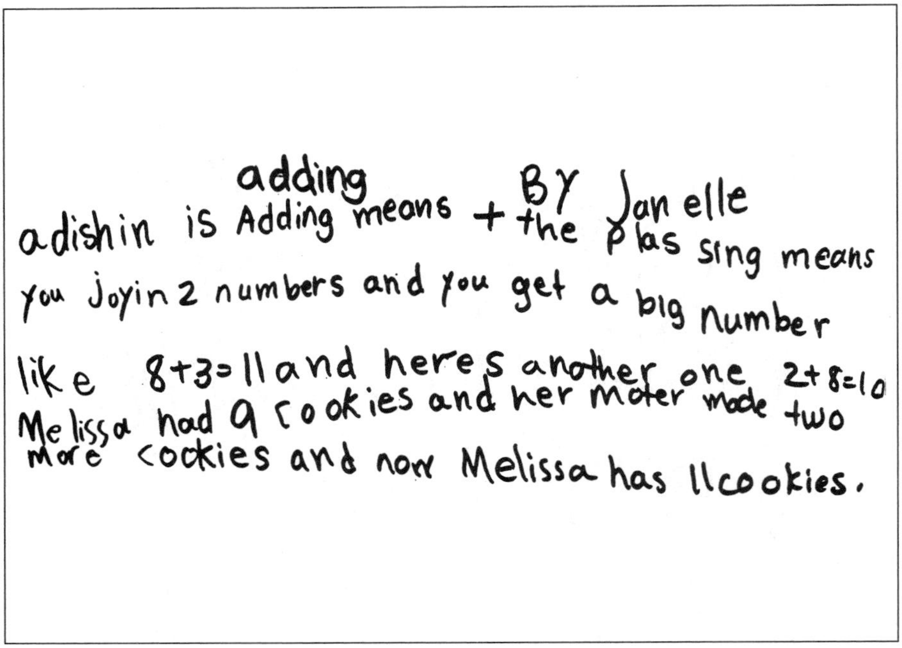

adding
adishin is Adding means + the plas sing means By Janelle
you joyin 2 numbers and you get a big number
like 8+3=11 and heres another one 2+8=10
Melissa had 9 cookies and her moter made two
more cookies and now Melissa has 11cookies.

Figure 18–3

Janelle's writing

changes they saw in logs; eventually, the writing included the revision in their thinking as blossoms appeared.

On the first day Chad wrote: "It looks like something that blooms and dies again. It has branches. It has leaves. It looks like any other plant and its branches are skinny and it looks like a plant from a flower shop." And the next day: "Since yesterday it has changed a lot. It used to have leaves on it. But now it has one flower on it. My guess about it is it's a flower bush!" And after the weekend: "On Friday it had only a little bit of flowers. Since Saturday and Sunday it has bloomed. Now it has hundreds of flowers on it. It looks like a flower bush that were picked out of a flower garden. I think they are buttercups."

Troy wrote: "I think it is a pussywillow that hasn't bloomed yet—that is a late bloomer." (Troy had just learned to read Robert Kraus' book, *Leo the Late Bloomer*.) And five days later: "It bloomed a lot of flowers. It could have been a pussy willow that bloomed though."

On the sixth day Courtney slipped a note on my desk that said: "Forsythia. My grandmother told me. I asked her what was a plant that had yellow flowers." Later, Courtney explained her process to the class. "Well, I asked my grandma. I told her what it looked like after I'd watched it a few days and she said forsythia. But I wanted to be sure, so then I asked a couple more people. I asked my mom and my Aunt Debbie and they both said forsythia so I figured it probably was." Courtney's observations and questioning led her not only to seek an answer but also to validate her answer with more than one source.

In late spring, after I read Roald Dahl's *James and the Giant Peach* to the class, we went to the library to learn more about the six creatures from that book: ladybug, spider, earthworm, centipede, grasshopper, and glowworm. The librarian and I helped the children locate poetry books, nonfiction books, junior encyclopedias, and study prints. We asked the children to look and read until they were "filled up," then to close their books and to write what seemed important. In the ensuing noise and bustle (this was NOT a quiet library time!) we overheard comments from the children.

Jon told one classmate after another, "The ladybug was named after Mary, Jesus's mother."

Jeff said, "I wrote something I think is important. You see this is about the earthworm and how it eats soil."

From Colleen: "I just learned that spiders have *nine eyes*!"

"Centipedes can be poisonous. Did you know that?" asked Jack. He read the encyclopedia to prove his point.

We took many of the books back to the classroom and set up a shelf for each creature. Among the materials we kept there were writing folders where children placed contributions: poems and illustrations they had collected or information they had written after reading about a particular insect. The children frequently gathered in pairs or small groups to read through the folders and discuss the ideas. Children brought books and artifacts from home to add to the shelves—everything from spiders and caterpillars in jars to a stuffed centipede. A teacher in another room became involved and shared spider webs he had sprayed and captured on black paper.

The children's thinking processes were evident in their writing. Katie wrote a page on spiders (an interest of hers from our reading of *Charlotte's Web*) that began: "Spiders hang from their silk when they want to see a closer view" (Figure 18–4). When I stopped to talk with Katie as she worked, she said, "I just wondered *why* a spider would drop down on a strand of silk and then I remembered Charlotte did that when she wanted to see the big pig at the fair and so I think that it might be so they can get a closer view."

Katie continued writing about spiders: "Some spider are poisonous like this. It is black and little of red on its body." She drew a spider. "Spiders have two parts. Spiders have jaws to suck blood out of the insect. Some spiders are good and eat grasshoppers because grasshoppers are bad."

Katie had drawn on information from another folder, where Jeff had recorded the devastation grasshoppers can cause to entire fields. Katie concluded her notes on spiders with a reference back to *Charlotte's Web*: "Spiders die before their babies hatch. And I think that is sad."

Their inquiries extended outside of school. One rainy morning Ted came into the classroom and wrote: "On my way to school I saw a puddle. In the

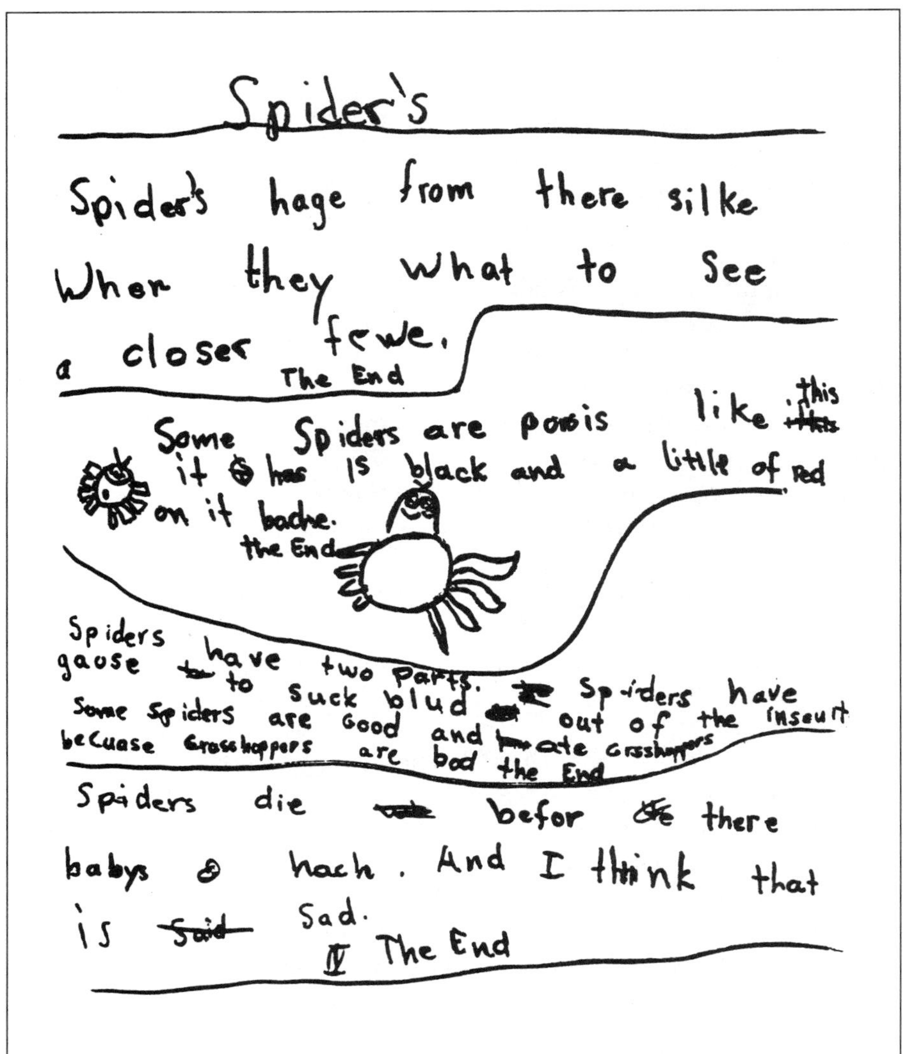
Spider's

Spider's hage from there silke
When they what to See
a closer fewe.
The End

Some Spiders are posis like this
it has is black and a little of red
on it bache.
the End

Spiders
gause have two parts.
to suck blud Spiders have
out of the inseurt
Some Spiders are Good and ate Grasshoppers
because Grasshoppers are bad the End

Spiders die befor there
babys hach. And I think that
is Sad.
The End

Figure 18–4

Katie's writing

puddle I saw a worm this big. [Ted illustrated just how big with a drawing.] I thought a worm needed to live in dirt. But it was water. It looked like its skin was pulling off" (Figure 18–5). Ted's writing led to class speculation as to why we see worms in puddles, why they come out on rainy mornings. A couple of weeks later, David reported reading that earthworms drink through their skin. Since earthworms also need air, the speculation went, they probably come up to get a drink and a breath of fresh air since it gets so muddy underground when it rains.

I saw more evidence that the children took their questioning attitude outside of the classroom when we visited the Philadelphia Academy of Natural

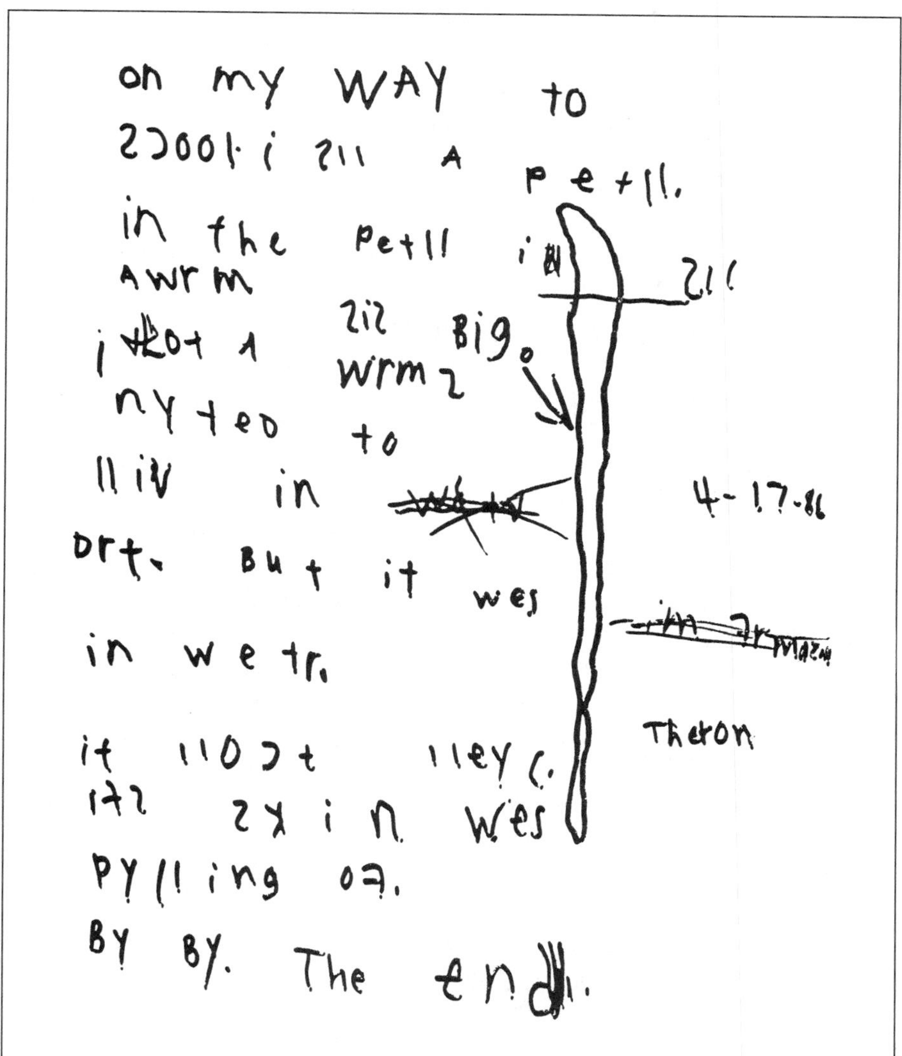

on my WAY to
in the
it wes
By By. The end.
4-17-86
Theron

Figure 18–5

Ted's writing

Sciences. Jon looked at a stuffed rhinoceros, commented that it resembled a dinosaur, and wondered if the rhinoceros evolved from the dinosaur. "Hmmm? How could you find out?" I asked.

Jon smiled, and without further prompting walked over to the attendant and asked. "No," came the answer, followed by an explanation: the dinosaur was a reptile and the rhinoceros is a mammal. Jon thanked the attendant and reported the information back to the group. Later he saw a picture of a dinosaur with bright reds and oranges on its head and said, "Look! There's *red* dinosaurs!" The curator explained to Jon a new theory regarding dinosaur colors. As we walked away Jon made a comment that referred to Amanda's writing about dinosaurs, which had been written nearly two months before. "Amanda was right. They could be any color!"

The importance of talking to peers was evident in many learning situations. On the morning after we visited a dentist's office, I asked children to write what they learned, share that writing with a classmate, and then write some more. Later I asked the children if this procedure had been helpful. Laura answered, "Yes! I talked to six people. At first I only knew this much about the dentist [she indicated a page of writing], but now I know this much!" She spread her arms full length.

Writing, talking, questioning, sharing, reading, thinking, and learning together became the expected norm for approaching a topic. When we began our China unit, I turned the recording of concepts on chart paper over to the children. Small groups sat on the floor negotiating and composing statements about pandas after viewing filmstrips or hearing books read aloud. Each group shared the chart they produced with the entire class, which prompted more inquiry about pandas. Children also kept individual logs on China. On the last day of school, small groups sat around the room sharing ideas from their China logs. As I walked around the room, I heard Mark reading to his peers: "Pandas like honey. They take honey from bees. Bees can't sting them because they have tough fur."

Jared responded, "No, not tough skin. They have tough inside their mouths! Remember, the film told us."

Mark answered, "Oh yeah, that's right." He stopped to make a change on his page. "I wonder if they have tough skin too. Probably they do or they'd get stung on their fur. I could look it up."

Reflecting on the Year

From the tentative beginnings, when I first asked children to write about a planetarium visit, until year's end, the children demonstrated time and again their ability and eagerness to question, to theorize, to explore, and to learn. Writing about their learning brought a new energy into the entire school day. The following year, I started children writing about science and social studies topics much earlier than February, and another group took up the inquiry process with equal enthusiasm. However, in the spring, I repeated the same activity with the insects from *James and the Giant Peach* only to discover that neither the children nor I felt the same energy as the previous year. We soon abandoned the project, and I confronted afresh the reality that not only every child, but also every group will be different and that carrying an activity from one year to another is not a good idea.

As we worked with these curricular areas, we used writing to express thinking. We'd read and talked about numerous books together during literature time and many children also read these books on their own. Children often returned from scheduled library visits with books they checked out on a current curricular topic. A highly significant factor in all of these studies, however, was *talk*.

Learning results, I believe, from an intrinsic need, inherent in each child, to understand the world and make sense of experiences. Children are natural and self-motivated learners who make connections to that which they perceive as relevant and dismiss that which is irrelevant to them at a particular time. I saw that children's learning was both developmentally and experientially based, that the interplay of physical maturation and life experiences was unique for each child, and that learning resulted from each new encounter with the world. Children are learning all the time, but I cannot assume that they interpret experiences as I anticipated they might. I had come to these beliefs (which I continue to revise and refine) through professional reading, attending conferences, being a reader and writer myself, and most of all, through observing children in the classroom and asking them to tell me how they worked and why they made the decisions they made. Motivation was not something I did to them; children motivated themselves. I could only establish the environment and tone for them to take the risks of plunging into new areas of learning. I am reminded of Janet Emig's words: "That teachers teach and children learn, no one will deny, but to believe that children learn because teachers teach and only what teachers explicitly teach is to engage in magical thinking" (1983, 135).

Using an Inquiry Approach

I began units of study by asking the children what they know about a particular topic and what more they want to explore. At one time I would have dismissed this procedure as inappropriate for first graders. After all, how would these little kids know what to study? How could I possibly manage a couple dozen first graders going in different directions? But children have shown me differently.

Social Studies

About ten days into the new school year we began our study of communities. I taped three sheets of chart paper to the chalkboard and labeled them "rural," "suburban," and "urban." I defined these terms and asked the children for characteristics of these three kinds of communities. In the next thirty to forty-five minutes, they produced lists that spilled over to second sheets of chart paper. When we were done, the children had listed all the concepts about urban, suburban, and rural communities outlined in the district curriculum guide intended to cover several class periods. In Lancaster County, Pennsylvania, it is almost impossible to travel even a short distance without encountering all three kinds of communities, and the children had paid attention to the world around them. The talking gave language to that experience. The pooling of knowledge within the group helped everyone. And it helped me know where to begin rather than spending time presenting concepts children already understood.

At the end of discussion on this day, I asked the children what they wanted to know more about in regard to these three different communities. For a minute no one responded. Then one brave little guy raised his hand and said, "What I really want to know is how do they fight fires in the country?"

"You mean on farms?" I asked.

"No, what I mean is how do they fight fires way out in the country, like in Yellowstone Park, 'cuz I been seeing these fires on TV, on the news, and you can't get a fire truck there. At least I don't *think* you can get a fire truck there very easy."

Wow! I would never have thought of this idea. The rest of the class responded immediately. The television news clips they had seen just didn't match their knowledge of firefighting learned from their experiences both in and out of school. We began searching for information. The library had no resources on this particular question, so we began collecting newspaper and magazine articles and reporting the news we saw on television. I learned too and learning *with* the children was invigorating.

Our Ecology Unit

A couple of weeks later I launched our ecology unit. The school district had just added this topic to the first-grade curriculum, and a limited number of resource materials were available through the school. When we began talking about ecology that day I had done no planning, gathered no library books, made no teacher centers, selected no activities. Secretly I was glad for the opportunity to carve out a total unit of study *with* the children. I did have an agenda of my own: I wanted to address farm preservation in Lancaster County, for we have some of the richest farmland in the world, much of which is being converted into shopping centers and housing developments. I opened this new topic by asking the children, "What does ecology mean to you?"

"Pollution"—specifically, "litter"—came the reply. "How come there's so much litter?" "Where does it come from?" "How come people litter?" The room burst into a frenzy of talk about litter. I had "done litter" since the early seventies when this topic first came around in curriculum units, so studying litter did not hold near the interest for me as did firefighting in Yellowstone

Park. Yet the class clearly wanted to explore the issue of litter. "We could pick up litter," someone suggested. However, our custodian maintains litter-free school grounds, and the manicured lawns in our neighborhood were immaculate. Then I had an idea, discussed it with the children, and before the day's end we'd composed a letter to parents asking each family to spend fifteen minutes collecting litter and to send this litter to school the following Friday. "Parent involvement," I told myself, but in truth I hadn't thought this through too carefully.

Not Friday, but Monday morning the bags started arriving. "My mother says you can have this now," said one little boy. All week the bags accumulated. The janitor rolled his eyes but went along with me when I explained that he couldn't throw these bags into the dumpster until Friday. That Friday afternoon we spread butcher paper on the floor and I donned work gloves (the litter was too sordid to allow the children to rummage through it) and began sorting. The children sat around the paper directing the placement of each item into specific piles. Debris from fast-food restaurants constituted a big hunk of this litter, but there also was a car battery pulled from a creek, a multitude of rusted cans and broken bottles, and a large assortment of one-of-a-kind articles. We sorted, categorized, and counted. "How about we make a graph?" I asked the class. We had been making graphs in math class and this seemed a perfect way to demonstrate a purposeful use of graphing. Scowls suddenly appeared on several faces.

"Why should we do that?" asked one little girl, "We can see right here which one has more."

"We already got a graph. It's all this stuff."

"But what about showing other people who aren't here?" I prodded.

"Na-aw," came the consensus.

I realized I had work to do to help these children understand that one purpose of a graph is to communicate with others, but now wasn't the moment to address this. They saw no purpose in such an activity.

"Look at all this yucky stuff. Don't you just wish you could do something?" came a quiet comment from Marcy.

"Yeah, this is awful."

"Well, what would you like to do?" I asked.

"You could write a letter to everyone in the school," suggested Mark.

"I'm not going to do that for you," I replied with playful outrage.

"Oh. Yeah. Well, we could write letters to everyone," came a suggestion.

Then a buzz of discussion broke out, and within a few seconds the children realized the enormity of such a task. Then I told the children about a petition, what it was, how it worked, its purpose. They decided to write a petition and chose two children to draft the document. A few days later, after returning to the class for input and discussing language that would persuade and not demand that others stop littering, the class agreed on their petition. With the children gathered around me on the floor, I recopied the final draft onto a large scroll of paper. The children watched closely. I pointed out the format for a letter of petition, the necessity for correct spelling and punctuation, and the advantage of easily read handwriting. Every child learned to read the petition. Then they signed up for committees and, with a box containing a sampling of their litter, went around to the other classrooms where they read their petition and requested signatures. When they finally posted the petition in the hall, everyone in the school—including every cook, custodian, secretary, even some parent volunteers—had signed it.

The integration of our curriculum had developed from the children's interests and questions. Collecting litter had led to: counting and categorizing, writing with the persuasive language of a petition, learning the form of a letter of petition, handwriting, spelling, punctuation, reading, public speaking, etc. It took place within a community learning together. However, we didn't make a graph!

We went on to explore other kinds of pollution and their effect on our world, and the children made a connection to the fires of Yellowstone that had destroyed a part of the environment. I got my bit in about farm preservation, though I had to be content only to raise the children's awareness; there was minimal interest in my topic. Long after we moved on to other curricular issues, the children maintained their inquisitiveness regarding ecological issues, specifically litter, occasionally bringing in newspaper articles, checking out related library books, reporting something they'd heard on television. In the spring, when they noticed candy wrappers on the playground, they determined that they needed to get their petition out to remind others not to litter. They also became keenly aware of the power of the written word through the use of a petition. When I read Tomie dePaola's *The Art Lesson* to them in the spring, part of their response was outrage toward Tommy's teacher for allowing only one sheet of paper to her students. "Yeah, if you did that, we'd write a petition and give it to Mr. Feltman!" they announced. When we studied China at the year's end, the question of democracy came up. "Some of those students want democracy," Matt commented in one discussion.

"What's that mean—democracy?" I asked.

"It means you get to choose," said Jeff. "You get to vote." Jeff began exploring his budding awareness of democracy but then had difficulty clarifying further.

"Why don't they just write a petition for what they want?" asked Adam.

And then these six-year-olds sat in amazement as I explained, as a beginning of an answer to their question, that a petition would probably not be tolerated in a country such as China. Through classroom experience these children had began to learn something of the meaning of democracy.

Guidelines for Approaching Curricular Studies

As I think of teaching curricular units today, I know that I could never go back to a file of activities repeated year after year. There are some guidelines that I apply to explore the topics of adopted curriculum.

- *Raising questions is an important beginning.* This question raising is always a different process. Sometimes, a particular book or film we've shared evokes questions. Or, I may begin with lists as I did with the urban/rural/suburban unit. Sometimes we freewrite on a specific topic and then talk. But the beginning objective is to raise questions from which we plunge into a topic. It's not the answers that are as important as the directions they take us in and the new questions they raise.
- *Writing for the purpose of thinking and exploring is a key component.* This writing differs from the writing we do in writing workshop. In this writing everyone's exploring the same topic initially. Also, the writing is not revised and edited, though later it may be used as a resource for writing that is crafted for an audience. We use the term *learning logs* (though *journals* or *notebooks* or another term might be just as appropriate) to differentiate this writing from our pieces in writing workshop. We write after reading books, seeing films and videos, going on field trips, etc. Sometimes we take "logs" on field trips and stop to write, sketch, or diagram what we've experienced or observed. We write after group discussions or after sharing log writing with others. We use logs to respond to open-ended questions and then discuss ideas. Sometimes small groups work together on chart paper to "log" their responses to a video. The writing is remembering, connecting, reflecting, observing, hypothesizing, and more.
- *Children's literature contributes to investigation.* I read many books related to topics of study. We compare information in books, check copyrights, examine the author's perspective, question facts. The books provide information and also models of the range of ways authors present nonfiction information. In addition to straightforward reporting, some weave information into narratives, others into biography (even the biography of a cactus in *Cactus Hotel*), still others use unusual formats such as *NBA by the Numbers*, which presents information on basketball in the format of a counting book. We even found books with stories showing a child using a "learning log" like ours (*An Island Scrapbook* and *A Desert Scrapbook*).

- *Writing to communicate information to other audiences occurs.* The children's investment in topics of inquiry leads them to select aspects of these topics for writing in writing workshop. I also make writing assignments by asking children to read through their logs and then to write a focused piece from the ideas and information recorded in the log. Some children experiment with various genres as they work on this assignment, using the models we've seen in children's literature. This assigned writing helps children synthesize a broad range of information and often raises new questions in the ongoing learning process.
- *Talk is a key component through all of this learning.* We talk after writing in logs, write again, then talk some more. We talk as we read books. We talk to question, speculate, predict, confirm, clarify, wonder, consider, and on and on. Children report that talk helps them. "When I was working with my group, because of stuff they said I remembered some things I forgot," Morgan says. "Before we talked about what we wrote in our logs I only knew this much," Jon reports, indicating the length of his writing, "but afterwards I knew *this* much." He indicates two more pages of writing. I confer with children as they write in logs, responding just as I do in writing workshop by focusing on the children's ideas. In fact, the experience of working in a writing workshop provided a strong foundation for the children to talk about topics.

The Internet provides a vast resource for finding information. When I worked beside Michelle DeCamp in her classroom in Old Forge, New York, children located and printed out Internet articles on topics. We asked them to read the articles until they felt they had sufficient information in their heads, then set the articles aside and write their thoughts as well as relevant information. Crucial teacher conferences as they read and wrote enabled them to clarify their emerging thoughts, untangled confusion as they struggled to comprehend difficult material, and led them away from merely copying from articles. Once again, talk, between teacher and child and among the children themselves, was crucial in thinking and learning. John Dewey said, "Learning is a social process." Children who are invested in learning, as inquiry approaches help achieve, demonstrate this to be true time and again.

Reflections

My risk taking paid off. I watched children invest in subject matter and acquire factual knowledge at levels that far outpaced my previous approach to teaching content units. Even more important, they developed broad concepts and ways of thinking about issues. I came to understand that integration is not something I as a teacher plan and implement, but rather something that occurs *within* learners. When curricular units are broadly framed and begin with the children, building on what they know, connections between all the disciplines occur. Reading and writing and talking and listening really are tools for learning, regardless of the topic.

I still occasionally pull activities from my resource files, but only when there is a specific need that arises from the children's questions. When the children speculated about the size of dinosaurs, for instance, we first looked up this information in books, then went to the playground and measured dinosaur lengths. We focused attention on answering the children's questions about dinosaur sizes because this was information they cared about learning, not because the activity is one that's done in dinosaur units.

I want children to learn to question and to understand that answers to those questions—like the world itself—are always changing. I found a model for this approach for content studies in Patricia Lauber's book *The News About Dinosaurs.* Lauber structures the book by presenting facts of what was once believed about dinosaurs followed by sections with the heading "The News Is . . ." where she tells how our theories have changed as we uncover more information. I believe that it is important to help children understand that what we believe today may be disproved tomorrow, that our theories about the world, our understanding, our knowledge are finite. Learning is based on a continuous process of theory making, testing, revising, and new theory making.

I've only skimmed the surface in reporting the active involvement with learning that goes on in my classroom in content-area studies. Like teaching reading and writing, I teach science, math, and social studies with a responsive teaching approach. I know I'll probably never repeat the litter activity with another class, not because of the messiness of bringing litter into the room, but because I understand now that activities must be purposeful to be effective. To discover what is purposeful learning, I must start by listening to the children. As a teacher I have expertise to share with children, but when, what, and how depends on the children. This kind of teaching demands more of me than any of my elaborate activities and intricate planning. It requires me not only to have a solid understanding of how to help children find information but also to be aware of the learning styles, experience levels, and thought processes of each of my students. Since those individual attributes are continuously in flux, I've got to be attentive so that I can help children take their learning further. It's a pretty invigorating way to teach.

CONSIDERING STUDENT PROGRESS

CHAPTER 19

Documenting Student Growth

Before I moved into reading and writing workshops, I looked at student achievement, in large part, by the way children completed worksheets and tests. So to record writing and reading development in workshops, initially I pulled a list of skills from the curriculum and set up an elaborate notebook to document when I saw children using the various skills. My plan to record skill development this way was faulty, for there was no one day when a child suddenly began writing complete sentences, or using a phonetic skill or any other language convention. Individual learning was too recursive for such specific documentation. And, noting discrete skills, or even testing comprehension through short passages with questions, provided scant information about a child's progress. Much more was going on as they read and wrote each day than any arbitrary list could capture; the whole was greater than the sum of the parts. What's more, the information I did glean provided little help in making decisions about what to teach and when. As these facts became obvious, I had a sinking feeling about all the children who had passed through my classroom in past years: could they really read? They passed the tests, but I now knew that that didn't mean they *could* read, let alone prove that they were *readers*! "One of the problems with 'meaningful' assessment and evaluation is that it's easy to have the pieces look like they are in place without having any impact on instruction and learning. . . . Assessment must promote learning, not just measure it" (Routman 2000, 558).

I came to realize that the primary *purpose* of record keeping is to help me *understand* the learning process of individual children, thus guiding instruction and providing data on each child's development to communicate to parents. I wanted to know the *children* as individual learners. To these ends, I needed to know what my students did, how they learned and why they made the decisions they did as they worked. I became what Yetta Goodman calls a "kidwatcher." "Kidwatching," Goodman (1985) writes, "is used as a slogan to reinstate and legitimatize the significance of professional observation in the classroom. . . . The best way to gain insight into language learning is to observe children using language to explore all kinds of concepts in art, social studies, math, science, or physical education" (10–11).

Therefore, a pivotal part of my teaching is closely observing children *as they work in the classroom on a day-to-day basis,* in order both to note their progress and struggles and to inform my teaching approaches. I keep brief notes on children's learning efforts, trying to be as specific as possible. I quickly learned that record keeping, to be effective, had to be efficient. Too much recording becomes burdensome, requiring extensive sifting of data later, but too little provides inadequate documentation and leads to generalizing about intricate learning processes. For instance, during reading workshop, I carry a one-page sheet of paper as I confer with students where I note strategies children use, suggestions I give them, and comments they make that indicate how they are decoding and comprehending. Just the process of noticing and recording plays a major role in showing me the children's development, but I also take time to reflect through journal writing on particular surprises, concerns, or wonderings that surface. Kidwatching procedures such as this provide documentation of student growth over time, create a unique picture of each child as a learner, and enable me to share detailed accounts of a child's actual progress rather than numbers or phrases that are open to varied interpretations.

This kind of observing and documenting has helped me be responsive to the children in a multitude of teachable moments. For example, in a reading conference as a child reads a few words to me I can quickly see if the book is too difficult—or too easy. "I'm not sure this is the best book for you right now. Let's find another; I'll help you," I'll say to a child and take a moment to search out an appropriate title with the child, thus demonstrating *how* to do so independently. A child struggles on a word, rereading because the passage doesn't make sense, but ignoring the final letters in the troubling word; I say, "Let me show you something that will help," and then take a moment to explain the use of ending sounds in the word in question. My brief notes on these interactions contribute to the ongoing record of each child and to my knowledge of each learner. Nancy Johnson (2001) writes, "The most effective teachers are those who make the best teaching decisions possible . . . the most beneficial teaching decisions are those that are thoughtfully considered, grounded in knowledge about reading processes and experience teaching reading, and *based upon individual students*" (40). Observations help me know children and respond to the diversity of learning styles, interests, and needs at the appropriate time.

Though still faced with the reality of report cards, where I must grade thirty items on a 1 to 5 scale, and required to administer a standardized test in the spring, I work toward documenting the children's ongoing development with specific information to share with parents. My report card grades have always been based on more than tests and the accuracy of worksheets and drills; my subjective knowledge of each child plays a part in the grades my students receive. Documenting provides important data to substantiate these grades. Instead of *telling* others *about* a child through scores or my judgment, I try to show a picture of each child, allowing others to *see* a child's progress. When I place more emphasis on the child as an individual rather than comparing the child to others, so do the parents. We focus on individual growth from a perspective of success rather than from a deficiency model.

Perhaps most important, I learned through kidwatching how assessment is deeply embedded in the day-to-day process of teaching and learning and involves everyone—teachers, students, and parents. I am far more comfortable with this approach to documenting and reporting student growth than one that places me in the position of authority on the learner or by determining growth by measurement tools alone. Kidwatching advances valuing of the learner and takes into account context, which is essential to understanding the growth of individual learners.

Recording Writing and Reading Development

I set up two simple forms to use during conferences in reading and writing workshops. In Chapters 4 and 7, I shared my "Conference Checklist" for writing workshop. To jot quick notes, I devised a single record sheet where I could record notes for the entire class on any given day by sectioning one sheet of paper into blocks and writing each child's name in the corner of a block. I file these record sheets chronologically in a class reading folder. Since each child's notation appears at the same place on each page, I can quickly peruse the records, get a chronological record and also see a given child's work in relationship to other children on a particular day. I use this form one or two days a week for writing and maybe three days a week for reading. I found it too time-consuming and burdensome to use the record sheet every day—too much energy on taking notes rather than listening to children.

To further record reading and writing development, I prepare two folders for each child before school opens, one for reading and one for writing. I color-code the folders (red for reading and blue for writing) and keep them on my center table for easy access. Inside the writing folder I staple blank paper for anecdotal records and a form devised for taking notes during publishing conferences. In similar fashion, the reading folder has paper for anecdotal records and a form for recording notes when children read books to me. The folders also provide a place for filing additional documents or data that contribute to the picture of a child's reading or writing development such as dialogue letters with parents, test results, etc. I keep the forms simple and tweak them from year to year to make them easy to use. (See Appendices B and E.)

Writing Folders

Traditionally, products have been the way to determine student achievement. Final products can be examined in isolation, but the context surrounding any piece of writing enriches my understanding of a child's development. When I saw this fuller picture, I knew I couldn't possibly grade individual papers. Instead, I began looking at growth over time and considering all that children said and did as they wrote. Product *and* process are essential to documenting student growth. The writing folders I keep are an attempt to show both product and process.

My writing folders do not take the place of the writing folder the children keep. Children's folders hold the majority of their writing. My folders hold drafts of published pieces of writing (the writing that a child has worked to revise and edit for an audience), notes from the publishing conferences, and anecdotal notes such as specific revisions and language skills I've taught. I file notes children write to me, as well as vacation journals here. When parents plan a family vacation and request their child's "work" to take along, I send a book parents and child can read together and a stapled booklet of blank paper for the child to write in during the absence. Jody requested such a booklet for Christmas vacation. He returned it in January with the title,

"Christmas Day and Another Day." Eventually, this vacation journal went into his writing folder as additional documentation of his involvement in writing.

On the anecdotal record sheet in the writing folders, I jot down significant incidents relating to a child's writing. Usually, I make a quick note during the workshop to remind myself and then record it later so that this note taking does not rob time from conferences in the workshop itself. I end up with extensive notes on some children and brief notes on others. I go though these anecdotal notes periodically and reflect on *all* the children, especially considering those for whom notes are minimal. I've come to trust that the volume of notes has little correlation to my knowledge about a particular child. It is the *anomalies* that I want to understand, and writing helps me reflect on those anomalies. I can't hope to record everything that happens with a child's writing, but short notes written when events occur provide specific information and also spark my memories of those moments.

My notes and samples of children's writing over the course of the school year provide a developmental picture of each child as a writer. For example, from the writing samples, my notes, and journal reflections I am able to construct the following vignette of Jenny as a writer. In addition to the brief narrative, I've included snippets of my notes, journal reflections, and follow-up lessons informed, in part, by Jenny's writing.

In notes on Jenny the first week of school I describe her as "exuberant, energetic, and very social: smiling, sunny disposition, gets along well with peers. Says school is 'hard.'" I described her classroom work in these words: "cooperative, follows procedures willingly," "struggles with math—last to finish assignments," "says 'I can't read any words—just my name.'" In her writing the first week of school she drew and labeled pictures only after my urging in writing conferences. In mid-September Jenny produced the piece of writing shown in Figure 19–1.

SEPTEMBER 14 Jenny writes *T* for table, *F* for food, *F* for fork, and *ME* to indicate herself. In conference she tells me about the good chicken her mom fixed the night before. I suggest she write a sentence. She tells me she can't because writing makes her hand hurt. I leave. When I return she has written, "I like chicken" and reads the sentence to me. She throws up her hands and says, "I did it. I didn't know I could. But I did it. I wrote a whole sentence." Going out the door that afternoon Jenny says, "I'm gonna tell my mom I wrote a whole sentence today."

I recorded this anecdote in my notes, including her comments. I also noted: "Encouragement paid off. J. talked all day about her sentence!"

SEPTEMBER 22 Jenny draws a school bus (bus No. 14) with her mom behind the wheel and herself seated in the front seat (Figure 19–2). She tells me

Figure 19–1

Jenny's writing, September 14

her mom was the substitute bus driver this day and she got to ride the entire route. She reads her sentence, "I am riding a bus-a and my mom is driving z bus-a." (Spoken language matches the sounds of letters she has written.)

Teacher Notes: Big day—important topic. Points accurately to letters as she reads and spoken language matches the sounds of letters she wrote. Told names of everyone in the bus windows. Picture important.

Follow-Up Lessons: capital letters and periods for sentences, adding more information through additional sentences. (Note: these lessons were based on observations of the entire class, not just Jenny.)

Figure 19–2

Jenny's writing, September 22

OCTOBER 21 Jenny draws a car loaded with people, suitcases, and pets. She spends most of her time writing the sentences on a separate page (Figure 19–3). She reads them to me, pausing to reread and use context to figure the words out and inserting "mi" in the first line when she notices the sentence does not make sense without that word. Then she reads through the piece: "Me and my mom are going to California, my dad and Tara and Mack. I like to go to California. Do you like to go to California?" She points to the question mark and says, "I put one of them things like you showed us," referring to the mini-lesson that day. She says she crossed out the question mark at the end

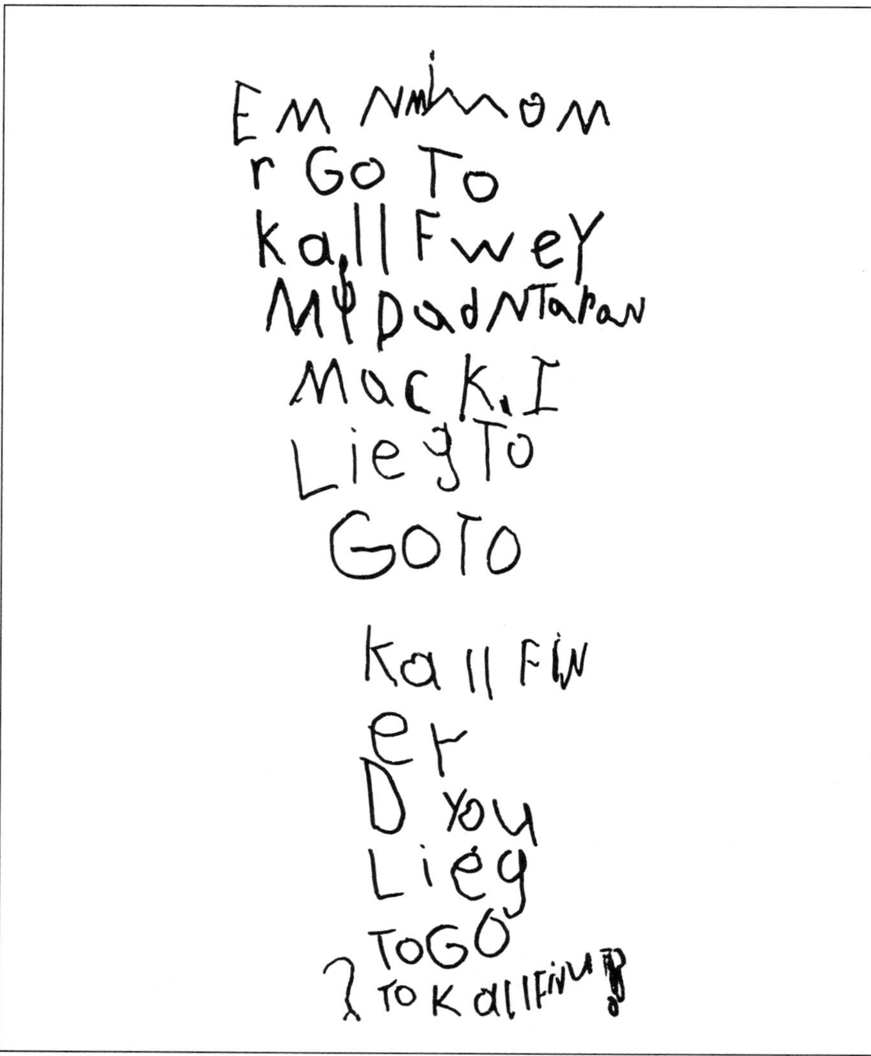

Figure 19–3

Jenny's writing, October 21

and moved it to the other end of the line because it was difficult to see in the binding of the writing book.

Teacher Notes: Rereading her writing shows her how to read—knows what she writes, uses letters and context, rereads when "messes up." Family themes important—especially Mom.

NOVEMBER 11 Jenny writes a book about her mom (Figure 19–4). Each segment is on a different page of a small, prestapled booklet. She has trouble reading the entire piece because her fluency in putting ideas on paper outpaces her spelling development. Together we figure out most of the piece. Showing

I hiad my.
Mom
I Lite.
tohp my
mom.

My mom.
is pi the
Lr e E.
nin the
wmh N.

MoM
me clen.
crie C
tiwise doer?

Wie dwe
moms
taGa wrke
hehe.

Mom
can
doie a the
Firvs. heny
Sme
tiem.

Mom
Pat
.Knde
to
Bade

Figure 19–4

Jenny's writing, November 11

her how to skip words and use context and the initial letter is the main strategy we use—plus Jenny's memory of her ideas. The book reads:

> I help my Mom. I like to help my Mom.
>
> Mom can clean [undecipherable].
>
> Mom can do a fire in the fireplace sometime. [Jenny uses words more than once when she reads this sentence.]
>
> My mom is putting the laundry in the washing machine. Why do Moms go to work? Huh?
>
> Moms put kids to bed.

Teacher Notes: Mom topic again. Voice!—sounds just like J. talking! J. worked hard to read this. Needed help figuring out some words. Context helps. Conscientious use of capitals and punctuation. There's a zig-zag pace to her reading and writing growth—she writes more than she can easily read back; earlier, writing was ahead of reading.

Follow-Up Lessons: strategies for reading one's writing; reread for making sense; show J.'s writing as example of including specific information.

EARLY DECEMBER Over a week's time Jenny writes a book about herself that is several pages long. The particular page shown in Figure 19–5 has a drawing of her reading in the classroom, the circular conference table, and the other children seated at their desks. The words read, "I like to read. Do you like to read? Ten Little Bears." She inserts the *e* on the end of *like* when she edits the book for publishing. *Ten Little Bears* refers to a book she has learned to read.

Teacher Notes: Fluent and confident. Spelling improving (class work on spelling patterns and her reading).

FIRST WEEK IN FEBRUARY Jenny writes about her dog (Figure 19–6). She draws the scene outside her home and then writes, "My dog likes to dig to hide his bones." She reads her writing without difficulty. She explains a page with five dogs on it (see Figure 19–7): "First I drew this one (number 1) then

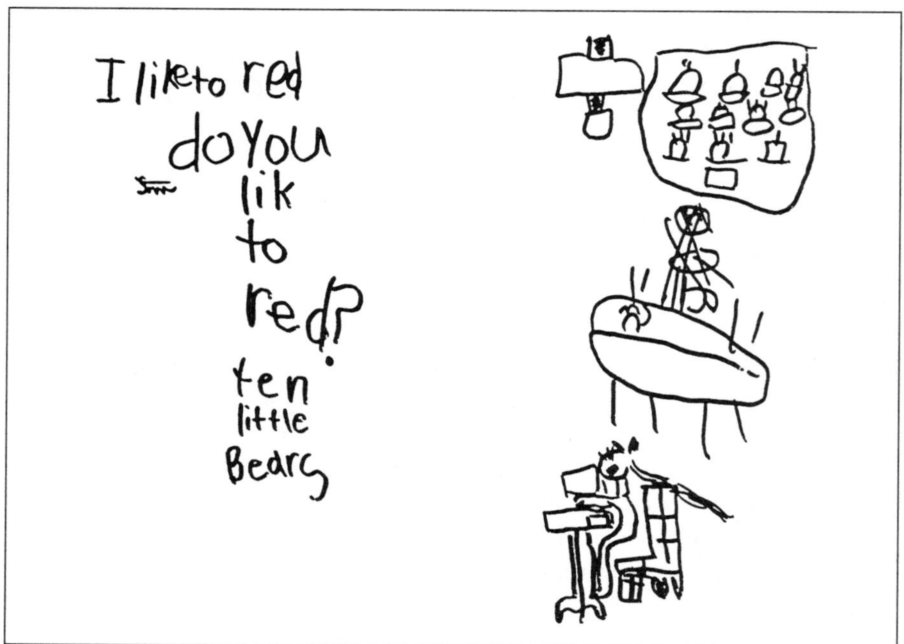

Figure 19–5

Jenny's writing, early December

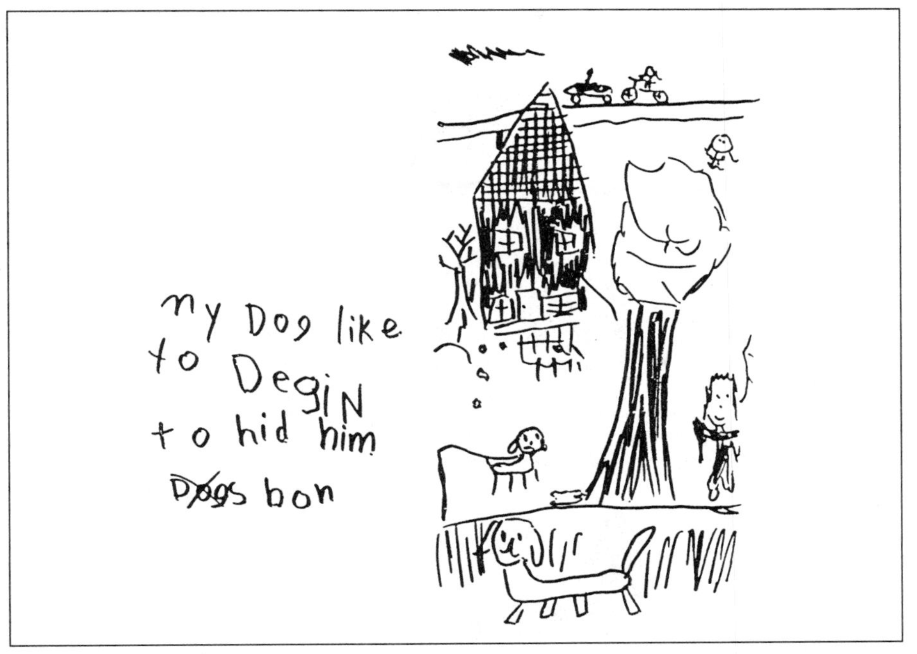

my Dog like
to Degin
to hid him
Dogs bon

Figure 19–6

Jenny's writing, February

I thought I could do it better and so then I drew this one . . . I revised." Jenny added the numbers at my request so that we would recall the order in which the dogs developed.

Teacher Journal: Jenny revised by *drawing*. Astounding! All the revision lessons have been on writing, but she took the concept to her drawing. This is a reminder how important drawing is for kids and how a child will choose the best way for herself. I think J. felt revision was less risky with drawing; she's quite comfortable drawing, less so writing—though she's come a long way from Sept.! It's interesting that she "revised" the drawing so many times.

Follow-Up Lessons: Share J.'s example with everyone and work on concept of revision as "re-seeing" in our minds.

EARLY APRIL Jenny writes about her mom for Mother's Day (Figure 19–8). This page, one of ten, reads, "My mom cooks chicken. Whenever my Mommy fixes chicken she acts like one and she says, 'BOK.'" Using her picture dictionary, Jenny corrected the spelling of "chicken" to edit her piece for publication.

Teacher Reflections: "Mom" topic a thread through J.'s writing all year—so she wrote this with ease. Rereads and makes corrections. Drawing still important to her. She's brought the confidence and exuberance that is Jenny to her writing.

Follow-Up Lessons: editing strategies (line out), quotation marks.

Figure 19–7

Jenny's revisions of her dog drawings, February

LATE MAY Jenny again writes about her mother (Figure 19–9). An excerpt: "My mom loves me. She will not give me away. Maybe for a $100. Would you?"

JUNE 7, THE LAST WEEK OF SCHOOL Jenny continues writing about her mother. One page she writes that day (Figure 19–10) reads, "My mom is so, so, so, so, so, so, so, so great at cooking chicken and meat too."

Teacher Reflections: Jenny is a writer and reader. The processes of both r. and w. complemented each other throughout her development. I believe that writing definitely helped her develop strong reading skills. She says. "I

Figure 19–8

Jenny's writing, April

5/24

my mom loves me She will not a way give me may-be a$100 2 too for whod you.

Figure 19–9

Jenny's writing, May

My mom is soso
so so so sososo
grate at cooking
chicken and met
too.

Jenny
June

Figure 19–10

Jenny's writing, June

love to read." She's not intimidated by more advanced readers in the class. She uses a range of reading strategies. She spells following phonetic rules though irregular spellings still throw her. She writes extended pieces with solid information and uses basic conventions of written language.

The teacher-maintained record folders are my first resource for examining a child's development as a writer. If I want to delve deeper, I go to the folders the children keep that hold all of their writing. All writing remains in the classroom until the last day of school, is easily accessible, and provides a history of a writer's development.

Reading Folders

Reading development is more challenging to record because reading leaves no tangible product as does writing. A list of titles a child reads over the course of a year is a beginning, but I want more information. I set up reading folders similar to the writing folders. On a record sheet I called "Reading Record" (see Appendix E), I note *what* a child reads, *how* the child reads (the struggles, successes, strategies used), *why* the child chose a particular reading material or abandoned it, and the *child's responses* to what he or she reads (thoughts and feelings about characters, actions, author's style and the connections the child makes to personal experience). In the beginning of the year, first graders need to read *to* someone, a process parallel to the publication process in writing. I spend part of my time during two or three reading workshops a week (and during morning free play, indoor recess, etc.) listening to children read books that they have practiced and polished for fluent oral reading. When children read to me, I jot notes on the Reading Record sheet in their folder. The children quickly came to expect me to write while they read. Later, when the task of listening to young readers grows, I show volunteers how to write observations as they listen.

Learning about running records and miscue analysis taught me much about understanding and documenting reading development as I listened to children read. Marie Clay developed running records as a means of analyzing a child's reading. I'm not doing an intensive analysis of a child's reading, but I am noting how the child reads—the miscues, the corrections, the strategies used. Ken Goodman developed miscue analysis, a system that examines the type of miscues readers make, analyzing them for the strategies the reader uses. Describing the significance of miscues in beginning readers, Frank Smith (1988) wrote:

> Children will strive for sense even when they learn to read (provided the material they are expected to learn from has some possibility of making sense in the first place). The mistakes that are made are sometimes called *miscues* rather than *errors* to avoid the connotation that they are something bad (Goodman 1965). Such misreadings show that these beginning readers are attempting to read in the way fluent readers do, with sense taking priority over individual word identification. Of course, reading with minimal attention to individual words will sometimes result in misreadings that do make a difference to meaning, but one of the great advantages of reading for meaning in the first place is that one becomes aware of mistakes that make a difference to meaning. An important difference between children who are doing well in reading and those who are not is not that good readers make fewer mistakes, but that they go back and correct the mistakes that make a difference. (151–52)

Both running records and miscue analysis provide information to inform instruction. For more information on these systems I recommend *The Art of Teaching Reading* by Lucy Calkins (2001); *Miscue Analysis Made Easy: Building on Student Strengths* by Sandra Wilde (2000); and *Conversations: Strategies for Teaching, Learning, and Evaluating* by Regie Routman (2000).

I found that lack of time prevented me from doing extensive formal running records or miscue analysis on children's reading. The importance of these systems was seeing what could be learned from them and modifying them for my use. I am interested in miscues students make as they read, what they do about those miscues, and what that indicates about their developing reading strategies. I am also interested in strategies children use when they come to words they don't readily know. Finally, I want to know how the child understands what is read, not just a literal retelling, but thoughts, feelings, and connections with the text.

As the children read, I note children's miscues and reading strategies with my own shorthand system. For miscues I write the word the child uttered, a slash, then the correct word much the way one might write a mathematical fraction. Then I note in abbreviated form what the child did following such a miscue. My system has evolved to this:

m.m.—maintains meaning

s.c.—self-corrects (after which I note the particulars)

skip—a child skips a word entirely (if child returns to the word, usually because meaning was lost, I note any strategies I observe)

pic.—uses picture clues

ctx.—uses context clues

s.o.—sound out (often I write the word underlining the part of the word where the child used phonetic clues; e.g., <u>bl</u>anket—the child used the *bl* blend)

stop—I interrupt because the oral reading does not make sense. "What did you say?" or "Does that make sense?" or "Hey, I don't get that," I ask in an outrageous and playful tone and then note what the child says and does.

IDK—to record the "I don't know" answer I often get from children when I first ask a question. I usually respond to the child by saying, "That's something to think about" as a way of setting expectations for future reading.

This coding system emerged as I listened to the children and keeps changing as I work with it. Had I derived a system ahead of time or followed a system designed by someone else, using it effectively would have been difficult.

During this reading time, I also ask children questions designed to get at their thinking. I want them to articulate their processes as well as their comprehension. So I ask questions such as:

How did you choose this book?

What struggles or problems did you have when you learned to read this?

How did you solve those problems?

What do you think about this book? story? ending?

Tell me about your favorite part?

What were you thinking as you read this? What do you think now?

What will you read next?

Of course, I avoid falling into a routine set of questions. I often ask, "How did you figure that out?" after a child corrects a miscue as a means of helping the child become aware of personal strategies. I've found that self-awareness of one's strategies leads readers to value them and use them again. My questions open up conversations with children about books and reading. Children internalize these questions and soon come to reading time ready to talk about their reading. As we chat, I jot down key comments they make. I find that my questions and our talk quickly develop into serious conversation that is part of both reading instruction and evaluation.

By year's end, I have a record of approximately twenty reading experiences with each child. An entry from Jamie's mid-February reading of *Drummer Hoff* is an example of these reading records (Figure 19–11). The predictable language, the rhyme, and the rhythm all supported his reading, and when he read *Mayor* for *General*, he immediately corrected himself. When I asked him how he knew the word, he replied, "*General* begins with *G* and ends with *L*, so then I could get it."

The notes on Jamie's reading do not include all the books he read. Just as I cannot read everything the children write, so I cannot listen to them read or even talk with them about everything they read. First graders dip into lots of books, reading pages here and there, chatting about books with their friends.

Date 2-13 Title Drummer Hoff

Observations: Corporal Bammer – s.c. "I thought it was Corp. Bam."
Mayor —"No!" s.c. to "General" How? "General starts with G + it also ends with L."

Reader Comments: "I like this book. I like cannons and stuff."
"This was in the olden times 'cuz they don't shoot canons today.

Future Plans: IDK

Figure 19–11

Teacher's notes on Jamie's reading

I'm convinced that the independence in the workshops contributes to their developing as independent readers who choose to read on their own. They reread and practice some books, polishing these titles to read aloud to others. I do not require them to perfect everything they read any more than I require them to revise, edit, and publish everything they write. To mold them into such a rigid structure would limit the children's reading development. I try to let the children lead. Noting reading behaviors helps me understand children's progress and, in the end, reassures me of growth. In the first year of reading workshop, one little fellow read and reread a page on ships from a book he brought from home. The text was difficult. When I suggested other books, he shrugged them off. After three weeks he set his book aside to try something new. I admired his perseverance and I suspect that the idea of finishing this reading had come from his older siblings. Certainly he learned much from working with one page, but I know he lost interest in the meaning of the words he read. I wondered how much he would have achieved if he had moved on to other reading material earlier and then returned to the book he so wanted to read. However, it was important to let him come to this decision for himself. I made suggestions but left the final choice to him. He became an excellent reader. Taking notes through these three weeks helped me see the *child's* perspective and kept me from intruding on his process.

"I want to understand and remember how you read," I explain to the children, "so I'll be taking notes." The children accept the recording as part of the workshop. Occasionally I ask a child to repeat something of particular interest: "Would you say that again?" The children take a keen interest in these notes and sometimes pause to ask, "Did you get that all down?" Of course, I can't capture everything that is said; I'd lose the interaction with the child. We pause, make eye contact, and chat during the reading. Glenda Bissex once told me that if something was important, it would appear again and again. Remembering her words gave me permission to relax, listen, and focus first on the child and second on recording. I don't need to record everything. Interestingly, I found that rereading the notes was not critical; the *process of recording* helped me remember the experience and better understand that child.

Interviews

Even young children can articulate the decisions they make as they read and write. About midpoint of my first year with workshops, I began interviewing children about their progress—a process that naturally evolved from our daily conferences. Those first interviews provided so much information about individual learning that in subsequent years I added interviews to the documenting process. Hearing Carolyn Burke (1984), Mary Ellen Giacobbe and

Nancie Atwell (1985) speak about interviews helped me refine my interview questions. However, the thrust of all interviews is not the questions but rather the talk by the learner.

I try to interview each child three times a year. Here are three interviews with Greg. The first took place during the first week of school.

MRS. A: Can you read?

GREG: Ummm, some. [hesitant answer]

MRS. A: How did you learn?

G: From my dad reading to me at night.

MRS. A: What does someone do to learn to read?

G: Saying words and practicing. [pause] I know a lot of opposites I can read.

MRS. A: Can you write?

G: Yeah. [no further comment on writing even in response to questions]

MRS. A: Who do you know who's a good reader?

G: My dad and my mom.

MRS. A: What makes them good?

G: My dad can read a book about Nicolas Knock. It's a two-night book! My mom, she reads funny stories and stuff like that.

MRS. A: A two-night book?

G: Yeah.

MRS. A: Anything else?

G: No.

MRS. A: Well, who do you know who's a good writer?

G: My dad. He writes most of the checks and stuff.

Greg added that *Nicolas Knock* was his favorite book. As opening interviews go, Greg was pretty talkative in comparison to most of the children, though not especially reflective about reading and writing. In mid-December he had this to say:

MRS. A: Can you read and write?

G: Yeah! I just started a new story today. It's about when Max came over to my house yesterday.

MRS. A: I see. How do you choose your topics for writing?

G: Well, most of the time I write about what I've done. That's stuff like I chose to write about when Max came over yesterday because it was fun and it had some interesting story parts in it, like when we started to put the new roof on my tree house. It has just one roof that we didn't like so we took some of my wood out and we nailed it on. So the rain won't get in it and rot it.

MRS. A: I see. What can you do now in writing that you couldn't do when school started?

G: Hmmm, that's a hard question. [pause] Well, most of the things I do now that I didn't do when school started is think about like what I did more and I sound out more words than I did when school started. Stuff like that.

MRS. A: If you had to tell somebody what was most important about writing, what would you tell them?

G: Hmmm, that's a good question. [pause] I'd tell them that if you want to be a writer then you have to, most of the time, do a good job on the pictures and stuff—if you can draw pictures. You also have to get your stories to make sense. Like if, say somebody wrote a story and like they said, "I went down to the store" and they put the same thing in again, that wouldn't make sense.

MRS. A: If they said it twice. So what would you do, if you were them?

G: Well, I'd take one of them out. That way it wouldn't say, "I went down to the store. I went down to the store." That would be silly.

MRS. A: Anything else that writers do that you're able to do?

G: Well, hmmm. Well, most writers don't make stories that don't have much information. Like when I write. I put information in. That's what I do.

MRS. A: Well, tell me about reading.

G: Well, when school started I couldn't read that much books as I can now.

MRS. A: How'd you learn to read them?

G: Sounding out the words. There's one thing I've learned with most of the books is to keep them for awhile. Like in reading workshop, most of the time I read the same book. If it's too hard for me, I keep practicing it until I get the words right.

MRS. A: So you keep practicing it?

G: Yeah.

MRS. A: What's your favorite book that you've learned to read?

G: Hmmm, favorite book. *Chester.*

MRS. A: What are you wanting to learn to do next in reading?

G: Read some more harder books.

MRS. A: How about in writing?

G: I'd like to try to spell harder words, to get them right.

MRS. A: Okay, thank you very much Greg.

Like his classmates, Greg had begun to articulate his processes of writing and reading. At this point in the year, most of the children spoke more precisely about writing than reading, and almost all expressed a concern about learning to spell correctly. I took notes during both the September and December interviews and ran a tape recorder as backup. Making frequent eye contact and encouraging the children through nonverbal communication was an important part of the interviewing process. For the final interviews at the end of the year, I typed as children spoke, occasionally asking them to pause while I caught up. I only had to ask an opening question for each child to launch into free-flowing talk about reading, writing, and learning, as this interview in the first week of June shows.

MRS. A: Tell me about yourself as a reader.

GREG: I basically learned to read by getting books that I remembered about from other places. I remembered *This Old Man* by remembering the song and if I got stuck on a word, I would remember the song and then I would put the word in place that I would think of and I would use the letters and sounds and probably make out the word. Sometimes I would remember the word from when you read it in the class and then I would memorize it so I would use it in other books. Sometimes I would sound out, but sometimes I come to a word when sound out does not work. Like in *The Boy That Held Back the Sea* [the part where] he was trying to get the guards to believe him that there were pirate ships. I couldn't get the word "arouse." I kept figuring what could it be and then when I read it to you, you told me and then I remembered it when I read to my mom and dad.

MRS. A: How do you choose books?

G: I prefer to pick certain books that I like. See, what I do is read two or three pages to see if the book's too hard or too easy. Most of the time now they're too easy.

MRS. A: What's your all-time best book?

G: *Sailing with the Wind.* It makes me think about sailing and their boat almost hit the rocks. It makes me think of when our boat almost tipped over.

MRS. A: What will you do to become an even better reader?

G: Read harder books. I listen to my dad read almost every night and I watch him where he is on the pages and I think of the words he's reading and I try to figure them out myself. When we come to a different chapter, I try to read the chapter title myself.

MRS. A: Tell me about yourself as a writer.

G: I learned to write by writing little stories and I remembered more and did more and I wrote longer and better stories. I wrote about what happens in school and on weekends and some adventures. One thing I want to write about is Mother's Day—how I felt and what it was like, our Mother's Day party. And our Chinese dinner. I also like to write about how to make things and how to do things.

MRS. A: What is your best piece of writing?

G: I think it's "Sailing a Model Boat." It makes me feel like I'm sailing on that little boat and it makes me feel like that boat's real and it might hit another boat or that a propeller might cut up my boat.

MRS. A: What would you tell someone who asked you about becoming a reader and a writer?

G: I would tell them it's important to become a better reader and take books out of the library and buy your own books. If I was to tell them how to become a better writer I'd say, write stories. Don't copy these stories, write about information from books you read. If you learned something, you could put that in your story because that's your information now. Don't write a boring story. Write one that you think readers would like to read. Boring books would say: "Me and my dad went fishing. We had fun. I had fun. My dad had fun. We didn't catch any fish. We went home." If it was a good story it would be: "One day my dad and I went fishing. We didn't catch anything but we had fun trying. At 6 o'clock we went home. My mom was happy to see me again." It wouldn't just go on and on. It would have a good ending and good beginning so it would get the reader hooked and unhooked.

MRS. A: Do you have a favorite author?

G: Yes. Thomas Locker because he writes good books and I like his pictures a lot!

Finding time in a busy school day to interview children isn't easy. During the first week of school I squeeze interviews in during morning free play and at random moments throughout the day—even recess. Often, later in the year, I'm able to interview when a student teacher is in charge of the class. By late spring, the children capably continue their reading or writing while I interview classmates.

Initial interviews in September require much coaxing from me to draw out even one- or two-word answers. Some of the children are eager to sit down with me, some are slightly reluctant, but almost all of them seem baffled by my questions. Had I not experienced the richness of end-of-year interviews, I might have become pretty discouraged. I must be content to wait and to trust. I listen and respond to the child during the interview, rather than think ahead about questions I want to ask. It helps me to remember that good interviews get children talking openly about reading and writing rather than answering a string of questions. I believe that the questions I continually ask children all year about their processes—How did you do that? Tell me how you figured that out?—contributed to the development of them as reflective learners and is one reason interviews became effective tools.

The purpose of interviews is to learn from and about children: their perspective on reading and writing. In the beginning I suspect that I was searching for absolute answers about the children's learning to relieve my anxieties and help me standardize these new teaching practices. Instead, I learned from the children that they are as unique as they are alike. No absolutes. No standardization. I have noticed some patterns, however. For instance, children who have difficulty thinking of someone who is a good reader are often struggling readers while fluent readers quickly recall a model. For example, in response to the question, "Who's a good reader that you know? Amy immediately replied, "My Mom. She reads all day when I'm at school." Jack shrugged, looked around the room, and finally said, "Hmm, Amy, I think Amy's a good reader."

The children's talk in interviews helps me understand each learner a little better, understanding that improves my total response to that child. For the children, a brief, focused time to talk about their learning permits them to give language to experience. I see children pause to think, then talk about their experiences and understanding of those experiences. This same process, in condensed form, occurs during the daily writing and reading conferences. In fact, it is these conferences, where children talk about the reading and writing they are doing, that enable children to develop a reflective stance toward learning. Interviews enhance this reflective perspective and extend self-evaluation. Interviews provide opportunity to bring it all together—for both the children and me.

SELF-EVALUATION

Interviews help children reflect on their learning and articulate the process of that learning. So do questions during our workshops that ask how or why learners make particular decisions as they read or write. Usually, those decisions are below conscious awareness at first, but the questioning—asking children to think and communicate—enables children to develop an awareness of those processes. Self-awareness leads to self-evaluation and, in turn, thoughtful decision making. I knew that our continual classroom inquiries about process helped the children internalize self-evaluation, but I was surprised when Tiffany chose to write a piece about how she wrote (Figure 19–12). Her piece made me more aware of the importance of giving children the opportunity to examine their own processes.

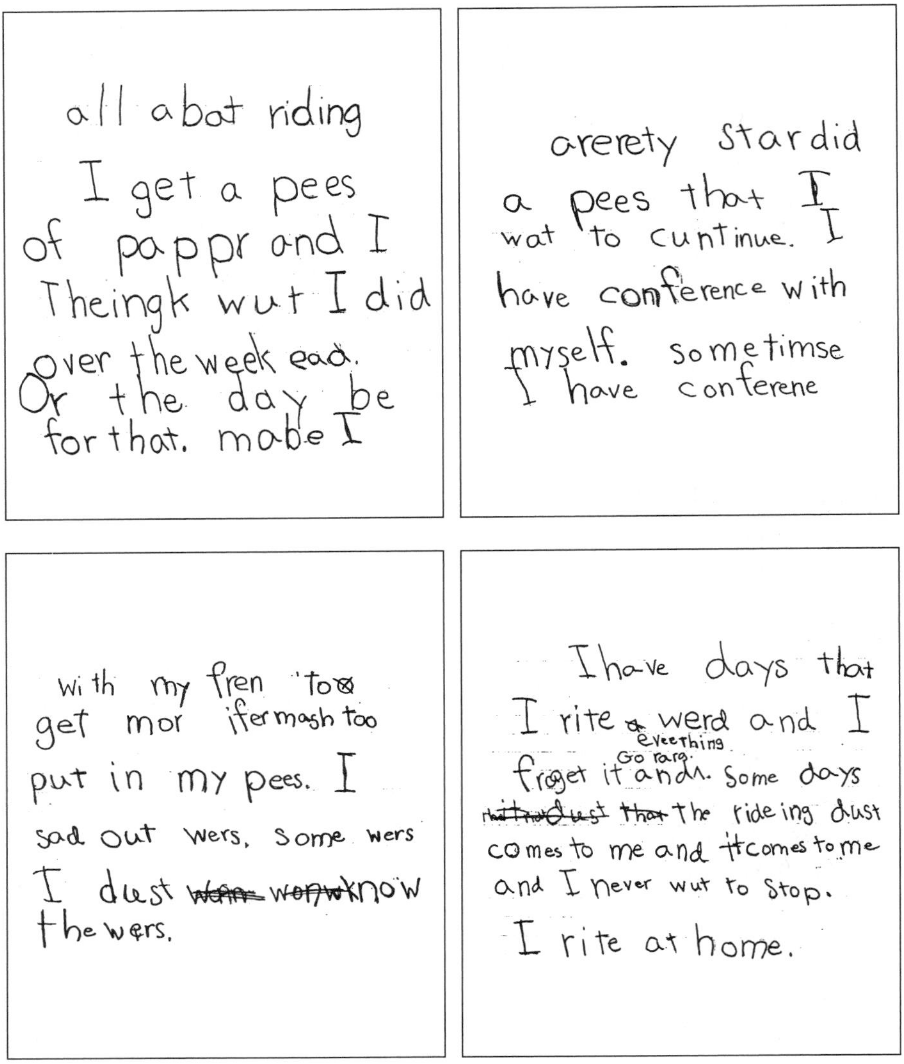

all abat riding
I get a pees of pappr and I Theingk wut I did over the week ead. Or the day be for that. mabe I

arerety stardid a pees that I wat to cuntinue. I have conference with myself. sometimse I have conferene

with my fren too get mor ifermash too put in my pees. I sad out wers, Some wers I dust know the wers.

I have days that I rite werd and I froget it and everething Go rarg. Some days The rideing dust comes to me and it comes to me and I never wut to stop.
I rite at home.

Figure 19–12

Tiffany's writing about writing

I developed a procedure to help children increase their self-awareness. Occasionally at the end of a writing or reading workshop, I ask the children, "How did writing (or reading) go for you today? I'd like you to think about that a moment and give me a number from one to three. One means it was a great day for writing. Two means an okay day. Three means this was just one of those days when writing didn't go very well. We've all had those days!" I read the class role and the children reply with a number. They know that in this classroom we all have good days and days when we struggle and that there's no penalty for "bad" days, so they report honestly. Because they write *every day*, they are able to self-evaluate and they often explain why a day was a "one," "two," or "three" day. I experienced the power of this brief self-reflection one day when I asked the children to self-evaluate after a writing workshop.

Matt gave himself a three and then added, "You want to know why it was a 'three'? Well, because I just published my new book. I did all the illustrating, and today I wasn't sure what I'd write about. I started a new piece about playing at my friend's, but it wasn't going so good and then I just started talking and I didn't get much done."

"What could you do about that?" piped up Lisa.

"Hmm, well I guess tomorrow I'll start a new piece. I'll think about it tonight," Matt replied.

Jody told the group, "Three. 'Cuz all I could do was draw pictures of micromachines."

The children nodded in empathy. "Some days are like that. You can't write the words," someone comments.

Matt and Jody were the only children who gave themselves a "three" and their self-evaluation, as usual, was congruent with my observations. For most of the children, this had been a good writing day. Then Stacy asked, "I'd like to know what it was for you, Mrs. Avery. What was it like for you talking to people about their writing today?"

Her question took me a bit by surprise. "Well, I'll tell you," I answered slowly (I needed a moment to think), "it started out as a three because I was sorta tired, but then it got to be a one because I listened to so many good stories." As I spoke, I became aware that the energy of the community had raised my enthusiasm this day. Giving myself a number required me to be precise in my evaluation, but, like Matt and Jody, I needed to explain my number.

I ask the children to do this self-evaluation only sporadically and I do not record or average these numbers to determine a final evaluation. The purpose is to encourage self-reflection. The children understand that it is okay to have a three, and I think they see that everyone works and learns at varying paces.

At the end of one school year, the district language arts committee decided that a sample of each student's writing would be placed in the language arts folder that went on to the next teacher. Teachers had three options for deciding which piece of writing should be used as a sample:

1. The teacher makes the selection.
2. The teacher and student hold a conference and mutually agree on the sample.

3. The student selects the sample and attaches a written summary explaining why the student selected this piece.

I chose the third option, delighted for the opportunity to involve the children in another self-evaluation strategy. The children plunged into the exercise with vigor. Some children immediately knew what they wanted to select while others browsed through the writing for a day or so before making a decision. All children chose pieces about special times or special interests. The pieces often represented an achievement felt by the child as a writer.

- "This piece is good because I think it has a good lead," wrote one girl. Her lead read, "My sister Erin said, 'Help me with the dishes.' I said, 'NO!' [underlined four times] She said, 'want to fight for it?' I said, 'Yes I do!'" I remembered this young author's delight in writing the conversation between Erin and herself and how much the class had enjoyed that opening to her story.
- "It is a good piece because authors put in funny things and I did that." Kelly's story, "The Lady," was about an incident of seeing a woman's slip fall down in public. The piece had evoked ripples of laughter from the class.
- "'I Was in the Hospital.' It took me so long. It was probably so long that it took me 11 days to finish it." This child had missed several weeks of school due to an emergency appendectomy and, of all the topics she wrote about over the course of the year, this one had consumed the most effort.

Many of the children explained that their pieces represented a topic that was important.

- "I like this piece because it is a neat piece. It is one of my favorite toys. It is my best piece of writing. It has a good part about putting my micromachine toy together. I didn't even know how to put the stickers on, then my dad put it together. My dad had to switch the stickers around."
- "I think 'The Accident' is my best piece of writing because it is about my dad having an accident. That makes the reader feel sad and it has good pictures."

Some children wrote about how the writing affected them.

- "'Chinese Acrobats.' I like this piece because they were so talented and it really makes me think about China today. It has a lot of information and I like the piece because it is good and well written [and] because it makes me feel stuff."

- "'When I Got My Duck' because I like the way it sounds to me and the way it feels to me. It is real perfect to me. I love it."

Most children did not choose pieces that I would have selected and it was difficult watching them pass over what I considered to be their best pieces. Yet they all chose solid, well-written pieces. Looking closely, I noticed that the children's criteria for selecting a "best" piece were grounded not only in objective criteria for a quality piece of writing but also in subjective valuing—the writing held special significance for that child. In the process of choosing a particular piece, the children revealed a bit more about themselves as learners and as individuals, and I couldn't help thinking how established standards for "good work" fail to consider the student's perspective. Don Graves (1991) writes, "The child is the most important evaluator in the entire chain of evaluation that leads from child to teacher, principal, system, state, and national exam. If the child plays no major role in the scheme, then the system fails" (175). I saw through this exercise of selecting a piece of writing that children can provide important data about their own learning. Much energy surrounded this self-reflective process. The children chatted for days about their choices and why they chose them. They listened to classmates explain their choices and nodded in understanding and appreciation. The children gained more from this activity than just selecting a piece of writing for the language arts folder.

This concept of self-evaluation and self-reflection can be expanded with the use of student-developed portfolios. I was first introduced to this form of self-evaluation as an instructor during a summer institute for teachers at the University of New Hampshire. Jane Hansen, then a professor at UNH, had worked on portfolios with teachers and students in the Manchester, New Hampshire, schools. In her research project, children and their teachers compiled portfolios by self-selecting items (not just pieces of writing) that showed who they were as literate individuals. They also wrote about the items in the portfolio and why they were included. Jane shared this method of self-evaluation at the institute and inspired me to ask the teachers in the writing group I headed to compile portfolios. "Let your portfolio show who you are as a literate person and what you can contribute to a learning community," I directed, and I compiled my own portfolio with them.

While working on my portfolio, I talked to my son Tim, who told me of his recent job search. For the first time in his engineering career, prospective employers asked for a portfolio. In addition to letters of reference from current or former employers, prospective employers wanted descriptions of projects Tim had worked on. They wanted his thoughts about what had gone well, what he'd learned, what he'd do differently. Tim's experience introduced me to new ways of evaluation in the business world, supporting the practicality of developing portfolios in school.

I asked my first graders what it was like for them to choose their best pieces of writing. They provided answers like, "Great!" "Fun!" "You really had to *think*." "It was hard to choose." I know I'll want to continue exploring the process of self-evaluation with children. Reflecting on my learning about portfolios, I've compiled the following list of reminders for myself as I help children compile portfolios.

1. *The portfolio has a focus.* Questions to consider: What is the purpose of this portfolio? What is it meant to communicate? Who is the audience?
2. *Every item in the portfolio is included for a reason that the learner can articulate.* Articulating reasons encourages reflection and thoughtful selection.
3. *A portfolio has breadth as well as depth.* For example, in my own portfolio I focused on teaching and young children, but also included photos of crewel embroidery kits I had designed and an item representing volunteer work in my community. Both items reveal skills I bring to my teaching, but they also show something of me beyond my role as teacher.
4. *Portfolios are ever-changing.* One item in my portfolio is a list of ten books that have had a strong influence on me. (I found it important to set a limit.) Some books have remained constant on that list while I change others; portfolios will change because we change.
5. *Portfolios include thoughtful choices.* I noticed while compiling my own and watching other teachers select items for portfolios that we all had an inclination to include too much. Too many items become overwhelming for the reader. It might be helpful to negotiate a maximum number of items to encourage careful choices.
6. *Portfolios are for self-reflection and communication.* Because self evaluation is the basis of the entire process, I would not grade these portfolios nor place any other value judgments on them. I realized with my own portfolio that its significance is in the insight I gained and that sharing the insights became a basis of communication with others. For anyone to impose a grade would negate the process; had I anticipated a grade as I compiled my portfolio, the portfolio would have been quite different, and I would have lost a degree of investment in the entire process.

I want to guard against standardizing portfolios for then I'd jeopardize honest self-reflection and evidence of individual diversity that are their strength. Portfolios provide a means for student self-evaluation and provide another aspect in the ongoing process of understanding learners and their learning.

CASE STUDIES

Learning to document student progress in new ways took time and stretched me professionally. One technique that helped was conducting case studies in which I followed one or two children in the classroom very closely, documenting their growth in depth. One teacher doesn't have time for intense documentation on every child in the classroom but when I looked closely at one or two individuals, I discovered that I saw the other children as well. The process of looking closely at one child taught me how to keep efficient, yet detailed records. Most important, the case study approach taught me how to look at learning with goals of understanding rather than judging and valuing rather than evaluating.

Glenda Bissex (1980), my teacher in how to do case studies, writes that "case studies can only disprove the universality of generalizations; we cannot generalize from one case too many. Conversely, we cannot presume to know an individual in terms of generalizations drawn from groups. In our schools, we usually teach to groups, though children (like the rest of us) learn as individuals in the context of groups" (39).

Collecting data for a case study provides another way of looking at student growth. Close observation of children as they work in the classroom helps me put first priority on the learner rather than on the curriculum. When I do that, I find I can accomplish a more effective job of bringing the learner and the curriculum together.

TESTS

Testing will always be a part of our classrooms. However, it's important for teachers to keep tests in perspective, especially with regard to their use with young children. Yes, tests can give us information about a child's learning, but tests also have severe limitations.

When I moved to reading and writing workshops, the school district required that I give students the tests from the adopted reading program throughout the year and a standardized test in late spring. Our district maintained a low profile on testing, recognizing its limitations especially with regard to testing young children. However, everyone (myself included) felt we need the reassurance of the children's achievement with an "objective" tool.

Over the first few years I used the periodic tests from two different reading programs. (The change to a second came when the district made a change in reading programs.) A major part of the first set of tests consisted of stories with comprehension questions. Also, each test included discrete skills out of context, such as matching words with the same vowel sounds. I had taught these skills and the children used them when they read and wrote. That is, after all, what the skills are for! But to prepare children for the test, I showed them how to use these skills on worksheets—something they hadn't done before. The children consistently produced solid results on these tests. I believe this was because they were aggressive readers, with a range of strategies and able to tackle unknown words efficiently as they read for meaning.

The second test was written in the controlled vocabulary of that particular reading program and the children complained. "I don't understand this." "It doesn't make sense." "There aren't enough words." The preprimer test alone was nearly twenty-five pages long. In addition to the significant amount of time we devoted to test taking, I found that the results gave no real information about student progress. On the second test, even I had to look up the answer for a three-sentence story that asked for the "main idea." With administrators' approval, I eventually abandoned the reading program tests.

Testing with the California Achievement Test initially raised my anxiety because this type of test was new for us. I knew the children were good readers, but I had no idea how they would deal with a standardized test. I led them through a few worksheets so they would understand how to handle multiple-choice questions, fill in answer bubbles, etc. I knew they needed specific instruction on the format of tests and in "test thinking." My initial fears subsided when CAT scores in the group ranged from the 76th to 99th percentiles. Early on, I *needed* test scores to confirm that the children's progress matched that of previous classes. In time, I came to see that testing was important, but that it was not the central indicator of the children's or my success.

However, these testing experiences over several years' time truly opened my eyes to the reality of tests, their limitations, and how to approach test taking with my students. I quickly saw that tests provide only a small portion of the information about children and their learning. More significant information came from the documentation I gleaned in the classroom as children read and wrote and talked. This specific information helped me make specific teaching decisions. It provided solid information to share with parents in conferences. The tests gave me only a fleeting glimpse of one moment in time. Test results are subject to influence by many factors (the day before a test we even suggest kids get a good night's sleep and eat a good breakfast), yet we've often regarded the results as the ultimate authority on learning and teaching. I learned not to let tests take more authority than they ought and to be thorough in demonstrating children's learning through other means.

As limited as test results are to the total picture, the results can be helpful only if teachers and students receive more than scores. I remember asking a child to tell me about her answer on a comprehension question. This six-year-old explained with perfect logic why she selected her answer (a wrong answer). She had outthought the test! Tests have helped me see patterns in children's learning such as the child who answered all comprehension questions correctly but had difficulty with the phonics sections. Tests can be one more source of information in understanding learners. However, I've heard more than one teacher lament that she and the children only see scores and have no idea what errors are made. For tests to be helpful, we need to know exactly what errors were made. When I share test results with parents, I show them the child's actual test or a sample. When parents see the questions the test asks and their child's errors, I've found that the amount of significance they attach to the test diminishes. Feedback on the test is important to me, to the parents, and to test takers themselves—the children.

I learned that all tests are not created equal. Some tests are better than others: more fair, better written, providing better information. It's important for teachers and districts to look at tests and determine if they are appropriate and if they test what we teach. Tests need to match the adopted curriculum of local school districts or else they are in danger of mandating that curriculum. And curriculum in our democracy is a matter that belongs to local decision making.

Learning test-taking skills and understanding "test thinking" is something that I needed to teach. It's much like lawyers who go to law school, but then take a test-prep course before they take the bar exam. I don't think that this means cramming for the test or dropping all instruction to "teach for the test." There's a big difference in "teaching for the test" and learning how to take a test. The best ways I know to prepare students for reading and writing tests are to read and write every day and receive instruction during these activities. To get ready for tests, we then provide students with strategies for using their reading and writing skills in test-taking situations. I have deep concern about the quality of instruction and learning when teachers feel compelled to "teach for the test" because test results have become the final authority on teaching and learning. I believe that one reason my children did well on tests was because of all the reading and writing they did *every day* and the commitment we all made to *learning*, and no one viewed the tests as the absolute bottom line.

To get a handle on test-taking skills, a group of teachers and I used an old test to take the state writing test ourselves. Even those in the group who were good writers felt the pressure of time to organize their thoughts, present ideas clearly, and tend to mechanics. From this experience we compiled test-taking ideas to share with students:

- Read everything before beginning and reread after writing and adjust.
- Take time to think and plan before you begin.
- Write, using what you've learned about good writing.
- Maintain a focus—find a central idea and keep it simple.
- Relax.

We also felt it was important to have students do practice tests with time frames, to practice using writing prompts, and to discuss the qualities that scorers will be looking for when the test is read—including neatness. A teacher who scored state writing tests said, "They say handwriting doesn't count but it does. You can't help but be influenced if something is hard to decipher." The strategies we arrived at were important but just as important was our experience of taking a test ourselves and the conversation afterward. Professional conversations around test taking are essential as we address our issues with tests. I recommend Regie Routman's *Conversations* (2000) for discussion of ways to conduct such professional interactions.

Among the professional organizations that have spoken out about testing is the National Council of Teachers of English. In 1989, English and language arts teachers passed a resolution on the testing of young children, calling for an immediate end to "the use of norm-referenced, multiple-choice, standardized tests for children in preschool and the primary grades." Part of the background statement of this resolution stated that "scores on standardized tests reflect neither the diversity of children's preschool experiences nor the range of their development. Nevertheless, test results may be used to assign young children to curricular tracks. The use of scores by school boards, administrators, and teacher committees, . . . prompts teachers to replace sound educational practices with undesirable efforts to prepare children in preschool and the primary grades."

In 1998, an NCTE Resolution On Testing and Equitable Treatment stated that "many testing programs do not account for differently-abled learners or for learners for whom English is not their first language." The resolution went on to condemn "the wholesale usurpation of the English language arts curriculum by excessive attention to test preparation . . . [and] the use of assessment instruments in English with students who are not sufficiently proficient in English." The resolution supported "ongoing teacher and student critique of test making and test taking . . . the use of alternative forms of assessment in order to ensure equitable treatment of all students [and] . . . teacher-developed, contextualized, and reasonable instruction regarding test-taking practices for students."[1]

The issues surrounding testing and evaluation will continue. As this is written, testing issues have moved into the political arena and the views of educators are minimized. We cannot back away. As professionals our responsibility is to advocate for what is best for children and their learning. This includes learning about testing and evaluation and participating in the conversations on these issues that so affect the children.

---

1. Full text of NCTE Resolutions and other position statements are available at <http://www.NCTE.org>.

CHAPTER 20

Reporting Student Growth

When I taught high school English, I spent a weekend every nine weeks averaging student grades with an adding machine. The machine tape curled across the floor with the all-important number for each student: the final average for the marking period. When I saw Roger's grade I remember thinking, "This can't be right! Roger's not failing English!" Yet, the numbers said he was. When it came time to transfer grades to report cards, I put a passing mark on Roger's report card—a grade that wasn't a gift. As Roger's teacher, I had knowledge about his progress that wasn't reflected by the numbers in my grade book. I knew those numbers provided only part of the information about his achievement. I understood even then that learning cannot be measured by numbers in the same way that we measure physical stature. Still, I was nervous about Roger's report card because I knew that, if questioned, I couldn't prove that passing grade. I had no documentation of any student's school progress other than the numbers and checks in the grade book. Numbers were the basis of grading. Teacher knowledge didn't count.

As a first-grade teacher I didn't keep a grade book full of numbers. However, I did assign worksheets and workbook exercises, administer tests, and, every nine weeks, determine grades based on student success in the programs of instruction. Through the years I watched those grades take on increasing significance. Children counted the number of A's and played one-upmanship with peers. Parents rewarded top grades with money or toys. I noticed how grades encouraged children to view themselves in comparison to others. Some students convinced themselves they were better than others, while others perceived themselves as failures.

I believe grading results in unrealistic perceptions of self, threatens self-esteem, and pressure on children for perfection. Children believe that the goal of school is receiving good grades, an attitude that hinders learning. "Does this count?" they ask when teachers give assignments. One evening on the television show *Jeopardy* the host asked a contestant, a teacher of eighth-grade gifted students, "What do eighth-grade gifted students think about most?" "Grades," came the *immediate* reply. In my own classroom a little boy announced, "You have to get all ones (1 equals A) in first grade so that you can go to Princeton College."

Just as we can use a variety of ways to document student growth, there are options for reporting student progress. Although a few schools have found innovative ways to break away from the traditional report-card grading, most of us still are tied to some type of report card. I believe that the report card is just one mechanism for communicating about students. When we use a variety of reporting methods, no one method carries all the weight or becomes disproportionately important to teachers, students, schools, and parents.

Report Cards

When it came time to complete report cards that first year, I asked our reading coordinator, Rose Stetler, how she might suggest I mark our district's report card. Assigning numbers to children's progress wasn't congruent with the dynamic learning going on in my classroom. Rose and I agreed to eliminate marking the reading level, which was demonstrated by drawing an arrow up a scale to indicate the book in the reading program in which the child was currently working. Since we weren't using the program, the scale was not applicable. As to the rest of the report card, she advised me, "Mark it just as you always have." Rose's reply helped me examine how I did mark report cards. I had never really thought it through. The district report card for primary grades at that time listed thirty items to be marked on a 1 to 5 scale, 1 representing outstanding and 5, poor. When I thought about it, I had to acknowledge that my grades were very subjective. I also realized that I had procedures and a philosophy of sorts for marking report cards that I need not change. This is what it looks like.

I take the entire batch of report cards home on a day when I feel really good about the class, not the evening of an approaching snowstorm or a day when everything's been crazy. I plan for a chunk of time when I can record all the grades for all the children in one sitting. If I can't do it in one sitting I break up the report card into sections and do one section for all the children at one time. To determine the grade, I read the skill I'm to grade ("Comprehends what is Read," as an example) and think about the child in relationship to that phrase. I determine a number from my knowledge and understanding of the child. The number must convey my honest and realistic perceptions of the child's progress and also must encourage the child. Some grades are clear-cut while for others I need to look back at notes in my reading and writing folders. I try to avoid comparing children although I know that my knowledge of all of the children is part of my frame of reference when I view each individual child.

When I've finished marking the cards, I put them away for a few days. Just before the report cards go to parents I read through them and attempt to look at each report from the perspective of the individual child and his or her parents. Will the parents and child understand what I intend to communicate? Will they see strengths and areas to develop? Most important, will this report card encourage the child as a learner? Just as I believe an important goal of writing or reading conferences is to encourage the writer or reader to want to write or read again, so I believe one goal of a report card is to encourage the child to want to come back to school the next day and the next, and want to continue learning in this community. While reviewing the grades, I write the narrative paragraph that goes at the bottom of the report card.

I know I have made and always will make some mistakes. A mother called me after her daughter took home her report card. "We've got a problem," she said, "there are so many tears here over the math grade." I couldn't even recall what math grade I had given, so I went back to look at the records. I had made a mistake and a higher grade was in order. I could only apologize. However, I believe that most of the grades I give are more fair, more supportive of learning, and less prone to error than those I assigned when I was trying to be clinically objective and averaging numbers. Can we really be objective with report cards? I think not. Our principal devoted a faculty meeting to report cards one year, and as we tenuously ventured our philosophies about giving grades, we discovered that each of us had our individual ideas. The great myth was that we all did it the same and that we all placed the same value on the A's, B's, C's, etc., or that it was even possible to do so. I came away from that meeting realizing how important it was to explain to parents our individual philosophies about report cards.

Children do not always understand the language of the report card. I spent time with first graders talking about the several reading grades on their report cards—"word attack," "understands what is read," etc. When I taught fourth grade, I photocopied a report card and asked the children to grade themselves. I discovered that they too had no idea what many of the words and phrases on the report card meant. I had to go through each item and define it in terms of classroom work. Interestingly, when the group marked their report cards, they came pretty close to matching the grades I had written the night before.

Report cards are changing. Many schools have moved away from letter or numerical grades in favor of checklists, especially for young children. Some districts are substituting narratives for graded report cards. To cope with the time requirement of writing narratives for an entire class, they're looking at building a structure for the narrative (topics to address, for example) and cutting back on the number of times a year these kinds of report cards are given. In one district the teachers prepared a checklist report card and, at an administrator's suggestion, added a brief narrative. When it came time to use the report card, the teachers asked if they could skip the checklist. They needed the checklist as a guide for the narrative, but the checklist, like letter and numerical grades, needed much explaining. They chose to eliminate the checklist and write just a narrative.

PARENTS

At Back-to-School Night in September, I talk to parents about the structure of our classroom and the approach to writing and reading that their children are experiencing. I explain invented spelling and discuss the concept of meaning making as the basis of reading. All of the children's writings since the first day of school are on their desks for parents to examine. On a bulletin board is the writing each child did on the first day of school. This display allows parents to see their child's work in relation to others in the class. I explain to parents why all the writing will stay in school and invite them to stop by to see this writing any time. I also explain why children will not be bringing home the papers (worksheets) that they are accustomed to seeing as schoolwork. Our "work" is actual reading and writing, I explain, not just exercises on the little parts of reading and writing. I introduce my lending library for parents, which includes books and articles on topics such as invented spelling and the teaching of writing and reading as a meaning-making process. I give parents a one-page handout with suggestions that encourage parents to continue the natural practices they've begun at home. I also distribute two brochures prepared by the National Council of Teachers of English: "Helping Your Child Become a Better Writer" and "Elementary School Practices." Both pamphlets are written in jargon-free language and are helpful to parents.

I try to keep in touch with parents through the letters that accompany the reading children take home, with phone calls, and by maintaining an open-door policy. Often parents stop in the room for a brief moment before or after school. I've learned that not all parents are comfortable coming to school. One father finally came for the fall conference after breaking several appointments. This large, burly man and I sat on small chairs at a low table while I showed him his son's reading and writing. He fidgeted while he listened but said little; he never looked at me. "School's important," he finally commented, "I want my boy to do good in school." He took the report card and left, obviously anxious to be on his way. I could only wonder at the experiences that made him so very uncomfortable in a classroom. However, there was no doubt in my mind of his strong commitment to his son and to education.

Dialogue Letters with Parents

One means of establishing communication with parents is dialogue letters, described in Chapter 13. Not every parent wrote letters when children took books home to read to them and none wrote every time, but over the course of the year we exchanged several hundred letters. I viewed the letter exchange as an invitation for parent involvement and a way to maintain communication. The letters from parents gave me information about children's reading development. Also, through their letters, I saw parents evolve in their understanding of reading. Here's the first and last letter from a thick pack from one parent.

> September 19
>
> We thoroughly enjoy listening to N. read. She has a love for reading that we share and it heartens us to see our daughter share this joy. N's determination to solve words she is unfamiliar with brings pride to us. Her pride in her own reading gives us many rewards. Her attention to detail (sight words) could use work but for the most part we couldn't be more pleased with her progress.
>
> C. and M. G.

May 23

Dear Carol,

Again, it was a great pleasure to hear N. read these two moving stories. The story *When I Was Young in the Mountains* was especially endearing. N. felt very strongly that she would not like a dead snake around her neck or in her swimming area. We discussed okra and diarrhea. Also, outhouses came up. She knew their use. The baptism in the river was compared to the baptisms she is familiar with. She felt happy that the young girl was so confident.

The second story was a step-by-step discussion of the give/take, gain/loss, love and thanks way of life. She felt I looked like the Mom in *A New Coat for Anna*. The combing and dying of the wool were new ideas to her. She noticed that two of the celebrants at the Christmas party had their payments on (garnet necklace and gold watch). N. appreciated the Mother's efforts and the pride of the new coat felt by the protagonist. Anna's gratefulness was appropriate according to N. These books were good.

Warmly, C. L. G.

Dialogue letters also provide a means of addressing parent concerns and questions. One child's mother wrote in September: "We enjoyed listening to him read this book but when we asked him the same words outside of the book, he did not know them. I think he has just memorized this book." In my reply, I explained that memory plays a part in learning to read and that I'd rather a child read by memorizing words in a meaningful context rather than learn by memorizing a list of words. These letters provide a vehicle for me to address issues before they escalate. In addition, I learn much that helps me understand and appreciate the children and the individual cultures of their homes.

I make every effort to answer parent letters on the day I receive them. I write my replies quickly—spontaneously—and send them home that afternoon. I photocopy my note, staple the copy to the parent letter, and file both in the child's reading folder. I want a record in case anyone questions what I've written (though no one ever has). If a parent writes a short letter, I keep my reply short. If the parent's letter is a page long, I write a page. At the end of the first year of writing these, one mother wrote, "I've really appreciated these letters this year. I especially like that your letters, like mine, aren't perfect. You're willing to scratch out and continue writing. I know that you write these during lunch and when the children are in music just as I write mine at the breakfast table or before I shut off the light at night. If you had taken the time to write polished, typewritten letters I probably would never have written back to you." I realized that communication with parents needs to be down-to-earth and unpretentious.

I started using dialogue letters with parents several years after initiating writing and reading workshops. The letters opened up a whole new area of communication with parents and their views of school and learning, and I found myself wishing I had initiated letter writing sooner. However, I know that I wasn't ready. In the beginning I had my hands full just learning to manage the new structures in my classroom and the intricate process of listening and responding to children. Like the children, I needed time to learn too.

Parent Conferences and Responses

Parent conferences are scheduled at our school in November and teachers give the first report cards to parents at those conferences. The report card used to be the center of the conference, and we discussed every grade. Now I usually begin by asking the parents to tell me about their child: how they see the child's response to school, their opinion of their child's interests and learning style, and any questions they have about the child and school. Although parents are far more of an authority on their child than I, our observations about the children's personalities almost always match. "That's the way my boy's been since he was a baby," is a comment I've heard many times when I share my observations. As we chat, I gain a fuller picture of the child and try to present a realistic picture of the child in the classroom by showing accomplishments and by raising any concerns I have. I avoid comparing the child to other children. When I give the parent the report card at the first parent conference, I say, "Take this with a grain of salt. I want you to know that if I did these grades next week, it's likely they'd all be different." I explain my philosophy about report cards, how I mark them, and what I hope this particular report card will communicate to the child. Then, I share the child's writing and my observations of his or her reading. Because of the letters and the reading the child has taken home, and because many parents have seen their children writing on their own at home (a frequent occurrence when children work in daily writing workshops in school), there are usually no real surprises in the report cards. As a result parent conferences are rarely stressful for me or the parents. Many teachers today include children in parent conferences. I know of one fifth-grade teacher who spends time before conferences helping students reflect on their learning. When the parents come to school, the child leads the conference. I'd like to incorporate this concept into future parent conferences in first grade.

I did try student-led conferences with my fourth graders. These take some planning and require work ahead of time but they are well worth the effort.

As a group we determined what would be important to share with parents. The class agreed on the following:

- Writing folders—showing favorite pieces and talking about achievements and goals as writers
- A list of books they'd read; read aloud a section from their current reading
- Math folders and explanations of what they've learned
- A current science project and the writing that accompanied it
- Behaviors in school (this one was the most difficult for many but the class was adamant that it had to be included)
- Goals: one or two goals they wanted to work on the next marking period

We planned and rehearsed these conferences in the classroom. The results surprised us all. The children came through with flying colors, the parents loved it, and the format seemed to make the entire evaluation process more important to the children.

Getting parent feedback on the school year is important. Just before school ended one year I sent home a form titled "Parent Evaluation of a Child's Progress." On the first page were ten questions related to school progress; parents were to circle a choice of three answers: almost always, some of the time, not yet. I asked the children to complete the same questions in school. As I compiled the results, I saw a remarkable congruence between the child's, the parent's, and my perceptions of learning. On a second page of the parent evaluation, I invited parents to write comments on the strengths and weaknesses of this approach to reading and writing and to express any concerns or suggestions. Over three-fourths of the parents wrote responses. The following are a sampling of their comments.

"I must admit at first I thought this approach to reading was questionable, but since November I can see nothing but strengths. I see a great enthusiasm for reading and books. [My child] chooses her books often (at the library) by the author. She can tell me why she likes the book—picking a specific passage that she liked rather than saying generally it was a good book. She has the confidence to pick up any book and begin to read it or try rather than only reading from the 'reading book' or books she has brought home from school. This was a great year for [my child]. She has a lot of confidence in herself and isn't as hesitant to try new things. She is learning to record her ideas, put them on paper, [be] in touch with her thoughts."

"[My child's] success is a result of *his* effort and the effort of *his* teacher, a very human being. [My child] is very much aware of how the class work *evolved* as a result of the students' efforts. [My child] has an excellent self-image in relation to his reading and writing. Last year in 1st grade [my child] found the prepackaged reading program a standard that was very hard to keep up with."

"Reading big words is so important for [my child] because using just 1st grade vocabulary is so limiting to comprehension. There is a flow to [my child's] reading and writing that is not emphasized in the basal program. This flow may be just as important as the specific skills that seem so inhibitory when taught each skill in isolation."

"My daughter . . . loves to read and does so constantly. She began chapter books by October. Her fascination with illustrations reflects her own interest in Art and her new awareness of the genre itself (illustrations). She discusses certain authors with such aplomb that I must remind myself she is only six. Her desire and determination to tackle and unlock vocabulary in the stories is strong. She has experienced many foreign notions and ideas from the grand assortment of authors as well. The moral aspects of some stories reflect strongly on your choices and have aided in reaffirming or discovering how she correctly perceives her own morals."

"Trying to be extremely objective I can see no weaknesses in learning to read with this approach. Among the strengths I would include diversity of material and instilling a love for reading at an earlier age due to a 'non drill like' learning environment. I wouldn't change a thing."

Three concerns surfaced in the parent responses:

> "The weakness I see is in his spelling. I work with him at home on this and he seems to be getting it, although slowly."
>
> "Will this approach be carried through into second grade? If not, will it be a difficult transition for the child to switch to another learning approach?"
>
> "As parents we had no benchmark to compare [our child's] progress. We did not know what was considered normal progress, therefore at times we did not know what [our child's] weaknesses were and how we could or should help her. Was [our child] getting the reading help she needed? Also we had no means to tell how [our child] was progressing [in relation] to her peers . . . in the other first-grade classes." (This comment came from the parents of a strong student—one I had no concerns about—showing me that I must tell parents when I have no concerns.)

I've heard these concerns before but hearing them again—if only from a few people—communicates that these issues continue to be important for parents. Usually these concerns come from parents who are sending their first child to school, reminding me that education of the community at large is an ongoing task. I hope parents and I can grow in our understanding of each other for the sake of our common interest in the child. For my part, I've found it helpful to attempt to negate the traditional role of teacher as authority by communicating directly and clearly. That's not always easy. Several years ago an articulate mother with more than one college degree wrote a note: "I finally actually saw what you folks call 'word attack.' When he came to a word he didn't know I really saw how he 'attacked' that word to get it." I was appalled at my own insensitivity in falling into educational jargon that blocked communication. How many other terms, acronyms, phrases like "word attack" did I casually rattle off in conversations with parents? I've made a concerted effort to eliminate educational jargon in all parent/teacher interactions.

The Teacher's Role in Evaluating Progress

A couple of years ago, after wrestling with the terms *evaluation* and *assessment* and *report cards* and *accountability*, I brainstormed a list of ideas, writing them down just as they came to me, in order to help me think through what it was I believed about this incongruous mess! Across the top of my paper I wrote: My Attitudes About Evaluation. Then I crossed out "Evaluation" and wrote "Assessment," then I crossed out this word and finally just put a big question mark and continued. What I wanted to do was put on paper some guidelines to myself as I approached all these ticklish issues. Here's my list (unedited) from that time.

1. Look at development and growth—avoid a deficiency model.
2. Recognize that learning/growth patterns are uneven, recursive, and individual.
3. Examine the growth of the individual—avoid comparison with others.
4. Set goals—with students—but be flexible. Remember: growth may go in unpredictable directions; avoid measuring against predetermined standards.
5. Recognize the limitations of tests.
6. Include student self-evaluation.
7. Recognize that *all* assessment procedures and tools have an element of subjectivity and bias—including my own methods.

As a classroom teacher, I must give feedback (for want of a better term). Writing out what I believed helped me clarify my underlying philosophy of evaluation. This exercise helped me refine the ways I document children's learning and influenced my communications with both parents and children. I felt some relief from the stress of attempting to match the richness of learning in the classroom to the traditional but inadequate practices of examining student achievement. I found it personally important to articulate not only *what* I did, but *why*.

The terms *evaluation* and *assessment* often carry heavy connotations of judgment, leading to a focus on weakness rather than strength, deficiency rather than growth, failure rather than success. My role as a teacher and learner with children is not to stand in judgment of their growth but to provide honest and helpful responses. I can do that through several modes of communicating with both parent and child. I look to the following four broad areas to provide information about children's learning:

1. documents of the children's work over time, such as writing samples, and reading records
2. student self-evaluation that includes a strong component of self-reflection
3. observations and insights of parents
4. teacher observations of specific behaviors and reflection on the meaning of those behaviors

The underlying purposes of gathering and sharing any information about children's growth in the classroom is to *understand* each child's process as a learner and to *communicate* with both parent and child.

REFLECTIONS

During the first years with reading and writing workshops, evaluation issues, specifically report cards, troubled me. Traditional modes of evaluation just weren't congruent with the responsive teaching of the workshops. A friend told me a story from her personal experience that expresses the difficulty. My friend needed to move to a new office space for her growing business. Though she searched and searched, she could find nothing suitable until she realized that she was searching for a space similar to what she currently had. Once she realized that the new space could be different, that it did not have to replicate the past, she realized that lots of possibilities existed. "I was limited by my own vision of the way it had to be," she said. In the same way, I recognize that my vision of report cards and evaluation—in fact of many changes in my classroom—was restricted in the beginning by established practices. "Kidwatching" rescued me! When I looked and listened in my classroom I envisioned new ways of teaching and learning. The children were my teachers. Evaluation is not an activity that occurs from a test, after producing a product, or at the end of a marking period. Instead it is an ongoing and integral aspect of the teaching/learning process that guides me—the teacher—in making daily decisions about instruction. When I understood that evaluation/assessment is woven into everything that occurs in the classroom, the incongruence fell away and I viewed evaluation as an ally, helping me understand the children.

Conclusion

The last morning arrives. The room sparkles through streams of sunlight, and refreshing morning air flows through open windows. The children run from the school buses, shouting, singing, some still squabbling. Many bring me gifts: garden flowers, a gift certificate for books, a wooden apple. Monica slips me a copy of *Charlotte's Web* and Ellen presents a book she's authored and published at home about first grade. The children cluster around to help me tear away the wrapping paper; it's like Christmas morning, except they are both Santa and child. And they're just as boisterous as they were on the first day. Cory's gone, and so are Carrie and Eric. Do I miss them? Maybe—individually. But in the group? No. The group dynamics improved as each one left. Our community is shaped by all of us, and even one angry, frustrated child can make life difficult for everyone. It's not been an easy year and I have a jumble of feelings now that it's over.

A visitor asked the children one day what was good about this class and they told her about reading and writing—all the good stuff. When she asked what wasn't so good they told her they were noisy. True. They've been noisy all right—sometimes downright argumentative and nasty with each other. Somehow we've weathered it all.

There have been good moments and success stories: the class applauding Cory's reading, Michael's and Natalie's becoming readers after such slow beginnings. But there are also trouble spots. Mark seems to have stood still in the last two months, no longer taking risks. Bradley is still smart-alecky. And Darren? He tells me he hates writing. I think he hates reading too. This way of teaching can't solve all classroom problems. But it's better than it was—better than it was for George who had shared the birth of butterflies years earlier.

We start the last day by reading the final chapter of *Charlotte's Web.* When I close the book the children and I exchange smiles; no words are necessary. In writing workshop the children continue to begin new pieces, to revise others. That we won't be back tomorrow doesn't seem to enter their heads. I marvel. We clean out our desks and pack up before gathering on the rug for our last literature time. We are reading and talking when the loudspeaker comes on. The principal says his good-byes and a student helper begins calling buses earlier than expected. The children hurry to gather their things. I put down the book unfinished. Our time together has run out. In a few minutes they are out the door and gone. The community that took so long to come together vanishes. Or does it? I never know what vestiges are left.

I remember comments by my son Nathan, who has been visiting my classroom since he was fifteen. "I don't get it Mom. I mean, what's the big deal? What you do is so simple." What a fine compliment. The methodology is simple—much simpler than it was in George's class. Yet what's occurred here is far from simplistic; it's intricately complex. We've not been learning about reading and writing, math, and all the rest, but *been* readers and writers and mathematicians and scientists. We're not getting ready for life; we're living life now. I think on this and I realize that it's not the lessons I teach or the achievement children make or the content we cover. It's the surprises—the unexpected, indefinable moments that distinguish our time together. I saw the first glimmers of such moments in the children's writing. When I first began writing workshop, I knew so little about teaching writing: I could do nothing but listen and respond and struggle and rejoice with writers. Slowly those first glimmers grew brighter. The children taught me how to teach and how to learn.

When I took that journey years ago to learn about teaching writing through reading, I thought I'd come home with the door wide open—everything clear and revealed. I came home with the door open a crack. Now, after all these years, I realize that we never really "get there." Teaching is a matter of being a learner and learning is a lifetime experience. I know that my beliefs about learning and teaching continue to be shaped by all of my experiences and the relationships with others that are part of those experiences—my home and family, the work of researchers and educators, my daily observations and reflections in the classroom. Learning to teach is an ongoing process.

Still, every teacher faces pressures to "nail it down," "do it right," and produce better and better test scores. I suspect there will always be outside interests attempting to determine what is right or best. In many ways, children and schools have become pawns in political battles and big business interests (testing and reading programs are definitely big business!). No one group, committee, or individual has the final definite "answer" about how best to teach. Anyone who's taught knows that effective teaching is done through decisions made on a day-by-day and minute-by-minute basis and always with children's needs leading the way.

On my wall beside me as I write is a framed illustration signed by Gary and Ruth Paulsen from their book *Worksong*. In the illustration, a teacher or librarian is reading to children and in the corner are the words, "Whatever you are, whatever you do, let it be for the children." I once thought teaching without a reading program was "foolish and irresponsible." Such was the educational climate of that time. In truth, teaching without a program turned out to be the most responsible teaching I could muster because it ensured that my efforts, though not perfect, were for the children. Times change; new issues confront. But the Paulsens' words ring true: "Whatever you are, whatever you do, let it be for the children."

Afterword: Laura's Legacy

May 8, 1987

We celebrate Mother's Day in our first-grade classroom this Friday afternoon. The children perform a play for their mothers entitled "The Big Race," the story of the tortoise and the hare. Laura is the "turtle" who wins the race.

A few minutes later Laura reads aloud the book she has authored about her mother. The group laughs as she reads about learning to count with her cousins when she was three years old. Laura writes: "I was learning six. Then my Mom came in and asked what we were doing. I said, 'I'm learning sex!'" Laura's mother is delighted. The reading continues with a hilarious account of a family squabble between Mom and Dad over a broken plate. Laura concludes the anecdote, "So then I just went in and watched TV." Laura looks at me and smiles as she pauses, waiting for her audience to quiet before she goes on. I wink at her; I know she is thinking, "Wait till they hear the next part. It's the funniest of all." She reads about a llama spitting in Mom's eye on a visit to the zoo. Laura's way with words has brought delight to everyone. I remember a week earlier when Laura and I sat to type her draft and she said, "This is the best part. I put it last so that everyone will feel happy at the end."

May 9, 1987

Saturday night, around 11:45 P.M., a light bulb ignites fabric in a closet outside Laura's bedroom. Laura wakes. She cannot get through the flames, and by the time firefighters reach her it is too late. Laura dies. No one else is injured.

May 11, 1987

The children and I gather on our Sharing Rug in the classroom on Monday morning. I have no plans. We start to talk. There are endless interruptions until Michael says, "Mrs. Avery, can we shut the door so people stop bothering us?" So Michael shuts the door. "Are you going to read us the newspapers?" they ask. "Is that what you'd like?" "Yes," comes the unanimous response. The children huddle close; a dozen knees nuzzle against me. I read aloud the four-paragraph story on the front page of the *Sunday News* that accompanies a picture of our Laura sprawled on the lawn of her home with firefighters working over her. I read the longer story in Monday morning's paper that carries Laura's school picture. We cry. We talk and cry some more. And then we read Laura's books—writings which Laura determined were her best throughout the year and which were "published" to become part of our classroom library. These books are stories of Laura and her family, stories with titles such as "My Dad Had a Birthday" and "When My Grandmother Came to My House." Laura's voice comes through loud and clear with its sense of humor and enthusiasm. We laugh and enjoy her words. "Laura was a good writer," they say. "She always makes us laugh when we read her stories." Then Dustin says, "You know, it feels like Laura is right here with us, right now. We just can't see her."

A short time later we begin our writing workshop. Every child chooses to write about Laura this day. Some write about the fire, some write memories of Laura as a friend. I write with them. After forty-five minutes it is time to go to art, and there are cries of disappointment at having to stop. We will come back to the writing. There will be plenty of time. The last five weeks of school will be filled with memories of Laura as we work through our loss together. The children will decide to leave her desk in its place in the room because "it's not in our way, and anyway, this is still Laura's room even if she's not really here anymore." Laura's mother and little brother will come in to see us. On the last day they will bring us garden roses that Laura would have brought. Laura will always be a part of us, and none of us will ever be the same.

In the days immediately following Laura's death and in the weeks since then certain thoughts have been rattling around in my head: I'm so glad that I teach the way I do. I'm so glad I really knew Laura. I know that I can never again teach in a way that is not focused on children. I can never again put a textbook or a "program" between me and the children. I'm glad I knew Laura so well. I'm glad all of us knew her so well. I'm glad the classroom context allowed her to read real books, to write about real events and experiences in her life, to share herself with us and to become part of us and we of her. I'm grateful for a classroom community that nurtured us all throughout the year and especially when Laura was gone. Laura left a legacy. Part of that legacy is the six little published books and the five-inch-thick stack of paper that is her writing from our daily writing workshops. When we read her words, we hear again her voice and her laughter.

APPENDIX A

Conference Checklist

Name	*Mon*	*Tues*	*Wed*	*Thur*	*Fri*	*Mon*	*Tues*	*Wed*	*Thur*	*Fri*	*Comments*

Mini-lessons:

Code:
- ✔ Good conference
- – Weak conference
- ~ Not sure
- ☺ Shared this day
- ★ Publishing conference
- P Published this day

APPENDIX B

Publishing Conference Record

Name ______________________________

Date ______________ Title __________________________________

Peer Participants:
Conference Notes:

Skills/Strategies/Techniques Addressed:

Content Related:

Language/Mechanics:

Date ______________ Title __________________________________

Peer Participants:
Conference Notes:

Skills/Strategies/Techniques Addressed:

Content Related:

Language/Mechanics:

APPENDIX C

Directions for Bookbinding

Materials Needed:

Cardboard or cereal boxes
Rubber cement
Decoupage roller
Lightweight oaktag
Sewing machine with a large needle, or a stapler

1. Cut two pieces of cardboard the size you wish the finished book to be.* Score each piece by holding a ruler approximately ⅜″ from the edge that will be the spine and drawing a sharp knife along the edge of the ruler.

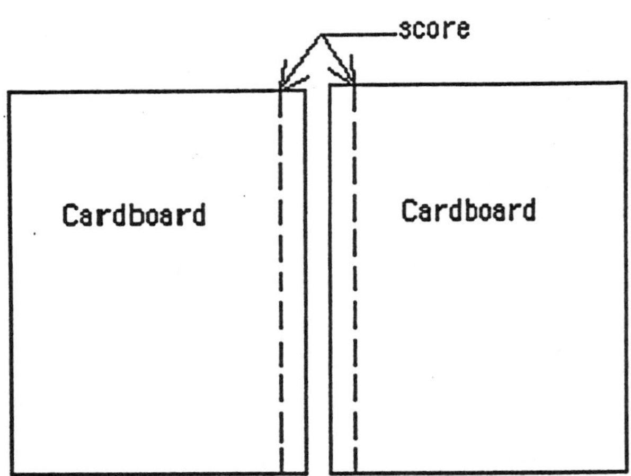

2. Cut a piece of wallpaper large enough to leave a 1″ border around all four sides when the two pieces of cardboard are placed side by side with approximately ¼″ space between them.

*To make large blank books cut cardboard in 9″ by 12″ pieces. Follow steps 1–4 leaving a slightly wider space between the cardboard sections (step 2). Cut lightweight oaktag approximately 16″ by 11″, or large enough to cover inside of cover when opened. Glue oaktag to inside of cover. Count out 15–20 sheets of 17½″ by 11″ paper (available at office supply stores). Fold paper in half and staple into the spine of the book. (Use a long armed stapler or a saddle-stitch stapler if available.)

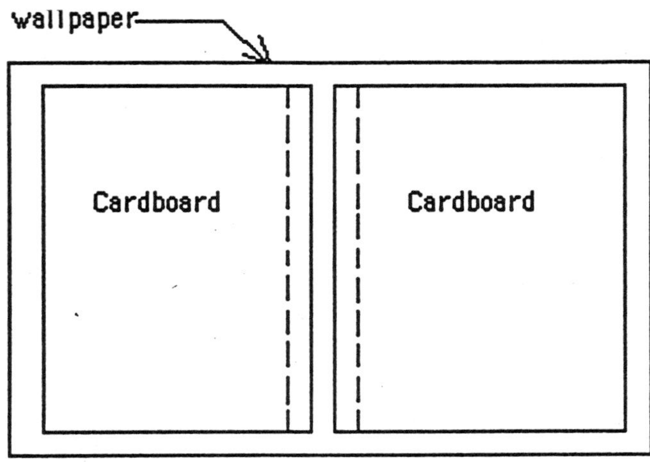

3. Fold the wallpaper in half to form a crease along what will become the spine of the book. Open the wallpaper and, with score lines facing up and placed in the center, glue the two pieces of cardboard to the wallpaper, leaving the ¼″ space between them. Use rubber cement for gluing.
4. Fold the 1″ edges of the wallpaper over the cardboard and glue in place. Do the corners first, then the sides. Going over the glued surfaced with a decoupage roller helps sharpen edges and spread the glue under the wallpaper, thus eliminating air pockets.

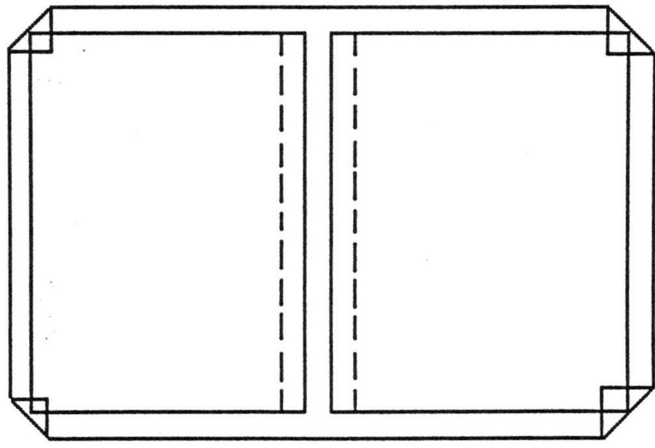

5. Cut the paper for the book pages to fit inside the book. Cut a piece of lightweight oaktag twice the width of the book pages and fold it around the pages after typing has been done. Staple or sew through the oaktag and book pages to make an oaktag-covered booklet. (If

you use staples, place them close together.) Allow the child to illustrate the book before completing the next step.

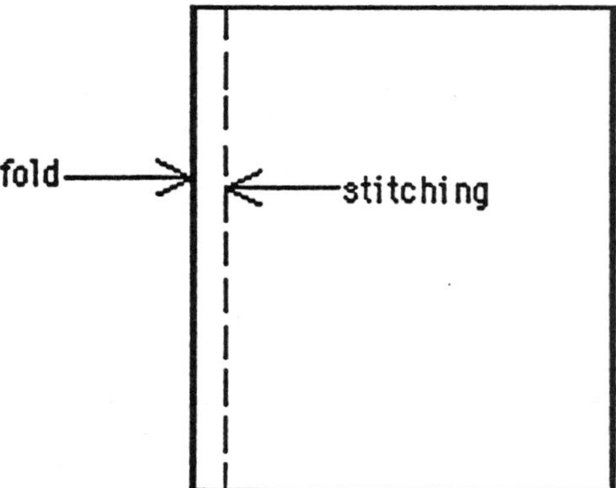

6. Fold the cardboard bookcover on score lines to make cover bend at the spine. Open cover. Glue oaktag-covered booklet to cover with rubber cement.

APPENDIX D

Reading Conference Notes (Whole Class)

	Date: ____________

APPENDIX E

Reading Record (Individual)

Name ______________________

Date ____________ Title ______________________

Observations:

Reader Comments:

Strategies/Skills Addressed:

Date ____________ Title ______________________

Observations:

Reader Comments:

Strategies/Skills Addressed:

Date ____________ Title ______________________

Observations:

Reader Comments:

Strategies/Skills Addressed:

APPENDIX F

Strategies and Skills of Written Language

The following list represents the particular language skills that I addressed with my first-grade classes. The degree of proficiency with these skills was, of course, a factor of the individual development of each child. However, all children were introduced to these skills through classroom instruction as they read real books and wrote real texts.

Alphabetic Knowledge, Phonemic Awareness, Concepts of Print

- Ability to recognize twenty-six letters, upper- and lowercase, when not in relationship to entire alphabet
- Ability to recall and write twenty-six letters, upper- and lowercase
- Ability to discern that individual words are made up of units of sound (phonemic awareness)
- Ability to attend to the sounds of language (phonological awareness)
- Awareness of left-to-right, top-to-bottom arrangement of print
- Awareness of spacing between words

Phonetic Elements

Ability to identify and use the letter-sound relationship of the following when reading and writing:

- Consonant letters sounds: beginning, medial, final
- Consonant clusters (blends) at word beginnings: *bl, br, cl, cr, dr, fl, fr, gl, gr, pl, pr, sl, sm, sn, sp, spr, st, sw, tr, tw.*
- Digraphs: *ch, sh, th, wh, qu*
- Vowel sounds: long and short
- "R" controlled vowels: *ar, or, er, ir, ur*
- Vowel digraphs:

  ow as in *how*, *ow* as in *low*

  oe as in *toe*

  ea as in *bread*, *ea* as in *bead*

oo as in *look, oo* as in *stood*

oy as in *boy*

oi as in *coin*

ou as in *loud*

ee as in *feed*

igh as in *light*

ai as in *main*

ay as in *say*

- Silent initial consonants: *kn, wr*
- *C* as in *circus, c* as in *cat*
- *G* as in *game, g* as in *giraffe*

Structural Analysis

- Word endings:

  ed as in *wanted, d* as in *moved,* /t/ sound as in *liked,*

  ing

  er
- Doubling final consonants before endings: *running*
- Dropping final *e* before endings: *making*
- Changing *y* to *i* before endings: *tried*
- Compound words
- Common word families and rhyming e.g.: *at*
- Contractions
- Homonyms
- Synonyms
- Antonyms
- Word referents (pronouns)
- Multi-meaning words
- Plurals: es, s, irregular
- Possessive: 's

Punctuation

- Period: at end of sentence and after abbreviations
- Question mark
- Exclamation mark

- Quotation marks
- Comma: in greeting and salutation of letters and in a sequence within a sentence
- Colon

Genres

- Fiction and nonfiction (understanding of difference)
- Wordless picture books
- Poetry
- Songs in picture-book format
- Riddles
- Folktales and fairy tales
- Fantasy
- Biography and autobiography
- Jokes and riddles
- "How-to" articles

Study Skills

- Picture dictionaries
- Children's dictionaries
- Children's encyclopedias
- Labels
- Diagrams
- Maps
- Table of contents
- Index
- Internet use
- Note taking
- Library research
- Planning and organizing

Comprehension Attitudes and Skills

- Understands written language; conveys meaning
- Follows written directions
- Can verify a statement

- Understands factual and literal knowledge from a passage
- Draws conclusions from given facts
- Draws inferences from a passage: cause-and-effect relationship; implied meaning
- Recalls what has been read aloud
- Recalls what has been read independently
- Places events in correct sequence
- Recalls where to find answers to specific details from a passage
- Predicts outcomes and revises predictions
- Identifies central themes or main ideas in passages
- Discerns development of fictional characters
- Recognizes plot development and has a sense of story
- Distinguishes real from fanciful content
- Views reading and writing as significant activities
- Sees reading and writing as positive experiences

Oral and Silent Reading Skills

- Develops a sight vocabulary in an ongoing manner
- Ability to use a range of strategies in an integrated manner to figure out unknown words

  Letter/sound clues

  Context clues

  Syntax clues

  Visual clues

  Meaning clues
- Uses phrasing that conveys meaning (not word-by-word) when reading aloud
- Uses voice intonation to convey meaning when reading aloud
- Uses punctuation when reading aloud
- Reads fluently while maintaining a focus on meaning

Writing Skills

- Views writing as a meaning-making process
- Conveys meaning through drawings, letters, words, sentences, paragraphs

- Rereads writing to determine if it makes sense and/or conveys intended meaning
- Revises writing to convey meaning

  Adds letter, words, or chunks of information

  Moves words or chunks of information

  Deletes letters, words, or chunks of information
- Organizes information into a meaningful whole
- Sequences information in a meaningful manner
- Develops appropriate beginnings and endings
- Develops focused pieces of writing
- Includes essential and supporting information
- Strives to use effective words: specific nouns, strong verbs, only essential adjectives and adverbs
- Explores various genres
- Develops a spelling vocabulary of frequently used words
- Uses phonetic and visual strategies to spell unknown words
- Uses punctuation and capitalization conscientiously
- Accomplishes some final editing of finished pieces

APPENDIX G

Children's Books

Child-Tested Favorites

The danger in any list of books is that it's impossible to include every favorite or address every topic, interest, or perspective one would like to include. My lists of books are forever changing. This list includes some old titles and some new titles but all the selections have been favorites with *children.*

Alborough, Jez. *Duck in a Truck*

Aliki. *Spoken Memories*

Alter, Anna. *Estelle and Lucy*

Asbjornsen, Peter C., and Jorgen Moe. *The Three Billy Goats Gruff*

Bateman, Robert. *Safari*

Bordon, Louise. *The Day Eddie Met the Author*

Brooks, Bruce. *NBA by the Numbers*

Brown, Marc. *Arthur* series

Brown, Ruth. *Toad*

Burton, Virginia Lee. *The Little House*

Camp, Lindsay. *The Biggest Bed in the World*

Carle, Eric. *Papa, Please get the moon for me*

Carle, Eric. *The Grouchy Ladybug*

Carle, Eric. *The Very Hungry Caterpillar*

Cooney, Barbara. *Miss Rumphius*

Creech, Sharon. *Fishing in the Air*

Cronin, Doreen. *Click, Clack, Moo, Cows That Type*

Croswell, Ken. *See the Stars*

Crotty, K. M. *Dinosongs: Poems to Celebrate a T. Rex Named Sue*

Cuyler, Margery. *100th Day Worries*

Dahl, Roald. *James and the Giant Peach*

dePaola, Tomie. *26 Fairmont Avenue*

dePaola, Tomie. *The Art Lesson*

Eglielski, Richard. *Buz*

Ehlert, Lois. *Red Leaf, Yellow Leaf*

Ehlert, Lois. *Snowballs*

Ehlert, Lois. *Waiting for Wings*

Erickson, Russell. *A Toad for Tuesday*

Falconer, Ian. *Olivia*

Feiffer, Jules. *Bark George*

Fleishman, Paul. *Westlandia*

Fox, Mem. *Koala Lu*

Fox, Mem. *Tough Boris*

French, Vivian. *Growing Frogs*

Gag, Wanda. *Millions of Cats*

Galdone, Paul. *The Little Red Hen*

George, Jean Craighead. *Dear Rebecca, Winter Is Here*

Gibbons, Gail. *My Soccer Book*

Gollub, Matthew. *Cool Melons—Turn to Frogs*

Henkes, Kevin. *Chrysanthemum*

Henkes, Kevin. *Lilly's Purple Plastic Purse*

Henkes, Kevin. *Wemberly Worried*

Jackson, Alison. *I Know an Old Lady Who Swallowed a Pie*

Jenkins, Martin. *The Emperor's Egg*

Jones, Evan and Mal. *Good Night, Sleep Tight: A Poem for Every Night of the Year*

Kellogg, Steven. *The Missing Red Mitten*

Kraus, Robert. *Little Louie the Baby Bloomer*

Krupp, E. C. *The Rainbow and You*

Lester, Julius. *Julius Lester's Sumptuously Silly, Fantastically Funny Fables*

Lester, Julius. *Sam and the Tigers*

Lichentenheld, Tom. *Everything I Know About Pirates*

Linch, Tanya. *My Duck*

Lionni, Leo. *Fish Is Fish*

Lionni, Leo. *Swimmy*

Lobel, Arnold. *Frog and Toad* series

Marcus, Leonard. *Author Talk*

Marshall, James. *Little Red Riding Hood*

Martin Jr., Bill. *Beasty Story*
Martin Jr., Bill. *Brown Bear, Brown Bear, What Do You See?*
McCloskey, Robert. *Blueberries for Sal*
McCloskey, Robert. *Make Way for Ducklings*
McPhail, David. *Edward and the Pirates*
Milne, A. A. *Winnie the Pooh*
Munsch, Robert. *Aaron's Hair*
Munsch, Robert. *Get Out of Bed!*
Munsch, Robert. *Thomas' Snowsuit*
Myers, Christopher. *Wings*
Pinkney, Jerry. *Sam and the Tigers*
Pinkney, Sandra. *Shades of Black*
Polacco, Patricia. *Mr. Lincoln's Way*
Polacco, Patricia. *The Bee Tree*
Ray, Mary Lyn. *Mud*
Rogers, Sally. *Earthsong*
Root, Phyllis. *One Windy Wednesday*
Rosenberg, Liz. *Monster Mama*
Rylant, Cynthia. *Poppleton* series
Rylant, Cynthia. *Scarecrow*
Rylant, Cynthia. *The Relatives Came*
Rylant, Cynthia. *When I Was Young in the Mountains*
Sciescka, Jon, and Lane Smith. *Squids Will Be Squids*
Sendak, Maurice. *Where the Wild Things Are*
Shannon, David. *No! David*
Silverstein, Shel. *Where the Sidewalk Ends*
Simon, Seymour. *Animals Nobody Loves*
Steptoe, John. *Mufaro's Beautiful Daughters: An African Tale*
Stevens, Janet, and Susan Stevens Crummel. *Cook-a-Doodle-Doo!*
Stevenson, Robert Louis. *My Shadow*
Taback, Simms. *Joseph Had a Little Overcoat*
Van Allsburg, Chris. *Two Bad Ants*
Viorst, Judith. *Alexander and the Terrible, Horrible, No Good, Very Bad Day*
Viorst, Judith. *Earrings*
West, Colin. *I Don't Care Said the Bear*

White, E. B. *Charlotte's Web*
Williams, Sue. *Let's Go Visiting*
Wood, Audrey. *The Napping House*
Yolen, Jane. *Color Me a Rhyme*
Yolen, Jane. *How Do Dinosaurs Say Good Night?*
Yolen, Jane. *Letting Swift River Go*
Zelinsky, Paul. *Rumpelstiltskin*

Works Cited

Anderson, R. C., P. T. Wilson, and L. G. Fielding. 1988. "Growth in Reading and How Children Spend Their Time Outside of School." *Reading Research Quarterly* 23(3): 285–303.

Arbuthnot, May Hill. 1964. *Children and Books,* 3d ed. Glenview, IL: Scott, Foresman.

Au, Kathryn H. 2000. "Literacy Instruction for Young Children of Diverse Backgrounds." In *Beginning Reading and Writing,* edited by Dorothy S. Strickland and Lesley Mandel Morrow. New York: Teachers College Press and Newark, DE: The International Reading Association.

Avery, Carol. 1987. "First Grade Thinkers Become Literate." *Language Arts,* 64: 611–18.

———. 1989. "From the First: Teaching to Diversity." In *Stories to Grow On,* edited by Julie Jensen. Portsmouth, NH: Heinemann.

Babbitt, Natalie. 1990. "Protecting Children's Literature." *The Horn Book,* 66: 696–703.

Bissex, Glenda. 1980. *GNYS AT WRK: A Child Learns to Write and Read.* Cambridge, MA: Harvard University Press.

Braunger, Jane, and Jan Patricia Lewis. 1997. *Building a Knowledge Base in Reading.* Portland, OR: Northwest Regional Educational Laboratory's Curriculum and Instruction Services.

Burke, Carolyn. 1984. Presentation at convention of the National Council of Teachers of English. Detroit, Michigan.

Calkins, Lucy McCormick. 1986. *The Art of Teaching Writing.* Portsmouth, NH: Heinemann.

———. 2001. *The Art of Teaching Reading.* New York: Addison-Wesley.

Clay, Marie M. 1998. *By Different Paths to Common Outcomes.* York, ME: Stenhouse.

Coles, Robert. 1989. *The Call of Stories.* Boston: Houghton Mifflin.

Condon, Mark W. F., and Michael McGuffee. 2001. *Real ePublishing, REALLY PUBLISHING!* Portsmouth, NH: Heinemann.

Cunningham, Patricia. 1995. *Phonics They Use—Words for Reading and Writing.* 2d ed. New York: Harper Collins College.

Dahl, Karin L., Patricia L. Scharer, Lora L. Lawson, and Patricia R. Grogan. 2001. *Rethinking Phonics: Making the Best Teaching Decisions.* Portsmouth, NH: Heinemann.

Donaldson, Margaret. 1978. *Children's Minds.* New York: W. W. Norton.

Eide, Priscilla. 2001. "Coping with Change: Educational Reform in Literacy Practice." In *Primary Voices*, 9(3): 15–20.

Elbow, Peter. 1973. *Writing Without Teachers.* New York: Oxford University Press.

Emig, Janet. 1983. *The Web of Meaning: Essays on Writing, Teaching, Learning, and Thinking.* Portsmouth, NH: Boynton/Cook.

Fletcher, Ralph, and JoAnn Portalupi. 1998. *Craft Lessons: Teaching Writing K–8.* Portland, ME: Stenhouse.

———. 2001. *Writing Workshop: The Essential Guide.* Portsmouth, NH: Heinemann.

Fountas, Irene C., and Gay Su Pinnell. 1996. *Guided Reading: Good First Teaching for All Children.* Portsmouth, NH: Heinemann.

Fox, Mem. 1990. "There's a Coffin in My Office." *Language Arts*, 67: 468–72.

Fulwiler, Toby. 1985. "Writing and Learning, Grade Three." *Language Arts*, 62: 55–59.

Garan, Elaine M. 2001. *Resisting Reading Mandates: How to Triumph with the Truth.* Portsmouth, NH: Heinemann.

Giacobbe, Mary Ellen. 1982. "Teaching Writing in the Elementary School." Presentations at Martha's Vineyard, Massachusetts.

———. 1991. "A Letter to Parents About Invented Spelling." In *Workshop 3: The Politics of Process*, edited by Nancie Atwell. Portsmouth, NH: Heinemann.

Giacobbe, Mary Ellen, and Donald Graves. 1983–85. Workshops for the Pennsylvania Department of Education, Harrisburg, Pennsylvania.

Giacobbe, Mary Ellen, and Nancie Atwell. 1985. "Reading, Writing, Thinking and Learning." Presentations at Martha's Vineyard, Massachusetts.

———. 1986–88. Workshops for the Pennsylvania Department of Education, Harrisburg, Pennsylvania.

Goodman, Kenneth S. 1965. "A Linguistic Study of Cues and Miscues in Reading," *Elementary English.*

Goodman, Yetta M. 1985. "Kidwatching: Observing Children in the Classroom." In *Observing the Language Learner*, edited by Angela Jaggar and M. Trika Smith-Burke. Newark, DE: The International Reading Association; Urbana, IL: National Council of Teachers of English.

Graves, Donald H. 1978–81. Articles initiated for the Committee on Research, National Council of Teachers of English at the Writing Process Laboratory, University of New Hampshire, Durham, New Hampshire, published in the "Research Update" section of *Language Arts.*

———. 1982. *A Case Study Observing the Development of Primary Children's Composing, Spelling, and Motor Behaviors During the Writing Process. NIE-G-78-0174.* Washington, DC: National Institute of Education.

———. 1983. *Writing: Teachers and Children at Work.* Portsmouth, NH: Heinemann.

———. 1984. "The Enemy Is Orthodoxy." In *A Researcher Learns to Write.* Portsmouth, NH: Heinemann.

———. 1991. *Build a Literate Classroom.* Portsmouth, NH: Heinemann.

———. 2001. *The Energy to Teach.* Portsmouth, NH: Heinemann.

Harste, Jerome C., Virginia A. Woodward, and Carolyn L. Burke. 1984. *Language Stories and Literacy Lessons.* Portsmouth, NH: Heinemann.

Holdaway, Don. 1979. *The Foundations of Literacy.* New York: Scholastic.

Hopkins, Lee Bennett. 1991. "'Leave Me Alone,' Cries the Poem." *Perspectives,* 7(3): xii–xv.

Huck, Charlotte. 1986. "To Know the Place for the First Time." *The Bulletin* (spring): 69–71.

Jensen, Julie, ed. 1989. *Stories to Grow On.* Portsmouth, NH: Heinemann.

Johnson, Nancy J. 2001. "Coping with Constraint: Reflecting on Responsibilities," in *Primary Voices,* 9(3): 37–43.

King, Stephen. 2000. *On Writing.* New York: Scribner.

Kitagawa, Mary M. 2000. *Enter Teaching! The Essential Guide for Teachers New to Grades 3–6.* Portsmouth, NH: Heinemann.

Lloyd-Jones, Richard, and Andrea A. Lunsford. 1989. *The English Coalition Conference: Democracy through Language.* Urbana, IL: National Council of Teachers of English.

Martin, Ann M. 1989. "Letters From Readers." In *Workshop I: Writing and Literature,* edited by Nancie Atwell. Portsmouth, NH: Heinemann.

Mills, Heidi, Timothy O'Keefe, and Diane Stephens. 1991. *Looking Closely: Exploring the World of Phonics in One Whole Language Classroom.* Urbana, IL: National Council of Teachers of English.

Mooney, Margaret. 1990. *Reading To, With, and By Children.* New York: Richard C. Owens.

Moustafa, Margaret. 1998. "Whole-to-Parts Phonics Instruction." In *Practicing What We Know,* edited by Constance Weaver. Urbana, IL: National Council of Teachers of English.

———. 2000. *Beyond Traditional Phonics: Research Discoveries and Reading Instruction.* Portsmouth, NH: Heinemann.

Murray, Donald M. 1982. *Learning by Teaching: Selected Articles on Writing and Teaching.* Portsmouth, NH: Boynton/Cook.

———. 1985. *A Writer Teaches Writing,* 2d ed. Boston: Houghton Mifflin.

———. 1991. *The Craft of Revision.* Fort Worth, TX: Holt, Rinehart and Winston.

National Council of Teachers of English. 1989. *A Handbook on Public Communication.* Urbana, IL: NCTE.

Newkirk, Thomas. 1989. *More Than Stores: The Range of Children's Writing.* Portsmouth, NH: Heinemann.

Newkirk, Thomas, with Patricia McLure. 1992. *Listening In: Children Talk About Books (and other things).* Portsmouth, NH: Heinemann.

Opitz, Michael F., and Michael P. Ford. 2001. *Reaching Readers: Flexible and Innovative Strategies for Guided Reading.* Portsmouth, NH: Heinemann.

Parkes, Brenda. 2000. *Read It Again: Revisiting Shared Reading.* Portland, ME: Stenhouse.

Paterson, Katherine. 1990. "Heart in Hiding." In *Worlds of Childhood: The Art and Craft of Writing for Children,* edited by William Zinsser. Boston: Houghton Mifflin.

Portalupi, JoAnn, and Ralph Fletcher. 2001. *Nonfiction Craft Lessons: Teaching Information Writing, K–8.* Portland, ME: Stenhouse.

Report of the National Reading Panel: Teaching Children to Read: An Evidence-Based Assessment of the Scientific Research Literature on Reading and Its Implications for Reading Instruction. Reports of the Subgroups. 2000. Washington, DC: National Institute of Child Health and Human Development.

Rogers, Carl R. 1969. *Freedom to Learn.* Columbus, OH: Merrill.

Rosenblatt, Louise. [1938] 1976. *Literature as Exploration.* New York: Noble and Noble.

———. 1978. *The Reader the Text and the Poem.* Carbondale, IL: Southern Illinois University Press.

———. 1980. "What Facts Does This Poem Teach You?" *Language Arts* (April): 386–94.

———. 1991. "Literature—S. O. S.!" *Language Arts* (68): 444–48.

Routman, Regie. 2000. *Conversations: Strategies for Teaching, Learning, and Evaluating.* Portsmouth, NH: Heinemann.

Sendak, Maurice. 1990. "Visitors from My Boyhood." In *Worlds of Childhood: The Art and Craft of Writing for Children,* edited by William Zinsser. Boston: Houghton Mifflin.

Short, Kathy G., and Caroline Burke. 1991. *Creating Curriculum: Teachers and Students as a Community of Learners.* Portsmouth, NH: Heinemann.

Smith, Frank. 1982. *Writing and the Writer.* New York: Holt, Rinehart and Winston.

———. 1988. *Understanding Reading,* 4th ed. Hillsdale, NJ: Lawrence Erlbaum.

Snow, Catherine E., M. Susan Burns, and Peg Griffin, eds. 1998. *Preventing Reading Difficulties in Young Children.* National Research Council. Washington, DC: National Academy Press.

Stafford, William. 1986. You *Must Revise Your Life.* Ann Arbor, MI: University of Michigan Press.

Strickland, Dorothy S. 1998. *Teaching Phonics Today: A Primer for Educators.* Newark, DE: The International Reading Association.

Teale, William H. 1984. "Reading to Young Children: Its Significance for Literacy Development." In *Awakening to Literacy,* edited by Hillel Goelman, Antoinette A. Oberg, and Frank Smith. Portsmouth, NH: Heinemann.

Teale, William H., and Junko Yokota. 2000. "Beginning Reading and Writing: Perspectives on Instruction." In *Beginning Reading and Writing,* edited by Dorothy S. Strickland and Lesley Mandel Morrow. New York: Teachers College Press and Newark, DE: The International Reading Association.

Trelease, Jim. 1982. *The Read-Aloud Handbook.* New York: Penguin.

Tunnell, Michael O., and James S. Jacobs. 1989. "Using 'Real' Books: Research Findings on Literature-Based Reading Instruction." *Reading Teacher* 42(7): 470–77.

Veatch, Jeannette. 1964. *How to Teach Reading with Children's Books.* New York: Teacher's College Bureau.

———. 1966. *Reading in the Elementary School.* New York: Ronald Press.

Vygotsky, Lev S. 1978. *Mind in Society: The Development of Higher Psychological Processes.* Cambridge, MA: Harvard University Press.

Weaver, Constance. 1988. *Reading Process and Practice from Socio-linguistics to Whole Language.* Portsmouth, NH: Heinemann.

Wells, Gordon. 1986. *The Meaning Makers: Children Learning Language and Using Language to Learn.* Portsmouth, NH: Heinemann.

Wilde, Sandra. 1997. *What's a Schwa Sound Anyway? A Holistic Guide to Phonetics, Phonics, and Spelling.* Portsmouth, NH: Heinemann.

———. 2000. *Miscue Analysis Made Easy: Building on Student Strengths.* Portsmouth, NH: Heinemann.

Zinsser, William. 1990. *On Writing Well,* 4th ed. New York: Harper & Row.

Children's Books Cited

Adams, Pam, illus. 1975. *This Old Man.* New York: Grosset & Dunlap.

Aliki. 1979. *The Two of Them.* New York: Greenwillow.

Asbjornsen, Peter C., and Jorgen Moe. 1957. *The Three Billy Goats Gruff.* Illustrated by Marcia Brown. New York: Harcourt.

Atwater, Richard, and Florence Atwater. 1938. *Mr. Popper's Penguins.* New York: Little, Brown.

Bang, Molly. 1980. *The Grey Lady and the Strawberry Snatcher.* New York: Four Winds.

———. 1991. *Yellow Ball.* New York: Morrow.

Barton, Byron. 1989. *Bones, Bones, Dinosaur Bones.* New York: HarperCollins.

———. 1981. *Building a House.* New York: Greenwillow Books.

Berger, Barbara. 1984. *Grandfather Twilight.* New York: Philomel.

Brooks, Bruce. 1997. *NBA by the Numbers.* New York: Scholastic.

Brown, Marc. 1976. *Arthur's Nose.* New York: Atlantic/Little, Brown.

———. 1986. *Arthur's Teacher Trouble.* Boston: Atlantic Monthly Press.

———. 1988. *Arthur's Valentine.* Boston: Little, Brown.

Brown, Marc, and Leurene Krasny. 1986. *Dinosaur's Divorce: A Guide for Changing Families.* New York: Little, Brown.

Brown, Ruth. 1987. *Our Puppy's Vacation.* New York: Dutton.

Browne, Anthony. 1986. *The Piggybook.* New York: Knopf.

Bruce, Lisa. 1999. *Fran's Flower.* London: Bloomsbury.

Bunting, Eve. 1987. *Ghost's Hour, Spook's Hour.* New York: Clarion.

Burton, Virginia Lee. 1942. *The Little House.* New York: Houghton Mifflin.

Carle, Eric. 1969. *The Very Hungry Caterpillar.* New York: Philomel.

———. 1977. *The Grouchy Ladybug.* New York: Philomel.

———. 1986. *Papa, please get the moon for me.* New York: Philomel.

Carrick, Carol. 1976. *The Accident.* New York: Clarion.

———. 1977. *The Foundling.* New York: Clarion.

———. 1983. *Patrick's Dinosaur.* New York: Clarion.

Cleary, Beverly. 1965. *The Mouse and the Motorcycle.* New York: Morrow.

Cooney, Barbara. 1982. *Miss Rumphius.* New York: Viking.

Cowley, Joy. 1980. *Mrs. Wishy Washy.* Aukland, New Zealand: Shortland.
Dahl, Roald. 1961. *James and the Giant Peach.* New York: Knopf.
Delaney, A. 1988. *The Gunnywolf.* Retold and illustrated. New York: Harper & Row.
dePaola, Tomie. 1973. *Nana Upstairs and Nana Downstairs.* New York: Viking.
———. 1975. *Strega Nona.* New York: Prentice Hall.
———. 1978. *Pancakes for Breakfast.* New York: Harcourt Brace Jovanovich.
———. 1981. *One Foot, Now the Other.* New York: Putnam.
———. 1988. *Tomie dePaola's Book of Poems.* New York: G. P. Putnam's.
———. 1989. *The Art Lesson.* New York: Putnam.
Eggar, Bettina. 1986. *Marianne's Grandmother.* New York: Dutton.
Ehlert, Lois. 1988. *Planting a Rainbow.* New York: Harcourt Brace Jovanovich.
Emberley, Barbara. 1967. *Drummer Hoff.* New York: Prentice Hall.
Ford, Meila. *Little Elephant*. 1984. New York: Greenwillow.
Fox, Mem. 1988. *Koala Lu.* New York: Harcourt Brace Jovanovich.
Freeman, Don. 1968. *Corduroy.* New York: Viking.
Frost, Robert. 1978. *Stopping by a Woods on a Snowy Evening.* Illustrated by Susan Jeffers. New York: Dutton.
Galdone, Paul. 1968. *Henny Penny.* New York: Seabury.
———. 1973. *The Little Red Hen.* New York: Seabury.
———. 1975. *The Gingerbread Boy.* New York: Seabury.
Guiberson, Brenda. 1991. *Cactus Hotel.* New York: Henry Holt.
Haley, Gail. 1986. *Jack and the Bean Tree.* New York: Crown.
Harste, Jerome C., and Janet L. Goss. 1981. *It Didn't Frighten Me.* School Book Fairs.
Hest, Amy. 1995. *In the Rain with Baby Duck.* Cambridge, MA: Candlewick.
Hutchins, Pat. 1972. *Good Night, Owl!* New York: Macmillan.
Isadora, Rachel. 1979. *Ben's Trumpet.* New York: Greenwillow.
Jeffers, Susan. 1974. *All the Pretty Horses.* New York: Macmillan.
Knight, Eric. 1940. *Lassie Come Home.* Philadelphia: John C. Winston.
Kraus, Robert. 1971. *Leo the Late Bloomer.* New York: Thomas Crowell.
———. 1985. *Where Are You Going, Little Mouse?* New York: Lothrop, Lee & Shepard.
Krauss, Ruth. 1949. *The Happy Day.* New York: Scholastic.
Langstaff, John. 1974. *Oh, A-Hunting We Will Go.* New York: McElderry.
Lauber, Patricia. 1986. *Volcano.* New York: Bradbury.
———. 1989. *The News About Dinosaurs.* New York: Bradbury.
Lobel, Arnold. 1970. *Frog and Toad Are Friends.* New York: Harper & Row.
———. 1975. *Owl at Home.* New York: Harper & Row.
Locker, Thomas. 1987. *The Boy Who Held Back the Sea.* New York: Dial.
MacLachlan, Patricia. 1983. *Seven Kisses in a Row.* New York: Harper & Row.
———. 1985. *Sarah, Plain and Tall.* New York: Harper & Row.
Marshall, James. 1987. *Little Red Riding Hood.* New York: Dial.

———. 1988. *Goldilocks.* New York: Dial.
Martin, Bill, Jr. 1983. *Brown Bear, Brown Bear, What Do You See?* New York: Holt, Rinehart and Winston.
———. 1991. *Polar Bear, Polar Bear, What Do You Hear?* New York: Henry Holt.
McCloskey, Robert. 1941. *Make Way for Ducklings.* New York: Viking.
———. 1948. *Blueberries for Sal.* New York: Viking.
McDermott, Gerald. 1992. *Zomo the Rabbit.* San Diego: Harcourt Brace Jovanovich.
Minarik, Elsie. 1968. *A Kiss for Little Bear.* New York: Harper & Row.
Munsch, Robert. 1980. *The Paper Bag Princess.* Toronto: Annick.
———. 1985. *Mortimer.* Toronto: Annick.
———. 1986. *Love You Forever.* Scarborough, Ontario: Firefly.
Paulsen, Gary. 1997. *Worksong.* Illustrated by Ruth Wright Paulsen. New York: Harcourt Brace & Co.
Schwartz, Alvin. 1984. *In a Dark, Dark Room and Other Scary Stories.* New York: Harper & Row.
Scott, Foresman & Company. 1976. *The Bus Ride.* Glenview, IL: Scott Foresman.
———. 1976. *Catch That Frog.* Glenview, IL: Scott Foresman.
———. 1976. *Ten Little Bears.* Glenview, IL: Scott Foresman.
Sendak, Maurice. 1963. *Where the Wild Things Are.* New York: Harper & Row.
———. 1967. *Higglety Pigglety Pop!* New York: Harper & Row.
Steptoe, John. 1987. *Mufaro's Beautiful Daughters: An African Tale.* New York: Lothrop, Lee & Shepard.
Turner, Ann. 1985. *Dakota Dugout.* New York: Macmillan.
———. 1987. *Nettie's Trip South.* New York: Macmillan.
Twain, Mark. 1936. *Tom Sawyer.* New York: Heritage Press.
Van Allsburg, Chris. 1988. *Two Bad Ants.* Boston: Houghton Mifflin.
Ward, Cynthia. 1988. *Cookie's Week.* New York: G. P. Putnam's.
White, E. B. 1952. *Charlotte's Web.* New York: Harper & Row.
Wood, Audrey. 1984. *The Napping House.* New York: Harcourt Brace Jovanovich.
Wright-Frierson, Virginia. 1996. *A Desert Scrapbook.* New York: Simon & Schuster.
———. 1998. *An Island Scrapbook.* New York: Simon & Schuster.
Yolen, Jane. 1987. *Owl Moon.* New York: Philomel.
———. 2000. *How Do Dinosaurs Say Good Night?* New York: The Sky Blue Press.
Zelinsky, Paul O. 1986. *Rumpelstiltskin.* New York: Dutton.
Zemach-Berson, Kaethe. 1988. *The Funny Dream.* New York: Greenwillow.
Ziefert, Harriet. 1986. *A New Coat for Anna.* New York: Knopf.

Index

Academic environment
  curriculum, 58, 413–414
  grouping of children, 59–60
  lesson plans, 61–62
  record keeping, 61, 417–448
  reporting student growth, 449–460
  scheduling, 58–59
  social climate, 62
The Accident, 226, 263, 334
Aesthetic reading, 240, 247
Aliki, 232, 265, 266
All the Pretty Horses, 328
Alphabetic knowledge, skills list of, 473
American Sign Language, 370
An Island Scrapbook, 413
Anderson, R. C., 270
Arbuthnot, May Hill, 229
The Art Lesson, 263, 412
Art supplies, 53–54
The Art of Teaching Reading, 431
Arthur's Nose, 287
Arthur's Teacher Trouble, 323
Arthur's Valentine, 294
Asbjornsen, Peter, 13
Astronomy, writing in, 400–401
Atwell, Nancie, 158, 292, 435
Au, Kathryn, 393
Authors
  inspirations of, 263–264
  perspective of, 165–180
  studying about, 262–265
Awakening to Literacy, 216

Babbitt, Natalie, 266
Bags, Cans, Pots and Pans, 300
Bang, Molly, 231, 352, 354
Barton, Byron, 333
Ben's Trumpet, 281
Berger, Barbara, 234
Beyond the Hill, 333
Bissex, Glenda, 8, 9, 123, 124, 318, 338, 445
Blueberries for Sal, 221, 257
Bones, Bones, Dinosaur Bones, 272
Bookbinding, 468–470
Books
  breadth of, 225–227
  children's adaptations of, 256–262
  children's appreciation for, 249–267
  for classroom, 229–230, 236
  discussions of, 242–248
  experiencing, 239–242
  genres of, 230–234
  lists of, 234–235
  nonfiction, 232
  novels, 232–234
  poetry, 230–231
  for reading aloud, 225–230
  for reading workshops, 286–289
  selection of, 227–229
  wordless, 231–232
Borwick, Barbara, 376, 394
The Boy Who Held Back the Sea, 335, 437
Braunger, Jane, 345
Bridwell, Norman, 306
Brooks, Bruce, 304
Brown Bear, Brown Bear, What Do You See?, 256, 336
Brown, Marc, 262, 294
Brown, Marcia, 13
Brown, Ruth, 212
Browne, Anthony, 247

Bruce, Lisa, 218
Bruner, Jerome, 338
Building blocks, in classroom, 54
Building a House, 281, 323, 333
Bunting, Eve, 245, 334, 335
Burke, Carolyn, 38, 45, 65, 399, 434
Burns, M. Susan, 270, 343, 361
Burton, Virginia Lee, 250
The Bus Ride, 327, 332

Cactus Hotel, 413
California Achievement Test, 446
Calkins, Lucy, 3, 110, 170, 304, 343, 394, 431
The Call of Stories, 248
Carle, Eric, 13, 14, 18, 244, 250, 257, 262–263, 361
Carrick, Carol, 226, 263, 334, 335
Case studies, use of, 445
Catch That Frog, 332
Charlotte's Web, 36, 225, 233, 256, 289, 405
Children
- appreciation for literature by, 249–267
- backgrounds of, 23, 29–31
- classroom grouping of, 59–60
- desire for reading, 313–314
- giving choices to, 75
- native writing talents of, 2–3, 4–5
- need for approval of, 159–163
- reading choices of, 272–273
- reading strategies of, 314–318
- uniqueness of, 6–7

Children and Books, 229
Children's Minds, 162
Choice, importance of, 75
Classroom
- as academic environment, 58–62
- arrangement of, 54–57
- library in, 52–53, 229–230
- multimedia aids in, 53–54
- as physical environment, 52–57
- structure of, 49–51

Classroom community
- acclimation to, 28–29, 46–47
- evolution of, 47
- listening in, 46
- literature in, 38–40
- rule setting in, 40–41
- shared experiences in, 31–33
- social climate of, 62
- teacher role in, 37–38
- tone of, 27–28
- trust in, 47

Clay, Marie, 224, 318, 357, 431
Coles, Robert, 248
Comprehension, skills list of, 475–476
Condon, Mark, 183
Consonant blends, teaching, 344–345
Context clues, 317
Conversations: Strategies for Teaching, Learning, and Evaluating, 432, 448
Cookie's Week, 12, 18, 19, 315, 322–323, 328
Cooney, Barbara, 226
Craft Lessons, 136
Curriculum
- adherence to, 58
- approach to, 413–414
- writing and, 399–412

Dahl, Karin, 341, 394
Dahl, Roald, 405
Dakota Dugout, 263
Deaf children, learning characteristics of, 369–370
Death, coping with, 464–465
Demonstrating strategies
- charts and lists in, 357–358
- grammar, 356–357
- handwriting lessons, 359–360
- importance of, 351
- during mini-lessons and conferences, 360–361
- reading aloud, 352–354
- spontaneous demonstrations, 354–355
- word of the day, 355–356
- word games in, 359

dePaola, Tomie, 12, 231, 263, 266, 328, 412
A Desert Scrapbook, 413
Digraphs
- teaching, 346
- vowel, 346–349

Dinosaur's Divorce, 262, 334

Documentation
  aids to, 419–420
  conference checklists, 466
  concerns regarding, 417–418
  purpose of, 418
  reading folders, 430–434
  reading records, 433–434
Donaldson, Margaret, 162
Downs, Tracy, 373
Drama props, in classroom, 54
Drummer Hoff, 433

Ecology, inquiry approach to, 410–412
Editing skills
  mini-lesson on, 118
  in publishing, 203–204
  spelling, 368
Efferent reading, 239
Egan, Judy, 70
Eggar, Bettina, 266
Ehlert, Lois, 328
Elbow, Peter, 127
Emig, Janet, 8, 9, 66, 213, 396
The Energy to Teach, 9
Environment
  academic, 58–62
  enabling, 66
  physical, 52–57
Evaluation
  case studies, 445
  faults of traditional methods of, 459–460
  interviews for, 432–439
  miscue analysis, 432
  reading folders, 430–434
  self-, 439–444
  teacher role in, 458–459
  tests, 445–448
  writing folders, 420–430

Fielding, L. G., 270
Fletcher, Ralph, 136
Focusing, of writing, 133–134
Folktales
  characteristics of, 255
  use in classroom, 251–255
Ford, Michael, 304, 305
The Foundling, 263
Fountas, Irene, 304
Fox, Mem, 250, 256
Fran's Flower, 218
Freedom to Learn, 31
Frog and Toad, 230, 249, 292
Frost, Robert, 86, 246, 283
Fulwiler, Toby, 399

Galdone, Paul, 253
Games
  in classroom, 54
  word, 358–359
Garan, Elaine, 343
Genres, skills list of, 475
Ghost's Hour, Spook's Hour, 245, 287, 334
Giacobbe, Mary Ellen, 3, 8, 9, 35, 46, 53, 61, 75, 77, 78, 110, 135, 144, 148, 158, 170, 292, 362, 434
Gingerbread Boy, 254
Goldilocks and the Three Bears, 241, 244, 247, 261
Good Night, Owl, 292
Goodman, Ken, 431
Goodman, Yetta, 256, 418
Grammar learning, 356–357
Grandfather Twilight, 234
Graves, Donald, 2, 6, 7, 8–9, 33, 46, 65, 110, 120, 139, 144, 162, 170, 305, 339, 443
The Grey Lady and the Strawberry Snatcher, 231
Griffin, Peg, 270, 343, 361
The Grouchy Ladybug, 250, 257
Group sharing, 70–72
  case study of, 165–170
  discouraging rote responses in, 173–174
  encouraging of, 172
  procedures for, 166
  starting, 170–172
Growth reporting
  parent communication, 452–458
  report cards, 419, 449–452
Guided reading, 298
  described, 299–302
  planning for, 304–305
  purposes of, 302–304, 311
The Gunnywolf, 254, 255
GYNS AT WRK, 9

Haley, Gail, 39, 40
Handwriting, learning of, 359–360
Hansen, Jane, 217, 443
The Happy Day, 333
Harold and the Great Stag, 306
Harste, Jerome, 38, 45, 65
Henny Penny, 254
Higglety Pigglety Pop, 226
Holdaway, Don, 216, 224
Hopkins, Lee Bennett, 266
How Do Dinosaurs Say Goodnight?, 392
Huck, Charlotte, 229, 236, 266
Hutchins, Pat, 292

I Know an Old Lay Who Swallowed a Fly, 222
In a Dark, Dark Room and Other Scary Stories, 245
In the Rain with Baby Duck, 373
Information
  importance of, 130–131
  revision by adding, 129
Inquiry approach
  to ecology, 410–412
  to social studies, 409–410
Intelligence testing, 29
Interviews
  to evaluate students, 434–439
  to guide students, 432–434
It Didn't Frighten Me, 332, 336

Jack and the Bean Tree, 39, 40
Jacobs, James, 216
James and the Giant Peach, 234, 405, 408
Jeffers, Susan, 283
Johnson, Nancy, 419

The Karate Test, 282
Kellogg, Steven, 263
Kindergarten
  classroom activities in, 394
  classroom community in, 373–375
  importance of, 396–397
  mini-lessons for, 386–387
  reading in, 392–396
  revision in, 387–390
  skills taught in, 395
  writing in, 374–383
King, Stephen, 136
A Kiss for Little Bear, 247, 335
Koala Lu, 250
Krasny, Levrene, 262
Kraus, Robert, 257, 404

Language, conventions of, 114
Language learning
  demonstrating strategies in, 350–361
  integrated nature of, 340–342
  phonics, 9, 269–270, 341–349, 360
  word structures, 349–350
Lauber, Patricia, 232, 415
Learning strategies
  individual nature of, 312–313, 338–339
  for new words, 316–317
  pointing to words, 315–316
  practicing, 318
  retelling, 314–315
  using memory, 314–315
Learning to read
  case studies of, 321–337
  desire for, 313–314
  effects of, 337–339
  skills for, 319–320
  strategies for, 314–318
  universal capability for, 312–313
Learning by Teaching, 135
Leo the Late Bloomer, 404
Lesson plans, 61–62
Lewis, Jan, 345
Library
  children's work in, 208
  classroom, 52–53
  literature choice for, 229–230
Listening, 137–138
  case study of, 174–177
  goals of, 177–178
  importance of, 46, 163–164
  learning about, 139
  questions in response to, 145–147
  settings for, 139–144
Literature
  book lists and, 234–235
  breadth of, 225–227
  children's adaptations of, 256–262
  children's appreciation for, 249–267
  for classroom, 229–230, 236
  discussions of, 242–248

Literature (*cont.*)
experiencing, 239–242
genres of, 230–234
nonfiction, 232
novels, 232–234
poetry, 230–231
for reading aloud, 225–230
for reading workshops, 286–289
selection of, 227–229
wordless picture books, 231–232
Literature circles, 298
beginning, 306
described, 305–306
in first grade, 306–310
purpose of, 311
structure of, 310
Little Elephant, 392
The Little Engine That Could, 119
The Little House, 250
The Little Red Hen, 251, 253, 254
Lobel, Arnold, 230, 249, 292
Locker, Thomas, 335
Looking Closely, 349
Love You Forever, 221

MacLachlan, Patricia, 225, 247, 263
Magic Tree House books, 229
Make Way for Ducklings, 53, 220
Marianne's Grandmother, 266, 322
Marshall, James, 247, 261
Martin, Ann, 265
Martin, Bill, Jr., 256, 277
Math, writing in, 401–403
McCloskey, Robert, 53, 220, 221, 257
McDermott, Gerald, 228
McGuffee, Michael, 183
McLure, Patricia, 316
Media equipment, in classroom, 54
Memory, in learning to read, 314–315, 316
Milligan, Spike, 221
Mills, Heidi, 349
Minarik, Elsie, 247
Mini-lessons
characteristics of, 110–112
demonstrations in, 360–361
direct presentation in, 115
on editing skills, 118
effectiveness of, 110–111
example of, 108–100
first writing workshop, 66–68
group participation in, 116–117
importance of, 136, 138
integrative, 134–135
kindergarten-level, 386–387
presentation of, 115–118
presentation of past experiences, 117–118
for reading, 291–293
on revision, 120–134
role playing in, 115–116
student participation in, 116
suggested topics for, 112–115, 118–120
teacher's role in, 117
Miscue analysis, 432–433
Miscue Analysis Made Easy, 431–432
Miss Rumphius, 226
Moe, Jorgen, 13
Mooney, Margaret, 304
Mortimer, 226, 294
"Mother Doesn't Want a Dog," 221
The Mouse and the Motorcycle, 330
Moustafa, Margaret, 349, 394
Mr. Popper's Penguins, 233
Mrs. Wishy Washy, 221
Mufaro's Beautiful Daughters, 272, 317
Munsch, Robert, 221, 226, 261, 294
Murray, Don, 120, 122, 135, 145

The Napping House, 295, 321
NBA by the Numbers, 304, 413
Nettie's Trip South, 264
Newkirk, Thomas, 75, 316
The News About Dinosaurs, 415
Nicolas Knock, 435
Nonfiction, use in classroom, 232
Nonfiction Craft Lessons, 136
Novels, use in classroom, 232–234

Oh! A-Hunting We Will Go, 222, 272
O'Keefe, Timothy, 349
On Writing, 136
On Writing Well, 135
One Foot, Now the Other, 257
Onset
defined, 349
teaching, 360
Opitz, Michael, 304, 305

Our Puppy's Vacation, 212
Owl at Home, 292
Owl Moon, 308

Pancakes for Breakfast, 231
Papa, please get the moon for me, 18, 19
The Paper Bag Princess, 261
Parents
  communication with teachers, 452–453
  conferences with, 455–458
  dialogue letters with, 453–455
Parkes, Brenda, 224
Partner reading, 293–294
Paterson, Katherine, 225, 291
Patrick's Dinosaur, 307
Patterned language, in learning to read, 315
Paulsen, Gary and Ruth, 461
Peer conferences, 148
Phonetic clues, 317
Phonics, 360
  differing views on, 342–343
  importance of, 9, 269–270, 341
  learning about, 344–349
  skills list of, 473–474
Phonological awareness, skills list of, 473
Physical environment
  classroom arrangement, 54–57
  classroom library, 52–53
  learning resources, 53–54
Picture clues, 316
The Piggybook, 247
Pinnell, Gay Su, 304
Piper, Walter, 119
Plagiarism, 156–157
Planetarium, visits to, 399–401
Planting a Rainbow, 328
Poetry, use in classroom, 230–231
Polar Bear, Polar Bear, What Do You Hear?, 277
Popular culture, affecting writing, 157–158
Portalupi, JoAnn, 136
Portfolios, 443
  guidelines for choosing, 444
Practicing, for reading, 318
Praise, as two-edged sword, 159–163
Preventing Reading Difficulties in Young Children, 270
Print concepts, skills list of, 477
Publishing
  author's party, 206–208
  bookbinding, 468–470
  case studies of, 184–203
  conference record, 467
  conferring before, 187–196
  editing for, 203–204
  final corrections for, 205–206
  as instructional tool, 203–206
  kindergarten-level, 391–392
  planning for, 184–187
  process of, 182–183
  revising for, 204–205
Punctuation, skills list of, 474–475
Puppets, in classroom, 54
Puzzles, in classroom, 54

Reading
  aesthetic vs. efferent, 239–240
  children's affinity for, 272
  effective, 319–321
  first-grade examples of, 321–337
  fostering engagement, 237–239
  guided, 298–305
  learning of, 312–339. *See also* Learning to read
  meaning and, 246–248
  mini-lessons for, 291–293
  partner, 293–294
  phonics in, 269–270
  prescriptive approach to, 5–6
  purpose of, 285
  readers' responses to, 237–248
  recordkeeping of, 471, 472
  self-selected, 274–276
  shared, 224–225
  and skills acquisition, 265–267
  skills list of, 476
  strategies for, 289–291
Reading aloud, 5, 215–216
  choice of literature for, 225–230
  as demonstration, 217–220, 352–354
  listening to, 294–297
  performers of, 224
  procedures for, 222–224
  research on, 216–217

Reading aloud (*cont.*)
shared reading, 224–225
time management for, 220–222
Reading folders, 430–434
Reading workshop
choice of literature for, 286–289
choice of reading strategies for, 289–291
conferences in, 276–281
example of, 11–22
feedback in, 273–274, 276–277
goals of, 297
guiding questions in, 279–281
listening in, 294–297
routine in, 36–37
optimal scheduling for, 36
structure of, 271–276
student appreciation of, 399
teaching strategies in, 270–271, 281–285
Real ePublishing, REALLY PUBLISHING!, 183
Recess
relation to classroom, 44–45
student behavior during, 41
Record keeping, 61
aids to, 419–420
conference checklists, 466
concerns regarding, 417–418
purpose of, 418
reading folders, 430–434
reading records, 433–434
Reluctant writers, 97–98
avoidance by, 99–100
emotional factors, 100–101
encouragement of, 104–107
physical factors, 99
remedying, 150–156
styles of learning and, 101–104
Report cards, 419
attitudes about, 450–451
practical issues regarding, 450–452
A Researcher Learns to Write, 6
Resisting Reading Mandates: How to Triumph with the Truth, 343
Retelling, as strategy for learning to read, 314–315
Revision
adding information, 129
case study of, 121–124
demonstrating, 130–134
focusing, 133–134
importance of, 120, 122–123
kindergarten-level, 387–390
of "list" stories, 131–133
making deletions, 129–130
in publishing, 204–206
rereading and, 127–129
teaching of, 120–121
Rhyming words, 349
Rime
defined, 349
teaching of, 360
Rogers, Carl, 31
Rosenblatt, Louise, 239, 240, 241, 242, 245, 247, 266, 313
Routine, value of, 36–37
Routman, Regie, 224, 304, 351, 418, 432, 448
Rule setting, shared, 40–41
Rumpelstiltskin, 253, 273

Sailing with the Wind, 437
Sarah, Plain and Tall, 225, 247
Scheduling
aids to, 59
constricting effect of, 22–23
demands on, 58–59
sample form, 60
Schwartz, Alvin, 245
Science, writing in, 403–408
Self-evaluation
benefits of, 443–444
guidelines for, 444
offering opportunities for, 442–443
of skills, 439–442
Sendak, Maurice, 53, 226, 264
Seven Kisses in a Row, 263
Shared experiences, 31–34
Shared reading, 224–225
Short, Kathy, 399
Smith, Frank, 431
Snow, Catherine, 270, 343, 361
Snow White, 245
Social studies, inquiry approach to, 409–410
Spelling
development of, 365–366
in editing, 368
mechanisms and strategies for, 369

teaching of, 361–365
word wall for, 366–368
writing and, 365, 368
Stafford, William, 145
Steele, Luci, 324, 325
Stephens, Diane, 349
Stetler, Rose, 2–3, 450
Stopping by a Wood on a Snowy Evening, 86, 246–247, 283
Stories to Grow On, 12
Strega Nona, 272
Strickland, Dorothy, 349
Structural analysis, skills list of, 474
Structure
of academic environment, 58–62
establishment of, 49–51
importance of, 51
physical environment, 52–57
Study skills, skills list of, 475
Sustained Silent Reading (SSR), 272, 273

Talking, importance to writing, 414
Teacher research, 9
Teaching
assumptions underlying, 65–66
evaluating progress, 458–459
expectations in, 23–25
need for consistency in, 8
need for responsiveness in, 7–8
prerequisites for success in, 11–12
theories and, 24
Teale, William, 216, 217, 224, 393
Ten Little Bears, 315
Tests
equity issues regarding, 448
limitations of, 445–446
skills for taking, 447–448
use of, 446–447
"This Is Just to Say," 221
This Old Man, 316, 323, 437
"A Thousand Hairy Savages," 221
The Three Billy Goats Gruff, 13, 14, 16, 18, 221, 243, 254, 294
The Tiny Family, 306
Traditional teaching
autocratic aspect of, 37
curriculum in, 58
report cards, 419, 449–452
rituals in, 6
tests, 445–448
Trust, importance of, 47
Tunnell, Michael, 216
Turner, Ann, 263
Twain, Mark, 242
Two Bad Ants, 246
The Two of Them, 266

Usage, teaching, 359

Van Allsburg, Chris, 246
Veatch, Jeannette, 8, 33
The Very Hungry Caterpillar, 13, 14, 16, 18, 243, 261, 272, 282, 325, 361
Viorst, Judith, 221
Visual cues, 317
Vocabulary learning
context clues for, 317
multiple clues in, 317
phonetic clues for, 317
picture clues for, 316
visual cues for, 317
word of the day, 355–356
word games, 358–359
word play, 359
Volcano, 232
Vowels
digraphs of, 348, 349
teaching, 346–348
Vygotsky, Lev, 138

Weaver, Connie, 351
The Web of Meaning, 9
Wells, Gordon, 216, 230
Where Are You Going, Little Mouse?, 257
Where the Wild Things Are, 53, 226, 257, 264
White, E.B., 36, 225, 256
Wilde, Sandra, 363, 432
Wilder, Laura Ingalls, 370
Williams, William Carlos, 221
Wilson, P. T., 270
Woodward, Virginia, 38, 45, 65
Woodworth, Wendy, 175–176
Word games, 359
Word play, 359
Word structures, teaching, 349–350

Word wall, for teaching spelling, 367–368
Wordless picture books, use in classroom, 231–232
Worksong, 461
Writing
and astronomy, 400–401
author's perspective on, 165–180
avoiding offensive content in, 158–159
background for, 66–68
children's, 256–262
children's perspectives on, 211–212
as communication, 125, 414
and content-area studies, 399–409, 414–415
desirable qualities of, 113–114, 209–211
enabling environment for, 66
first-grade examples of, 79–96
in kindergarten, 374–375
kindergarten examples of, 375–383
and learning to read, 318–321, 392–396
and math, 401–403
plagiarism, 156–157
popular culture reflected in, 157–158
procedural issues in, 112
process of, 209
publishing and, 181–213
purposes of, 413
reference works on, 135–136
of reluctant writers, 97–107
and science, 403–408
setting tone, 34–36
"showing not telling," 124–127
skills list of, 476–477
solving problems in, 150–156
strategies for, 112
talking and, 414
variability of, 7
Writing conferences, 68–70
in kindergarten, 385–386
peer, 148
problem solving during, 150–156
procedures for, 144–145, 163–164
questions to ask during, 145–147
record keeping for, 148–150, 466
roving, 139–144
Writing folders, 420–430
Writing: Teachers and Children at Work, 7
Writing workshop
conferences in, 68–70, 384–386
continuity in, 72
establishing, 63–74
for kindergarten, 384–391
large-group sharing in, 70–72
managing, 74–78, 107
materials for, 23, 52–53, 76–78, 385
prerequisites for success of, 8
purpose of, 76
sharing in, 166
student appreciation of, 399
student involvement in, 35
teacher's role in, 178–180
teaching strategies in, 270–271
time frame of, 75–76, 384

Yellow Ball, 352
Yokota, Junko, 217, 224, 393
Yolen, Jane, 392

Zartman, Carol, 99
Zelinsky, Paul, 253
Zinsser, William, 135
Zomo the Rabbit, 228